1949–1990
DEUTSCHE DEMOKRATISCHE REPUBLIK
BUNDESREPUBLIK DEUTSCHLAND
Deutschland
DÄNEMARK
Sylt
Nordfriesische Inseln
Helgoland
Ostfriesische Inseln
Nordsee
Ostsee
Rügen
Fehmarn
Flensburg
SCHLESWIG-HOLSTEIN
Husum
Kiel
Puttgarden
Neumünster
Lübeck
Bad Segeberg
Stralsund
Rostock
Greifswald
Wismar
MECKLENBURG-VORPOMMERN
Neubrandenburg
Müritz
HAMBURG
Hamburg
Reinbek
Schwerin
Bremerhaven
Emden
BREMEN
Westerstede
Elsfleth
Worpswede
Bremen
Oldenburg
Lüneburg
LÜNEBURGER HEIDE
Elbe
Prenzlau
Oder
Schwedt
POLEN
NIEDERSACHSEN
Wittenberge
Salzwedel
Celle
BERLIN
Berlin
Havel
Stendal
Hannover
Wolfsburg
Potsdam
Frankfurt (Oder)
NIEDERLANDE
Osnabrück
Braunschweig
Hildesheim
BRANDENBURG
Weser
Hameln
Magdeburg
Münster
Bielefeld
HARZ
NORDRHEIN-WESTFALEN
Detmold
SACHSEN-ANHALT
Wittenberg
Halberstadt
Dessau
Cottbus
Spree
Gelsenkirchen
Dortmund
Essen
Bochum
Duisburg
Ruhr
Düsseldorf
Wernigerode
Göttingen
Eisleben
Saale
Halle
Neiße
Kassel
Sondershausen
Wurzen
Leipzig
Mühlhausen
SACHSEN
Meißen
Bautzen
Dresden
Bergisch-Gladbach
Köln
Aachen
Donrath
Bonn
Eisenach
Weimar
Erfurt
Jena
Gera
Chemnitz
Zwickau
Marburg
THÜRINGEN
THÜRINGER WALD
Rudolstadt
ERZGEBIRGE
WESTERWALD
Giessen
Rhein
HESSEN
Fulda
Suhl
Plauen
BELGIEN
Koblenz
EIFEL
RHEINLAND-PFALZ
Bacharach
Wiesbaden
Frankfurt a. M.
Mainz
Main
Bayreuth
Elbe
Bingen
Mosel
Trier
LUXEMBURG
Bamberg
Würzburg
TSCHECHISCHE REPUBLIK
Worms
Kaiserslautern
Weinheim
Ochsenfurth
Erlangen
SAARLAND
Mannheim
Heidelberg
Nürnberg
BÖHMER WALD
Saarbrücken
Neckar
Rothenburg
BAYERN
Ansbach
BAYERISCHER WALD
Karlsruhe
Regensburg
Stuttgart
Baden-Baden
Plochingen
Donau
Isar
Passau
Tübingen
SCHWARZWALD
Ulm
FRANKREICH
BADEN-WÜRTTEMBERG
Augsburg
Inn
München
Freiburg
Bad Krozingen
Starnberger See
Chiemsee
Tegernsee
ÖSTERREICH
Kaufbeuren
Kempten
BAYERISCHE ALPEN
Konstanz
Lindau
Bodensee
ALLGÄU
Berchtesgaden
Oberstdorf
Garmisch-Partenkirchen
LIECHTENSTEIN
SCHWEIZ
0 50 100 150 km
0 50 100 mi

Instructor's Annotated Edition

Neue Horizonte

For
Royal Kemper
Best wishes and
Viel Spaß beim
Lernen!
David
Dollenmayer

Instructor's Annotated Edition / Fifth Edition

Neue Horizonte

A First Course in German Language and Culture

David B. Dollenmayer

Worcester Polytechnic Institute

Thomas S. Hansen

Wellesley College

Houghton Mifflin Company Boston New York

Director, Modern Language Programs: E. Kristina Baer
Development Manager: Beth Kramer
Development Editor: Harriet Dishman
Assistant Editor: Angela Schoenherr
Senior Project Editor: Helen Bronk
Senior Production/Design Coordinator: Jennifer Waddell
Manufacturing Manager: Florence Cadran
Marketing Manager: Patricia Fossi

Cover Design: Deborah Azerrad Savona
Cover Photograph: B. Schmid/Tony Stone Images

Printed in the U.S.A.

Library of Congress Catalog Card Number: 98-72016

Instructor's Annotated Edition ISBN: 0-395-90983-X
Student Edition ISBN: 0-395-90960-0

123456789-WOC-02 01 00 99 98

Contents

Instructor's Guide

The Instructor's Annotated Edition (IAE) of ***Neue Horizonte***, Fifth Edition, is an expanded version of the Student Text. The IAE begins with an Instructor's Guide that describes the program and its objectives, suggests teaching techniques for the various components, and offers a sample lesson plan. The text that follows the Instructor's Guide is exactly what your students have in their edition, except for the marginal instructor's annotations, printed in blue, which do not appear in the student edition. Student annotations are printed in black and appear both in the Student Text and the IAE. It would be helpful to familiarize yourself with the Preface that begins on page xv of the Student Text before continuing to read this Instructor's Guide.

Overview of Neue Horizonte

Neue Horizonte, Fifth Edition, is a beginning German text designed for students at both two-year and four-year colleges and universities. It is designed as a four-skills approach to learning German and is suitable for use in a course sequence of two semesters or three quarters. In institutions where language classes meet only three hours a week, it may sometimes be appropriate to use the text over three semesters, depending on the goals of the curriculum.

The complete program consists of the Student Text, the Instructor's Annotated Edition, the Workbook/Laboratory Manual, the Cassette Program, the Instructor's Resource Manual, the ***Neue Horizonte*** video, the Overhead Transparencies, the Situation Cards, the ***Neue Horizonte Now***! CD-ROM, the ***Neue Horizonte*** web site, and text-specific student software (the ***Neue Horizonte*** Computer Study Modules for Macintosh® and Windows®).

All components are integrated with the Student Text, but they are flexible enough to be adapted to various teaching environments, teaching styles, and variations in the number of contact hours.

New to the Fifth Edition

- ***Neue Horizonte***, Fifth Edition, conforms to the German spelling reform. An **Almanach** in **Kapitel 4** describes the major changes and discusses the controversy surrounding the new spelling. Instructor's annotations draw attention to particular details.
- Each reading is now followed by a new feature: **Nach dem Lesen** (*post-reading activities*). These engage students in the cultural theme of the chapter through realia-based activities, games, and content questions.
- New cultural information appears throughout the text, and maps, photos, realia, and statistics have been updated. **Kapitel 16** contains a completely new reading that uses the cartoons of the German caricaturist Marie Marcks to explore women's roles in family and society.

- Marginal icons for the **Almanach** in the Table of Contents alert users to the ***Neue Horizonte*** web site. This site provides activities that link students and teachers to contemporary material on the language and cultures of the German-speaking countries available on the World Wide Web.

Objectives of the Program

The goal of ***Neue Horizonte*** is twofold: it aims to teach students how to communicate in German and how to do so as accurately as possible. The authors believe that the goals of communicative and grammatical competency are ultimately inseparable. The text therefore embraces an eclectic methodology that both demands accuracy in controlled exercises and encourages free expression in communicative exercises. Instructors using various methodologies will find ***Neue Horizonte*** flexible, comprehensive, and adaptable to their individual styles.

Neue Horizonte presents a comprehensive introduction to the grammatical structures of German along with a basic vocabulary of approximately 1,600 high-frequency words and phrases. The book provides ample material to develop listening, speaking, reading, and writing skills. Through the **Dialoge**, **Lesestück**, **Situationen aus dem Alltag**, and **Almanach** sections, each chapter also introduces students to everyday life in German-speaking countries, as well as to several topics of central importance to twentieth-century Germany and Europe. Students learn to recognize and reflect upon differences in values, social organization, and human relations between German culture and their own.

The following are some attainable proficiency goals for a two-semester German course using ***Neue Horizonte***:

Speaking

1. Pronunciation of all of the sounds of German accurately enough to be understood by a native speaker of the language.
2. Expression of ideas using the active vocabulary and simple sentences in the present, perfect, and future tenses (as well as the simple past of **sein**, **haben**, and the modals), and the most common subjunctive forms.
3. Active control of verb-final word order in short subordinate clauses.
4. Occasional use in spontaneous speech of longer subordinate clauses.

Listening

1. Accurate recognition of all the sounds of German.
2. Comprehension of ideas expressed through the vocabulary and grammatical structures presented in ***Neue Horizonte***.

Reading

1. Understanding of simple German prose on nontechnical subjects.
2. Intelligent guessing of unfamiliar vocabulary using context clues.

Writing

1. Ability to write (in class and without a dictionary) a paragraph in German about a familiar topic so that a native speaker could understand it without difficulty. Such paragraphs may contain major errors in areas such as verb-subject agreement and adjective endings, but must be comprehensible.
2. Ability to write (outside of class) a paragraph in German about a familiar topic so that the ideas are comprehensible to a native speaker upon first reading. This paragraph should contain no major errors.

Culture

1. Elementary knowledge of important aspects of everyday culture in the German-speaking countries. For example, climate and geography, family life, school and university life, jobs, and urban life. Awareness of the major differences and similarities between German and North American culture.

2. Some comprehension of the cultural and historical differences among the Federal Republic, Austria, and Switzerland.
3. Elementary knowledge of some important issues in contemporary German life: the environment, integration of the five new German **Länder** into the Federal Republic, coming to terms with the National Socialist past, the position of foreigners in Germany, and women's roles in family and society.

Text Organization and Teaching Suggestions

Neue Horizonte, Fifth Edition, consists of an **Einführung** and sixteen chapters. At the end of the textbook are two appendices: Appendix 1 is an answer key to the **Videoecke** exercises, and Appendix 2 is a list of strong and irregular verbs introduced in the text. These are followed by German-English and English-German vocabularies and an index to the grammatical and communicative topics of the text.

Einführung

This introductory chapter is divided into three levels (**Stufe 1**, **2**, **3**), which should be covered during the first three days of class. The chapter is designed to give students communicative possibilities at the very beginning of their study of German. For easy visual reference, boxes highlight the basic words and phrases students need to learn. Assign the material in these boxes as homework for the second and third class days. At this point, students should be concentrating on entire phrases for communication rather than on individual phonemes. The complete introduction to German phonology in the cassette program should be assigned over the first two weeks of class. Be sure students use the Workbook/Laboratory Manual in conjunction with the Sounds of German section on the first cassette. Practice pronunciation for 5–10 minutes per class meeting during this time.

Dialoge

The dialogues in each chapter present conversational exchanges using colloquial German in everyday situations. They include most of the grammatical structures to be learned in the chapter in short, ready-to-use expressions. Most of the dialogues are brief enough to be assigned for memorization, if desired. They can also be varied and embellished to fit students' personal communication. You can either introduce the dialogues in class, with books open, or assign students to hear them first in the language laboratory. Whether or not students memorize them, it is imperative that they do not just read the dialogues silently, but rather say them aloud with a partner. Explain to students that the dialogues contain grammar structures presented in the **Grammatik** sections, while the grammar explanations often draw their example sentences from the dialogues. All the vocabulary in the dialogues is for active acquisition.

Dialogue Translations

These are equivalents of the German dialogues in idiomatic English. Alert students to the fact that they are not literal, word-for-word translations. Their purpose is to convey an immediate understanding of dialogue content even before students have studied the new structures in the **Grammatik** section.

Wortschatz 1

The two **Wortschatz** sections of each chapter contain all the vocabulary that students are expected to master for active use. The first of these, **Wortschatz 1**, contains all new vocabulary introduced in the dialogues, as well as lexical items not used in the dialogues but needed later in the chapter. Nouns are grouped by gender as an aid to memorization. Antonyms are presented under the rubric **Gegensätze**, and the section **Mit anderen Worten** introduces colloquial synonyms of new vocabulary. These are defined in German rather than English.

In the first days of the course, give students tips on learning vocabulary and reiterate them frequently. For example, tell students to recite new vocabulary aloud for a maximum of ten to fifteen minutes at a sitting. This is most profitably done with a classmate and promotes cooperative learning. Flash cards can be a valuable aid to learning because they are portable, require students to write the words, and allow them to randomize order.

Spend a minute of class time pointing out specific words and modeling ones with unusual or difficult pronunciation. A good time to spot-check current and previously learned vocabulary is early in the class period, before introducing new material.

Variationen

This section uses material from the dialogues to encourage students to express their own thoughts, ideas, and experiences. It should be done in class after students have listened to and practiced the dialogues at home. The first **Variation** is always a set of **Persönliche Fragen** based on the dialogues that ask students to talk about themselves. This is a good chance for students to see how material from the dialogues can be varied to talk about their own experiences. Other exercises in this section, called **Partnerarbeit**, emphasize student-to-student communication. The instructor should move around the classroom, listening and offering help when it is needed, while monitoring grammatical accuracy.

Lyrik zum Vorlesen

Students can have fun while practicing their pronunciation and intonation with the poem or song in each chapter. The emphasis here is on **Vorlesen**. If possible, students should listen to the recorded version of these texts on the Cassette Program and then read them aloud in class. In early chapters these poems are quite simple. Later, more challenging texts relate directly to the chapter's cultural topics. Unfamiliar vocabulary is glossed. The instructor's annotations suggest simple, interpretive questions in English or German. In some cases, you may want to ask students to memorize the poem or song. Students gain confidence from this preparation.

Grammatik und Übungen

The **Grammatik** section presents the grammar topics of the lesson succinctly, in terms simple enough for students to understand on their own. Tables and diagrams make explanations as visual as possible. New or difficult grammatical concepts are defined and often illustrated with English examples before the German is introduced. Assign this section for students to read carefully before coming to class, so that minimal class time is spent on grammar explanations in English. Set aside five minutes at the beginning of the class hour for students' questions. Each grammar point is followed by oral exercises to be done in class.

The Fifth Edition of ***Neue Horizonte*** includes three kinds of exercises:

- **Übungen** are instructor-directed and reinforce grammar at the most mechanical level. As often as possible, the direction line establishes a context, and the exercise consists of a brief conversational exchange between instructor and student. Most **Übungen** are preceded by a **Beispiel** that should be said chorally by the entire class. The **Beispiel** can be done with books open, but books should then be closed for the remainder of the exercise. (Occasional open-book exercises are labeled **Mit offenen Büchern**.) In doing the **Übungen**, grammatical accuracy should be required. The headset icon next to an exercise, along with an annotation referring users to the Laboratory Manual, indicates that this exercise is recorded verbatim on the Cassette Program:

 **Lab Manual**, Kap. 5, Üb. 2.

In some cases the Cassette Program has a variation on the same grammar topic:

 **Lab Manual**, Kap. 5, Var. zur Üb. 2.

Assign these taped exercises along with the **Grammatik** sections in the Student Text as part of the students' preparation for class.

Other written exercises presenting additional practice of the grammar and vocabulary of the chapter are offered in the Workbook. Students are guided at the appropriate time to each exercise in the Workbook by a pen icon and a student annotation:

 **Workbook**, Kap. 15, H.

- **Gruppenarbeiten** are to be done either by the whole class or by groups of students with minimal direction by the instructor. The simplest type of **Gruppenarbeit** is the so-called **Kettenreaktion** in which one student, for instance, says what she likes to eat, then asks the next student what he likes to eat. The instructor should intervene only if several students continue making the same error (for example, **"Was esst du gern?"**). Other **Gruppenarbeiten** ask students to use German communicatively in a carefully controlled context. Here, the instructor should move from group to group, giving help as needed or requested, but not checking grammatical accuracy as long as students are communicating adequately with each other.
- **Partnerarbeiten** require students to work in pairs. Since students tend to sit in the same seat in each class, thereby choosing the same partner each time, you should decide whether you want students to work with various partners by changing the seating arrangement from time to time. In the **Partnerarbeiten** students are given considerable communicative freedom. Again, the instructor should be available for help with both vocabulary and structures, but should have a high tolerance for grammatical errors.

All three types of exercises have German direction lines whenever possible. Many are based on line art or realia.

- **Notes on Usage and Fragewörter:** Features of spoken German, such as flavoring particles, compressed forms (**ich hab'**), and colloquialisms that are more related to usage than grammar, are highlighted in yellow boxes. These *Notes on Usage* appear whenever appropriate throughout the chapter. Question words (**Fragewörter**) are also highlighted in boxes.

Vor dem Lesen

- **Tipps zum Lesen und Lernen:** This pre-reading section consists of three parts:

  Tipps zum Vokabelnlernen give students tips on topics such as noun suffixes, recognizing gender, and easily learned classes of words such as the adverbs

morgens, **nachmittags**, and **mittwochs**. This section is often accompanied by an **Übung** that may be done in class or as homework.

Leicht zu merken lists easily recognized cognates from the reading that follows but does not give their English equivalents. (The English definitions are, however, included in the end vocabularies.) If the stress of the German word falls on a different syllable from that of its English cognate, this is indicated in the right-hand column (e.g., **Universität**). Especially in the early weeks of the course, it is advisable to go over this list briefly in class. Students should be encouraged not just to recognize these cognates, but to become accustomed to how they are formed and pronounced. This vocabulary is not assumed to be part of the students' active vocabulary.

Einstieg in den Text provides a variety of activities designed to facilitate reading comprehension. In early chapters, students are given tips on how to approach a foreign language text in which they do not understand every word. In later chapters they are asked to concentrate on examples of structures they have just learned, such as passive voice or relative clauses. They are sometimes asked to reflect on their own knowledge of or feelings about a topic such as environmental pollution before reading about it. This section can be assigned as homework or covered in class.

- **Wortschatz 2** is structurally identical to **Wortschatz 1**. It contains the vocabulary needed to understand the reading and do the end-of-chapter activities (**Zum Schluss**). As in **Wortschatz 1**, students must memorize this active vocabulary.

Lesestück

The **Lesestück** is the centerpiece of each chapter's cultural theme. Words or phrases that are not active, as well as grammatical structures that have not yet been taught, are glossed in the margins. Selected passages can be read aloud in class for practice in pronunciation and sentence intonation. Since recordings of the **Lesestück** selections are included on the Cassette Program, students can also practice reading them aloud in the language laboratory or at home. It may also be useful to have students translate selected passages into English.

Two chapters contain authentic texts: *Zwei Denkmäler* by Anna Seghers (**Kapitel 12**), and *Wer ist ein Türke?* by Şinasi Dikmen (**Kapitel 15**). The reading in **Kapitel 16** is based on cartoons by Marie Marcks.

Nach dem Lesen

New to the Fifth Edition, these post-reading activities engage students in the cultural theme of the chapter through realia-based activities, games, and content questions. Some material requires students to make educated guesses based on context clues. These activities provide a relaxed approach to the cultural theme following the work on the **Lesestück**.

Situationen aus dem Alltag

The vocabulary and activities in this section build a bridge between presentation of culture and survival skills. For example, after students have read about German city life in **Kapitel 8**, they make the transition to interpersonal communication by working in groups to find their way around a city and order food in a restaurant. The thematically grouped vocabulary introduced in **Situationen aus dem Alltag** is not considered active and is therefore not recycled in subsequent chapters. Instructors may choose whether or not to assign and test this vocabulary.

Zum Schluss

The oral and written exercises in this section, entitled respectively **Sprechen wir miteinander**! and **Schreiben Sie zu Hause**, synthesize the cultural material, grammar, and vocabulary of the chapter. The oral exercises contain both **Partnerarbeit** and **Gruppenarbeit** and challenge students to use what they have learned in communicative situations. The written exercises range from fairly mechanical grammar-based exercises, to English-to-German translation sentences, to essay topics for free composition. Instructors may choose to assign all or just some of these exercises.

Videoecke

The **Videoecke** section appears after **Zum Schluss** in every even-numbered chapter, integrating the ***Neue Horizonte*** video with the Student Text. The ***Neue Horizonte*** video generally follows the sequence of grammar and vocabulary in the Student Text. It also introduces additional high-frequency vocabulary.

Each **Videoecke** contains the following elements:

- A brief summary in German, accompanied by a context-setting video still, introduces the characters and action of the video episode. Only familiar vocabulary and structures are used.
- **Wortschatz zum Video** highlights some new vocabulary important to the video episode. The vocabulary is not considered active in the Student Text and instructors may choose whether to have students learn it or not. The words do, however, appear in the end vocabularies of the Student Text.
- The activities that follow are designed to increase students' understanding and enjoyment of the episode by encouraging them to integrate viewing and listening. After pre-viewing activities, students can watch the video without sound to sharpen their comprehension of non-verbal cues. (The icon for sound-off activities appears on the left.) Students can work with the **Videoecke** outside of class. Parts of episodes can also be shown in class and the exercises done by the entire group or in pairs. Repeated viewing of the video may be necessary to do some of the exercises. Answers to the activities are found in Appendix 1 at the end of the book. Above all, the video should be a source of enjoyment for the students.

Almanach

This section supplements each chapter's cultural presentation in various ways. In some chapters, the **Almanach** provides information in English on the chapter topic (for example, vital statistics of the Federal Republic of Germany, Austria, and Switzerland; or information on schools, political parties, or foreign residents). This section provides the kind of detail that is part of the cultural repertoire of a native speaker but impossible to convey in elementary readings in German. Other **Almanach** entries provide pieces of authentic realia such as help-wanted ads, a brochure for a Berlin bus line, and a page from a Youth Hostel guide. Instructor's annotations suggest ways to implement these in classroom activities.

Appendices

Appendix 1: Answer Key to **Videoecke** Activities
Appendix 2: Principal Parts of Strong and Irregular Verbs

Make sure students understand the organization and usefulness of the end matter—appendices, end vocabularies, and index—from the beginning of the course.

End Vocabularies

The German-English vocabulary contains the following:

- All active vocabulary items from **Wortschatz 1** and **2**, keyed to the chapter in which they are introduced (for example, 10-1 = **Kapitel 10**, **Wortschatz 1**). A few items introduced in the **Grammatik** are keyed in the following way: 10-G = **Kapitel 10**, **Grammatik**). Make sure students understand that these codes tell them whether they should already know the word they are looking up.
- All cognates introduced in the **Leicht zu merken** parts of the **Tipps zum Lesen und Lernen** sections are keyed to the chapter in which they are introduced (for example, 3-TLL = **Kapitel 3**, **Tipps zum Lesen und Lernen**).
- All the optional additional vocabulary items from the **Situationen aus dem Alltag**, keyed to the chapter in which they are introduced (for example, 16-SA = **Kapitel 16**, **Situationen aus dem Alltag**).
- All the optional vocabulary items from the **Wortschatz zum Video** sections, keyed to the **Videoecke** sections in which they are introduced (for example, 8-VID = **Videoecke** in **Kapitel 8**).

The English-German vocabulary contains the same items, but without references to chapters.

A list of abbreviations used throughout ***Neue Horizonte*** can be found at the beginning of the German-English vocabulary on p. 488.

Student Annotations

Annotations for the student are printed in the margin of the Student Text. These annotations also appear in the Instructor's Annotated Edition (IAE). They not only provide cross-references to the Workbook/Laboratory Manual and Cassette Program, but also offer study hints, cultural and historical notes, contrasts and similarities to English, and interesting word histories. Student annotations also recall the communicative and cultural goals of the chapter. Tell students that these annotations provide commentary for their guidance and enjoyment.

Instructor's Annotations

The instructor's annotations are printed in blue in the IAE only and have several functions:

- Methodological hints suggest how to orchestrate an exercise or activity, remind instructors of additional vocabulary from previous chapters that can be used to expand an exercise, provide variations on exercises or additional activities, and offer simple interpretive questions for some of the poems and readings.
- Additional details are presented for some grammar topics. These go beyond the simplifications inevitable in a first-year text and anticipate questions students may ask. Contrasts or similarities to English are often suggested.
- Cross-references are provided to related grammar and cultural topics elsewhere in the book.
- Suggested German translations for the section **Wie sagt man das auf Deutsch?** are given in the second half of the book.
- Occasional reminders of pronunciation and stress are provided for instructors whose native language is not German.

Program Components

Workbook/Laboratory Manual

The Workbook section of this manual provides a variety of writing exercises and activities that use and recombine the vocabulary and grammatical structures in the corresponding chapters of the Student Text. Illustrations vary the pace of the activities and can be used as the basis of class discussions. After **Kapitel 4**, **8**, **12**, and **16**, a **Zusammenfassung und Wiederholung** section summarizes the grammatical and functional topics of the preceding four chapters in schematic and tabular form. Grammar concepts are grouped by categories such as verb forms, noun morphology, adjective formation, and sentence structure. Idiomatic, communicative phrases are grouped by function: greetings, parting formulae, comparing, expressing preferences, etc. Each **Zusammenfassung und Wiederholung** section ends with a *Test Your Progress*—a self-test for students to diagnose their individual areas of strength and weakness.

The Laboratory Manual begins with the *Sounds of German* section on phonology. Each chapter then contains dialogue-based exercises, listening comprehension activities, pronunciation sections, directed exercises for grammar and vocabulary reinforcement, word and phrase stress exercises, and dictations to be done in conjunction with the Cassette Program. An Answer Key for both the Workbook and Laboratory Manual sections is provided for self-correction.

Cassette Program

The Cassette Program for ***Neue Horizonte***, Fifth Edition, available for student purchase, is fully supported by the Laboratory Manual. The Cassette Program begins with recorded material for the preliminary chapter, the **Einführung**, which includes a complete presentation of German pronunciation. Students should listen to and practice the *Sounds of German* section within the first few days of class and refer to it as needed throughout the year. The **Einführung** portion of the Cassette Program concludes with a section on classroom expressions.

For each of the sixteen regular chapters, the Cassette Program contains the following recorded material:

- **Dialoge**: The dialogues of the chapter, with pauses for student repetition.
- **Fragen zu den Dialogen:** True-false and multiple-choice questions that check comprehension of the dialogues.
- **Hören Sie gut zu!:** A dialogue for listening comprehension that does not appear in either the textbook or the Laboratory Manual. This dialogue recycles vocabulary and grammatical structures from previous chapters and is followed by comprehension questions (in English in **Kapitel 1** and **2**; in German in **Kapitel 3–16**). Students hear these questions on the cassettes and must answer them in writing in the Laboratory Manual.
- **Übung zur Aussprache:** A section in **Kapitel 1–8** that practices sounds that pose particular difficulty. Students repeat minimal word pairs and sentences containing the targeted sounds.
- **Lyrik zum Vorlesen:** The poems printed in the corresponding textbook section.
- **Üben wir!:** Selected exercises from the Student Text, with pauses for repetition, as well as variations on textbook exercises.
- **Üben zur Betonung:** Practice of stress in words or phrases. Cognates and words borrowed from other languages such as *Chance*, *Garage*, and *interviewen* are

presented here. Material from the **Leicht zu merken** list of the textbook's **Lesestück** section is also emphasized, thus recycling items that are not necessarily considered active but are easy for students to remember and to make part of their passive vocabulary.

- **Lesestück:** The textbook's reading selection read at normal speed. Because the **Lesestück** is not intended for repetition, the text is read without pauses.
- **Diktat:** Dictation sentences that include the chapter's grammatical points and vocabulary items from **Wortschatz 1** and **2**. Students should not do the dictation until they have discussed the **Lesestück** in class.

The **Dialoge**, **Fragen zu den Dialogen**, **Hören Sie gut zu!**, **Übung zur Aussprache**, and **Lyrik zum Vorlesen** sections reinforce the material in the opening parts of the corresponding textbook chapter. They can be done before students have begun the chapter's **Grammatik**. The **Üben wir!** section of the Cassette Program should accompany study of the **Grammatik**. The remaining sections of recorded material for each chapter reinforce materials in the latter part of the corresponding textbook chapter and should not be done until students have completed at least the **Lesestück** and the **Situationen aus dem Alltag** sections.

Neue Horizonte Video

Filmed in Berlin, the ***Neue Horizonte*** video enables students to see and hear native German speakers interact in authentic settings. The video consists of eight modules, each approximately five minutes in length, that correlate to the **Videoecke** sections of the Student Text. Each module contains a live segment that follows the everyday activities of a group of students in Berlin and a documentary segment, **Welle Magazin**, related to the module's theme. The language used in the modules reflects the grammar and vocabulary sequence of ***Neue Horizonte***, as well as topics related to the textbook's dialogues and **Situationen aus dem Alltag** sections.

Instructor's Resource Manual

This component contains the Testing Program and the complete transcripts of the Cassette Program and the ***Neue Horizonte*** Video. The Testing Program provides a test for the **Einführung** and each of the sixteen regular chapters. Each test includes a listening section and draws upon the skills of reading, writing, and culture as it checks the mechanics of grammar and vocabulary. Two complete final exams, one for **Kapitel E–8**, the other for **Kapitel 9–16**, are also provided.

Neue Horizonte Computer Study Modules

This text-specific software package is available in Macintosh® and Windows® versions. It offers additional chapter-by-chapter, computer-aided practice of the structures and vocabulary of the textbook.

Neue Horizonte NOW! CD-ROM

Developed in collaboration with Transparent Language, Inc., and Windows® and Macintosh® compatible, the ***Neue Horizonte*** **NOW!** CD-ROM uses an interactive approach to teach students vocabulary, grammar, and culture. The program includes dialogues, vocabulary, and cultural notes and is correlated by chapter with the textbook.

Neue Horizonte Web Site

The ***Neue Horizonte*** **Web Site** links students and teachers to contemporary material on the language and cultures of the German-speaking countries available on the World Wide Web.

Overhead Transparencies

The Overhead Transparency package features 28 transparencies designed to practice the vocabulary, grammar, and culture of selected textbook chapters and to stimulate class discussions. The transparencies appear without labels, to make them more flexible and useful for classroom work. In addition, the Overhead Transparencies package includes the textbook's full-color maps. Each map is offered without labels and accompanied by an overlay with the names of all geographical features.

Situation Cards Kit

This useful, easy-to-implement classroom tool aids instructors in the testing, practice, and evaluation of students' oral skills. Each of the 120 cards focuses on a realistic, clearly defined communicative task. The cards are sequenced in order of increasing difficulty, and an accompanying Instructor's Guide provides an index to aid in the correlation of the cards to the Student Text.

Instructor's Resource Kit

This conveniently boxed supplement contains the Instructor's Resource Manual, the Overhead Transparencies, and the Situation Cards Kit.

Sample Lesson Plan

The following lesson plan assumes an elementary class meeting four times a week during a 13-week semester, allowing a total of 52 hours of class time to cover eight chapters per semester. Depending on how much time is spent on administration, testing, review, and the **Einführung** chapter, this schedule allows for 5–6 class hours per regular chapter. Instructors may also want to budget class time for each of the **Videoecke** sections that appear in each even-numbered chapter. Instructors with academic calendars organized on the quarter system can use this same lesson plan as a guide. They should plan on completing **Kapitel E–5** in the first quarter, **Kapitel 6–11** in the second quarter, and **Kapitel 12–16** in the third quarter.

In courses meeting three times a week, the instructor can reduce or eliminate activities as necessary in order to cover the material in a semester or quarter. Exercises not covered in class can be assigned as written homework. Many of the **Übungen** are included in the Cassette Program and can be assigned as work in the language laboratory or at home. Alternatively, the last four chapters of ***Neue Horizonte*** can form the core of a third-semester course.

This sample lesson plan for the first nine class days represents a three-hour presentation of the **Einführung** and a five-hour presentation of **Kapitel 1**, with an in-class test on Day 9. It also integrates assignments in the Workbook/Laboratory Manual, which are thoroughly cross-referenced in the Student Text.

Week 1: Day 1

1. First day of the new course. Spend ten minutes getting to know students, handing out the syllabus, and discussing the importance of the language laboratory. Spend another five minutes describing the structure of the semester's work and the goals of the course. Wait until you begin **Kapitel 1** to give students an overview of the ***Neue Horizonte*** textbook and its ancillaries. Describe the goals and activities of the first three days. Tell students they will learn to speak some basic German without having to learn formal grammar. Open books to p. 1 and point out the communicative goals of the **Einführung**.
2. Proceed to **Stufe 1** (p. 2). Work with open books on this first day. Model the greetings and conversations and have students repeat them chorally and individually. The minimal grammar explanations (e.g., some personal endings of verbs in the present tense) need not be covered in class but can be assigned for review outside of class. Students will learn to greet each other, find out each other's names, say how they are today, name some classroom objects and the days of the week, and say good-bye. When covering classroom vocabulary on p. 6, have students close their books. Before class, make large labels for classroom objects (e.g., **die Tafel**) and attach them to the objects as you say them. Have students repeat chorally and individually: **Das ist die Tafel**. Correct pronunciation as necessary.
3. Homework: Have students listen to the mini-dialogues from **Stufe 1** of the **Einführung** that students have already done once in class, in the language laboratory, or at home using their cassettes. Point out that the vocabulary and phrases in **Wortschatz** boxes are to be memorized. (Most students will have learned these expressions already by working with them in class.) Have students

read the short explanations of grammatical points (some verb endings, German equivalents of *the*, etc.) in **Stufe 1**. Tell them that **Stufe 2** will be done at the next class meeting and that they can preview it if they have time.

Week 1: Day 2

1. Books closed, spend 5–10 minutes reviewing material from Day 1: greetings, classroom objects, etc. Model an exchange with a student using **Sie**, then have a student pair repeat it using **du**. Then have entire class do the exchange in pairs. Use **Partnerarbeit 9** to review classroom objects and people.
2. Open books and move to new material in **Stufe 2**: the alphabet and spelling, more about feelings and moods, and weather vocabulary. Again, move from instructor-centered model to work in student pairs. Speak as much German as possible. Students can understand commands such as **Machen Sie bitte Ihre Bücher auf** if you perform the action while saying the command.
3. Homework: Listen to the **Einführung**, **Stufe 2** material on the Cassette Program. Review **Stufe 2** in the Student Text, memorizing the boxed material. Tell students that **Stufe 3** will be done in the next class meeting and that they can preview it if they have time. Have students read the **Almanach** section (*Profile of the Federal Republic of Germany*) at the end of the **Einführung**.

Week 1: Day 3

1. Books closed, spend 5–10 minutes reviewing material from **Stufe 1** and **2**. Ask students in English what they learned from the **Almanach** that they hadn't known about Germany.
2. Open books and begin **Stufe 3**: counting to 20, telling time, saying where one comes from and where one lives, and naming the months. Bring in a classroom clock to practice telling time.
3. Go over the *Useful Classroom Expressions*, p. 18. Read them aloud for pronunciation practice. Tell students they do not need to memorize these expressions. Make sure they understand that the **Wortschatz** section at the end of the **Einführung** contains all the vocabulary they should have learned from the chapter.
4. Dedicate the last 5–10 minutes to a preview of **Kapitel 1**. Briefly go through the format of the chapter as well as the communicative and cultural goals highlighted on its opening page. Read and have students repeat at least two of the new dialogues.
5. Homework: Review **Stufe 3** of the **Einführung** on the Cassette Program. Prepare for chapter test on the **Einführung**. Listen to dialogues for **Kapitel 1** on the cassettes and read through **Wortschatz 1**. Memorize one dialogue for recitation in class. This can be assigned to student pairs with each partner responsible for one part. Answer the **Fragen zu den Dialogen** in the Laboratory Manual and listen to and answer the questions about the additional dialogue, entitled **Hören Sie gut zu!** Tell students to bring their Workbook/Laboratory Manuals to the next class meeting in order to begin work with the *Sounds of German* section.

Week 1: Day 4

1. Chapter test on the **Einführung** (optional).
2. Practice dialogues in **Kapitel 1**, first as a **Partnerarbeiten** with books closed. Then have pairs model the dialogues. Ask students if they have any questions on structures in the dialogues or on the vocabulary. Do **Variationen A–E** with closed books whenever possible.

3. Talk about the structure of **Wortschatz 1** (grouping by word category, plural abbreviations, etc.). Help students memorize vocabulary (always learn articles with nouns, say words aloud, etc.).
4. Beginning today, and for the next two weeks or so, work on the *Sounds of German* for five minutes a day. This introduction to German phonetics is found in the **Einführung** section of the Laboratory Manual and Cassette Program.
5. Homework: Use the Cassette Program and the Laboratory Manual to review the *Sounds of German*. Listen to the **Übung zur Aussprache** on the cassette for **Kapitel 1**. Continue to memorize **Wortschatz 1**. Read the **Grammatik** section, pp. 26–29: *Personal pronouns* and *Verbs: Infinitive and present tense*. Prepare specific **Übungen** for the next class. Remind students that exercises marked with the headphone icon are on the Cassette Program, either verbatim or in variation. (Exercises such as **Übung 2**, **Kettenreaktion**, on p. 28 can be done only in class.) Write out **Übung 1** and **Übung 3** for practice of verb forms.

Week 2: Day 5

1. Collect homework. Have the class warm up by reviewing material from the **Einführung**, such as telling time and discussing the weather.
2. Continue work on the *Sounds of German*.
3. Continue to work on **Kapitel 1** dialogues for 5–10 minutes. Have students work in pairs.
4. Have students read **Lyrik zum Vorlesen** (with books open). They can also hear these poems on the Cassette Program.
5. Do **Grammatik Übungen 1–4** with books closed.
6. You may choose to do **Partnerarbeit C** from **Zum Schluss** at this point.
7. Briefly preview grammar for the next class.
8. Homework: In the Workbook, do **Kapitel 1**, **Übungen A–C**. Use the Cassette Program to review the *Sounds of German* and the **Lyrik zum Vorlesen** sections covered in class. Continue to memorize **Wortschatz 1**. Prepare for a brief vocabulary quiz during next class. Read the **Grammatik** section, pp. 30–33: *Noun gender and pronoun agreement, Noun plurals, Nominative case*. Using the Cassette Program, prepare **Übungen** for the next class. Assign some **Übungen** as written homework.

Week 2: Day 6

1. Give students a brief quiz on **Wortschatz 1**.
2. Have the class warm up with material from previous days.
3. Continue to work on the *Sounds of German*.
4. Do **Grammatik Übungen 5–10** with books closed where possible. Review nouns for classroom objects as examples of gender and plural endings.
5. Preview **Tipps zum Lesen und Lernen**, **Leicht zu merken**, **Wortschatz 2**, and the **Lesestück**. A good technique is to make an overhead transparency of the **Lesestück** and refer to it as you work through the suggestions in **Einstieg in den Text**, p. 38.
6. Homework: Do Workbook, **Kapitel 1**, **Übungen D–F**. Use the Cassette Program to review the *Sounds of German* covered in class. Read the **Grammatik** section, pp. 33–36: *The sentence: German word order, The flavoring particle* **ja**. Using the Cassette Program, prepare **Übungen** for the next class. Assign some **Übungen** as written homework. Read **Tipps zum Lesen und Lernen** and listen to and read **Wie sagt man *you* auf Deutsch?**, p. 39. Begin learning the vocabulary in **Wortschatz 2**.

Week 2: Day 7

1. Continue to work on the *Sounds of German*.
2. Do **Grammatik Übungen 11–14**.
3. Do the **Partnerarbeit** on the feminine ending **-in**, p. 37, in pairs, then spot-check pronunciation with the entire class.
4. **"Wie sagt man *you* auf Deutsch?"** is short enough to be read aloud in class by the students. Do **Nach dem Lesen**.
5. If there is time, you can also do the **Situationen aus dem Alltag** in class, since students are familiar with the **du/Sie** distinction by now.
6. Homework: Do Workbook, **Kapitel 1**, **Übungen G–J**. Review **Wortschatz 1** and continue to learn **Wortschatz 2**. Assign students to prepare some or all of the **Sprechen wir miteinander!** exercises for the next class. Assign one or more of the **Schreiben Sie zu Hause** exercises as written homework. It is suggested that students always translate the **Wie sagt man das auf Deutsch?** sentences, since they are a good review of grammar covered in the chapter. Students can write a sentence apiece on the blackboard as they come into the next class hour and then correct them together. Read the **Almanach** section, *Where is German spoken?*

Week 2: Day 8

1. Spot-check **Wortschatz 2**.
2. Continue work on the *Sounds of German*.
3. Do the **Situationen aus dem Alltag** if you didn't do it on the previous class day.
4. Spend most of class on the **Sprechen wir miteinander!** activities.
5. Spend 5–10 minutes correcting the **"Wie sagt man das auf Deutsch?"** sentences on the blackboard.
6. During the last five minutes of class, discuss in English the **Almanach** section *Where Is German Spoken?* in conjunction with the endpaper maps.
7. Homework: Prepare for the chapter test. Vocabulary focus will be on **Wortschatz 2**. Do the **Übung zur Betonung** and the **Diktat** in the Laboratory Manual and bring the completed Workbook/Laboratory Manual to the next class.

Week 3: Day 9

1. Chapter test on **Kapitel 1**.
2. During the last 10–15 minutes of class, go over **Kapitel 2** chapter goals, model and have students repeat new dialogues. Anticipate main grammar points (accusative case, possessive adjectives) as they occur in dialogues.
3. Homework: Read and listen to dialogues in **Kapitel 2** of the Cassette Program. Do the **Fragen zu den Dialogen** and **Hören Sie gut zu!** in the Laboratory Manual.

Teaching Techniques for Oral Exercises

Devoting part of each class to rapid oral drill with books closed can be an effective way to help students speak German sentences with reasonably accurate rhythm and intonation. As the book progresses, the sentences get longer. Drilling can be an important step toward accurate and comprehensible utterances in free conversation. Drill also helps students develop some degree of automatic control over grammatical structures, so that when speaking extemporaneously they can concentrate more and more on the content rather than grammar.

In order for such oral exercises to be truly effective, instructors need to understand a few techniques. Most drills involve the transformation of an original sentence. The instructor should first model the original sentence, then make sure that students can accurately say the utterance they will be called upon to transform. This stage is crucial: when students do not control the model sentence, the drill will be ineffective. It is also important for teachers to confirm a correct answer by repeating it in a loud, clear voice to insure that all students have heard the correct response. Ideally, the class should repeat the instructor's confirmation.

Since the rhythm and pace of a drill are crucial to keeping the class on its toes, instructors should not wait for volunteers after the cue. Rather they should call on a student to respond. For the same reason, instructors should not call on students in any predictable pattern, such as going in rows or in a circle.

Here are some of the most common types of drills used in the text, along with sample scripts. The abbreviations used are I = Instructor, C = Class (group response), and S = Student (individual response).

Person-Number Substitution

I: Wiederholen Sie bitte: Ich sehe einen Mann.
C: Ich sehe einen Mann.
I: Du.
S: Du siehst einen Mann.
(I: Du siehst einen Mann.) *May be omitted.*
C: Du siehst einen Mann.
I: Wir
S: Wir sehen einen Mann. (etc.)

Noun Substitution

I: Wiederholen Sie bitte: Ich brauche das neue Auto.
C: Ich brauche das neue Auto.
I: Buch
S: Ich brauche das neue Buch.
(I: Ich brauche das neue Buch.) *May be omitted.*
C: Ich brauche das neue Buch.
I: Wagen
S: Ich brauche den neuen Wagen. (etc.)

The instructor can check for meaning by asking for some of the sentences to be translated from English to German.

I: How do you say *I need a new car*?
S: Ich brauche das neue Auto.
I: I need the new newspapers.
S: Ich brauche die neuen Zeitungen.

Progressive Substitution Drills

These drills ask the student to restate a sentence cumulatively, element by element. For each cue, the student must recognize which element must be changed.

I: Wiederholen Sie bitte: Sie saß in einem kleinen Zimmer.
C: Sie saß in einem kleinen Zimmer.
I: Wohnung
S: Sie saß in einer kleinen Wohnung.
C: Sie saß in einer kleinen Wohnung.
I: groß
S: Sie saß in einer großen Wohnung.
C: Sie saß in einer großen Wohnung.
I: Wagen. (etc.)

Expansion Drills

Expansion drills require the student to add an element to a base sentence and to make the changes required. Expansion drills help the student produce progressively longer utterances and are particularly useful for teaching modal auxiliaries and attributive adjectives.

I: Wiederholen Sie bitte: Wir haben ein Haus.
C: Wir haben ein Haus.
I: schön
S: Wir haben ein schönes Haus.
(C: Wir haben ein schönes Haus.) *May be omitted.*
I: alt
S: Wir haben ein schönes altes Haus. (etc.)

Transformation Drills

Transformation drills differ from substitution and expansion drills. The cue is not a new semantic element, but rather a command to transform the sentence, e.g., from one tense to another or from active to passive voice. Although transformation drills may seem mechanical, transformations often occur in conversational exchanges.

A: Essen deine Geschwister jetzt?
B: Nein, sie haben schon gegessen. (*present to perfect tense*)
A: Können Sie mir bitte das Frühstück bringen?
B: Ja, es wird sofort gebracht! (*active to passive voice*)

Transformation drills are especially useful in presenting new tenses. Since the student must know the original sentence thoroughly in order to transform it, choral repetition of the model sentence is essential. Here is a sample transformation drill for the perfect tense.

I: Let's change these sentences from present tense to the perfect. Wiederholen Sie bitte: Hans kauft ein Buch.
C: Hans kauft ein Buch.
I: Perfekt?
S: Hans hat ein Buch gekauft.

(I: Hans hat ein Buch gekauft.) *May be omitted.*
C: Hans hat ein Buch gekauft.
I: Sie gehen weg.
C: Sie gehen weg.
I: Perfekt?
S: Sie sind weggegangen. (etc.)

Response Drills

Response drills use the patterns question-and-answer or statement-and-rejoinder and thus come closer to authentic communication than the more mechanical drills described above. These drills can be led by the instructor or by a student. ***Neue Horizonte*** is particularly rich in response drills of various kinds. The following response drill from **Kapitel 12** practices comparison of adjectives and adverbs. The grammatical structure is given, but the student has a free choice of vocabulary.

I or S: Was fährt schneller als ein Fahrrad?
S: Ein Auto fährt schneller (als ein Fahrrad).
I or S: Was fährt langsamer als ein Zug?
S: Ein Motorrad fährt langsamer als ein Zug.

Free-Response Exercises and Activities

The ultimate goal of ***Neue Horizonte*** is to enable students to use German to express themselves and obtain information. Free-response exercises and activities are found both in the **Grammatik** and the end-of-chapter exercises in the section entitled **Zum Schluss**. Within each grammar topic, exercises progress from instructor-directed drills (**Übungen**) to guided conversation (**Partnerarbeit**). The **Sprechen wir miteinander!** activities found in the **Zum Schluss** section provide conversational exchanges, role-playing, and interviews, which let students communicate with each other in situations that are freer than those in the **Grammatik** section. Sometimes these situations relate to the cultural topic of the chapter. In **Kapitel 16**, for example, students are given the choice of three role-playing situations that reflect contemporary concerns of women. Other **Sprechen wir miteinander!** activities are closely related to new grammar topics. After they have learned the adjective ending system in **Kapitel 9**, for example, students are asked to prepare an oral description of a photograph or picture from a magazine for presentation to their classmates.

The **Schreiben Sie zu Hause** section of **Zum Schluss** contains both structured and free-response activities. The former always includes an English-to-German translation exercise entitled **Wie sagt man das auf Deutsch?** The latter includes a variety of written activities, which include letters and postcards, fantasy questions such as planning one's ideal city (**Kapitel 8**), and topics for brief essays in which students can reflect on the cultural issues of the chapter.

Neue Horizonte

Fifth Edition

Neue Horizonte

A First Course in German Language and Culture

David B. Dollenmayer

Worcester Polytechnic Institute

Thomas S. Hansen

Wellesley College

Houghton Mifflin Company Boston New York

Director, Modern Language Programs: E. Kristina Baer
Development Manager: Beth Kramer
Development Editor: Harriet Dishman
Assistant Editor: Angela Schoenherr
Senior Project Editor: Helen Bronk
Senior Production/Design Coordinator: Jennifer Waddell
Manufacturing Manager: Florence Cadran
Marketing Manager: Patricia Fossi

Cover Design: Deborah Azerrad Savona
Cover Photograph: B. Schmid/Tony Stone Images

For permission to use copyrighted material, grateful acknowledgment is made to the copyright holders listed on pages 527–528, which are hereby considered an extension of this copyright page.

Printed in the U.S.A.

Library of Congress Catalog Card Number: 98-72016

Student Edition ISBN: 0-395-90960-0
Instructor's Annotated Edition ISBN: 0-395-90983-X

123456789-WOC-02 01 00 99 98

About the Authors

David B. Dollenmayer is Professor of German at the Worcester Polytechnic Institute (Worcester, Massachusetts). He received his B.A. and Ph.D. from Princeton University and was a Fulbright fellow at the University of Munich. He has written on the 20th-century writers Alfred Döblin, Joseph Roth, Christa Wolf, and Ingeborg Bachmann, and is the author of *The Berlin Novels of Alfred Döblin* (Berkeley, CA: University of California Press, 1988).

Thomas S. Hansen is Professor of German and Chairman of the German Department at Wellesley College (Wellesley, Massachusetts). He received his B.A. from Tufts University, studied six semesters at the University of Tübingen, and received his Ph.D. from Harvard University. His current research focuses on the 20th-century writer Arno Schmidt and on German-American literary relations. He is the author (with Burton R. Pollin) of *The German Face of Edgar Allan Poe: A Study of Literary References in His Works* (Columbia, SC: Camden House, 1995).

Contents

Kapitel 2

Kapitel 3

Kapitel 4 Land und Leute 98

Kapitel 10 Deutschland im 20. Jahrhundert 276

Kapitel 11 Deutschland nach der Mauer 308

WWW

Kapitel 13 Die Schweiz 372

Kapitel 14 Österreich 398

WWW

Preface

Neue Horizonte, Fifth Edition, is a comprehensive first-year German program for college and university students. With it you will learn the basic structures and vocabulary of German by practicing the four skills of speaking, listening, reading, and writing. In addition, you will learn about the culture of contemporary Germany, Austria, and Switzerland.

The goal of the program is to help you achieve a basic level of linguistic proficiency in German. Such proficiency includes both communicative competence—that is to say, speaking the language in order to communicate thoughts, ideas, and feelings—and grammatical accuracy. ***Neue Horizonte*** prepares you either to continue with an intermediate course in German, or to go directly to a German-speaking country. There, after a period of acclimatization, you will be able to communicate in most everyday situations and to continue to build on what you have already learned.

In addition, the text aims to excite your curiosity and help you view your own culture through the prism of another, thereby expanding your intellectual horizons in the spirit of the Austrian philosopher Ludwig Wittgenstein when he wrote, "Die Grenzen meiner Sprache sind die Grenzen meiner Welt." (*The boundaries of my language are the boundaries of my world.*)

The Student Text

Neue Horizonte consists of an introductory chapter and sixteen regular chapters.

Einführung (Introductory chapter)

From the very first day of the course, you begin talking with your fellow students in German. In this chapter you will learn greetings and farewells. You will also learn basic vocabulary such as the names of classroom objects, the days of the week, and the months of the year. In addition, you will learn how to spell, count to twenty, tell time, talk about the weather, and tell how you feel and where you are from.

Chapter Organization

Each of the sixteen regular chapters contains the following sections:

Dialoge und Variationen (Dialogues and Variations)

The **Dialoge** introduce new vocabulary and structures through idiomatic conversations in everyday situations. There are two or three dialogues per chapter, most short enough to be memorized, with English translations printed on the following page. The **Variationen** follow up with activities that encourage you to build on and vary the material in the dialogues. When a dialogue is closely related to the ***Neue Horizonte*** video, this is signaled by a video icon that appears in the margin.

Wortschatz 1 und Wortschatz 2 (Vocabulary 1 and Vocabulary 2)

Each chapter contains two lists of words and phrases for you to learn. **Wortschatz 1** (*Vocabulary 1*) comes early in the chapter, following the dialogues. **Wortschatz 2** comes later, just before the reading selection. Words are arranged alphabetically by parts of speech. In addition, nouns are arranged by gender to facilitate learning. Each **Wortschatz** also includes useful expressions (**Nützliche Ausdrücke**), antonyms (**Gegensätze**), as well as a section called **Mit anderen Worten** (*In other words*). Here some of the colorful idioms frequent in the everyday speech of native Germans are defined using German you already know. These include, for instance, intensified forms of adjectives such as **blitzschnell** (*quick as lightning*) and colloquialisms such as **prima** (*great!*). By the end of ***Neue Horizonte*** you will have acquired a total active lexicon of about 1,600 words and phrases.

Lyrik zum Vorlesen (Poetry for reading aloud)

Each chapter includes a poem related to its cultural theme. This may be used both for pronunciation and intonation practice and for simple interpretive discussion. Unfamiliar vocabulary is glossed in the margins.

Grammatik (Grammar)

Grammar explanations in ***Neue Horizonte*** are brief but complete and do not presuppose familiarity with English grammatical terms. So that class time can be devoted to communication, you should study the grammar carefully outside of class.

The sequence of in-class activities moves from theory to practice. The **Übungen** (*Exercises*) are directed by your instructor and briefly reinforce the grammar you have studied on your own. These are followed by activities called **Gruppenarbeit** and **Partnerarbeit** (*Group work* and *Work with partners*) in which you use German with more freedom and creativity on your way toward communicative competence.

Vor dem Lesen (Before the reading)

This pre-reading section offers tips for learning and expanding your German vocabulary. Lists of easily recognized cognates (e.g., **Universität**) are given under the heading **Leicht zu merken** (*Easy to remember*). Strategies for approaching the reading selection that follows are also provided.

Lesestück (Reading selection)

The **Lesestück** is the core of the cultural presentation of each chapter. In Chapters 1–8 it provides basic information on daily life in the German-speaking countries. Topics include the family, secondary schools, geography and climate, work and professions, university study, travel, and urban life. The readings of Chapters 9–16 address important topics in twentieth-century German history and culture. These include the Weimar era, the legacy of World War II, and German reunification, as well as issues of intense current concern such as the environment, foreigners living and working in Germany, and the status of women in modern society. The readings in Chapters 13 and 14 are devoted to Switzerland and Austria, respectively. Chapters 12 and 15 present authentic, unedited nonfiction texts by the modern writers Anna Seghers and Şinasi Dikmen. Chapter 16 features satirical cartoons by Marie Marcks. In each chapter, the section **Nach dem Lesen** (*After the reading*) includes content questions as well as a variety of activities related to the topic of the reading.

Situationen aus dem Alltag (Situations from everyday life)

This section contains activities and optional vocabulary that emphasize "survival skills" for everyday situations such as using public transportation, eating in restaurants, introducing oneself in various social situations, and expressing feelings. When these situations are the subject of a ***Neue Horizonte*** video module, this is indicated by the video icon (shown on the left).

Zum Schluss (In conclusion)

The oral and written exercises in this section integrate and combine the grammatical, lexical, and cultural material of the chapter in communicative and interactive contexts. The final written exercise of each chapter, entitled **Wie sagt man das auf Deutsch?** (*How do you say that in German?*), asks you to translate brief colloquial conversations from English to German. In this way you can verify your mastery of the grammar and vocabulary you have learned in the chapter.

Videoecke (Video corner)

The **Videoecke** follows the **Zum Schluss** section in every even-numbered chapter of ***Neue Horizonte***, Fifth Edition. It contains pre-viewing and viewing activities to increase your understanding and enjoyment of the ***Neue Horizonte*** video program that accompanies the text. You can find an answer key to these activities in Appendix 1 at the end of this book.

Almanach (Almanac)

The final section provides more detailed information in English on the cultural topic of the chapter or presents authentic material in German related to the chapter's theme. For example, in Chapter 3 you will learn more about the school system in German-speaking countries, while in Chapter 8 you will work with a city bus brochure.

Student Annotations

Student annotations are printed in black in the margins. These annotations serve several purposes. They not only provide cross-references to the Workbook/Laboratory Manual and Cassette Program, but also offer learning hints, cultural and historical notes, contrasts and similarities to English, interesting ' histories, and statements of communicative and cultural goals.

Reference Section

Neue Horizonte includes the following appendices:

Appendix 1: An answer key to the **Videoecke** exercises that appear in every even-numbered chapter.

Appendix 2: A table of the principal parts of the strong and irregular verbs introduced in the book.

Both the German-English and the English-German end vocabularies include all the active vocabulary in the **Wortschatz** sections, as well as the optional vocabulary from the **Situationen aus dem Alltag** and the **Videoecke** sections.

For quick reference, the book ends with a comprehensive index to grammatical and communicative topics included in the text.

The Workbook/Laboratory Manual and the Cassette Program

The Workbook/Laboratory Manual and the Cassette Program for ***Neue Horizonte***, Fifth Edition, are fully integrated with the Student Text. The textbook includes extensive cross-references to the ancillary components. The Cassette Program and its coordinated Laboratory Manual are an integral part of the ***Neue Horizonte*** program. The cassettes are available for individual purchase at a special student price.

In order to use the Workbook/Laboratory Manual to best advantage, follow the sequence suggested in the marginal cross-references in your Student Text. Each cross-reference is identified by an icon referring either to the Workbook or to the Laboratory Manual and Cassette Program.

The pen icon directs you to written exercises in the Workbook. These offer further practice of the vocabulary and grammar presented in each chapter.

The headphone icon directs you to the Cassette Program and the Laboratory Manual. All the **Dialoge**, **Lyrik zum Vorlesen**, and **Lesestücke** from the Student Text are recorded on the cassettes, which also include numerous grammar exercises. Some of these are identical to exercises in the Student Text, while others are variations on them.

An especially valuable feature of the Workbook is the **Zusammenfassung und Wiederholung** (*Summary and review*) section located after every four chapters. This section contains condensed grammar summaries and reviews useful vocabulary expressions. It includes a self-correcting test called *Test Your Progress* that you can use to review the preceding quarter of the textbook.

The Neue Horizonte *Video*

Shot entirely on location in Berlin, the ***Neue Horizonte*** video contains eight modules, each of which corresponds to two chapters of the Student Text.

Each module opens with scenes of Germany related to the module's cultural theme. There follow several minutes of a continuing story, performed by German actors using idiomatic language. Each module concludes with a **Welle Magazin** segment in which further footage shows aspects of German culture and life. For students who wish to view the video at their own convenience, the ***Neue Horizonte*** video is available for purchase at a special discount price.

The eight **Videoecke** sections in the Student Text are designed for use with the eight modules of the ***Neue Horizonte*** video. In addition, when a video module is particularly closely related to a dialogue or a **Situation aus dem Alltag** section in the Student Text, a video icon (shown here on the left) signals that fact and alerts you to the possibility of viewing this module again at this point.

The Neue Horizonte *Computer Study Modules*

Available in Macintosh® and Windows® formats, this text-specific software offers additional, computer-aided practice of the structures and vocabulary of the Student Text. It also provides helpful error correction.

Neue Horizonte *NOW! CD-ROM*

Developed in collaboration with Transparent Language, Inc., and Windows® and Macintosh® compatible, the ***Neue Horizonte*** **NOW!** CD-ROM is a learning tool that helps you to work at your own pace, practicing listening, speaking, reading, and writing through interactive games and activities. This program includes text dialogues, vocabulary, and cultural notes and is correlated by chapter with the textbook.

Neue Horizonte *Web Site*

The multifaceted, text-specific ***Neue Horizonte*** **Web Site** features a self-testing section for practice and a task-based activity section. It also links you to contemporary material on the language and cultures of the German-speaking countries available on the World Wide Web.

Look for this icon next to the **Almanach** headings in the **Contents**.

Acknowledgments

We wish to express our special gratitude to Ellen Crocker of the Massachusetts Institute of Technology for countless suggestions for improvement of the text and better coordination with the Workbook/Laboratory Manual and Cassette Program. Thanks to Harriet Dishman and Simone Berger of Elm Street Publications for their unfailing attention to detail, as well as to the expert editorial team at Houghton Mifflin Company, particularly Helen Bronk and copyeditor Karen Hohner. Thanks also to our colleagues and students at Wellesley College, Worcester Polytechnic Institute, and the Massachusetts Institute of Technology who have used and improved ***Neue Horizonte*** along with us, as well as to our users whose comments and criticisms have helped to make it better from edition to edition.

We wish to thank especially the following colleagues and institutions for their advice and help.

Prof. Jutta Arend, College of the Holy Cross and Worcester Polytechnic Institute

Prof. John Austin, Georgia State University Deutsche Schule, Washington, D.C.

Prof. Sharon DiFino, University of Florida at Gainesville

Prof. Wighart von Koenigswald, Universität Bonn, and the Hessisches Landesmuseum, Darmstadt, Germany

Prof. Jean Leventhal, Wellesley College

Prof. Thomas Nolden, Wellesley College

Prof. Michael Ressler, Boston College

Prof. Ute Trevor, Arbeitskreis DaF in der Schweiz

Prof. Margaret Ward, Wellesley College

In addition, we would like to thank the following colleagues who reviewed the manuscript at various stages of its development:

Prof. Margaret Klopfle Devinney, Temple University

Prof. Monika R. Dressler, University of Michigan

Prof. Enno Lohmeyer, University of Kansas

Prof. James R. McIntyre, Colby College

Prof. Guenter Georg Pfister

Prof. Ann Ulmer, Carleton College

Prof. Gretchen Van Galder-Janis, Johnson County Community College

Prof. Elizabeth I. Wade, University of Wisconsin at Oshkosh

We welcome reactions and suggestions from instructors and students using ***Neue Horizonte***. Please feel free to contact us.

Prof. David B. Dollenmayer
Department of Humanities and Arts
Worcester Polytechnic Institute
Worcester, Massachusetts 01609-2280
E-mail: dbd@wpi.edu

Prof. Thomas S. Hansen
Department of German
Wellesley College
Wellesley, Massachusetts 02482
E-mail: thansen@wellesley.edu

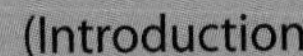

(Introduction) EINFÜHRUNG

Communicative Goals

- Greeting people and asking their names
- Identifying classroom objects
- Saying good-bye
- Learning the days of the week and months of the year
- Spelling in German
- Describing how you feel
- Talking about the weather
- Counting to 20
- Telling time
- Telling where you are from

The first three class meetings should be spent on this three-step **Einführung**, which concentrates on basic oral communication and thus has no written activities in the **Workbook**. Page through **Stufe 1–3** with students, showing them the kind of material they will be learning. Point out the student annotations and the vocabulary in shaded boxes. This vocabulary will be considered *active* in subsequent chapters. **Stufe 1** contains most of the new active vocabulary, including classroom items. Allow students to spread vocabulary learning over the first three class days and do not quiz the vocabulary until they have completed all three **Stufen**.

You will be the students' most important model for pronunciation. German phonetics are covered systemically at the beginning of the tape program (see the **Einführung** in the **Lab Manual**). Assign a few new sounds each day during the first weeks of the course.

Stufe 1 (Step 1)

■ Guten Tag! (Hello!)

The shaded boxes in this **Einführung** (*Introduction*) contain useful words and phrases that you should memorize. You will find a complete list of this vocabulary on p. 19.

Say the greetings aloud and have students repeat them, both chorally and individually. Follow this procedure with all the dialogues in the **Einführung**.

German speakers greet each other in various ways. What greeting you use depends on the time of day:

Guten Morgen!	*Good morning!* (until about 10:00 A.M.)
Guten Tag!	*Hello!* (literally: "*Good day.*" Said after 10:00 A.M.)
Guten Abend!	*Good evening!* (after 5:00 P.M.)

where you live:

Grüß Gott!	*Hello!* (in southern Germany and Austria)

and how well you know each other and what the social situation is:

Hallo! / **Tag!**	*Hi!* (informal greetings)

Lab Manual Einführung dialogues in Stufe 1. Complete introduction to the sounds of German at the end of the **Einführung** cassette.

Refer students to the Preface for an explanation of the icons.

■ **1** ■ **Gruppenarbeit: Guten Tag!** (Group work) When German speakers meet friends and acquaintances, they not only greet each other, but they also shake hands. Greet the students next to you in German. Don't forget to shake hands!

■ **2** ■ **Partnerarbeit: Was sagen diese Leute?** (Work with partners: What are these people saying?) With a partner, complete the following dialogues by saying them aloud.

German has no equivalent to English *Ms.* One can avoid **Fräulein** by using **Frau** for all young women. In restaurants a waitress is frequently called by saying **Bedienung, bitte!** (*Service, please!*).

Herr = *Mr.*
Frau = *Mrs. or Ms.*
Fräulein = *Miss*

1. ______, Herr Lehmann!
   ______, Frau Schmidt!

2. ______, Brigitte!
   ______, Heinz!

3. _____, Fräulein Schröder!
   _____, Frau Königstein!

4. _____, Peter!
   _____, Ute!

If necessary, point out geographical clue on road sign.

Work with open books, use choral repetition.

5. _____, Franz!
   _____, Joseph!

■ **Wie heißen Sie?** (What's your name?)

You: *du* or *Sie*?

German has two forms of the pronoun *you*. If you're talking to a relative or good friend, use the familiar form **du**. University students often call each other **du** even when they're meeting for the first time. If you're talking to an adult whom you don't know well, use the formal **Sie**.

When you meet people for the first time, you want to learn their names. Listen to your instructor, then repeat the following dialogue.

A: **Hallo, ich heiße Anna. Wie heißt du?**	*Hello, my name is Anna. What's your name?*
B: **Hallo Anna. Ich heiße Thomas.**	*Hello Anna. My name's Thomas.*
A: **Freut mich, Thomas!**	*Pleased to meet you, Thomas.*

You can hear these dialogues on the tape accompanying the **Einführung**.

If you're meeting an adult who is not a fellow student, the dialogue would go like this:

A: **Ich heiße Schönhuber und wie heißen Sie?**
B: **Guten Tag, Herr Schönhuber. Ich heiße Meyer.**
A: **Freut mich, Herr Meyer.**

Beginning in Kap. 1, verb paradigms will list the formal second person together with the third-person plural: **sie, Sie heißen**.

heißen: ______'s name is

German verbs have endings that must agree with the subject of the sentence:

ich heiß**e**	*my name is* (literally: *I am called*)
du heiß**t** Sie heiß**en**	*your name is*
er heiß**t**	*his name is*
sie heiß**t**	*her name is*
Wie heißt du? **Wie heißen Sie?**	*What's your name?* (literally: *How are you called?*)

Move from pair to pair and correct pronunciation as needed.

3 Partnerarbeit: Wie heißt du? Practice the first dialogue at the bottom of p. 3 with a partner. Substitute your own names for Anna and Thomas, and don't forget to switch roles.

After students have met each other, you can model the **Sie-** form in instructor-student exchanges:
I: Ich heiße Mencken und wie heißen Sie?
S: Ich heiße Bob McGrath.
Students will get consistent practice with all 2nd person forms if **I–S** exchanges use **Sie** and **S–S** exchanges use **du/ihr**. **Ihr** will be introduced in Kap. 1.

4 Gruppenarbeit: Ich heiße ... Now introduce yourself to three or four people in class you don't know. Use **du** and don't forget to shake hands.

Wie heißt du?

Wie heißt er?

Wie heißt sie?

Variation: **Heißt er Robert? Heißt sie Anna?** Your rising intonation will let students know that these are questions, and you can add: … , **ja oder nein?**

■ 5 ■ Gruppenarbeit: Wie heißt … ? Your instructor will ask you the names of other students. If you can't remember someone's name, just ask that person, **Wie heißt du?**

■ Wie geht's? (How are you?)

dir or *Ihnen*?

informal	Wie geht's **dir**?	(literally) *How goes it for you?*
formal	Wie geht es **Ihnen**?	

Say the dialogues aloud and have students repeat them.

After you've said hello, you want to find out how someone is. With a relative or fellow student, the conversation goes like this:

A: **Wie geht es dir, Franz?** — *How are you, Franz?*
B: **Sehr gut, danke. Und dir?** — *Very well, thanks. And you?*
A: **Prima, danke.** — *Great, thanks.*

With other adults, the exchange goes like this:

A: **Wie geht es Ihnen heute, Frau Müller?** — *How are you today, Mrs. Müller?*
B: **Leider nicht so gut.** — *Unfortunately, not so well.*
A: **Oh, das tut mir Leid.** — *Oh, I'm sorry.*

■ 6 ■ Partnerarbeit: Wie geht's? With a partner, practice the two preceding dialogues several times until you can say them with books closed.

■ 7 ■ Partnerarbeit: Wie geht's dir? Complete this dialogue with a new partner. You're both students or good friends and so say **du** or **dir** to each other.

A: Hallo! Wie geht's dir heute, ______ ?
B: ______ , danke. Und ______ ?
A: ______ , danke.

■ 8 ■ Partnerarbeit: Wie geht es Ihnen? Now you have a more formal relationship. Use **Ihnen** instead of **dir**.

A: Guten Tag, Frau/Herr ______ . Wie geht es ______ heute?
B: Leider ______ .
A: Oh, ______ .

Was ist das? (What is that?)

In items 1–4, the first word refers to a university classroom (professor and student), while the second word in parentheses refers to a secondary school classroom (teacher and pupil). **Student** in German *always* means *university student*.

1. der Professor (der Lehrer)
2. die Professorin (die Lehrerin)
3. der Student (der Schüler)
4. die Studentin (die Schülerin)
5. die Tafel
6. der Tisch
7. die Uhr
8. die Wand
9. das Fenster
10. der Stuhl
11. die Tür
12. die Landkarte
13. das Poster
14. die Kreide
15. der Wischer

Additional vocabulary: **das Lineal** (*ruler*), **der Filzstift** (*felt-tip pen*), **der Füller** (*fountain pen*), **die Tinte** (*ink*), **der Kuli** (*ballpoint pen*), **das Rollo** (*or* **Rouleau**) (*window shade*).

1. das Buch
2. das Heft
3. das Papier
4. der Bleistift
5. der Kugelschreiber
6. der Radiergummi

Plural forms are introduced in Kap. 1. Plurals for these nouns are given in a student annotation on page 31. They are also in the glossary.

Say these dialogues aloud with books closed and have students repeat them. Point to each object as you say its name. Write each article + noun on the board as you say it, or make signs before class and tape them to each object as you say its name.

A:	**Was ist das?**	*What is that?*
B:	**Das ist der Tisch.**	*That's the table.*
	das Buch.	*the book.*
	die Tafel.	*the blackboard.*

The = *der, das* or *die*

Every German noun belongs to one of three classes, traditionally called *masculine*, *neuter*, and *feminine*. The form of the definite article (**der**, **das**, **die** = *the*) shows which class each noun belongs to. This article *must* be learned with each noun.

masculine	**der** Mann	*the man*
	der Stuhl	*the chair*
neuter	**das** Kind	*the child*
	das Buch	*the book*
feminine	**die** Frau	*the woman*
	die Tafel	*the blackboard*

A: **Wer ist das?** — *Who is that?*
B: **Das ist Thomas.** — *That's Thomas.*
die Professorin. — *the (female) professor.*
der Professor. — *the (male) professor.*
die Studentin. — *the (female) student.*
der Student. — *the (male) student.*

The **-in** suffix denotes a female.

■ 9 ■ Partnerarbeit: Was ist das?

Work together and see how many people and things in the room you can identify.

A: Was ist das?
B: Das ist der/das/die ______.

A: Wer ist das?
B: Das ist ______.

Question words

wie?	*how?*
was?	*what?*
wer?	*who?*

Auf Wiedersehen!

■ Auf Wiedersehen! (Good-bye!)

There are several expressions you can use when leaving.

Tschüss is derived from Spanish *adiós*.

In Austria, the informal expression **Servus** means both *hi* and *so long*. In Switzerland, instead of **Guten Tag**, one says **Grüezi** formally and **Hoi** informally.

Auf Wiedersehen!	*Good-bye!*
Tschüss!	*So long!* (informal, among friends)
Schönes Wochenende!	*(Have a) nice weekend!*
Danke, gleichfalls!	*Thanks, same to you! (You too!)*
Bis morgen!	*Until tomorrow!*
Bis Montag!	*Until Monday!*

Lab Manual Einführung, The days of the week.

Practice the days of the week with students. Students learn them quickly. Teach: **Heute ist Montag. Morgen ist Dienstag** and then the other days. Ask students tomorrow: **Ist heute Dienstag? Was ist morgen?** (Review all the days.)

Assign pronunciation on tape for homework before next class day.

The letter **ß** represents the unvoiced *s*-sound. It follows long vowels and diphthongs. In Switzerland **ss** is used instead of **ß**.

■ Die Wochentage (Days of the week)

Montag	*Monday*
Dienstag	*Tuesday*
Mittwoch	*Wednesday*
Donnerstag	*Thursday*
Freitag	*Friday*
Samstag (in southern Germany) / **Sonnabend** (in northern Germany)	*Saturday*
Sonntag	*Sunday*

■ 10 ■ Gruppenarbeit: Auf Wiedersehen! At the end of class, turn to your neighbors and say good-bye until next time. Tell your instructor good-bye too.

Stufe 2

Lab Manual Einführung, The alphabet.

In addition to this alphabet, German also has three vowels modified by a symbol called the **Umlaut: ä, ö, ü**.

Call students' attention to the headphone icon. Indicate which part of the tape program they should listen to at this point.

■ Das Alphabet

The name of almost every letter in German contains the sound ordinarily represented by that letter. You should memorize the German alphabet. Listen to the alphabet on the tapes and to your instructor.

a	ah	**j**	jot	**s**	ess
b	beh	**k**	kah	**t**	teh
c	tseh	**l**	ell	**u**	uh
d	deh	**m**	emm	**v**	fau
e	eh	**n**	enn	**w**	weh
f	eff	**o**	oh	**x**	iks
g	geh	**p**	peh	**y**	üppsilon
h	hah	**q**	kuh	**z**	tsett
i	ih	**r**	err	**ß**	ess-tsett

Notes on capitalization:

- All nouns are capitalized, wherever they occur in the sentence.
- Adjectives denoting nationality are *not* capitalized.

deutsch	*German*	**kanadisch**	*Canadian*
amerikanisch	*American*	**schottisch**	*Scottish*

Lab Manual Einführung, Variations on dialogues in Stufe 2.

Tell students to spell thus: **schön** is **S-C-H-Ö** (not **O Umlaut) N**. After ***Partnerarbeit***, ask individuals: **Wie schreibt man Buch (Tisch usw.)?** Correct student pronunciation of letters.

■ 11 ■ Partnerarbeit: Wie schreibt man das? (How do you spell that?)

A. Ask each other how you spell your names. Write the last name as your partner spells it, then check to see whether you've written it correctly.

A: Wie heißt du?
B: Ich heiße Jay Schneider.
A: Wie schreibt man Schneider? — *How do you spell "Schneider"?*
B: Man schreibt das S-C-H-N-E-I-D-E-R. — *You spell it . . .*

B. Now turn to the classroom objects pictured on p. 6. One partner spells four or five of the objects pictured; the other partner says each word as it is spelled. Then switch roles.

BMW = Bayerische Motorenwerke (*Bavarian Motor Works*), **MP** = Militärpolizei, **ISBN** = Internationale Standardbuchnummer, **EKG** = Elektrokardiogramm, **BASF** = Badische Anilin- und Sodafabrik (*Baden Aniline and Soda Factory*).

■ 12 ■ Gruppenarbeit: Wie sagt man das? (How do you say that?)

Here are some abbreviations used in both English and German. Take turns saying them in German:

VW	BMW	ISBN	BASF
IBM	MP	EKG	TNT
USA	PVC	CD	

■ 13 ■ Gruppenarbeit: Wie spricht man das aus? (How do you pronounce that?)

A. Let's move from individual letters to pronouncing entire words in German. Here are some well-known German surnames. Take turns saying them aloud.

The **u** in **Luther** is short.

Fahrenheit	Kissinger	Nietzsche	Bach
Jung	Freud	Luther	Schönberg
Diesel	Ohm	Zeppelin	Schwarzenegger
Beethoven	Röntgen	Bunsen	Goethe
Hesse	Mozart	Schiffer	Pfeiffer

B. Now here are some words that English has borrowed from German. Caution: in English, their pronunciation has been anglicized. Be sure to pronounce them in German, and see if you know what they mean.

Flak = acronym for **Fliegerabwehrkanone** (*anti-aircraft gun*).

Angst	Kindergarten	Spiel
Ersatz	Kitsch	Strudel
Flak	Leitmotiv	Wanderlust
Gestalt	Poltergeist	Weltanschauung
Gesundheit	Rucksack	Zeitgeist
Hinterland	Schmalz	Zwieback

■ Wie geht's?

With books open, ask individual students how they are.

Now let's move beyond the basics of "How are you?" "I'm fine" and find out more detail about how you're feeling.

A: **Wie geht's heute? Bist du guter Laune?**	*How are you today? Are you in a good mood?*
B: **Nein, ich bin nicht guter Laune. Ich bin schlechter Laune.**	*No, I'm not in a good mood. I'm in a bad mood.*

You will learn the complete present tense of **sein**, including plural forms, in **Kapitel 1**.

sein to be

The most frequently used verb in German is **sein**. It is very irregular in the present tense.

ich **bin**	*I am*
du **bist** / Sie **sind**	*you are*
er **ist**	*he is*
sie **ist**	*she is*

■ Negation

Nicht (*not*) is placed in front of the adjective it negates:

A: Bist du müde?	*Are you tired?*
B: Nein, ich bin **nicht** müde.	*No, I'm not tired.*

Wie geht's?

Es geht mir gut. *(I'm fine.)*

Ich bin ...
- **guter Laune** *(in a good mood).*
- **munter** *(wide-awake, cheerful).*
- **fit** *(in good shape).*

Das freut mich! *(I'm glad!)*

Es geht mir nicht so gut. *(I'm not so well.)*

Ich bin ...
- **schlechter Laune** *(in a bad mood).*
- **müde** *(tired).*
- **krank** *(sick).*
- **sauer** *(ticked off, sore).*

Das tut mir Leid. *(I'm sorry.)*

■ 14 ■ Gruppenarbeit Describe these six people in German.

Er *(oder)* sie ist ______ .

■ 15 ■ Partnerarbeit With a partner, complete the following dialogues.

GERTRUD: Grüß Gott, Melanie! Wie geht's ______ heute?
MELANIE: Hallo, Gertrud. Leider geht's mir ______ gut. Ich bin heute ______ .
GERTRUD: Oh, ______ .

FRAU PABST: Guten Tag, Herr Hauser! Wie geht es ______ ?
HERR HAUSER: Guten Tag, Frau Pabst! Sehr gut, danke. Ich bin heute ______ !
FRAU PABST: Oh, ______ !

■ 16 ■ Gruppenarbeit: Bist du ... ? Form groups of three or four for this guessing game. Each person in turn acts out one of the adjectives listed on page 10. The others ask questions until they guess what the mood is.

Overcome students' inhibitions by first acting out some of these moods yourself.

A: Bist du müde?
B: Nein, ich bin nicht müde.
C: Bist du ... ?
B: Ja, ich bin ...

■ Das Wetter (The weather)

The weather is a frequent topic of conversation everywhere.

A: Wie ist das Wetter heute?
B: Es ist **herrlich** (*great, terrific*). ODER (*or*)
Es ist **furchtbar** (*terrible*).

Es ist kühl. Es ist warm. Es ist kalt. Es ist heiß.

Scheint die Sonne heute? *Is the sun shining today?*

Ja, die Sonne scheint. *Yes, the sun is shining.*

Nein, es regnet. *No, it's raining.*

■ 17 ■ Partnerarbeit: Wie ist das Wetter heute? Chat briefly with a partner about today's weather. Use the words and phrases above.

Emphasize spelling and pronunciation of **-ig** in **windig**, **sonnig**, etc.

More Weather Words

Es ist heute wolkig.	*Today it's cloudy.*
neblig.	*foggy.*
sonnig.	*sunny.*
windig.	*windy.*
Es regnet.	*It's raining.*
Es schneit.	*It's snowing.*

Ask students: **Wie ist das Wetter in Europa? Wie ist es in Wien?**

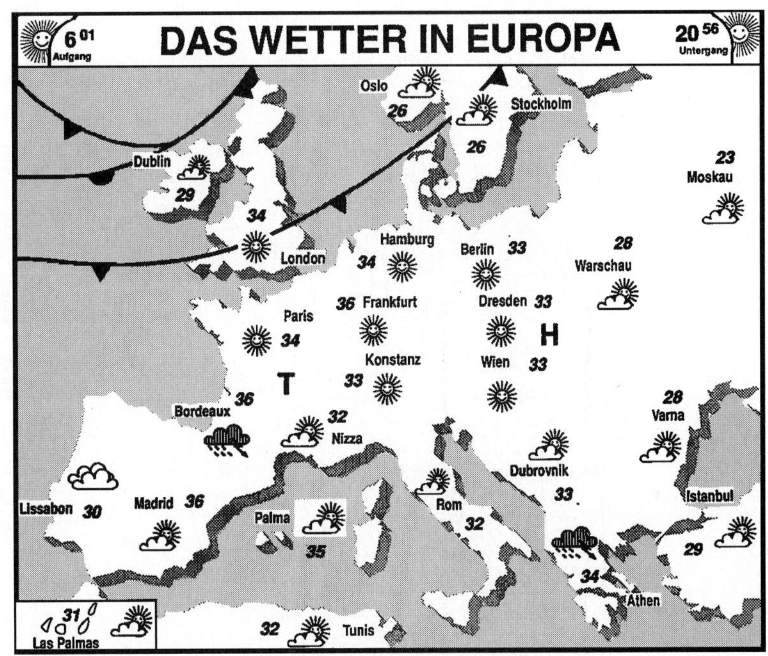

Guess the meaning of **Aufgang** and **Untergang**. What season is this?
Ist es heiß oder kalt? (Die Temperatur ist Celsius!)

Wie ist das Wetter in Berlin?
Ist es Sommer oder Winter?

18 **Gruppenarbeit: In Oslo ist es ...** Describe the weather in the following places.

Wie ist das Wetter in ...

Oslo?

Cannes?

Boston?

Berlin?

Hamburg?

Be sure to recycle **Auf Wiedersehen**, etc., at the end of the class hour.

Stufe 3

Wie viele? (How many?)

Lab Manual
Einführung, The numbers.

Practice 0–20 aloud with students.

Bring in or find in classroom collections of 20 or fewer objects. Point to them and say: **Wie viele sind hier?**

0	null	11	elf
1	eins	12	zwölf
2	zwei	13	dreizehn
3	drei	14	vierzehn
4	vier	15	fünfzehn
5	fünf	16	sechzehn
6	sechs	17	siebzehn
7	sieben	18	achtzehn
8	acht	19	neunzehn
9	neun	20	zwanzig
10	zehn		

If students ask: It is not as idiomatic to use **was** in this question.

Two of these numbers include an area code beginning with 0. When dialing German numbers from abroad, the zero is omitted. For example, to dial the Dortmund number from the U.S., dial 011 (international operator), 49 (country code), then the area code 231 (without zero), and then the local number 82 34 45. 49 is the country code for Germany, 43 for Austria, 41 for Switzerland.

■ 19 ■ Gruppenarbeit: Wie ist die Telefonnummer? (What is the telephone number?) Read these business telephone numbers aloud.

NATURKOST · NATURKOSMETIK
belladonna
BERGMANNSTR. 101
694 3731

mitfahr zentrale
Berlin 15
030-8827606

SCHALLPLATTEN + CD's
ANKAUF · VERKAUF · TAUSCH
Ständiger Barankauf von LP's + CD's (Sammlungen)
LP's ab 4 DM
Sl ab 1 DM
Mo–Fr 12.00–18.30
Sa 10.00–14.00
Bergmannstraße 10
Telefon: 6 93 19 98

Dortmund
0231/82 34 45
82 20 67

EIGENER ABSCHLEPPDIENST
K. Walter
VORM. ZINNEKER
1230 WIEN, BREITENFURTERSTR. 213
804 21 42
Autokosmetik
KAROSSERIE-FACHWERKSTÄTTE
Einbrenn-und Sonderlackierung

Lab Manual Einführung dialogues in Stufe 3.

You may want to teach the pronunciation **zwo** for **zwei** when giving telephone numbers.

■ 20 ■ Kettenreaktion: Wie ist deine Telefonnummer? (Chain reaction: What's your telephone number?) Follow the model. One student asks the next.

BEISPIEL: (Example)
A: Wie ist deine Telefonnummer?
B: Meine Telefonnummer ist ______. Wie ist *deine* Telefonnummer?
C: ______.

Wie viel Uhr ... will be introduced in Kap. 7. Bring in a classroom clock with moveable hands and practice other times.

■ Wie spät ist es bitte? (What time is it, please?)

Es ist drei Uhr.

Es ist Viertel nach sieben.

Es ist Viertel vor zehn.

Es ist ein Uhr. ***or*** Es ist eins.

Es ist elf (Minuten) nach zehn.

Es ist vierzehn vor acht.

The half hour is counted in German in relation to the following full hour, not the preceding hour as in English.

Es ist halb acht.
(literally) *It is halfway to eight.*

„Wie spät ist es?" (Turmuhr [*tower clock*] und Sonnenuhr in Würzburg)

■ 21 ■ Partnerarbeit: Wie spät ist es bitte? Take turns asking each other for the time.

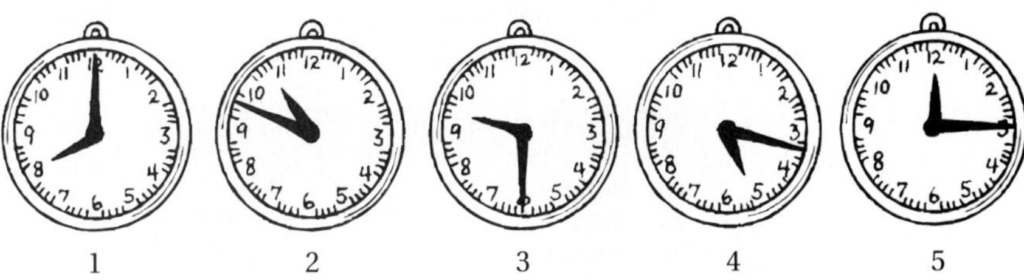

■ Persönliche Fragen (Personal questions)

Write names of other countries on the board as needed.
Expansion: After **Gruppenarbeit**, ask students **Woher kommt er/sie?**

Question words	
woher?	*from where?* (origin)
wo?	*where?* (location)

When you meet people, you usually want to find out some basic facts about them, such as where they come from. Listen to the following dialogue and repeat it after your instructor.

Woher kommst du? connotes *Where were you born?*

The only American states with separate German names are **Kalifornien** and **Pennsylvanien,** and states beginning with **Nord-** or **Süd-,** as in **Südkarolina**.

A:	**Woher kommst du?**	*Where do you come from?*
B:	**Ich komme aus Minnesota.**	*I come from Minnesota.*
A:	**Wo wohnst du jetzt?**	*Where do you live now?*
B:	**Ich wohne jetzt in Kalifornien.**	*I'm living in California now.*

	kommen	*to come*		wohnen	*to live*
ich	komm**e**	*I come*	ich	wohn**e**	*I live*
du	komm**st**	*you come*	du	wohn**st**	*you live*
Sie	komm**en**	*you come*	Sie	wohn**en**	*you live*
er	komm**t**	*he comes*	er	wohn**t**	*he lives*
sie	komm**t**	*she comes*	sie	wohn**t**	*she lives*

■ 22 ■ Gruppenarbeit: Woher? Walk around the classroom and find out what cities, states, or foreign countries your classmates are from. Your instructor can help you with the German names of other countries. Then find out where your classmates live, on campus or otherwise.

Write on board: **in der Stadt / zu Hause / mit Freunden zusammen / auf dem Campus**.

A: Woher kommst du?
B: Ich komme aus ______ .
A: Wo wohnst du jetzt?
B: Ich wohne in Davis Hall.

Question word	
wann?	*when?*

Listen to the dialogue and repeat it after your instructor.

A: Wann hast du Geburtstag?	*When is your birthday?* (literally: *When do you have birthday?*)
B: Ich habe im Januar Geburtstag.	*My birthday is in January.*

	haben		*to have*
ich	**habe**		*I have*
du	**hast**	}	*you have*
Sie	**haben**	}	
er	**hat**		*he has*
sie	**hat**		*she has*

Lab Manual Einführung, The months.

The stress is on the second syllable in **Apríl** and **Augúst**.

Die Monate (The months)

im Januar	im Juli
im Februar	im August
im März	im September
im April	im Oktober
im Mai	im November
im Juni	im Dezember

After **Kettenreaktion**, ask students: **Wann hat er/sie Geburtstag?**

■ 23 ■ Kettenreaktion Find out in what months your classmates were born.

BEISPIEL: A: Wann hast du Geburtstag?
B: Ich habe im _____ Geburtstag. Wann hast *du* Geburtstag?
C: _____ .

Lab Manual Einführung, The sounds of German and Useful classroom expressions.

These sentences are not for active student use at this point. They will become familiar through frequent use.

This is useful classroom vocabulary. You need not memorize these expressions.

■ Useful classroom expressions

Wie sagt man „the book" auf Deutsch?	*How do you say "the book" in German?*
Man sagt „das Buch".	*You say "das Buch."*
Übersetzen Sie bitte.	*Please translate.*
Wiederholen Sie bitte.	*Please repeat.*
Üben wir!	*Let's practice!*
Machen Sie Nummer drei, bitte.	*Please do number three.*
Alle zusammen, bitte.	*All together, please.*
Sie sprechen zu leise.	*You're speaking too softly.*
Sprechen Sie bitte lauter.	*Please speak more loudly.*
Sie sprechen zu schnell.	*You're speaking too fast.*
Sprechen Sie bitte langsamer.	*Please speak more slowly.*
Wie bitte?	*I beg your pardon? What did you say?*
Antworten Sie bitte auf Deutsch!	*Please answer in German.*
Das ist richtig.	*That's correct.*
Das ist falsch.	*That's incorrect.*
Verstehen Sie das?	*Do you understand that?*

Wortschatz (Vocabulary)

The following list contains all the words and expressions from the **Einführung** that you need to know.

Greetings

Grüß Gott! Hello! (*in southern Germany and Austria)*
Guten Abend! Good evening!
Guten Morgen! Good morning!
Guten Tag! Hello!
Hallo! / **Tag!** Hi!

Partings

Auf Wiedersehen! Good-bye!
Bis morgen. Until tomorrow.
Schönes Wochenende! Have a nice weekend!
Danke, gleichfalls! Thanks, same to you!
Tschüss! So long!

Days of the week

Montag Monday
Dienstag Tuesday
Mittwoch Wednesday
Donnerstag Thursday
Freitag Friday
Samstag/Sonnabend Saturday
Sonntag Sunday

Courtesy titles

Frau Mrs./Ms.
Fräulein Miss
Herr Mr.

Question words

wann? when?
was? what?
wer? who?
wie? how?
wie viele? how many?
wo? where?
woher? from where?

Personal questions, feelings, and emotions

Wie heißen Sie? / Wie heißt du? What's your name?
Wie geht es Ihnen? / Wie geht es dir? How are you?
Ich bin guter / schlechter Laune. I'm in a good / bad mood.
Ich bin munter / müde. I'm wide-awake, cheerful / tired.
fit in good shape
krank sick
sauer ticked off, sore
Das freut mich. I'm glad.
Das tut mir Leid. I'm sorry.

Time and place

Wie spät ist es bitte? What time is it, please?
Woher kommst du? Where do you come from?
Wann hast du Geburtstag? When is your birthday?

Classroom words

der Lehrer, die Lehrerin (school) teacher
der Professor, die Professorin professor
der Schüler, die Schülerin pupil, student (*pre-college*)
der Student, die Studentin (university) student
der Bleistift pencil
der Kugelschreiber ballpoint pen
der Radiergummi rubber eraser
der Stuhl chair
der Tisch table
der Wischer blackboard eraser
das Buch book
das Fenster window
das Heft notebook
das Papier paper
das Poster poster
die Kreide chalk
die Landkarte map
die Tafel blackboard
die Tür door
die Uhr clock, watch
die Wand wall

Months of the year

Januar	**Juli**
Februar	**August**
März	**September**
April	**Oktober**
Mai	**November**
Juni	**Dezember**

The weather

Wie ist das Wetter heute? How's the weather today?
Es regnet / schneit. It's raining / snowing.
Es ist herrlich / furchtbar. It's great / terrible.
heiß hot
kalt cold
kühl cool
warm warm
neblig foggy
sonnig sunny
windig windy
wolkig cloudy

Profile of the Federal Republic of Germany

Area:	357,000 square kilometers; 138,000 square miles
Population:	83.5 million, or 234 people per square kilometer (605 per square mile)
Currency:	Deutsche Mark; 1 DM = 100 Pfennige
Major Cities:	Berlin (largest city, official capital, pop. 3.5 million); Bonn (pop. 311,000); Munich (pop. 1.3 million); Frankfurt am Main (pop. 629,000); Hamburg (pop. 1.6 million); Cologne (pop. 1 million); Düsseldorf (pop. 577,000); Leipzig (pop. 500,000); Stuttgart (pop. 581,000); Dresden (pop. 481,000)
Religions:	Protestant: 45%; Catholic: 37%; other: 18%

In 1945 the victorious Allies divided defeated Germany into four zones of occupation: American, British, French, and Soviet. Their original intention was to denazify and reunite Germany. But by 1949 the ideological tensions of the Cold War led to the creation of two German states. The Federal Republic of Germany in the West and the German Democratic Republic in the East existed side by side for 41 years. The reunification of 1990 merged one of the most affluent capitalist countries with one of the most prosperous socialist countries from the Eastern bloc. The former GDR was divided into five new states (*Länder*) of the Federal Republic.

Today, the unified nation has an area slightly smaller than Montana. The Federal Republic is the most populous and economically one of the strongest countries in the European Union.

But the revolutionary changes in Germany are still difficult to assess. Forty years of state ownership and lack of competition left eastern Germany's industry obsolete and unable to compete in the Western marketplace. The infrastructure of the former GDR is being modernized and its industry privatized, a process that has caused inflation in the entire country and high rates of unemployment in the former East German workforce. Unification has thus come at a high price to German taxpayers. Germans east and west must continue to make economic sacrifices to resolve their differences and achieve genuine national unity.

Assign **Almanach** as homework. Devote 5–10 minutes of class to a discussion of it in English. Ask students what they associate with "Germany." What information new to them did the **Almanach** contain? Have them use the statistics to contrast Germany with their native countries. (**USA** area: 9,372,614 sq. km.; population: 254.1 million; religions: 52% Protestant, 26.2% Catholic; **Canada** area: 9,970,610 sq. km.; population: 26.9 million; religions: 46.5% Catholic, 41.2% Protestant.

Wie geht es Ihnen?

Communicative Goals

- Making statements
- Asking yes/no questions
- Asking for information: when, why, who, where, what, etc.

Cultural Goal

- Understanding the social implications of German forms of address

Chapter Outline

- **Lyrik zum Vorlesen**
  Kinderreime, Zungenbrecher
- **Grammatik**
  Personal pronouns
  Verbs: Infinitive and present tense
  Noun gender and pronoun agreement
  Noun plurals
  Nominative case
  The sentence: German word order
  The flavoring particle *ja*
- **Lesestück**
  Wie sagt man „you" auf Deutsch?
- **Situationen aus dem Alltag**
  Sie oder *du*?
- **Almanach**
  Where Is German Spoken?

Introduce students to the structure of each chapter. Leaf through Kap. 1 together, pointing out section headings and what they mean. Repeat German rubrics together.

Dialoge

(Dialogues)

Lab Manual Kap. (Kapitel) 1, Dialoge, Fragen, Hören Sie gut zu!, Üb. (Übung) zur Aussprache [**ch**].

In colloquial German **guten Morgen!**, **auf Wiedersehen!**, and **guten Tag!** are often shortened to **Morgen!**, **Wiedersehen!**, and **Tag!**

If students ask about word order of **kommen ... zurück**, separable prefixes are introduced in Kap. 5.

One or two of the dialogues can be assigned for memorization. Students can then say them in pairs in class (books closed).

Words can be grouped for brief pronunciation practice, e.g., **September**, **Sonne**, **Suppe** (voiced **s**); **Tag**, **Kind** (unvoiced final consonant); **typisch**, **Tschüss** (**ü**).

In Eile

HERR LEHMANN: Guten Morgen, Frau Hauser!
FRAU HAUSER: Morgen, Herr Lehmann. Entschuldigung, aber ich bin in Eile. Ich fliege um elf nach Wien.
HERR LEHMANN: Wann kommen Sie wieder zurück?
FRAU HAUSER: Am Mittwoch – also dann, auf Wiedersehen!
HERR LEHMANN: Wiedersehen! Gute Reise!

Die Mensa

KARIN: Tag, Michael!
MICHAEL: Hallo, Karin! Wie ist die Suppe heute?
KARIN: Sie ist ganz gut. – Übrigens, arbeitest du viel im Moment?
MICHAEL: Nein, nicht sehr viel. Warum fragst du?
KARIN: Ich gehe heute Abend zu Horst. Du auch?
MICHAEL: Ja, natürlich.
KARIN: Prima! Also tschüss, bis dann.

Typisch für September

FRAU BACHMANN: Guten Tag, Frau Kuhn! Wie geht's?
FRAU KUHN: Tag, Frau Bachmann! Sehr gut, danke, und Ihnen?
FRAU BACHMANN: Danke, auch gut. Was machen die Kinder heute?
FRAU KUHN: Sie spielen draußen, das Wetter ist ja so schön.
FRAU BACHMANN: Ja, endlich scheint die Sonne. Aber vielleicht regnet es morgen wieder.
FRAU KUHN: Das ist typisch für September.

„Wie ist die Suppe heute?"

Wortschatz 1 (Vocabulary 1)

Verben (Verbs)

arbeiten to work
fliegen to fly
fragen to ask
gehen to go; to walk
kommen to come
machen to make; to do
regnen to rain
scheinen to shine; to seem
sein to be
spielen to play
wohnen to live; to dwell

In this book, nouns are grouped by gender for easier learning. Always learn the article and the plural along with the singular of each noun. Don't just learn **Kind** = *child,* but rather **das Kind**, **die Kinder**.

Substantive (Nouns)

der **Herr, -en** gentleman
  Herr Lehmann Mr. Lehmann
der **Morgen, -** morning
der **September** September
der **Tag, -e** day

das **Büro, -s** office
das **Kind, -er** child
das **Wetter** weather
(das)**Wien** Vienna

die **Frau, -en** woman; wife
  Frau Kuhn Mrs./Ms. Kuhn
die **Mensa** university cafeteria
die **Sonne** sun
die **Straße, -n** street, road
die **Suppe, -n** soup

City names are neuter in German but are seldom used with the article. In such cases, the article is given in parentheses in the **Wortschatz**.

Adjektive und Adverbien (Adjectives and adverbs)

auch also, too
da there
dann then
draußen outside
endlich finally
gut good; well
  ganz gut pretty good; pretty well
heute Abend this evening, tonight
hier here
morgen tomorrow
natürlich natural(ly); of course
schön beautiful(ly)
sehr very
typisch typical(ly)
vielleicht maybe, perhaps
wieder again

German has no equivalent for the English adverbial ending *-ly*. For example, the German word **natürlich** can mean both *natural* and *naturally* (similarly, **gut** means both *good* and *well*).

Andere Vokabeln (Other words)

aber but
also well
bis until; by
  bis dann until then; by then
danke thanks
für for
in in
ja yes; *untranslatable "flavoring particle," see p. 36.*
nach to (*with cities and countries*)
nein no
nicht not
übrigens by the way
um (*prep.*) at (*with expressions of time*)
und (*conj.*) and
usw. (= **und so weiter**) etc. (= and so forth)

There is a complete list of abbreviations on p. 488.

viel (*pron.*) much, a lot
warum? why?
wie (*conj.*) how; like, as
zu (*prep.*) to (*with people*); too (*as in* "too much")
zurück back

Nützliche Ausdrücke (Useful expressions)

am Mittwoch (Donnerstag usw.) on Wednesday (Thursday, etc.)
Entschuldigung! Pardon me! Excuse me!
Gute Reise! (Have a) good trip!
im Moment at the moment
in Eile in a hurry
Prima! Terrific! Great!

Gegensätze (Opposites)

gut ≠ schlecht good ≠ bad
hier ≠ da here ≠ there
schön ≠ hässlich beautiful ≠ ugly
der Tag ≠ die Nacht day ≠ night
viel ≠ wenig much, a lot ≠ not much, little

Study hint: learn antonyms in pairs. They are all active vocabulary.

Mit anderen Worten (In other words)

prima = sehr gut
wunderschön = sehr schön

Be sure to integrate phonetic practice from the tape program and **Laboratory Manual**. We suggest systematic overview and classroom practice of German phonetics during the first two weeks, then continuing focus on difficult sounds throughout the course. (The tape program for Kap. 1 focuses on front vs. back **ch**.) Include classroom phonetics practice during the first two days of work on each new chapter.

In a Hurry

MR. L: Good morning, Ms. Hauser.
MS. H: Morning, Mr. Lehmann. Forgive me, but I'm in a hurry. I'm flying to Vienna at eleven.
MR. L: When are you coming back again?
MS. H: On Wednesday. Well then, good-bye.
MR. L: Bye. Have a good trip!

English translations are idiomatic, not always word-for-word.

The University Cafeteria

K: Hi, Michael!
M: Hello, Karin! How's the soup today?
K: It's pretty good. By the way, are you working a lot at the moment?
M: No, not very much. Why do you ask?
K: I'm going to Horst's tonight. You too?
M: Yes, of course.
K: Great! Well, so long until then.

Typical for September

MRS. B: Hello, Mrs. Kuhn. How are you?
MRS. K: Hi, Mrs. Bachmann. Very well, thanks, and you?
MRS. B: Thanks, I'm fine too. What are the kids doing today?
MRS. K: They're playing outside—the weather is so nice.
MRS. B: Yes, the sun is finally shining. But maybe it will rain again tomorrow.
MRS. K: That is typical for September.

Variationen (Variations)

Since instructors pose the **Persönliche Fragen** to the students, the questions are in the **Sie**-form throughout the book. You may choose to use the **du**-form.

■ A ■ Persönliche Fragen (Personal questions)

1. Wo wohnen Sie?
2. Wie geht es Ihnen heute?
3. Arbeiten Sie viel im Moment?
4. Was machen Sie heute Abend?

Asking for information is a communicative goal.

■ B ■ Partnerarbeit (Work with a partner)

Now ask each other the same questions as in **Variation A**. Use the **du**-form.

■ C ■ Partnerarbeit: Wann fliegst du?

The clock faces show departure times from the Frankfurt airport. Ask each other when you're flying to various places.

Vary times on your own classroom clock. Vary questions: **Wann arbeiten Sie heute Abend? Wann gehen Sie zu Karin? Wann kommen Sie zurück?**

BEISPIEL: Wann fliegst du nach Sydney?
Ich fliege um halb acht.

1. nach Prag

2. nach Moskau

3. nach Kopenhagen

4. nach Madrid

5. nach Toronto

6. nach Singapur

Review greetings from **Einführung**. When doing with students, recycle **Danke, gleichfalls.** After **I–S** practice, may be done **S1–S2**, with partners doing as many simple exchanges as possible.

D **Übung** (Exercise) Respond to these greetings and farewells.

1. Guten Morgen!
2. Wie geht es Ihnen?
3. Guten Tag!
4. Auf Wiedersehen!
5. Gute Reise!
6. Tschüss, bis dann.
7. Tag!
8. Hallo!
9. Schönes Wochenende!

E **Übung: Und Sie?** To each question, respond that you feel the same way.

If students ask why they may not say **Ich bin auch** (*I am too*), explain that the copulative (linking) verb **sein** in German *must* have a predicate nominative to complete its meaning.

BEISPIEL: Richard ist heute guter Laune. Und Sie?
Ja, *er* ist guter Laune und *ich* bin es auch.

1. Maria ist fit. Und Sie?
2. Herr Schrödinger ist krank. Und Sie?
3. Frau Bachmann ist munter. Und Sie?
4. Christian ist guter Laune. Und Sie?
5. Wir sind schlechter Laune. Und Sie?
6. Ich bin heute sauer. Und Sie?

Lyrik zum Vorlesen (Poetry for reading aloud)

In each chapter this section presents some short selections of original German poetry (**Lyrik**), rhymes, or song texts for your enjoyment. Read them aloud. Don't worry about understanding everything. The emphasis here is on the *sound* of German.

Lab Manual Kap. 1, Lyrik zum Vorlesen.

Kinderreime (Children's rhymes)

Traditional counting-out rhymes

Eins zwei drei,
du bist frei°. — free
Vier fünf sechs,
du bist weg°. — out
Sieben acht neun,
du musst's sein°. — you are it

Ich heiße Peter, du heißt Paul.
Ich bin fleißig°, du bist faul°. — hard-working / lazy

Children's alphabet rhyme

A b c d e f und g,
h i j k l m n o p,
q r s t u v w,
x y z und o weh°,
jetzt kann ich das ABC°.

o weh = oh my
now I know the ABC

Zungenbrecher°

Tongue twisters

Ulm lies on the Danube River in the southern state of Baden-Württemberg. Its famous Gothic church has the highest spire in the world at 161.6 meters (530 ft.).

In Ulm, um Ulm°
und um Ulm herum°.

In Ulm, around Ulm,
and round about Ulm.

Fischers Fritz fischt frische Fische.
frische Fische fischt Fischers Fritz°.

Fischer's (boy) Fritz fishes fresh fish.
Fresh fish is what Fischer's Fritz fishes.

Grammatik

(Grammar)

Emphasize stress: **Grammátik.**

Personal pronouns

Personal pronouns as the subject of a sentence:

	Singular		Plural	
1st person	**ich**	*I*	**wir**	*we*
2nd person	**du** **Sie**	*you* (familiar) *you* (formal)	**ihr** **Sie**	you (familiar) *you* (formal)
3rd person	**er** **es** **sie**	*he, it* *it* *she, it*	**sie**	*they*

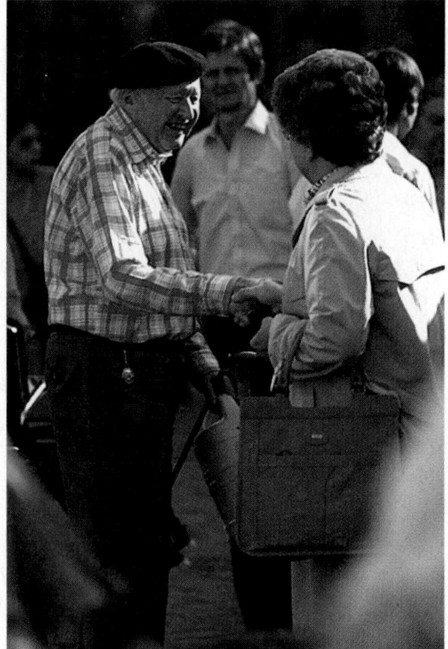

„Tag, Frau Breitenkamp! Wie geht es Ihnen?"

■ The three ways to say *you* in German

Understanding the social implications of German forms of address is the cultural goal of this chapter.

Students will get continual practice with all 3 forms if **I–S** and **S–I** exchanges use **Sie** and **S–S** exchanges use **du/ihr**.

German has three words for the subject pronoun *you*: **du**, **ihr**, and **Sie**.

The familiar pronouns **du** (*singular*) and **ihr** (*plural*) are used when addressing children, family members, close friends, animals, and the deity. Members of certain groups (students, blue-collar workers, soldiers, athletes) converse among themselves almost exclusively with **du** and **ihr**. People on a first-name basis usually use **du** with each other. In conversation with German speakers, allow them to establish which form is used.

The formal **Sie** is used when addressing one or more adults who are not close friends of the speaker. In writing, **Sie** meaning *you* is distinguished from **sie** meaning *they* by always beginning with a capital letter.

The pronoun **ich** is not capitalized except when it is the first word in a sentence.

Verbs: Infinitive and present tense

If students ask: A verb is a word expressing an action (**fliegen**), a condition (**sein**), or a mental state (**meinen**).

■ The infinitive

German verbs are found in a dictionary in the infinitive form. In English the infinitive is usually preceded by *to*.

to play *to hike*

In German, the infinitive consists of the verb stem plus the ending **-en** or **-n**.

spiel-	**spielen**	*to play*
wander-	**wandern**	*to hike*

■ Present-tense endings

A German verb has various endings in the present tense, depending on its subject.

Das Kind spiel**t** draußen.	*The child plays outside.*
Die Kinder spiel**en** draußen.	*The children play outside.*

In order to form the present tense of a German verb, first find the stem by dropping the infinitive ending **-en** or **-n**:

komm- ~~en~~

Then add the personal endings:

Stem + Ending		Present Tense		
ich	komm-**e**	ich	komme	*I come*
du	komm-**st**	du	kommst	*you come* (familiar singular)
er, es, sie	komm-**t**	er, es, sie	kommt	*he, it, she comes*
wir	komm-**en**	wir	kommen	*we come*
ihr	komm-**t**	ihr	kommt	*you come* (familiar plural)
sie, Sie	komm-**en**	sie	kommen	*they come*
		Sie	kommen	*you come* (formal singular and plural)

The verb ending will help you distinguish between **sie** = *she* (**sie kommt**) and **sie**, **Sie** = *they*, *you* (**sie**, **Sie kommen**). The verb ending for third-person plural and the polite *you*-form is always the same. From now on they will be listed together in verb paradigms: **sie**, **Sie kommen**.

Lab Manual Kap. 1, Üb. 1, 3; Var. (Variationen) zu Üb. 1, 3.

Workbook Kap. 1, A, B.

To distinguish **sie** (*she*) from **sie** (*they*) without resorting to English, point to a female student or to a group of students. Var.: **Ich gehe/spiele morgen.** To elicit formal **Sie**, point to yourself.

Prepare by writing on board **Wo wohnen Sie?** and then asking students. After the chain has gone on for a while, ask students who have not yet participated: **Wo wohnt er/sie?**, pointing to students who have already answered.

■ 1 ■ Übung: Wer kommt morgen? Say who is coming tomorrow, using the pronouns cued.

BEISPIEL: ich
Ich komme morgen.

1. er
2. Sie (*you*)
3. wir
4. sie (*they*)
5. sie (*she*)
6. du
7. ich
8. ihr

■ 2 ■ Kettenreaktion: Wo wohnst du? Say where you live and then ask the next student.

BEISPIEL: Ich wohne in Atlanta. Wo wohnst du?
Ich wohne in ________ .

■ Regular variations in personal endings

Verbs with stems ending in **-d**, **-t**, or a consonant cluster such as **-gn** require an **-e-** before the **du**, **er**, and **ihr** endings to make them pronounceable.

arbeiten	stem: **arbeit-**			**regnen** stem: **regn-**
ich	arbeite	wir	arbeiten	
du	arbeit**e**st	ihr	arbeit**e**t	es regn**e**t
er, es, sie	arbeit**e**t	sie, Sie	arbeiten	

■ **3** ■ **Übung: Wer arbeitet heute?** Tell who is working today, using the cued pronoun or name.

BEISPIEL: wir
Wir arbeiten heute.

Ask students: **Arbeiten Sie heute?** Then tell them to ask each other: **Arbeitest du heute?**

1. ich
2. Herr Lehmann
3. sie (*they*)
4. du
5. ihr
6. Sie (*you*)
7. wir
8. Michael

■ **4** ■ **Gruppenarbeit: Was machst du heute? (*4 Studenten*)** Ask each other what you're doing today.

A: Was machst du heute, Katrin?
B: Ich fliege nach Wien. Was machst du heute?
C: Ich ______ . Was machst du heute?

To emphasize lack of progressive forms in German, ask students for German equivalents of short English cues derived from the dialogues: I am flying to Vienna. When are you coming back? Are you working? I'm going to Horst's. Are they playing outside?

To practice present tense with future meaning, add *tomorrow* to the sentences in the previous annotation.

■ English and German present tense compared

German present tense is equivalent to three English forms:

ich gehe { *I go* / *I am going* / *I do go* }

■ Present tense with future meaning

In German the present tense often expresses future meaning, especially when another element in the sentence makes the future meaning clear.

Ich fliege um elf nach Wien.	*I'm flying to Vienna at eleven.*
Mittwoch bin ich wieder zurück.	*I'll be back Wednesday.*

Note that English often uses the present progressive (*I'm flying*) for the same purpose.

Because students infrequently use **ihr** in class, it needs practice. Review and write on board adjectives describing feelings from page 10. In groups of three, students take turns asking, **Seid ihr ______ ?** Other two respond.

■ The verb *sein*

Like *to be* in English, the verb **sein** is irregular; its forms must be memorized.

ich	**bin**	*I am*	wir	**sind**	*we are*
du	**bist**	*you are*	ihr	**seid**	*you are*
er, es, sie	**ist**	*he, it, she is*	sie, Sie	**sind**	*they, you are*

Prima leben und sparen

Noun gender and pronoun agreement

You have learned that German has three genders for nouns, shown by the definite article (**der, das, die**). When a pronoun replaces a noun (*the chair* = *it*), it must have the same gender.

Wo ist **der** Stuhl?	**Er** ist hier.	*It's here.*
Wo ist **das** Buch?	**Es** ist hier.	*It's here.*
Wo ist **die** Tafel?	**Sie** ist hier.	*It's here.*

Note that **er**, **es**, and **sie** can all mean *it*.

Note also the similarities between the definite article and its corresponding pronoun.

de**r** Stuhl → **er**
da**s** Buch → **es**
die Tafel → **sie**

Plural forms do not show gender. The definite article **die** is used with all plural nouns, and the pronoun **sie** replaces all plural nouns.

Wo sind **die** Stühle?
Wo sind **die** Bücher? } **Sie** sind hier. *They are here.*
Wo sind **die** Tafeln?

Lab Manual Kap. 1, Üb. 5; Var. zur Üb. 5.

Workbook Kap. 1, C, D.

5 **Übung** Answer the questions affirmatively. Use a pronoun.

BEISPIEL: Ist Rolf heute guter Laune?
Ja, er ist heute guter Laune.

1. Ist das Buch gut?
2. Ist Frau Schmidt sehr müde?
3. Spielen die Kinder draußen?
4. Ist das Wetter typisch für September?
5. Scheint die Sonne heute?
6. Sind Karin und Michael Studenten?
7. Ist die Suppe gut?
8. Ist der Tag schön?

6 **Partnerarbeit: Hier oder da?** Partner A asks where the things in the left-hand column are. Partner B answers with the correct pronoun, pointing to the object. Reverse roles for the right-hand column.

BEISPIEL: A: Wo ist die Tafel?
B: Sie ist da.

das Buch	der Radiergummi
das Heft	das Fenster
die Tür	der Professor/die Professorin
der Bleistift	der Tisch
die Wand	der Stuhl
die Landkarte	das Poster

Here are the nouns you learned in the **Einführung** with their plurals:
der Lehrer, - / die Lehrerin, -nen
der Professor, -en / die Professorin, -nen
der Schüler, - / die Schülerin, -nen
der Student, -en / die Studentin, -nen
der Bleistift, -e
das Buch, ¨er
das Fenster, -
das Heft, -e
der Kugelschreiber, -
das Poster, -
der Stuhl, ¨e
die Tafel, -n
der Tisch, -e
die Tür, -en
die Uhr, -en
die Wand, ¨e

Noun plurals

The most common plural ending for English nouns is *-s* or *-es*: chair, chair*s*; dish, dish*es*. Some nouns have irregular plurals: man, *men*; mouse, *mice*; child, *children*; sheep, *sheep*.

German has a much greater variety of plural forms. There is no one basic rule, nor is any one form the most common. The following list gives examples of all the plural forms.

	Singular	*Plural*
No change	der Lehrer	die Lehrer
Umlaut added to stem vowel	die Mutter	die M**ü**tter
Add ending **-e**	der Tisch	die Tisch**e**
Umlaut + ending **-e**	der Stuhl	die St**ü**hl**e**
Add ending **-er**	das Kind	die Kind**er**
Umlaut + ending **-er**	das Buch	die B**ü**ch**er**
Add ending **-en**	die Frau	die Frau**en**
Add ending **-n**	die Straße	die Straße**n**
Add ending **-s**	das Büro	die Büro**s**

If students ask: A noun is a word that names a person (**Frau Braun**, **Kind**, **Hermann**), a place (**Wien**), a thing or animal (**Sonne**, **Tag**), or an idea or quality (**Solidarität**).
Review classroom objects from **Einführung**, p. 6, and teach their plurals.

Dictionaries and vocabulary lists customarily use an abbreviation to indicate the plural. An umlaut above the hyphen indicates that the stem (stressed) vowel is umlauted in the plural.

Dictionary entry	*You must learn*
der **Lehrer, -**	der **Lehrer**, die **Lehrer**
die **Mutter, ¨**	die **Mutter**, die **Mütter**
der **Tag, -e**	der **Tag**, die **Tage**
der **Stuhl, ¨e**	der **Stuhl**, die **Stühle**

Lab Manual Kap. 1, Üb. 7, 8.

Workbook Kap. 1, E.

7 Übung Look at the following nouns and say aloud both the singular and plural forms with their articles.

1. das Kind, -er
2. das Büro, -s
3. der Tisch, -e
4. die Mutter, ¨
5. die Tafel, -n
6. die Straße, -n
7. der Stuhl, ¨e
8. die Frau, -en

Turn to the German–English Vocabulary at end of book, pp. 488–508, for more practice with plurals.

8 Übung Make the subjects plural. Change the verbs accordingly.

BEISPIEL: *Der Herr kommt* um elf.
Die Herren kommen um elf.

1. Das Büro ist sehr schön.
2. Die Frau fliegt nach Wien.
3. Das Kind kommt heute Abend.
4. Die Straße ist sehr schön.
5. Das Buch ist gut.
6. Der Lehrer arbeitet morgen im Büro.
7. Der Tag ist schön.

Nominative case

The definite article in German, unlike English *the*, shows the *gender* (masculine, neuter, or feminine), *number* (singular or plural), and *case* of the noun it is used with. As a result, German has many forms that all correspond to *the* in English.

Emphasize vowel length in **den** (as opposed to **denn**). Both words are active vocabulary in Kap. 2.

The case of a noun or a pronoun signals its function in the sentence. German has four cases: nominative, accusative, dative, and genitive. The article used with the noun shows its case.

Der Schüler fragt den Lehrer.	*The pupil asks the teacher.*
Der Lehrer fragt **den** Schüler.	*The teacher asks the pupil.*

Nominative case		*Accusative case*
der Schüler		**den** Schüler
subject	vs.	*direct object*
person asking		*person being asked*

This chapter uses only the nominative case, which is the case for the subject of a sentence and for a predicate nominative (see page 33).

■ Definite article in the nominative case

You have already learned the definite articles (*the*) in the nominative:

	Singular	*Plural*
masculine	**der** Mann	**die** Männer
neuter	**das** Kind	**die** Kinder
feminine	**die** Frau	**die** Frauen

■ Indefinite article in the nominative case

Like the definite article, the indefinite article (*a, an*) shows the gender, number, and case of the noun it is used with. Here are the indefinite articles in the nominative:

	Singular	*Plural*
masculine	**ein** Mann	Männer
neuter	**ein** Kind	Kinder
feminine	**eine** Frau	Frauen

Note: Masculine and neuter singular indefinite articles are identical in the nominative: **ein** Mann, **ein** Kind. The indefinite article has no plural:

Ein Kind ist hier. → Kinder sind hier.

The personal pronouns you have learned in this chapter (**ich**, **du**, *etc.*) are all in the nominative case.

Add plurals: **Was sind das?** Teach students to answer: **Das sind ...**

■ 9 ■ Übung: Was ist das? Say what your instructor is pointing to. Use the indefinite article.

BEISPIEL: PROFESSORIN: Was ist das?
STUDENTIN: Das ist **ein** Fenster.

Predicate nominative is confusing for students, who often write sentences like **Herr Braun ist einen Lehrer.** Explain that **sein** is a linking verb that functions like an equal sign, with nouns on each side in the nominative.

■ Use of the nominative case

The subject of the sentence is always in the nominative case. Notice that the subject does not have to come at the beginning of the sentence.

Der Herr ist in Eile.	*The gentleman is in a hurry.*
Endlich kommt **die Suppe**.	*The soup is finally coming.*
Morgen fliegt **sie** zurück.	*She's flying back tomorrow.*

Other linking verbs (**bleiben** *to remain*; **heißen** *to be called*; **werden** *to become*) also take the predicate nominative. You will learn them later.

A predicate nominative is a noun that refers to the same person or thing as the subject of the sentence. It follows the subject and the linking verb **sein**.

Das ist **Frau Schmidt**.	*That is Mrs. Schmidt.*
Paul ist **ein Kind**.	*Paul is a child.*

Remember to always use nominative case after the verb **sein**.

Lab Manual Kap. 1, Var. zur Üb. 10.

Workbook Kap. 1, F.

■ **10** ■ **Gruppenspiel** (Group game): **Was ist das? Wer ist das?** One student leads the game. The rest are divided into two teams. The leader points to an object or a person in the room and asks:

Wer / Was ist das?
Das ist ein(e) / der / das / die ________.

Teams answer alternately. The team with the most correct answers wins.

The sentence: German word order

Making statements is a communicative goal.

If students ask: A sentence must contain a subject and an inflected verb.

■ Statements: Verb-second word order

In declarative sentences (statements) in English, the subject almost always comes immediately before the verb phrase.

subject verb
We **are going** to Richard's tonight.

Other elements may precede the subject-verb combination:

Tonight **we are going** to Richard's.

In German statements, only the verb has a fixed position. *The verb is always the second element.*

1	2	3	4
Wir	**gehen**	heute Abend	zu Richard.

This is an ironclad rule that must be learned well. If an element other than the subject begins the sentence, the verb *remains* in second position and the subject then *follows* the verb. Note the difference from English, where the subject always precedes the verb.

You may want to tell students that personal pronouns come either in first position or immediately after the verb.

1	2	3	4
Heute Abend	**gehen**	wir	zu Richard.
Zu Richard	**gehen**	wir	heute Abend.

A time phrase (**heute Abend**) or a prepositional phrase (**zu Richard**) may consist of two or more words, but counts as *one* grammatical element.

Initial **ja**, **nein**, **und**, and **aber** do *not* count as first elements.

0	1	2	3
Ja,	wir	gehen	zu Richard.
Aber	wir	gehen	zu Richard.

First position is generally used to restate what's being talked about. A new element with information value—the answer to a question, for instance—is usually placed at the end of the statement.

Was machen wir?	Wir gehen **zu Claudia**.
Was machen wir heute Abend?	Heute Abend **gehen wir zu Claudia**.
Wann gehen wir zu Claudia?	Zu Claudia gehen wir **heute Abend**.

Workbook Kap. 1, G.

■ **11** ■ **Übung** Restate the sentences, beginning with the word or phrase in italics.

BEISPIEL: Ich arbeite *übrigens* viel.
Übrigens arbeite ich viel.

1. Die Lehrerin geht *morgen* zu Frau Bachmann.
2. Die Sonne scheint *endlich* wieder.
3. Es regnet *heute*.
4. Wir fliegen *um elf* nach Wien.
5. Das ist *vielleicht* die Straße.
6. Ich arbeite viel *im Moment*.
7. Die Suppe ist *heute* ganz gut.
8. Es regnet *natürlich* viel.

■ Questions

Asking yes/no questions and asking for information are communicative goals.

A humorous equivocation in German is **jein**: *"yes and no."*

There are two main types of questions in German:

- Yes/no questions are answered by **ja** or **nein**. In a yes/no question, the verb is always the first element.

Ist Andrea hier?	*Is Andrea here?*
Arbeitet sie in Berlin?	*Does she work in Berlin?*
Kommst du wieder zurück?	*Are you coming back again?*

- Questions asking for information start with a question word (*what, how, when, etc.*) and have the same verb-second word order as statements.

1	2		
Was	macht	er?	*What is he doing?*
Wie	geht	es Ihnen?	*How are you?*
Wann	kommen	Sie wieder zurück?	*When are you coming back again?*

Wohin is introduced in Kap. 3.

Here are some question words:

wann	*when*	**Wann** kommt sie zurück?
warum	*why*	**Warum** fragst du?
was	*what*	**Was** macht er?
wer	*who*	**Wer** ist das?
wie	*how*	**Wie** geht es dir?
wo	*where*	**Wo** wohnen Sie?
woher	*from where*	**Woher** kommt ihr?

Do not confuse **wer** (*who*) and **wo** (*where*)!

Lab Manual Kap. 1, Üb. 12.

Workbook Kap. 1, H, I, J.

Next stage: Have students generate their own yes/no questions for each other.

■ **12** ■ **Übung** Change these statements to yes/no questions.

BEISPIEL: Stefan arbeitet in Stuttgart.
Arbeitet Stefan in Stuttgart?

1. Das ist typisch für September.
2. Ihr geht wieder zu Karin.
3. Es regnet.
4. Herr Hauser fliegt nach Berlin.
5. Frau Kuhn kommt auch.
6. Du arbeitest viel im Moment.
7. Er ist sehr in Eile.
8. Der Herr kommt am Mittwoch zurück.

■ **13** ■ **Übung** Ask the questions for which the following statements are answers:

BEISPIEL: Das ist der Professor.
Wer ist das?

1. Er fliegt um elf.
2. Die Lehrer sind im Büro.
3. Das ist Frau Bachmann.
4. Das ist die Mensa.
5. Die Suppe ist gut, danke.
6. Sie kommt aus Deutschland.

■ Time before place

In German, adverbs like **heute** and adverbial phrases like **nach Wien** *must* come in the sequence *time before place*. The usual sequence in English is exactly the reverse: *place before time*.

	time	place		place	time
Sie fliegt	morgen	nach Wien.	*She's flying to*	*Vienna*	*tomorrow.*
Wir gehen	heute Abend	zu Horst.	*We're going to*	*Horst's*	*tonight.*

Next stage: Have students generate their own questions.

■ **14** ■ **Übung: Heute oder morgen?** Answer with a complete sentence, using either **heute** or **morgen**.

BEISPIEL: Wann gehen Sie zu Stefanie?
Ich gehe heute zu Stefanie.

1. Wann fliegt Stefan nach Wien?
2. Wann geht Frau Bachmann zu Frau Kuhn?
3. Wann spielen die Kinder draußen?
4. Wann kommt Herr Lehmann zurück?

The flavoring particle ja

German adds various kinds of emphasis to sentences by using intensifying words known as "flavoring particles." These can seldom be directly translated into English, but it is important to become familiar with them and understand the intensity, nuance, or "flavor" they add to a sentence.

One flavoring particle frequently used in declarative sentences (i.e., statements) is **ja**. As a flavoring particle, **ja** does not mean *yes*, but rather adds the sense of *after all, really*.

In the third dialogue at the beginning of this chapter, Frau Kuhn says about her children:

Sie spielen draußen, das Wetter ist **ja** so schön.	*They're playing outside—the weather really is so beautiful.*

The flavoring particle **ja** is usually placed immediately after the verb and personal pronouns. Here is how **ja** might be added to some other sentences from the dialogues:

Ich bin **ja** in Eile.	*I'm in a hurry, after all.*
Ich gehe **ja** heute Abend zu Horst.	*I'm going to Horst's tonight, you know.*

Vor dem Lesen (Before the reading)

Tipps zum Lesen und Lernen (Tips for reading and studying)

■ **Tipps zum Vokabelnlernen** (Tips for learning vocabulary)

The feminine suffix ***-in*** You've learned that German has two different nouns to distinguish between a male and a female.

Professor/Professorin	Lehrer/Lehrerin
Schüler/Schülerin	Partner/Partnerin
Student/Studentin	

If students ask: The titles **Frau Professor** and **Frau Doktor** do not show **-in** ending, but: **Sie ist Professorin.**

The suffix **-in** always denotes the female, and its plural is always **-innen**.

-in	*-innen*
die Studentin	die Studentinnen

■ **Partnerarbeit: Wie heißt der Mann, wie heißt die Frau?** With a partner, fill in the blanks. Say the words aloud as you write them.

Note the stress shift: **Profes'sor / Professo'rin.**

Mann	*eine Frau?*	*zwei Frauen?*
1. Amerikaner	*Amerikanerin*	*Amerikanerinnen*
2. Tourist	______	______
3. Nachbar (*neighbor*)	______	______
4. Lehrer	______	______
5. Professor	______	______
6. Schüler	______	______
7. Student	______	______
8. Partner	______	______

Lab Manual Kap. 1, Üb. zur Betonung.

■ Leicht zu merken (Easy to remember)

Leicht zu merken vocabulary is not used actively in drills or exercises. Although it will not be glossed in the readings, it *does* appear in both glossaries at the end of the book. Practice pronunciation with students. Get them used to the stress patterns of these cognates. Remind them that **formell** can mean either *formal* (*adj.*) or *formally* (*adv.*).

German has many words that look so much like their English equivalents that you can easily guess their meanings. Both languages have borrowed many of these words from Latin or French. When such words occur in the readings, they are previewed in this special section called **Leicht zu merken**. If the German word is stressed on a different syllable than the English, this will be indicated to the right. You should have no trouble guessing the meanings of these cognates:

formell	for<u>mell</u>
die **Solidarität**	Solidari<u>tät</u>
der **Tourist**	Tour<u>ist</u>

These pre-reading exercises help you to acquire the skill of reading a text in a foreign language. Always work through them carefully before beginning to read the **Lesestück**. The most valuable technique is *re*-reading a foreign language text as many times as possible.

Preview reading before assigning it as homework. Walk students through these reading tips.

■ Einstieg in den Text (Getting into the text)

Here are some tips to help you get the most out of the reading (**Lesestück**) in each chapter.

- Read the title. How does it anticipate the text? The title "Wie sagt man *you* auf Deutsch?," for example, lets you know that the text is about the various forms of second-person address. You have already used these.
- Read out loud the new active vocabulary for the reading (**Wortschatz 2**). Try to identify similarities between English and German forms that will help you remember the words; for example, **grüßen** (*greet*), **Haus** (*house*), **Gruppe** (*group*); **freundlich** (*friendly*), **oft** (*often*).
- Read the text once aloud without referring back to the vocabulary. Do not try to translate as you read. Your purpose is to get a rough idea of content from the key words you recognize in each paragraph. For example, in the first paragraph of the following reading, you will recognize the words **Touristen**, **Deutschland**, and **Amerikaner**. A good working assumption is that the paragraph deals with tourists in Germany.
- Once you have a general idea of the content of each paragraph, read the text at least one more time, again without trying to translate. Your objective this time is to begin to understand the text on the sentence level. The marginal glosses (marked by the degree sign°) will help you to understand words and phrases not for active use.
- Read and try to answer the **Nach dem Lesen** questions that follow the reading. Refer back to the text only if necessary.

Wortschatz 2

Verben

bedeuten to mean, signify
 Was bedeutet das? What does that mean?
duzen to address someone with **du**
grüßen to greet, say hello
meinen to be of the opinion, think
sagen to say; to tell
siezen to address someone with **Sie**
(stimmen) das stimmt that's right, that's true
studieren to attend a university; to study (*a subject*); to major in

Substantive

der **Amerikaner, -** American (*m.*)
der **Deutsche, -n** German (*m.*)

Note the abbreviations *m.* (for *masculine*) or *f.* (for *feminine*) after **Amerikaner**, **Deutsche**, and other nouns. There is a complete list of abbreviations on p. 488.

der **Schüler, -** primary or secondary school pupil (*m.*)
der **Student, -en** university student (*m.*)
der **Tourist, -en** tourist (*m.*)

(das) **Deutschland** Germany
das **Haus, ¨er** house

die **Amerikanerin, -nen** American (*f.*)
die **Deutsche, -n** German (*f.*)
die **Gruppe, -n** group
die **Klasse, -n** class; grade
die **Schule, -n** school
die **Schülerin, -nen** primary or secondary school pupil (*f.*)
die **Studentin, -nen** university student (*f.*)
die **Touristin, -nen** tourist (*f.*)

Note the plural form of **Haus—Häuser**: the first vowel of a diphthong is umlauted.

Adjektive und Adverbien

freundlich friendly
höflich polite(ly)
immer always
oft often
so so; like this
viele many
wahrscheinlich probably
ziemlich fairly, quite

Andere Vokabeln

einander (*pron.*) each other
man one (*indefinite pronoun*)
miteinander with each other
oder (*conj.*) or
zueinander to each other

Note on **man**: This pronoun is often best translated with *we, you,* or *they*: **Das sagt man oft.** = *They (people) often say that.* See p. 86 for a complete explanation.

Nützliche Ausdrücke

zum Beispiel for example
auf Deutsch in German

Gegensätze

immer ≠ nie always ≠ never
oft ≠ selten often ≠ seldom

Lab Manual Kap. 1, Lesestück.

Wie sagt man „you" auf Deutsch?

When working with the reading, it is useful to know **das Wort** and **die Zeile**.

Touristen in Deutschland sagen oft, die Deutschen sind sehr freundlich und höflich. Das stimmt, aber wahrscheinlich meinen viele Amerikaner auch, die Deutschen sind ziemlich formell.

Frau Bachmann und Frau Kuhn sind zum Beispiel Nachbarinnen°. Sie wohnen im selben° Haus und sind auch miteinander befreundet°, aber Frau Bachmann fragt nicht: „Wie geht es dir, Gisela?" Nein, sie sagt: „Wie geht es Ihnen, Frau Kuhn?" Sie grüßen einander formell.

Wie ist es in der Schule? In allen° Klassen – von Klasse eins bis Klasse dreizehn – duzen die Lehrer ihre° Schüler. Die Schüler siezen die Lehrer natürlich immer.

Das Du ist auch ein Ausdruck der° Solidarität. Für die Studenten bedeutet es: Wir sind eine Gruppe. Karin und Michael, zum Beispiel, studieren.[1] Sie sagen von Anfang an° „du" zueinander.

neighbors
im selben = in the same / on friendly terms
all
their
Ausdruck der = expression of
von ... = from the beginning

In **Kapitel 5** you will learn why line 8 reads **in *der* Schule** even though **Schule** is feminine.

1. Note that **studieren** means to attend college or university and is not used to describe a student's daily activity of studying. Thus, *I'm studying* (i.e., doing homework) *tonight* is translated as **Ich *arbeite* heute Abend,** or **Ich *lerne* heute Abend.**

Diese Studenten sagen „du" zueinander.

Some laid-back teachers in the upper grades allow their students to say **du** to them.

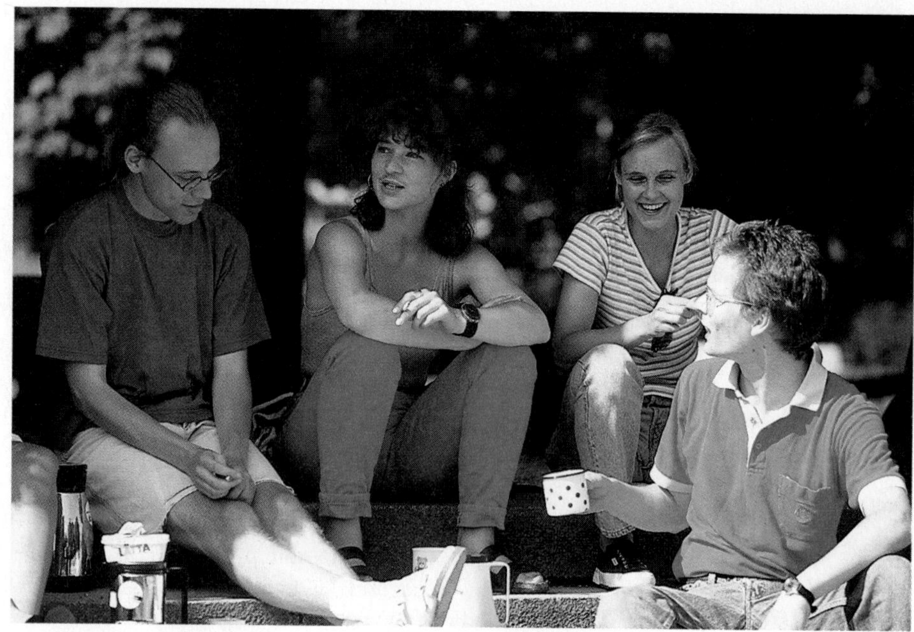

Nach dem Lesen (After the reading)

A **Richtig oder falsch?** (True or false?)

1. Lehrer duzen die Schüler bis Klasse zehn.
2. Karin und Michael sind Schüler.
3. Frau Kuhn und Frau Bachmann sagen „du" zueinander.

B **Antworten Sie auf Deutsch.** (Answer in German.)

1. Was meinen Touristen: Wie sind die Deutschen?
2. Duzen die Schüler die Lehrer in Deutschland?
3. Siezt Karin Michael?
4. Was bedeutet das Du für Studenten?

For a thorough discussion of the use of second-person forms, see Werner Besch, *Duzen, Siezen, Titulieren* (Göttingen: Vandenhoeck & Ruprecht, 1996).

C **Was sagt man?** (What do you say?) Sie sind Student oder Studentin. Zu wem (*to whom*) sagen Sie „Sie", zu wem sagen Sie „du"?

Situationen aus dem Alltag

(Situations from everyday life)

Partnerarbeit: *Sie* oder *du*?

Frau Professor Ullman

Herr Kuhn

Karoline und Dieter Flessner

Niklas Schuhmacher

1. Take turns asking the people pictured
   a. what their names are.
   b. whether they're working at the moment.
   c. whether they're tired today.
   d. where they live.
   e. where they work.
2. Partner A plays one of the people pictured above and responds to Partner B's questions. Then Partner B plays another of these people and answers Partner A's questions.

   BEISPIEL: A: Wo wohnen Sie, Herr Kuhn?
   B: Ich wohne in Wien.
3. Now ask each other three personalized questions using the **du**-form.

Zum Schluss

(In conclusion)

Lab Manual Kap. 1, Diktat.

These final exercises use vocabulary from both **Wortschatz** sections of the chapter and should be used after reading the **Lesestück**. They are designed to be a culmination and review of the chapter rather than to be used while covering the grammar.

Sprechen wir miteinander! (Let's talk together!)

A **Partnerarbeit: Ist es wahrscheinlich?** Partner A uses the cues to ask questions. Partner B responds, beginning with one of the three adverbs in the right-hand column.

BEISPIEL: fliegen / Berlin?
A: Fliegst du nach Berlin?
B: Vielleicht fliege ich nach Berlin.

Partner A	*Partner B*
gehen / zu Marion?	Natürlich …
studieren / in Konstanz?	Wahrscheinlich …
arbeiten / im Moment?	Vielleicht …
kommen / zurück?	
wohnen / hier?	
fliegen / nach Leipzig?	

■ B ■ Partnerarbeit: An welchem Tag? (On which day?) Review the days of the week together as a class. Then use the cues below to ask each other questions. Your partner answers with any day of the week, beginning the sentence with **Am ...**

BEISPIEL: wann / kommen / zurück?
A: Wann kommst du zurück?
B: Am Dienstag komme ich zurück.

1. wann / arbeiten?
2. wann / haben / Deutsch?
3. wann / gehen / zu Gisela?
4. wann / fliegen / nach Hamburg?
5. wann / kommen / zurück?
6. wann / spielen / Tennis?

Open-book exercise. Vocabulary not introduced for active use. Gets students used to recognizing cognates. Have them pronounce the list before exercise begins.

■ C ■ Partnerarbeit: Seid ihr auch so? With your partner, look at the following adjectives you can use to describe your personality. You shouldn't have trouble understanding them, because they all have English cognates. Ask each other questions to find out which of these characteristics you have in common. Make a list of three or four characteristics you share.

BEISPIEL: Ich bin sehr emotional. Bist du auch emotional?
Ja, ich bin (immer / oft / ziemlich / sehr) emotional.
or: Nein, ich bin (selten / nicht / nie) emotional.

emotional	modern	kreativ	konservativ
sentimental	aktiv	dynamisch	objektiv
subjektiv	kompetent	progressiv	optimistisch
pessimistisch	naiv	athletisch	exzentrisch
intelligent	clever		

■ D ■ Gruppenarbeit Now go with your partner to another pair of students and ask questions to find out how they describe themselves. Use the words listed in exercise C.

BEISPIEL: GRUPPE A: Seid ihr auch emotional?
GRUPPE B: Nein, wir sind nicht emotional, wir sind ... Und ihr?

Ask **Wie ist / sind: das Wetter / die Studenten hier / die Mensa / Ihr Deutschbuch / die Touristen / der Professor / die Professorin.**

■ E ■ Übung: Wie ist das Wetter im Januar? Was machen Sie am Montag? Answer the following questions. The lists of vocabulary will give you some ideas.

BEISPIEL: Wie ist das Wetter im Januar?
Es ist kalt. / Es schneit viel.

Was machen Sie am Montag?
Ich arbeite mit Karl.

1. Wie ist das Wetter im ________ ?

schön	kalt	herrlich	heiß	kühl
windig	sonnig	neblig	wolkig	

2. Was machen Sie am ________ ?

arbeiten fliegen spielen gehen

Schreiben Sie zu Hause. (Write at home.)

Students can write this dialogue in pairs in class and then read it aloud.

■ F ■ Zwei Studenten im Gespräch (Two students in conversation) Write a dialogue using the following cues. You will need to provide verb endings, correct word order, etc.

ULLI: Tag / Dieter! du / arbeiten / morgen?
DIETER: Nein. warum / du / fragen?
ULLI: morgen / wir / gehen / zu Hans. du / kommen / auch?
DIETER: natürlich / ich / kommen

■ G ■ Was machst du? Answer each question according to the cue in English. Answer appropriately for the way you're addressed (**Was machst du? Ich fliege … Was macht ihr? Wir fliegen …**).

BEISPIEL: Was machst du morgen? (*flying to Vienna*)
Ich fliege morgen nach Wien.

1. Was macht ihr heute? (*going to Stefan's*)
2. Was machst du im Moment, Richard? (*working a lot*)
3. Was machen Sie, Frau Gruber? (*attending the university*)
4. Was machst du, Regina? (*playing outside*)
5. Was macht ihr am Mittwoch, Rolf und Helene? (*flying to Hamburg*)
6. Was machen Sie, Frau Bachmann? (*greeting Mrs. Kuhn*)

■ H ■ Antworten Sie bitte auf Deutsch! (Please answer in German.) Answer the yes/no questions affirmatively and with complete sentences.

1. Was machst du heute Abend?
2. Bist du in Eile?
3. Fliegt der Professor nach New York?
4. Wer wohnt hier?
5. Regnet es wieder?
6. Was machen wir im Moment?
7. Arbeitest du vielleicht morgen?
8. Ist das typisch?

■ I ■ Wie sagt man das auf Deutsch?

1. When are you coming back, Jürgen and Katrin?
2. We are coming back tomorrow.

3. Excuse me, are you in a hurry?
4. Yes, I'm going to Helene's.

5. She says the Germans are friendly.
6. Yes, that's right.

7. How are you, Herr Beck?
8. Fine thanks, and you?

9. The sun is shining again.
10. Good! We'll work outside.

Where is German Spoken?

German is the language of the Federal Republic of Germany, Austria, Liechtenstein, and portions of Switzerland, Luxembourg, the South Tyrol in northern Italy (until 1919 part of Austria), and Belgium. Linguistic enclaves of German speakers in the U.S.A. (notably the Amish in Pennsylvania), Canada, Brazil, Africa (especially in Namibia, once the German colony of South West Africa), and Australia bring the number of native German speakers to around 121 million. In 1993, 20 million people were studying German as a second language. Of these, 13 million were eastern Europeans.

The following statistics on the world's major languages include both native and second-language speakers in 1994. Notice that the names of almost all languages in German end with **-sch**.

Chinesisch	1 Milliarde 18 Millionen
Englisch	470 Millionen
Hindustani	418 Millionen
Spanisch	401 Millionen
Russisch	288 Millionen
Arabisch	219 Millionen
Portugiesisch	182 Millionen
Japanisch	126 Millionen
Französisch	124 Millionen
Deutsch	121 Millionen
Italienisch	63 Millionen

eine Milliarde = (American) *billion;*
eine Billion = (American) *trillion.*

Look at the map on the inside back cover. Ask students in which countries German is spoken as a principal language, in which it is spoken by minorities. Discuss briefly such topics as why German was an official language in Namibia, why there are German speakers in Northern Italy (South Tyrol ceded to Italy after Austria's defeat in W.W. I) and North America (Mennonites and Amish fled religious persecution in the 18th century), German emigration in 19th and 20th centuries. Have them pronounce the German names for other world languages.

Familie und Freunde

Communicative Goals

- Talking about the family
- Saying what belongs to whom
- Counting above 20

Cultural Goal

- Learning about German family life

Chapter Outline

- **Lyrik zum Vorlesen**
  „Du bist mein"
- **Grammatik**
  The accusative case
  More on verbs in the present tense
  Possessive adjectives
  Cardinal numbers above 20
- **Lesestück**
  Die Familie heute
- **Situationen aus dem Alltag**
  Die Familie
- **Videoecke**
  Ist das Zimmer noch frei?
- **Almanach**
  Die ganze Familie

Dialoge

Lab Manual Kap. 2, Dialoge, Fragen, Hören Sie gut zu!, Üb. zur Aussprache **[z/s]**.

First dialogue: Dependent word order is used here only because it's parallel to English.

Listen carefully to the tapes and your instructor for the difference in the pronunciation of **denn** (short vowel) and **den** (long vowel).

The video screen icon signals that related material appears in the video program.

Pronunciation practice: Use dialogue phrases to review front vs. back **ch (ich suche, er kennt dich, in München, ich brauche ein Zimmer, ziemlich groß)** and **z (meine Zeitung, ziemlich groß, ein Zimmer)**. The tape program for Kap. 2 focuses on **z** vs. **s**.

Pronunciation of **hab'**: **b** becomes unvoiced **p**.

Most common elision occurs when the personal ending **-e** is followed by a word beginning with a vowel.

Have students ask each other short questions with **denn**. They may respond with any appropriate answer.

Wer liest die Zeitung?

VATER: Kurt, ich suche meine Zeitung. Weißt du, wo sie ist?
SOHN: Deine Zeitung? Ich lese sie im Moment.
VATER: Was liest du denn?
SOHN: Ich lese einen Artikel über unsere Schule.

Ich hab' eine Frage

ANNETTE: Katrin, ich hab' eine Frage. Kennst du den Mann da drüben?
KATRIN: Wen meinst du denn?
ANNETTE: Er spricht mit Stefan. Ich sehe, er kennt dich.
KATRIN: Natürlich kenn' ich ihn – das ist mein Bruder Max!
ANNETTE: Ach, du hast auch einen Bruder! Ich kenne nur deine Schwester.

Georg sucht ein Zimmer

GEORG: Kennst du viele Leute in München?
STEFAN: Ja, meine Familie wohnt da. Warum?
GEORG: Ich studiere nächstes Semester dort und brauche ein Zimmer.
STEFAN: Unser Haus ist ziemlich groß. Sicher haben meine Eltern ein Zimmer frei.
GEORG: Fantastisch! Vielen Dank!
STEFAN: Bitte, bitte. Nichts zu danken.

Notes on Usage: Unstressed *e* and *denn*

***Dropping unstressed* e** In informal conversation, Germans often drop the unstressed ending **-e** in the first-person singular.

Katrin, ich **hab'** eine Frage.
Natürlich **kenn'** ich ihn.

***The flavoring particle* denn** Probably the most frequently used flavoring particle is **denn**. It adds an element of personal interest to a question. **Denn** is never stressed and usually comes immediately after the verb and personal pronouns.

Was liest du **denn**?
Wen meinst du **denn**?
Wer ist **denn** das?

Wortschatz 1

Verben

brauchen to need
essen (isst) to eat
haben to have
heißen to be called
  Er heißt Max. His name is Max.
kennen to know, to be acquainted with
lesen (liest) to read
  lesen über (+ *acc.*) to read about
meinen to mean
nehmen (nimmt) to take
sehen (sieht) to see
sprechen (spricht) to speak, to talk
  sprechen über (+ *acc.*) to talk about
suchen to look for; to seek
wissen (weiß) to know (*a fact*)

Substantive

der **Artikel, -** article
der **Bruder, ̈-** brother
der **Freund, -e** friend
der **Mann, ̈-er** man; husband
der **Sohn, ̈-e** son
der **Vater, ̈-** father

das **Fleisch** meat
das **Gemüse** vegetables
das **Obst** fruit
das **Semester, -** semester
das **Zimmer, -** room

die **Familie, -n** family
die **Frage, -n** question
die **Schwester, -n** sister
die **Zeitung, -en** newspaper

die **Eltern** (*pl.*) parents
die **Leute** (*pl.*) people

Adjektive und Adverbien

(da) drüben over there
dein (*fam. sing.*) your
dort there
frei free; unoccupied
groß big; tall
mein my
nur only
sicher certain, sure
unser our

Andere Vokabeln

ach oh, ah
bitte you're welcome
denn *flavoring particle, see p. 46*
mit with
über (+ *acc.*) about
wen? whom?
wessen? whose?
wie viele? how many?

The preposition **über** means *about* with verbs like *to say, tell, write, read, laugh,* etc.

Nützliche Ausdrücke

Fantastisch! Fantastic!
vielen Dank many thanks, thanks a lot
nächstes Semester next semester
Nichts zu danken! Don't mention it!

Gegensätze

danke ≠ bitte thank you ≠ you're welcome
groß ≠ klein big; tall ≠ little; short

Verbs: Explain that forms in parentheses are 3rd-person sing. Conjugate present tense of **essen** on blackboard.

Remind students of the other definition of **meinen** (**Wortschatz 1-2**). Rule of thumb: Things *signify*: **Was *bedeutet* das?** People *have opinions, think*: **Was *meinst* du?**

DIE BANK
FÜR LEUTE
VON HEUTE

Who's Reading the Newspaper?

FATH.: Kurt, I'm looking for my newspaper. Do you know where it is?
SON: Your newspaper? I'm reading it at the moment.
FATH.: What are you reading?
SON: I'm reading an article about our school.

I Have a Question

A: Katrin, I have a question. Do you know that man over there?
K: Whom do you mean?
A: He's talking with Stefan. I see he knows you.
K: Of course I know him—that's my brother Max!
A: Oh, you have a brother too! I only know your sister.

Georg Is Looking for a Room

G: Do you know many people in Munich?
S: Yes, my family lives there. Why?
G: I'm studying there next semester and need a room.
S: Our house is pretty big. I'm sure my parents have a room free.
G: Fantastic! Thanks a lot!
S: You're welcome. Don't mention it.

Variationen

■ A ■ Persönliche Fragen

1. Wie viele Studenten kennen Sie hier? Wie heißen sie?
2. Stefans Haus ist ziemlich groß. Ist Ihr Haus auch groß oder ist es klein? Wie viele Zimmer hat es?
3. Stefan kommt aus München. Woher kommen Sie?
4. Kurt liest die Zeitung im Moment. Lesen Sie auch eine Zeitung? Oft oder nur selten? Wie heißt sie?

■ B ■ Partnerarbeit: Wie heißt ... ? Help each other recall the names of other students in the class.

A: Wie heißt die Studentin (*oder* der Student) da drüben?
B: Sie/er heißt ...

■ C ■ Partnerarbeit: Wen kennst du hier? Ask your neighbor whom he or she knows in class and how well.

A: Wen kennst du hier?
B: Ich kenne ...
A: Kennst du ihn (*oder* sie) gut?
B: Ja, sehr gut. (*oder*: Nein, nicht sehr gut.)

Vielleicht sprechen die Frauen über das Wetter. Was sagen sie zueinander?

■ D ■ Partnerarbeit: Was suchst du? Tell what you're looking for. Try to remember the correct gender of these nouns, then put them into the corresponding column.

Buch	Stuhl	Professor
Bleistift	Kugelschreiber	Professorin
Heft	Landkarte	Zeitung
Uhr		

Ich suche:

meinen (masculine)	**mein** (neuter)	**meine** (feminine)
__________	__________	__________
__________	__________	__________
__________	__________	__________
__________	__________	__________
__________	__________	__________

Now use each of these objects in the following conversation.

A: Was suchst du?
B: Ich suche meinen/mein/meine _____ .
A: Er/es/sie ist nicht hier.

■ E ■ Gruppenarbeit: Was brauchen wir? (*4 Studenten*) You and three friends are going to Munich to study. Decide together on some things you'll need.

Wir brauchen:

einen (masculine)	**ein** (neuter)	**eine** (feminine)
__________	__________	__________
__________	__________	__________
__________	__________	__________
__________	__________	__________

Lyrik zum Vorlesen

Lab Manual Kap. 2, Lyrik zum Vorlesen.

This is one of the earliest surviving love poems in German. It was found in the Latin text of a letter written ca. 1160 A.D. by a lady to her lover. The original medieval German has been translated into modern German.

Du bist mein

Du bist mein, ich bin dein.	
Des sollst du gewiss sein°.	**Des ...** = of that you can be certain
Du bist verschlossen°	locked up
In meinem Herzen°,	heart
Verloren° ist das Schlüsselein°:	lost / little key
Du musst immer drinnen° sein.	inside

Grammatik

The accusative case

In **Kapitel 1** you learned the forms and functions of the nominative case. In this chapter you will learn the accusative case. The direct object of a verb is in the accusative.

The direct object

The direct object is the thing or person acted upon, known, or possessed by the subject.

Reemphasize the pronunciation of **den**.

Subject (nominative)		*Direct object (accusative)*	
Sie	lesen →	das Buch.	*They're reading the book.*
Anna	kennt →	meine Eltern.	*Anna knows my parents.*
Karl	hat →	einen Bruder.	*Karl has a brother.*

The indefinite article **ein** has no plural form. Therefore, the possessive adjective **mein-** (*my*) is used to show the plural endings.

The accusative is identical in form to the nominative *with the exception of the masculine singular articles.*

	Nominative	*Accusative*
masc:	Hier ist **der** / **ein** Bleistift.	Ich habe **den** / **einen** Bleistift.
neut:	Hier ist **das** / **ein** Zimmer.	Ich habe **das** / **ein** Zimmer.
fem:	Hier ist **die** / **eine** Zeitung.	Ich habe **die** / **eine** Zeitung.
plur:	Hier sind **die** / **meine** Bücher.	Ich habe **die** / **meine** Bücher.

For **Übung 1**, use objects the students have with them.

Use only neuter and feminine objects: **Buch**, **Zeitung**, **Heft**, **Uhr**, **Landkarte**, **Haus**, **Zimmer**, **Frage**, **Schwester**, **Büro**.

Workbook Kap. 2, A, B.

1 **Übung: Wer hat ein Deutschbuch?** Your instructor asks who has various things. Say that you have them.

BEISPIEL: Wer hat ein Deutschbuch?
Ich habe ein Deutschbuch.

Lab Manual Kap. 2, Var. zu Üb. 2, 3.

2 **Übung: Was sehen Sie?** Name five things you see in the picture.

BEISPIEL: Ich sehe einen Tisch.

Übungen 1 and **2** practice accusative with indefinite article, **Übung 3** with definite article.

3 Kettenreaktion: Was brauchst du? Ask other students what things they need.

BEISPIEL: A: Was brauchst du?
B: Ich brauche den/das/die ______. Und was brauchst du?
C: Ich brauche ...

Fragewort

The accusative form of the question word **wer** is **wen**:

Wen kennst du in München? *Whom do you know in Munich?*

Accusative of the personal pronouns

Be sure to learn all forms of the accusative personal pronouns.

Singular			Plural		
nom.	acc.		nom.	acc.	
ich	**mich**	*me*	wir	**uns**	*us*
du	**dich**	*you*	ihr	**euch**	*you*
er	**ihn**	*him, it*			
es	**es**	*it*	sie; Sie	**sie, Sie**	*them; you*
sie	**sie**	*her, it*			

Workbook Kap. 2, C, D, E.

Übung 4: Use familiar classroom vocabulary: **Stuhl**, **Bleistift**, **Kuli**, **Buch**, **Heft usw**.

4 Übung: Brauchen Sie etwas? Your instructor asks whether you need something. Say that you do need it.

BEISPIEL: Brauchen Sie den Stuhl?
Ja, ich brauche ihn.

Lab Manual Kap. 2, Var. zur Üb. 5.

Model this exchange with a student before it is done in pairs.

5 Partnerarbeit: Wen kennst du hier? Conduct the following dialogue with your partner, naming as many students in your class as possible.

A: Wen kennst du hier?
B: Ich kenne Barbara/Robert.
A: Ich kenne sie/ihn auch.
B: Wen kennst *du* hier?

Tell students you will be addressing each other in **du**-form for this exercise. Make eye contact with the student you want to answer the question. Point to that student and another for **ihr** and **euch**, to yourself and another student for **wir** and **uns.** For sentences 9 and 10, tell students: **Jetzt bin ich wieder der Professor, wir sagen *Sie*.** Show that **Sie** can be singular or plural by pointing either to one or to several students.

6 Übung: Fragen Answer the questions affirmatively.

BEISPIEL: Suchst du mich?
Ja, ich suche dich.

1. Kennst du mich?
2. Brauchst du uns?
3. Seht ihr uns?
4. Kenne ich dich?
5. Kenne ich euch?
6. Fragst du mich?
7. Brauche ich dich?
8. Brauche ich euch?
9. Kennen Sie mich?
10. Kenne ich Sie?

More on verbs in the present tense

■ Contraction of *du*-form: *heißen*

Verbs with stems ending in **-s**, **-ß**, or **-z** contract the **du**-form ending **-st** to **-t**. In these verbs, the **du**-form and the **er**-form are identical. You used some of the forms of **heißen** in the **Einführung**. Here is the complete conjugation in the present tense.

heißen *to be called*		stem: **heiß-**	
ich	heiße	wir	heißen
du	**heißt**	ihr	heißt
er, es, sie	heißt	sie, Sie	heißen

■ Verbs with stem-vowel change *e* to *i* or *ie*

Two English verbs umlaut in pronunciation (but not in spelling) in 3rd-pers. sing.: *do* (*she does*) and *say* (*he says*).

Some German verbs change their stem vowel in the **du-** and **er-**forms of the present tense.

e → i		**sprechen**	*to speak*
ich	spreche	wir	sprechen
du	**sprichst**	ihr	sprecht
er, es, sie	**spricht**	sie, Sie	sprechen

e → ie		**sehen**	*to see*
ich	sehe	wir	sehen
du	**siehst**	ihr	seht
er, es, sie	**sieht**	sie, Sie	sehen

e → ie		**lesen**	to read
ich	lese	wir	lesen
du	**liest**	ihr	lest
er, es, sie	**liest**	sie, Sie	lesen

Stem-vowel change will be indicated in the **Wortschatz** sections by inclusion of the **er**-form: **sehen (sieht)** *to see*. Two other verbs in this group are **essen,** *to eat*; and **nehmen**, *to take*. Note that **nehmen** changes not only its stem vowel but also some consonants.

essen	*to eat*	**nehmen**	*to take*
ich	esse	ich	nehme
du	**isst**	du	**nimmst**
er, es, sie	**isst**	er, es, sie	**nimmt**

Lab Manual Kap. 2, Var. zur Üb. 7.

Workbook Kap. 2, F.

After students are done, add 3rd-person singular: I: **Ich esse Suppe, was essen Sie?** S1: **Ich esse Fleisch.** I: **Was isst sie?** S2: **Sie isst Fleisch.** I: **Und was essen Sie?** (pointing to 2 students) SS: **Wir essen Brot.**

■ 7 ■ Kettenreaktion

1. Say what you eat, then ask the next person.

   BEISPIEL: Ich esse Fleisch, was isst du?

2. Say what you read, then ask the next person.

   BEISPIEL: Ich lese den *Spiegel,* was liest du?

Tell students they can lie about which languages they speak. Practice pronunciation with example sentence. Consonant clusters in **sprichst** are difficult.

3. Say what languages you speak and then ask the next person.

   BEISPIEL: Ich spreche ______, was sprichst du?

Chinesisch	Französisch
Italienisch	Englisch
Polnisch	Japanisch
Schwedisch	Spanisch
Deutsch	Russisch

Model for the students first, emphasizing accusative:
I: Ich sehe ein Buch. (alle zusammen)
Ich sehe einen Tisch. (alle zusammen)
Ich sehe eine Tafel. (alle zusammen)
Was sehen Sie?
When students do chain exercise with vowel change, you may choose to tolerate high error frequency in accusative endings.

4. Say what you see. The next student repeats what you see, then adds something new.

   BEISPIEL: A: Ich sehe ein Fenster.
   B: Sie sieht ein Fenster und ich sehe eine Tafel.

■ The verb *wissen*

The verb **wissen** (*to know*) is irregular in the present singular. Its forms must be memorized.

Emphasize 3rd-pers. sing. of **wissen**. Students will tend to add **-t**.

ich	**weiß**	wir	wissen
du	**weißt**	ihr	wisst
er, es, sie	**weiß**	sie, Sie	wissen

Both the first-person singular and the third-person singular lack endings: **ich weiß**, **er weiß**.

The difference between **wissen** and **kennen** parallels that between French **savoir** and **connaître** and Spanish **saber** and **conocer**. Cf. Scots English *ken: to know* (a person or thing); also "beyond my ken": *beyond my knowledge.*

wissen* vs. *kennen Both **wissen** and **kennen** may be translated as "to know," but **wissen** means "to know a fact" and **kennen** means "to be familiar, acquainted with" and is used when the direct object is a person or place.

Weißt du, wer das ist?	*Do you know who that is?*
Ja, ich **kenne** ihn sehr gut.	*Yes, I know him very well.*
Kennen Sie Berlin, Herr Brandt?	*Do you know Berlin, Mr. Brandt?*
Nein, nicht sehr gut.	*No, not very well.*

Workbook Kap. 2, G.

■ 8 ■ Übung: *Wissen* oder *kennen*?

BEISPIEL: ich / Georg
Ich kenne Georg.

1. er / Michael
2. wir / Berlin
3. Katrin / wo ich wohne
4. ihr / was sie macht
5. ich / Stefan und Annette
6. du / München
7. ich / wer das ist
8. die Schüler / was der Lehrer meint

■ The verb *haben*

The verb **haben** (*to have*) is irregular in the present singular.

ich	habe	wir	haben
du	**hast**	ihr	habt
er, es, sie	**hat**	sie, Sie	haben

Lab Manual Kap. 2, Var. zu Üb. 9.

Point to individual students, a group of students, yourself, the student you are asking, etc.

9 **Übung: Wer hat die Zeitung?** Your professor asks you who has the newspaper, while pointing to somebody. Say that that person has the newspaper.

BEISPIEL: Wer hat die Zeitung? (*points to Sean*)
Sean hat sie.

Possessive adjectives

Learn all forms of the possessive adjectives.

Point out that there are three possessive adjectives corresponding to the three second-person pronouns: **dein**, **euer**, **Ihr** = *your*.

Point out to students that just as **er** and **sie** mean *it* when they replace masculine and feminine nouns like **der Tisch** and **die Straße**, so **sein** and **ihr** can mean *its*:
der Tisch → ***seine*** **Farbe**
die Tür → ***ihre*** **Farbe**

Singular			Plural		
personal pronoun	**possessive adjective**		**personal pronoun**	**possessive adjective**	
ich	**mein**	*my*	wir	**unser**	*our*
du	**dein**	*your*	ihr	**euer**	*your*
er es sie	**sein** **sein** **ihr**	*his; its* *its* *her; its*	sie; Sie	**ihr; Ihr**	*their; your*

Note that formal **Ihr** (*your*), like formal **Sie** (*you*), is always capitalized.

Possessive adjectives must agree with the nouns they modify in case, number, and gender. This agreement is shown by endings. As the following table shows, the endings of the possessive adjectives are the same as the endings of **ein**. Possessive adjectives are therefore called **ein**-words.

Ending of **ein**-words				
	masc.	**neut.**	**fem.**	**plur.**
nom.	ein mein ihr unser euer	ein mein ihr unser euer	ein**e** mein**e** ihr**e** unsr**e** eur**e**	(*no plural*) mein**e** ihr**e** unsr**e** eur**e**
acc.	ein**en** mein**en** ihr**en** unsr**en** eur**en**	ein mein ihr unser euer	ein**e** mein**e** ihr**e** unsr**e** eur**e**	(*no plural*) mein**e** ihr**e** unsr**e** eur**e**

The **e** *must* be dropped from **euer** (→ **euren**) and *may* be dropped from **unser**.

Note: The **-er** on **unser** and **euer** is *not* an ending, but part of the stem. When **euer** and **unser** take endings, the second **-e-** of the stem is dropped.

Das ist **unser** / **euer** Bruder. Das ist **unsre** / **eure** Schwester.

Note: The endings for nominative and accusative possessive adjectives are identical *except in the masculine*.

Das ist mein Bruder. Und das ist meine Schwester.

Start by telling students they should use the **du**-form when addressing you in **Übung 10.** Point to your book (S: **dein Buch**), book of student you're asking (S: **mein Buch**), or other students' books (**sein Buch, ihr Buch**). To elicit **euer**, hold your book and point to yourself and another student. For **unser**, point to yourself and student you're asking. Then say: **Ich bin wieder der Professor. Jetzt sagen Sie „Sie" zu mir.** Pay special attention to **ihr / Ihr** (*her, their/your*). Variation: **Wessen Zeitung ist das?** (Bring in a German newspaper.)

Variation: Point to student's possessions and ask whether they belong to someone else: **Ist das *sein* Heft? Nein, das ist *mein* Heft.** Etc.

Masculine nominative	*Masculine accusative*
Das ist mein Bruder.	Ich sehe mein**en** Bruder.
Das ist ihr Bruder.	Sie sieht ihr**en** Bruder.
Das ist unser Bruder.	Wir sehen unsr**en** Bruder.
Das ist euer Bruder.	Ihr seht eur**en** Bruder.

Fragewörter

wer?	*who?*
wen?	*whom?*
wessen?	*whose?*

Lab Manual Kap. 2, Var. zu Üb. 10, 11.

10 **Übung: Wessen Buch ist das?** Tell your instructor whose book is being pointed to.

BEISPIEL: Wessen Buch ist das?
Das ist *mein* Buch.

Workbook Kap. 2, H, I, J, K.

Saying what belongs to whom is a communicative goal.

11 **Übung: Wessen Freund kennen Sie?** Tell your instructor whose friend you know.

BEISPIEL: Wessen Freund kennen Sie?
Ich kenne *seinen* Freund.

Variation zu Übung 11: Wessen **Mutter**, **Eltern**. Cue possessive adjectives by pointing to yourself, females, males, and more than one person.

Cardinal numbers above 20

The English nursery rhyme "Sing a Song of Sixpence" contains the phrase "four-and-twenty blackbirds." German forms the cardinal numbers above twenty in the same way: 24 = **vierundzwanzig**.

Counting above 20 is a communicative goal.

20	zwanzig	30	dreißig
21	einundzwanzig	31	einunddreißig (usw.)
22	zweiundzwanzig	40	vierzig
23	dreiundzwanzig	50	fünfzig
24	vierundzwanzig	60	sechzig
25	fünfundzwanzig	70	siebzig
26	sechsundzwanzig	80	achtzig
27	siebenundzwanzig	90	neunzig
28	achtundzwanzig	100	hundert
29	neunundzwanzig	1 000	tausend

4 982 viertausendneunhundertzweiundachtzig

German uses a period or a space where English uses a comma to divide thousands from hundreds, etc. German numbers above twelve (**zwölf**) are seldom written as words, except on checks. When they *are* written out, each number is one continuous word.

German	***English***
4.982 oder 4 982	4,982

German uses a comma where English uses a decimal point. The comma is read as **Komma**.

0,5 (null Komma fünf)	0.5 (zero point five)

Workbook Kap. 2, L.

Further practice: **Ich bin 1963 geboren. Wann sind Sie geboren?** Students answer with year only.

12 Übung Read these numbers aloud in German.

26	1 066	3 001
69	533	0,22
153	985	3,45
4 772,08	48	71
1992	1971	1800

Was kostet das?

Wie weit ist es nach Garmisch-Partenkirchen?

Sign directs drivers to **Ortsmitte** (*town center*), where tourist information (**i**) is available.

Lesestück

Lab Manual Kap. 2, Üb. zur Betonung.

Vor dem Lesen

Tipps zum Lesen und Lernen

Tipps zum Vokabelnlernen

Compound nouns A characteristic feature of German is its formation of compound nouns from two or more nouns. You should get used to analyzing these words and should learn to identify their component parts. You will frequently see similarities to English compound nouns.

Hausfrau	*housewife*
Hausarbeit	*housework*

Often a connecting **-(e)s-** or **-(e)n-** is inserted between the components.

das **Eigentum** (*property*) + die **Wohnung** (*apartment*) = die **Eigentumswohnung** (*condominium*)

der **Bund** (*federation*) + die **Republik** = die **Bundesrepublik**

die **Familie** + die **Diskussion** = die **Familiendiskussion**

The gender of the *last* component noun is *always* the gender of the entire compound.

das **Haus** + die **Frau** = die **Hausfrau**

das **Wort** + der **Schatz** = der **Wortschatz**
(*word*) (*treasure*) (*vocabulary*)

Practice pronunciation.

Leicht zu merken

die **Alternative, -n**	Alternative
der **Konflikt, -e**	Konflikt
(das) **Nordamerika**	
normal	normal
relativ	
sozial	sozial
traditionell	traditionell

Einstieg in den Text

- Review the tips for reading on page 38 in **Kapitel 1**.
- The following text is entitled "Die Familie heute." This gives you a good idea of what sort of information to expect.
- Before reading, recall the vocabulary you already know that relates to the topic of family, e.g., **Bruder**, **Schwester**, etc.
- *Guessing from context* The first sentence of a paragraph—the topic sentence—announces the primary topic of what follows. Look at page 61, line 8 of "Die Familie heute." **Die typische Familie** is the topic of this paragraph. Later in the paragraph comes this sentence:

  Fast alle Familien besitzen ein Auto und einen Fernseher.

  The words that are probably immediately comprehensible to you are **alle Familien** and **Auto**. Knowing the topic, you can make an educated guess at the meaning of **fast** and **besitzen**. Such educated guessing, or finding context clues, is very important when reading texts with many unfamiliar words.

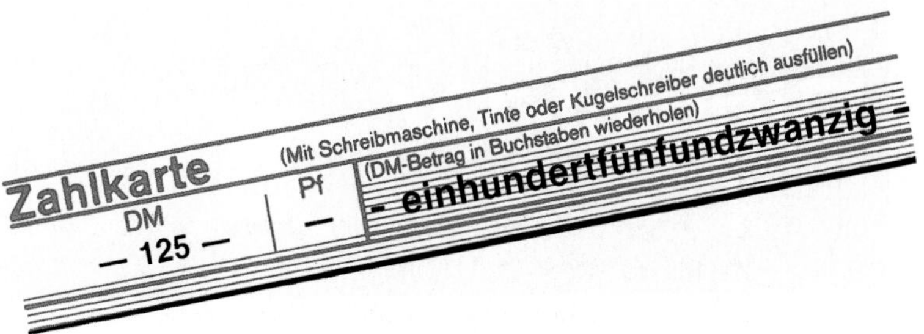

Wortschatz 2

Verben

besitzen to own
bleiben to stay, remain
finden to find
geben (gibt) to give
kochen to cook
leben to live; to be alive
verdienen to earn

Substantive

der **Beruf, -e** profession, vocation
der **Fernseher, -** TV set
der **Großvater, ¨** grandfather
der **Onkel, -** uncle

das **Auto, -s** car
das **Essen** food; meal
das **Geld** money
das **Klischee, -s** cliché
das **Problem, -e** problem

die **Arbeit** work
die **Bundesrepublik (Deutschland)** the Federal Republic (of Germany)
die **BRD** the FRG
die **Diskussion, -en** discussion
die **Großmutter, ¨** grandmother
die **Hausfrau, -en** housewife
die **Mutter, ¨** mother
die **Rolle, -n** role
die **Stelle, -n** job, position
die **Tante, -n** aunt
die **Tochter, ¨** daughter

die **Großeltern** (*pl.*) grandparents

Model pronunciation: **berufs-tätig**.

Adjektive und Adverbien

anders different
berufstätig employed
deutsch German
fast almost
jung young
manchmal sometimes
mehr more
nicht mehr no longer, not any more
noch still
noch ein another, an additional
sogar even, in fact
überall everywhere
wenigstens at least
wichtig important

Andere Vokabeln

alle (*pl.*) all; everybody
niemand nobody, no one
zwischen between

Nützliche Ausdrücke

es gibt (+ *acc.*) there is, there are
das sind (*pl. of* **das ist**) those are
zu Hause at home

Gegensätze

jung ≠ alt young ≠ old
niemand ≠ jemand no one ≠ someone
wichtig ≠ unwichtig important ≠ unimportant

Mit anderen Worten

Kinder sagen:
Vati = Vater
Mutti = Mutter
Oma = Großmutter
Opa = Großvater

Emphasize difference between **leben** (*to be alive*) and **wohnen** (*to dwell*).

Die Familie heute

Lab Manual Kap. 2, Lesestück.

„Der Vater hat einen Beruf und verdient das Geld, die Mutter ist Hausfrau. Sie bleibt zu Hause, kocht das Essen und versorgt° die Kinder." Die Klischees kennen wir schon. Heute stimmen sie aber nicht mehr, wenigstens nicht für junge[1] Familien in Deutschland. Dort ist die Rollenverteilung° oft anders. Viele Frauen sind berufstätig oder suchen eine Stelle. Tagsüber° ist manchmal niemand zu Hause. Oft machen der Mann und die Frau die Hausarbeit gemeinsam° und in Familiendiskussionen haben die Kinder heute auch eine Stimme°.

Die typische Familie ist relativ klein: Ein oder zwei Kinder, das ist normal. Manchmal wohnen auch die Großeltern mit ihnen zusammen°. Viele Familien in der Bundesrepublik haben ein Haus oder eine Eigentumswohnung°. Fast alle Familien besitzen ein Auto und einen Fernseher. Ihr Lebensstandard° ist sogar oft höher als° in Nordamerika.

Aber gibt es denn keine° Probleme? Natürlich! Man findet in Deutschland, wie überall, Konflikte zwischen Eltern und Kindern. Nach dem Schulabschluss° suchen junge Leute manchmal Alternativen wie das Zusammenleben° in Wohngemeinschaften°. Aber für die Mehrheit° bleibt die traditionelle Familie – Mutter, Vater und Kinder – noch die wichtigste° soziale Gruppe.

takes care of
assignment of roles
during the day
jointly
voice
mit ... = with them
condominium
standard of living / **höher als** = higher than
no
Nach ... = after secondary school / living together
communal living groups / majority / most important

Learning about German family life is the cultural goal of this chapter.

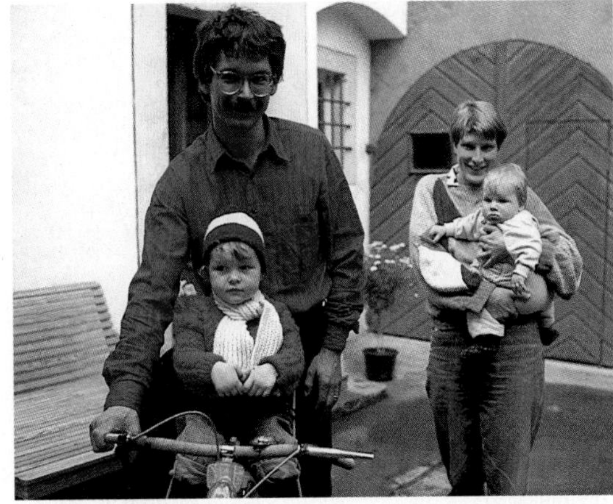

Junge Familie aus Eibelstadt. Wie alt sind die Kinder?

Stress that adjective endings must be pronounced: **junge Familien, die typische Familie**.

Nach dem Lesen

Students will need help with the professions or jobs of their parents. Insist on their asking in German: **Wie sagt man** *lawyer* **auf Deutsch?** After the questionnaires are completed, ask selected students to report their findings to the class.

■ **A** ■ **Partnerarbeit: Fragebogen** (Questionnaire) You are a German sociologist studying American family life. Use the questionnaire below to interview your partner. Be ready to report the information that you collect to the class.

1. **Großeltern**: Leben sie noch? ja / nein
2. **Mutter**: wie alt? _______ berufstätig? ja / nein Beruf? _______
3. **Vater**: wie alt? _______ berufstätig? ja / nein Beruf? _______

1. Line 3 **junge**: When German adjectives are used before nouns they have endings, most often **-e** or **-en**. You will learn how to use these endings actively in **Kapitel 9**.

4. **Geschwister**: wie viele Brüder? _______ wie alt? _______
   wie viele Schwestern? _______ wie alt? _______
5. **Autos:** wie viele? _______
6. **Fernseher**: wie viele? _______
7. Wer kocht das Essen? _______
8. Wer macht die Hausarbeit? _______
9. Wer liest die Zeitung? _______
10. Besitzt Ihre Familie ein Haus? ja / nein

■ B ■ Antworten Sie auf Deutsch.

1. Was sind die Klischees über die traditionelle Familie?
2. Was suchen heute viele Frauen?
3. Haben Familien in Deutschland viele Kinder?
4. Besitzen alle Familien in Deutschland ein Haus?

Situationen aus dem Alltag

Talking about the family is a communicative goal.

■ Die Familie

Here is some useful vocabulary for talking about your family. Words you already know from **Wortschatz** sections are listed without English equivalents; new supplementary vocabulary is listed with definitions.

Additional vocab.: **die Stiefmutter** (*stepmother*), **der Stiefvater** (*stepfather*).

This vocabulary focuses on an everyday topic or situation. Your instructor may assign some supplementary vocabulary for active mastery.

die **Großeltern**
die **Großmutter, ¨**
  die **Oma, -s** — *grandma*
der **Großvater, ¨**
  der **Opa, -s** — *grandpa*
die **Eltern**
die **Mutter, ¨**
  die **Mutti, -s** — *mama, mom*
der **Vater, ¨**
  der **Vati, -s** — *papa, dad*
der **Sohn, ¨e**
die **Tochter, ¨**

die **Geschwister** (*pl.*)	*siblings, brothers and sisters*
der **Bruder, ¨**	
die **Schwester, -n**	
der **Onkel, -**	
die **Tante, -n**	
die **Kusine, -n**	*cousin* (f.)
der **Vetter, -n**	*cousin* (m.)

Workbook Kap. 2, M, N, O.

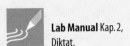

Lab Manual Kap. 2, Diktat.

geb. = geboren (*born*)

Reviews third-person possessive adjectives and family members.

■ A ■ Übung: Wer ist in der Familie? Answer the questions about Sylvie, Felix, and their families.

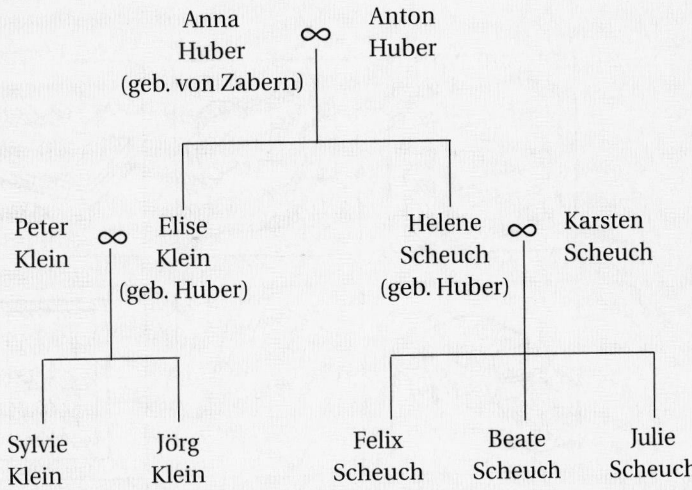

1. Das ist Sylvie Klein. Sie hat eine Mutter und …
   Wer ist Peter Klein? … Er ist ihr Vater.
   Wer ist Elise Klein?
   Wer ist Jörg?
   Wer sind Anna und Anton Huber?
2. Das ist Felix Scheuch. Er hat einen Vater und …
   Wer sind Beate und Julie? Karsten Scheuch? Helene Scheuch? Elise Klein?
3. Machen Sie einen Stammbaum (*family tree*) für Ihre Familie.

If students don't prepare this as homework, they may have pictures in their wallets that they can use on the spot.

■ B ■ Gruppenarbeit: Familienfotos (*4 oder 5 Studenten*) Bring to class photographs or your own drawing of some of your family members. Tell the others in the group about the people in the picture.

Zum Schluss

Tell students that **es gibt** is used to say what's there *(There are two windows in our room)*, but not to point to it demonstratively (*There's the window:* **Dort ist das Fenster).** Encourage the use of plurals and numbers **(Hier gibt es 12 Stühle, drei Fenster, einen Tisch).**

Sprechen wir miteinander!

A **Gruppenarbeit: Was gibt es hier?** Say what's in your classroom.

BEISPIEL: Hier gibt es ______.

B **Partnerarbeit: Was siehst du?** Take turns saying what you see in the pictures.

BEISPIEL: Ich sehe ein Auto.

C **Gruppenarbeit (*3 oder 4 Personen*)** How many answers can you give to the following questions?

After students make their lists, question individuals at random: **Laurie, was lesen Sie denn?** Correct accusatives through repetition.
S: **Ich lese ein Artikel.**
I: **Ach, Sie lesen einen Artikel.**
S: **Ja, ich lese einen Artikel.**

1. *Was liest du denn?*
   Ich lese ______.
   ______.
   ______.
   ______.
2. *Was kochst du?*
   Ich koche ______.
   ______.
   ______.
   ______.
3. *Wen kennst du?*
   Ich kenne ______.
   ______.
   ______.
   ______.
4. *Was suchst du?*
   Ich suche ______.
   ______.
   ______.
   ______.
5. *Was brauchst du denn?*
   Ich brauche ______.
   ______.
   ______.
   ______.
6. *Was siehst du denn?*
   Ich sehe ______.
   ______.
   ______.
   ______.

■ **D** ■ **Gruppenarbeit (*3 Personen*)** A German student from Rostock is visiting America and doesn't understand much English. Student A is a reporter asking questions. Student B interprets for the German visitor (student C).

BEISPIEL: A: Where is she from?
B: Woher kommst du denn?
C: Ich komme aus Rostock.

1. Where does his/her family live?
2. Does it rain there often?
3. What's his/her mother's name?
4. Is he/she employed?
5. Are his/her grandparents alive?
6. Whom does he/she know here?

Schreiben Sie zu Hause.

■ **E** ■ Write sentences using the cues provided. Add verbs, articles, and endings to verbs and possessive adjectives where necessary.

BEISPIEL: ich / suchen / mein / Geschwister
Ich suche meine Geschwister.

1. kennen / du / mein / Bruder?
2. Frau Huber / lesen / Artikel
3. unser / Mutter / haben / Beruf
4. dein / Eltern / auch / berufstätig?
5. mein / Familie / besitzen / Fernseher
6. Karin / suchen / ihr / Bruder
7. sehen / du / unser / Professor?
8. kennen / ihr / Mann / da drüben?

Students may do this dialogue in pairs, at home, or in class. They may also add another exchange and perform the entire dialogue for the class.

■ **F** ■ Construct dialogues from the following cues (a double slash indicates a comma).

1. Sie / kennen / Berlin?
   ja // mein / Familie / wohnen / dort. warum / Sie / fragen?
   ich / studieren / im Oktober / da / und / suchen / Zimmer
2. wie / du / heißen?
   ich / heißen / Klaus
   wen / du / suchen / denn?
   mein / Bruder. du / wissen // wo / er / sein?

■ G ■ *Wissen oder kennen?* Choose the correct equivalent of the verb *to know.*

A: ________ du den Mann da drüben?
B: Natürlich ________ ich ihn.
A: ________ du, wie er heißt?
B: Ja, er heißt Wolf Breisacher.

C: Ich ________ München gut.
D: Das ________ ich. Du kommst ja aus München!
C: ________ du Julian Wegener? Er studiert dort.
D: Wirklich? Ich ________ ihn nicht gut, aber ich ________, er wohnt in München.

■ H ■ Wie sagt man das auf Deutsch?

1. Her family is quite typical.
2. Their name is Schölz and they live in Munich.
3. Does her brother work, or is he looking for a job?
4. He's studying in Heidelberg.

5. I'm looking for my newspaper.
6. Fritz has it.
7. He's reading an article.

8. Where are your children, Mr. Asch?
9. They're at home.

10. When are you eating, children?
11. Probably at six.

Videoecke

1 Ist das Zimmer noch frei? (00:00)

Katrin nimmt das Zimmer.

Tell students that in the video episodes they will initially encounter some structures and vocabulary not yet covered in *Neue Horizonte*. Since students cannot expect to understand all the spoken German, they should rely in part on visual cues to follow the episode. In order to show how effective visual cues are, it is often worthwhile to show each episode first without sound. Pause often and have students speculate about what is going on.

Katrin Berger aus Leipzig studiert in Berlin. Sie braucht ein Zimmer und findet eine Adresse, wo ein Zimmer frei ist. Das Zimmer ist in der Wohnung von Familie Bachmann. Katrin geht hin (there) *und findet das Zimmer schön. Es kostet auch nicht viel und sie nimmt es. Sie ist nicht in Eile und trinkt mit Bachmanns zusammen eine Tasse Kaffee.*

Wortschatz zum Video

kosten	*to cost*
mieten	*to rent*
zeigen	*to show*
das **Bett, -en**	*bed*
der **Garten, ¨**	*garden, yard*
der **Wandschrank, ¨e**	*cupboard, closet*
gern	*gladly, with pleasure*
hell	*bright*
eine Tasse Kaffee	*a cup of coffee*
ein Stück Kuchen	*a piece of cake*

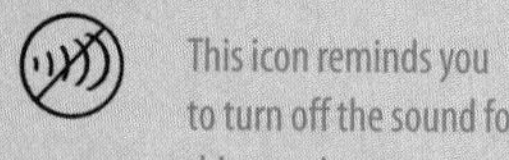

This icon reminds you to turn off the sound for this exercise.

■ A ■ Was sehen Sie im Video? Watch video Module 1 (00:20–03:58) once without sound. Check off in the list below the things you see in the video.

Ich sehe …

_____ 1. ein Auto
_____ 2. einen Tisch
_____ 3. einen Fernseher
_____ 4. die Mutter
_____ 5. den Großvater
_____ 6. Bücher
_____ 7. ein Fenster
_____ 8. ein Radio

■ B ■ Was hören Sie? Now watch the same section with sound, checking off the words you hear. Try to guess the meanings of the ones you haven't yet learned.

_____ 1. Universität
_____ 2. Bruder
_____ 3. Balkon
_____ 4. Biologie
_____ 5. Rostock
_____ 6. Großvater
_____ 7. Sofa
_____ 8. Schwester

■ C ■ Wer macht das? Wer sagt das? Choose the person who does or says the following.

1. _____ zeigt Katrin das Zimmer.

   a. Herr Bachmann b. Frau Bachmann c. Sabrina

2. „Ich habe Zeit."

   a. Stefan b. Herr Blum c. Fräulein Berger

3. _____ studiert in Heidelberg.

   a. Frau Bachmanns Tochter b. Frau Bachmanns Sohn c. Katrin

4. „Kennst du Berlin schon?"

   a. Harald b. Stefan c. Herr Bachmann

■ D ■ Richtig oder falsch? Indicate whether each statement is **richtig (R)** or **falsch (F)**.

1. Das Zimmer ist nicht groß genug (*enough*).	R	F
2. Die Kinder spielen draußen.	R	F
3. Das Zimmer kostet DM 400 im Monat.	R	F
4. Im Zimmer gibt es einen Fernseher.	R	F
5. Katrin isst ein Stück Kuchen.	R	F
6. Katrin kommt aus Leipzig.	R	F

E **Welle Magazin: Was sehen Sie?** Read through the list below. Then watch the **Welle Magazin** (04:03–05:26) and check off the rooms and things you see in the video.

Ich sehe …

_____ 1. die Garage (*garage*)
_____ 2. das Badezimmer (*bathroom*)
_____ 3. den Garten
_____ 4. eine Blumenvase (*vase of flowers*)
_____ 5. das Esszimmer (*dining room*)
_____ 6. die Küche (*kitchen*)
_____ 7. einen Schreibtisch (*desk*)
_____ 8. den Keller (*cellar*)
_____ 9. das Schlafzimmer (*bedroom*)
_____ 10. einen Computer
_____ 11. den Dachboden (*attic*)

This newspaper advertisement lists an apartment and a house for rent. How much of the descriptions can you guess from context?

Wohnungsmarkt

3-ZIMMER-WOHNUNG
zu vermieten, frisch gestrichen, moderne Küche, nahe Universität. Tel. 09 11/35 24 03

HAUS ZU VERMIETEN
4 Schlafzimmer, Möbel, Moltkestr. 66/Ecke Engelstr., Tel. 02 41/52 31 22

Die ganze Familie (The whole family)

Der Vater, der heißt Daniel,
der kleine Sohn heißt Michael,
die Mutter heißt Regine,
die Tochter heißt Rosine.

Der Bruder, der heißt Kristian,
der Onkel heißt Sebastian,
die Schwester heißt Johanna,
die Tante heißt Susanna.

Der Vetter, der heißt Benjamin,
die Kusine, die heißt Katharin,
die Oma heißt Ottilie—
nun kennst du die Familie!

Have one student read the poem aloud while others look at the family tree. Ask questions in German about the relationships and dates on the family tree: **Wie heißen die Töchter von Daniel und Regine? Wessen Sohn ist Sebastian? Wer ist Benjamins Vetter? Wann ist Ottilie geboren?** Possessive forms of proper names are parallel to English.

In 1997, these were the most popular names for newborn children according to the **Gesellschaft für deutsche Sprache** (Society for the German Language):

Namen für Mädchen			*Namen für Jungen*		
Sarah	Julia	Maria	Christian	Michael	Daniel
Marie	Lisa	Laura	Lukas	Felix	Alexander
Anna / Anne	Sophie	Vanessa	Tobias	Kevin	Maximilian
Lena	Jessica	Michelle	Tom	Marcel	Jan
			Philipp	Paul	Florian
			Erik		

Parents do not have absolute freedom in choosing names for their children. A name may be rejected by the government registry office if it does not clearly indicate the child's sex or if it is deemed to "endanger the well-being of the child."

Die Familie ist zusammen. Sie trinken Kaffee und sprechen miteinander.

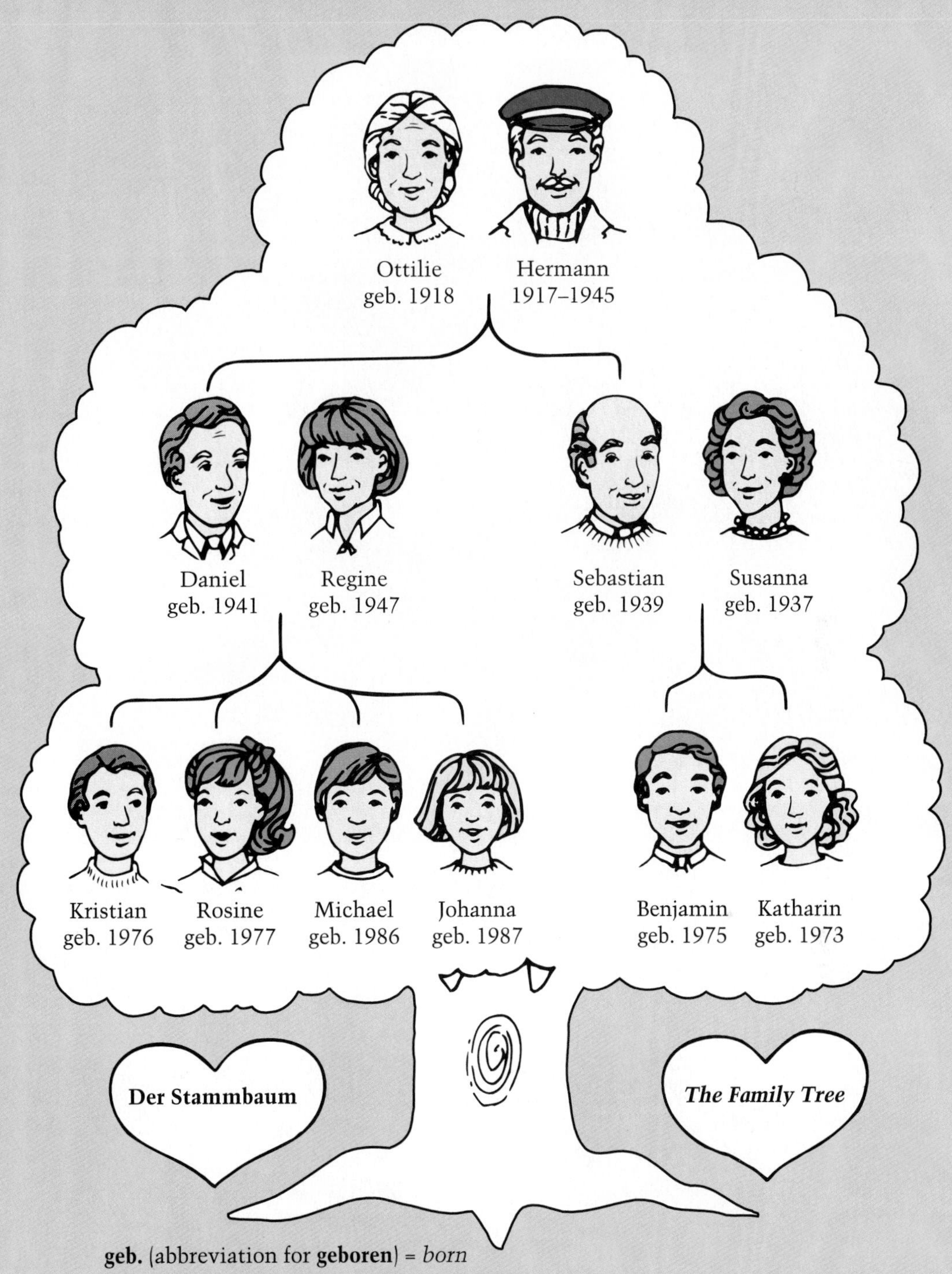

geb. (abbreviation for **geboren**) = *born*

KAPITEL 3

Jugend und Schule

Communicative Goals

- Negating statements and questions
- Contradicting someone
- Requesting confirmation
- Expressing opinions
- Talking about clothing

Cultural Goal

- Learning about German schools

Chapter Outline

- **Lyrik zum Vorlesen**
  „Bruder Jakob" und Rätsel
- **Grammatik**
  The predicate
  Modal verbs
  Verbs with stem vowel change *a* to *ä*, *au* to *äu*
  Negation with *nicht* (not)
  Negation with *kein*
  Expecting an affirmative answer: *nicht wahr*?
  Contradicting a negative statement or question: *doch*
  The indefinite pronoun *man*
- **Lesestück**
  Eine Klassendiskussion
- **Situationen aus dem Alltag**
  Kleidung und Farben
- **Almanach**
  A Note about Schools in German-speaking Countries

Dialoge

Lab Manual Kap. 3, Dialoge, Fragen, Hören Sie gut zu!, Üb. zur Aussprache **[o/ö]**.

Two cities in Germany are named Frankfurt. They are distinguished by the rivers on which they are situated: Frankfurt am Main (Frankfurt a. M. or Frankfurt/Main) in the state of Hessen; and Frankfurt an der Oder (Frankfurt a. d. O. or Frankfurt/Oder) in the state of Brandenburg.

Innsbruck is the capital city of the mountainous Austrian province of Tyrol (German **Tirol**). German place names often have topographical significance. **Die Brücke** = *bridge;* this city was originally a settlement at "the bridge over the Inn River." See the map in the front of the book.

Um Gottes Willen! Although **Gott** means *God,* this exclamation is not offensive in German, but is the social equivalent of *For heaven's sake* or *Oh, my gosh.*

Pronunciation practice: Tape program focuses on **o** and **ö**. Use dialogues to review these sounds in class (long **o**: **oder**, **schon**, **was ist los**, **Mitbewohner**; short **o: doch, noch, um Gottes Willen**; long **ö**: **zwölf**; short **ö: möchte**.

Du hast es gut!

Tell students that **Hinterwalden** is the German equivalent of **Nowheresville, Podunk,** or **Resume Speed**.

Renate besucht ihre Freundin Monika.

MONIKA: In Frankfurt hast du es gut, Renate! Hier in Hinterwalden ist es stinklangweilig.
RENATE: Dann musst du mich bald besuchen. Oder hast du keine Lust?
MONIKA: Doch, ich möchte schon nach Frankfurt, aber ich habe leider kein Geld.
RENATE: Das verstehe ich schon, aber bis Juni kannst du sicher genug verdienen.

Draw students' attention to the inverted word order in **Das verstehe ich schon** and **Das schaff' ich leicht**.

Eine Pause

Kurt und Stefan fahren nach Innsbruck.

KURT: Wir müssen noch eine Stunde nach Innsbruck fahren.
STEFAN: Können wir eine Pause machen? Ich möchte ein bisschen laufen.
KURT: Ich auch. Da drüben kann man halten, nicht wahr?
STEFAN: Ja. (*Sie halten.*) Mensch! Der Berg ist wahnsinnig steil!
KURT: Was ist denn los? Bist du nicht fit?
STEFAN: Doch! Das schaff' ich leicht.

Heute habe ich leider keinen Wagen

CAROLA: Klaus, wie spät ist es denn?
KLAUS: Um Gottes Willen! Es ist schon halb zwölf.
CAROLA: Musst du jetzt nach Hause?
KLAUS: Ja, und ich muss zu Fuß gehen. Heute habe ich leider keinen Wagen.
CAROLA: Warum denn nicht?
KLAUS: Mein Mitbewohner hat ihn heute Abend. Er hat viel zu tun.

Note on Usage: The flavoring particle *schon*

As a flavoring particle, **schon** is often used to strengthen, confirm, or reinforce a statement. It adds the sense of *really, indeed.* In the first dialogue, Monika protests:

Ich möchte **schon** nach Frankfurt, aber ich habe leider kein Geld.	*I really would like to go to Frankfurt, but unfortunately I don't have any money.*

Renate answers:

Das verstehe ich **schon** ...	*I certainly understand that . . .*

Wortschatz 1

Verben

Go over conjugation with students: ich *tue*, du *tust*, er/sie *tut*.

besuchen to visit
dürfen (darf) may, to be allowed to
fahren (fährt) to drive; to go (*by vehicle*)
halten (hält) to stop (*intrans.*); to hold
können (kann) can, to be able to
laufen (läuft) to run; to go on foot, walk (*colloq.*)
ich möchte I would like to
müssen (muss) must, to have to
schaffen (*colloq.*) to handle, manage; to get done
schlafen (schläft) to sleep
sollen (soll) should, to be supposed to
tragen (trägt) to carry; to wear
tun to do
verstehen to understand
wollen (will) to want to

Berg: cf. English *iceberg.*

Substantive

der **Berg, -e** mountain
der **Wagen, -** car
der **Mitbewohner, -** roommate (*m.*)

die **Freundin, -nen** friend (*f.*)
die **Minute, -n** minute
die **Pause, -n** break; intermission
eine Pause machen to take a break
die **Stunde, -n** hour; class hour
die **Deutschstunde** German class
die **Mitbewohnerin, -nen** roommate (*f.*)

Adjektive und Adverbien

bald soon
fit in shape
genug enough
jetzt now
langweilig boring
leicht easy; light (*in weight*)
leider unfortunately
schon already, yet
spät late
steil steep
wahnsinnig (*colloq. adv.*) extremely, incredibly
wahr true

Andere Vokabeln

doch yes I *do*, yes I *am*, etc. (*contradictory*, see p. 86)
kein not a, not any, no
nichts nothing
wie lange? how long?
wohin? where to?

Kein has the same endings as **ein.** See p. 84.
Practice pronounciation of **nichts** by first adding vowels to its end, then eliminating them: **nich-zu, nich-ze, nichts.**

Practice pronunciation of **bisschen.**

Nützliche Ausdrücke

ein bisschen a little; a little bit; a little while
Ich habe keine Lust. I don't want to.
Mensch! Man! Wow!
nach Hause home (*as destination*)
Ich fahre nach Hause. I'm driving home.
nicht (wahr)? isn't it?, can't you?, doesn't he?, etc.
Um Gottes Willen! For heaven's sake! Oh, my gosh!
Was ist los? What's the matter?; What's going on?
zu Fuß gehen to go on foot, walk

Gegensätze

langweilig ≠ interessant boring ≠ interesting
leicht ≠ schwer light; easy ≠ heavy; difficult, hard
nichts ≠ etwas nothing ≠ something
spät ≠ früh late ≠ early

Mit anderen Worten

stinklangweilig = sehr, sehr langweilig
wahnsinnig (*colloq.*) **= sehr, sehr**

Contrast **zu Hause** and **nach Hause.**

You've Got It Made!

Renate is visiting her friend Monika.

M: You've got it made in Frankfurt, Renate. It's really boring here in Hinterwalden.
R: Then you have to visit me soon. Or don't you want to?
M: Sure I do. I really would like to go to Frankfurt, but unfortunately I don't have any money.
R: I certainly understand that, but surely you can earn enough by June.

A Break

Kurt and Stefan are driving to Innsbruck.

K: We still have an hour to drive to Innsbruck.
S: Can we take a break? I'd like to walk a bit.
K: Me too. We can stop over there, can't we?
S: Yes. (*They stop.*) Man, the mountain is really steep!
K: What's the matter? Aren't you in shape?
S: Sure! I can manage that easily.

Unfortunately, I Don't Have a Car Today

C: Klaus, what time is it?
K: Oh, my gosh! It's already 11:30.
C: Do you have to go home now?
K: Yes, and I have to walk. Unfortunately I don't have a car today.
C: Why not?
K: My roommate has it tonight. He has a lot to do.

Draw students' attention to different pattern of modals in 3rd sing.: no **-t**.

Variationen

■ A ■ Persönliche Fragen

1. Wo sind Sie zu Hause?
2. Gibt es da viel zu tun oder ist es langweilig?
3. Brauchen Sie heute einen Wagen oder gehen Sie zu Fuß?
4. Besitzen Sie einen Wagen?
5. Sind Sie fit oder nicht?
6. Haben Sie genug Geld?

Übung B gives students an initial sense of how modals work.

■ B ■ Übung

1. Kurt möchte ein bisschen laufen. Ich möchte zu Hause bleiben.
   Was möchten Sie denn machen?
   Ich möchte ________ .

2. Kurt und Stefan wollen da drüben halten. Ich will nach Hause laufen.
   Was wollen Sie denn machen?
   Ich will ________ .

3. Klaus muss morgen arbeiten. Ich muss kochen.
   Was müssen Sie denn morgen machen?
   Ich muss ________ .

■ C ■ Partnerarbeit: Doch!

Contradict what your partner says, using **doch**.

BEISPIEL: Du besuchst mich nicht!
Doch, ich besuche dich!

1. Du bist nicht fit!
2. Der Tourist kommt nicht aus Amerika!
3. Du verstehst mich nicht!
4. Wir arbeiten heute nicht!
5. Die Studenten gehen nicht nach Hause!
6. Robert ist nicht dein Freund!
7. Der Berg ist nicht steil!
8. Es ist nicht spät!

Lyrik zum Vorlesen

Lab Manual Kap. 3, Lyrik zum Vorlesen.

Bruder Jakob

This round for four voices comes originally from France, but is sung by children all over the world. In German, **Frère Jacques** is called **Bruder Jakob**.

Bruder Jakob, Bruder Jakob!
Schläfst° du noch? Schläfst du noch? — sleep
Hörst du nicht die Glocken°? — bells
Hörst du nicht die Glocken?
Ding, ding, dong. Ding, ding, dong.

Rätsel (Riddles)

Rhyming riddles are very old forms of oral popular literature. The solutions to these two are shown by the accompanying illustrations.

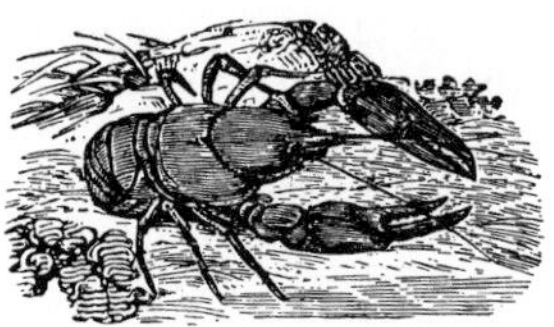

(der Hummer)

Rot° und gut, — red
hat Fleisch° und kein Blut°. — flesh / blood

(die Schnecke)

Ich gehe alle Tage° aus — every day
und bleibe doch in meinem Haus.

This discussion of the predicate anticipates analysis of the position of **nicht** and sentence-final elements like dependent infinitives and past participles.

The predicate

In both German and English, all statements and questions contain a subject (S) and an inflected verb (V):

S V Ich arbeite viel.	S V *I work a lot.*
V S Schläfst du?	V S *Are you sleeping?*

The verb by itself, however, is not always adequate to express the entire action or condition in which the subject is involved. For example, consider the simple statement:

Stefan ist jung.

Stefan is the subject and **ist** is the verb. When taken by themselves, however, the words

Stefan ist

are not a meaningful utterance. The verb **sein** must be completed, in this case by the adjective **jung**. **Sein** may also be completed by a noun in the nominative case.

Stefan ist **mein Bruder**.

In both cases, the verb and its complement together make up the entire verbal idea, or predicate. That's why adjectives and nouns that follow the verb **sein** are called *predicate adjectives* and *predicate nominatives.*

Various kinds of words and phrases can complement verbs to form the complete predicate. For instance, in the sentence

Ich trage Jeans.

the verb **trage** is completed by the direct object **Jeans.** In the sentence

Ich möchte laufen.

the modal verb **möchte** is completed by the infinitive **laufen**. You will learn about modal verbs like **möchte** in the following section.

The English modal system has no past tense for verbs like *must* and *may*; instead, English speakers say *had to* and *was allowed to*. The German system is much more regular.

Modal verbs

There is a group of six verbs in German called *the modal verbs*. They do not express an action or condition by themselves, but rather the subject's *attitude* or *relation* to the action expressed by another verb.

Wir **müssen** noch eine Stunde **fahren**.	*We still **have to drive** for an hour.*
Bis Juni **kannst** du genug **verdienen**.	*By June you **can earn** enough.*

The modal verb **müssen** (*have to*) indicates that it is *necessary* for the subject (**wir**) to perform the action of driving (**fahren**). **Müssen** is the first part of the predicate, and the infinitive **fahren** is the second part of the predicate. The German modals are:

		Expresses
dürfen	*to be allowed to, may*	permission
können	*to be able to, can*	ability
müssen	*to have to, must*	necessity
sollen	*to be supposed to, should*	obligation
wollen	*to want to; to intend to*	desire; intention
(ich) **möchte**	*(I) would like to*	inclination, desire

Möchte (*would like to*) is a subjunctive form of the modal verb **mögen** (*to like*), which you will learn in the next chapter.

Lehrer und Schüler

The modal auxiliaries take no endings in the **ich**- and **er**-forms, and most have a changed stem vowel in the singular.

Point out similarity to the present-tense singular conjugation of **wissen** (stem-vowel shift, no ending in 1st and 3rd person).

dürfen *to be allowed to*			
ich	**darf**	wir	dürfen
du	**darfst**	ihr	dürft
er, es, sie	**darf**	sie, Sie	dürfen

Darf ich draußen **spielen**?
May I play outside?

können *to be able to*			
ich	**kann**	wir	können
du	**kannst**	ihr	könnt
er, es, sie	**kann**	sie, Sie	können

Wir **können** da drüben **halten**.
We can stop over there.

müssen *to have to*			
ich	**muss**	wir	müssen
du	**musst**	ihr	müsst
er, es, sie	**muss**	sie, Sie	müssen

Heute **muss** ich zu Fuß **gehen**.
Today I have to go on foot.

wollen *to want to*			
ich	**will**	wir	wollen
du	**willst**	ihr	wollt
er, es, sie	**will**	sie, Sie	wollen

Willst du jetzt **essen**?
Do you want to eat now?

Notice that only **sollen** does not have a stem-vowel change in the singular.

sollen *to be supposed to*			
ich	soll	wir	sollen
du	sollst	ihr	sollt
er, es, sie	soll	sie, Sie	sollen

Sollen wir eine Pause **machen**?
Should we take a break?

Notice that **möchte** has endings different from the other modal verbs.

For **ich mag**, etc., see Kap. 4. If students ask, **möchte** is a subjunctive form (indicated in English by *would*). The subjunctive is taught systematically in Kap. 14, but **möchte** is so frequent that students should learn it now.

ich möchte *I would like to* (infinitive: **mögen**)			
ich	möchte	wir	möchten
du	möchtest	ihr	möchtet
er, es, sie	möchte	sie, Sie	möchten

Ich **möchte** dich **besuchen**.
I would like to visit you.

In contrast to German, some English modals require a dependent infinitive with *to* (*I want **to read***), while others do not (*I can **read***).

The modal verb is *always* the inflected verb in the sentence. The complementary infinitive (which is the second part of the predicate) comes at the end of the sentence. Note the difference from English, in which the dependent infinitive immediately *follows* the modal verb.

Wir **können** da drüben **halten**.	*We **can stop** over there.*
Das **muss** ich für morgen **lesen**.	*I **have to read** that for tomorrow.*
Marie **soll** ihre Eltern **besuchen**.	*Marie **is supposed to visit** her parents.*

It is important to get used to this two-part predicate, since it is a central structural feature of German sentences.

Lab Manual Kap. 3, Var. zu Üb. 1, 4.

Workbook Kap. 3, A, B, C.

Point out that in German, the infinitive comes *last* in such phrases: **Monika besuchen** = *to visit Monika* or *visiting Monika.*

Variation: Students will now be able to ask each other similar questions and give free responses.

■ 1 ■ Übung: Was möchten Sie heute tun? Here are some things people in the dialogues on p. 73 are doing.

Monika besuchen	Geld verdienen
nach Frankfurt fahren	eine Pause machen
ein bisschen laufen	da drüben halten
nach Hause fahren	zu Fuß gehen

Choose from these activities to answer the following questions.

BEISPIEL: Was möchten Sie heute tun?
Ich möchte Monika besuchen.

1. Was können Sie heute tun?
2. Was müssen Sie heute tun?
3. Was möchten Sie heute tun?

■ 2 ■ Gruppenarbeit: Was willst du machen? (*4 Studenten*) Ask each other about what you intend to do or be. This list will provide some ideas. What others can you find?

BEISPIEL: Was willst du denn machen?
Ich will in Deutschland studieren, und du?

eine Familie haben	Freunde in Europa besuchen
viel Geld verdienen	fit sein
berufstätig sein	eine Pause machen
ein Haus besitzen	in Deutschland studieren
nach Hause fahren	

■ Omission of the infinitive

Certain infinitives may be omitted from sentences with modal verbs when they are clearly implied.

- **haben**

Möchten Sie ein Zimmer [**haben**]?	*Would you like (to have) a room?*

- **machen, tun**

If students ask: **machen** and **tun** should be considered roughly synonymous at this point. They will encounter idioms (**Das macht nichts, Es tut mir Leid**) where only one is correct.

Das kann ich leider nicht [**machen/tun**].	*Unfortunately I can't (do that).*

- verbs of motion (**gehen, fahren, fliegen, laufen**) when destination is expressed

Musst du jetzt nach Hause [**gehen, fahren**]?	*Do you have to go home now?*

- **sprechen**, in the following expression:

Kannst du Deutsch?	*Can you speak German?*
Ja, ich kann Deutsch.	*Yes, I can speak German.*
Ich kann auch Dänisch.	*I can also speak Danish.*

For review, come back to these later and have students generate the German from English cues: I: Do you want to go home now? S: **Willst du jetzt nach Hause?**

■ 3 ■ Übung: Wie sagt man das auf Englisch?

1. Wollen Sie jetzt nach Hause?
2. Er kann das noch nicht.
3. Willst du meinen Bleistift?
4. Mein Vater will das nicht.
5. Sie können schon gut Deutsch.
6. Möchten Sie das Geld?
7. Darf man denn das?
8. Wann wollen Sie nach Amerika?

Wohin (*where to?*) is analogous to the question word **woher**? (*from where?*): **Woher kommst du?**

Fragewort	
wohin?	*where to?*

Prepare students for work in pairs by modeling the country names and eliciting a couple of free responses: **Wohin wollen *Sie* denn im Februar?**

■ 4 ■ Partnerarbeit: Wohin wollen wir im Februar? By the time the semester break comes in mid-February, many German students want to travel where it is warm. Use the map of Europe on the inside back cover to plan such a trip with your partner.

BEISPIEL: A: Wohin willst du im Februar?
B: Ich will nach ... Wohin willst du?

Verbs with stem-vowel change a *to* ä, au *to* äu

Some verbs change their stem-vowel in the following ways:

Practice pronunciation of **du hältst**. Stem-changing verbs whose stem ends in **-t** do *not* insert **-e-** between stem and personal ending: **du hältst, er hält** (in the latter form, the ending **-t** merges with the **-t** of the stem).

a → ä	fahren *to drive; to go by vehicle*		
ich	fahre	wir	fahren
du	**fährst**	ihr	fahrt
er, es, sie	**fährt**	sie, Sie	fahren

	halten *to hold; to stop*		
ich	halte	wir	halten
du	**hältst**	ihr	haltet
er, es, sie	**hält**	sie, Sie	halten

Other verbs in this group are: **schlafen** (**schläft**), *to sleep*; **tragen** (**trägt**), *to carry, wear.*

au → äu	laufen *to run*		
ich	laufe	wir	laufen
du	**läufst**	ihr	lauft
er, es, sie	**läuft**	sie, Sie	laufen

Lab Manual Kap. 3, Var. zur Üb. 5.

Workbook Kap. 3, D.

■ 5 ■ Kettenreaktion Say how you get home, then ask your classmates how they get home.

BEISPIEL: A: Ich fahre nach Hause. Fährst du auch nach Hause?
B: Nein, ich laufe nach Hause. Läufst du auch nach Hause?
C: Ja, ich laufe auch nach Hause. Läufst du ...

Fragewort
wie lange? *how long?*

6 **Kettenreaktion** Wie lange schläfst du?

BEISPIEL: Ich schlafe acht Stunden. Wie lange schläfst du?

7 **Gruppenarbeit: Mit offenen Büchern** (With open books) Tell one thing that you're wearing, then one thing the person next to you is wearing.

BEISPIEL: Ich trage ________ und er/sie trägt heute ________ .

These and other items of clothing will be introduced on page 92.

Negating statements and questions is a communicative goal.

Negation with nicht *(not)*

Nicht is used to negate a sentence.

Sabrina ist meine Schwester.	*Sabrina is my sister.*
Sabrina ist **nicht** meine Schwester.	*Sabrina is **not** my sister.*

For a preview and summary of German negation, see **Zusammenfassung und Wiederholung I**, in the Workbook.

In the preceding example, the position of **nicht** is exactly the same as the position of *not* in English. In most German sentences, however, this will not be the case. Here are some preliminary guidelines for the position of **nicht**.

In English, *not* almost always follows the inflected verb immediately.

- **Nicht** usually *follows* the subject, verb, direct object, and all personal pronouns.

Ich kenne deinen Freund **nicht**.	*I don't know your friend.*
Er sagt das **nicht**.	*He doesn't say that.*
Wir besitzen das Auto **nicht**.	*We don't own the car.*
Deine Schwester kennt mich **nicht**.	*Your sister doesn't know me.*

Some expressions of definite time: **jetzt**, **heute**, **heute Abend**, **morgen**, **am Mittwoch**.

- **Nicht** usually *follows* expressions of definite time.

Sie können heute Abend **nicht** kommen.	*They can't come tonight.*
Hans arbeitet jetzt **nicht**.	*Hans isn't working now.*

Lab Manual Kap. 3, Üb. 8, 9.

Workbook Kap. 3, E.

■ 8 ■ Übung Negate these sentences by adding **nicht**.

1. Kurt besucht seinen Bruder.
2. Ich kenne eure Mutter.
3. Frau Schmidt besucht uns morgen.
4. Monika macht das heute Abend.
5. Ich verstehe ihn.
6. Am Donnerstag kochst du.
7. Er liest sein Buch.
8. Mein Großvater schläft.
9. Das schafft er.

Review the explanations of the predicate on p. 77 and of predicate nominatives on p. 33.

Emphasize that the predicate is the inflected form of an "entire verbal idea," i.e., not **sein**, but **steil sein** (**Der Berg ist** is not a possible sentence). In **Monika verdient genug**, what's being asserted is not that she earns, but that she earns *enough*. The entire verbal idea is **genug verdienen** (*to earn enough*).

Some expressions of indefinite time: **bald**, **spät**, **früh**, **immer**, **oft**.

- **Nicht** *precedes* complements that constitute the second part of the predicate. These include:

1. Predicate adjectives

Der Berg ist **steil**.	*The mountain is **steep**.*
Der Berg ist **nicht** steil.	*The mountain is **not** steep.*

2. Predicate nominatives

Das ist **Herr Blum**.	*That is **Mr. Blum**.*
Das ist **nicht** Herr Blum.	*That is not Mr. Blum.*

3. Adverbs of manner, indefinite time, and place

Margit geht **zu Fuß**.	*Margit is going **on foot**.*
Margit geht **nicht** zu Fuß.	*Margit is**n't** going on foot.*
Er besucht mich **oft**.	*He **often** visits me.*
Er besucht mich **nicht** oft.	*He does**n't** visit me often.*
Sie wohnt **hier**.	*She lives **here**.*
Sie wohnt **nicht** hier.	*She does**n't** live here.*

4. Prepositional phrases that show destination (**nach Wien, nach Hause**) or location (**in Berlin, zu Hause**)

Sie geht **nach Hause**.	*She's going **home**.*
Sie geht **nicht** nach Hause.	*She's **not** going home.*
Er arbeitet **in Berlin**.	*He works **in Berlin**.*
Er arbeitet **nicht** in Berlin.	*He does**n't** work in Berlin.*

5. Infinitives complementing modal verbs

Er kann mich **sehen**.	*He can **see** me.*
Er kann mich **nicht** sehen.	*He can**'t** see me.*

Make sure students understand that in **Übung 9** they are simply negating statements, while **Übung 10** is a conversational exchange.

9 **Übung** Negate these sentences by adding **nicht**.

1. Das Wetter ist schön.
2. Ich kann dich besuchen.
3. Ich möchte Berlin sehen.
4. Der Berg ist steil.
5. Wir wollen halten.
6. Frau Mackensen ist unsere Lehrerin.
7. Ich muss nach Hause gehen.
8. Margit läuft gut.
9. Er kann mich sehen.

10 **Partnerarbeit: Unsere neue Mitbewohnerin** You're both getting a new roommate. Take turns asking each other questions about her. Answer them all negatively.

BEISPIEL: A: Kennt unsere Mitbewohnerin Berlin?
B: Nein, sie kennt Berlin nicht.

1. Kommt sie aus Dresden?
2. Ist sie freundlich?
3. Arbeitet sie heute Abend?
4. Studiert ihr Bruder in Leipzig?
5. Kennst du ihn?
6. Muss sie nach Hause?
7. Fährt sie bald nach Hause?
8. Schläft sie viel?
9. Ist das ihr Auto?
10. Ist sie oft schlechter Laune?

Negation with kein

Kein (*not a, not any, no*) is the negative of **ein**. It negates nouns preceded by **ein** or nouns not preceded by any article.

Morgen will ich ein Buch lesen.	*I want to read a book tomorrow.*
Morgen will ich **kein** Buch lesen.	*I don't want to read a book tomorrow.*
Hier wohnen Studenten.	*Students live here.*
Hier wohnen **keine** Studenten.	*No students live here.*

Emphasize the concept of **ein**-words (students have now learned them all). They will still tend to put predicate nominatives into the accusative (**Herr Beck ist keinen Lehrer**).

Kein is an **ein**-word and takes the same endings as **ein** and the possessive adjectives.

Das ist { **ein** Fernseher. / **kein** Fernseher. / **unser** Fernseher. }

Er hat { **einen** Wagen. / **keinen** Wagen. / **meinen** Wagen. }

Nicht and **kein** are mutually exclusive. In any given situation, only one will be correct. If a noun is preceded by the definite article or by a possessive adjective, use **nicht** rather than **kein** to negate it.

Ist das die Professorin?	*Is that the professor?*
Nein, das ist **nicht** die Professorin.	*No, that's not the professor.*
Ist das eure Professorin?	*Is that your professor?*
Nein, das ist **nicht** unsere Professorin.	*No, that's not our professor.*
Ist sie Professorin?	*Is she a professor?*
Nein, sie ist **keine** Professorin.	*No, she's not a professor.*

Lab Manual Kap. 3, Üb. 11; Var. zur Üb. 11.

Workbook Kap. 3, F, G.

■ **11** ■ **Übung** Negate the sentence, using **kein**.

1. Meine Familie besitzt einen Wagen.
2. Maria hat heute Geld.
3. Hier gibt es ein Problem.
4. Hier wohnen Studenten.
5. Morgen gibt es eine Diskussion.
6. Herr Meyer hat Kinder.

Variation: Students can ask each other **Hast du ...** or **Trägst du ...** about clothing on p. 82. Warm-up/review on following day as teacher–student exchange: **Haben Sie eine Schwester/einen Wagen?** Encourage use of **leider** where appropriate.

■ **12** ■ **Übung** Respond negatively to these questions, using **kein** or **nicht**.

BEISPIEL: Hat Barbara einen Freund? Nein, sie hat keinen Freund.
Ist das ihr Freund? Nein, das ist nicht ihr Freund.

1. Haben Sie einen Freund in Oslo?
2. Haben Sie Freunde in Washington?
3. Ist das der Professor?
4. Verdient er Geld?
5. Sehen Sie das Haus?
6. Ist das seine Freundin?
7. Suchen Sie das Buch?
8. Suchen Sie ein Buch?

■ **13** ■ **Partnerarbeit: Meine Familie** Ask each other about your families. (For family members, see pp. 62–63.)

BEISPIEL: A: Hast du einen Sohn?
B: Nein, ich habe keinen Sohn.

Requesting confirmation is a communicative goal.

Nicht wahr? can only follow positive statements.

The tag question **oder?** can be attached to either positive *or* negative statements: **Du hast kein Geld mehr, *oder*? Du hast noch Geld, *oder*?**

Expecting an affirmative answer: nicht wahr?

Nicht wahr? (literally, "not true?"), when added to a positive statement, anticipates confirmation (English: *doesn't she? wasn't he? wasn't it? didn't you?* etc.). In spoken German, you may shorten it to **nicht**?

Heute ist es schön, **nicht wahr**?	*It's beautiful today, isn't it?*
Sie studieren in Freiburg, **nicht**?	*You're studying in Freiburg, aren't you?*
Gisela kennst du, **nicht wahr**?	*You know Gisela, don't you?*

Point to an object and assert that it is something else. Throw in an occasional correct assertion. Students can then repeat this as a **Partnerarbeit**.

■ **14** ■ **Übung: Das ist ein Tisch, nicht wahr?** Contradict your instructor if necessary.

BEISPIEL: Das ist ein Tisch, nicht wahr?
Nein, das ist kein Tisch, das ist ein(e) ______ .

Übung 15 may be assigned as written homework.

■ **15** ■ **Übung: Wie sagt man das auf Deutsch?**

1. You have a car, don't you?
2. You're learning German, aren't you?
3. You'll visit me soon, won't you?
4. He's in good shape, isn't he?
5. We can work today, can't we?
6. You can understand that, can't you?

Contradicting a negative statement or question: doch

Contradicting someone is a communicative goal.

Si serves the same function in French.

To contradict a negative statement or question, use **doch** instead of **ja**.

Ich spreche nicht gut Deutsch.	*I don't speak German well.*
Doch, Sie sprechen sehr gut Deutsch!	*Yes you do, you speak German very well.*
Kennst du Ursula nicht?	*Don't you know Ursula?*
Doch, ich kenne sie sehr gut!	*Sure, I know her very well.*

Lab Manual Kap. 3, Var. zur Üb. 16.

Initial **doch** does not count as the first element in determining word order. See p. 34.

■ 16 ■ Übung: Doch! Contradict these negative statements and questions, beginning your response with a stressed **doch**.

BEISPIEL: Schaffst du das nicht?
Doch, ich schaffe das!

1. Wir wollen nicht halten.
2. Wir haben nicht genug Geld.
3. Hast du keinen Bruder?
4. Es ist nicht sehr spät.
5. Kannst du kein Deutsch?
6. Willst du nicht zu Fuß gehen?

This is the reverse of the game in **Übung 14**. This time, you're indicating that things are *not* what they in fact are. When students are good at this, you can mix the two forms or students can do it on their own.

■ 17 ■ Übung Contradict your instructor if necessary.

BEISPIEL: Das ist kein Tisch.
Doch! Natürlich ist das ein Tisch!

The indefinite pronoun man

On serves the same function in French.

The indefinite pronoun **man** refers to people in general rather than to any specific person. Although the English indefinite pronoun *one* may sound formal in everyday speech, **man** does not sound this way in German. It is used in both colloquial and formal language. It is often best translated into English as *people, they, you,* or even *we.*

You can use **man** only as the subject of a sentence, and only with a verb in the third-person singular.

In Deutschland sagt **man** das oft.	*They often say that in Germany.*
Das muss **man** lernen.	*You've got to learn that.*
Das weiß **man** nie.	*One never knows.*

Do not confuse **man** with **der Mann** (*the man*).

Der Mann spricht Deutsch.

Hier spricht man Deutsch.

■ 18 ■ **Übung** Change the subject to **man**.

1. In Hinterwalden können die Leute nicht genug verdienen.
2. Um elf Uhr machen wir eine Pause.
3. Hoffentlich können wir drüben halten.
4. Hier können Sie gut essen.
5. Dürfen wir hier schlafen?

Übung 19 may be assigned as written homework. You could ask students to add a few more such general statements of their own invention.

■ 19 ■ **Übung: Wie sagt man das auf Deutsch?** Use **man** as the subject.

1. In America we don't say that.
2. You've got to stop here.
3. One has to do that.
4. People say there are problems here.
5. Can we go on foot?

Vor dem Lesen

Tipps zum Lesen und Lernen

■ Tipp zum Vokabelnlernen

Masculine nouns ending in **-er** have the same form in the plural.

Singular	*Plural*
der Lehrer	die Lehrer
der Amerikaner	die Amerikaner
der Schüler	die Schüler
der Europäer	die Europäer
der Pullover	die Pullover
der Computer	die Computer

Tell students that loan words from other languages usually do take plural **-s: Hotel**, **Büro**, **Auto**, **Kino**.

Resist the temptation to add an **-s** as in the English plural (*two pullovers*). Remember that *very few* German nouns take **-s** in the plural.

■ ■ ■ **Übung** Answer your instructor's questions with the plural form.

1. Wie viele Computer besitzt die Universität?
2. Wie viele Amerikaner sind hier im Zimmer?
3. Wie viele Schüler kennen Sie?
4. Wie viele Europäer studieren hier?
5. Wie viele Pullover besitzen Sie?

Lab Manual Kap. 3, Üb. zur Betonung.

■ Leicht zu merken

international	international	der **Sport**	
die **Jeans** (*pl.*)		das **System, -e**	System
optimistisch	optimistisch	das **Schulsystem**	Schulsystem
pessimistisch	pessimistisch	das **Theater**	Theater

Einstieg in den Text

1. The speakers in the following **Klassendiskussion** express opinions about their recent trip. Notice how often they preface opinions with such phrases as **Ich finde**, ... or **Man meint**, ... *(I think ..., People think ...)*.
2. Remember that word order in German is in some ways freer than in English. It is true that the verb must be in second position in statements. In place of the subject, however, an object, an adverb, or some other element can be in first position. You will often find sentences beginning with the direct object:

Das finde ich auch.	*I think so too.* (literally: *I find that too.*)
Das kann ich verstehen.	*I can understand that.*

The clue to understanding such sentences is the personal ending of the verb. Words like **habe** and **finde** are obviously first person and go with the subject pronoun **ich**.

Wortschatz 2

You may want to teach **schwänzen** (*to cut a class*).

Verben

besprechen (bespricht) to discuss
entscheiden to decide
hassen to hate
hören to hear
lachen to laugh
lernen to learn
schreiben to write
singen to sing

Substantive

der **Europäer, -** European (*m.*)
der **Fuß, ⸚e** foot
zu Fuß on foot
der **Mantel, ⸚** coat
der **Pullover, -** pullover, sweater
also: der **Pulli, -s**
der **Schuh, -e** shoe
der **Turnschuh** sneaker, gym shoe
(das) **Amerika** America
(das) **Deutsch** German (*language*)
(das) **Englisch** English
(das) **Europa** Europe
das **Gymnasium,** die **Gymnasien** secondary school (*prepares pupils for university*)
das **Hemd, -en** shirt
das **Kleid, -er** dress; *pl.* = dresses *or* clothes
die **Angst, ⸚e** fear
Angst haben to be afraid
die **Europäerin, -nen** European (*f.*)
die **Farbe, -n** color
die **Hausaufgabe, -n** homework assignment
die **Hose, -n** trousers, pants
die **Jacke, -n** jacket
die **Musik** music
die **Reise, -n** trip
eine Reise machen to take a trip
die **Sprache, -n** language
die **Fremdsprache** foreign language

Gymnasium derives from Greek for the place where athletes trained (**gymnos** = *naked*). The word was later generalized to mean *place of study*.

die **Umwelt** environment
die **Welt, -en** world
die **Zeit, -en** time
die **Pommes frites** (*pl., pronounced "Pomm fritt"*) French fries

Adjektive und Adverbien

ähnlich similar
also thus, for that reason
amerikanisch American
darum therefore, for that reason
dunkel dark
ehrlich honest
eigentlich actually, in fact
fremd strange, foreign
neu new
schnell fast
toll (*colloq.*) great, terrific

Basic meaning of **toll**: *mad, crazy* (**das Tollhaus** = *madhouse*).

Angst from Latin *angustiae* = a narrow constriction. English has borrowed **Angst** from German and uses it to mean *anxiety, existential fear*.

Farben

blau blue
braun brown
bunt colorful, multicolored
gelb yellow
grau gray
grün green
rot red
schwarz black
weiß white

Nützliche Ausdrücke

bitte please
Das finde ich auch. I think so too.
gar nicht not at all
Stimmt schon. That's right.

Gegensätze

dunkel ≠ hell dark ≠ light
hassen ≠ lieben to hate ≠ to love
lachen ≠ weinen to laugh ≠ to cry
neu ≠ alt new ≠ old
schnell ≠ langsam fast ≠ slow
Stimmt schon. ≠ Stimmt nicht. That's right. ≠ That's wrong.

Wie bitte? = *I beg your pardon? What did you say?* Remind studens that **bitte** also means *You're welcome.*

Mit anderen Worten

uralt = sehr, sehr alt
blitzschnell = sehr, sehr schnell

Additional vocabulary: **die Note, -n** (*grade*). Grades in German schools are numbers, not letters (1–6 = A–F), and are feminine: **Ich habe eine Eins in Mathe.**

Lab Manual Kap. 3, Lesestück.

Eine Klassendiskussion

Learning about German secondary schools is the cultural goal of this chapter.

Last spring class 12a from the Kepler Gymnasium in Hannover visited a high school in California. Now they are discussing their impressions of the States with their teacher, Herr Beck; they also plan to write an article for their school newspaper.[1]

Notice the flavoring particle **ja** (lines 2 and 6) conveying the meaning *after all*.

HERR BECK: Können wir jetzt unsere Amerikareise ein bisschen besprechen? Rolf, möchtest du etwas sagen? – Ach, er schläft ja wieder. (*Alle lachen.*)

ROLF: Meinen Sie mich? Entschuldigung! Unsere Reise? Sie war° doch toll.

KIRSTEN: Das finde ich auch. Die Amerikaner sind wahnsinnig freundlich und jetzt weiß ich, die Schüler in Amerika sind eigentlich gar nicht so anders. Dort trägt man ja auch Jeans und Turnschuhe, hört Rockmusik, singt dieselben Schlager° und isst Pommes frites.

HERR BECK: Stimmt schon, aber haben die amerikanischen Schüler auch ähnliche Probleme wie ihr?

ANDREAS: Ach, wissen Sie, alle Schüler hassen Hausaufgaben! (*Alle lachen.*) Nein, aber im Ernst°, wir sind alle manchmal pessimistisch. Man meint, man kann später° keine Arbeit finden, und auch die Umweltprobleme sind heute international. Auch in Amerika haben die Schüler manchmal ein bisschen Angst.

HERR BECK: Das kann ich verstehen, muss ich ehrlich sagen. Aber gibt es denn keine Unterschiede° zwischen hier und dort?

KIRSTEN: Doch, natürlich! Dort besuchen° alle Schüler die Highschool, bis sie 18 sind. Mit zehn Jahren müssen wir aber entscheiden: Gymnasium, Realschule oder Hauptschule.[2] Die zwei Schulsysteme sind also ganz anders.

was
dieselben Schlager = the same hits
seriously
later
differences
here: attend

Assign **Almanach** (p. 97) as homework before assigning this **Lesestück**.

1. The **Gymnasium** in German-speaking countries has 13 grades. Class 12a is one of several parallel 12th-grade classes in the **Gymnasium**. Students stay in the same group for several years and take all their classes together. German 13th-graders are between 18 and 20 years old.
2. See *Almanach*, p. 97.

Die Schülerin hat eine Frage. (Hannover)

CHRISTA: Ich finde, wir müssen hier mehr und schneller° lernen. Deutschland ist in Mitteleuropa° und hat viele Nachbarländer°. Darum müssen wir ja Fremdsprachen lernen. Viele Europäer können z.B. gut Englisch, aber relativ wenige Amerikaner lernen Fremdsprachen. Andererseits° macht man an der Schule[1] in Amerika mehr Sport, Musik und Theater.

faster / Central Europe / neighboring countries / on the other hand

HERR BECK: Jetzt haben wir leider keine Zeit mehr. Aber morgen können wir unseren Artikel über die Reise für die Schülerzeitung schreiben. Auf Wiedersehen bis dann.

Nach dem Lesen

A **Unterschiede und Ähnlichkeiten** (differences and similarities) Which statements apply to schools in Germany, which apply to schools in America, which apply to both (**beide**)?

	Deutschland	*USA*	*beide*
1. Die Schüler hören gern Rockmusik.	_____	_____	_____
2. Man trägt oft Jeans und Turnschuhe.	_____	_____	_____
3. Die Schule hat 13 Klassen.	_____	_____	_____
4. Fremdsprachen sind sehr wichtig.	_____	_____	_____
5. Sport, Musik und Theater sind sehr wichtig.	_____	_____	_____
6. Mit zehn Jahren müssen Schüler die Schule wählen (*choose*).	_____	_____	_____

1. **an der Schule** = *at school.* The article **der** indicates that **Schule** is in the dative case, which you will learn about in **Kapitel 5**.

Have students count the courses and read the schedule aloud. Correct pronunciation. Help them with **Geschichte** and **Erdkunde** (**Das heißt auch Geographie**). Ask questions such as: **Wie viele Stunden Französisch hat er pro Woche? Wann kann er früh nach Hause gehen? Wann kann er lange schlafen?**

■ B ■ Ein Stundenplan Fabian Becker ist ein Schüler in Klasse 13 im Keplergymnasium. Hier sehen Sie seinen Stundenplan für die Woche. Sie können sehen, ein Schüler in Deutschland hat viele Fächer (*subjects*). Wie viele Fächer hat er? Wie viele Fremdsprachen und naturwissenschaftliche Fächer (*science courses*) hat er? Was hat er am Montag und Dienstag? Welche (*which*) Hausaufgaben muss er am Mittwochabend machen?

Wie ist sein Stundenplan anders als (*different from*) der Stundenplan in amerikanischen Schulen?

Zeit	Montag	Dienstag	Mittwoch	Donnerstag	Freitag
7^{45} - 8^{30}	–	–	Französisch	Biologie	–
8^{35} - 9^{20}	Englisch	Mathematik	Französisch	Biologie	–
9^{30} - 10^{15}	Religion	Politik / Erdkunde	Deutsch	Mathematik	Mathematik
10^{20} - 11^{05}	Deutsch	Chemie	Deutsch	Religion	Politik / Erdkunde
11^{25} - 12^{10}	Sport	Biologie	Geschichte	Englisch	Englisch
12^{15} - 13^{00}	Sport	Biologie	–	Französisch	Geschichte
13^{00} - 14^{00}	(Orchester)				
14^{00} - 14^{45}	Biologie				
14^{50} - 15^{35}	Französisch				
15^{40} - 16^{25}	Französisch		Chemie		
16^{30} - 17^{15}			Chemie		
17^{20} - 18^{05}					

Activity to promote recall of material: Make **Unterschiede** and **Ähnlichkeiten** columns on the board and get students to list differences and similarities.

■ C ■ Antworten Sie auf Deutsch.

1. Sind die Schüler in Amerika sehr anders oder sind sie ähnlich?
2. Was trägt man zum Beispiel in Amerika und auch in Deutschland?
3. Was isst man auch dort?
4. Was hassen alle Schüler?
5. Warum sind viele Schüler manchmal pessimistisch?
6. Warum müssen die Deutschen Fremdsprachen lernen?
7. Was schreibt die Klasse für ihre Schülerzeitung?

Situationen aus dem Alltag

Talking about clothing is a communicative goal.

■ Was soll ich heute tragen?

This vocabulary focuses on an everyday topic or situation. Words you already know from **Wortschatz** sections are listed without English equivalents; new supplementary vocabulary is listed with definitions. Your instructor may assign some supplementary vocabulary for active mastery.

You already know some of this vocabulary.

die **Kleidung**	*clothing*
1. der **Anzug, ⸚e**	*suit*
2. die **Bluse, -n**	*blouse*
3. die **Brille** (*sing.*)	*glasses*
4. der **Handschuh, -e**	*glove*
5. das **Hemd, -en**	
6. die **Hose, -n**	
7. der **Hut, ⸚e**	*hat*
8. die **Jacke, -n**	
9. das **Kleid, -er**	
10. die **Krawatte, -n**	*tie*
11. der **Mantel, ¨**	
12. der **Pulli, -s**	
13. der **Rock, ⸚e**	*skirt*
14. der **Schuh, -e**	
15. die **Tasche, -n**	*pocket; handbag, shoulder bag*
16. das **T-Shirt, -s**	*T-shirt*
17. der **Turnschuh, -e**	
18. der **Regenschirm, -e**	*umbrella*
19. die **Mütze, -n**	*cap*

Other items of clothing: **der Regenmantel**, **die Armbanduhr**, **das Kostüm** (*woman's suit*), **der Stiefel**, **die Sandale**, **das Jackett** (*sport coat*). Another popular Americanism: **das Sweatshirt, -s**.

■ A ■ Gruppenarbeit: Was tragen Sie heute?

BEISPIEL: PROFESSOR: Was tragen Sie heute, Mary?
STUDENTIN: Ich trage ______ und ______.

■ B ■ Partnerarbeit: Was trägst du heute?

BEISPIEL: A: Was trägst du heute, Mary?
B: Ich trage ______ und ______. Was trägst du?

■ C ■ Gruppenarbeit: Was tragen Sie in diesen Situationen?

Weather vocabulary from **Einführung**.

BEISPIEL: Es regnet.
Dann trage ich ...

1. Es regnet. (Es schneit. Es ist windig.)
2. Die Sonne scheint und es ist sehr warm.
3. Sie müssen eine Stelle suchen.
4. Sie und Ihre Mitbewohner machen heute Abend eine Party.

Use the flags to practice colors, pronunciation, geography, and the constituency of the European Union. Model **Partnerarbeit**, reviewing **sein/ihr** distinction: point to individuals and ask **Welche Farbe hat ihr/sein Sweatshirt?** Model pronunciation of **orange**.

■ Welche Farbe hat das?

The prefixes **dunkel** and **hell** may be added to the colors you have learned in **Wortschatz 2**.

dunkelblau = *dark blue*
hellgrün = *light green*

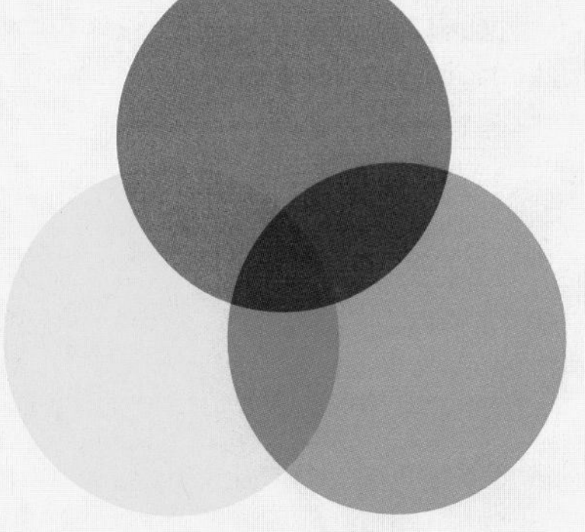

Three more colors that may be useful:

rosa *pink*
lila *violet, lavender*
orange *orange*

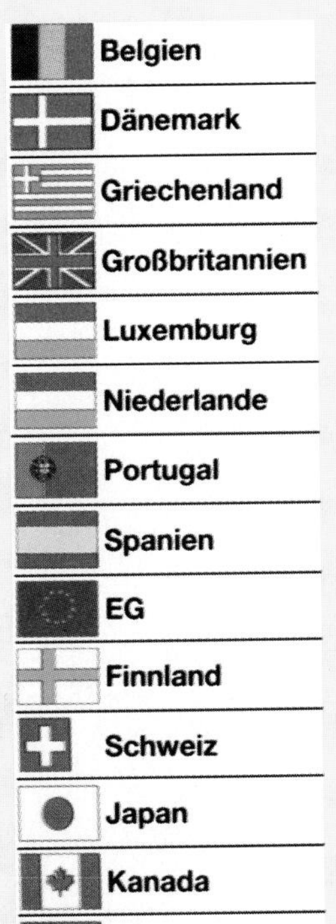

■ D ■ Übung Welche Farben haben diese Fahnen (*flags*)?

Frankreich

BEISPIEL: Frankreich: rot, weiß, blau

Deutschland: ______, ______, ______ [*gold*]
Österreich: ______, ______, ______
Schweden: ______, ______
Italien: ______, ______, ______
Irland: ______, ______, ______

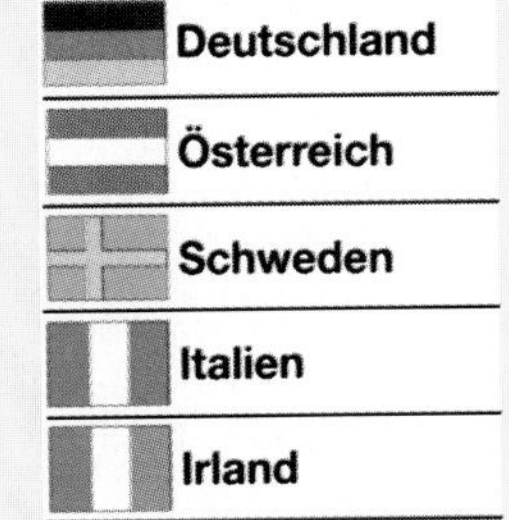

■ E ■ Partnerarbeit Ask each other about the colors of various things in the classroom and of clothing people are wearing.

BEISPIELE: Welche Farben hat die Landkarte?
Sie ist ______.

Welche Farbe hat Peters Hemd?
Sein Hemd ist ______.

Zum Schluss

Workbook Kap. 3, H, I, J, K, L.

Lab Manual Kap. 3, Diktat.

Sprechen wir miteinander!

A Übung Answer each question in the negative, making sure to use **nicht** or **kein** correctly.

1. Haben Sie heute Abend Hausaufgaben?
2. Machen Sie Ihre Hausaufgaben heute Abend?
3. Können wir jetzt arbeiten?
4. Sind Ihre Freunde fit? Sind Sie fit?
5. Machen Sie im Dezember eine Reise?
6. Wollen Sie das?
7. Hören Sie mich?
8. Lachen die Kinder laut?
9. Haben Sie Angst?
10. Tragen Sie eine Mütze?
11. Ist ihre Hose grün?
12. Fahren Sie oft nach Hause?

Übung A, item 11: Point to a female student.

You may want to assign two sentences from **Übung B** as written homework after students have done it orally.

B Gruppenarbeit: Mit offenen Büchern (*3 oder 4 Studenten*) Take turns changing each sentence by substituting the new elements provided.

BEISPIEL: Ich möchte morgen nach Berlin. (wollen)
A: Ich will morgen nach Berlin. (Wien)
B: Ich will morgen nach Wien.

1. Ich möchte morgen nach Berlin.
   wollen
   München
   müssen
   wir
   Kopenhagen
   nächstes Semester
2. Im Juni kannst du viel Geld verdienen.
   müssen
   September
   ich
   haben
   wollen
3. Wir können da drüben halten.
   sollen
   eine Pause machen
   ich
   möchte
   arbeiten
   zu Hause
4. Er geht jetzt nach Hause.
   fahren
   morgen
   Max
   bald
   ihr

Unser Kind soll gesund sein.

Expressing opinions is a communicative goal.

■ C ■ **Gruppenarbeit: Was meinen Sie? (*4 Personen*)** Here are some topics of conversation and some adjectives. Using the verbs **meinen** and **finden**, take turns expressing opinions about these topics. Others in the group agree or disagree.

BEISPIEL: A: Ich finde (meine), die Umwelt ist wichtig.
B: Das finde (meine) ich auch. *oder*
Das finde (meine) ich nicht.

Schulen in Amerika	schön/hässlich
Schulen in Deutschland	wichtig/unwichtig
Rockmusik	interessant/langweilig
klassische Musik	toll
die Umwelt	prima
Fremdsprachen	stinklangweilig
Hausaufgaben	wahnsinnig gut

■ D ■ **Gruppenspiel: Stimmt nicht! (*3 Personen*)** Play this game with two other people. One says something obviously false. The others contradict that statement and give the correct information. Then the next player takes a turn.

BEISPIEL: ________ Kirsten trägt heute einen Pulli.
________ Stimmt nicht! Sie trägt keinen Pulli! Sie trägt eine Bluse.

■ E ■ **Partnerarbeit: Interview – *heute und morgen*** Interview each other. Give as many answers as possible to the following questions.

1. Was möchtest du heute Abend machen? Ich möchte ________ .
2. Was musst du morgen machen? Morgen muss ich ________ .
3. Was willst du in 10 Jahren (*in 10 years*) machen? In 10 Jahren will ich ________ .

Schreiben Sie zu Hause.

■ F ■ Udo is throwing a party, but nobody can come. Finish writing him the following note explaining why. There are some cues to help you.

Lieber Udo (*Dear Udo*),
leider kann niemand zur Party kommen. Monika muss zu Hause bleiben.
Klaus ...

Klaus / müssen / für morgen / machen / seine Hausaufgaben
Ruth / möchten / fahren / nach Berlin
Peter und Ute / wollen / besuchen / ihre Tante / in Wien
Herr Beck / können / leider / finden / seinen Anzug / nicht
Andreas / dürfen / nicht so spät / kommen / nach Hause
ich / wollen / gar nicht / kommen

G Finish the following dialogue by completing the sentences.

ANNA: Hallo Klaus!
KLAUS: ________ , wie geht's?
ANNA: ________ . Was machst du denn heute?
KLAUS: Heute muss ich ________ . Und du?
ANNA: Heute soll ich ________ , aber ich will ________ . Also tschüss!
KLAUS: Tschüss Anna!

Now compose your own dialogue of three or four exchanges.

H Wie sagt man das auf Deutsch?

1. Wouldn't you like to stay a bit?
2. Unfortunately, I have to work this evening.
3. What do you have to do?
4. I have to read a book and an article.

5. Don't you have any friends in Hinterwalden?
6. Yes, I do. Unfortunately they're quite boring.
7. Then you have to visit us soon.

8. You want to come to Berlin, don't you?
9. Yes. I can't stay in Hinterwalden.
10. Why not? Aren't there any jobs there?
11. Yes, but not enough. I want to look for a job in Berlin.

Almanach

A Note about Schools in German-speaking Countries

The public school systems in Germany, Austria, and Switzerland all differ from American public schools in the degree to which they track pupils. Relatively early in their schooling, children are steered toward apprenticeships, commercial training, or preparation for university study. In the Federal Republic of Germany, each **Land** (state) has authority over its own school system. In all **Länder**, children attend four years of elementary school (**Grundschule**) together. At the end of the fourth, fifth, or sixth grade (depending on the **Land**), they are then tracked into separate schools. The decision is made on the basis of grades and conferences between teachers and parents.

There are three possibilities: the **Hauptschule**, the **Realschule**, or the **Gymnasium**. The first two are oriented respectively toward trades and business and prepare the pupils for various forms of apprenticeship and job training. The **Gymnasium** is the traditional preparation for university study. After passing their final examination, called the **Abitur** in Germany and the **Matura** in Austria and Switzerland, pupils may apply to a university.

Since 1971, there has been some experimentation in the Federal Republic with **Gesamtschulen** (unified schools) comprising all three types of secondary schools. These schools resemble American high schools, in that pupils need not make their important decision at the age of ten, but can wait until they are sixteen. **Gesamtschulen**, however, comprise only a small percentage of the total number of secondary schools.

DUDEN
für
SCHÜLER

Once students have read both the **Lesestück** and the **Almanach**, contrast the German system with the ones they know. What are the advantages and disadvantages? Have any of them been or known exchange students? Supplement discussion with realia such as German schoolbooks; mention that children carry their books home every day in **Schulranzen**; the school day is over before lunch; children stay together in the same class group through several grades.

KAPITEL 4

Land und Leute

Communicative Goals

- Making suggestions and giving commands
- Expressing likes, dislikes, and preferences
- Discussing weather, climate, and landscape

Cultural Goal

- Learning about the climate and geography of Germany

Chapter Outline

- **Lyrik zum Vorlesen**
  „Die Jahreszeiten"
- **Grammatik**
  Prepositions with the accusative case
  Suggestions and commands: The imperative
  The verb *werden*
  Negating *schon* and *noch*
  Equivalents of English *to like*
  Sentence adverbs
  Gehen + infinitive
- **Lesestück**
  Deutschland: Geographie und Klima
- **Situationen aus dem Alltag**
  Klima, Wetter und Landschaft
- **Videoecke**
  Ohne Frühstück geht's nicht!
- **Almanach**
  The Common Origin of German and English; The German Spelling Reform

Dialoge

Lab Manual Kap. 4, Dialoge, Fragen, Hören Sie gut zu!, Üb. zur Aussprache **[r]**.

Am See

FRAU MÜLLER: Wollen Sie noch einmal schwimmen gehen, Frau Brinkmann?
FRAU BRINKMANN: Nein, lieber nicht. Ich bin ein bisschen müde. Und das Wasser ist so wahnsinnig kalt. Gehen Sie doch ohne mich.
FRAU MÜLLER: Möchten Sie vielleicht lieber Karten spielen?
FRAU BRINKMANN: Ja, gerne!

Kitzbühel is a popular skiing and hiking resort in Tirol (Austria).

Winterurlaub

RICHARD: Möchtest du im Winter nach Österreich?
EVA: Super! Fahren wir doch im Januar nach Kitzbühel.
RICHARD: Hoffentlich können wir noch ein Hotelzimmer bekommen.
EVA: Ich glaube, es ist noch nicht zu spät.

Das Frühstück originally meant the piece (**das Stück**) of bread eaten early (**früh**) in the morning.

Morgens um halb zehn

ANITA: Also tschüss! Ich muss jetzt weg.
BEATE: Warte mal! Ohne Frühstück geht's nicht! Iss doch wenigstens ein Brötchen.
ANITA: Leider habe ich keine Zeit mehr. Mein Seminar beginnt um zehn und unterwegs muss ich noch ein Heft kaufen.
BEATE: Nimm doch das Brötchen mit. Später wirst du sicher hungrig.
ANITA: Du hast Recht. – Also, bis nachher!

Beim Bäcker kauft man frische Brötchen.

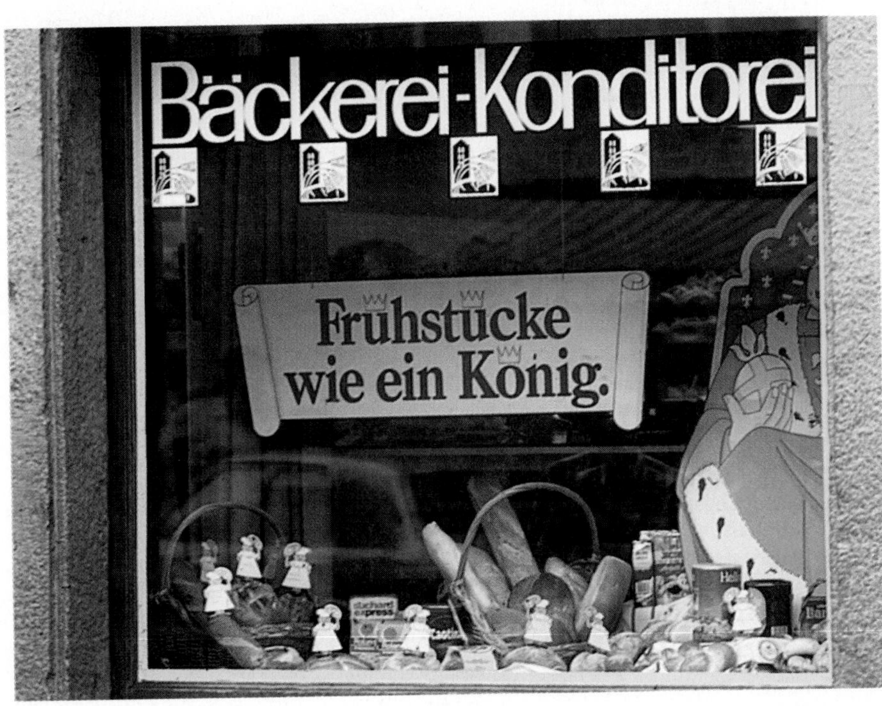

Pronunciation practice: Tape program focuses on uvular vs. vocalic **r**. Use dialogues to review these sounds in class. Uvular **r**: **Frau Brinkmann, fahren, Österreich, Brötchen, du hast Recht**. Vocalic **r**: **lieber nicht, Wasser, Karten spielen, gerne, im Winter, super, warte mal, unterwegs, mein Seminar**.

Wortschatz 1

Verben

beginnen to begin
bekommen to receive
frühstücken to eat breakfast
(etwas oder jemand) gern haben to like something or someone
glauben to believe; to think
kaufen to buy
mögen (mag) to like
schwimmen to swim
warten to wait
werden (wird) to become, to get (*in the sense of* "become")

Don't confuse **bekommen** (*to receive*) with **werden** (*to become*).

Substantive

der **See, -n** lake
am See at the lake
der **Urlaub, -e** vacation (*from a job*)
der **Winter, -** winter
im Winter in the winter

das **Brötchen, -** roll
das **Frühstück** breakfast
zum Frühstück for breakfast
das **Hotel, -s** hotel
(das) **Österreich** Austria
das **Seminar, -e** (*university*) seminar
das **Wasser** water

die **Karte, -n** card; ticket; map

Brötchen (called **Semmeln** in southern Germany and Austria), crusty rolls baked fresh daily, are the most common breakfast food.

Adjektive und Adverbien

einmal once
noch einmal once again, once more
gern(e) gladly, with pleasure
Gott sei Dank thank goodness
hoffentlich I hope . . .
hungrig hungry
kalt cold
lang(e) long; for a long time
lieber (+ *verb*) prefer to, would rather
Ich spiele lieber Karten. I'd rather play cards.
morgens (*adv.*) in the morning(s)
müde tired, weary
nachher later on, after that
noch nicht not yet
selbstverständlich it goes without saying that . . ., of course
später later
super (*colloq.*) super, great
unterwegs on the way; en route; on the go
weg away, gone
zusammen together

The final **-e** on **gerne** is optional; **gern** and **gerne** mean the same thing.

Andere Vokabeln

doch (*flavoring particle with commands, see p. 104*)
durch through
gegen against
mal (*flavoring particle with commands, see p. 104*)
mit along (with me, us, etc.)
ohne without
um around; at ()

We avoid translating **hoffentlich** as *hopefully* (**hoffnungsvoll**). Suggest: *One can only hope . . .*

Nützliche Ausdrücke

Bis nachher! See you later!
Es geht. It's all right. It's possible. It can be done.
Es geht nicht. Nothing doing. It can't be done.
Lieber nicht. I'd rather not. No thanks. Let's not.
Recht haben to be right
Du hast Recht. You're right.
Warte mal! Wait a second! Hang on!

Gegensätze

kalt ≠ **heiß** cold ≠ hot
kaufen ≠ **verkaufen** to buy ≠ to sell
lang ≠ **kurz** long; for a long time ≠ short; for a short time
zusammen ≠ **allein** together ≠ alone

Mit anderen Worten

todmüde = sehr müde
super = fantastisch = prima = sehr gut

Tell students that **Recht haben** may only have a human subject. Cf. **Das stimmt**.

At the Lake

MRS. M: Do you want to go swimming again, Mrs. Brinkmann?
MRS. B: No, I'd rather not. I'm a little tired. And the water is so awfully cold. You go without me.
MRS. M: Maybe you'd rather play cards?
MRS. B: Yes, gladly!

Winter Vacation

R: Would you like to go to Austria this winter?
E: Great! Let's go to Kitzbühel in January!
R: I hope we can still get a hotel room.
E: I don't think it's too late yet.

9:30 in the Morning

A: So long then. I've got to go now.
B: Wait a second! Not without breakfast! Eat a roll at least.
A: Unfortunately I have no more time. My seminar begins at ten, and on the way I still have to buy a notebook.
B: Take the roll along. Later you're sure to get hungry.
A: You're right . . . Well, see you later!

Variationen

■ A ■ Persönliche Fragen

1. Frau Brinkmann und Frau Müller spielen gern Karten. Was machen Sie gern?
2. Spielen Sie gern Karten oder gehen Sie lieber schwimmen?
3. Frau Brinkmann sagt, sie ist ein bisschen müde. Sind Sie heute müde?
4. Wohin wollen Sie im Winter?
5. Essen Sie immer Frühstück oder haben Sie manchmal keine Zeit?
6. Essen Sie gern Brötchen?
7. Wann beginnt die Deutschstunde?
8. Anita muss ein Heft kaufen. Was müssen Sie heute kaufen?

May also be done as instructor-led **Übung** with books closed or **Partnerarbeit** with books open.

■ B ■ Gruppenarbeit: Gegensätze (*Mit offenen Büchern*)

Contradict each other.

BEISPIEL: A: Fremdsprachen sind unwichtig.
B: Nein, sie sind wichtig.

1. 8.00 Uhr ist zu früh.
2. Dieses Buch ist langweilig.
3. Dieses Zimmer ist schön.
4. Wir kennen jemand in München.
5. Bernd hasst Rockmusik.
6. Du trägst oft Turnschuhe.
7. Sie sind immer müde.
8. Ich esse sehr langsam.

STARTEN SIE RICHTIG!
Machen Sie Ihr Studium zum Start in eine erfolgreiche Zukunft – mit der
Frankfurter Allgemeine
ZEITUNG FÜR DEUTSCHLAND

Good as written assignment after doing **Übung C** in class. Tell students to choose 2–3 exchanges and expand them into 4-line dialogues.

■ C ■ Partnerarbeit: Wie kann man antworten?

For each sentence in the left column choose appropriate responses from the right column.

1. Gehen wir noch einmal schwimmen!
2. Das Wasser ist zu kalt!
3. Ohne Frühstück geht's nicht.
4. Es gibt keine Hotelzimmer mehr.
5. Spielen wir zusammen Karten!
6. Das schaffst du leicht.
7. Bist du hungrig?
8. Ein Hotelzimmer mit Frühstück kostet 250 Mark!
9. Du kommst wieder zu spät.
10. Mensch, bin ich müde.

Super!
Du hast Recht.
Stimmt schon.
Stimmt nicht.
Das finde ich auch.
Gar nicht!
Es tut mir Leid.
Was ist denn los?
Um Gottes Willen!
Nichts zu danken.
Mensch!
Fantastisch!
Doch!
Prima!
Gerne!

Mensch, bin ich todmüde!

Now choose one of the exchanges above and expand it into a mini-dialogue. Prepare to say it for the whole class.

BEISPIEL: A: Es gibt keine Hotelzimmer mehr.
B: Um Gottes Willen! Was machen wir denn?
A: Ich weiß nicht. Hoffentlich ...

Lyrik zum Vorlesen

Viele deutsche Kinder lernen dieses traditionelle Gedicht (*poem*) über die Jahreszeiten.

Lab Manual Kap. 4, Lyrik zum Vorlesen.

Die Jahreszeiten°

	seasons
Es war° eine Mutter,	there was
Die hatte° vier Kinder:	who had
Den Frühling, den Sommer,	
Den Herbst und den Winter.	
Der Frühling bringt Blumen°,	flowers
Der Sommer bringt Klee°,	clover
Der Herbst, der° bringt Trauben°,	it / grapes
Der Winter bringt Schnee°.	snow

Grammatik

No German prepositions take nominative case, which is used only for the subject of a sentence and for predicate nominatives (see p. 33).

In spoken German, **durch**, **für**, and **um** often contract with the article **das**: **durchs**, **fürs**, **ums**.

Students should memorize this list so they can recite it in their sleep. Because **bis** is usually used with time phrases, it rarely shows the accusative case. However: **bis nächsten Dienstag**, **bis nächstes Wochenende**.

Prepositions with the accusative case

Prepositions are a class of words that show relationships of space (*through* the mountains), time (*until* Tuesday), or other relationships (*for* my friend, *without* any money). A preposition with the noun or pronoun that follows it is called a prepositional phrase. German prepositions are used with nouns in specific grammatical cases. Here is the list of prepositions that are always followed by the accusative case. Learn this list by heart.

bis	*until, by*	Wir warten **bis Dienstag**.
		Ich muss es **bis morgen** lesen.
durch	*through*	Er fährt **durch die Berge**.
für	*for*	Sie arbeitet **für ihren Vater**.
gegen	*against*	Was hast du **gegen mich**?
	around, about (with times)	Karl kommt **gegen drei**.
ohne	*without*	Wir gehen **ohne dich**.
um	*around* (the outside of)	Das Auto fährt **um das Hotel**.
	at (with times)	Karl kommt **um drei**.

Workbook Kap. 4, A, B.

Übung 1: Several different students should answer each question. If students need cues, suggest relatives (**Bruder**, **Schwester**) and words like **Freund**, **Professorin**, **Mitbewohner**.

■ 1 ■ Übung: Für wen?

Sie suchen eine Karte. Für wen suchen Sie sie?
Ich suche sie für mein-________ .
Sie machen heute das Frühstück. Für wen machen Sie es?
Ich mache es für mein-________ .

Lab Manual Kap. 4, Var. zur Üb. 2.

Replace names with those of students in class. May be continued as **Partner-** or **Gruppenarbeit** with free-response questions. In sentence 4 of **Übung 2**, point toward yourself and another student as you say **uns**, thus eliciting **Nein, ohne Sie**.

■ 2 ■ Übung: Ich mache das allein.

Your instructor asks if you do things with other people in your class. Say that you do everything without them. Use pronouns in your answer.

1. Spielen Sie mit Richard Karten? Nein, ohne ________ .
2. Arbeiten Sie morgen mit Ingrid zusammen? Nein, leider ohne ________ .
3. Gehen Sie mit Robert und Susan schwimmen?
4. Frühstücken Sie am Mittwoch mit Patrick?

3 Übung: Wohin fährt Monika?

Monika is going to drive through various locations. Tell where she's driving. Use a complete sentence.

Sie fährt durch ________ .
Dann fährt sie durch ________ .

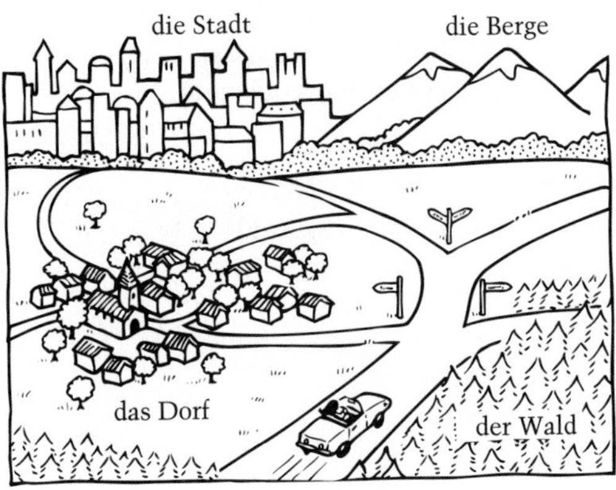

Übung 4 may be assigned as written homework.

4 Übung: Wie sagt man das auf Deutsch?

1. Are you for me or against me?
2. I'd like to take a trip around the world.
3. I hope I can do it without my parents.
4. She's looking for a card for her grandfather.
5. Let's drive through the mountains.

Making suggestions and giving commands are communicative goals.

Suggestions and commands: The imperative

The imperative form of German verbs is used either to make suggestions ("Let's go swimming") or to give commands ("Wait!").

"Let's do something": The *wir*-imperative

Fahren wir nach Österreich.	***Let's go*** *to Austria.*
Spielen wir Karten.	***Let's play*** *cards.*

The **wir**-imperative has the same word order as a yes/no question, but at the end of the sentence, the voice drops instead of rising. Compare the following intonation curves:

Gehen wir nach Hause?　　Gehen wir nach Hause!

In the first dialogue on page 99, Frau Brinkmann uses the **Sie**-imperative: ***Gehen Sie* doch ohne mich.**

"Do something": The *Sie*-imperative

Fahren Sie nach Österreich.	*Go to Austria.*
Bitte **besuchen Sie** mich im Mai.	*Please visit me in May.*

Doch can also add a note of impatience: **Lass das doch!** It all depends on tone of voice.

Bitte also turns an imperative into a polite request: **Gehen Sie *bitte* nach Hause.**

Note on punctuation: German uses an exclamation mark to add emphasis to commands.

Note on Usage: Flavoring particles *doch* and *mal*

doch ***(why don't you . . .)*** You can soften a command to a suggestion by adding the unstressed flavoring particle **doch**.

Gehen Sie nach Hause!	*Go home!*
Gehen Sie **doch** nach Hause.	*Why don't you go home.*

mal You can make a command more peremptory by adding the unstressed flavoring particle **mal**.

Warte!	*Wait!*
Warte **mal**!	*Wait a second!*
Hören Sie **mal**!	*Just listen here!*

Lab Manual Kap. 4, Üb. 5; Var. zu Üb. 6, 7.

For additional practice with the **Sie**-imperative, write a list of verbs on the board and have students use them to tell you to do things.

■ 5 ■ Übung: Machen Sie das doch! Encourage your instructor to go ahead and do something.

BEISPIEL: Ich möchte eine Reise machen.
Machen Sie doch eine Reise!

1. Ich möchte Brötchen kaufen.
2. Ich möchte eine Pause machen.
3. Ich möchte nach Hause gehen.
4. Ich möchte Tennis spielen.
5. Ich möchte Frau Klein besuchen.
6. Ich möchte meinen Wagen verkaufen.

Übung 6 reviews negation with **nicht** and **kein**; it may be assigned as written homework.

■ 6 ■ Übung: Nein, machen Sie das nicht! Now tell your instructor *not* to do the things listed in **Übung 5**.

BEISPIEL: Ich möchte nach Hause gehen.
Nein, gehen Sie nicht nach Hause!

■ 7 ■ Gruppenarbeit: Ja, machen wir das! Here are some activities you could do today. Take turns suggesting them to each other.

BEISPIEL: schwimmen gehen
A: Gehen wir heute schwimmen!
B: Ja, machen wir das! *oder* Nein, lieber nicht.

jetzt frühstücken	eine Reise machen
Karten spielen	eine Pause machen
eine Zeitung kaufen	nach Hause laufen
zu Hause arbeiten	den Wagen verkaufen

Now suggest other things to do today.

■ 8 ■ Übung: Wie sagt man das auf Deutsch? (*Mit offenen Büchern*) Use the **Sie**- or **wir**-imperative.

1. Let's go swimming.
2. Buy a notebook.
3. Let's discuss our trip.
4. Learn a foreign language.
5. Please speak slowly.
6. Don't sleep now.
7. Let's walk a little bit.
8. Don't wear that.

Imperative forms for *du* and *ihr*

To give commands or make suggestions to people whom you address with **du**, you need to learn the forms of the **du-** and **ihr-**imperatives.

The* du*-imperative The **du**-imperative of most verbs is simply the verb stem without ending.

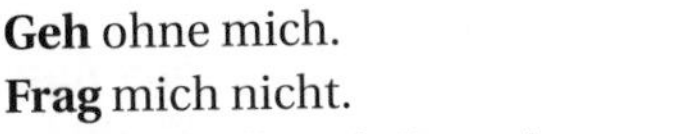

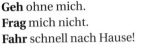

Geh ohne mich.	*Go without me.*
Frag mich nicht.	*Don't ask me.*
Fahr schnell nach Hause!	*Drive home quickly!*
Sei nicht so langweilig.	*Don't be so boring.*

Note: The pronoun **du** is *not* used with the **du**-imperative!

If the verb changes its stem vowel from **e** to **i(e)**, the *changed* stem is used:

Verb	*Statement*	*du-imperative*
lesen	Du **liest** das für morgen.	**Lies** das für morgen.
geben	Du **gibst** Peter das Buch.	**Gib** Peter das Buch.
essen	Du **isst** ein Brötchen.	**Iss** ein Brötchen.

Note that the stem-vowel change **a(u)** to **ä(u)** does *not* appear in the *du*-imperative:

fahren	Du **fährst** nach Hause.	**Fahr** nach Hause.
laufen	Du **läufst** zu schnell.	**Lauf** nicht so schnell!

Verb stems ending in **-d** or **-t** add an **-e** to the stem:

According to Duden, the **du**-imperative takes the ending **-e** in all cases (**trinke, komme, gehe**). However, the ending is usually dropped in colloquial speech. Final **-e** is retained in verbs whose stem ends in **-d**, **-t**, or **-n**: **rede, arbeite, öffne**.

Arbeite nicht so viel.	*Don't work so hard.*
Warte doch!	*Wait!*

Lab Manual Kap. 4, Var. zu Üb. 9, 10; Üb. 11.

For later review, give these as English cues for student–student interaction. For example:
I: Ask her whether you should do that.
S1: **Soll ich das tun?**
S2: **Ja, tu das.**

9 **Übung: Ja, tu das doch!** Your instructor plays the part of your friend Beate. Tell her to go ahead and do the things she asks about.

BEISPIEL: Soll ich da drüben halten?
Ja, halte doch da drüben.

1. Soll ich Englisch lernen?
2. Soll ich mit Hans sprechen?
3. Soll ich Peter das Buch geben?
4. Soll ich schnell laufen?
5. Soll ich hier warten?
6. Soll ich Pommes frites essen?
7. Soll ich etwas singen?
8. Soll ich zu Fuß gehen?
9. Soll ich eine Zeitung lesen?
10. Soll ich eine Jacke tragen?

Wie bitte? Was sollen wir essen?

■ 10 ■ Partnerarbeit: Nein, lieber nicht. Now tell your partner *not* to do the things listed in **Übung 9**. This time, do *not* use **doch**.

BEISPIEL: Soll ich drüben parken?
Nein, park nicht drüben.

The* ihr-*imperative The **ihr**-imperative is identical to the present-tense **ihr**-form, but without the pronoun.

Present tense	***ihr**-imperative*
Ihr **bleibt** hier.	**Bleibt** hier.
Ihr **singt** zu laut.	**Singt** nicht so laut.
Ihr **seid** freundlich.	**Seid** freundlich.

Reminder: **Sie-** and **wir-** imperatives include the pronoun; **ihr-** and **du-** imperatives do not.

■ 11 ■ Übung: Sollen wir das machen?

A. Your instructor plays one of a group of children and asks what they all should do.

BEISPIEL: Sollen wir bald nach Hause kommen?
Ja, kommt doch bald nach Hause.

Be sure students use the flavoring particle **doch** in their answers.

1. Sollen wir Karten spielen?
2. Sollen wir das Buch lesen?
3. Sollen wir nach Hause laufen?
4. Sollen wir die Brötchen essen?

B. Now tell them what not to do.

BEISPIEL: Sollen wir nach Hause kommen?
Nein, kommt nicht nach Hause.

1. Sollen wir Jeans tragen?
2. Sollen wir heute kommen?
3. Sollen wir hier bleiben?
4. Sollen wir das sagen?

■ Imperative of *sein*

The verb **sein** is irregular in the **Sie**- and **wir**-imperatives (the **du**- and **ihr**-forms are regular):

Seien Sie bitte freundlich, Herr Kaiser.	*Please be friendly, Mr. Kaiser.*
Seien wir freundlich.	*Let's be friendly.*
Seid freundlich, Kinder.	*Be friendly, children.*
Sei freundlich, Rolf.	*Be friendly, Rolf.*

Lab Manual Kap. 4, Var. zur Üb. 12.

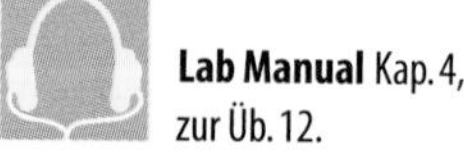

Workbook Kap. 4, C.

■ 12 ■ Übung: Sei doch ... !

A. Tell the following people to be honest.

BEISPIEL: Richard
Sei doch ehrlich, Richard!

1. Kinder
2. Herr Bachmann
3. wir
4. Barbara

Übung 12 may be assigned as written homework.

B. Now tell them not to be so boring.

BEISPIEL: Herr Stolze
Seien Sie doch nicht so langweilig, Herr Stolze!

1. Ute
2. Frau Klein
3. Thomas und Beate
4. wir

■ 13 ■ Übung: Wie sagt man das auf Deutsch? *(Mit offenen Büchern)* Use the **du**-imperative.

1. Please be honest.
2. Wear your jeans.
3. Please read the article.
4. Give Anita your notebook.

Now use the **ihr**-imperative.

5. Ask me later.
6. Please wait here.
7. Work together.
8. Don't be so pessimistic.

The only German verbs that are irregular in the present tense are **werden, sein, haben, wissen,** and the modal verbs. You have now learned them all.

Tell students that **werden** is another linking verb followed by the predicate nominative. Students tend to say: **Ich möchte einen Lehrer werden.**

The verb werden

The verb **werden** (*to become*) is irregular in present tense **du-** and **er-**forms.

ich	werde	wir	werden
du	**wirst**	ihr	werdet
er, es, sie	**wird**	sie, Sie	werden

Werden is a frequently used verb. Its basic English equivalent is to *become, get.* It can be translated in various ways, depending upon context.

Es **wird** kalt.	*It's getting cold.*
Ihre Kinder **werden** groß.	*Your children are getting big.*
Meine Schwester will Professorin **werden**.	*My sister wants to become a professor.*
Am Montag **werde** ich endlich 21.	*I'm finally turning 21 on Monday.*

■ 14 ■ Übung: Wer wird müde? Say who is getting tired.

BEISPIEL: Barbara
Barbara wird müde.

1. wir
2. die Kinder
3. meine Mutter
4. ihr
5. du
6. ich

To review **werden** later in chapter, come back to these sentences as English cues, but change elements. Examples:
1. It'll get hot on Tuesday.
2. When will she be 20?
3. It's getting cold out.
4. The newspaper is getting interesting.
5. My friend wants to be a professor.

■ 15 ■ Übung: Wie sagt man das auf Englisch?

1. Morgen wird es heiß.
2. Wann wirst du denn zwanzig?
3. Draußen wird es warm.
4. Das Buch wird endlich interessant.
5. Meine zwei Freunde wollen Lehrer werden.

Negating schon *and* noch

■ Negation of *schon*

The negations of **schon** (*already, yet*) are:

noch nicht	*not yet*
noch kein- [+ *noun*]	*not a* [+ noun] *yet*
	not any [+ noun] *yet*

Here are some examples of questions followed by negative answers.

Sind Sie **schon** hungrig? Nein, **noch nicht**.	*Are you hungry yet?* *No, not yet.*
Wollt ihr **schon** gehen? Nein, wir wollen **noch nicht** gehen.	*Do you want to leave already?* *No, we don't want to leave yet.*
Hast du **schon** Karten? Nein, ich habe **noch keine** Karten.	*Do you have tickets yet?* *No, I don't have any tickets yet.*
Kauft er **schon** einen Wagen? Nein, er kauft **noch keinen** Wagen.	*Is he already buying a car?* *No, he's not buying a car yet.*

Lab Manual Kap. 4, Üb. 16, 17.

Students need practice with these negations. Difficulties stem from the multiple English equivalents (**schon** = *already, yet;* **nicht mehr** = *not any more, no longer;* **Hast du noch Geld?** = *Do you still have money?/Do you have any more money?*). Concentrate on drilling German rather than contrasting with English. Students will need to review this over the next few weeks.

In **Übung 17**, the short answers would all be **Nein, noch nicht.** Complete-sentence answers, however, must use **noch kein-** [+ *noun*].

Übungen 16–18 may be done as **Partnerarbeit** or as written assignment after having been done in class. Partners can improvise their own exchanges based on these models.

■ 16 ■ Übung: Nein, noch nicht. Answer the following questions about Katrin Berger negatively, saying that things haven't happened yet.

1. Ist Katrin schon da?
2. Studiert sie schon in Berlin?
3. Kennt sie Frau Bachmann schon?
4. Beginnt das Semester schon?
5. Will sie schon essen?

■ 17 ■ Übung Say you don't have any of these things yet.

1. Haben Sie schon Kinder?
2. Haben Sie schon eine Karte?
3. Haben Sie schon ein Hotelzimmer?
4. Besitzen Sie schon einen Wagen?
5. Haben Sie schon Angst?
6. Besitzen Sie schon einen Computer?

■ Negation of *noch*

The negations of **noch** (*still*) are:

nicht mehr	*not any more, no longer*
kein- [+ *noun*] **mehr**	*no more* [+ noun], *not any more* [+ noun]

Here are some examples of questions followed by negative answers:

Regnet es **noch**? Nein, **nicht mehr**.	*Is it still raining?* *No, not any more.*

Studiert Rita **noch**?	*Is Rita still a student?*
Nein, sie studiert **nicht mehr**.	*No, she's no longer a student.*
Hast du **noch Geld**?	*Do you have any more money?*
Nein, ich habe **kein Geld mehr**.	*No, I haven't got any more money.*
Können wir **noch Karten** bekommen?	*Can we still get tickets?*
Leider habe ich **keine Karten mehr**.	*Unfortunately I have no more tickets.*

Lab Manual Kap. 4, Üb. 18, 19; Var. zu Üb. 18, 19.

Workbook Kap. 4, D.

■ 18 ■ Übung Answer these questions negatively.

1. Wohnen Sie noch zu Hause?
2. Können Sie noch warten?
3. Ist es draußen noch kalt?
4. Ist Ihr Wagen noch neu?
5. Geht Ihre Uhr noch?
6. Können Sie uns noch besuchen?

■ 19 ■ Übung Answer these questions negatively.

1. Hat er noch Arbeit?
2. Haben Sie noch Zeit?
3. Hat Ihre Großmutter noch einen Wagen?
4. Ist er noch ein Kind?
5. Gibt es noch Probleme?
6. Hören Sie noch Rockmusik?

Equivalents of English to like

Expressing likes, dislikes, and preferences is a communicative goal.

Gern is etymologically related to English *yearn*.

■ Verb + *gern(e)* = to like to do something

Ich **schwimme gern**.	*I like to swim.*
Sie **geht gern** zu Fuß.	*She likes to walk.*
Hören Sie **gerne** Musik?	*Do you like to listen to music?*

Gern(e) generally comes immediately after the subject and verb. The negation of **gern** is **nicht gern**.

Ich schwimme **nicht gern**.	*I don't like to swim.*

Lab Manual Kap. 4, Var. zu Üb. 20, 22.

■ 20 ■ Partnerarbeit: Ich höre gern Musik. Take turns saying what you like to eat (**essen**), read (**lesen**), play (**spielen**), and listen to (**hören**). Here are some suggestions.

BEISPIEL: Ich höre gern Rockmusik. Und du?

Jazz	Fußball	Frühstück
Pizza	Brötchen	Volksmusik
Mozart	Zeitungen	Bücher
Tennis	Tischtennis	Lyrik (*poetry*)

■ 21 ■ Kettenreaktion: Was machen Sie gern? Was machen Sie lieber?

A: Ich spiele gern Tennis.
B: Sie spielt gern Tennis, aber ich lese lieber Bücher.
C: Er liest gern Bücher, aber ich ______ lieber ______ .
usw.

■ *Mögen* or *gern haben* = to like someone or something

Ich **habe** dich sehr **gern**.
Ich **mag** dich sehr.
} *I like you very much.*

Negation: Ich habe dich **nicht gern**.
Ich mag dich **nicht**.

Mögen is a modal verb. Its present-tense forms are:

mögen	*to like (something)*		
ich	**mag**	wir	mögen
du	**magst**	ihr	mögt
er, es, sie	**mag**	sie, Sie	mögen

Use **mögen** or **gern** + *verb* to say what you like to eat: **Ich mag die Suppe heute** and **Brötchen esse ich gern.** Do not use **gern haben** for food.

Unlike the other modals, it is usually used without an infinitive.

Ich **mag** Maria.	*I like Maria.*
Mögen Sie die Suppe nicht?	*Don't you like the soup?*

■ **22** ■ **Übung** Tell who likes Frau Brandt. Use the appropriate form of **mögen**.

BEISPIEL: die Schüler
Die Schüler mögen Frau Brandt.

1. du
2. wir
3. Franz
4. meine Eltern
5. ich
6. ihr

Correct errors such as: **Ich habe Schwimmen gern** by saying **Ach, Sie schwimmen gern. Ich schwimme auch gern.**

■ **23** ■ **Übung: Was haben Sie gern?** Say which things and people you like or dislike. Here are some ideas. Add some of your own. Use **gern haben** or **mögen**.

meine Mitbewohner
das Mensaessen
den Winter
Hausaufgaben
die Uni
meine Arbeit
meine Geschwister
Fremdsprachen

■ Summary: Three German equivalents for *to like*

Distinguish carefully among the three German equivalents for English *to like*:

You may want to teach students that **möchte** is frequently used with **gern: Ich möchte gern nach Österreich.**

- **Möchte** means *would like to* do something and is used with a complementary infinitive (which may sometimes be omitted, see p. 80):

  Ich **möchte** Innsbruck besuchen.
  Ich **möchte** nach Innsbruck (fahren).

- A *verb* + **gern** means *to like to do something.*

  Ich spiele **gern** Karten.

  Möchte expresses a wish for something, while a *verb* + **gern** makes a general statement about your likes or dislikes:

Ich **möchte** Karten spielen.	*I would like to play cards.*
Ich spiele **gern** Karten.	*I like to play cards.*

- **Mögen** or **gern haben** means *to like* people or things and is used with a noun or pronoun:

  Ich **mag** Professor Jaeger.
  Ich **habe** ihn **gern**.

■ 24 ■ Übung: Wie sagt man das auf Deutsch?

1. I like the soup.
2. I like to eat soup.
3. I would like the soup.
4. They would like to study in Germany.
5. Karl doesn't like to wait.
6. Do you like Professor Lange?
7. Our children like to play outside.
8. We would like to drive home.
9. I don't like that.
10. I like her.

Students may need reminding that adverbs are usually defined as words that modify a verb, an adjective, or another adverb, and answer the question **wie**.

Sentence adverbs

Sentence adverbs modify entire sentences and express the speaker's attitude toward the content of the whole:

Natürlich bin ich morgens müde.	***Of course*** *I'm tired in the morning.*
Du hast **sicher** genug Geld.	*You* ***surely*** *have enough money.*
Leider habe ich keine Zeit mehr.	***Unfortunately*** *I have no more time.*
Gott sei Dank ist es nicht mehr so heiß.	***Thank goodness*** *it's not so hot any more.*
Du kannst mich **hoffentlich** verstehen.	***I hope*** *you can understand me.*
Selbstverständlich mag ich Pizza.	***Of course*** *I like pizza.*
Übrigens habe ich kein Geld mehr.	***By the way,*** *I don't have any more money.*

Lab Manual Kap. 4, Var. zur Üb. 25.

Workbook Kap. 4, E.

Übung 25 may also be done as a **Partnerarbeit** using **du**.

■ 25 ■ Übung: Selbstverständlich! Answer these questions emphatically. Show that your answer is obvious by beginning it with **Selbstverständlich ...** or **Natürlich ...**

BEISPIEL: Lernen Sie Deutsch?
Selbstverständlich lerne ich Deutsch!

1. Frühstücken Sie bald?
2. Sind Sie hungrig?
3. Haben Sie Zeit für mich?
4. Möchten Sie nach Österreich?
5. Schwimmen Sie gern?
6. Spielen Sie gern Karten?

■ 26 ■ Übung: Leider! Answer these questions. Show that you regret having to answer "yes" by beginning your answer with **Ja, leider ...**

BEISPIEL: Regnet es noch?
Ja, leider regnet es noch.

1. Schneit es noch?
2. Haben Sie viele Fragen?
3. Sind Sie sehr müde?
4. Ist der Berg sehr steil?
5. Gehen Sie ohne mich?
6. Ist das Wasser zu kalt?

Segelboot im Hafen von Lindau (Bodensee)

Gehen + *infinitive*

The verb **gehen** is often used with an infinitive as its complement.

Sie **geht** oft **schwimmen**.	*She often goes swimming.*
Gehen wir noch einmal **schwimmen**!	*Let's go swimming again!*
Ich **gehe** mit Dieter **schwimmen**.	*I'm going swimming with Dieter.*

The complementary infinitive **schwimmen** is the second part of the predicate and comes at the end of the sentence.

Note what happens when the entire verbal idea **schwimmen gehen** (*to go swimming*) is used as the complement of a modal verb:

Wir wollen heute **schwimmen gehen**.	*We want to go swimming today.*

■ 27 ■ Partnerarbeit: Dann geh doch ...! Partner A reads the sentences on the left. Partner B then tells partner A what to do, choosing an appropriate activity from the right-hand column.

BEISPIEL: A: Ich bin müde.
B: Dann geh doch schlafen!

1. Ich muss Geld verdienen.	arbeiten gehen
2. Ich bin hungrig.	schlafen gehen
3. Ich möchte gern fit bleiben.	essen gehen
4. Ich bin müde!	Tennis spielen gehen

Lesestück

Vor dem Lesen

Tipps zum Lesen und Lernen

Tipps zum Vokabelnlernen

- Note that all four compass points are masculine:

der Norden	der Osten
der Süden	der Westen

Remember that the days, seasons, and the months are also masculine:

der Montag	der Januar
der Dienstag	der Februar
der Mittwoch	der März
der Donnerstag	der April
der Freitag	der Mai
der Samstag (oder Sonnabend)	der Juni
der Sonntag	der Juli
	der August
der Frühling	der September
der Sommer	der Oktober
der Herbst	der November
der Winter	der Dezember

Haupt is derived from Latin *caput* (head).

- The prefix **Haupt-** is attached to nouns and adds the meaning *main, chief, primary, principal, most important.*

die **Haupt**regionen	*the principal regions*
die **Haupt**frage	*the main question*
die **Haupt**stadt	*the capital city*
die **Haupt**rolle	*the leading role*
die **Haupt**straße	*the main street*

Lab Manual Kap. 4, Üb. zur Betonung.

Kolonie: Both this word and the city name Cologne (German **Köln**) are derived from Latin *colonia*. The Roman emperor Claudius named the city Colonia Agrippinensis in A.D. 50 after his wife Agrippina. Its strategic position on the Rhine made it the capital of the Roman colony *Germania Inferior*.

Leicht zu merken

die **Alpen**	
barbarisch	
die **Geographie**	Geographie
geographisch	
die **Kolonie, -n**	Kolonie
der **Kontrast, -e**	Kontrast
die **Kultur, -en**	Kultur
mild	
die **Region**	Region
der **Rhein**	
wild	
zirka	

Rivers in German are generally **die**. Exceptions are **der Rhein**, **der Main**, **der Inn**, **der Lech**, **der Neckar**, and foreign rivers (**der Nil**, **der Mississippi**) except those ending in **-a** or **-e** (**die Themse**, **die Rhone**).

Children in Southern Germany learn: **Iller, Isar, Lech und Inn / fließen zu der Donau hin.**

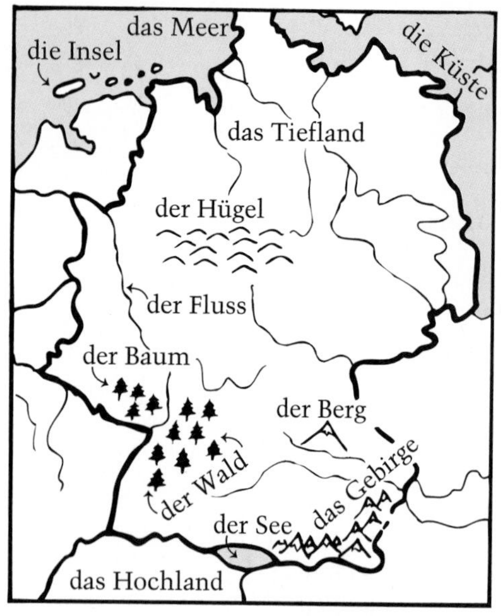

Einstieg in den Text

The reading in this chapter builds on familiar vocabulary about the weather (**das Wetter**) and discusses climate and geography (**Klima und Geographie**).

Study this map and try to guess the meanings of the new words.

The word **Wein** is not of Germanic origin but was introduced by the Romans (Latin *vinum*) along with viniculture. The word **Bier** comes from Latin *bibere* (*to drink*). The Germanic word for beer is preserved in English *ale*, which was brewed without hops. The medieval cloister breweries first added hops to the beverage.

Wortschatz 2

Conjugate present tense of **wandern** on board. Point out **-n** instead of **-en** in first- and third-person plural.

Verben

beschreiben to describe
fließen to flow
liegen to lie; to be situated
trinken to drink
wandern to hike; to wander

Frühling: also **das Frühjahr.**

Substantive

der **Baum, ⸚e** tree
der **Fluss, ⸚e** river
der **Frühling** spring
der **Herbst** fall, autumn
der **Hügel, -** hill
der **Norden** the North
der **Osten** the East
der **Schnee** snow
der **Sommer** summer
der **Süden** the South
der **Wald, ⸚er** forest

The obvious cognates in points of the compass and seasons (**der Herbst**, English *harvest*) recall common Germanic designations for time and space.

der **Wein, -e** wine
der **Westen** the West

das **Bier, -e** beer
(das) **Italien** Italy
das **Klima** climate
das **Land, ⸚er** country
das **Leben** life
das **Lied, -er** song
das **Volkslied, -er** folk song
das **Märchen, -** fairy tale
das **Meer, -e** sea
das **Tal, ⸚er** valley

die **Landschaft, -en** landscape
die **Schweiz** Switzerland
die **Stadt, ⸚e** city

Adjektive und Adverbien

flach flat
hoch high
immer noch / noch immer still (*intensification of* **noch**)
modern modern
nass wet, damp
schrecklich terrible
sonnig sunny
trocken dry

Andere Vokabeln

von from

Nützliche Ausdrücke

im Süden (im Norden usw.) in the South (in the North, etc.)
im Winter (im Sommer usw.) in the winter (in the summer, etc.)

Gegensätze

modern ≠ altmodisch modern ≠ old-fashioned
nass ≠ trocken wet ≠ dry

Lab Manual Kap. 4, Lesestück.

Deutschland: Geographie und Klima

Cultural goal: Learning about the climate and geography of Germany.

Für die alten Römer° war° das Leben in der Kolonie Germania nicht sehr schön. Der Historiker° Tacitus (zirka 55 bis 115 n.Chr.°) beschreibt das Land als° kalt und neblig°. Über die Germanen° schreibt er: „Sie sind ohne Kultur, haben keine Städte und leben im Wald. Sie sind wild und barbarisch, wie ihr Land."

Das moderne Deutschland liegt in Mitteleuropa und die „wilden Germanen" wohnen heute zum größten Teil° in der Stadt.[1] Es gibt keinen Urwald° mehr, aber der Wald ist immer noch typisch und wichtig für die Landschaft in Deutschland, Österreich und der Schweiz. Am Sonntag wandert man gern durch die Wälder und die Kinder hören auch heute noch gern Märchen wie „Hänsel und Gretel" oder „Schneewittchen".[2] In solchen° Märchen und auch in deutschen Volksliedern spielt der Wald eine große Rolle.

Auch das Klima in Deutschland ist Gott sei Dank nicht so schrecklich, wie° Tacitus meint. Selbstverständlich ist es nicht so warm und sonnig wie in Italien, aber das deutsche Klima ist eigentlich ziemlich mild. In den Flusstälern wird es zum Beispiel im Winter nicht sehr kalt. Die großen Flüsse – der Rhein, die Weser, die Elbe und die Oder – fließen durch das Land von Süden nach Norden. Nur die Donau° fließt von Westen nach Osten. Am Rhein und an der° Donau trinkt man gern Wein; die Römer brachten° den Weinbau° nach Deutschland. Die Deutschen trinken also nicht nur Bier.

Romans / was
historian / **nach Christus** = A.D. / as / foggy / Germanic peoples

zum ... = for the most part of / primeval forest

such

so ... wie = as . . . as

Have students locate rivers on the map inside the front cover.

the Danube River
am and **an der** = on the
brought / viniculture

Familienwanderung im Regen

1. **Die Germanen** were the ancient tribes that the Romans called collectively *germani*. The word **Deutsch** comes from Old High German **diot** (*people*). The French applied the name of one tribe, the *alemanni*, to the whole people: *les Allemands*.
2. *Snow White*. Other folk tales are **Dornröschen** (*Sleeping Beauty*), **Rotkäppchen** (*Little Red Riding Hood*), **Aschenputtel** (*Cinderella*), and **Der Froschkönig** (*The Frog King*).

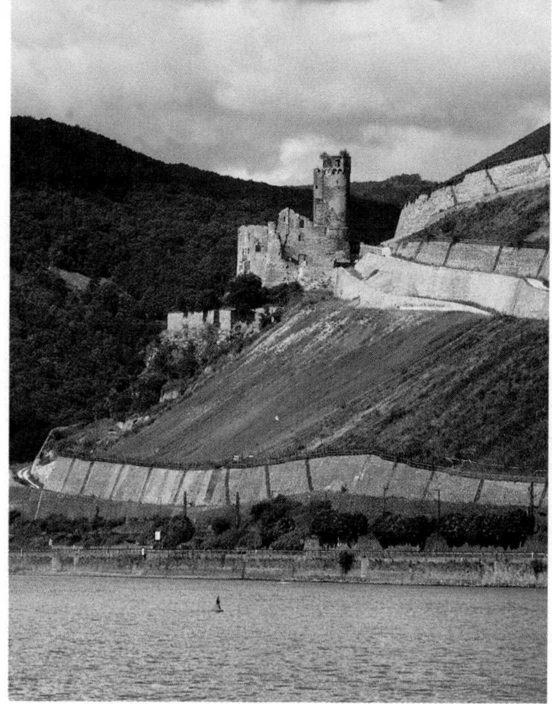

Burgruine (*castle ruin*) Ehrenfels am Rhein

Es gibt in Deutschland drei geographische Hauptregionen. Im Norden ist das Land flach und fruchtbar und ohne viele Bäume. Hier beeinflusst° das Meer – die Nordsee und die Ostsee – Landschaft und Klima. Diese° Region nennt man das Norddeutsche Tiefland°. In der Mitte des Landes° gibt es aber viele Hügel und kleine Berge. Man nennt diese Region das Mittelgebirge°. Im Süden liegt das Hochgebirge° – die Alpen. Hier gibt es natürlich viel Schnee im Winter, denn° die Berge sind sehr hoch. Deutschlands höchster° Berg ist die Zugspitze (2 963 m). Man sieht also, in Deutschland gibt es viele Kontraste: Stadt und Land, Wald und Feld°, Berge und Meer.

influences
this
North German lowlands / **In ...** In the middle of the country / central mountains / high mountains / because / highest / field

Nach dem Lesen

■ A ■ Partnerarbeit: Märchen Take turns reading aloud these descriptions of well-known **Märchen**. Then match the descriptions with the silhouettes on the next page. Use context to help you guess unknown vocabulary.

1. Vier Freunde – ein Esel, ein Hund, eine Katze und ein Hahn – sind alt und können nicht mehr arbeiten. Also gehen sie zusammen nach Bremen. Dort wollen sie Straßenmusikanten werden und so ihr Brot verdienen.
2. Eine Frau isst Rapunzeln (*lamb's lettuce, a leafy salad vegetable*) aus dem Garten ihrer Nachbarin. Diese Nachbarin ist aber eine Hexe. Die Hexe nimmt die erstgeborene Tochter der Frau und schließt sie in einen Turm.
3. Ein kleines Mädchen bringt ihrer kranken Großmutter Kuchen und Wein. Sie muss durch einen Wald, aber im Wald wartet ein Wolf. Der Wolf frisst die Großmutter und das Mädchen auf.
4. Eine Familie ist sehr arm und hat nicht genug zu essen. Die Stiefmutter zwingt den Vater, seine Kinder im Wald zu lassen. Bruder und Schwester finden dort ein kleines Haus aus Brot, Kuchen und Zucker. Dort wohnt aber eine böse Hexe und sie will die Kinder essen.

■ **B** ■ **Antworten Sie auf Deutsch.**

1. Wie beschreibt Tacitus die Kolonie Germania?
2. Was ist noch immer typisch für die Landschaft in Deutschland?
3. Was macht man gern am Sonntag?
4. Wie ist das Klima in Deutschland?
5. Ist es so warm und sonnig wie in Italien?
6. Wo trinkt man viel Wein?
7. Wie ist das Land im Norden?
8. Wo gibt es viel Schnee im Winter?
9. Wie heißen die drei geographischen Hauptregionen?

■ C ■ Partnerarbeit: Tacitus modern – Gespräch (conversation) **mit einem römischen Historiker** Tacitus has returned to modern Germany. Work in pairs. Correct his outdated impressions by completing the following dialogue, then perform it for your classmates.

TACITUS: Ihr Germanen seid alle furchtbar barbarisch.
REAKTION: Das stimmt gar nicht mehr! Wir sind heute ______________________ .

TACITUS: Euer Klima ist schrecklich, immer kalt und neblig.
REAKTION: ______________________ .

TACITUS: Ihr lebt ja alle im Wald wie die wilden Tiere (*animals*).
REAKTION: ______________________ .

TACITUS: Ihr trinkt nur Bier und keinen Wein. Das finde ich barbarisch.
REAKTION: ______________________ .

Situationen aus dem Alltag

Discussing weather, climate, and landscape is a communicative goal.

■ Klima, Wetter und Landschaft

You already know some of these words from the introductory chapter (see pp. 12–13).

This vocabulary focuses on an everyday topic or situation. Words you already know from **Wortschatz** sections are listed without English equivalents; new supplementary vocabulary is listed with definitions. Your instructor may assign some supplementary vocabulary for active mastery.

Klima und Wetter

die **Luft** *air*
der **Regen** *rain*
  regnerisch *rainy*
  Es regnet.
der **Schnee**
  Es schneit.
der **Wind** *wind*
  Es ist windig.
wolkig
neblig
sonnig
windig
kalt ≠ **heiß**
warm ≠ **kühl**
nass ≠ **trocken**
mild

Landschaft

der **Baum, ¨e**
der **Berg, -e**
der **Hügel, -**
  hügelig hilly
  bergig *mountainous*
der **Wald, ¨er**
das **Meer, -e**
das **Tal, ¨er**

■ A ■ Gruppenarbeit: Sprechen wir über Klima und Landschaft. Beschreiben Sie die Landschaft in diesen Fotos.

1.

2.

3.

If students need prompting, ask: **Ist die Landschaft in Foto Nummer 1 flach? Wo findet man diese Landschaft, im Norden? Welche Farben sehen Sie?**

■ B ■ Partnerarbeit: Landschaft und Klima, wo ich wohne Find out where your partner comes from and ask about the climate and geography there.

BEISPIEL: Woher kommst du denn?
Wie ist das Klima dort im Sommer?
Kannst du die Landschaft beschreiben?

Zum Schluss

Sprechen wir miteinander!

Lab Manual Kap. 4, Diktat.

Workbook Kap. 4, F, G, H.

■ A ■ Partnerarbeit: Sei doch (nicht) ...! Give your partner some ideas for self-improvement. Take turns telling each other how you should be (or not be).

BEISPIEL: Sei doch ehrlich!
Sei doch nicht sauer!

guter Laune	sauer	höflich
schlechter Laune	munter	fit
glücklich	freundlich	ehrlich

■ B ■ Partnerarbeit: Nein, das darfst du nicht! Ask your partner for permission to do something. Your partner tells you to do something else. The list will help you get started. Then try inventing some of your own exchanges.

BEISPIEL: zu Hause bleiben? (draußen spielen)
A: Darf ich zu Hause bleiben?
B: Nein, spiel doch draußen!

nach Hause fahren? (zu Fuß gehen)
Tennis spielen? (deine Hausaufgaben machen)
jetzt Pizza essen? (bis heute Abend warten)

■ C ■ Partnerarbeit: Macht das bitte für uns! Machen Sie zusammen eine Liste: Was können andere Studenten für Sie machen? Seien Sie kreativ!

BEISPIEL: Sie können für uns ...
die Bücher tragen
die Hausaufgaben schreiben
usw.

Sie und Ihr Partner sagen jetzt zu zwei anderen Studenten, sie sollen etwas für Sie machen. Die anderen antworten **ja** oder **nein**.

BEISPIEL: A + B: Jennifer und Brian, tragt bitte die Bücher für uns.
C + D: Ja, O.K., das machen wir gern für euch. *oder*
Nein, das wollen wir nicht machen.

Expressing likes and dislikes is a communicative goal.

Übung D: Put 4 lists on board, entitled: **mögen/gern haben, nicht mögen/nicht gern haben, gern tun, nicht gern tun.** These titles will help distinguish between *liking something/someone* and *liking to do something.*

■ D ■ Gruppenarbeit Say what you like and don't like about university life. Also say what you like and don't like to do. Your instructor will write your responses on the board.

BEISPIEL: Ich habe meine Mitbewohnerin sehr gern.
Ich mag das Essen nicht.

■ E ■ Gruppenarbeit: Was wollen wir denn machen? Planen wir einen Urlaub. Lesen wir zusammen diese Anzeigen für Ferienorte. Hier gibt es sehr viel zu tun! Was machen Sie gerne? Was machen Sie lieber? Wollen wir schwimmen oder wandern gehen?

Die Landschaft für Aktivurlaub und echte Erholung

Wandern, Tennis, Reiten, Wintersport, heilklimatischer Jahreskurort, Luftkurort, Kur- und Höhenbäder, beheiztes Freibad, Schwarzwälder Gastlichkeit, sonnige Höhenlage.

Schreiben Sie zu Hause.

Übung F: Remind students that they cannot write about what things were like in the past, but only about Tacitus's impressions of the present. Remind them not to confuse **die Germanen** with **die Deutschen.**

■ F ■ Fantasiefrage You are the Roman historian Tacitus. You have returned to contemporary Germany to update your impressions. Write in German about the country. What do people still (**noch**) do or no longer (**nicht mehr**) do? What plays a role in modern life? How are things nowadays, such as the cities, the wine, etc.?

■ G ■ Write sentences using the elements below. You may have to add words.

1. wer / wollen / wandern / durch / Berge?
2. er / möchten / fahren / ohne / sein / Freund
3. leider / wir / haben / kein / mehr / Brötchen (*pl.*)
4. du / können / vier Uhr / gehen / schwimmen
5. wir / gehen / zusammen / durch / Tal
6. im Winter / ich / mögen / die Berge

H Wie sagt man das auf Deutsch?

With this chapter you have completed the first quarter of ***Neue Horizonte.*** For a concise review of the grammar and idiomatic phrases in chapters 1–4, you may consult the **Zusammenfassung und Wiederholung 1** (*Summary and Review 1*) of your Workbook. The review section is followed by a self-correcting test.

1. The sun is shining and the water is warm. Let's go swimming.
2. I don't want to go swimming yet. Go without me.
3. But I don't like to swim alone.
4. Do you like the winter, Stefan?
5. No, I don't like it any more.
6. I don't like to walk through the snow.
7. Wait here, Sabrina and Harald.
8. We don't want to wait.
9. I hope that you still have money.
10. Unfortunately, I don't have any more money.
11. Can you do something for me?
12. Unfortunately, I have to go home now.

Videoecke

2 Ohne Frühstück geht's nicht! (5:29)

Es ist schon acht Uhr, aber die Studentin Katrin Berger schläft noch. Harald will sie darum wecken (wake)*. Katrin ist in Eile und muss schnell weg – ihr Seminar beginnt ja um 10. Aber Herr Blum meint, sie muss noch etwas essen. Seinen Regenschirm soll Katrin auch mitnehmen* (take along)*. Es soll heute regnen. Katrin geht weg, aber dann beginnt der Regen und sie muss zurückkommen und den Schirm holen* (get)*.*

Wortschatz zum Video

aufstehen	*to get up*
wecken	*to wake (someone) up*
die **Butter**	*butter*
das **Ei, -er**	*egg*
die **Erdbeermarmelade**	*strawberry jam*
die **Wurst, ¨e**	*sausage*
vorher	*before that*
Ich bin spät dran.	*I'm late.*
Setzen Sie sich.	*Sit down.*
eine Tasse Tee	*a cup of tea*

■ **A** ■ **Was sehen Sie im Video?** Watch video Module 2 (5:43–8:36) once without sound. Check off in the list below what you see in the video.

Ich sehe ...

_____ 1. ein Ei
_____ 2. Pommes frites
_____ 3. eine Zeitung
_____ 4. Tee
_____ 5. Kaffee
_____ 6. Marmelade
_____ 7. einen CD-Spieler
_____ 8. Bier
_____ 9. Frau Bachmann

■ **B** ■ **Was hören Sie?** Now watch the same section with sound, checking off the words you hear. Try to guess the meanings of the ones you haven't yet learned.

_____ 1. früh
_____ 2. aufstehen
_____ 3. Brot
_____ 4. Brötchen
_____ 5. Tee
_____ 6. Heft
_____ 7. Regenmantel
_____ 8. Regenschirm

C **Wer macht das? Wer sagt das?** Choose the person who does or says the following.

a. Harald | b. Katrin | c. Herr Blum
d. Frau Bachmann | e. Stefan

1. ____________ schläft ein bisschen zu lange.
2. ____________ sagt: „Ich muss weg!"
3. ____________ sagt: „Nimm doch ein Brötchen mit."
4. ____________ muss schnell ein Buch kaufen.
5. ____________ besitzt keinen Regenschirm.

D **Richtig oder falsch?** Indicate whether each statement is **richtig (R)** or **falsch (F)**.

1. Es ist Viertel vor acht. R F
2. Harald geht Katrin wecken. R F
3. Katrin isst ein Ei. R F
4. Vor ihrem Seminar muss Katrin ein Buch kaufen. R F
5. Herr Blum ist heute in Eile. R F
6. Katrin braucht keinen Regenschirm. R F

E **Was ist die beste Lösung?** Complete the sentence with the best word or phrase.

1. Tschüss, Kinder. Ich muss jetzt ____________.

   a. kaufen b. studieren c. gehen

2. Nehmen Sie doch ____________ ein Ei oder Butter und Wurst.

   a. hoffentlich b. wenigstens c. um 9 Uhr

3. Sie sollten aber einen Regenschirm ____________!

   a. vergessen b. finden c. mitnehmen

4. Ich habe ein Seminar ____________.

   a. am Donnerstag b. um halb elf c. um zehn

5. ____________ muss ich noch ein Buch kaufen.

   a. Früher b. Vor c. Vorher

F **Welle Magazin: Was sehen Sie?** Read through the list below. Then watch the **Welle Magazin** (8:38–9:30) and check off the words and things you see in the video.

Ich sehe ...

_____ 1. Eduscho (*brand of coffee*)
_____ 2. Berliner Morgenpost (eine Berliner Zeitung)
_____ 3. eine Schule
_____ 4. Zum Imbiss (ein Restaurant, wo man schnell essen kann)
_____ 5. die Familie Bachmann im Garten
_____ 6. Konditorei (Hier kann man Kaffee und Kuchen bekommen.)
_____ 7. eine Küche

Almanach

The Common Origin of German and English

Although Tacitus thought the Germanic tribes had "always been there," in fact, they originated in the Baltic region around the second millenium B.C. As the Roman Empire began to collapse in the fourth century A.D., the Germanic peoples migrated south, a movement that continued for nearly two hundred years. The **Germani** (as they were called by the Romans) displaced the Celts from the heart of the European continent, pushing them as far west as Ireland. The Romans temporarily halted Germanic expansion southward by establishing their own northern frontier, a series of fortifications called the **limes**, literally the "limits" or boundaries of their empire. Remains of the **limes** can be seen in Germany today. Contemporary dialects and regional differences within the German-speaking countries have their origins in the various Germanic tribes of the early Middle Ages.

Thanks to the migration of the Germanic Angles and Saxons to the British Isles in the fifth century A.D., the Germanic language that was to evolve into modern English was introduced there. German and English thus share a common origin. Some other languages included in the Germanic family are Yiddish, Dutch, Flemish, Norwegian, Swedish, Danish, and Icelandic. You will easily recognize cognates (words that have the same etymological root) in English and German, although different meanings may have developed. These words can be readily identified by some regularly occurring consonant shifts. Try guessing the English equivalents for the following words:

German	*English*	*Related words*
z	**t**	zehn = ten
		Herz =
ss	**t**	Wasser =
		groß =
pf	**p**	Pflanze =
ff	**p** or **pp**	Schiff =
		Pfeffer und Salz =
ch	**k**	machen =
		Milch =
t	**d**	Tag =
		Tür =
d	**th**	du =
		drei =
		Pfad =

Hochdeutsch (*High German*) is the official, standardized language of the German-speaking countries. It is the language of the media, the law, and education, and is based on written German (**Schriftdeutsch**). Educated native speakers are bi-dialectal, knowing their local dialect and High German, which they may speak with a regional accent.

The cognate of **du** is *thou*. Mention regional dialects and their continued importance. See if students can find English cognates for these words they know: **fließen** (*float, fleet*); **Tal** (*dale*); **hoffen** (*hope*); **durch** (*through*); **kurz** (*curt*); **schwarz** (*swarthy*); **Kleid** (*cloth, clothing*); **hassen** (*hate*); **sprechen** (*speak*); **Zeitung** (*tidings*). Point out how one finds etymological information in a good dictionary.

The German Spelling Reform

English speakers are used to alternate spellings. In particular, most of us are aware that there are variant British and American spellings of a number of words (*jail/gaol, tire/tyre, theater/theatre*). Thus, you may be surprised that the German-speaking countries have an officially approved set of spelling rules. German spelling was codified in 1902 in a set of 212 rules. Compared to English, you will find that German spelling is very phonetic, that is, every letter stands for only one or at the most two sounds. For instance, German **o** represents the long or the short version of a single vowel sound, whereas English *o* represents a different sound in each of the following words: *to, woman, women, hold, world, long, got.* In German, it is almost always possible to sound out a new word correctly according to the pronunciation rules you have learned.

In spite of German's already straightforward spelling, however, language experts from the German-speaking countries have been working for the past 15 years or so on a reform aimed at making the orthography even more rational. After years of discussion and revision, the new spelling was agreed to by the governments of Austria, Germany, and Switzerland in July 1996. The new rules (112 instead of the 212 of 1902) have been taught in schools since 1998–1999, although the old spelling will continue to be allowed until 2005. You are learning the new spelling in this edition of ***Neue Horizonte***.

Although the spelling reformers during their deliberations solicited opinion from the general public and especially from professional writers, most German authors were caught off guard by the announcement of the new rules. Many of them signed a declaration of protest and call to resistance against the reform at the Frankfurt Book Fair in October 1996. But although some authors have threatened to refuse permission to reprint their works in the reformed orthography, the **Rechtschreib-reform** appears to be inevitable.

In fact, the reform doesn't change German spelling very much. It has been characterized as a **Reförmchen**—*a reformlet*—by some critics. Many regret that the reformers were not able to agree on the elimination of noun capitalization and of the letter **ß**, the two major features that make German spelling different from that of other languages that use the Latin alphabet. The Swiss Germans have not used the diagraph-S for years and the reform allows them to continue to use **ss** instead.

Although you are learning German in the new spelling, you will inevitably encounter the old spelling as well when you travel in Europe or read German books and magazines printed before 1998. The main differences you will notice are the following:

1. In the new spelling, the letter **ß** is used only when an unvoiced, hissing *s*-sound (rather than a voiced, buzzing *s*-sound) follows a long vowel or diphthong:

   Klasse (short **a** followed by unvoiced *s*)
   Straße (long **a** followed by unvoiced *s*)
   Nase (long a followed by voiced *s*)

In the old spelling, **ß** occurred in other cases as well. You need only remember that this letter always represents the unvoiced *s*-sound, both in the old and the new spelling. Here are some examples of the changes:

New spelling	*Old spelling*
dass	daß
ich muss	ich muß
der Fluss	der Fluß

2. In the new spelling, several noun + verb combinations are written apart, whereas they used to be written together.

New spelling	*Old spelling*
Rad fahren	radfahren
Ski laufen	skilaufen

3. In unchanging idiomatic phrases, some nouns are now capitalized that used to be written lower case:

New spelling	*Old spelling*
auf Deutsch	auf deutsch
heute Morgen	heute morgen
morgen Abend	morgen abend

KAPITEL 5

Arbeit und Freizeit

Communicative Goals

- Talking about work and professions
- Showing, giving, and telling things to people
- Asking about prices in shops
- Saying when and for how long things happen

Cultural Goal

- Learning about the world of work in Germany

Chapter Outline

- **Lyrik zum Vorlesen**
  Richard Dehmel, „Der Arbeitsmann"
- **Grammatik**
  Dative case
  Dative personal pronouns
  Word order of noun and pronoun objects
  Prepositions with dative case
  Verbs with separable prefixes
  Verbs with inseparable prefixes
  Time phrases in accusative case
- **Lesestück**
  Drei Deutsche bei der Arbeit
- **Situationen aus dem Alltag**
  Berufe
- **Almanach**
  Stellenangebote (*Help Wanted Ads*)

Lab Manual Kap. 5, Dialoge, Fragen, Hören Sie gut zu!, Üb. zur Aussprache **(l)**.

Pronunciation practice: Tape program focuses on **l**. Use dialogues to review this sound in class: **Lehrling; lernst du; Laden; Brezeln; willst du; die Schule verlassen; ich will; schlecht; ich hab' die Nase voll; ich möchte lieber.**

DM 6,80 is pronounced **sechs Mark achtzig**.

Lehrling: apprentice in training, colloquially called **Azubi** (acronym for the official term **Auszubildender** = *person to be trained*).

Duration is covered systematically in Kap. 10. However, **seit** + *present tense* occurs frequently in the **Lesestück** of Kap. 5. To familiarize students with this structure now, try the following complete-sentence exchanges. To avoid the need for dative endings, tell students to answer with a month or a year: **Seit wann studieren Sie hier? / kennen Sie mich? / lernen Sie Deutsch? / spielen Sie ein Musikinstrument?**

Der neue Bäckerlehrling kommt an

Morgens um 6.00. Georg macht die Bäckerei auf.

MARTIN: Morgen. Ich heiße Martin Holst. Ich fange heute bei euch an.
GEORG: Morgen, Martin. Mein Name ist Georg. Den Chef lernst du gleich kennen.
MARTIN: Ist gut. Seit wann arbeitest du denn hier?
GEORG: Erst seit einem Jahr. Komm jetzt mit und ich zeige dir den Laden.

Beim Bäcker

VERKÄUFERIN: Was darf's sein, bitte?
KUNDE: Geben Sie mir bitte sechs Brötchen und ein Bauernbrot.
VERKÄUFERIN: (*Sie gibt ihm das Brot.*) So, bitte sehr. Sonst noch etwas?
KUNDE: Sind diese Brezeln frisch?
VERKÄUFERIN: Ja, von heute Morgen.
KUNDE: Dann geben Sie mir doch sechs Stück. Wieviel kostet das bitte?
VERKÄUFERIN: Das macht zusammen DM 6,80, bitte sehr.
KUNDE: Danke. Auf Wiedersehen.
VERKÄUFERIN: Wiedersehen.

Schule oder Beruf?

VATER: Warum willst du denn jetzt die Schule verlassen? Deine Noten sind ja ganz gut und du hast nur noch ein Jahr.
KURT: Aber das Abitur brauch' ich nicht. Ich will ja Automechaniker werden.
VATER: Sei nicht so dumm! Als Lehrling verdienst du schlecht.
KURT: Aber ich hab' die Nase einfach voll. Ich möchte lieber mit den Händen arbeiten.
VATER: Quatsch! Du schaffst das Abitur und ich schenke dir ein Motorrad. Einverstanden?
KURT: Hmmm.

Note on Usage: *Seit wann?*

Seit wann **arbeitest** du hier? *How long **have** you **worked** here?*

English uses perfect tense (*have worked*) for a situation beginning in the past but still continuing. German uses present (**arbeitest**).

„bei Heinz Holl"
Spezialitäten Restaurant für Kenner
Geöffnet: Mo. - Sa. 19.00 -2.00 Uhr
1 Berlin 31
Damaschkestraße 26
Tel.: 3231404
Tischbestellungen erbeten!

Wortschatz 1

Remind students of root meanings of these verbs: **machen** vs. **aufmachen**, **stehen** vs. **aufstehen**, etc.

See p. 138 for an explanation of the raised dot in **an·fangen** and other verbs.

Verben

an·fangen (fängt an) to begin, start
an·kommen to arrive
an·rufen to call up
auf·hören (mit etwas) to cease, stop (*doing something*)
auf·machen to open
auf·stehen to stand up; to get up; get out of bed
kennen lernen to get to know; to meet
kosten to cost
mit·kommen to come along
schenken to give (*as a gift*)
stehen to stand
verlassen (verlässt) (*trans.*) to leave (*a person or place*)
zeigen to show

Substantive

der **Automechaniker, -** auto mechanic
der **Bäcker, -** baker
der **Bauer, -n** farmer
der **Chef, -s** boss
der **Kunde, -n** customer (*m.*)
der **Laden, ¨** shop, store
der **Lehrling, -e** apprentice
der **Name, -n** name

das **Abitur** final secondary school examination
das **Brot** bread
  das **Bauernbrot** dark bread
das **Jahr, -e** year
das **Motorrad, ¨er** motorcycle
das **Stück, -e** piece
  sechs Stück six (*of the same item*)

die **Bäckerei, -en** bakery
die **Brezel, -n** soft pretzel
die **Chefin, -nen** boss (*f.*)
die **Deutsche Mark (DM)** the German mark
die **Hand, ¨e** hand
die **Kundin, -nen** customer (*f.*)
die **Nase, -n** nose
die **Note, -n** grade
die **Woche, -n** week

Adjektive und Adverbien

dumm dumb
einfach simple, easy
erst not until; only
fertig (mit) done, finished (with); ready
frisch fresh
gleich right away, immediately
heute Morgen this morning
voll full

Andere Vokabeln

als as a
  als Lehrling as an apprentice
  als Kind as a child
dies- this, these
dir (to *or* for) you
euch (to *or* for) you (*pl.*)
jed- each, every
wem? to *or* for whom?
wie viel? how much?

Dies- and **jed-**: These words (*this, every*) always take endings (**dieser, jede**, etc.).

Präpositionen mit Dativ

The eight prepositions below are followed by dative case. See **Grammatik**, p. 136.

aus out of; from
außer except for; besides
bei at; at the home of
  bei euch with you, at your place (*i.e., where you work or live*)
mit with
nach after
seit since (*temporal*)
von from; of; by
zu to

Nützliche Ausdrücke

Ist gut. (*colloq.*) O.K.; Fine by me.
Was darf es sein? What'll it be? May I help you?
Bitte sehr. Here it is. There you are.
Sonst noch etwas? Will there be anything else?
Das macht zusammen ... All together that comes to . . .
Ich habe die Nase voll. I'm fed up. I've had it up to here.
Quatsch! Baloney! Nonsense!
Einverstanden. Agreed. It's a deal. O.K.

Gegensätze

an·fangen ≠ auf·hören to start ≠ to stop
auf·machen ≠ zu·machen to open ≠ to close
dumm ≠ klug dumb ≠ smart, bright
einfach ≠ schwierig simple ≠ difficult
voll ≠ leer full ≠ empty

Mit anderen Worten

das Abi = das Abitur (*Schülerslang*)
blöd = dumm

Point out that in the dialogue, **Einverstanden?** is a question: *Is it a deal?*

The New Baker's Apprentice Arrives

Six A.M. Georg is opening the bakery.

M: Morning. My name is Martin Holst. I'm starting here today.
G: Morning, Martin. My name is Georg. You'll meet the boss soon.
M: O.K. How long have you been working here?
G: Only for a year. Now come with me and I'll show you the shop.

At the Baker's

*CL: May I help you?
**CU: Give me six rolls and one loaf of dark bread, please.
CL: (*She gives him the bread.*) There you are. Anything else?
CU: Are these pretzels fresh?
CL: Yes, from this morning.
CU: Then give me six of those. How much is that, please?
CL: Together that comes to six marks eighty.
CU: Thank you. Good-bye.
CL: Bye.

*CL = Clerk
**CU = Customer

School or Profession?

F: Why do you want to leave school now? Your grades are pretty good and you've only got one more year.
K: But I don't need the **Abitur**. I want to be an auto mechanic.
F: Don't be so dumb. You won't earn much as an apprentice.
K: But I'm fed up. I'd rather work with my hands.
F: Nonsense! You pass your **Abitur** and I'll give you a motorcycle. Is it a deal?
K: Hmmm.

Variationen A1: When working with closed books, write paradigm for response on board: **Er schenkt mir** ______ . Ask question of several students.

Variationen

■ A ■ Persönliche Fragen

1. Der Vater schenkt Kurt ein Motorrad. Was schenkt Ihnen Ihr Vater? Er schenkt mir ______ .
2. Kurt sagt, das Abitur braucht er nicht. Was brauchen *Sie* nicht?
3. Kurt hat nur noch ein Jahr und dann ist er mit der Schule fertig. Wie viele Jahre haben Sie noch an der Universität?
4. Kurt arbeitet gern mit den Händen. Arbeiten Sie auch gern mit den Händen?
5. Martin lernt den Chef gleich kennen. Wen möchten *Sie* kennen lernen?
6. Sechs Brezeln und ein Bauernbrot kosten DM 6,80. Was kosten 12 Brezeln und zwei Bauernbrote?

"The Germans have an inhuman way of cutting up their verbs. Now a verb has a hard enough time of it in this world when it's all together. It's downright inhuman to split it up. But that's just what those Germans do. They take part of a verb and put it down here, like a stake, and they take the other part of it and put it away over yonder like another stake, and between these two limits they just shovel in German."

Mark Twain

Asking about prices in shops is a communicative goal.

■ B ■ Partnerarbeit: Was darf's sein? (*Mit offenen Büchern*) Partner A spielt den Verkäufer oder die Verkäuferin, Partner B spielt eine Kundin oder einen Kunden. Für das Semester müssen Sie viel kaufen. Spielen Sie diesen Dialog zusammen. Hier sehen Sie, was man kaufen kann.

A: Guten Tag. Was darf's denn sein, bitte?
B: Zeigen Sie mir bitte ________ .
A: Bitte sehr.
B: Was kostet denn ________ ?
A: Das kostet ________ .
B: Ich möchte gern ________ , ________ und ________ kaufen.
A: Das macht zusammen DM ________ , bitte sehr.

Lyrik zum Vorlesen

Richard Dehmel worked as a journalist in Berlin and was active in progressive literary circles. The language of his revolutionary lyric poetry was influenced by the philosopher Friedrich Nietzsche. In this poem an **Arbeitsmann** (*day laborer*) contrasts his family's life of toil and deprivation with the freedom, beauty, and fearlessness of the swallows that he and his child see on a Sunday walk.

Lab Manual Kap. 5, Lyrik zum Vorlesen.

Der Arbeitsmann

Wir haben ein Bett°, wir haben ein Kind,
Mein Weib!°
Wir haben auch Arbeit, und gar zu zweit°,
Und haben die Sonne und Regen und Wind.
Und uns fehlt nur eine Kleinigkeit°,
Um so frei zu° sein, wie die Vögel° sind:
Nur Zeit.

bed
mein Weib = meine Frau
und ... = and even together
uns ... = we lack only a small thing
um ... zu = in order to / birds

Wenn wir sonntags° durch die Felder° gehn, Mein Kind, Und über den Ähren weit und breit° Das blaue Schwalbenvolk blitzen sehn°, Oh, dann fehlt uns nicht das bisschen Kleid, Um so schön zu sein, wie die Vögel sind: Nur Zeit.	on Sundays / fields **über** ... = above the grain far and wide **Das** ... = see flocks of blue swallows flashing
Nur Zeit! wir wittern° Gewitterwind°, Wir Volk°. Nur eine kleine Ewigkeit°; Uns fehlt ja nichts, mein Weib, mein Kind, Als all das, was durch uns gedeiht°, Um so kühn° zu sein, wie die Vögel sind. Nur Zeit!	smell / stormwind common folk eternity **Als** ... = except for all that prospers through us daring

Richard Dehmel (1863–1920)

Dative case

The dative case is the case of the indirect object in German. An indirect object is the person or thing *for* whom an action is performed or *to* whom it is directed.

Dative comes from **datus**, a form of the Latin verb **dare** (*to give*). The etymology highlights an important function of dative case: to designate the receiver of something given.

Sie gibt **ihm** das Brot.	*She gives him the bread.* (or) *She gives the bread to him.*

English shows the indirect object by means of word order and in some cases also uses a preposition (*to* him, *for* the teacher).

1 Übung Identify the direct object and the indirect object in the following English sentences.

1. We owe him a debt of gratitude.
2. I'm buying my father a necktie.
3. Tell me what you think.
4. We're cooking spaghetti for the kids.
5. Peel me a grape.
6. To whom did you say that?

Die Arbeit in der Bäckerei fängt früh an.

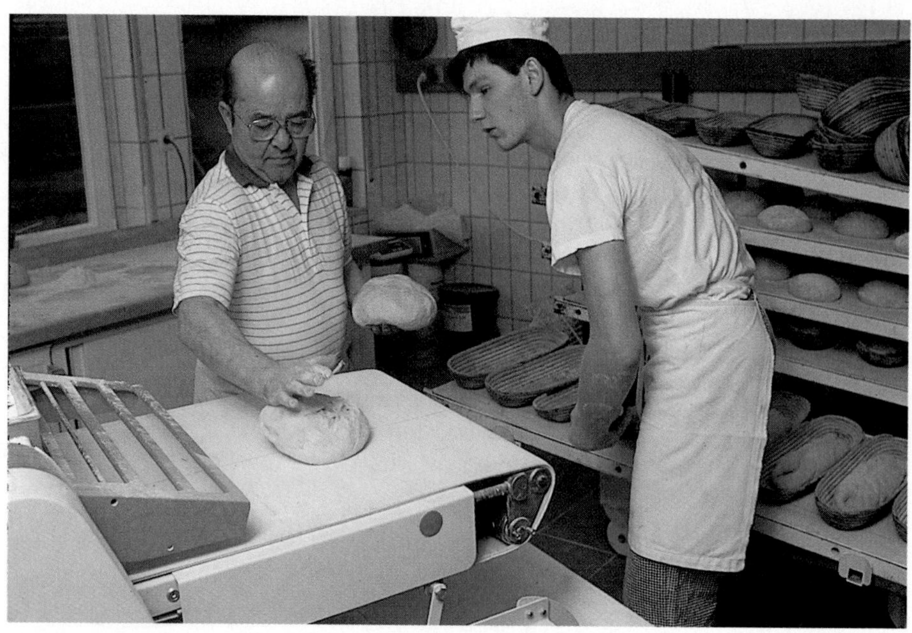

■ German versus English indirect object

You can recognize the dative case by the form of the personal pronoun (e.g., **dir** = *to/for you*) or of the article or possessive adjective used with a noun (**dem** Lehrer = *to/for the teacher*, **ihrer** Tochter = *to/for her daughter*).

German does *not* use a preposition to show the indirect object. It is signalled by case alone.

Here are some verbs you already know that can take a dative and an accusative object in the same sentence: **sagen (Sag mir etwas); geben (Ich gebe dir 2 Mark); kochen; tragen; schreiben; singen; kaufen; verkaufen; beschreiben; schenken; zeigen.**

ind. obj. *dir. obj.* Ich kaufe **dir das Motorrad**.	*I'll buy you the motorcycle.* *I'll buy the motorcycle for you.*
ind. obj. *dir. obj.* Sag **dem Lehrer Guten Morgen**.	*Tell the teacher good morning.* *Say good morning to the teacher.*
ind. obj. *dir. obj.* Sie gibt **ihrer Tochter das Geld**.	*She's giving her daughter the money.* *She's giving the money to her daughter.*

Showing, giving, and telling things to people are communicative goals.

The German case system allows more flexibility in word order than does English. The following sentences all say basically the same thing, with some minor shifts in emphasis.

Sie gibt **ihrer Tochter das Geld**.
Sie gibt **das Geld ihrer Tochter**.
Das Geld gibt sie **ihrer Tochter**.
Ihrer Tochter gibt sie **das Geld**.

By mastering the case endings, you can always find your way through such sentences and understand what they mean.

Forms of the dative case

The definite article, indefinite article, possessive adjectives, and **dies-** all share the same set of dative endings. The chart below shows these dative forms, as well as the nominative and accusative forms of the definite article (the cases you have already learned).

	masc.	neut.	fem.	plural
nom. acc.	der Vater den Vater	das Kind	die Frau	die Leute
dat.	-em **dem** Vater dies**em** Vater ein**em** Vater unser**em** Vater	-em **dem** Kind dies**em** Kind ein**em** Kind dein**em** Kind	-er **der** Frau dies**er** Frau ein**er** Frau sein**er** Frau	-en -n **den** Leute**n** dies**en** Leute**n** kein**en** Leute**n** mein**en** Leute**n**

Note: *All nouns* in the dative plural add an **-n** to the noun itself (**den** Leute**n**, **den** Hände**n**), except those nouns already ending in **-n** (**den** Fraue**n**) and those ending in **-s** (**den** Hotel**s**).

Fragewörter

wer? *who?*
wen? *whom?* (direct object)
wessen? *whose?*
wem? *to* or *for whom?* (indirect object)

Wem geben Sie das Geld? ***To whom** are you giving the money?*

Lab Manual Kap. 5, Var. zur Üb. 2.

Workbook Kap. 5, A.

Reviews family members. With large classes, substitute new direct object, e.g., **Wem schenkst du einen Regenschirm?**

2 **Übung: Wem soll sie es geben?** Beate kann ihr Brötchen nicht essen. Wem soll sie es geben?

BEISPIEL: die Lehrerin
Sie soll es der Lehrerin geben.

Feminine
1. ihre Freundin
2. ihre Schwester
3. die Professorin
4. die Chefin

Neuter and masculine
5. ein Kind
6. ihr Freund
7. der Lehrer
8. mein Vater
9. dieser Automechaniker

Plural
10. die Kinder
11. diese Leute
12. die Studenten
13. ihre Freunde

To review family vocabulary, see pp. 62–63.

Übung 3: Also good as written assignment. Have students invent sentences of their own using **sagen, verkaufen,** and **singen**.

3 **Kettenreaktion: Wem schenkst du den Pulli?** Sie kaufen einen schönen Pulli für jemand in Ihrer Familie. Wem schenken Sie ihn?

BEISPIEL: A: Wem schenkst *du* den Pulli?
B: Meiner Schwester. Wem schenkst *du* den Pulli?
C: Mein-________. Wem ... ?

Das gebe ich dir, aber was gibst du mir?

■ 4 ■ Übung: Wie sagt man das auf Deutsch? Benutzen Sie (*Use*) den du-Imperativ.

BEISPIEL: Buy the child a book.
Kauf dem Kind ein Buch.

1. Buy your sister a book.
2. Give my parents the money.
3. Describe the problem to the mechanic.
4. Write your mother a card.
5. Cook the food for your friends.
6. Show my friend the city.

Dative personal pronouns[1]

The following table lists the dative personal pronouns and reviews their nominative and accusative forms as well.

Singular				Plural			
nom.	*acc.*	*dat.*		*nom.*	*acc.*	*dat.*	
ich	mich	**mir**	*to/for me*	wir	uns	**uns**	*to/for us*
du	dich	**dir**	*to/for you*	ihr	euch	**euch**	*to/for you*
er	ihn	**ihm**	*to/for him*				
es	es	**ihm**	*to/for it*	sie	sie	**ihnen**	*to/for them*
sie	sie	**ihr**	*to/for her*	Sie	Sie	**Ihnen**	*to/for you*

Note the similarities between the third-person dative pronouns and the dative endings of the articles and possessive adjectives.

ihm → **dem** Mann, **meinem** Kind
ihr → **der** Frau, **seiner** Schwester
ihnen → **den** Freunden, **unseren** Kindern

Point to several students to elicit **ihnen**, to yourself for **Ihnen** or **dir**, to yourself and another student for **Ihnen** or **euch**.

■ 5 ■ Übung: Kaufen wir Brot. Sie wollen Brot kaufen. Ihre Professorin möchte wissen, **wem** Sie es kaufen.

BEISPIEL: Wem kaufen Sie das Brot? (*points to another student*)
Ich kaufe es *ihm* / *ihr*.

Lab Manual Kap. 5, Var. zur Üb. 6.

Workbook Kap. 5, B, C.

Be sure to monitor each pair for correct forms.

■ 6 ■ Partnerarbeit: Kaufst du mir etwas? Taking turns and using the cues below, ask your partner what he or she will do for you.

BEISPIEL: Kaufst du mir eine Brezel?
Ja, ich kaufe dir eine Brezel *oder*
Nein, ich kaufe dir keine Brezel.

dein Motorrad verkaufen
deine Fotos zeigen
deine Reise beschreiben
Geld schenken
eine Karte kaufen
ein Brötchen geben (gibst)

1. Note that English pronouns do not have different forms for the direct object and the indirect object, whereas German pronouns (except **uns** and **euch**) do.

*I see **him**.*	Ich sehe **ihn**.
*I'm giving **him** the book.*	Ich gebe **ihm** das Buch.

Word order of noun and pronoun objects

Verbs such as **geben**, **schenken**, **kaufen**, **beschreiben**, **sagen**, and **zeigen** often have two objects. The first is usually the person (in the dative case) *to whom* something is given, shown, etc., or *for whom* something is done. The second object is the thing (in the accusative case) that is being given, shown, bought, etc.

Ich zeige **meiner Freundin den Laden**.	*I'm showing my girlfriend the shop.*

If one of the objects is a pronoun, it precedes the noun object.

Ich zeige **ihr den Laden**.	*I'm showing her the shop.*
Ich zeige **ihn meiner Freundin**.	*I'm showing it to my girlfriend.*

If both objects are pronouns, the accusative must precede the dative. (Note the similarity to English word order.)

Ich zeige **ihn ihr**.	*I'm showing it to her.*

Any personal pronouns that are not in the first position are placed *immediately after the inflected verb.*

Note the third example: the direct-object pronoun (**uns**) even precedes the noun subject (**dein Opa**).

Ich gebe **ihm** mein Buch.	*I'm giving **him** my book.*
Ich gebe **es** meinem Bruder.	*I'm giving **it** to my brother.*
Kann **uns** dein Opa anrufen?	*Can your grandpa phone **us**?*

If more than one personal pronoun follows the verb, they come in the order *nominative, accusative, dative.* Again, this is just like English word order: *subject pronoun, direct-object pronoun, indirect-object pronoun.*

Ich gebe **es Ihnen** heute.	*I'm giving **it to you** today.*
Heute gebe **ich es Ihnen**.	*Today **I'm** giving **it to you**.*

Lab Manual Kap. 5, Var. zur Üb. 7.

Workbook Kap. 5, D.

Repeat the entire question each time.

7 Übung: Wem schenken Sie das Buch? You've bought copies of your favorite novel as presents. Your instructor will ask whom you're giving it to. Answer the questions affirmatively, using pronouns.

BEISPIEL: Wem schenken Sie das Buch? Schenken Sie es Ihrer Mutter?
Ja, ich schenke es ihr.

Schenken Sie es ...

1. Ihrem Vater?
2. den Kindern?
3. Ihrem Freund?
4. Ihrer Mitbewohnerin?
5. mir?
6. uns?

MERIAN zeigt Ihnen die Welt.

As with the list of accusative prepositions (p. 102), you must learn this list until you can repeat it in your sleep.

You may want to add *made out of*: **aus Metall**.

Bei sometimes has the meaning *near*, which is infrequent except in such expressions as **Bebenhausen bei Tübingen**. Use of **bei** to set a scene (**beim Essen**) or *while ... -ing* (**beim Ski laufen**) is introduced in Kap. 11. **Ich habe kein Geld bei mir** (= *on me*).

mit also = *by means of*: **mit dem Bus, Zug**

Stress contrast with English in use of article in time phrases: **nach der Arbeit, nach dem Essen, nach dem Frühstück.**

Over the next few days, spot-check dative and accusative prepositions with short cues in English: *She's looking out the window. He's at work. I work with them. They work for my brother.*

bis zu followed by dative = *up until* or *as far as*

More work on equivalents for the directional *to* in Kap. 8, p. 231.

zu = *for* in certain phrases: **zum Frühstück, Geburtstag**

Prepositions with dative case

The dative case is also used for the object of the following prepositions.

aus	*out of* *from* (native country, city or region)	Sie sieht **aus** dem Fenster. Ich komme **aus** Amerika.	*She's looking out of the window.* *I'm from America.*
außer	*except for* *besides, in addition to*	**Außer** ihm sind wir alle hier. **Außer** ihm wohnt auch sein Bruder hier.	*We're all here except for him.* *Besides him, his brother lives here too.*
bei	*in the home of* *at*	Ich wohne **bei** meiner Tante. Er ist **bei** der Arbeit.	*I live at my aunt's.* *He's at work.*
mit	*with*	Ich arbeite **mit** den Händen.	*I work with my hands.*
nach	*after* *to* (with country and city names)	**Nach** der Arbeit bin ich manch-mal müde. Wir fahren **nach** England.	*After work I'm sometimes tired.* *We're going to England.*
seit	*since* (referring to time) *for*	**Seit** dem Tag mag ich ihn nicht mehr. Ich arbeite **seit** einem Jahr hier.	*Since that day I haven't liked him.* *I've worked here for a year.*
von	*from* *of* *by*	Das Buch habe ich **von** meiner Mutter. Er ist ein Freund **von** mir. Das ist ein Buch **von** Hermann Hesse.	*I got that book from my mother.* *He's a friend of mine.* *That's a book by Hermann Hesse.*
zu	*to* (people and some locations)	Ich gehe **zur** Schule und dann **zu** meinen Freunden.	*I'm going to school and then to my friends' house.*

■ Contractions

The following contractions are standard.

bei dem	→ **beim**	Brezeln kaufe ich immer **beim** Bäcker.
von dem	→ **vom**	Ich komme gerade **vom** Chef.
zu dem	→ **zum**	Ich muss schnell **zum** Professor.
zu der	→ **zur**	Ich gehe jetzt **zur** Schule.

Lab Manual Kap. 5, Var. zur Üb. 8.

Workbook Kap. 5, E.

If students are already confident of dative forms, **Übung 8** could be done as **Partnerarbeit** or with student leading it as a **Gruppenarbeit**.

■ 8 ■ Übung: Bei wem wohnen Sie? Sie sind alle Studenten in Tübingen. Sie wohnen aber nicht im Studentenwohnheim (*dormitory*). Sagen Sie Ihrem Professor oder Ihrer Professorin, bei wem Sie wohnen.

BEISPIEL: Bei wem wohnen Sie?
Bei meinem Freund.

Tante	Freundin	Bruder	Großeltern
Familie	Vater	Freund	Frau König

■ 9 ■ Kettenreaktion: Zu wem gehst *du*? Say whom you are going to see, then ask another student.

BEISPIEL: PROFESSOR/IN: Zu wem gehen Sie?
A: Ich gehe zu meiner Familie. Zu wem gehst *du*?
B: Ich gehe zum Bäcker. Zu wem ...

Automechaniker	Bäckerin	Lehrling
Professorin	Automechanikerin	Amerikaner
Professor	Eltern	Familie
Chef	Amerikanerin	Bäcker

Prepare **Übung 10** by demonstrating how to answer: **Mit wem gehe ich schwimmen? Mit ihnen** (*point to group*), **mit ihm** (*point to male*), **mit ihr** (*to female*). Vary with: **Mit wem gehen Sie wandern / Tennis spielen / essen?**

■ 10 ■ Übung: Mit wem gehen Sie schwimmen? Sie gehen mit Freunden aus der Deutschstunde schwimmen. Sagen Sie, mit wem Sie schwimmen gehen.

BEISPIEL: PROFESSOR/IN: Mit wem gehen Sie schwimmen?
STUDENT/IN: (*points to one or more other students in the class*)
Mit ihr/ihm/ihnen.

Verbs with separable prefixes

Point out that the prefix system is a central morphological feature of German. A single infinitive can acquire different meanings by adding prefixes to one stem. The same feature exists in English, but with Latin roots, e.g., *attract, detract, subtract, extract.*

The meanings of many English verbs can be changed or modified by the addition of another word.

to find → *to find out*
to look → *to look up*
to burn → *to burn down*
to hang → *to hang around*

Likewise, the meanings of many German verbs are modified—or even changed completely—by the addition of a prefix to the root verb.

stehen	*to stand* →	**auf**stehen	*to stand up; get out of bed*
kommen	*to come* →	**mit**kommen	*to come along*
hören	*to hear* →	**auf**hören	*to cease, stop*
fangen	*to catch* →	**an**fangen	*to begin*

Similarly:

ankommen	*to arrive*
anrufen	*to call up*
aufmachen	*to open*
kennen lernen	*to get to know, meet*
zurückkommen	*to come back*

Note that although **kennen lernen** is written as two words, the first element **kennen** behaves like a separable prefix.

Such verbs are called *separable-prefix verbs*. Separable-prefix verbs have the primary stress on the prefix (**an**kommen, **auf**hören).

In the present tense and the imperative, the prefix is *separated* from the verb and placed at the end of the sentence or clause. It is the second part of the predicate.

Ich **stehe** morgen sehr früh **auf**.	*I'm getting up very early tomorrow.*
Wann **stehst** du **auf**?	*When are you getting up?*
Stehen Sie bitte **auf**!	*Please get up!*
Steht ihr denn bald **auf**?	*Are you getting up soon?*

When a verb with a separable prefix complements a modal verb, the separable prefix is again attached to the root verb infinitive at the end of the sentence or clause.

Without a modal	***With a modal***
Er **fängt** morgen **an**.	Er soll morgen **anfangen**.
Sie **kommt** bald **zurück**.	Sie möchte bald **zurückkommen**.

Note: Separable prefixes will be indicated in the **Wortschatz** sections by a raised dot between prefix and root verb: **an·fangen**. This symbol is often used in textbooks, though *not* in conventional German spelling.

Lab Manual Kap. 5, Var. zu Üb. 11, 12.

Workbook Kap. 5, F, G.

After first time through this exercise as I–S exchange, try it as S–S exchange. Instructor cues with: *Tell your neighbor to start on Wednesday*. Remind students that **doch** softens commands, suggesting: *Why don't you ... ?* or *Go ahead and ...*

■ 11 ■ Übung Ihre Professorin sagt, Sie sollen etwas machen. Antworten Sie, Sie können es nicht machen.

BEISPIEL: Fangen Sie doch heute an.
Ich kann heute nicht anfangen.

1. Hören Sie doch auf.
2. Kommen Sie doch mit.
3. Machen Sie das Fenster auf.
4. Rufen Sie doch Ihre Mutter an.
5. Stehen Sie bitte auf.
6. Kommen Sie bitte heute zurück.

■ 12 ■ Übung Ihr Professor sagt, Sie müssen etwas machen. Sie antworten, Sie sind einverstanden.

BEISPIEL: Sie müssen um sieben aufstehen.
Einverstanden, ich stehe um sieben auf.

1. Sie müssen jetzt anfangen.
2. Sie müssen früh aufstehen.
3. Sie müssen um acht aufmachen.
4. Sie müssen Helena anrufen.
5. Sie müssen aufhören.
6. Sie müssen gleich mitkommen.

■ 13 ■ Partnerarbeit: Mach das bitte für mich.

1. **aufmachen** Partner A asks partner B to open various things, and B agrees.

BEISPIEL: A: Mach doch ________ auf.
B: Gut, ich mache ________ auf.

Buch	Laden	Rucksack	Zeitung
Fenster	Tür	Tasche	

2. **anrufen** Partner B tells A to call up various relatives and friends. Partner A doesn't want to.

BEISPIEL: B: Ruf doch dein-________ an.
A: Aber ich will mein-________ nicht anrufen.

Onkel	Tante	Freundin	Lehrer
Bruder	Schwester	Großeltern	Professorin
Mutter	Vater	Geschwister	

3. **Um 7 Uhr** Partner A wants to know when B is going to do various things. Partner B answers with the time.

BEISPIEL: A: Wann kommst du denn zurück?
B: Um 7 komme ich zurück.

ankommen	mit deiner Arbeit aufhören
zurückkommen	morgens aufstehen
anfangen (fängst ... an)	den Chef kennen lernen

Warte, ich komme auch mit!

Verbs with inseparable prefixes

There are also German verbs with *inseparable* prefixes. These prefixes *never* separate from the root verb. You can tell them from separable prefixes in these ways:

- They are *never* stressed.
- They have no independent meaning of their own, while separable prefixes resemble other parts of speech such as prepositions (**mit**kommen) and adverbs (**zurück**kommen).

The inseparable prefixes are: **be-**, **emp-**, **ent-**, **er-**, **ge-**, **ver-**, and **zer-**. Here are the verbs with inseparable prefixes that you have already learned: **bedeuten**, **beginnen**, **bekommen**, **beschreiben**, **besitzen**, **besprechen**, **besuchen**, **entscheiden**, **verdienen**, **verlassen**, **verstehen**.

■ 14 ■ Übung Say these verb pairs aloud to practice the difference between stressed separable prefixes and unstressed inseparable prefixes. Then complete the following sentences with the appropriate verb.

Inseparable	*Separable*
verstehen	**auf**stehen
beschreiben	**auf**schreiben (*to write down*)
gehören (*to belong to*)	**auf**hören
bekommen	**mit**kommen
erfahren (*to find out*)	**ab**fahren (*to depart*)

1. Ich ______ dich nicht. (*understand*)
   Ich ______ um 7 Uhr ______. (*get up*)
2. ______ Sie es bitte! (*describe*)
   ______ Sie es bitte ______! (*write down*)
3. Harald ______ heute ein Motorrad. (*is getting*)
   Bernd ______ heute ______. (*is coming along*)

Saying when and for how long things happen is a communicative goal.

Remember that when a time phrase uses a preposition, that preposition will govern the case of the noun: **seit dem Tag** *since that day;* **nach einer Stunde** *after an hour.*

Time phrases in accusative case

Here are some time phrases telling *when* or *how often* something occurs or *how long* it goes on. The nouns in these phrases are in the *accusative case.*

Wann?

diesen Freitag	dieses Semester	diese Woche
diesen Herbst	dieses Jahr	
diesen März		

Ich studiere **dieses Semester** in Konstanz. — *I'm studying in Konstanz this semester.*

Diese Woche ist Thomas krank. — *Thomas is sick this week.*

Wann / Wie oft?

jeden Morgen	jedes Semester	jede Minute
jeden Abend	jedes Jahr	jede Stunde
jeden Tag		jede Woche
jeden Montag		
jeden Mai		
jeden Sommer		

Remember that expressions of time (**jeden Tag**) precede expressions of place or destination (**zum Bäcker**).

Wir gehen **jeden Tag** zum Bäcker. — *We go to the baker's every day*

Er fährt **jedes Jahr** nach Amerika. — *He goes to America every year.*

Wie lange?

einen Tag	ein Jahr	eine Minute	drei Tage
		eine Stunde	zwei Semester

Wir bleiben **einen Tag** in London. — *We're staying in London for a day.*

Ich studiere **ein Semester** in Köln. — *I'm studying in Cologne for a semester.*

Note that the German equivalent of "*for* a day" is simply **einen Tag** without a preposition.

Übung 15: Also good as written assignment. Variation for free response: Ask personalized questions using **wann**, **wie oft**, and **wie lange**.

■ **15** ■ **Übung** (*Mit offenen Büchern*) Supply the missing time phrases cued in English.

1. Wie oft stehen Sie um 7 Uhr auf?
   Ich stehe _______ um 7 Uhr auf. (*every day*)
2. Wann rufen Sie Ihre Eltern an?
   Ich rufe sie _______ an. (*this Wednesday*)
3. Wie lange bleiben Sie in Tübingen?
   Ich bleibe _______ dort. (*a year*)
4. Wann arbeitest du denn mit Karl zusammen?
   Wahrscheinlich arbeite ich _______ mit ihm zusammen. (*this week*)
5. Wie lange wartet ihr noch?
   Wir warten noch _______ vor der Bäckerei. (*for an hour*)
6. Hoffentlich kannst du lange bei uns bleiben.
   Nein, leider kann ich nur _______ bei euch sein. (*one day*)
7. Wann ist das Klima bei euch besonders schön?
   Das Wetter ist _______ mild und sonnig. (*every October*)
8. Wann kann ich Sie besuchen, Herr Wahrig?
   _______ um 9 Uhr bin ich frei. (*every Tuesday*)

Lesestück

Vor dem Lesen

Tipps zum Lesen und Lernen

■ Tipps zum Vokabelnlernen

Remember that singular masculine nouns ending in **-er** have the same form in the plural: **der Arbeiter**, **die Arbeiter**. Feminine forms ending **-erin**, however, do have a plural ending: **die Arbeiterin**, **die Arbeiterinnen**.

Agent nouns Both English and German add the suffix **-er** to a verb stem to form a noun that denotes a person who performs the action (agent). In German, the additional ending **-in** indicates that the agent is female.

arbeiten	→ **der Arbeiter / die Arbeiterin**	*to work*	→ *worker*
lesen	→ **der Leser / die Leserin**	*to read*	→ *reader*

Sometimes an umlaut is added in the agent noun:

If students ask, **Anfänger** is not gender specific.

anfangen	→ **Anfänger**	*to begin*	→ *beginner*
tragen	→ **Briefträger**	*to carry*	→ *letter carrier*
backen	→ **Bäcker**	*to bake*	→ *baker*
handeln	→ **Buchhändler**	*to trade, deal*	→ *bookseller*

Students can generate agent nouns. Instructor says: "Tell me what group likes to do the following: Wer trinkt gern Bier?" (Answer: Biertrinker trinken gern Bier.)
I: Wer fängt jetzt an? (Die Anfänger ...)
I: Wer steht gern früh auf? (Frühaufsteher ...)
I: Wer arbeitet viel? (Arbeiter ...)
I: Wer schwimmt gern? (Schwimmer ...)
I: Wer wandert gern durch die Berge? (Wanderer ...)

■ **A** ■ **Übung** Was machen diese Leute?

1. Herr Kropf ist Kaffeetrinker.
2. Frau Baumann ist Zeitungsleserin.
3. Wir sind alle Anfänger.
4. Albert ist Frühaufsteher.
5. Frau Hanselmann ist Buchhändlerin.

Briefträgerin in Bielefeld (Nordrhein-Westfalen)

Adverbs of time German adds an **-s** to the names of the days or parts of the day to form adverbs showing regular or habitual occurrence.

morgens	*in the mornings, every morning*
nachmittags	*in the afternoons, every afternoon*
abends	*in the evenings, every evening*
nachts	*at night, every night*
montags	*Mondays, every Monday*
dienstags	*Tuesdays, every Tuesday*
usw.	*etc.*

Note: These words are *adverbs*, not nouns, and are therefore not capitalized.

Specify answers with **montags**, **morgens**, etc. or allow free responses (may get **um 7 Uhr**, etc.). Possible further **Partnerarbeit**: Ask each other about your regular activities.
BEISPIEL: **Was machst du morgens (nachmittags, abends, samstags)?**

■ **B** ■ **Übung** Wann machen Sie das?

BEISPIEL: Wann essen Sie Brötchen?
Morgens esse ich Brötchen.

1. Wann haben Sie Deutsch?
2. Wann trinken Sie Kaffee?
3. Wann machen Sie Ihre Hausaufgaben?
4. Wann gehen Sie zum Bäcker?
5. Wann rufen Sie Ihre Familie an?

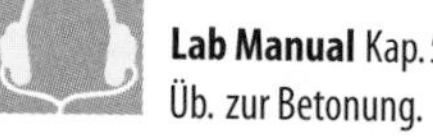

Lab Manual Kap. 5, Üb. zur Betonung.

Model pronunciation of **Journalist**.

Korsika (*Corsica*) is a French island in the Mediterranean. See map on the inside of the back cover.

■ Leicht zu merken

campen	(pronounced **kämpen**)
die **Industrie, -n**	Industrie
der **Journalist, -en**	Journalist
(das) **Kanada**	
der **Korrespondent, -en**	Korrespondent
(das) **Korsika**	
der **Partner, -**	
realistisch	
der **Supermarkt**	
die **Universität, -en**	Universität
die **USA** (*pl.*)	

Einstieg in den Text

The title "Drei Deutsche bei der Arbeit" lets you know that the reading will focus on three individuals and their work. What sorts of things would you expect to learn about people's personal and professional lives from such a reading? You can apply to this text the familiar question words that you have been using to ask about each other's lives.

Before reading the whole text, skim the third portrait and see if you can quickly find answers to the following questions:

Wie heißt dieser Mann?
Wie alt ist er?
Was macht er?
Wo wohnt er?
Wer sind die anderen (*other*) Menschen in seiner Familie?

Let these questions guide your reading for information as you work through the entire text.

Wortschatz 2

Verben

ab·holen to pick up, fetch, get
aus·sehen (sieht aus) to appear, look (happy, tired, fit, etc.)
Du siehst schrecklich aus. You look terrible.
berichten to report
ein·kaufen to shop for; to go shopping
fern·sehen (sieht fern) to watch TV
reisen to travel
schließen to close
spazieren gehen to go for a walk
sterben (stirbt) to die
vergessen (vergisst) to forget
vorbei·kommen to come by, drop by

schließen: *synonym* = **zumachen**

Substantive

der **Arbeiter, -** worker
der **Fußball** soccer
der **Reiseführer, -** (travel) guide book
der **Roman, -e** novel
der **Stadtplan, ¨-e** city map
der **Stress** stress

das **Bild, -er** picture; image
das **Dorf, ¨-er** village
(das) **Frankreich** France
das **Geschäft, -e** business; store
das **Mittagessen** midday meal, lunch
das **Schaufenster, -** store window
das **Wochenende, -n** weekend
am Wochenende on the weekend
das **Wort** word (*2 plural forms*: **die Worte**: words in a context; **die Wörter**: unconnected words, as in a dictionary)
das **Wörterbuch, ¨-er** dictionary

die **Buchhandlung, -en** bookstore
die **Fabrik, -en** factory
die **Freizeit** free time
die **Mannschaft, -en** team
die **Muttersprache, -n** native language
die **Postkarte, -n** postcard
die **Stimme, -n** voice
die **Wanderung, -en** hike
die **Zeitschrift, -en** magazine

die **Lebensmittel** (*pl.*) groceries

The word **Frankreich** recalls the original empire of the Franks (**die Franken**), a Germanic tribe that settled mainly west of the Rhine. The greatest Frankish king was Charlemagne (**Karl der Große**), 747–814 A.D.

Adjektive und Adverbien

abends (in the) evenings
aktuell current, topical
besonders especially
bunt colorful
fleißig industrious, hard-working
französisch French
meistens mostly, usually

Gegensätze

fleißig ≠ **faul** industrious ≠ lazy

Mit anderen Worten

stressig (*colloq.*) = **mit viel Stress**

Am Schreibtisch arbeiten

Drei Deutsche bei der Arbeit

Lab Manual Kap. 5, Lesestück.

Learning about the world of work in Germany is the cultural goal of this chapter.

Man sagt über die Deutschen, sie leben für ihre Arbeit. Stimmt das heute noch? Unsere Beispiele zeigen ein anderes° Bild.

different

Christine Sauermann, Buchhändlerin

Christine Sauermann ist 35 Jahre alt, geschieden°, und hat einen jungen Sohn Oliver (10 Jahre alt). Sie ist seit sieben Jahren berufstätig und besitzt seit fünf Jahren eine Buchhandlung in der Altstadt° von Tübingen.[1] Zwei Angestellte° arbeiten für sie im Laden.

divorced
old city / employees

Das Geschäft geht gut, denn° viele Touristen gehen durch die Altstadt spazieren und Studenten kommen auch jeden Tag vorbei. Mit den neuesten° Romanen sieht ihr Schaufenster immer bunt aus. Den Studenten verkauft sie Wörterbücher und Nachschlagewerke°, aber die Touristen kaufen meistens Reiseführer, Stadtpläne und Postkarten von der Stadt.

because
newest
reference works

Morgens macht sie um 9 Uhr auf und abends um 6 Uhr zu. Von 1 Uhr bis 3 Uhr macht sie Mittagspause°. Sie schließt den Laden, holt Oliver von der Schule ab und geht mit ihm nach Hause. Dort kocht sie das Mittagessen und kauft später dann noch Lebensmittel im Supermarkt ein.[2]

midday break

Außer sonntags arbeitet Christine Sauermann jeden Tag sehr fleißig in ihrem Laden. In ihrer Freizeit möchte sie also Erholung° vom Stress. Darum macht sie gern Wanderungen mit ihrem Sohn zusammen. Diesen Sommer zum Beispiel gehen sie zusammen in Schottland° campen.

relaxation
Scotland

Es ist schon spät, aber die Buchhandlung ist noch offen. (München)

1. Most German cities and towns have an **Altstadt** (*old city*) in their centers, which may date from the Middle Ages. They are often pedestrian zones. **Tübingen** is a university town on the Neckar River about twenty miles south of Stuttgart. The university was founded in 1477.
2. Many small shops and businesses close from 1:00 to 2:30 or 3:00 P.M., but this practice is less common nowadays in large cities. The noon meal is traditionally the main meal of the day.

Jörg Krolow (22 Jahre alt), Fabrikarbeiter

Jörg Krolow arbeitet seit einem Jahr als Mechaniker in einer Autofabrik in Dortmund.[1] Die Arbeit ist schwer, aber gut bezahlt°. Nach der Arbeit trinkt er oft ein Bier mit Freunden zusammen oder sieht fern. Am Wochenende spielt er im Sportverein° Fußball.

paid
sports club

Wie die meisten° deutschen Arbeiter in der Schwerindustrie ist Krolow in einer Gewerkschaft°. Sie sichert° jedem Mitglied° einen guten Lohn° und gibt den Arbeitern eine Stimme im Aufsichtsrat.[2]

most
union / assures / member / wage

Krolow hat wie die meisten Deutschen° fünf Wochen Urlaub im Jahr. Dieses Jahr will er im Sommer mit seiner Freundin nach Korsika. Im Oktober fährt seine Fußballmannschaft nach Amiens,[3] der Partnerstadt von Dortmund, und spielt dort gegen einen französischen Fußballklub.

wie ... = like most Germans

Klaus Ostendorff (53 Jahre alt), Journalist

Klaus Ostendorff ist Korrespondent bei der Deutschen Presseagentur° in Nordamerika. Seit fünfzehn Jahren berichtet er über die USA und Kanada für Zeitungen und Zeitschriften in Deutschland. Seine Artikel geben den Lesern ein realistisches Bild von beiden° Ländern.

wire service
both

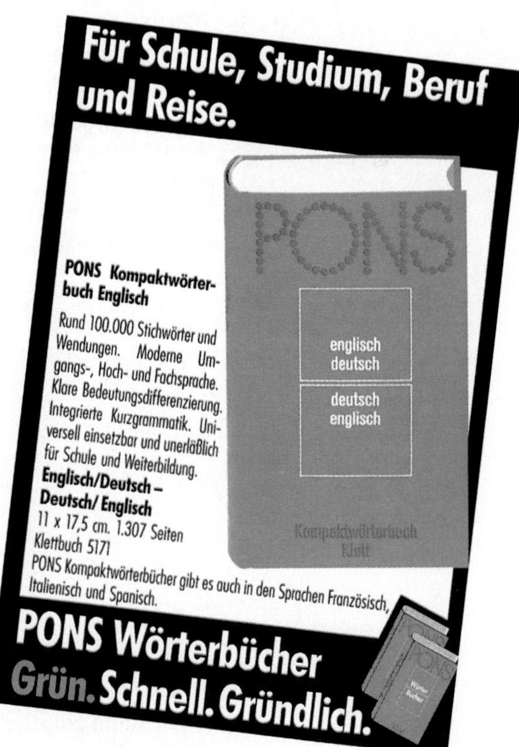

1. An industrial city in North Rhine-Westphalia. See map on the inside of the front cover.
2. **Aufsichtsrat** = board of directors. Historically, the ability of West German trade unions to elect up to 50% of the board of directors of large companies brought a high degree of cooperation between management and labor, very few strikes, and a high standard of living for union members. West Germany's economic growth ensured low unemployment rates. Since German unification in 1990, however, unemployment in the new eastern **Bundesländer** has been high, and many workers have left the unions.
3. Northern French city on the Somme River. Many such partnerships exist between European cities.

Im Moment schreibt Ostendorff einen Artikel über das Waldsterben° in Nordamerika. Dieses Problem ist in Deutschland besonders aktuell: Auch in Europa bedroht° der saure° Regen die Wälder.

Ostendorff lebt mit seiner Frau Martina und ihren drei Kindern in Washington. Die Kinder sollen ihre Muttersprache nicht vergessen und darum spricht die Familie zu Hause meistens Deutsch. Die Kinder besuchen das deutsche Gymnasium in Washington und reisen im Sommer nach Deutschland. Dort macht die ganze° Familie Urlaub bei den Großeltern. Sie wohnen in einem Dorf in den Bayerischen° Alpen.

death of the forests
threatens / acid
whole
Bavarian

Nach dem Lesen

■ A ■ Antworten Sie auf Deutsch.

1. Wo arbeitet Christine Sauermann?
2. Wie lange ist sie schon berufstätig?
3. Wer sind ihre Kunden und was kaufen sie bei ihr?
4. Wie sieht ein typischer Tag für Frau Sauermann aus?
5. Was macht sie gern in ihrer Freizeit?
6. Was macht Jörg Krolow in seiner Freizeit?
7. Wohin fährt er im Urlaub?
8. Über was schreibt Klaus Ostendorff im Moment?
9. Wie ist seine Familie anders als die Familie von Christine Sauermann oder Jörg Krolow?
10. Warum sprechen Ostendorff und seine Frau zu Hause meistens Deutsch?

MIT FREUNDEN,
SURFBRETTERN,
PICKNICK-
KOFFER,
MOUNTAIN-
BIKES UND
EINEM HUND.

■ B ■ Wer macht was? In the left-hand column are some jobs and professions; in the right-hand column are some statements about what people in these jobs do. For each job, find the statement that describes it best.

Bäcker, Bäckerin	Schreibt Artikel für Zeitungen und Zeitschriften.
Fabrikarbeiter, Fabrikarbeiterin	Arbeitet schwer, verdient aber nichts.
Hausmann, Hausfrau	Lehrt an einer Universität
Journalist, Journalistin	Repariert Maschinen, z. B. Autos.
Lehrer, Lehrerin	Bäckt Brote und Brötchen.
Mechaniker, Mechanikerin	Unterrichtet (*teaches*) an einer Schule.
Professor, Professorin	Arbeitet in einer Fabrik.

■ **C** ■ **Die Deutsche Schule Washington (DSW)** Klaus Ostendorffs Kinder besuchen die Deutsche Schule Washington. Hier sehen Sie Informationen über die Schule. Was ist die Unterrichtssprache (*language of instruction*)? Welche (*which*) Fremdsprachen kann man lernen? In welchen Klassen sind sie fakultativ (*elective*), in welchen sind sie Pflicht (*a requirement*)? An welchen Feiertagen (*holidays*) gibt es keine Schule? Wann haben die Schüler Ferien (*vacations*)?

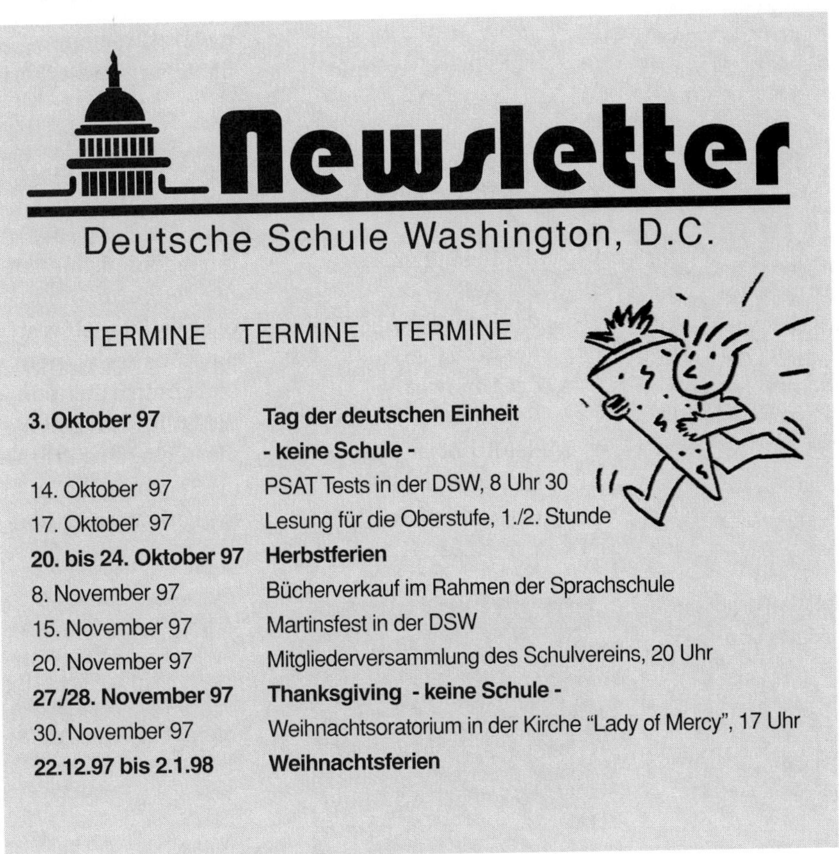

Newsletter

Deutsche Schule Washington, D.C.

TERMINE TERMINE TERMINE

3. Oktober 97	**Tag der deutschen Einheit - keine Schule -**
14. Oktober 97	PSAT Tests in der DSW, 8 Uhr 30
17. Oktober 97	Lesung für die Oberstufe, 1./2. Stunde
20. bis 24. Oktober 97	**Herbstferien**
8. November 97	Bücherverkauf im Rahmen der Sprachschule
15. November 97	Martinsfest in der DSW
20. November 97	Mitgliederversammlung des Schulvereins, 20 Uhr
27./28. November 97	**Thanksgiving - keine Schule -**
30. November 97	Weihnachtsoratorium in der Kirche "Lady of Mercy", 17 Uhr
22.12.97 bis 2.1.98	**Weihnachtsferien**

Situationen aus dem Alltag

This vocabulary focuses on an everyday topic or situation. Words you already know from **Wortschatz** sections are listed without English equivalents; new supplementary vocabulary is listed with definitions. Your instructor may assign some supplementary vocabulary for active mastery.

■ Berufe

Was sind Sie von Beruf? *What is your profession?*

Here are some other professions you can use in the following exercises.

Cf. **Zahnarzt**; **Kinderarzt** (ask students to guess German word for *pediatrician*).

Landwirt is the modern designation for someone who makes a living in **Landwirtschaft**. **Der Bauer** has historical connotation of *peasant* (cf. **die Bauernkriege**), a meaning preserved in **der Bauer**, *pawn* (the chess piece).

der **Arzt, ¨e**	die **Ärztin, -nen**	*physician*
der **Elektrotechniker, -**	die **Elektrotechnikerin, -nen**	*electrician* or *electrical engineer*
der **Geschäftsmann** (*pl.*) **Geschäftsleute**	die **Geschäftsfrau, -en**	*businessman/business-woman*
der **Ingenieur, -e**	die **Ingenieurin, -nen**	*engineer*
der **Kellner, -**	die **Kellnerin, -nen**	*waiter/waitress*
der **Krankenpfleger, -**	die **Krankenschwester, -n**	*nurse*
der **Künstler, -**	die **Künstlerin, -nen**	*artist*
der **Landwirt, -e**	die **Landwirtin, -nen**	*farmer*
der **Politiker, -**	die **Politikerin, -nen**	*politician*
der **Rechtsanwalt, ¨e**	die **Rechtsanwältin, -nen**	*lawyer*
der **Schriftsteller, -**	die **Schriftstellerin, -nen**	*writer*
der **Verkäufer, -**	die **Verkäuferin, -nen**	*salesperson*

Wer arbeitet hier? Lesen Sie die Schilder (*signs*).

Talking about work and professions is a communicative goal.

The German word **der Job** (short **o**) is used colloquially for temporary employment; the verb **jobben** = *to hold a temporary job*. **Im Sommer jobbe ich als Kellnerin.**

Writing assignment after oral work in class: Student chooses one of the professions on p. 148, names a person, and writes about the person, using these questions as guides.

■ A ■ Fragen: Was wissen Sie über diese Berufe?

1. Wer braucht das Abitur?
2. Wer muss für seinen Beruf studieren?
3. Wer macht eine Lehre (*apprenticeship*)?
4. Wer verdient gut? Wer verdient relativ schlecht?
5. Wer hat viel Freizeit? Wer hat nicht viel Freizeit?
6. Wer hat flexible Arbeitszeiten?
7. Wer arbeitet oft nachts / morgens / abends?
8. Wer arbeitet draußen?
9. Wer braucht vielleicht einen Computer bei der Arbeit?
10. Wer arbeitet meistens allein, wer mit anderen Menschen zusammen?

Mit Menschen zu tun haben

Handwerklich arbeiten

Im Labor arbeiten

Article is also omitted with religious & political affiliations: **Er ist Katholik/Sozialist**, and after **sein**, **werden**, **bleiben** (i.e., for predicate nouns). Cf. **Mein Bruder wird Lehrer.** vs. **Ich kenne den Lehrer.** Contrast: **Er ist Lehrer** vs. **Er ist der Lehrer** (specificity added). Article is not omitted when adjective adds specificity: **Fr. Gerhard ist die/eine berufstätige Amerikanerin.** Negation: **Ich bin kein Arzt** (or) **Ich bin nicht Arzt.**

Note on Usage: Stating profession or nationality

Ich will Automechaniker werden.	*I want to become* ***an*** *auto mechanic.*
Frau Gerhard ist Amerikanerin.	*Ms. Gerhard is* ***an*** *American.*

German does not use an indefinite article before the noun.

■ B ■ Gruppendiskussion: Was willst du werden, und warum? (*4 Studenten*)

First tell each other what you want to do after college. Then ask questions about each other's career plans.

BEISPIEL: A: Ich möchte Lehrer werden.
B: Verdienen Lehrer genug Geld?
C: Sind deine Eltern Lehrer?
D: Wo möchtest du denn arbeiten?
usw.

Tell students to try to figure out jobs by themselves, using cognates and context clues.

■ C ■ Partnerarbeit mit dem Almanach: Suchen wir eine Stelle.

Sie und Ihr Partner brauchen Geld und suchen Stellen für den Sommer. Im Almanach (S. 154) sind einige Stellenangebote (*job offers, help wanted ads*) aus deutschen Zeitungen. Besprechen Sie sie zusammen. Was möchten Sie gern machen? Was möchten Sie lieber nicht machen?

Zum Schluss

Sprechen wir miteinander!

Lab Manual Kap. 5, Diktat.

Workbook Kap. 5, H, I.

A **Gruppenarbeit: Was zeigst du mir? (*4 oder 5 Personen*)** Use a verb from the list below to ask other students what they are going to do for you. Other students use a noun from the list to answer. After asking each person in the group, a new questioner starts over with a different verb.

BEISPIEL: Was kaufst du mir, Joanne?
Ich kaufe dir einen Fernseher.
Vielen Dank! Was ________ du mir, Steve?

Verbs	*Nouns*	
kaufen	Mantel	Hemd
beschreiben	Wagen	Mittagessen
kochen	Artikel	Buch
geben	Stadtplan	Stadt
schenken	Fernseher	Roman
zeigen	Brot	Tasche
verkaufen	Auto	Zeitung
	Brötchen	Zeitschrift
	Wörterbuch	Uhr
	Motorrad	

B **Partnerarbeit: Nein, das stimmt nicht! (*Mit offenen Büchern*)** Take turns contradicting each other.

BEISPIEL: Dieser Wagen ist *neu*!
Nein, das stimmt nicht. Dieser Wagen ist *alt*!

1. Wir holen die Kinder *früh* ab.
2. Hamburg liegt in *Süddeutschland*.
3. Jetzt *fangen* wir *an*.

4. Der Lehrling *schließt* den Laden.
5. Der Chef möchte *etwas* sagen.
6. Wir essen *viel*.
7. Ich glaube, *jemand* wohnt da drüben.
8. Meine Nase ist *hässlich*.
9. Diese Jacke ist *altmodisch*.
10. Diese Übung ist *schwer*.

Answers to **Übung C**: (1) **stinklangweilig**, (2) **Oma**, (3) **wahnsinnig**, (4) **blitzschnell**, (5) **todmüde**, (6) **wunderschön**.

■ C ■ Gruppenarbeit: Mit anderen Worten With books closed, the class forms two teams. The instructor says a sentence, and the first team to think of a more colorful or colloquial way to say the same thing gets a point.

BEISPIEL: Heute ist es *sehr sehr* kalt.
Heute ist es *wahnsinnig* kalt.

1. Der Film ist *sehr langweilig*.
2. Ich schenke meiner *Großmutter* ein Foto von mir.
3. Roberts VW ist *sehr* alt.
4. Die Autos fahren *sehr schnell* durch die Stadt.
5. Heute bin ich *sehr sehr müde*.
6. Die Berge in Österreich sind *sehr schön*.

■ D ■ Partnerarbeit: Sprechen Sie miteinander! Take turns asking each other the following questions. Choose your responses from the list of words below. Then ask some questions of your own.

(der)	Tag, Morgen, Nachmittag, Abend Montag, Dienstag usw. Januar, Februar, März usw. Winter, Frühling, Sommer, Herbst
(das)	Semester, Jahr, Wochenende
(die)	Stunde, Woche

1. Wie oft gehst du schwimmen?
   Ich gehe jed-________ schwimmen.
2. Wie oft isst du Brezeln?
   Brezeln esse ich ________ .
3. Wann fährst du nach Europa?
   Ich fahre dies- ________ nach Europa.
4. Wann studierst du in Konstanz?
   Ich studiere ________ in Konstanz.
5. Wie lange bleibst du in München?
   Ich bleibe ein- ________ da.
6. Wie viele Stunden schläfst du am Wochenende?
   Am Wochenende schlafe ich ________ .

Lab Manual Kap. 5, Ex. on professions and nationalities.

■ E ■ Gruppenarbeit: Bist du Amerikaner/in? Choose a profession or nationality (**Bäcker**, **Studentin**, **Amerikaner**, etc.). Don't tell anyone else what you are. Speak to as many of your classmates as possible and guess what they are until you find the right answer.

BEISPIEL: Bist du Bäckerin?
Nein, ich bin nicht (oder) keine Bäckerin.
Bist du ________ ?

Schreiben Sie zu Hause.

F **Der Arbeitstag** Gerd hat eine neue Stelle. Er schreibt seinen Eltern und beschreibt ihnen einen typischen Arbeitstag. (Use the cues to reconstruct his letter.)

Liebe Mutti, lieber Vati!

aufstehen / morgens / 7.00
Arbeit / anfangen / 8.30
ich / arbeiten / mit / mein Freund Kurt / zusammen
Laden / zumachen / 6.00
nach / Arbeit / ich / gehen / Bier / trinken
nach / Essen / fernsehen / oft / ein bisschen
abends / ich / sein / todmüde

Euer Gerd

G Fill in the blanks with the correct dative ending or dative personal pronoun.

1. Ich wohne seit ein-________ Monat bei mein-________ Tante in Tübingen.
2. Mit ________ (*her*) gehe ich fast jeden Tag einkaufen.
3. Sie bekommt oft Briefe von ihr-________ Freunden und ihr-________ Bruder.
4. Sie schreibt ________ (*them*) oft Postkarten mit Bilder-________ von d-________ Stadt.
5. Nach d-________ Seminar gehe ich mit mein-________ Freunden Fußball spielen.

H **Berufsberatung** (Career counseling) Frau Friedrichsen, a career counselor (**Berufsberaterin**), is advising her client, Herr Liebig. Fill in Herr Liebig's answers to her questions.

FRAU F: Also Herr Liebig, sagen Sie mir bitte: Arbeiten Sie lieber mit Menschen oder allein?
HERR L: ________________________________
FRAU F: Sagen Sie mir etwas über Ihre Familie. Wie viele Kinder haben Sie?
HERR L: ________________________________
FRAU F: Ist Ihre Frau auch berufstätig?
HERR L: Ja.
FRAU F: Und was ist sie von Beruf?
HERR L: ________________________________
FRAU F: Was machen Sie besonders gern in Ihrer Freizeit?
HERR L: ________________________________
FRAU F: Wie viel wollen Sie verdienen?
HERR L: ________________________________
FRAU F: Also, Herr Liebig, vielleicht sollen Sie ________ werden.

Students are limited to present tense, even if they are writing about a job they had in the past.

I Aufsatzthema (Essay topic): **Beschreiben Sie Ihre Arbeit**! You have read about the lives of three working Germans. Write a page about your own job or your parents' jobs. How is working in this country different from what you have read about working in Germany?

J Wie sagt man das auf Deutsch?

1. When are you getting up tomorrow?
2. At six. I have to leave the house early.
3. Why? What are you doing?
4. I'm driving with my girlfriend to Munich.

5. What are you doing on the weekend?
6. I don't know yet. Why do you ask?
7. Can you come by? A student from Germany is visiting me.
8. Gladly. I'd like to meet him.
9. I want to show him the city tomorrow.
10. Good. I'll come by at ten.

Use these ads to show students how to infer meaning from context clues. Have them read ads aloud. How many agent nouns can they find? Explain new vocabulary as needed (**Informatiker**). Point out the orthographic shorthand of gender-inclusive endings. Send students on an information hunt with questions like: **Wo braucht man eine/n Stadtplaner/in? Wo kann eine junge Frau als Aupairmädchen arbeiten? Für welchen Job muss man früh aufstehen?**

Stellenangebote (Help Wanted Ads)

These help-wanted ads from the German press range from unskilled labor (**Zeitungsträger/in**) to highly specialized professionals (**Statistiker/in**). Note the English business and computer jargon in the technical fields.

Marketing Forschung

Marketing-Forschung und -Beratung der Markenartikelindustrie ist unser Tätigkeitsfeld. Die vergangenen Jahre waren durch eine stetige Expansion gekennzeichnet. Für die Zukunft haben wir uns ehrgeizige Ziele gesetzt.
Zur Erweiterung unseres Mitarbeiterstabes suchen wir jüngere Damen und Herren (auch Berufsanfänger) als:

STATISTIKER/IN

Sind Sie Frühaufsteher?

Wir bieten Ihnen — auch nebenberuflich — gute Verdienstmöglichkeiten als

Zeitungsträger(in)

Folgender Zustellbezirk ist zur Zeit unbesetzt:

Usingen-Eschbach

Bitte schreiben Sie uns, besuchen Sie uns, oder rufen Sie uns an unter Telefon-Nr. 06081/94032.

Frankfurter Rundschau

Vertriebsabteilung
Agentur Doris Görlich
Am Hebestumpf 11, 6393 Wehrheim 1

Der Caritasverband für die Stadt Köln e. V.
sucht eine(n)

qualifizierte(n) Mitarbeiter(in)

im

Sozialdienst für Italiener

Zur Aufgabe gehören die Beratung in sozialen Angelegenheiten italienischer Mitbürger und die Arbeit mit Gruppen und Vereinen.

Wir stellen uns vor, daß ein italienischer Mitarbeiter/in mit qualifizierter pädagogischer Ausbildung und sehr guten Deutsch-Kenntnissen für diese Aufgaben ebenso in Frage kommt wie deutsche Sozialarbeiter/Sozialpädagogen/innen mit sehr guten Kenntnissen der italienischen Sprache und der Kultur und dem Lebensstil Italiens.

Wir erwarten die Zugehörigkeit zur katholischen Kirche und aktive Teilnahme an ihrem Leben.

Caritasverband für die Stadt Köln e. V.
Große Telegraphenstr. 35, 5000 Köln 1

Wir suchen dringend eine
Haushälterin
die bei uns wohnen und unsere drei Kinder betreuen kann.
Herr und Frau Adda, privat 0211/614208, Büro 0211/393041.

STADT HERTEN

Die Stadt Herten (70000 EW), Kreis Recklinghausen, sucht zum baldmöglichen Eintritt eine(n)

STADTPLANER(IN)

– Bes.Gr. A 15 –

als Amtsleiter(in) des Stadtplanungsamtes.

Au-pair-Mädchen für 2 Kinder in Dublin gesucht, Tel.: 07391/2189.

Leitende/n Ärztin/Arzt (Dr. med.)

Wir wünschen uns eine engagierte Persönlichkeit, die die Grundsätze unserer Organisation im Hinblick auf die Sorge und Verantwortung für behinderte Menschen mitträgt.

Für ein erstes Gespräch stehen wir Ihnen ab 3. 8. 87 gern telefonisch unter der Rufnummer 0421/23 83-211 oder 221 zur Verfügung.

Ihre Bewerbung erbitten wir an den **Geschäftsführer.**

REICHSBUND BERUFSBILDUNGSWERK GMBH
Kitzbühler Straße 1 · 2800 Bremen 33

Software-Engineering
Datenbanken
Informationssysteme

Informatiker
Mathematiker
Physiker
Ingenieure

n
bstän-
siert in
ganz-
ikolas-
)00 ab

nt

Hilfe im
Betreu-

ückflug,
)0,– DM

Niederlassun
nell expandie
n Vertrieb un
otechnologie.

Interatom GmbH
Postfach
5060 Bergisch Gladbach 1

INTERATOM

nöglichen Eintrittstermin suchen wir

Mikrobiologen/innen

als Spezialisten für die Sparte Fermentation bundesweit.

Wir erwarten: biochemische/mikrobiologische/molekularbiologische universitäre Ausbildung, gute

An der Universität

Communicative Goals

- Talking about events in the past
- Writing a letter in German

Cultural Goal

- Learning about German student life and the university system

When previewing grammar of this chapter, call students' attention to Table of Strong Verbs, p. 164. Tell them not to panic. Point out that it is only the boldfaced past participles that are new. Give them plenty of time to learn this list.

Chapter Outline

- **Lyrik zum Vorlesen**
  Johann Wolfgang von Goethe, „Wanderers Nachtlied"
- **Grammatik**
  Simple past tense of *sein*
  Perfect tense
  Two-way prepositions
  Masculine N-nouns
- **Lesestück**
  Ein Brief aus Freiburg
- **Situationen aus dem Alltag**
  Das Studium; Das Studentenzimmer
- **Videoecke**
  Wie war deine Vorlesung?
- **Almanach**
  Universities in the German-Speaking Countries

Dialoge

Lab Manual Kap. 6, Dialoge, Fragen, Hören Sie gut zu!, Üb. zur Aussprache (**b**, **d**, **g** / **p**, **t**, **k**).

Karin sucht ein Zimmer

STEFAN: Hast du endlich ein Zimmer gefunden?
KARIN: Nee, ich suche noch. Leider habe ich keinen Platz im Studentenwohnheim bekommen.
STEFAN: Du! Gestern ist bei uns in der WG die Helga ausgezogen. Also, jetzt ist ein Zimmer frei. Willst du zu uns?
KARIN: Super! Meinst du, das ist möglich?
STEFAN: Selbstverständlich!

Dormitory space is scarce in Germany. Students frequently live together in apartments called **Wohngemeinschaften** (abbreviated **WG**).

Am Semesteranfang

CLARA: Wo warst du denn so lange?
EVA: In der Bibliothek und später in der Buchhandlung.
CLARA: Hast du mir ein Vorlesungsverzeichnis mitgebracht?
EVA: Ja, ich hab's auf den Schreibtisch gelegt.
CLARA: Ach ja, da liegt es unter der Zeitung. Wie viel hat's denn gekostet?
EVA: Vier Mark fünfzig, aber ich schenk's dir.
CLARA: Das ist wirklich nett von dir! Vielen Dank!

German students buy their course catalogues every semester in local bookstores.

An der Uni in Tübingen

PETRA: Hast du den Peter schon kennen gelernt?
KLAUS: Ist das der Austauschstudent aus Kanada?
PETRA: Ja. Er kann fantastisch Deutsch, nicht?
KLAUS: Ich glaube, er hat schon zwei Semester in Konstanz studiert.
PETRA: Ach, darum!

German students calculate time spent at the university in semesters rather than years.

Konstanz is a city on Lake Constance (**der Bodensee**) with a university founded in 1966.

Model pronunciation of **Austauschstudent**. Contrast stress in **warum'?** and **dárum**.

Pronunciation practice: Tape program focuses on unvoicing of **b**, **d**, and **g**. Use dialogues to review these sounds in class: **endlich**, **selbstverständlich**, **hab's**, **Schreibtisch**, **gelegt**, **liegt**.

Note on Usage: Definite article with names

In informal, colloquial speech, Germans often use the definite article with proper names. The dialogues contain two examples of this:

Gestern ist bei uns in der WG **die** Helga ausgezogen.	*Yesterday Helga moved out of our apartment.*
Hast du **den** Peter schon kennen gelernt?	*Have you met Peter yet?*

Wortschatz 1

Verben

aus·ziehen, ist ausgezogen[1] to move out
bringen, hat gebracht to bring
legen to lay, put down
mit·bringen, hat mitgebracht to bring along, take along
ziehen, hat gezogen to pull

Substantive

der **Anfang, ¨-e** beginning
am Anfang at the beginning
der **Austauschstudent, -en, -en**[2] exchange student
der **Mensch, -en, -en** person, human being
der **Platz, ¨-e** place; space; city square
der **Schreibtisch, -e** desk

das **Bett, -en** bed
(das) **Kanada** Canada
das **Studentenwohnheim, -e** student dormitory
das **Vorlesungsverzeichnis, -se** university course catalogue

die **Bibliothek, -en** library
die **Universität, -en** university
an der Universität at the university
die **Vorlesung, -en** university lecture
die **Wohngemeinschaft, -en** communal living group, co-op apartment

Adjektive und Adverbien

gestern yesterday
möglich possible
nett nice
so lange for such a long time
wirklich real; really

Präpositionen mit Dativ oder Akkusativ

an to, toward; at, alongside of
auf onto; on, upon, on top of
hinter behind
in into, to; in
neben beside, next to
über over, across; above
unter under; beneath
vor in front of
zwischen between

Gegensätze

am Anfang ≠ am Ende at the beginning ≠ at the end
ausziehen ≠ einziehen to move out ≠ to move in
möglich ≠ unmöglich possible ≠ impossible

Mit anderen Worten

die **Uni, -s** (*colloq.*) = **Universität**
die **WG, -s** (*colloq.*) = **Wohngemeinschaft**
nee (*colloq.*) = **nein**

Have students memorize the 2-way prepositions as a block, as with accusative and dative lists. You may want to postpone memorization until work on the **Grammatik**, pp. 167–169.

Compare **bringen, gebracht** with *bring, brought*. English spelling with *gh* shows that past tense was originally pronounced with a back *ch* sound as in German.

Ziehen introduced here because it is root of **aus-, ein-, umziehen**. It also means *to move* when used with a directional: **1965 sind wir nach München gezogen.**

Karin Looks for a Room

S: Have you finally found a room?
K: Nope, I'm still looking. Unfortunately I didn't get a place in the dorm.
S: Hey! Yesterday Helga moved out of our apartment. So now there's a room free. Do you want to move in with us?
K: Terrific! Do you think it's possible?
S: Of course.

At the Beginning of the Semester

C: Where were you for so long?
E: In the library and later at the bookstore.
C: Did you bring me a course catalogue?
E: Yes, I put it on the desk.
C: Oh yeah, it's lying under the newspaper. How much did it cost?
E: Four marks fifty, but I'll give it to you for free.
C: That's really nice of you! Thanks a lot.

At the University in Tübingen

P: Have you met Peter yet?
K: Is that the exchange student from Canada?
P: Yes. He speaks fantastic German, doesn't he?
K: I think he's already studied two semesters in Konstanz.
P: So that's why!

1. For an explanation of the form **ist ausgezogen**, see **Grammatik**, pp. 160–163.
2. For an explanation of the second ending, see **Grammatik**, p. 171.

Variationen

■ A ■ Persönliche Fragen

1. Wo wohnen Sie: im Studentenwohnheim, bei einer Familie, in einer WG oder zu Hause bei Ihren Eltern?
2. Stefan wohnt in einer WG. Kennen Sie Studenten in WGs? Was ist dort anders als im Studentenwohnheim?
3. Eva kauft ein Vorlesungsverzeichnis. Was müssen Sie am Semesteranfang kaufen?
4. Eva schenkt Clara das Vorlesungsverzeichnis. Was schenken Sie Ihrem Mitbewohner oder Ihrer Mitbewohnerin?
5. An der Uni in Tübingen gibt es viele Austauschstudenten. Gibt es auch an Ihrer Uni Austauschstudenten? Woher kommen sie?

Übung B uses weak verbs to anticipate perfect tense formation. Students should be able to recognize verb and respond in present. Optional: To preview grammar, write **habe ... gewohnt** on board.

■ B ■ Übung: Das möchte ich auch.

Your instructor tells you something he has done. Say you would like to do that too.

BEISPIEL: A: Ich habe in Berlin gewohnt.
B: Ich möchte auch in Berlin wohnen.

1. Ich habe einen Sportwagen gekauft.
2. Ich habe um acht Uhr gefrühstückt.
3. Ich habe Karten gespielt.
4. Ich habe Russisch gelernt.
5. Ich habe eine Reise gemacht.

■ C ■ Übung: Was meinen Sie? Antworten Sie mit dem Gegensatz.

BEISPIEL: Finden Sie den Film *gut*?
Nein, ich finde ihn *schlecht*.

1. Soll man *spät* aufstehen?
2. Ist dieses Klassenzimmer zu *groß*?
3. Sind Fremdsprachen *unwichtig*?
4. Ist Deutsch *schwer*?
5. Soll man *immer* in Eile sein?
6. Spricht der Professor zu *langsam*?
7. Soll man *allein* arbeiten?
8. Sind die Studenten hier meistens *faul*?

Lyrik zum Vorlesen

Lab Manual Kap. 6, Lyrik zum Vorlesen.

Many composers have set this text to music. One of the most famous settings is Franz Schubert's Opus 96, No. 3 (D 768).

This brief poem from 1780 is perhaps the most famous in the German language. Goethe first wrote it on the wall of a forest hut where he was spending the night. The simplicity of its three main images (mountains, trees, and birds) and the evocative language of stillness make this a profound statement of the relationship between man and nature.

After working on 2-way prepositions, return to this text and point out 3 occurrences with dative showing location. This reinforces sense of rest and stasis.

Der junge Goethe

Wanderers Nachtlied

Tell students they can figure out the title.

Über allen Gipfeln°	mountain peaks
Ist Ruh°,	peace
In allen Wipfeln°	tree tops
Spürest° du	feel
kaum° einen Hauch°;	hardly / breath
Die Vögelein° schweigen° im Walde.	little birds / are silent
Warte nur, balde°	**balde = bald**
Ruhest° du auch.	rest

Johann Wolfgang von Goethe (1749–1832)

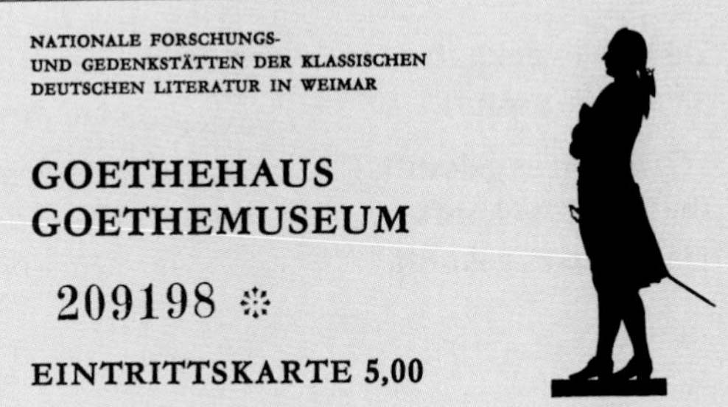

NATIONALE FORSCHUNGS- UND GEDENKSTÄTTEN DER KLASSISCHEN DEUTSCHEN LITERATUR IN WEIMAR

GOETHEHAUS
GOETHEMUSEUM

209198

EINTRITTSKARTE 5,00

Ask: **Wie heißt das Museum? Wo ist es? Wer hat hier gewohnt? Was kostet der Eintritt?**

Grammatik

Talking about events in the past is a communicative goal.

Simple past tense of sein

Up to now, you have been using the present tense of verbs to talk about events in the present. To talk about events in the past, German has two tenses. One is called the *perfect tense* and the other, the *simple past tense*. In spoken German, the perfect tense is usually used to talk about the past. You will learn how to use it in this chapter. The frequently occurring verb **sein**, however, is used more often in the simple past than in the perfect. It is therefore very useful for you to learn the following conjugation.

ich	**war**	*I was*	wir	**waren**	*we were*
du	**warst**	*you were*	ihr	**wart**	*you were*
er, es, sie	**war**	*he, it, she was*	sie, Sie	**waren**	*they, you were*

Lab Manual Kap. 6, Var. zur Üb. 1.

Workbook Kap. 6, A.

1 **Übung: Wo waren sie?** You all traveled in Europe last summer. Turn to the map at the back of the book. Tell your instructor where people were.

BEISPIEL: Wo war Eva?
Sie war in Belgien.

1. Wo war Clara?
2. Wo war Franz?
3. Wo warst du?
4. Wo waren die Studenten?
5. Wo war ich?
6. Wo wart ihr?
7. Wo waren wir?
8. Wo waren Sie?

Perfect tense

The perfect tense is composed of an *auxiliary verb* ("helping" verb) and a form of the main verb called the *past participle*. The auxiliary verb, either **haben** or **sein**, is conjugated to agree with the subject of the sentence. The past participle is a fixed form that never changes. The participle is placed at the end of the sentence or clause.

Conjugation with *haben*

Most German verbs use **haben** as their auxiliary verb. Here is a sample conjugation:

aux. *part.*	
Ich **habe** das Buch **gekauft**.	*I bought the book.* (or: *I have bought the book.)*
Du **hast** es **gekauft**.	*You bought it.*
Sie **hat** es **gekauft**.	*She bought it.*
Wir **haben** es **gekauft**.	*We bought it.*
Ihr **habt** es **gekauft**.	*You bought it.*
Sie **haben** es **gekauft**.	*They bought it.*

Reminder: Drop **-en** or **-n** from the infinitive to get the verb stem. Stems ending in **-d** or **-t** add **-et**: **arbeit-** (stem), **gearbeitet** (past participle).

Some instructors prefer the terms *t-verbs* (weak) and *n-verbs* (strong). Students may find it helpful to be reminded of the parallels in past tenses of English weak verbs: liv<u>ed</u>, work<u>ed</u>, lai<u>d</u>. Such a tense marker is called a *dental suffix* (i.e., pronounced at the front teeth).

legen: Students often confuse English *lay* and *lie*. It can't hurt to reinforce correct English usage: *lay, laid, laid* vs. *lie, lay, lain*. The usage for weak verb (destination) and strong verb (location) is identical in both languages.

Lab Manual Kap. 6, Var. zu Üb. 2, 4, 6, 8–11.

Workbook Kap. 6, B–F.

Past participles of weak verbs

There are two basic classes of verbs in German: the *weak* verbs and the *strong* verbs. They are distinguished by the way they form their past participle.

The weak verbs form their past participle by adding the unstressed prefix **ge-** and the ending **-t** or **-et** to the verb stem. Here are some examples of weak verbs you have already learned:

Infinitive	*Stem*	*Auxiliary + past participle*
arbeiten	arbeit-	hat **gearbeitet**
kaufen	kauf-	hat **gekauft**
kosten	kost-	hat **gekostet**
legen	leg-	hat **gelegt**
meinen	mein-	hat **gemeint**

Verbs ending in **-ieren** are *always* weak verbs. They do *not* add the prefix **ge-** in the past participle, just a **-t** to the stem.

studieren → studier- → hat **studiert**

Er hat in Freiburg **studiert**. *He studied in Freiburg.*

2 Übung: Was haben Sie gekauft und was hat das gekostet? You went on a shopping spree yesterday. Tell your instructor which of the things listed below you bought and what they cost.

1. eine Schreibmaschine (DM 949)
2. einen Taschenrechner (DM 39)
3. ein Vorlesungsverzeichnis (DM 4,50)
4. eine Espressomaschine (DM 129)

BEISPIEL: A: Was haben Sie gestern gekauft?
B: Ich habe ein-_______ gekauft.
A: Was hat das denn gekostet?
B: Das hat DM _______ gekostet.

Solar-Digital Taschenrechner nur 39,-

3 Partnerarbeit: Austauschstudenten Say where the exchange students come from and where they studied.

BEISPIEL: Nicole kommt aus Frankreich und sie hat in Leipzig studiert.

Name	*Heimat* (homeland)	*Universitätsstadt*
Nicole	Frankreich	Leipzig
Yukiko	Japan	Tübingen
Pedro	Spanien	Zürich
Cathleen	Irland	Wien
Matthew	Kanada	Berlin
Beth	USA	Konstanz

■ Past participles of strong verbs

Beginning in **Wortschatz 1** of this chapter, the past participle (and present-stem vowel change, when applicable) of each new strong verb is given following the infinitive.

Strong verbs in English also form past tenses by changing their root vowels and sometimes add the ending *-n: give, gave, given; see, saw, seen; stand, stood, stood; drink, drank, drunk; do, did, done.*

The strong verbs form their past participle by adding the prefix **ge-** and the suffix **-n** or **-en** to the verb stem. In addition, many strong verbs change their stem vowel. Some verbs also change consonants in the stem. For this reason, *the past participle of each strong verb must be memorized.* Here are some examples of strong verbs you have already learned:

Infinitive	*Auxiliary + past participle*
geben	hat **gegeben**
sehen	hat **gesehen**
stehen	hat **gestanden**
trinken	hat **getrunken**
tun	hat **getan**

Übung 4: Tell students they don't have to be truthful here. They should use any noun that comes to mind.

■ 4 ■ Übung: Was haben Sie gesehen? Was haben Sie gestern gesehen? Sagen Sie es der Gruppe.

BEISPIEL: A: Sagen Sie uns, was Sie gestern gesehen haben.
B: Ich habe ________ , ________ und ________ gesehen.

■ 5 ■ Kettenreaktion: Was hast du getrunken? You and your friends were thirsty yesterday. Each person says what he or she drank, then asks the next person.

BEISPIEL: A: Gestern habe ich ________ getrunken. Was hast du getrunken?
B: Ich habe ________ getrunken.

■ Conjugation with *sein*

Some German verbs use **sein** rather than **haben** as their auxiliary verb in the perfect tense.

Gestern **ist** die Helga ausgezogen. *Helga moved out yesterday.*

To take **sein**, a verb must fulfill two conditions:

1. It must be *intransitive* (i.e., it *cannot* take a direct object).
2. It must indicate *change of location or condition.*

Here are some examples of verbs with **sein** as their auxiliary:

Infinitive	*Auxiliary + participle*	
ausziehen	**ist ausgezogen**	
fliegen	**ist geflogen**	
gehen	**ist gegangen**	*change of location*
wandern	**ist gewandert**	
reisen	**ist gereist**	
aufstehen	**ist aufgestanden**	
sterben	**ist gestorben**	*change of condition*
werden	**ist geworden**	

As you can see, verbs with **sein** may be either weak (**gereist**) or strong (**geflogen**).

Two frequently used verbs are exceptions to the second rule: **sein** itself and **bleiben**. In the perfect tense, these verbs use **sein** as their auxiliary even though they don't show change of location or condition:

Wo **bist** du so lange **gewesen**?	*Where were you for so long?*
Wir **sind** bei unseren Freunden **geblieben**.	*We stayed with our friends.*

■ **6** ■ **Kettenreaktion: Wohin bist du gereist?** Alle haben sicher Reisen gemacht. Wohin sind *Sie* einmal gereist?

BEISPIEL: A: Ich bin nach Mexiko gereist. Wohin bist du gereist?
B: Ich bin ________ gereist.
(usw.)

■ **7** ■ **Übung: Was ist sie geworden?** You've all lost touch with your old school friend Karoline. Tell your instructor what you think she became.

BEISPIEL: Was glauben *Sie*?
Ich glaube, sie ist Ärztin geworden.

Manchmal arbeitet man zusammen am Referat.

There are about 200 strong or irregular verbs in German, many of low frequency. In *Neue Horizonte* you will learn about 70 frequently used ones. The strong verb forms are the result of a linguistic development in the Germanic languages that was completed hundreds of years ago. New verbs coined in German today are always regular weak verbs, often borrowed from English: **interviewen**, **formattieren**.

■ Table of strong verbs

The following table contains all the strong verbs that you have learned so far.[1] Review your knowledge of the infinitives and stem-vowel changes in the present tense. Note that the verbs with stem-vowel change in the present-tense **du-** and **er-**forms are *always* strong verbs. *Memorize the past participles.*

Infinitive	Stem-vowel change	Aux. + participle	English
anfangen	fängt an	**hat angefangen**	*to begin*
anrufen		**hat angerufen**	*to call up*
beginnen		**hat begonnen**	*to begin*
besitzen		**hat besessen**	*to possess*
bleiben		***ist* geblieben**	*to stay*
entscheiden		**hat entschieden**	*to decide*
essen	isst	**hat gegessen**	*to eat*
fahren	fährt	***ist* gefahren**	*to drive*
finden		**hat gefunden**	*to find*
fliegen		***ist* geflogen**	*to fly*
fließen		***ist* geflossen**	*to flow*
geben	gibt	**hat gegeben**	*to give*
gehen		***ist* gegangen**	*to go*
halten	hält	**hat gehalten**	*to hold; to stop*
heißen		**hat geheißen**	*to be called*
kommen		***ist* gekommen**	*to come*
laufen	läuft	***ist* gelaufen**	*to run*
lesen	liest	**hat gelesen**	*to read*
liegen		**hat gelegen**	*to lie*
nehmen	nimmt	**hat genommen**	*to take*
scheinen		**hat geschienen**	*to shine; to seem*
schlafen	schläft	**hat geschlafen**	*to sleep*
schließen		**hat geschlossen**	*to close*
schreiben		**hat geschrieben**	*to write*
schwimmen		***ist* geschwommen**	*to swim*
sehen	sieht	**hat gesehen**	*to see*
sein	ist	***ist* gewesen**	*to be*
singen		**hat gesungen**	*to sing*
sprechen	spricht	**hat gesprochen**	*to speak*
stehen		**hat gestanden**	*to stand*
sterben	stirbt	***ist* gestorben**	*to die*
tragen	trägt	**hat getragen**	*to carry; to wear*
trinken		**hat getrunken**	*to drink*
tun		**hat getan**	*to do*
vergessen	vergisst	**hat vergessen**	*to forget*
verlassen	verlässt	**hat verlassen**	*to leave*
werden	wird	***ist* geworden**	*to become*
ziehen		**hat gezogen**	*to pull*

1. Except for **anfangen**, **anrufen**, **besitzen**, **entscheiden**, **vergessen**, and **verlassen**, this list includes only the basic verb (e.g., **stehen** but not **aufstehen** or **verstehen**). See pp. 165–166 for the formation of past participles of verbs with separable and inseparable prefixes.

To warm up for this exercise, have students give *infinitive and auxiliary + participle* for verb cued in English.
I: *describe*
S1: beschreiben
S2: hat beschrieben. Then do the exercise with books closed.

Übungen 8 and 9: Also good as written assignment.

■ 8 ■ Übung: Heute und gestern Sie hören etwas über heute. Sie sagen, auch gestern ist es so gewesen.

BEISPIEL: A: Heute scheint die Sonne.
B: Auch gestern hat die Sonne geschienen.

1. Heute trägt Thomas einen Pulli.
2. Heute liegt die Zeitung da.
3. Heute tun wir das.
4. Heute singt er zu laut.
5. Heute nimmt Vater den Wagen.
6. Heute schließe ich den Laden.
7. Heute steht Markus draußen.
8. Heute liest du einen Artikel.
9. Heute essen wir um sieben.
10. Heute Abend wird es kalt.
11. Heute finden wir die Vorlesung gut.
12. Heute schlafen wir bis acht.
13. Heute läuft Christian durch den Wald.
14. Heute kommt ihr um neun Uhr.
15. Heute geben wir dem Kind ein Brötchen.
16. Heute hält das Auto hier.

■ Past participles of separable-prefix verbs

Verbs with separable (stressed) prefixes form their past participles by inserting **-ge-** *between* the prefix and the verb stem.

anfangen → hat **angefangen**
aufmachen → hat **aufgemacht**

Das Konzert hat um acht Uhr **angefangen**.	*The concert began at eight o'clock.*
Wann bist du denn **aufgestanden**?	*When did you get up?*
Wer hat den Laden **aufgemacht**?	*Who opened the store?*

■ 9 ■ Übung: Ich habe das schon gemacht! Ihr Professor sagt Ihnen, Sie sollen etwas tun. Sagen Sie, Sie haben es schon getan.

BEISPIEL: A: Machen Sie doch die Tür auf.
B: Ich habe sie schon aufgemacht.

1. Fangen Sie doch an.
2. Hören Sie doch auf.
3. Stehen Sie doch auf.
4. Kaufen Sie doch ein.
5. Machen Sie doch die Tür zu.
6. Rufen Sie doch Robert an.

To review inseparable prefixes, see p.139–140.

Other weak verbs with inseparable prefixes: **bedeuten, besuchen, verdienen, verkaufen.** Have students generate perfect: **hat bedeutet**, etc.

■ Past participles of inseparable-prefix verbs

Verbs with inseparable (unstressed) prefixes do *not* add the prefix **ge-** in the past participle.

berichten → hat **berichtet**
verstehen → hat **verstanden**

Sie hat uns über Amerika **berichtet**.	*She reported to us about America.*
Das habe ich nicht **verstanden**.	*I didn't understand that.*

■ 10 ■ Übung: Ich habe das schon getan! Ihr Professor sagt Ihnen, Sie sollen etwas tun. Sagen Sie, Sie haben es schon getan.

BEISPIEL: A: Beginnen Sie bitte.
B: Ich habe schon begonnen.

1. Beschreiben Sie die Landschaft.
2. Vergessen Sie das.
3. Besuchen Sie Ihre Großeltern.
4. Berichten Sie über Ihre Reise.
5. Besprechen Sie das Problem.
6. Verlassen Sie das Zimmer.

■ Perfect tense of mixed verbs

A handful of German verbs have the weak participle form **ge—t** but also change their stem. They are called "mixed verbs." The ones you have learned so far are:

bringen	hat **gebracht**
mitbringen	hat **mitgebracht**
kennen	hat **gekannt**
wissen	hat **gewusst**

Schon gehört? . . .
Nee, hab' ich nicht gewusst.

■ 11 ■ Partnerarbeit: Das habe ich schon gewusst! Take turns telling each other things. Respond either that you did or did not know that already.

BEISPIEL: A: Mark kommt aus Kanada.
B: Das habe ich schon gewusst! (*oder*)
Wirklich? Das habe ich nicht gewusst.

Variation: Students take turns telling and asking whom they visited. A: **Ich habe _____ und _____ besucht. Wen hast du besucht?** Similar activities: **Wie viel hast du verdient? Was hast du zum Geburtstag bekommen? Was hast du heute vergessen?**

■ 12 ■ Kettenreaktion: Was hast du heute mitgebracht? Say what you've brought with you to class today, then ask what the next student has brought.

BEISPIEL: A: Ich habe heute einen Bleistift mitgebracht. Was hast du mitgebracht?
B: Ich habe ein-________ mitgebracht.

■ The use of the perfect tense

The perfect tense is used much more frequently in German than it is in English. In spoken German, the perfect is the most frequently used tense for talking about events in the past. It is therefore often referred to as the "conversational past." English uses the simple past tense (one-word form) for the same purpose.

Sie **sind** gestern nach Berlin **geflogen**.	*They **flew** to Berlin yesterday.*
Ich **habe** die Zeitung um sieben **gelesen**.	*I **read** the newspaper at seven.*

Students usually can understand the distinction between location and destination but have trouble because they need to (1) make the distinction, (2) remember noun gender, and (3) remember correct article. Warm up with one classroom object at a time. Write on board: **Tisch**: **den/dem.** I: **Wohin lege ich das Heft?** Ss: **Auf/ hinter/neben/unter/vor den Tisch.** Repeat with **Zeitung**: **die/der** and **Buch**: **das/dem.**

There are no German equivalents for English past-tense progressive and emphatic forms.

Ich habe **gesprochen**. = { *I spoke.* / *I have spoken.* / *I was speaking.* / *I did speak.* }

Two-way prepositions

Review accusative prepositions, p. 102; dative prepositions, p. 136.

Memorize the list of two-way prepositions.

You have learned that some prepositions in German are always followed by an object in the accusative case, while others are always followed by an object in the dative case. A third group, called the "two-way prepositions," all show spatial relationships. They are followed by the *accusative* case when they signal *destination*, and by the *dative* when they signal *location*. In the example sentences in the table below, notice how the verb determines location or destination. Verbs like **stehen** and **sein** show location (*dative*); verbs like **fahren** and **gehen** show destination (*accusative*).

Some two-way prepositions can show non-spatial relationships, e.g., **über** + accusative = *about*: **Wir haben *über* unsere Amerikareise gesprochen.**

	Destination (accusative)	Location (dative)
Preposition	Answers *Wohin?*	Answers *Wo?*
an	***to, toward*** Hans geht **ans Fenster**. *Hans is walking toward the window.*	***at, alongside of*** Hans steht ***am Fenster***. *Hans is standing at the window.*
auf	***onto*** Wohin legt Inge das Buch? Sie legt es **auf den Tisch**. *She's putting it on the table.*	***on, on top of*** Wo liegt das Buch? Es liegt **auf dem Tisch**. *It's lying on the table.*
hinter	***behind*** Das Kind läuft **hinter das Haus**. *The child is running behind the house.*	***behind*** Das Kind steht **hinter dem Haus**. *The child is standing behind the house.*
in	***into, in*** Wo gehen die Studenten hin? Sie gehen **in die Mensa**. *They're going (in)to the cafeteria.*	***in*** Wo sind die Studenten? Sie sind **in der Mensa**. *They're in the cafeteria.*
neben	***beside, next to*** Leg dein Buch **neben die Zeitung**. *Put your book next to the newspaper.*	***beside, next to*** Dein Buch liegt **neben der Zeitung**. *Your book is next to the newspaper.*
über	***over, across*** Wir fliegen **über das Meer**. *We're flying across the ocean.*	***over, above*** Die Sonne scheint **über dem Meer**. *The sun is shining over the ocean.*
unter	***under*** Die Katze läuft **unter das Bett**. *The cat runs under the bed.*	***under, beneath*** Die Katze schläft **unter dem Bett**. *The cat sleeps under the bed.*
vor	***in front of*** Der Bus fährt **vor das Hotel**. *The bus is driving up in front of the hotel.*	***in front of*** Der Bus hält **vor dem Hotel**. *The bus is stopping in front of the hotel.*
zwischen	***between*** Er läuft **zwischen die Bäume**. *He's running between the trees.*	***between*** **Er steht zwischen den Bäumen**. *He's standing between the trees.*

You may want to teach: **unter** also = *among*: ***Unter*** **seinen Freunden sind viele Austauschstudenten.**

Note: The prepositions **an** and **in** are regularly contracted with the articles **das** and **dem** in the following way:

an das → **ans**	in das → **ins**
an dem → **am**	in dem → **im**

Woher can also mean *from what source*: **Woher hast du so viel Geld? Woher kennst du sie? Woher wissen Sie das?** *(How do you know that?)*

Fragewörter

The question words **wohin** and **woher** can be separated in the following way:

Wohin gehst du?	*oder*	**Wo** gehst du **hin**?
Woher kommen Sie?	*oder*	**Wo** kommen Sie **her**?

Workbook Kap. 6, G–J.

13 **Übung: *Wo* oder *wohin*?** Ihre Professorin fragt Sie, **wo** einige (*some*) Leute sind, oder **wohin** sie gehen. Antworten Sie mit **In der Mensa** oder **In die Mensa**.

1. Wo ist Karin?
2. Wo geht ihr jetzt hin?
3. Wo habt ihr gestern gegessen?
4. Wo sind Horst und Petra?
5. Wo hast du Wolf gesehen?
6. Wohin läuft Peter so schnell?

14 **Partnerarbeit: *Wo* oder *wohin*? (*Mit offenen Büchern*)** Ask each other questions about where things are lying or where they are being placed. Answer with **Auf dem Tisch** or **Auf den Tisch** as appropriate.

1. Wo liegt meine Zeitung?
2. Wohin soll ich das Geld legen?
3. Wo liegen die Karten für heute Abend?
4. Wohin hast du das Buch gelegt?
5. Wo liegt denn das Vorlesungsverzeichnis?

■ 15 ■ Übung: Wo war Martina heute? Martina war heute viel unterwegs. Sagen Sie, wo sie war.

BEISPIEL: Sie war in der Stadt.

#1: in der Stadt/auf der Straße, #4: auf der Straße/im Auto.

Lab Manual Kap. 6, Var. zur Üb. 16.

Augment **Übung 16** by having students use the verbs listed to ask each other simple **wo** or **wohin** questions, e.g., **Wohin gehen wir? Wo liest du gern?**

■ 16 ■ Gruppenarbeit (*Mit offenen Büchern*) Take turns replacing the verbs in the sentences below with new verbs from the list. Change the case of the prepositional object according to whether the verb you use shows destination or location. Choose three or four new verbs for each sentence.

gehen	liegen	warten	laufen	halten
arbeiten	fahren	lesen	wohnen	sein

1. Wir fahren in die Stadt.
2. Jutta steht hinter dem Haus.
3. Das Kind läuft unter den Tisch.
4. Hans steht am Fenster.
5. Wir sind im Zimmer.
6. Ich lese im Bett.

Suche für meinen Sohn (Jura-Stud., NR) z. 1. 9. od. 1. 10.
Zimmer mit Bad
od. 2-Zi.-App. zu mieten.
Tel. 02 11/40 03 76, Rückruf

NR = Nichtraucher.
Jura: See p. 178.

■ Note on the prepositions *an* and *auf*

You can use classroom objects to illustrate **auf** and **an** + *dat.*:
I: **Wo sitze/stehe ich?**
Ss: **Auf dem Stuhl./An der Tafel./Am Fenster./Auf dem Tisch.**

Explain to students that although **das Meer** is a horizontal surface, you are not driving onto it, but up to its edge, therefore **ans Meer**.

The prepositions **an** and **auf** do not correspond exactly to any English prepositions.

- **an** generally signals motion *toward* or location *at* a border, edge, or vertical surface.

Gehen Sie bitte **an die Tafel**.	*Please go to the blackboard.*
Wir fahren **ans Meer**.	*We're driving to the ocean.*
Sie steht **am Tisch**.	*She's standing at the table.*

- **auf** generally signals motion *onto* or location *upon* a horizontal surface.

Leg das Buch **auf den Tisch**.	*Put (or lay) the book on the table.*
Das Buch liegt **auf dem Tisch**.	*The book is (lying) on the table.*

■ 17 ■ Übung: Wo ist Hans? Wohin geht er? Sagen Sie, wohin Hans geht oder wo er steht.

■ 18 ■ Übung: *an* oder *auf*? Complete each sentence with **an** or **auf** and the appropriate article.

Wohin? Antworten Sie mit Präposition + *Artikel im Akkusativ.*

1. Karl geht ________ Tafel.
2. Legen Sie Ihren Mantel ________ Stuhl.
3. Marga fährt im Sommer ________ Meer.
4. Ich habe die Zeitung ________ Schreibtisch gelegt.

Wo? Antworten Sie mit Präposition + *Artikel im Dativ.*

5. Das Kind steht ________ Stuhl.
6. Karl wartet ________ Tür.
7. Das Haus liegt ________ Meer.
8. Das Essen ist schon ________ Tisch.

Jetzt neu in Ihrer Stadt

Students have learned the weak noun **der Name** (5-1) but the genitive **des Namens** can be taught along with **des Glaubens, Friedens, Willens, Herzens** in the second year.

With a few exceptions all German masculine nouns referring to persons or animals with plural in **-en** or **-n** are N-nouns (**Journalist** and **Korrespondent** occur in Kap. 5 **Lesestück**). Exceptions: **der Professor, der Vetter**.

Masculine N-nouns

A few masculine nouns take the ending **-en** or **-n** in all cases except the nominative singular. They are called "N-nouns."

	Singular	Plural
nom.	der Student	die Student**en**
acc.	den Student**en**	die Student**en**
dat.	dem Student**en**	den Student**en**

Dieser Student kennt München sehr gut.
Kennst du diesen Student**en**?
Ich habe diesem Student**en** einen Stadtplan verkauft.

A good rule-of-thumb is that a noun that is masculine, refers to a person or animal, and has the plural ending **-en** or **-n** is an N-noun. Here are the N-nouns you have already learned. The first ending is for all cases in the singular *except* nominative; the second ending is for all cases in the plural.

When **Herr** is used as a title (*Mr.*), it also must have the N-noun singular ending: **Das ist Herr Weiß;** *but* **Kennen Sie Herrn Weiß?**

der **Bauer, -n, -n**	*farmer*
der **Herr, -n, -en**	*gentleman; Mr.*
der **Journalist, -en, -en**	*journalist*
der **Kunde, -n, -n**	*customer*
der **Mensch, -en, -en**	*person, human being*
der **Student, -en, -en**	*student*
der **Tourist, -en, -en**	*tourist*

Lab Manual Kap. 6, Var. zur Üb. 19.

Workbook Kap. 6, K, L.

■ 19 ■ Partnerarbeit: Wer ist das? Ich kenne ihn nicht. Partner A asks who one of these men is; partner B answers. Partner A says he/she doesn't know this person. Switch roles for the next man.

BEISPIEL: A: Wer ist das?
B: Das ist ein Bauer.
A: Ich kenne diesen ________ nicht.
B: Wer ist das? (usw.)

Lesestück

Writing a letter is a communicative goal.

Have students read the letter aloud.

Give students index cards and have them write short postcards based on this model. Have them send their cards to students in other sections of the course.

The spelling reform eliminates the capitalization of second-person familiar forms in personal correspondence.

Vor dem Lesen

Tipps zum Lesen und Lernen

■ **Wie schreibt man eine Postkarte oder einen Brief auf Deutsch?**

Salutation: **-e** with a female name, **-er** with a male name

Place and date: day / month / year

Jena, den 20.5.99

Liebe Sabine, lieber Markus!

Hallo! Wie geht's euch denn? Gestern sind wir hier angekommen und haben schon eure Kusine Gertrud besucht. Sie und ihre Freunde sind wahnsinnig nett und haben uns sehr viel von Jena gezeigt.

Morgen fahren wir nach Berlin und sind dann Freitag wieder zu Hause.

Bis dann.

Viele herzliche Grüße von

Tanja und Fabian

Standard closing = *many cordial greetings*

Lab Manual Kap. 6, Üb. zur Betonung.

Leicht zu merken

automatisch	
der **Film, -e**	
finanzieren	finanzieren
das **Foto, -s**	
das **Konzert, -e**	Konzert
die **Party, -s**	
die **Philosophie**	Philosophie
praktisch	
privat	privat
das **Programm, -e**	Programm

Einstieg in den Text

Einen Brief lesen The following text is a letter written by a German student named Claudia in response to a letter from her American friend Michael, who is coming to Germany as an exchange student. Such informal letters between friends are more loosely structured and associative than formal prose. They tend to be halfway between spoken and written style. In Claudia's letter, for instance, you'll find conversational phrases and slang (e.g., "Ich kann dir eine Menge erzählen" or "Da staunst du wohl, oder?").

Claudia writes first about what she's studying, then tells a bit about student life in Freiburg and compares it to America. Then she describes the difficulty of finding a place to live and talks about the rich cultural life in Freiburg. It is clear that her letter is a response to what Michael has written her. She refers to his letter with the following phrases:

"Dein Brief ist gestern angekommen, ..." (line 6)

"Du schreibst, ... " (lines 6–7)

What do you think Michael wrote in his original letter? Claudia also asks some questions of him:

"Wie ist es denn bei dir? Bekommst du ... " (line 35)

How might Michael respond in his next letter to her?

The last question is assigned as written homework on p. 182.

In einer Vorlesung

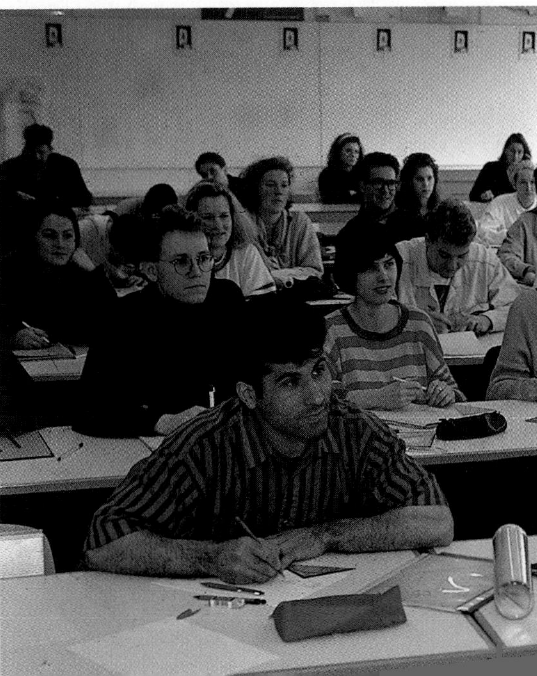

Wortschatz 2

feiern: Go over perfect: **hat gefeiert.**

Verben

antworten (+ *dat.*) to answer (*a person*)
Ich kann dir nicht antworten. I can't answer you.
aus·geben, hat ausgegeben to spend (*money*)
belegen to take (*a university course*)
bezahlen to pay for
enttäuschen to disappoint
erzählen to tell, recount
feiern to celebrate, have a party
schicken to send
sitzen, hat gesessen to sit
staunen to be amazed, surprised

Substantive

der **Ausweis, -e** I.D. card
Studentenausweis student I.D.
der **Brief, -e** letter
der **Bürger, -** citizen
der **Krieg, -e** war
der **Termin, -e** appointment

das **Ende, -n** end
das **Glück** happiness; luck
Glück haben to be lucky
das **Haar, -e** hair
das **Hauptfach, ¨er** major field (*of study*)
das **Kino, -s** movie theater
ins Kino gehen to go to the movies
das **Nebenfach, ¨er** minor field (*of study*)
das **Referat, -e** oral report; written term paper
das **Stipendium, Stipendien** scholarship, stipend
das **Studium** (university) studies
das **Tempo** pace, tempo

die **Antwort, -en** answer
die **Geschichte, -n** story; history
die **Klausur, -en** written test
die **Kneipe, -n** tavern, bar
die **Wohnung, -en** apartment

die **Ferien** (*pl.*) (school or university) vacation
die **Semesterferien** semester break

Glück haben means *to be lucky*, but **glücklich sein** means *to be happy*.

Der Urlaub is a vacation from a job. **Die Ferien** (always plural) is the term for school and university vacations.

Adjektive und Adverbien

billig inexpensive, cheap
gerade just, at this moment
je ever
kostenlos free of charge
lieb dear, nice, sweet
Das ist lieb von dir! That's sweet of you!
niedrig low
schlimm bad
sofort immediately, right away
sonst otherwise, apart from that
verantwortlich (für) responsible (for)
wohl probably

Andere Vokabeln

alles (*sing.*) everything
einige some
ein paar a couple (of); a few
selber or **selbst** by oneself (myself, yourself, ourselves, etc.)

Remember: **alle** (*pl.*) = *everybody*.

Nützliche Ausdrücke

das heißt that means, in other words
d.h. i.e. (= that is)
herzlich willkommen! Welcome! Nice to see you!
letzte Woche last week

Gegensätze

billig ≠ teuer cheap ≠ expensive
Glück haben ≠ Pech haben to be lucky ≠ to be unlucky
je ≠ nie ever ≠ never
der Krieg ≠ der Frieden war ≠ peace

Mit anderen Worten

die **Bude, -n** (*Studentenslang*) = **das Studentenzimmer**
eine Katastrophe = **eine schlimme Situation**
eine Menge (*colloq.*) = **viel**

herzlich willkommen: Contrast to **bitte sehr** (*you're welcome*).

Two German equivalents of English *bad*. **Schlecht**: an objective judgment. **Ich höre schlecht; schlecht geschlafen.** Also means *poor* in quality: **schlechtes Wetter; diese Äpfel sind schlecht. Schlimm** is more subjective and suggests "serious with the potential of worsening," i.e., serious: **schlimme Zeiten; es war damals nicht so schlimm; ein schlimmer Fehler.**

Lab Manual Kap. 6, Lesestück.

Ein Brief aus Freiburg[1]

Learning about German student life and the university system is the cultural goal of this chapter.

Claudia Martens hat gerade einen Brief von ihrem amerikanischen Freund Michael Hayward bekommen. Claudia war ein Jahr in Amerika als Austauschschülerin an Mikes Schule in Atlanta. Sie schickt ihm sofort eine Antwort.

Freiburg, den 20.2.99

Lieber Michael,

dein Brief ist gestern angekommen und ich möchte ihn sofort beantworten°. Du schreibst, du willst zwei Semester an der Uni in Freiburg Geschichte studieren. Das finde ich super! Ich studiere auch Geschichte, aber nur im Nebenfach. Mein Hauptfach ist eigentlich Philosophie. Letztes° Semester habe ich ein sehr interessantes Seminar über den Ersten Weltkrieg belegt. Vielleicht können wir im Herbst zusammen in die Vorlesung über Bismarck und die Gründerjahre[2] gehen.

answer (*trans.*)
last

Habe ich dir je über unser Universitätssystem und das Studentenleben bei uns berichtet? Die Semesterferien[3] haben gerade begonnen, also habe ich endlich ein bisschen Freizeit und kann dir eine Menge erzählen. Im Allgemeinen° ist das Tempo bei uns etwas langsamer und das Studium weniger° stressig als bei euch. Wir schreiben nicht so viele Klausuren und Referate und man ist als Student mehr für sich selbst° verantwortlich. Das heißt zum Beispiel, du kannst abends zu Hause sitzen und Bücher wälzen° oder mit Freunden in die Kneipe gehen. Erst am Semesterende musst du für das Seminar ein Referat schreiben; dann bekommst du einen Schein°. Bei einer Vorlesung gibt es weder Referate noch° Klausuren! Da staunst du wohl, oder°?

im Allgemeinen = in general
weniger = nicht so
für ... = for oneself
Bücher wälzen = hit the books
certificate of course credit
weder ... noch = neither . . . nor / = **nicht wahr?**

Wie du vielleicht schon weißt, sind unsere Unis staatlich°; das bedeutet, sie sind für uns Studenten fast kostenlos. Die Studiengebühren° sind sehr niedrig. Ansonsten° muss man praktisch nur für Wohnung, Essen, Bücher und Kleidung Geld ausgeben. Außerdem° bekommen viele Studenten auch das sogenannte° Bafög.[4] Wie finanzierst du eigentlich dein Jahr in Deutschland? Mit einem Stipendium, oder musst du alles selber bezahlen?

state-run
tuition fees / otherwise
in addition / so-called

Klausuren correspond more or less to American final examinations. The word **Prüfung** is not restricted to academe (**Meisterprüfung**). At universities, a **Prüfung** can have both oral and written parts and usually covers material learned in more than one course. Avoid the Anglicism **das Examen** for an *exam* in the classroom context. It is reserved for a comprehensive examination for a diploma or a degree (e.g., **das Staatsexamen**).

1. City in Baden-Württemberg between the Black Forest and the Rhine. The Albert-Ludwigs-Universität was founded in 1457.
2. **Otto von Bismarck** (1815–1898): German statesman and Prussian Chancellor, under whose leadership the German states were united into the German Empire in 1871. **Gründerjahre**: the "Founders' Years" refers to the period of 1870–1900, when many German businesses were established.
3. The German academic year has a **Wintersemester** that begins in mid-October and ends in mid-February. The **Sommersemester** begins in late April and ends in mid-July. The **Semesterferien** come between the two semesters.
4. Inexpensive government loans for university students in Germany are mandated by the Federal Education Support Law, or **Bundesausbildungsförderungsgesetz** (**Bafög**). This acronym has entered the university vocabulary.

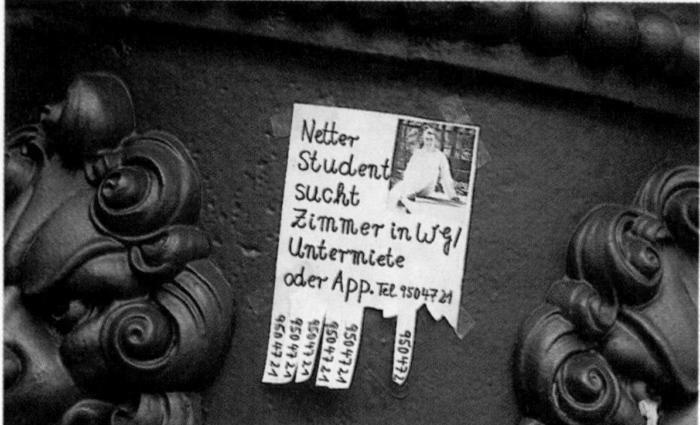

Wo möchte dieser Student wohnen? Kann man ihn anrufen?

Jedenfalls° ist das Essen in der Mensa immer billig und relativ gut, aber mit dem Wohnen ist es manchmal eine Katastrophe. Es gibt nicht genug Studentenwohnheime für alle Studenten und private Buden sind wahnsinnig teuer geworden. Die Wohnungsnot° ist besonders schlimm: Wir sind seit der Wiedervereinigung° überflutet von° Deutschen aus der ehemaligen° DDR und von den Aussiedlern aus Osteuropa.[1] Übrigens habe ich letztes Semester einigen Schulkindern aus zwei Aussiedlerfamilien Nachhilfestunden° in Deutsch gegeben, denn° diese neuen Bürger können oft nur wenig Deutsch.

in any case
housing shortage / reunification / inundated by / former
tutoring / because

Wie ist es denn bei dir? Bekommst du durch das Austauschprogramm automatisch einen Platz im Studentenwohnheim? Wenn nicht°, dann hast du Glück: Du kannst zu uns in die WG! Wir haben nämlich° nächstes Semester ein Zimmer frei und du bist herzlich willkommen. Michael, du bist immer so gern ins Kino und Konzert gegangen. Ich bin sicher, die Filme und Konzerte hier werden dich nicht enttäuschen°. Mit deinem Studentenausweis bekommst du im Theater, Kino und Museum immer eine Ermäßigung°.

wenn nicht = if not
you see
werden ... = will . . . disappoint
discount

Jetzt habe ich aber einen Termin beim Arzt und muss nachher für eine Party einkaufen. Wir feiern nämlich heute Abend das Semesterende. Also, genug für heute, aber ich schreibe dir bald wieder. Viele herzliche Grüße an dich und deine Familie.

Deine

Claudia

P.S. Ich hab' dir einen Stadtplan und ein paar Postkarten von der Altstadt beigelegt° und dazu° ein neues Foto von mir. Kennst du mich noch mit kurzen Haaren?

enclosed
in addition

mit kurzen Haaren: The plural form is usually used to describe someone's hair: **Jetzt hat sie kurze Haare**.

1. Citizens of the former German Democratic Republic and the **Aussiedler** (*emigrants*, ethnic Germans from other Eastern European countries) have a constitutional right to German citizenship. Many of them have flooded the German housing and employment markets since the dissolution of the Soviet bloc in the late 1980s.

Nach dem Lesen

A **Antworten Sie auf Deutsch.**

1. Wo hat Claudia Michael kennen gelernt?
2. Was will Michael in Freiburg studieren?
3. Wie ist das Tempo im Studentenleben in Freiburg?
4. Warum kostet das Studium in Deutschland nicht sehr viel?
5. Warum sind Studentenzimmer manchmal wahnsinnig teuer?
6. Was hat Claudia letztes Semester in ihrer Freizeit gemacht?
7. Wo kann Michael in Freiburg wohnen?
8. Was hat ihm Claudia außer einem Brief geschickt?
9. Was war für Michael neu auf dem Foto von Claudia?

B **Partnerarbeit: Michael und Claudia (*Mit offenen Büchern*)** Partner A spielt die Rolle von Claudia. Partner B spielt Michael und stellt Fragen über ihr Leben an der Uni. (Use the **Lesestück** for information but answer in your own words.)

Was studierst du denn?
Was belegst du dieses Semester?
Wann habt ihr Ferien?
Was kostet das Studium bei euch?
Was für ein Zimmer hast du?
Sag mir bitte: Wo kann ich nächstes Jahr wohnen?
Was gibt's denn zu tun in Freiburg?

Situationen aus dem Alltag

This vocabulary focuses on an everyday topic or situation. Words you already know from **Wortschatz** sections are listed without English equivalents; new supplementary vocabulary is listed with definitions. Your instructor may assign some supplementary vocabulary for active mastery.

Das Studium

Einige Wörter kennen Sie schon.

studieren an (+ *dat.*)	*to study at*
Ich studiere an der FU.	
(**= Freien Universität, Berlin**).	
die **Bibliothek, -en**	
das **Fach, ¨er**	*area of study, subject*
das **Hauptfach**, das **Nebenfach**	
die **Klausur, -en**	
das **Labor, -s**	*lab*
das **Referat, -e**	
ein Referat halten	*to give an oral report*
ein Referat schreiben	*to write a paper*
das **Semester, -**	
das **Sommersemester**	*spring term (usually April to July)*
das **Wintersemester**	*fall term (usually October to February)*
das **Seminar, -e**	
die **Vorlesung, -en**	
die **Wissenschaft, -en**	*science; scholarship; field of knowledge*

Note stress: **Labór.**

Die Bibliothek comes from Greek via Latin into German, an etymology that traces the origins of humanistic institutions. **Die Bücherei** used for public institutions (**Volks-, Stadtbücherei**); **Bibliothek** designates academic libraries.

Einige Studienfächer

Note that most academic disciplines are feminine.

Remember that this is optional vocabulary. Students will want to know how to say their own fields in German.

Additional vocabulary: **Völkerkunde** (or) **Anthropologie**, **Theologie**, **Amerikanistik** (*American studies*). In student slang, **WiWi** = **Wirtschaftswissenschaft** (*economics*). In Austria and Switzerland, **Jura** = **Jus**.

High-frequency idiomatic equivalent of *What are you taking this semester?* is **Was machst du dieses Semester?** Answer: **Ich mache ein Seminar** ***in*** **Kunstgeschichte** ***über*** **Dürer.**

die **Anglistik**	Anglistik	*English studies*
die **Betriebswirtschaft**		*management, business*
die **Biologie**	Biologie	*biology*
die **Chemie**	Chemie	*chemistry*
die **Elektrotechnik**		*electrical engineering*
die **Germanistik**	Germanistik	*German studies*
die **Geschichte**		*history*
die **Informatik**	Informatik	*computer science*
Jura (used without article)		*law*
die **Kunstgeschichte**		*art history*
die **Landwirtschaft**		*agriculture*
die **Linguistik**	Linguistik	*linguistics*
die **Mathematik**	Mathematik	*mathematics*
die **Medizin**	Medizin	*medicine*
die **Musikwissenschaft**		*musicology*
die **Pädagogik**	Pädagogik	*education*
die **Philosophie**	Philosophie	*philosophy*
die **Physik**	Physik	*physics*
die **Politikwissenschaft**		*political science*
die **Psychologie**	Psychologie	*psychology*
die **Soziologie**	Soziologie	*sociology*
die **Wirtschaftswissenschaft**		*economics*

Talking about university life is a communicative goal.

Model this with one student first (**Was belegen Sie denn dieses Semester?**). Then have students do as chain drill. To test comprehension, ask students to recall each others' majors.

Also good as written assignment.

A **Gruppenarbeit: Was studierst du denn?** Was ist Ihr Hauptfach und was belegen Sie dieses Semester?

BEISPIEL: Mein Hauptfach ist ________. Dieses Semester belege ich ________, ________ und ________. Was studierst denn du?

B **Partnerarbeit: Interview** Interview each other in more detail about your studies. Take notes if necessary, and be prepared to report to the whole class. Ask each other questions such as the following:

1. Was tust du lieber: Referate schreiben oder Referate halten? Wie oft musst du das tun?
2. Schreibst du deine Referate auf einem Computer?
3. Arbeitest du oft in der Bibliothek oder mehr im Labor?
4. Was willst du nach dem Studium machen?
5. Brauchst du Deutsch für dein Studium oder für deinen Beruf?
6. Wie finanzierst du das Studium? Bekommst du ein Stipendium?
7. Wohnst du im Studentenwohnheim oder privat?

Das Studentenzimmer

You can use this drawing to practice 2-way prepositions with dative: **Wo steht die Lampe, das Bett? usw.**

Ask students: **Können Sie auf diesem Bild eine Maus finden?**

sing.: **das Möbelstück**

Die Möbel (*pl.*) *furniture*

Dieses Zimmer ist **möbliert** (*furnished*).

1. das Telefon, -e
2. das Bett, -en
3. die Lampe, -n
4. der Teppich, -e
5. der Computer, -
6. der CD-Spieler, -
7. die CD, -s
8. das Radio, -s
9. das Bücherregal, -e
10. das Poster, -
11. der Spiegel, -
12. der Wecker, -
13. der Kleiderschrank, ¨-e
14. der Schlüssel, -
15. die Decke, -n
16. der Boden, ¨

Variation for written homework: Ask students to describe their own rooms. This can be done as a dialogue between roommates planning to furnish their room. Opinions differ about what they need, like, want, etc.

■ C ■ Gruppenarbeit: Beschreiben wir dieses Zimmer. Wie finden Sie dieses Zimmer? Ist es typisch für die Studentenzimmer bei Ihnen? Kann man hier gut wohnen? Wie sieht *Ihr* Zimmer aus? Was gibt es zum Beispiel *nicht* bei Ihnen?

Zum Schluss

Lab Manual Kap. 6, Diktat.

Workbook Kap. 6, Üb. M.

Talking about events in the past is a communicative goal.

Übungen A and **B** also good as written assignments.

Sprechen wir miteinander!

■ A ■ Gruppenarbeit: Was hat Maria letzte Woche gemacht? Maria studiert Philosophie an der Uni in Tübingen. Sie ist sehr gut organisiert. Das sieht man an ihrem Terminkalender für letzte Woche. Wo war sie letzte Woche und was hat sie gemacht?

BEISPIEL: Am Montag hat sie mit Thomas im Café Völter Kaffee getrunken.

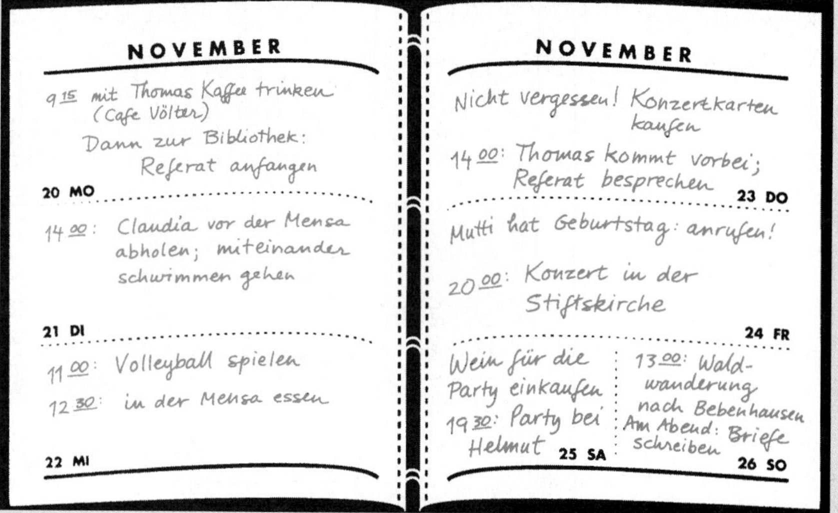

Have students prepare this the night before and bring their datebooks to class.

■ B ■ Gruppenarbeit: Was haben Sie letzte Woche gemacht? Jetzt machen Sie *Ihren* Terminkalender auf. Was haben *Sie* letzte Woche gemacht?

■ C ■ Gruppenarbeit: Wo im Klassenzimmer? Answer the questions about where the people and things are located in the classroom shown on p. 181. Then describe the locations of other people and objects.

BEISPIEL: Wo sitzt Herr Schröder?
Er sitzt auf dem Tisch (vor Marie usw.).

1. Wo sitzt Marie?
2. Wo steht Jutta?
3. Wo steht Karl?
4. Wo steht Gertrud?
5. Wo sitzt der Lehrer?
6. Wo steht Emil?
7. Wo liegt die Zeitung?
8. Wo sind diese Leute?

■ **D** ■ **Gruppenarbeit** Jetzt beschreiben Sie *Ihr* Klassenzimmer. Wo stehen oder sitzen die Menschen?

■ **E** ■ **Gruppenarbeit** Here is another picture of the same classroom, but now everyone is moving around and doing things. Tell where they are going and what they are doing. Describe any other actions you can.

1. Wohin legt Gertrud ihr Buch?
2. Wo geht Karl hin?
3. Wohin legt der Lehrer das Buch?
4. Wo geht Emil hin?
5. Wo geht Anna hin?

F **Gruppenarbeit: Wir möchten in die WG. (*4 Personen*)** Zwei Studenten sind schon Mitbewohner in einer WG und zwei andere Studenten wollen in diese WG. Die Mitbewohner interviewen die neuen Studenten über ihr Studium und ihre Interessen (*interests*).

Was studiert ihr?
Habt ihr je in einer WG gewohnt?
Warum wollt ihr bei uns wohnen? usw.

Die neuen Studenten haben auch einige Fragen:

Wie sehen die Zimmer aus?
Gibt es schon einen Schreibtisch im Zimmer? usw.

Schreiben Sie zu Hause.

Übung H: Remind students that their letter may now mix present and perfect tenses. In a multi-section course, have students in one section write letters to an imaginary friend (relative, etc.) of their choice. Deliver letters to students in section 2 and have them write letters back.

Letter-writing is a communicative goal.

G **Was habe ich letzte Woche gemacht?** In exercise A above you used Maria's appointment calendar to help you describe what she did last week, then in exercise B you described your own activities. Now write a paragraph in German describing what you did last week.

H **„Liebe Claudia, ..."** Claudias Brief an Michael Hayward haben Sie schon gelesen. In diesem Brief hat sie ihm das Studentenleben in Freiburg beschrieben. Jetzt spielen Sie die Rolle von Michael Hayward und schreiben Sie eine Antwort an Claudia. Beantworten Sie ihre Fragen und schreiben Sie über das Studentenleben bei Ihnen. Haben Sie andere Fragen an Claudia über Freiburg und das Studium dort? (Review »Wie schreibt man eine Postkarte oder einen Brief auf Deutsch" on p. 172.)

I **Wie sagt man das auf Deutsch?**

1. I've brought you a course catalogue.
2. Did it cost much?
3. No, it was cheap. Shall I put it on your desk?

4. The lecture began at ten o'clock.
5. Unfortunately, I arrived too late.
6. I stood behind my friends and didn't hear anything.

7. What did you study in Dresden?
8. History was my major but I also studied German.

9. Tonight we're going to the movies together.
10. I hope you haven't forgotten your student I.D.
11. No, it's in my pocket.
12. Good, let's go! We have to be there before 8:00 o'clock.

Videoecke

3 Wie war deine Vorlesung? (09:33)

Was macht ihr denn heute Abend?

In der Bibliothek lernt Stefan Su-Sin, eine Studentin aus China, kennen. Sie besprechen ihr Studium an der Uni. Dann kommt Katrin mit zwei Freunden vorbei. Heute Abend läuft ein neuer Film und sie wollen zusammen essen und dann ins Kino gehen. Eigentlich soll Stefan pauken (cram), *aber dann geht er doch mit.*

Wortschatz zum Video

pauken	*cram (student slang)*
Mathe	*math*
Echt?	*Really? (colloq.)*
Setz dich.	*Sit down.*
Viel Spaß noch!	*Have fun!*

A Was sehen Sie im Video? Watch video Module 3 (9:38–12:43) once without sound. Check off in the list below the words, things, and people you see in the video.

____ 1. Universitätsbibliothek
____ 2. Studenten liegen in der Sonne.
____ 3. eine Familie am Frühstückstisch
____ 4. Stefan und Katrin in der Mensa
____ 5. Hörsaal (*lecture hall*)
____ 6. einen Mann auf einem Fahrrad (*bicycle*)

B Wissen Sie die Antwort? Now watch video Module 3 with sound (9:38–12:43). Then answer these questions about what happens.

1. Wo lernt Stefan Su-Sin kennen?
2. Woher kommt Su-Sin?
3. Was studiert Stefan?
4. Wie war seine Vorlesung bei Professor Klemm?
5. Was wollen Katrin und ihre Freunde heute Abend machen?

C Wer sagt das? Choose the person who says the following.

a. Su-Sin   b. Stefan   c. Katrin   d. Professor Klemm

1. ____ sagt: „Meine Familie wohnt seit zwei Jahren in Berlin."
2. ____ sagt: „Ich muss lesen."
3. ____ fragt: „Wie war deine Vorlesung heute?"
4. ____ sagt: „Ich hab' so die Nase voll."
5. ____ sagt: „Ich hab' keine Zeit. Muss pauken. Mathe."
6. ____ sagt: „Wir können ja vorher zum Italiener essen gehen."

D Richtig oder falsch?

Indicate whether each statement is **richtig (R)** or **falsch (F)**.

1. Stefan findet seine Mathevorlesung langweilig. R F
2. Die Freunde wollen zusammen ins Theater gehen. R F
3. Su-Sin macht dieses Semester Biologie. R F
4. Stefan geht nicht mit ins Restaurant. R F
5. Professor Klemm scheint freundlich zu sein. R F
6. Stefan ist erst eine Stunde in der Bibliothek. R F

E Conversational exchanges For each sentence in the left column, find the appropriate response in the right column.

____ 1. Was studierst du denn?
____ 2. Das ist Su-Sin. Sie kommt aus Beijing.
____ 3. Stefan, kommst du mit?
____ 4. Wie findest du Berlin?
____ 5. Viel Spaß noch.

a. Leider nicht. Ich muss pauken.
b. Anglistik im Hauptfach und Geschichte im Nebenfach.
c. Danke, gleichfalls.
d. Freut mich, Su-Sin. Ich heiße Katrin.
e. Echt toll!

Almanach

Universities in the German-Speaking Countries

The university system is similar in all the German-speaking countries and differs in fundamental ways from that in the United States. All institutions of higher learning (**Hochschulen**) in Austria, Germany, and Switzerland are state-run and financed by taxes. Successful completion of the **Abitur** examination (called **Matura** in Austria and Switzerland) entitles a student to enroll in any university in the country. German universities do not have the general education or distribution requirements common at American colleges and universities; students begin their studies in a particular major. Some specialized schools (e.g., **Musikhochschulen**, **Kunsthochschulen**) and majors in high demand (e.g., medicine and management) have restricted enrollments.

Educational reforms in the 1960s and '70s led both to an increase in the number of students and more diversity in their socio-economic backgrounds. In 1950, for example, only 6% of German pupils completed the **Abitur**, and they were mostly the children of the upper middle class whose parents also had a university education. Today, the percentage of students in any given year who go on to university varies from about 16% in Switzerland to about 30% in Germany. Moreover, students who have not attended a **Gymnasium** can obtain a kind of **Abitur** that allows them to study at **Fachhochschulen**, which emphasize applied knowledge rather than theory. For example, one can study electrical engineering but not physics at a **Fachhochschule**, while hotel management is offered at some **Fachhochschulen,** not at universities.

The biggest difference from the United States is the fact that students pay almost no tuition. While a university education is thus feasible for almost everyone, the system has no strong financial incentive for students to complete their education quickly. In the past few years, universities have been encountering increasing fiscal difficulties. State education spending has not kept up with the needs of expanding institutions: faculties have not grown nearly as fast as student bodies, lecture halls and laboratories are often overcrowded, and libraries are unable to keep up with demand. Widespread but peaceful student strikes in Germany in late 1997 reflected growing discontent. In the coming years, legislators in the German-speaking countries must address both the structure and financing of higher education in order to maintain its high quality.

KAPITEL 7

Auf Reisen

Communicative Goals

- Expressing opinions, preferences, and polite requests
- Making travel plans and talking about traveling
- Talking on the telephone
- Telling time with the 24-hour clock

Cultural Goal

- Learning about traveling in Germany and Europe

Chapter Outline

- **Lyrik zum Vorlesen**
  Wilhelm Müller, „Wanderschaft"
- **Grammatik**
  Der-words and *ein*-words
  Coordinating conjunctions
  Verbs with dative objects
  Personal dative
  Using *würden* + infinitive
  Verbs with two-way prepositions
  Perfect tense of modal verbs
  Official time-telling
- **Lesestück**
  Unterwegs per Autostopp oder mit der Bahn
- **Situationen aus dem Alltag**
  Reisen und Verkehr
- **Almanach**
  Jugendherbergen (*Youth Hostels*)

Dialoge

Lab Manual Kap. 7, Dialoge, Fragen, Hören Sie gut zu!, Üb. zur Aussprache **[u/ü]**.

die Flasche: English cognate: *flask*.

der Straßenatlas: Most German drivers carry a bound road atlas of Western Europe rather than folding maps.

Pronunciation practice: Tape program focuses on **ü** versus **i** and **u**. Use dialogues to review these sounds in class: **Würden Sie**, **Wohin müssen Sie**, **Mein Zug**, **Urlaubsreise**, **Suchst du**, **unter meiner Jacke**, **zurück**.

Model and emphasize rising intonation when answering telephone: **Krogmann**?

Es tut mir Leid conveys sympathy or regret. Depending on the situation, **Entschuldigung** can also mean *sorry*: **Es tut mir Leid, dass ich Ihnen nicht helfen kann. Entschuldigung, ich habe Sie nicht verstanden.**

Am Bahnhof

Ein Student sieht eine alte Dame mit viel Gepäck und will ihr helfen.

STUDENT: Darf ich Ihnen helfen?
TOURISTIN: Ja, bitte! Würden Sie mir den Koffer tragen?
STUDENT: Gerne. Wohin müssen Sie denn?
TOURISTIN: Gleis drei. Mein Zug fährt um 15.00 Uhr ab.

Vor der Urlaubsreise

MARION: Suchst du die Thermosflasche?
THORSTEN: Nein, nicht die Thermosflasche, sondern den Straßenatlas. Ich glaube, ich habe ihn auf den Tisch gelegt.
MARION: Ja, hier liegt er unter meiner Jacke.
THORSTEN: Häng die Jacke doch auf, dann haben wir mehr Platz. Wir müssen unsere Reise nach Venedig planen.

Am Telefon

Marion ruft ihren Vater an. Es klingelt lange, aber endlich kommt Herr Krogmann ans Telefon.

HERR KROGMANN: Krogmann.
MARION: Hallo Papa! Hier ist Marion. Warum hast du nicht gleich geantwortet?
KROGMANN: Ach, Marion, seid ihr wieder zurück? Ich habe auf dem Sofa gelegen und bin eingeschlafen.
MARION: Oh, tut mir Leid, Papa.
KROGMANN: Das macht nichts. Ich habe sowieso aufstehen wollen. Wie war denn eure Reise?
MARION: Alles war wunderbar.

Am Bahnhof

Wortschatz 1

Verben

ab·fahren (fährt ab), ist abgefahren to depart, leave (*by vehicle*)
danken (+ *dat.*) to thank
ein·schlafen (schläft ein), ist eingeschlafen to fall asleep
gefallen (gefällt), hat gefallen (+ *dat.*) to please
  Das Buch gefällt mir. I like the book.
gehören (+ *dat.*) to belong to (a person)
hängen, hat gehängt (*trans.*) to hang
  auf·hängen to hang up
hängen, hat gehangen (*intrans.*) to be hanging
helfen (hilft), hat geholfen (+ *dat.*) to help
klingeln to ring
planen to plan
reservieren to reserve
setzen to set (down), put
stellen to put, place
würden (+ *infinitive*) would (do something)

Substantive

der **Bahnhof, ¨-e** train station
der **Koffer, -** suitcase
der **Straßenatlas** road atlas
der **Zug, ¨-e** train

das **Gepäck** luggage
das **Gleis, -e** track
das **Telefon, -e** telephone
(das) **Venedig** Venice

die **Flasche, -n** bottle
die **Thermosflasche** thermos bottle

Adjektive und Adverbien

sowieso anyway
wunderbar wonderful

Andere Vokabeln

sondern but rather, but . . . instead
welch- which

Nützliche Ausdrücke

Es tut mir Leid. I'm sorry.
Das macht nichts. That doesn't matter.
Das ist (mir) egal. It doesn't matter (to me). I don't care.
Das macht (mir) Spaß. That's fun (for me).
Wie viel Uhr ist es? = Wie spät ist es?

Often shortened in spoken German: **Tut mir Leid; Macht nichts; Mir egal.**

Gegensätze

ab·fahren ≠ an·kommen to depart ≠ to arrive
auf·stehen ≠ ins Bett gehen to get up ≠ to go to bed
ein·schlafen ≠ auf·wachen to fall asleep ≠ to wake up

The verbs in **Gegensätze** illustrate the meanings of some separable prefixes: **ab** = *away from*; **an** = *at*; **auf** = (*here*) *up* .

Alternative: **zu Bett gehen**.

Mit anderen Worten

Das ist mir Wurscht. (*colloq.*) = **Das ist mir egal.**

At the Train Station

A student sees an elderly woman with a lot of luggage and wants to help her.

S: May I help you?
T: Yes, please. Would you carry my suitcase?
S: Gladly. Where do you have to go?
T: Track three. My train leaves at 3:00 P.M.

Before the Trip

M: Are you looking for the thermos bottle?
T: No, not the thermos, but the road atlas. I think I put it on the table.
M: Yes, here it is, under my jacket.
T: Hang up the jacket, then we'll have more room. We've got to plan our trip to Venice.

On the Telephone

Marion is calling up her father. The phone rings a long time, but Mr. Krogmann finally comes to the telephone.

MR. K: Krogmann.
M: Hello, Dad. This is Marion. Why didn't you answer right away?
MR. K: Oh, Marion, are you back? I was lying on the sofa and fell asleep.
M: Oh, sorry, Dad.
MR. K: That doesn't matter. I wanted to get up anyway. How was your trip?
M: Everything was wonderful.

Variationen

■ A ■ Persönliche Fragen

With means of transportation **mit** = *by*: **Die Touristin fährt mit dem Zug.**

1. Sind Sie oft mit dem Zug gefahren? Wohin?
2. Fahren Sie gern mit dem Zug?
3. Die Touristin muss zu ihrem Zug. Wohin müssen Sie heute?
4. Thorsten und Marion brauchen einen Straßenatlas für ihre Reise. Was brauchen Sie für eine Reise?
5. Thorsten plant eine Reise nach Venedig. Planen Sie eine Reise in den Ferien? Wohin?
6. Schlafen Sie gern nachmittags wie Herr Krogmann?
7. Herr Krogmann schläft auf dem Sofa. Wo schlafen Sie lieber am Nachmittag, auf dem Sofa oder im Bett?

■ B ■ Reaktionen Respond to the statements and questions on the left with an appropriate phrase from the right.

1. Ich kann den Koffer nicht tragen.
2. Würden Sie mir bitte helfen?
3. Hast du das nicht gewusst?
4. Wo fährt denn Ihr Zug ab?
5. Waren die Hausaufgaben besonders schwer?
6. Wie war die Reise?
7. Wohin hast du den Atlas gelegt?
8. Wo liegt denn der Stadtplan?
9. Gehen wir zusammen einkaufen?
10. Was ist denn los?

Einverstanden!
Doch!
Oh, das tut mir Leid!
Das macht nichts!
Gerne!
Auf dem Tisch.
Gar nichts.
Auf das Sofa.
Das finde ich auch.
Bitte sehr.
Auf Gleis zehn.
Nee, gar nicht.
Wunderbar!

■ C ■ Übung: Im Reisebüro (At the travel agency) Im Reisebüro fragt man, ob Sie etwas machen wollen. Antworten Sie, Sie würden das gerne tun.

BEISPIEL: A: Wollen Sie ein Hotelzimmer reservieren?
B: Ja, ich würde gern ein Hotelzimmer reservieren.

1. Wollen Sie Ihren Mantel aufhängen?
2. Wollen Sie morgen abfahren?
3. Wollen Sie morgen Abend in Venedig ankommen?
4. Wollen Sie im Zug schlafen?
5. Wollen Sie mir Ihr Gepäck geben?
6. Wollen Sie Ihre Familie anrufen?

Lyrik zum Vorlesen

German Romantic literature uses nature images to evoke themes of yearning for the unknown, wandering, and love. The Romantic poets were obsessed with the illusory world of appearances expressed in moonlit nights, fog, and the forest. In the early 19th century **das Wandern** described the life of an itinerant journeyman. These were artisans who journeyed from town to town, gaining experience with different master craftsmen.

Wilhelm Müller's poem cycle "Die schöne Müllerin" (1820) is unified by the theme of the love of the journeyman for the miller's daughter. In this poem the youth is moved to **Wanderlust** by the mill itself with its rushing water and turning wheels. He ends by asking the miller and his wife for permission to depart.

Lab Manual Kap. 7, Lyrik zum Vorlesen.

Set to music by Franz Schubert, this poem is the first song in his cycle "Die schöne Müllerin," op. 5, no. 1 (D 795).

Wanderschaft°

Das Wandern ist des Müllers Lust°,
Das Wandern!
Das muss ein schlechter Müller sein,
Dem niemals fiel das Wandern ein°,
Das Wandern.

Vom Wasser haben wir's gelernt,
Vom Wasser!
Das hat nicht Rast° bei Tag und Nacht,
Ist stets° auf Wanderschaft bedacht°,
Das Wasser.

Das sehn wir auch den Rädern ab°,
Den Rädern!
Die gar nicht gerne stille stehn
Und sich mein Tag nicht müde drehn°,
Die Räder.

Die Steine selbst°, so schwer sie sind,
Die Steine!
Sie tanzen mit den muntern Reihn°
Und wollen gar noch schneller sein,
Die Steine!

O Wandern, Wandern, meine Lust,
O Wandern!
Herr Meister und Frau Meisterin,
Lasst mich in Frieden weiterziehn°
Und wandern!

Wilhelm Müller (1794–1827)

journeying

des ... = the miller's desire

dem ... = who has never thought of wandering

rest

stets = **immer** / intent

sehn ... see also from the wheels

Und ... = never tire of turning

Steine selbst = even the stones

cheerful dance

Lasst ... = let me go in peace

Grammatik

Der-*words and* ein-*words*

You have learned the definite and indefinite articles (**der** and **ein**) and similar words that precede nouns (**dies-**, **jed-**, **mein**, **kein**, **alle**). Such words are divided into two groups, the **der**-words and the **ein**-words, because of slight differences in their endings:

der-words		*ein-words*		
der, das, die	the	**ein**	a, an	
dies-	this, these	**kein**	no, not a	
jed-	each, every			
welch-	which	**mein**	my	*Possessive adjectives*
all-	all	**dein**	your	
		sein	his, its	
		ihr	her, its	
		unser	our	
		euer	your	
		ihr	their	
		Ihr	your	

Since the endings of the definite article (**der**, **das**, **die**) are slightly irregular, **dieser** is used here to review the **der**-word endings in the three cases you know so far.

der-word endings				
	masc.	neut.	fem.	plural
nom.	dies**er** Stuhl	dies**es** Buch	dies**e** Uhr	dies**e** Bücher
acc.	dies**en** Stuhl	dies**es** Buch	dies**e** Uhr	dies**e** Bücher
dat.	dies**em** Stuhl	dies**em** Buch	dies**er** Uhr	dies**en** Bücher**n**

The **ein**-words have the same endings as **der**-words *except in three cases* where they have *no* endings, as highlighted in the following table.

ein-word endings				
	masc.	neut.	fem.	plural
nom.	**mein** Stuhl	**mein** Buch	mein**e** Uhr	mein**e** Bücher
acc.	mein**en** Stuhl	**mein** Buch	mein**e** Uhr	mein**e** Bücher
dat.	mein**em** Stuhl	mein**em** Buch	mein**er** Uhr	mein**en** Bücher**n**

1 Übung Your instructor makes a statement. Student A asks which thing is meant. Student B answers.

BEISPIEL: Das Zimmer ist klein.
A: Welches Zimmer ist klein?
B: Dieses Zimmer ist klein.

1. Das Hemd ist teuer.
2. Die Turnschuhe sind neu.
3. Der Lehrling heißt Martin.
4. Die Gruppe fährt nach Europa.
5. Der Pulli ist hässlich.
6. Die Brötchen sind frisch.

Lab Manual Kap. 7, Var. zur Üb. 2.

Workbook Kap. 7, A.

Üb. 2: Tell students to listen carefully: the ending in the question is the same as in their answer. Drill **alle** by changing sentences thus: **Diese Berge sind steil. Aber nicht alle Berge sind steil.** (Omit number 4 for this transformation.)

Üb. 3 focuses on **der**-words with endings versus **ein**-words with and without endings. Other nouns you can use: **Heft**, **Tasche**, **Schuhe**, **Bücher**, **Bleistift**, **Kuli**, **Jacke**, **Handschuhe**, etc.

■ **2** ■ **Übung** Respond to each statement as in the example.

BEISPIEL: Dieser Berg ist steil.
Ja, aber nicht jeder Berg ist steil.

1. Dieser Koffer ist schwer.
2. Dieses Studentenwohnheim ist neu.
3. Dieser Zug fährt pünktlich ab.
4. Dieses Telefon klingelt zu laut.
5. Diese Thermosflasche ist teuer.
6. Dieser Tourist kann Deutsch.
7. Diese Vorlesung ist langweilig.

Tempelhofer Ufer 32
10963 Berlin
Tel. 030 / 264 95 2-0
Fax 030 / 262 04 37
JUGENDHERBERGE

■ **3** ■ **Übung** Your instructor wants to know what belongs to whom. Answer as in the examples.

BEISPIEL: A: Ist dieses Buch Ihr Buch?
B: Nein, dieses Buch ist sein Buch.
A: Welches Buch ist Ihr Buch?
B: Dieses Buch ist mein Buch.

Coordinating conjunctions

A clause is a unit containing a subject and an inflected verb. A simple sentence consists of one clause; a compound sentence has two or more clauses.

Coordinating conjunctions are words that join clauses that could each stand alone as a simple sentence. The coordinating conjunction joins them into a compound sentence.

Christa ist achtzehn. Ihr Bruder ist sechzehn.
Christa ist achtzehn **und** ihr Bruder ist sechzehn.

Kannst du das Fenster aufmachen? Soll ich es machen?
Kannst du das Fenster aufmachen **oder** soll ich es machen?

Do not confuse the conjunction **denn** with the flavoring particle used with questions: **Wo bist du denn so lange gewesen?**

Of the basic coordinating conjunctions, **denn** is least frequent. Because students tend to use it when they should use **weil**, we do not drill it extensively. **Denn** cannot begin a sentence, nor answer a **warum**-question.

The most common coordinating conjunctions in German are

und	*and*
oder	*or*
aber	*but, however*
sondern	*but rather, instead*
denn	*for, because*

Remember the iron-clad rule: The verb is always in second position in German statements. A coordinating conjunction is *not* counted as being in first position in its clause. The word order of the second clause is *not* affected by the coordinating conjunction.

0 1 2
Ute kommt nicht zu Fuß, **sondern** sie fährt mit dem Auto.

0 1 2
Ich kann dich erst am Abend anrufen, **denn** ich bin bis 7 in der Bibliothek.

0 1 2
Klaus muss bis drei arbeiten, **aber** dann kann er nach Hause.

The coordinating conjunctions are also used to join units smaller than a clause.

The spelling reform eliminates the comma before **und** and **oder** unless it is necessary to avoid ambiguity.

Ich habe einen Bruder **und** eine Schwester.
Möchtest du Wein **oder** Bier?
Dieser Laden ist gut, **aber** sehr teuer.
Barbara ist nicht hier, **sondern** in Italien.

Note on punctuation: There is *always* a comma before **aber**, **sondern**, and **denn**.

Lab Manual Kap. 7, Var. zu Üb. 4, 5.

Workbook Kap. 7, B, C.

■ 4 ■ Partnerarbeit Use **und**, **aber**, **oder**, or **denn** to join each sentence from column A to one from column B. Try to find the most logical pairings. Compare results with other students.

A	*B*
Meine Eltern kommen morgen.	Ich möchte sie dort besuchen.
Bist du krank?	Willst du in einer WG wohnen?
Gisela studiert in Freiburg.	Ich zeige ihnen meine Wohnung.
Ich bringe das Buch mit.	Mein Bruder wohnt auf dem Land.
Ich wohne in der Stadt.	Du sollst es lesen.
Ich bin jetzt in Eile.	Sie hat mir nicht geantwortet.
Willst du in der Mensa essen?	Mein Zug fährt gleich ab.
Willst du allein wohnen?	Wollen wir bei mir etwas kochen?
Ich habe Sabine gefragt.	Geht es dir gut?

(Example: Meine Eltern kommen morgen. —*und*→ Ich zeige ihnen meine Wohnung.)

■ *Aber* versus *sondern*

Aber and **sondern** are both translated with English *but*. Both express a contrast, but they are *not* interchangeable. **Sondern** must be used when *but* means *but . . . instead*, *but rather*.

Er bleibt zu Hause, **aber** sie geht einkaufen.	*He's staying home, but she's going shopping.*
Er bleibt nicht zu Hause, **sondern** geht einkaufen.	*He's not staying home,* ***but*** *is going shopping* ***instead****.*

Sondern *always* follows a *negative* statement and expresses *mutually exclusive alternatives*. Note that the clause following **sondern** often leaves out elements it has in common with the first clause. Such deletion is called *ellipsis*.

Er bleibt nicht zu Hause, sondern [er] geht einkaufen.
Das ist kein Wein, sondern [das ist] Wasser.
Käthe hat es nicht getan, sondern die Kinder [haben es getan].

■ 5 ■ Übung: *Aber* oder *sondern*? Combine each pair of simple sentences into a compound sentence, using **aber** or **sondern** as appropriate. Use ellipsis where possible.

1. Sie fliegt nach Italien. Ihr Mann fährt mit dem Zug.
2. Sie hasst mich nicht. Sie liebt mich.
3. Es ist noch nicht sieben Uhr. Er ist schon zu Hause.
4. Ich fahre nicht mit dem Auto. Ich gehe zu Fuß.
5. Ich trage keinen Mantel. Ich trage meine Jacke.
6. Bernd mag dieses Bier nicht. Lutz trinkt es gern.

Mit dem Fahrrad (*bicycle*) kann man billig reisen und auch fit bleiben. Woher kommen diese Radfahrer?

Word order: *nicht x, sondern y*

Notice how the position of **nicht** shifts when it is followed by **sondern**.

Ich kaufe den Mantel nicht.	*but*	Ich kaufe **nicht den Mantel**, sondern die Jacke.
Johanna arbeitet heute nicht.	*but*	Johanna arbeitet **nicht heute**, sondern morgen.

6 Übung: Nein, nicht x, sondern y. Answer these questions negatively, using **sondern**.

Allow short answers if you prefer: **Nein, nicht um sieben, sondern um zehn.** Next stage: Students ask questions of each other that must be answered negatively: **Ist dein Hemd *blau*?; Trägst du heute *Jeans*?; Heißt du *Katharina*?**

BEISPIEL: Wollen Sie *um sieben* frühstücken?
Nein, ich will nicht um sieben frühstücken, sondern um zehn.

1. Suchen Sie *die Thermosflasche*?
2. Gehen Sie *am Mittwoch* ins Kino?
3. Gehen Sie *mit Ursula* in die Stadt?
4. Gehen Sie mit Ursula in *die Stadt*?
5. Wollen Sie mir *die Fotos* zeigen?
6. Waren Sie *gestern* in der Bibliothek?

Verbs with dative objects

Review dative endings for **der**-words, p. 133, and dative forms of the personal pronouns, p. 134.

A few German verbs require an object in the dative case rather than the accusative. Two of these are **helfen** and **antworten**.

Ich sehe den Mann.	*I see the man.*
but:	
Ich helfe **dem** Mann.	*I'm helping the man.*
Du fragst die Frau.	*You ask the woman.*
but:	
Du antwortest **der** Frau.	*You answer the woman.*

This chapter introduces the following verbs with dative objects:

Glauben takes an accusative inanimate object, but a dative personal object: **Ich glaube das,** *but* **Ich glaube dir.** One can thus say: **Ich glaube dir das.** = I believe you when you say that.

antworten	*to answer* (someone)
danken	*to thank*
gefallen	*to please*
gehören	*to belong to*
glauben	*to believe* (someone)
helfen	*to help*

The dative object is usually a person.

Marie dankt **ihrem Lehrer.**	*Marie thanks her teacher.*
Wem gehört dieser Wagen?	*Who owns this car?* (Literally: *To whom does this car belong?*)
Diese Stadt gefällt **mir**.	*I like this city.* (Literally: *This city pleases me.*)

Note that **gefallen** is another way of saying to *like something*. However, since its literal meaning is *to please* (*someone*), the subject and object are the reverse of English. Remember that the verb must agree in number with the subject.

Die Vorlesungen gefallen **mir**. literally: *The lectures please me.*

I like the ***lectures***.

Lab Manual Kap. 7, Var. zur Üb. 7.

Workbook Kap. 7, D, E.

Üb. 7: Bring in other items to ask about.

■ 7 ■ Übung: Was gefällt Ihnen? Your instructor asks if you like various things. Say whether you do or do not.

BEISPIEL: Gefällt Ihnen das Wetter heute?
Ja, es gefällt mir. (*oder*) Nein, es gefällt mir nicht.

1. Gefällt Ihnen diese Stadt?
2. Gefällt Ihnen Ihr Hauptfach?
3. Gefällt Ihnen mein Hemd?
4. Gefällt Ihnen das Wetter heute?
5. Gefallen Ihnen die Vorlesungen an der Uni?
6. Gefallen Ihnen diese Bilder?
7. Gefallen Ihnen meine Schuhe?
8. Gefällt Ihnen dieser Film?

Üb. 8: Point to individuals and groups in the room to elicit all possible dative pronouns. (**Diese Leute helfen ihr, ihm, mir, ihnen, Ihnen**, etc.)

■ 8 ■ Übung: Wem helfen diese Leute? Diese Leute wollen heute helfen. Sagen Sie, wem sie helfen.

Üb. 9: Bring objects to class. Point to various personal possessions in the classroom. Students may answer with pronouns or names.

■ 9 ■ Übung: Wem gehört das Buch? Say what belongs to whom.

BEISPIEL: A: Wem gehört dieses Buch?
B: Es gehört mir. Es ist mein Buch.

■ 10 ■ Gruppenarbeit: Wer kann mir helfen? (*Mit geschlossenen Büchern*) Your instructor asks a general question. Redirect the question to a neighbor, who may answer positively or negatively.

BEISPIEL: Wer kann mir helfen?
A: Kannst *du* ihr helfen?
B: Nein, ich kann ihr nicht helfen.

Next stage after **Gruppenarbeit 10, Partnerarbeit**: Each pair is assigned a verb with dative object. Partners write short question-and-answer exchanges and read them aloud.

1. Wer glaubt mir?
2. Wer kann mir antworten?
3. Wem gehört dieser Rucksack?
4. Wem gefällt das Wetter heute?
5. Wer kann mir heute helfen?

Personal dative

You may also want to teach: **Mir ist schlecht. Mir ist kalt. Das passt mir nicht.**

The dative case is also used to indicate a person's involvement in or reaction to a situation. This *personal dative* is often translated by English *to* or *for*.

Ist es **Ihnen** zu kalt?	*Is it too cold **for you**?*
Es wird **mir** zu dunkel.	*It's getting too dark **for me**.*
Wie geht es **dir**?	*How are you?* (Literally: *How is it going **for you**?*)
Wie geht es **deiner Mutter**?	*How is **your mother**?*
Das ist **mir** egal.	*It's all the same **to me**.*
Das macht **mir** Spaß.	*That's fun **for me**.*

When personal dative is omitted, a statement is more absolute. Contrast **Es ist zu dunkel** with **Es ist mir zu dunkel**.

The personal dative may often be omitted without changing the basic meaning of the sentence.

Ist es zu kalt? Es wird zu dunkel. Wie geht es? Das macht Spaß.

It may *not* be omitted in the following idiom:

Das tut mir Leid. *I'm sorry about that.*

Lab Manual Kap. 7, Var. zur Üb. 11.

■ 11 ■ Übung: Ist es Ihnen zu kalt? Your instructor asks how you feel about something. Give your opinion, then ask your neighbor for an opinion.

BEISPIEL: Ist es Ihnen hier zu kalt?
A: Mir ist es nicht zu kalt. Und dir?
B: Mir ist es auch nicht zu kalt.

auch nicht = *not . . . either.*

1. Ist es Ihnen zu dunkel hier?
2. Ist Ihnen dieses Zimmer zu heiß?
3. Ist Ihnen dieses Buch zu teuer?
4. Ist Ihnen dieser Stuhl hoch genug?
5. Macht Ihnen Deutsch Spaß?
6. Ist Ihnen der Winter hier zu kalt?

Workbook Kap. 7, F.

■ 12 ■ Partnerarbeit: Reaktionen Make at least three statements (invented or real) about how things are going for you, what you're doing at the moment, etc. Your partner must decide whether to respond with indifference, sympathy, or enthusiasm. Then switch roles.

BEISPIEL: Ich habe morgen eine Klausur.
Oh, das tut mir Leid. (*oder*) Das ist mir egal.

Am Dienstag fahren wir nach Venedig.
Das finde ich toll!

Activity based on realia: Have students react similarly to other things: **mein Studium, mein Hauptfach, diese Stadt, dieses Wetter, der Winter, das Leben im Studentenwohnheim.**

Using würden + *infinitive*

Expressing opinions, preferences, and polite requests is a communicative goal.

To express opinions, preferences, and polite requests, **würden** is used with an infinitive.

Ich **würde** das nicht **machen**.	*I wouldn't do that.*
Was **würdest** du gerne **tun**?	*What would you like to do?*
Würden Sie mir den Koffer **tragen**?	*Would you carry my suitcase?*

Würden is the German equivalent of English *would*. It functions like a modal verb, with a dependent infinitive in final position. **Würden** is conjugated like **möchten** (see p. 78):

Ich **würde** sagen, ...	Wir **würden** sagen, ...
Du **würdest** sagen, ...	Ihr **würdet** sagen, ...
Er/sie **würde** sagen, ...	Sie/sie **würden** sagen, ...

■ 13 ■ Gruppenarbeit: Würden Sie bitte ... ? Ask your instructor to do a favor for you. Some possibilities are listed below.

Responses: **gerne**, **natürlich**, **es geht leider nicht**, **ich habe keine Zeit**. Variation: Students can ask each other with **du**-form.

BEISPIEL: Würden Sie bitte das Fenster schließen?

mir den Koffer tragen	für uns ein Foto machen
mir eine Brezel kaufen	Lebensmittel einkaufen
das Mittagessen kochen	Ihre Arbeit beschreiben
mir den Bahnhof zeigen	mir den Straßenatlas geben

■ 14 ■ Kettenreaktion: Ich würde gern ... Was würden Sie heute Abend gerne machen? Sagen Sie es und dann fragen Sie weiter.

BEISPIEL: Heute Abend würde ich gern ________. Und du?
Ich würde gern ________.

Verbs with two-way prepositions

Point out English parallels: *lay* and *set* (weak, transitive) vs. *lie* and *sit* (strong, intransitive).

There is an important group of verb pairs used with the two-way prepositions. One verb shows destination and always takes the accusative case. The other shows location and always takes the dative case.

Destination (accusative)	Location (dative)
Weak transitive verbs	*Strong intransitive verbs*
legen, hat gelegt *to lay (down), put* Ich lege das Buch **auf den Schreibtisch.** *I'm putting the book on the desk.*	**liegen, hat gelegen** *to lie, be lying* Das Buch liegt **auf dem Schreibtisch.** *The book is (lying) on the desk.*
setzen, hat gesetzt *to set (down), put* Sie setzt das Kind **auf den Stuhl.** *She's putting the child on the chair.*	**sitzen, hat gesessen** *to sit, be sitting* Das Kind sitzt **auf dem Stuhl.** *The child is (sitting) on the chair.*
stellen, hat gestellt *to place (down), put* Ich stelle die Flasche **auf den Tisch.** *I'll put the bottle on the table.*	**stehen, hat gestanden** *to stand, be standing* Die Flasche steht **auf dem Tisch.** *The bottle is (standing) on the table.*
hängen, hat gehängt *to hang up* Er hat die Karte **an die Wand** gehängt. *He hung the map on the wall.*	**hängen, hat gehangen** *to be hanging* Die Karte hat **an der Wand** gehangen. *The map hung on the wall.*

Ask students which verbs go with following objects when they are put or placed somewhere: **die Zeitung (legen); der Mantel (legen); die Kamera (stellen); der Bleistift (legen); das Bett (stellen); der Stuhl (stellen).**

Note that **hängen** has one infinitive form but a weak participle (**gehängt**) and a strong participle (**gehangen**).

Legen and **liegen** are used when objects are *laid down* or are *lying* in a horizontal position. **Stellen** and **stehen** are used when objects are *stood up* or are *standing* in a vertical position.

Ich **lege** das Buch auf den Tisch. — *I'm putting the book (down flat) on the table.*

but:

Ich **stelle** das Buch ins Bücherregal. — *I'm putting the book (upright) in the bookcase.*

Workbook Kap. 7, G, H.

■ 15 ■ Übung: Bei Frau Schneider zu Hause Frau Schneider is working around the house. Describe what she is doing in the left-hand pictures, then the results of her efforts in the right-hand pictures.

Repeat in the perfect tense: **Was hat Frau Schneider heute gemacht?**

Perfect tense of modal verbs

You know that modal verbs are used with a dependent infinitive.

Ich muss meinen Freund **anrufen**.	*I have to call my friend.*
Wir wollen nach Hause **gehen**.	*We want to go home.*

Here are the same sentences in the perfect tense:

Ich habe meinen Freund **anrufen müssen**.	*I had to call my friend.*
Wir haben nach Hause **gehen wollen**.	*We wanted to go home.*

A modal verb with a dependent infinitive uses its own *infinitive* form instead of a past participle to form the perfect tense.[1] The infinitive of the modal verb *follows* the dependent infinitive. This construction is called a "double infinitive."

Note that the modal verbs always use **haben** as their auxiliary in the perfect tense, regardless of the dependent infinitive.

Wir **sind** nach Hause gegangen.	*We went home.*
but:	
Wir **haben** nach Hause gehen wollen.	*We wanted to go home.*

Lab Manual Kap. 7, Üb. 16.

Workbook Kap. 7, I.

16 **Übung** Change these sentences from present to perfect tense.

BEISPIEL: Wir dürfen nicht laut singen.
Wir haben nicht laut singen dürfen.

1. Ich will meinen Stadtplan finden.
2. Meine Freundin muss ich heute anrufen.
3. Sie muss viel Geld ausgeben.
4. Ich kann den Bahnhof nicht finden.
5. Darf man Fotos machen?
6. Ich muss kein Referat schreiben.
7. Ich will dich nicht enttäuschen.

Realia activity: Ask: **Wo kann man Urlaub machen? Was kann man dort machen?** (supply: **Fahrräder**, *bicycles*) **Ist der Bauernhof in Nord- oder Süddeutschland? Wie weit ist es zur Ostsee?**

Urlaub auf dem Bauernhof
Ferien auf dem Lande

Seite 140 Marlene Jensen, Steinbergkirche
Einzelhof, ruhig und schön gelegen, Spielplatz, Tischtennis, Fahrräder, 7 km zur Ostsee, BAB-Abfahrt Tarp, Bahnstation Sörup.

1. All the modal verbs are mixed verbs and have past participles on the pattern **ge-** + *stem* + **-t** (**dürfen–gedurft**, **können–gekonnt**, **mögen–gemocht**, **müssen–gemusst**, **sollen–gesollt**, **wollen–gewollt**). These past participles, however, are used *only* when there is *no* dependent infinitive.

Das hat er nicht **gekonnt**.	*He wasn't able to do that.*
Sie hat mich nicht **gemocht**.	*She didn't like me.*
Das habe ich nicht **gewollt**.	*I didn't want that (to happen).*

Workbook Kap. 7, J.

Lab Manual Kap. 7, Üb. 17.

Official time-telling

You already know how to tell time in German (see p. 16). For official time-telling, however, there is another system. One gives the full hour and the number of minutes past it. In addition, rather than A.M. or P.M., the twenty-four hour clock is used. This is the way the time is given in the media, in train schedules, on announcements of events, etc. Subtract 12 to get the P.M. time as expressed in English.

Midnight can be both **0 Uhr** and **24.00 Uhr**. However, one minute past midnight is **0.01** (**null Uhr eins**).

Telling time with the 24-hour clock is a communicative goal.

Written	*Spoken*	*English*
1.40 Uhr	ein Uhr vierzig	*1:40* A.M.
7.55 Uhr	7 Uhr 55	*7:55* A.M.
13.25 Uhr	13 Uhr 25	*1:25* P.M.
20.00 Uhr	zwanzig Uhr	*8:00* P.M.

Brokerage 24

21.45 ist in Deutschland Schlafenszeit, in New York Börsenzeit, bei uns immer noch Orderzeit.

17 **Übung: Wie viel Uhr ist es?** Sagen Sie die Uhrzeit auf Deutsch.

BEISPIEL: 11:20 P.M.
Es ist 23.20 Uhr (dreiundzwanzig Uhr zwanzig).

1. 1:55 P.M.
2. 6:02 P.M.
3. 11:31 A.M.
4. 9:47 P.M.
5. 10:52 P.M.
6. 2:25 A.M.

Wann kann man Dr. Mehler donnerstags in der Praxis besuchen?

Dr. med. Ulrich Mehler
prakt. Arzt
Sprechzeiten:
Mo - Fr: 9 - 12 Uhr
Di + Fr: 16 - 18 Uhr
und nach Vereinbarung
Tel. 06031/12150
Praxis-Eingang

Lesestück

Vor dem Lesen

Tipps zum Lesen und Lernen

Tipps zum Vokabelnlernen

***Translating English* to spend** The reading passage in this chapter talks of spending time and money. Note the different verbs that German uses to distinguish between these two kinds of spending.

Zeit: verbringen

Wir ***verbringen*** unsere Ferien in den Alpen.	*We're spending our vacation in the Alps.*
Sie hat den Nachmittag zu Hause ***verbracht***.	*She spent the afternoon at home.*

Sparen (*to save*) is used with both time and money.

Geld: ausgeben

Wie viel muss man für ein Zimmer **ausgeben**?	*How much do you have to spend for a room?*
Wir haben sehr viel Geld **ausgegeben**.	*We spent a lot of money.*

Note the verbal noun in Wilhelm Müller's poem on p. 190: ***Das Wandern* ist des Müllers Lust.**

Verbal nouns Any German infinitive may act as a noun. It is then capitalized and is always neuter.

reisen → **das Reisen** (*traveling*)

Das Reisen ist heutzutage leicht. *Traveling is easy nowadays.*

These verbal nouns correspond to English gerunds (the form ending in **-ing**); some have additional, more specific meanings. For instance, **das Essen** means *eating* but also *food* and *meal*. Here are some other examples:

das **Fliegen**	*flying*
das **Lernen**	*learning, studying*
das **Leben**	*living; life*
das **Sein**	*being; existence*
das **Wissen**	*knowing; knowledge*

Lab Manual Kap. 7, Üb. zur Betonung.

Leicht zu merken

hektisch
der **Horizont, -e** Horizont
das **Instrument, -e** Instrument
die **Kamera, -s**
packen
spontan
das **Ticket, -s**
die **Wanderlust**

Das Ticket has been borrowed from English and is used mainly for airline tickets and international train travel. In a train, however, the conductor will say **Fahrkarten, bitte** (*Tickets, please*).

Practice pronunciation. **Wanderlust** is introduced as **Leicht zu merken**, but students may not be familiar with this loan word from German.

Einstieg in den Text

"Unterwegs per Autostopp oder mit der Bahn" describes how German young people travel in Europe. To gain a first impression of this text, simply skim it, do not read it. Look for familiar vocabulary that is related to travel. In addition, watch for context clues that point to new travel-related vocabulary. As you skim, also keep an eye out for obvious cognates such as **Instrument**.

After skimming the text, go back and read it through once completely. Use the following questions as a guide to highlight some main ideas. See whether you can answer them after a first reading.

Wie kann man durch Europa reisen?
Warum reisen diese Menschen gern?
Wie kann man beim Reisen Geld sparen?
Wo kann man unterwegs Menschen kennen lernen?
Wo kann man auf der Reise übernachten?

Wortschatz 2

Verben

aus·steigen, ist ausgestiegen to get out (*of a vehicle*)
benutzen to use
hoffen to hope
mit·nehmen (nimmt mit), hat mitgenommen to take along
quatschen (*colloq.*) to talk nonsense; to chat
sparen to save (*money or time*)
trampen (*pronounced „trämpen"*), **ist getrampt** to hitchhike
übernachten to spend the night
verbringen, hat verbracht (+ *time phrase*) to spend (*time*)

Substantive

der **Abend, -e** evening
am Abend in the evening
der **Platz, ¨-e** seat
der **Rucksack, ¨-e** rucksack, backpack

Remind students of **Quatsch** (Kap. 5); in reading, **quatschen** = *to chat.*

das **Ausland** (*sing.*) foreign countries
im Ausland abroad (*location*)
ins Ausland abroad (*destination*)
das **Ding, -e** thing
das **Flugzeug, -e** airplane
das **Foto, -s** photograph
ein Foto machen to take a picture
das **Ziel, -e** goal
Reiseziel destination

die **Bahn** railroad; railway system
die **Fahrkarte, -n** ticket (*for means of transportation*)
die **Freiheit, -en** freedom
die **Jugendherberge, -n** youth hostel
die **Tasche, -n** pocket; hand *or* shoulder bag

Adjektive und Adverbien

bequem comfortable
pünktlich punctual, on time
so so
sympathisch friendly, congenial, likeable
verrückt crazy, insane

Stress pronunciation of **bequem** and **so**.

Nützliche Ausdrücke

in der Nähe von near, nearby
egal wohin (wer, warum usw.**)** no matter where (who, why, etc.)

Gegensätze

aus·steigen ≠ ein·steigen to get out ≠ to get in

Mit anderen Worten

per Autostopp reisen = trampen

Das Ausland: English *outlandish* is parallel: something utterly foreign. Contrast destination vs. location of **ins Ausland vs. im Ausland**.

Unterwegs per Autostopp oder mit der Bahn

Lab Manual Kap. 7, Lesestück.

Mit dem Sommer kommt wieder die Wanderlust. Dann packt man den Koffer oder den Rucksack und macht eine Reise. Viele Menschen fahren mit dem eigenen° Wagen oder mit dem Flugzeug. Aber junge Leute mit wenig Geld in der Tasche wollen nicht so viel ausgeben. Sie fahren lieber mit der Bahn oder reisen per Autostopp. Ein paar erzählen uns hier von ihren Reiseerfahrungen°.

own

travel experiences

Adrienne, 18, Azubi° aus Kaisersaschern

„Trampen erweitert° den Horizont. Ich bin in den Sommerferien mit meinem Freund Markus nicht nur in Deutschland, sondern auch im Ausland getrampt. Wir haben Glück gehabt: Überall waren die Menschen sympathisch und wir haben auch eine Menge Geld gespart. In Italien war es einfach super. Ein Autofahrer hat uns von Venedig nach Florenz[1] mitgenommen. Er hat ein bisschen Deutsch verstanden und wir haben dann drei Tage bei seiner Familie gewohnt. Mit meiner Kamera habe ich ein paar schöne Fotos von seinen Kindern gemacht. Das hat uns Spaß gemacht und ich hoffe, wir können sie nächstes Jahr wieder besuchen. Ja, im Zug lernt man die Menschen einfach nicht so gut kennen."

= **Lehrling**

broadens

Azubi = Auszubildende/r

Learning about traveling in Germany and Europe is the cultural goal of this chapter.

Thomas, 21, Student aus Tübingen

„Ich trampe schon in der Nähe von Tübingen, aber für eine lange Reise würde ich immer ein Interrail-Ticket kaufen. Das kostet unter DM 500 für vier Wochen und man kann durch ganz Europa reisen. Mit diesem Ticket habe ich viel Freiheit: Da kann man spontan weg, egal wohin.

Tramper in der Nähe von Heidelberg.

1. Florence: city in Tuscany famous as a center of Italian Renaissance culture.

Freunde von mir benutzen den Zug als ‚rollendes° Hotel'. Am Tag besuchen sie eine neue Stadt. Am Abend steigen sie wieder ein und schlafen dann im Zug unterwegs zum nächsten° Reiseziel. Dieses Tempo ist mir aber zu hektisch. Ich übernachte lieber in der Jugendherberge und verbringe ein paar Tage in jeder Stadt."

rolling
next

Herbert, 29, Assistenzarzt° aus Ulm

„Früher bin ich viel per Autostopp gereist, aber heute würde ich das nicht mehr machen. Die Unsicherheit° ist mir zu stressig und ich habe nicht mehr so viel Freizeit. Das Reisen mit der Bahn gefällt mir, denn es ist sehr praktisch und bequem. Man geht einfach zum Bahnhof, kauft eine Fahrkarte und steigt in den Zug ein. Und man weiß, man kommt pünktlich an.

Im Abteil quatsche ich gern ein bisschen mit den Mitreisenden° über viele Dinge. Letztes Wochenende bin ich zum Beispiel nach Berlin gefahren. Neben mir hat ein Musikstudent aus Leipzig gesessen. Er ist in Wittenberg[1] ausgestiegen und ich habe ihm mit seinem Gepäck geholfen. Er hatte° nicht nur einen Rucksack und einen Koffer mit, sondern auch eine Bassgeige°. Für sein Instrument hat er einen zweiten° Platz reservieren müssen. Verrückt, nicht?"

resident (physician)
uncertainty
fellow passengers
had
double bass / second

Unterwegs mit der Bahn

Nach dem Lesen

A **Antworten Sie auf Deutsch.**

1. Wie kann man im Urlaub Geld sparen?
2. Wohin ist Adrienne getrampt?
3. Hat es ihr Spaß gemacht? Warum?

1. The composer Johann Sebastian Bach (1685–1750) spent the greater part of his life in **Leipzig** (in the state of Saxony). The church reformer Martin Luther (1483–1546) is buried in **Wittenberg** (in the state of Saxony-Anhalt).

Possible written assignment: **Sind Sie je getrampt? Wohin? Beschreiben Sie das.**

4. Wo kann man Menschen unterwegs kennen lernen?
5. Wie kann man mit der Bahn billig reisen?
6. Wie kann man den Zug als „rollendes Hotel" benutzen?
7. Wo kann man billig übernachten?
8. Warum würde Herbert heutzutage nicht mehr trampen?

■ B ■ Urlaub am Mittelmeer Nach dem langen kalten Winter machen viele Deutsche gern Urlaub am Mittelmeer, wo es warm und sonnig ist. Lesen Sie diese Beschreibungen von beliebten (*popular*) Urlaubszielen und dann suchen Sie diese Orte auf der Europakarte am Ende des Buches.

Kreta: die größte griechische Insel. Der Berg Ida erreicht eine Höhe von 2 456 m. Von 3000 bis 1200 v. Chr. war Kreta der Mittelpunkt der minoischen Kultur.

Korsika: französische Insel im Mittelmeer. Bergige Landschaft. Mildes Klima, Anbau von Kastanien, Oliven, Orangen und Wein. Bevölkerung spricht italienisch. Napoleon 1769 auf Korsika geboren.

Tunesien: eine Republik in Nordafrika. Landessprache: Arabisch. Im Norden Gebirge, im Süden Wüste mit Oasen. Viele Urlaubsorte an der Küste.

Türkei. Hauptstadt, Istanbul. Viele Türken wohnen und arbeiten in Deutschland und viele Deutsche machen gern Urlaub an der türkischen Mittelmeerküste.

TUNESIEN Djerba

Hotel Miramar Cesar Palace ■■■■■

— Komforthotel mit sehr guter Ausstattung —

Lage: Nur ca. 100 m bis zum weitläufigen, feinen Sandstrand, ca. 5 km bis Midoun und ca. 16 km nach Houmt Souk (Linienbushaltestelle am Hotel).
Ausstattung: Komfortable, elegant ausgestattete und vollklimatisierbare Hotelanlage mit Haupthaus und mehreren bungalowähnlichen Wohngebäuden, gepflegtem Garten, hübschem Swimmingpool mit Sonnenterrasse, Liegen (Auflagen gegen Geb.) und Schirmen, Pool-/Snackbar. Im Haupthaus schöne Empfangshalle im orientalischen Stil mit Rezeption. Ansprechend gestaltetes Speiserestaurant mit Nichtraucherzone, à la carte-Restaurant, Bar. Hallenbad. Tun. Kat.: 5 Sterne, 112 Zimmer. 1-2 Etagen. Kreditkarten: Euro-/Mastercard, Visa, Diners, Amex.

1 Wo. HP ab DM ***1051,-***

TÜRKISCHE RIVIERA

ALANYA / KONAKLI / KARABURUN

HOTEL
OBAKÖY
MODERNE FERIENANLAGE

LAGE:
Durch die Hauptstraße (Unterführung) vom weitläufigen Sandstrand getrennt und ca. 3 km vom Ortskern Alanyas entfernt (Dolmusverbindungen).

AUSSTATTUNG:
Empfangshalle mit Rezeption, Aufenthaltsraum, TV-Ecke (Sat.-Empfang), Mietsafe, Bar, Geschäfte, Speiserestaurant mit Terrasse, Swimmingpool, sep. Kinderbecken, Sonnenterrasse (Liegen u. Schirme inkl.) und Pool-/Snackbar.

ZIMMER:
Freundlich ausgestattete Zimmer mit Klimaanlage, Telefon, Sat.-TV, Radio, Fön, Minibar (gegen Gebühr), Bad oder Dusche/WC und Balkon.

VERPFLEGUNG:
Frühstück und Abendessen in Buffetform.

SPORT:
Beachvolleyball, Tischtennis und Fitness inkl., Billard, Sauna, Massage und Türkisches Bad gegen Gebühr.

UNTERHALTUNG:
Tagesanimation, abends gelegentlich Unterhaltungsprogramme.

ZUSATZINFORMATIONEN:
Landeskategorie 4 Sterne; 181 Zimmer, 6 Etagen, 1 Lift; Kreditkarten: Visa, Amex, Mastercard; Reinigung: täglich, Handtuch- und Bettwäschewechsel: 5 x pro Woche; Babybetten inkl.;
Tel.: 0090 242-5140700

1 WOCHE HALBPENSION AB DM 815,–

Situationen aus dem Alltag

This vocabulary focuses on an everday topic or situation. Words you already know from **Wortschatz** sections are listed without English equivalents; new supplementary vocabulary is listed with definitions. Your instructor may assign some supplementary vocabulary for active mastery.

■ Reisen und Verkehr (Travel and traffic)

Some of these words are already familiar.

Verben

ab·fahren ≠ an·kommen
ein·steigen ≠ aus·steigen
um·steigen to transfer, change (*buses, trains, etc.*)

Substantive

der **Bahnhof, ¨-e**
der **Bus, -se** *bus*
der **Flughafen, ¨** *airport*
der **Verkehr** *traffic*
der **Wagen, -**
der **Zug, ¨-e**

das **Auto, -s**
das **Flugzeug, -e**

die **Autobahn, -en** *expressway, high-speed highway*
die **Fahrkarte, -n**

ERHOLUNG AUF DEM RHEIN.
DIE BAHN BRINGT SIE ZUM SCHIFF.
KD Köln-Düsseldorfer DB Deutsche Bundesbahn

Debate continues about whether to impose a speed limit on the **Autobahn.** Many claim the present lack of a speed limit contributes to Germany's high accident rate.

Nützliche Ausdrücke

Ich fahre **mit dem Wagen.** ... *by car.*
mit dem Bus. ... *by bus.*
mit der Bahn. ... *by train.*
Ich fliege.

After repeating patterns, ask students: **Wie kann man nach Hamburg fahren?** (You may want to list means of transportation on board.) Then personalize: I: **Fragen Sie Ben, wie er nach Hamburg fährt.**
S1: Wie fährst du nach Hamburg?
S2: Ich fahre mit dem Bus/Ich trampe.

■ A ■ Partnerarbeit: Was habe ich zuerst gemacht? Here are eight statements about a train trip. Number them in the order that the events most likely happened. Then read them aloud in order.

_______ Ich habe im Zug mit der Frau neben mir gequatscht.
_______ Ich habe mir eine Fahrkarte gekauft.
_______ Ich habe im Zug einen guten Roman gelesen.
_______ Ich habe eine Reise ins Ausland machen wollen.
_______ Ich bin in den Zug eingestiegen.
_______ Ich habe mir eine Landkarte gekauft.
_______ Ich bin zum Bahnhof gegangen.
_______ Ich bin pünktlich angekommen.

Cue **Zuerst habe/bin ich ... und dann habe/bin ich ...**

Making travel plans and talking about traveling is a communicative goal.

■ B ■ Gruppenarbeit: Planen wir unsere Reise. (*4 Personen*) Planen Sie eine Reise nach Europa. Besprechen Sie diese Fragen zusammen. Benutzen Sie die Landkarte.

Welche Länder wollen wir besuchen?
Wie lange wollen wir bleiben?
Wie wollen wir durch Europa reisen? Mit der Bahn? Per Autostopp?
Wo wollen wir übernachten? In einer Jugendherberge? Im Hotel?
Was wollen wir mitnehmen? Machen wir eine Liste.
Haben wir etwas vergessen?

Have students draw up lists in German of things to take along.

Jetzt berichtet jede Gruppe über ihre Pläne.

Options: After working on this in class, individuals can turn in written version on following class day or partners can prepare together for performance in class.

■ C ■ Partnerarbeit: Rollenspiel Spielen Sie diese Situation mit Ihrem Partner. Partner A spielt den Autofahrer, Partner B spielt den Tramper. Der Tramper steht seit einer Stunde im Regen. Endlich hält ein Auto. Der Tramper steigt ein und spricht mit dem Fahrer über das Trampen und die Ferien.

Sie können Ihr Gespräch (*conversation*) dann der ganzen Klasse vorspielen.

■ D ■ Partnerarbeit: Wann kommt der Zug an? Sie arbeiten am Hauptbahnhof in Mannheim und geben Auskunft über die Züge. Eine Touristengruppe bittet um (*asks for*) Auskunft. Sie müssen die Antworten auf dem Fahrplan finden.

BEISPIEL: A: Entschuldigung, wann kommt der Zug aus Hamburg in Mannheim an?
B: Er kommt um 14.22 Uhr an.
A: Um wie viel Uhr fährt er in Hamburg ab?
B: Um 9.33 Uhr.

Mannheim Hbf (Hauptbahnhof)

	Ankunft (*arrivals*)			Abfahrt (*departures*)	
Zug-Nr.	*ab*[1]	*an*[1]	*Zug-Nr.*	*ab*	*an*
6342	Hamburg 9.33 Uhr	Mannheim 14.22 Uhr	1338	Mannheim 5.42 Uhr	Zürich 8.12 Uhr
7422	München 10.03 Uhr	Mannheim 13.10 Uhr	2472	Mannheim 6.06 Uhr	Nürnberg 9.33 Uhr
1387	Frankfurt 11.20 Uhr	Mannheim 12.01 Uhr	6606	Mannheim 7.55 Uhr	Straßburg 8.40 Uhr
7703	Wien 10.10 Uhr	Mannheim 17.56 Uhr	2203	Mannheim 10.12 Uhr	Innsbruck 15.46 Uhr
9311	Berlin 11.05 Uhr	Mannheim 19.16 Uhr	3679	Mannheim 13.23 Uhr	Prag 20.09 Uhr

1. **ab**: time and place of departure; **an**: time and place of arrival.

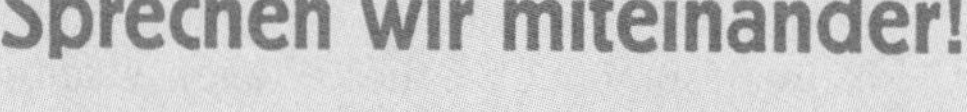

Zum Schluss

Workbook Kap. 7, K.

Lab Manual Kap. 7, Diktat.

Üb. A: Have groups compare lists. After lists have been made, ask: **Was gefällt Ihnen (nicht)? Warum gefällt es Ihnen (nicht)?**

Üb. B: Bring vertical objects (bottles, lamps, umbrella, coffee cup, etc.), horizontal objects (book, newspaper, etc.), things to hang up. May also review other 2-way prepositions (**Wo stehe ich jetzt?**). Student can also be performer of actions.

Talking on the telephone is a communicative goal.

Partnerarbeit C prepares students for the less guided improvisation in **D**. Could also be assigned as written work.

Sprechen wir miteinander!

■ A ■ Gruppenarbeit: Was gefällt euch hier? Was gefällt Ihnen an Ihrer Uni? Was gefällt Ihnen nicht? Machen Sie miteinander zwei Listen (*lists*).

das Essen in der Mensa
das Leben im Studentenwohnheim
die Vorlesungen
die Hausaufgaben
der Stress
die Studentenzeitung
usw.

■ B ■ Gruppenarbeit: Was mache ich jetzt? The class is divided into two groups. The instructor does various things, and each team in turn tries to describe the action. A correct answer scores a point. If your team answers incorrectly, the other team has a chance to describe the same action.

BEISPIEL: Was mache ich jetzt?
Sie stellen die Flasche auf den Stuhl.

■ C ■ Partnerarbeit: Am Telefon Situation: Barbara Hinrich phones her father to tell him when she's arriving this evening. He asks where she is and whether she's going to have dinner at home tonight. She says she's going to a restaurant with friends and won't be home until late. Her father says he'll see her later. They say good-bye (on the telephone: **Auf Wiederhören**).

Complete this conversation with your partner.

VATER: Hinrich.
BARBARA: Hallo ________! Hier ist ________.
VATER: Ach hallo ________! Wo ________?
BARBARA: ________.
VATER: Wirklich? ________?
BARBARA: ________.
VATER: Also, ________.
Auf Wiederhören, bis ________!
BARBARA: ________!

Freude für Tante Erna: Die ganze Familie ruft an.

Üb. D: Model first by improvising one conversation with a good student. Also good as written assignment.

■ **D** ■ **Partnerarbeit** Now choose one of the following situations and invent your own telephone conversation. Since long distance rates are expensive, be brief and convey as much information as efficiently as you can.

1. Phone a friend to report about your vacation abroad.
2. Phone home to say you have arrived somewhere.
3. Phone your roommate to say you've forgotten something.
4. Find out whether a youth hostel or hotel has room for you.

■ **E** ■ **Gruppeninterview: Wer ist schon weit gereist?** Wie viele Studenten haben schon eine lange Reise gemacht? Die anderen (*other*) Studenten interviewen sie und fragen zum Beispiel:

Wann? **Wohin?** **Mit wem?** **Warum?**

■ **F** ■ **Partnerarbeit: Was würdest du lieber machen?** Here are some choices you might make when traveling. Ask each other which you would rather do. State a preference and give a reason.

Expressing preferences is a communicative goal.

BEISPIEL:

sprechen

Ihre Muttersprache? eine Fremdsprache?

Ich würde lieber eine Fremdsprache sprechen, denn das macht mehr Spaß.

übernachten

im Hotel? in einer Jugendherberge?

reisen

per Autostopp? mit der Bahn?

mitbringen

einen Rucksack? einen Koffer?

eine Woche verbringen

in der Stadt? auf dem Land?

kennen lernen

Touristen aus Ihrem Land? Studenten aus dem Ausland?

sitzen

im Konzert? im Café?

Schreiben Sie zu Hause.

■ **G** ■ **Wanderlust** Complete the sentences below to form a short essay on traveling inexpensively.

1. Manchmal will ich einfach ...
2. Natürlich braucht man Geld für ...
3. Ohne viel Geld in der Tasche kann ...
4. Man kann aber immer ...
5. Das ist manchmal schön, denn ...
6. Mit meinem Interrail-Ticket kann ...
7. Ich würde wahnsinnig gern ...
8. Nächstes Jahr ...
9. Hoffentlich ist ...

H **Die Reise war super. Ein Brief nach Hause.** Auf Seite 204 im Lesestück hat Adrienne von ihrer Reise mit ihrem Freund erzählt. Natürlich hat sie im Ausland eigentlich viel mehr gemacht. Was hat sie ihren Eltern aus Italien geschrieben? Wie war es bei dieser Familie, warum hat es so viel Spaß gemacht usw.? Schreiben Sie Adriennes Brief nach Hause. (*Review letter-writing conventions in Kapitel 6, p. 172.*)

I Schreiben Sie das Gespräch (*conversation*) im Zug zwischen Herbert und dem Musikstudenten aus Leipzig. (Siehe S. 205.)

J **Wie sagt man das auf Deutsch?**

1. Did you take a trip this year?
2. Yes, we went to Venice.
3. Did you take the children along?
4. Yes, and they liked Italy very much. (*use* **gefallen**)

5. Does this suitcase belong to you?
6. Not to me, but to my brother.
7. Where should I put it?
8. Would you please put it under the table?

9. How's your husband?
10. He's not very well.
11. Oh, I'm sorry.

Ausflugsschiff (*excursion boat*) auf dem Bodensee.

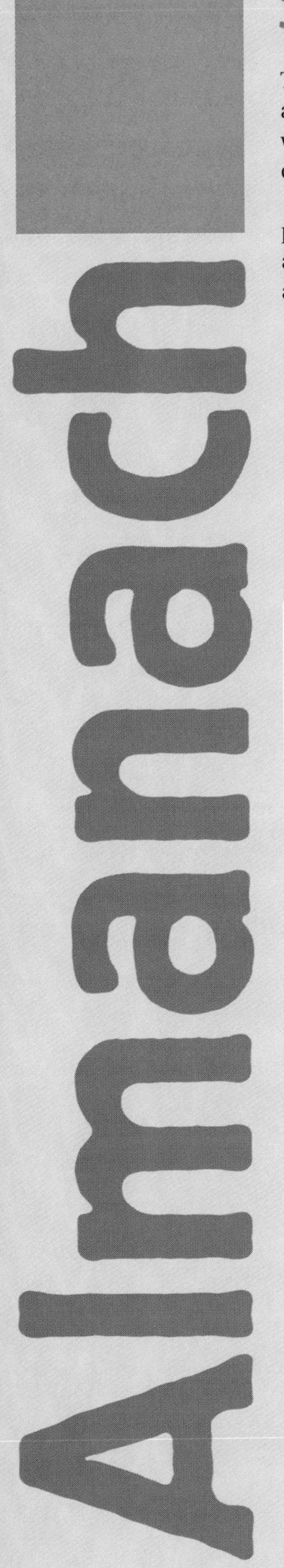

Jugendherbergen (Youth Hostels)

There are about 670 **Jugendherbergen** in Germany, 110 in Austria, 85 in Switzerland, and 13 in Luxembourg. They are meeting places for young travelers from all over the world. In addition to providing inexpensive food and lodging, they offer a variety of courses and organized trips.

Membership in the AYH (American Youth Hostels) entitles the cardholder to privileges in hostels all over the world. Membership costs as of 1995: under 17 years of age, \$10.00; 17–54, \$25.00; over 54, \$15.00. In Bavaria you must be under 26 years of age to stay in a youth hostel. To apply for membership, write to:

American Youth Hostels, Inc.
P.O. Box 37613
Washington, D.C. 20013–7613
(202) 783-6161

Here are some excerpts from the Youth Hostel handbook for Germany.

Berlin, Jugendgästehaus Berlin — 15, E 3

Anschrift: JGH Berlin, Kluckstraße 3, 10785 Berlin, ☎ 030/2611097, Fax: 030/2650383.
Herbergsväter: Hans-Martin Schwarz und Ingolf Keil.
Anreise: Auto: Stadtautobahn (Richtung Wilmersdorf/Schöneberg: Ausfahrt Innsbrucker Pl.), links, über Hauptstr. und Potsdamer Str. bis Lützowstr., dort links, Kluckstr. rechts einbiegen. Bahn: Bahnhof. Zoo-U-Bahn-Linie 1 (Richtung Schlesisches Tor) bis Kurfürstenstr. und 5 Min. Fußweg oder Bhf. Zoo und Bus 129 ab Haltestelle Kurfürstendamm/Joachimstaler Str. (Richtung Hermannplatz) bis JGH, Haltestelle "Gedenkstätte".
Lage: Innenstadt, am Rande des Tiergarten, nahe des Kulturforums.
Geeignet für: Familien (bedingt), Seminare, Tagungen, Lehrgänge (nach Absprache), Gruppen, Einzelgäste.
Raumangebot: 364 Betten, 5 Tagesräume, 6 Familienzimmer.
Freizeitmöglichkeiten: Fahrradausleihe (500 m entfernt), TT-Platten, Spaziergänge durch den Tiergarten mit Reichstag, Brandenburger Tor, Siegessäule, Kulturforum. Stadterkundungen auf kulturellem und historischen Gebiet, Gedenkstätte: Widerstand im 3. Reich,

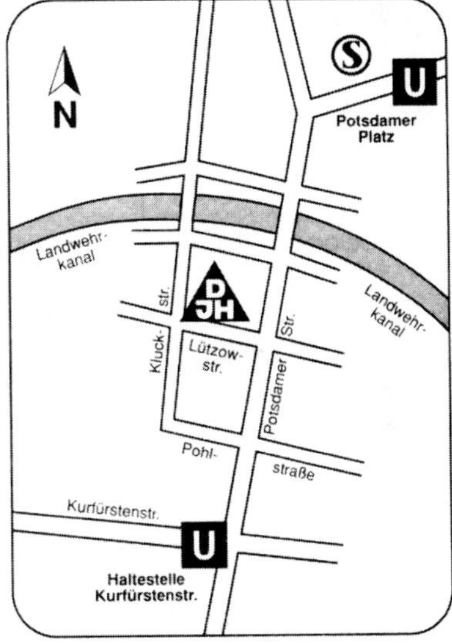

"Alternativszene" Kreuzberg, Berlin-Ost: historisches Zentrum (Nikolai-Viertel, Unter den Linden, Museumsinsel, Pergamonmuseum).

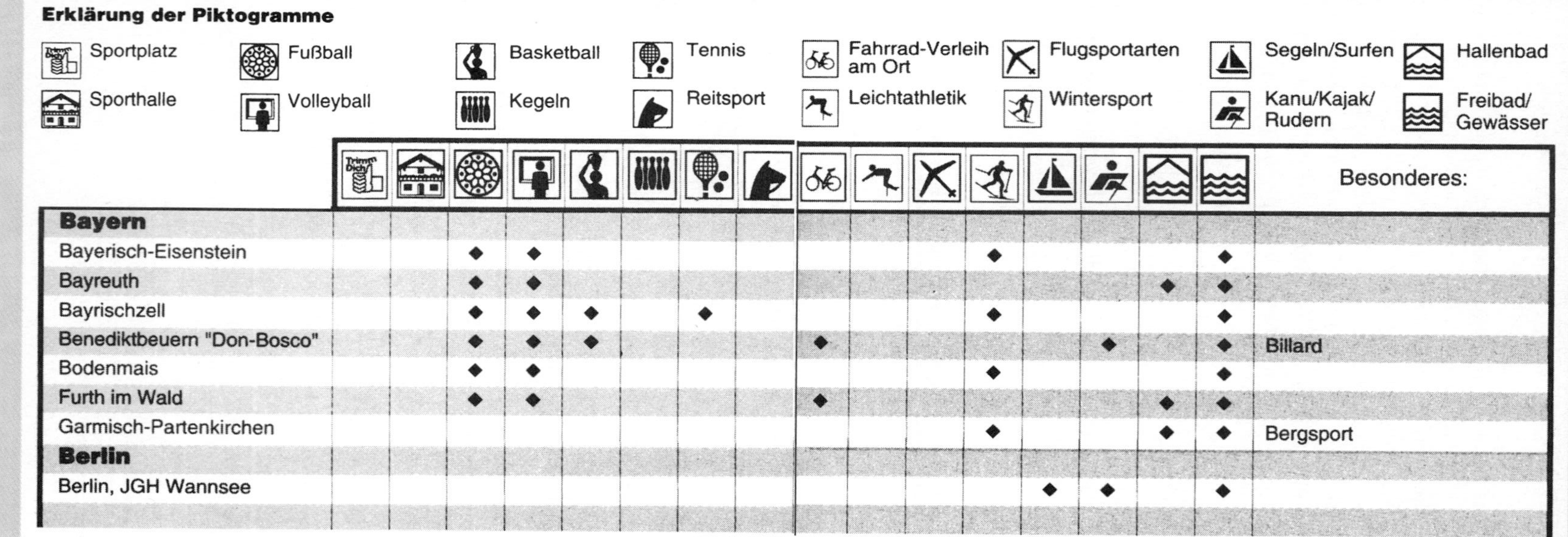

Erklärung der Piktogramme

Sportplatz · Sporthalle · Fußball · Volleyball · Basketball · Kegeln · Tennis · Reitsport · Fahrrad-Verleih am Ort · Leichtathletik · Flugsportarten · Wintersport · Segeln/Surfen · Kanu/Kajak/Rudern · Hallenbad · Freibad/Gewässer

	Sportplatz	Sporthalle	Fußball	Volleyball	Basketball	Kegeln	Tennis	Reitsport	Fahrrad-Verleih am Ort	Leichtathletik	Flugsportarten	Wintersport	Segeln/Surfen	Kanu/Kajak/Rudern	Hallenbad	Freibad/Gewässer	Besonderes:
Bayern																	
Bayerisch-Eisenstein			◆	◆								◆				◆	
Bayreuth			◆	◆											◆	◆	
Bayrischzell			◆	◆	◆		◆					◆				◆	
Benediktbeuern "Don-Bosco"			◆	◆	◆				◆					◆		◆	Billard
Bodenmais			◆	◆								◆				◆	
Furth im Wald			◆	◆					◆						◆	◆	
Garmisch-Partenkirchen												◆			◆	◆	Bergsport
Berlin																	
Berlin, JGH Wannsee													◆	◆		◆	

Have students read aloud the **Erklärung der Piktogramme**, guessing sports they don't know. Then ask questions based on the handbook page. **Was kann man in der Jugendherberge Bayreuth machen? Wo kann man bergsteigen?** Then have students figure out how to reserve a bed in the Berlin-Wannsee Youth Hostel and plan what to do while they're there. They may use a dictionary.

Das Leben in der Stadt

Communicative Goals

- Talking about food and shopping
- Discussing city life
- Asking for directions
- Ordering in a restaurant

Cultural Goal

- Learning about life in German cities

Chapter Outline

- **Lyrik zum Vorlesen**
  Heinrich Heine, „Die Loreley"
- **Grammatik**
  Subordinate clauses and subordinating conjunctions
  Infinitive constructions with *zu*
  Genitive case
  Nouns of measure, weight, and number
  Equivalents for English *to*
- **Lesestück**
  Aspekte der Großstadt
- **Situationen aus dem Alltag**
  Unterwegs in der Stadt; In der Konditorei
- **Videoecke**
  Gehen wir doch einkaufen!
- **Almanach**
  Mit dem Bus durch Berlin

Dialoge

Lab Manual Kap. 8, Dialoge, Fragen, Hören Sie gut zu!, Üb. zur Aussprache [**e/er**].

Remember: **DM 25,80** is spoken **fünfundzwanzig Mark achtzig**. Note on tipping: German restaurants automatically add 15% for service to the bill. When paying, however, it is customary to round up the bill.

Im Restaurant: Zahlen bitte!

KELLNERIN: So, hat es Ihnen geschmeckt?
GAST: Ausgezeichnet!
KELLNERIN: Möchten Sie noch etwas bestellen?
GAST: Nein, danke, ich möchte zahlen, bitte.
KELLNERIN: Sie haben Schnitzel, Pommes frites, einen Salat und ein Bier gehabt, nicht wahr?
GAST: Ja, und auch eine Tasse Kaffee.
KELLNERIN: Das macht zusammen DM 25,80, bitte sehr.
GAST: (*Gibt ihr DM 30*) 27 Mark.
KELLNERIN: Danke sehr, und drei Mark zurück.

Hat es Ihnen geschmeckt? (*How was everything?*) means literally *Did it taste good to you?*

Dialogue 1 contains new vocabulary, but no new grammar

Most Germans eat a hot meal at noon and a simple supper of cold cuts, bread, cheese, and salad in the evening.

Pronunciation practice: Tape program focuses on final **-e** versus final **-er**. Remind students to quickly retract their tongues when saying final **-er**. Use dialogues to review these sounds in class: **Danke, ich möchte zahlen, bitte**; **eine Tasse Kaffee**; **ich habe Hunger, das klingt lecker**.

Was brauchen wir noch?

DORA: Heute Morgen habe ich Max zum Abendessen eingeladen. Weißt du, ob er kommt?
FRANZ: Ja, aber er hat mir gesagt, dass er erst um halb sieben kommen kann. Wie viel Uhr ist es jetzt?
DORA: Halb sechs. Also muss ich noch schnell zum Supermarkt, um ein paar Sachen einzukaufen. Was brauchen wir noch?
FRANZ: Ein Kilo Kartoffeln, 200 Gramm Leberwurst, Käse, eine Flasche Rotwein und Obst zum Nachtisch.
DORA: Ist das alles?
FRANZ: Ich glaube schon.

Ein Stadtbummel

Marianne besucht ihren Freund Helmut in Köln. Er hat ihr die Stadt noch nicht gezeigt, weil es geregnet hat.

Du is used here as an attention-getter, equivalent to *hey, look*.

HELMUT: Du, der Regen hat endlich aufgehört! Hast du jetzt Lust einen Stadtbummel zu machen?
MARIANNE: Ja gerne. Aber ich hab' jetzt Hunger. Können wir zuerst essen?
HELMUT: Selbstverständlich! In der Nähe des Doms gibt es ein Lokal, wo wir griechisch essen können.
MARIANNE: Hmm, das klingt lecker!
HELMUT: Nachher können wir dann den Dom besuchen und von da ist es nicht mehr weit zum Kunstmuseum.

Wortschatz 1

Verben

bestellen to order
ein·laden (lädt ein), hat eingeladen to invite
klingen, hat geklungen to sound
schmecken to taste; to taste good
Wie schmeckt es dir? How does it taste? How do you like it?
zahlen to pay

Dom comes from Latin *domus ecclesiae* (*house of the congregation*).

Substantive

der **Bummel, -** stroll, walk
einen Stadtbummel machen to take a stroll through town
der **Dom, -e** cathedral
der **Durst** thirst
der **Gast, ¨e** guest; patron
der **Hunger** hunger
der **Kaffee** coffee
der **Kellner, -** waiter
der **Liter** liter
der **Nachtisch** dessert
zum Nachtisch for dessert
der **Salat, -e** salad; lettuce

Gender: ***der* Liter** seems to be preferred, though ***das* Liter** is also common.

das **Abendessen** supper, evening meal
zum Abendessen for dinner
das **Gebäude, -** building
das **Glas, ¨er** glass
das **Gramm** gram
das **Kilogramm** (*or* das **Kilo**) kilogram
(das) **Köln** Cologne
das **Lokal, -e** neighborhood restaurant or tavern
das **Museum, Museen** museum
das **Restaurant, -s** restaurant
das **Schnitzel, -** cutlet, chop

die **Kartoffel, -n** potato
die **Kellnerin, -nen** waitress
die **Kunst, ¨e** art
die **Sache, -n** thing; item
die **Tasse, -n** cup
die **Wurst, ¨e** sausage
die **Leberwurst** liverwurst

Adjektive und Adverbien

ausgezeichnet excellent
griechisch Greek
lecker tasty, delicious
weit far; far away
zuerst first, at first

Andere Vokabeln

dass (*sub. conj.*) that
noch etwas something else, anything more
ob (*sub. conj.*) whether, if
um ... zu in order to

Nützliche Ausdrücke

Durst haben to be thirsty
Hunger haben to be hungry
Lust haben (etwas zu tun) to want to (do something)
griechisch (italienisch, französisch usw.) essen to eat Greek (Italian, French, etc.) food
Ich glaube schon. I think so.

die Kunst comes from verb **können**, reminding of connection between art and ability. The meaning is preserved in **die Kochkunst**, **der Lebenskünstler**.

to eat supper = **zu Abend essen**

Point out negation: **keine Lust haben.**

In a Restaurant: Check please!

WAIT.: How was everything?
P: Excellent!
WAIT.: Would you like to order anything else?
P: No thanks. I'd like the check, please.
WAIT.: You had a cutlet, French fries, a salad, and a beer, right?
P: Yes, and also a cup of coffee.
WAIT.: All together that comes to 25 Marks 80, please.
P: (*Gives her DM 30*) 27 Marks.
WAIT.: Thank you, and three Marks change.

What Else Do We Need?

D: This morning I invited Max to supper. Do you know if he's coming?
F: Yes, but he told me that he couldn't come until 6:30. What time is it now?
D: 5:30. So I need to make a quick trip to the supermarket to buy a few things. What else do we need?
F: A kilo of potatoes, 200 grams of liverwurst, cheese, a bottle of red wine, and fruit for dessert.
D: Is that all?
F: I think so.

A Stroll Through Town

Marianne is visiting her friend Helmut in Cologne. He hasn't shown her around town yet, because it's been raining.

H: Hey look, the rain's finally stopped! Do you want to take a stroll through town now?
M: Sure. But I'm hungry now. Can we eat first?
H: Of course. Near the cathedral there's a place where we can eat Greek food.
M: Hmm, that sounds delicious!
H: Then we can visit the cathedral afterwards, and from there it's not far to the art museum.

in der Nähe (+ *gen.*) near, nearby
Zahlen bitte! (May I have the) check please!

You already know **in der Nähe von** (+ *dat.*).

Gegensätze

Ich glaube schon. ≠ Ich glaube nicht. I think so. ≠ I don't think so.
weit ≠ nah(e) far ≠ near
zuerst ≠ zuletzt at first ≠ finally, last of all

Mit anderen Worten

der Kram (*colloq.*) = **die Sachen; alte Sachen**

Contrast **zahlen**, denoting simply the act of handing over money, and **bezahlen** (Kap. 6), which adds the idea of discharging an obligation. **Im Restaurant: Zahlen bitte!** vs. **Bezahlen** = *to pay for:* **Ich bezahle das Essen.**

Käse des Monats:

Echter Käse aus Holland
holländischer Schnittkäse, 30% Fett i.Tr., 100 g **1.99**

Granny Smith Äpfel
Chile, Kl. I, neuerntig
1 kg **2.99**

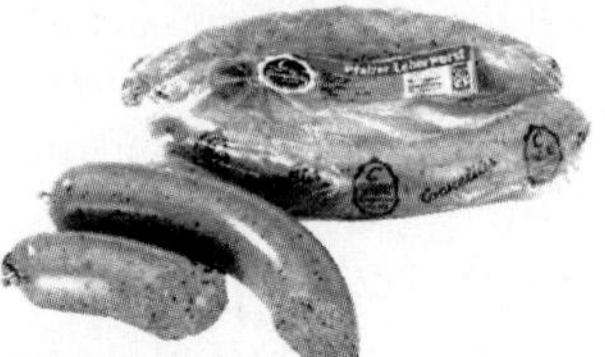

Unser SB-Wurst-Angebot:
Pfälzer Leberwurst
400-g-Packung **3.49**

Obstabteilung!

Griech. Victoria-Trauben
Hkl. I
1 kg **2.99**

Südafrik. Outspan-Orangen
Hkl. I
7er Netz **2.99**

Variationen

For items 1, 4, & 5, you may have to write vocabulary on board.

■ A ■ Persönliche Fragen

1. Haben Sie heute gefrühstückt? Was haben Sie denn gegessen? Hat's Ihnen geschmeckt?
2. Kennen Sie ein Lokal, wo man sehr gut essen kann? Wie heißt es?
3. Essen Sie gern griechisch? italienisch? französisch? deutsch?
4. Trinken Sie viel Kaffee? Was trinken Sie sonst?
5. Was essen Sie gern zum Nachtisch?
6. Laden Sie oft Freunde zum Abendessen ein?
7. Kaufen Sie im Supermarkt ein? Wie oft?
8. Marianne hat Lust einen Stadtbummel zu machen. Haben Sie Lust heute etwas zu machen? Was denn?
9. Gehen Sie gern ins Kunstmuseum? Welche Künstler (*artists*) mögen Sie?

```
15-08-90 #0000

GAST/TISCH # 161
2 PAELLA VAL.   *40.00
1 SCHNITZEL PA  *14.00
1 KINDERTELLER   *9.00
1 FL WASSER      *3.50
1 FL LIMO        *3.50
1 MÄRZEN 0.5     *2.80
1 WEIZEN         *3.50
1 MÄRZEN 0.3     *1.80
BROT             *2.00
BAR        *80.10
ENTH.MWST14%     *9.59

BESTEN DANK
COSTA DEL SOL
```

■ B ■ Übung: Raten Sie mal! (Take a guess!) Marianne und Helmut wollen einen Stadtbummel machen. Das heißt, sie haben ein bisschen Freizeit und können langsam durch die Stadt gehen. Um einen Bummel zu machen braucht man also Zeit. Raten Sie mal, was diese Wörter bedeuten:

1. Sie machen einen **Schaufensterbummel**.
2. Ich hab' ein bisschen Geld in der Tasche. Machen wir doch einen **Einkaufsbummel**.
3. Der Zug hat an jedem kleinen Bahnhof gehalten. Ich fahre nie wieder mit diesem **Bummelzug**!

4. Fritz studiert seit 13 Semestern an der Uni und ist immer noch nicht fertig. Er ist ein **Bummelstudent**!
5. Die Arbeiter arbeiten immer noch, aber sehr langsam. Sie machen einen **Bummelstreik**.

Reviews food vocabulary, personal dative, and prepares students for restaurant role-play later in chapter.

Talking about food is a communicative goal.

■ C ■ Partnerarbeit: Schmeckt es dir? Fragen Sie Ihren Partner, ob ihm etwas schmeckt.

BEISPIEL: A: Isst du gern Tomatensuppe?
B: Nein, das schmeckt mir nicht. (*oder*)
Ja, das schmeckt mir.

Käse	Kaffee
Bier	Brot
Pizza	Salat
Kartoffeln	Wiener Schnitzel
Pommes frites	griechisches Essen
Leberwurst	Wein

Lyrik zum Vorlesen

The cliff called the Loreley is on the Rhine River at its deepest spot. Heinrich Heine's famous poem "Ich weiß nicht, was soll es bedeuten" (1823) is a retelling of a Romantic legend invented by his contemporary Clemens Brentano (1778–1842). It recounts the tale of a siren who lures boatmen to their deaths at this place. Set to music by the composer Silcher, it achieved the status of a folk song.

Lab Manual Kap. 8, Lyrik zum Vorlesen.

Ich weiß nicht, was soll es bedeuten („Die Loreley")

Ich weiß nicht, was soll es bedeuten,
dass ich so traurig° bin;
ein Märchen aus alten Zeiten,
das kommt mir nicht aus dem Sinn°.

Die Luft ist kühl und es dunkelt°,
und ruhig° fließt der Rhein;
der Gipfel° des Berges funkelt°
im Abendsonnenschein.

Die schönste Jungfrau° sitzet°
dort oben° wunderbar,
ihr goldenes Geschmeide° blitzet°,
sie kämmt° ihr goldenes Haar.

Sie kämmt es mit goldenem Kamme°,
und singt ein Lied dabei°;
das hat eine wundersame°,
gewaltige° Melodei.

sad
das ... = das kann ich nicht vergessen
es dunkelt = es wird dunkel
peacefully
mountain top / glistens
most beautiful maiden / **sitzet = sitzt**
high above
jewelry / glistens
combs
comb
while doing so
= wunderbare
powerful

Heinrich Heine

Den Schiffer° im kleinen Schiffe°
ergreift es° mit wildem Weh°;
er schaut° nicht die Felsenriffe°,
er schaut nur hinauf in die Höh°.

Ich glaube, die Wellen° verschlingen°
am Ende Schiffer und Kahn°;
und das hat mit ihrem Singen
die Loreley getan.

Heinrich Heine (1797–1856)

sailor / boat
is gripped / longing
= **sieht** / submerged rock
up to the heights

waves / swallow
boat

Grammatik

Subordinate clauses and subordinating conjunctions

Subordinating conjunctions, like coordinating conjunctions, join two clauses together. The clause beginning with a subordinating conjunction, however, is *subordinate to*, or *dependent on*, the main clause. A subordinate clause is *not* an independent sentence.

When it answers a question, a subordinate clause can stand alone as a complete utterance: **Wie lange müssen wir warten? Bis der Regen aufhört.**

main clause	*subordinate clause*
I know	*that they still remember me.*

In the example above, the subordinate clause "that they still remember me" is not a complete sentence. In this chapter you will learn the following subordinating conjunctions:

bis	*until*
da	*since* (causal, not temporal)
dass	*that*
ob	*whether, if* (when it means *whether*)
weil	*because*
wenn	*if*

Causal meaning of *since*: Since it's raining . . . (**Da es regnet ...**); temporal meaning of *since*: Since November . . . (**Seit November ...**).

There is an increasing tendency in colloquial spoken German to use **weil** as a coordinating conjunction.

Five more subordinating conjunctions will be introduced in subsequent chapters: **obwohl**, **als**, **nachdem**, **bevor**, **damit**.

...für meine Familie tu' ich alles.
Aber was passiert, wenn mir was passiert?

Verb-last word order in the subordinate clause

Unlike coordinating conjunctions, which do not affect word order, subordinating conjunctions *move the inflected verb to the end of the subordinate clause.*

Review the coordinating conjunctions **und**, **oder**, etc. on pp. 192–194, which do *not* change word order in the second clause.

Wir essen um halb sieben.

Ich glaube, **dass** wir ▬ um halb sieben essen.
I think that we're eating at 6:30.

Brauchen wir noch etwas?

Weißt du, **ob** ▬ wir noch etwas brauchen?
Do you know whether we need anything else?

A subordinate cluase is always set off by a comma preceding the subordinating conjunction.

Ich habe gerade gegessen.

Ich habe keinen Hunger, **weil** ich ▬ gerade gegessen habe.
I'm not hungry because I've just eaten.

Ich habe Zeit.

Ich helfe dir, **wenn** ich ▬ Zeit habe.
I'll help you if I have time.

Lab Manual Kap. 8, Üb. 1, 2, 7; Var. zu Üb. 3, 5, 8.

Workbook Kap. 8, A–D.

Suggest that students substitute pronouns for nouns.

■ **1** ■ **Übung: Ich weiß, dass ...** Sie planen miteinander ein Abendessen. Ihre Professorin sagt Ihnen etwas. Sagen Sie, dass Sie das wissen.

BEISPIEL: Die Wurst ist teuer.
Ich weiß, dass sie teuer ist.

1. Wir essen um sieben.
2. Wir brauchen Rotwein.
3. Der Käse schmeckt gut.
4. Die Kinder wollen essen.
5. Tante Marie kommt zum Abendessen.
6. Wir haben keinen Salat.
7. Wir brauchen etwas zum Nachtisch.
8. Tante Marie trinkt keinen Kaffee.

■ **2** ■ **Übung: Ich weiß nicht, ob ...** Ihr Professor ist neu in dieser Stadt. Er hat viele Fragen, aber Sie wohnen auch nicht lange hier und können ihm keine Antworten geben.

BEISPIEL: Ist dieses Restaurant teuer?
Ich weiß nicht, ob es teuer ist.

1. Gibt es hier einen Automechaniker?
2. Ist dieses Hotel gut?
3. Ist die Uni weit von hier?
4. Gibt es eine Buchhandlung in der Nähe?
5. Kann man den Dom besuchen?
6. Kann man hier einen Stadtplan kaufen?

Model beforehand with a student or spot check after students have worked in pairs.

■ **3** ■ **Partnerarbeit: Warum lernst du Deutsch?** Ask each other why you do the things listed below. Give your reason, then ask the next question.

BEISPIEL: Warum lernst du Deutsch?
Ich lerne Deutsch, *weil* es interessant ist. Warum ... ?

Deutsch lernen	einen Rucksack tragen
zur Buchhandlung gehen	bis 9.00 schlafen
trampen	draußen sitzen
jetzt essen	keine Leberwurst essen
viel Kaffee trinken	früh aufstehen

WENN ALLES EGAL IST...

Straßenverkehr in Hamburg

■ Conditional sentences: If *x* is true, then *y* is true

A clause introduced by **wenn** is called a *conditional clause* because it states a condition. The main clause is then called the *result clause* because it states the expected result of the condition. The result clause may begin with an optional **dann** which does not affect word order.

> Wenn ich Zeit habe, helfe ich dir.
> Wenn ich Zeit habe, **dann** helfe ich dir.

■ 4 ■ Übung: Wenn ..., dann ...

May be prepared beforehand as written homework.

A. Complete these sentences by supplying a result clause:

1. Wenn wir Hunger haben, dann ...
2. Wenn du griechisch essen willst, dann ...
3. Wenn du mich morgen einlädst, dann ...

B. Now supply the conditional clause:

1. Wenn ... , dann können wir einen Stadtbummel machen.
2. Wenn ... , dann kannst du einen Nachtisch bestellen.
3. Wenn ... , dann müssen wir noch schnell einkaufen.

■ Question words as subordinating conjunctions

The question words (**wann**, **warum**, **was**, **wer**, etc.) act as subordinating conjunctions when they introduce an indirect question (i.e., a question restated as a subordinate clause).

question: Was brauchen wir zum Abendessen?

indirect question: Weißt du, was ▬▬ wir zum Abendessen brauchen?
Do you know what we need for supper?

question: Wer ist das?

indirect question: Ich kann Ihnen nicht sagen, wer ▬ das ist.
I can't tell you who that is.

Variation: After doing **Üb. 5** once through, change the question.
I: Wissen Sie, wer die Reise plant?

■ 5 ■ Übung: Die Tramper Ein Freund von Ihnen will mit anderen Studenten eine Reise per Autostopp machen. Ihr Professor hat Fragen über ihre Reise, aber Sie wissen die Antworten nicht.

BEISPIEL: Wer plant die Reise?
Ich weiß nicht, wer die Reise plant.

1. Wohin fahren die Tramper?
2. Wo wollen sie übernachten?
3. Warum trampen Ihre Freunde?
4. Wen wollen sie besuchen?
5. Wann kommen die Tramper zurück?
6. Was packen sie in den Rucksack?
7. Welche Städte besuchen sie?

■ Verbs with separable prefixes in subordinate clauses

You know that when a verb with a separable prefix is used in a main clause, the prefix is separated from the verb and placed at the end of the clause.

Dort **kaufe** ich immer **ein**.

In a subordinate clause, the verb moves to the end of the clause and the prefix is attached to it.

Weißt du, warum ich ▬▬ immer dort einkaufe?

■ 6 ■ Partnerarbeit: Wie lange müssen wir warten? Sie warten zusammen vor der Mensa. Sagen Sie einander (*each other*), bis wann Sie warten müssen. (*Use the cues below.*)

BEISPIEL: Wie lange müssen wir noch warten?
(der Bus / kommen)
Wir müssen warten, bis der Bus kommt.

1. der Regen / aufhören
2. Max / uns abholen
3. unsere Freunde / ankommen
4. die Vorlesung / anfangen
5. die Buchhandlung / aufmachen

■ 7 ■ Übung: Was hat sie gefragt? Die Professorin spricht zu leise (*quietly*). Student A hört sie nicht richtig und fragt Studentin B, was sie gesagt hat. Studentin B antwortet.

BEISPIELE: Wann stehen Sie auf?
A: Was hat sie gefragt?
B: Sie hat gefragt, wann du aufstehst.

Kommt Bernd vorbei?
A: Was hat sie gefragt?
B: Sie hat gefragt, ob Bernd vorbeikommt.

1. Wann fängt das Semester an?
2. Kommt Ingrid vorbei?
3. Warum geht Regine weg?
4. Bringt Maria die Kinder mit?
5. Hört die Musik bald auf?
6. Mit wem geht Hans spazieren?
7. Wo steigt man in die Straßenbahn ein?
8. Wo steigen wir aus?
9. Wer macht das Fenster zu?

■ Order of clauses in the sentence

Subordinate clauses may either follow or precede the main clause.

1 2
Ich spreche langsam, da ich nicht viel Deutsch gelernt habe.

1 2
Da ich nicht viel Deutsch gelernt habe, spreche ich langsam.

Students have trouble mastering this structure. Stress that the two verbs are in immediate proximity, write more examples on board, refer to this page in subsequent chapters.

Additional practice, ask: **Was machen Sie, wenn Sie Zeit haben?** Students answer, **Wenn ich Zeit habe, ...** They may use cues from **Üb. 3,** p. 221.

When the subordinate clause comes first, the *entire* subordinate clause is considered the first element in the sentence. The verb of the main clause therefore follows it immediately in second position. The two inflected verbs are directly adjacent to each other, separated by a comma.

subordinate clause *main clause*
Wenn ich Zeit **habe**, **gehe** ich ins Museum.
Ob er sympathisch **ist**, **weiß** ich nicht.

■ 8 ■ Übung Ihr Professor hat Fragen, aber Sie wissen die Antworten nicht.

BEISPIEL: Wie ist das Wetter?
Wie das Wetter ist, weiß ich nicht.

1. Wer ist das?
2. Wem gehört das?
3. Wohin fährt er?
4. Was kostet das?
5. Wie heißt sie?
6. Warum ist er müde?
7. Wessen Koffer ist das?
8. Wen kennt sie?

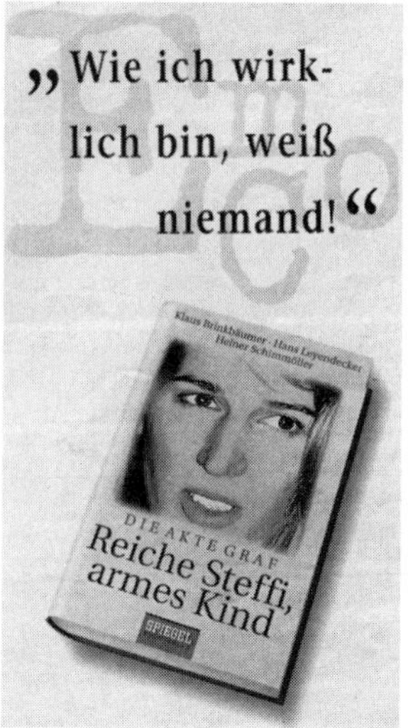

„Wie ich wirklich bin, weiß niemand!"
Die Akte Graf
Reiche Steffi, armes Kind

Üb. 9 variation: Students can supply different result clauses: **Da ich keine Zeit habe, komme ich nicht mit.**

9 **Übung: Ich mache heute keinen Stadtbummel.** You've decided not to take a stroll through town today. Use the cues below to explain why.

BEISPIEL: Es regnet noch.
Da es noch regnet, mache ich keinen Stadtbummel.

1. Ich habe keine Zeit.
2. Das Wetter ist schlecht.
3. Ich brauche nichts in der Stadt.
4. Ich gehe nicht gern allein.
5. Ich bin heute spät aufgestanden.
6. Ich habe zu viel Arbeit.

Infinitive constructions with zu

When used in a sentence, the German infinitive is frequently preceded by **zu**. For the most part, this construction parallels the use of the English infinitive with *to*:

One of the major changes in punctuation mandated by the spelling reform is the elimination of the comma setting off infinitive phrases with **zu**. However, commas may still be used to avoid misunderstandings: **Ich rate (,) ihm (,) zu helfen.**

Was gibt's hier **zu sehen**? — *What's there to see here?*
Hast du Zeit diesen Brief **zu lesen**? — *Do you have time to read this letter?*

Note especially the second sentence above. In German, the infinitive with **zu** comes at the end of its phrase. In English, the infinitive with *to* comes at the beginning of its phrase.

When a separable-prefix verb is used, the **zu** is inserted between the prefix and the stem infinitive.

ab**zu**fahren   spazieren **zu** gehen

Ich hoffe bald **abzufahren**. — *I hope to leave soon.*
Hast du Lust mit mir **spazieren zu gehen**? — *Would you like to go for a walk with me?*

Here are some cases in which the infinitive with **zu** is used:

- as a complement of verbs like **beginnen**, **anfangen**, **aufhören**, **helfen**, **hoffen**, **lernen**, **planen**, **scheinen**, and **vergessen**.

  Ich fange an **einen Brief zu schreiben**. — *I'm starting to write a letter.*
  Sie hofft **Geschichte zu studieren**. — *She's hoping to study history.*
  Ich habe vergessen **dir von meiner Reise zu erzählen**. — *I forgot to tell you about my trip.*

- as a complement of constructions like **Lust haben**, **Zeit haben**, and **Spaß machen**.

  Hast du Lust **einen Stadtbummel zu machen**? — *Do you want to take a walk through town?*
  Ich habe keine Zeit **einkaufen zu gehen**. — *I have no time to go shopping.*

- as a complement of many adjectives such as **dumm**, **einfach**, **schön**, and **wichtig**.

  Es ist sehr wichtig **das zu verstehen**. — *It's very important to understand that.*
  Es ist schön **dich wiederzusehen**. — *It's nice to see you again.*

Lab Manual Kap. 8, Var. zu Üb. 10, 13; Üb. 14.

Workbook Kap. 8, E, F.

■ 10 ■ Übung: Es macht mir Spaß ... Ihr Professor fragt, ob Sie etwas gerne machen. Antworten Sie ja oder nein.

BEISPIEL: Gehen Sie gern ins Museum?
Ja, es macht mir Spaß ins Museum zu gehen. (*oder*)
Nein, es macht mir keinen Spaß ins Museum zu gehen.

1. Trampen Sie gern?
2. Reisen Sie gern mit der Bahn?
3. Essen Sie gern im Restaurant?
4. Quatschen Sie gern am Telefon?
5. Spielen Sie gern Tennis?
6. Leben Sie gern in der Stadt?

■ 11 ■ Kettenreaktion: Was hast du vergessen? Sie haben alle vergessen etwas zu tun. Sagen Sie, was Sie vergessen haben, dann fragen Sie den nächsten Studenten.

BEISPIEL: A: Ich habe vergessen meine Hausaufgaben zu schreiben. Was hast du vergessen?
B: Ich habe vergessen ...

Diese Liste gibt Ihnen einige Möglichkeiten (*possibilities*):

to invite my friends	to shop
to order tickets	to buy potatoes
to order dessert	to show you my photographs

We prefer to continue to place a comma before **um ... zu** and **ohne ... zu**, although according to the spelling reform it is now optional.

■ Infinitives with *um ... zu* and *ohne ... zu*

um ... zu = *in order to*

Ich muss in die Stadt, **um Lebensmittel einzukaufen**.	*I have to go to town (in order) to buy groceries.*
Ich fahre nach Deutschland, **um Deutsch zu lernen**.	*I'm going to Germany in order to learn German.*

ohne ... zu = *without . . . -ing*

Sie ist abgefahren, **ohne mich zu besuchen**.	*She left without visiting me.*
Ich habe das Buch gelesen, **ohne es zu verstehen**.	*I read the book without understanding it.*

■ 12 ■ Übung Restate each sentence, changing the **weil**-clause to an **um ... zu** phrase and eliminating the modal verb and its subject.

BEISPIEL: Ich gehe in die Stadt, weil ich einkaufen will.
Ich gehe in die Stadt *um einzukaufen*.

1. Ich gehe ins Lokal, weil ich etwas essen will.
2. Sie sitzt am Fenster, weil sie die Straße sehen möchte.
3. Oft trampen Studenten, weil sie Geld sparen wollen.
4. Manchmal fährt man ins Ausland, weil man mehr lernen möchte.

■ 13 ■ Übung Sagen Sie, warum Sie etwas machen.

BEISPIEL: Warum gehen Sie zum Supermarkt?
Um Brot zu kaufen.

1. Warum gehen Sie zur Uni?
2. Warum gehen Sie nach Hause?
3. Warum arbeiten Sie diesen Sommer?
4. Warum sparen Sie Geld?
5. Warum rufen Sie Ihre Eltern an?
6. Warum gehen Sie ins Museum?

■ 14 ■ Übung Combine these sentences, changing the second one to an **ohne ... zu** phrase.

BEISPIEL: Er hat den Koffer genommen. Er hat mich nicht gefragt.
Er hat den Koffer genommen, ohne mich zu fragen.

1. Sie sind abgefahren. Sie haben nicht Auf Wiedersehen gesagt.
2. Ich arbeite in einem Geschäft. Ich kenne den Chef nicht.
3. Karin hat ein Zimmer gefunden. Sie hat nicht lange gesucht.
4. Geh nicht spazieren. Du trägst keinen Mantel.
5. Geh nicht weg. Du hast kein Frühstück gegessen.
6. Sie können nicht ins Konzert. Sie haben keine Karten gekauft.

Genitive case

The genitive case is the fourth and last case to be learned. It expresses possession (***John's** books*) or a relationship between two nouns marked in English by the preposition *of* (*the color **of your eyes***). Here are some examples of genitive phrases:

der Wagen **meiner Mutter**	***my mother's** car*
die Freunde **der Kinder**	***the children's** friends*
das Haus **meines Bruders**	***my brother's** house*
das Ende **des Tages**	*the end **of the day***
Egons Freundin	***Egon's** girlfriend*

Have students translate genitives in book titles.

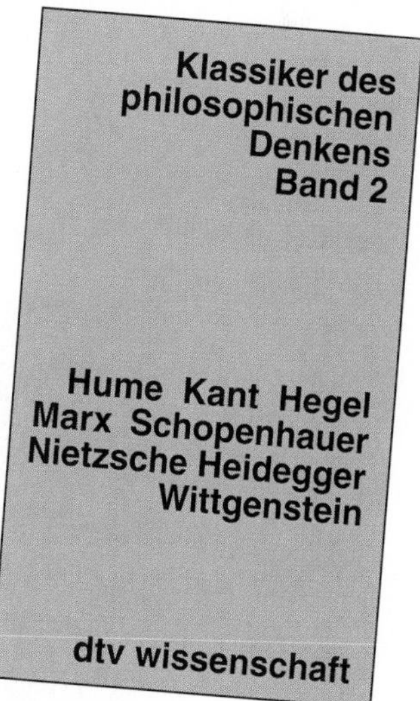

Review **der-** and **ein-**words on p. 191.

■ Forms of the genitive case

The **der**-words and the **ein**-words all share the same set of genitive endings. Nominative, accusative, and dative—the cases you have already learned—are included in the following table for comparison and review.

Table: Tell students that genitive of definite article is followed by various other **der-** and **ein-**words in the genitive in order to show that *all* have the same endings.

Genitive Case				
	masc.	neut.	fem.	plural
nom.	der Mann	das Kind	die Frau	die Leute
acc.	den Mann			
dat.	dem Mann	dem Kind	der Frau	den Leuten
gen.	-es -(e)s **des** Mann**es** **eines** Mann**es** **meines** Mann**es** **dieses** Mann**es**	-es -(e)s **des** Kind**es** **eines** Kind**es** **eures** Kind**es** **jedes** Kind**es**	-er **der** Frau **einer** Frau **Ihrer** Frau **welcher** Frau	-er **der** Leute **keiner** Leute **unserer** Leute **dieser** Leute

Notice in Dialogue 3, p. 216, **in der Nähe des Doms**; "**des Domes**" sounds archaic. Tell students they will gradually develop a feeling for this.

Review N-nouns on p. 171.

In addition to the genitive ending of the **der-** or **ein**-word, in the masculine and neuter singular *the noun itself adds the ending* **-s** (**des** Bahnhof**s**). Monosyllabic nouns such as **Mann** and **Kind** usually take the ending **-es** (**des** Mann**es**).

The masculine N-nouns, however, do *not* add an **-s** to the noun, but rather the same **-en** or **-n** ending as in the accusative and dative.

Kennen Sie die Freundin **meines Studenten**?	*Do you know my student's friend?*
Kennen Sie die Frau **dieses Herrn**?	*Do you know this gentleman's wife?*

Proper names ending in a sibilant (**-s**, **-ß**, **-x**, **-z**) add apostrophe rather than **s**: **Fritz' Hut**, **Marx' Werke**, **Strauß' Operetten**. This can be avoided with: **die Werke von Marx**, **die Operetten von Strauß**.

■ Use of the genitive case

In German, the genitive generally *follows* the noun it modifies, but in English, the possessive precedes the noun: **das Haus meines Bruders** (*my brother's house*). Proper names and kinship titles used as names, however, usually *precede* the nouns they modify, as in English: **Egons Freundin** (*Egon's girlfriend*), **Muttis Wagen** (*Mom's car*). Proper names simply add **-s** without an apostrophe in the genitive.

German uses the genitive case for both persons and things, whereas English usually reserves the possessive ending *'s* for people and animals and uses *of* for things.

das Haus **meiner Großmutter**	***my grandmother's** house*
die Häuser **der Stadt**	*the houses **of the city***

260.000 Langzeitarbeitslose eingestellt.

Nicht das Ende aller Probleme.

Aber ein wichtiger Schritt.

Lab Manual Kap. 8, Üb. 15; Var. zur Üb. 16.

Workbook Kap. 8, G, H.

Üb. 15: Stage 2: Contextualize forms by asking questions with these phrases used in expanded answer. I: **Wessen Haus ist das?** S: **Das ist das Haus eines Arztes. Wessen Mantel ... ?** etc. (Omit nos. 7, 11, 12). Note that in nos. 9 & 10 students must manipulate N-nouns for the first time.

■ 15 ■ Übung Change these noun phrases from nominative to genitive.

BEISPIEL: der Zug
des Zuges

1. ein Arzt
2. mein Freund
3. unser Vater
4. die Lehrerin
5. das Kind
6. die Leute
7. jede Uni
8. deine Mutter
9. der Student
10. dieser Herr
11. das Essen
12. diese Zimmer

Note on Usage: *von* + dative

German uses **von** + *dative* where English uses **of** + *possessive*:

a friend of my brother's	**ein Freund von meinem Bruder**
a cousin of mine	**eine Kusine von mir**
Is Max a friend of yours?	**Ist Max ein Freund von dir?**

Üb. 16: If students ask, tell them to think of these phrases as the subjects of potential sentences. Use nominative for the noun that is modified by the genitive phrase or by **von** + *dative* (nos. 17 & 18). Also good as written assignment. Have students use each phrase in a complete sentence.

Üb. 16: No. 12: Place names in the genitive may either precede or follow the noun they modify: **die Städte Europas** or **Europas Städte**.

■ 16 ■ Übung: Wie sagt man das auf Deutsch?

BEISPIEL: *your girlfriend's sister*
die Schwester deiner Freundin

1. the walls of my room
2. the end of the week
3. Karl's major
4. the children's pictures
5. the history of the war
6. his brother's house
7. her sister's boyfriend
8. the cities of Switzerland
9. a student's letter
10. the rooms of the house
11. Maria's students
12. the cities of Europe
13. the windows of this room
14. your mother's car
15. the history of these countries
16. Grandpa's clock
17. a friend of yours
18. a student of mine

■ Prepositions with the genitive

You've already memorized the accusative, dative, and two-way prepositions on pp. 102, 136, and 167. Remember that no prepositions take the nominative case.

In spoken German **trotz** and **wegen** are frequently used with the dative case, but the genitive is considered more correct, especially with **wegen**.

There is a small group of prepositions that take the genitive case.

statt or **anstatt**	*instead of*	Schreib eine Karte **statt eines Briefes**.
trotz	*in spite of, despite*	**Trotz des Wetters** sind wir ans Meer gefahren.
während	*during*	**Während der Woche** fährt er oft in die Stadt.
wegen	*because of, on account of*	**Wegen meiner Arbeit** kann ich nicht mitkommen.

Note: **Statt** and **anstatt** are interchangeable and equally correct.

Assign **Üb. 17** as written work. Remind students of word order: verb in second position immediately after prepositional phrase.

17 Übung Form prepositional phrases with the elements provided and give English equivalents. Then complete the sentences in your own words.

BEISPIEL: während / Sommer
während des Sommers (*during the summer*)
Während des Sommers habe ich gearbeitet.

1. trotz / Wetter
2. während / Ferien
3. statt / Stadtplan
4. wegen / mein / Mutter
5. wegen / mein / Studium
6. trotz / Arbeit
7. während / Tag
8. anstatt / Hotel

18 Übung: Warum tun Sie das? Ihre Professorin möchte wissen, warum Sie etwas tun. Sagen Sie es ihr. Die Liste von Gründen (*reasons*) hilft Ihnen.

BEISPIEL: Warum arbeiten Sie so viel?
Wegen meines Studiums.

Studium	Eltern	Wetter
Klausur	Schnee	Klima
Arbeit	Regen	Stress

1. Warum bleiben Sie heute zu Hause?
2. Warum wollen Sie im Süden wohnen?
3. Warum dürfen Sie heute Abend nicht mitkommen?
4. Warum brauchen Sie Ferien?
5. Warum brauchen Sie manchmal Aspirin?
6. Warum wollen Sie heute draußen sitzen?

Nouns of measure, weight, and number

German noun phrases indicating measure and weight do not use a preposition. Equivalent English phrases use *of*.

ein Glas Bier	*a glass* ***of*** *beer*
eine Flasche Wein	*a bottle* ***of*** *wine*
eine Tasse Kaffee	*a cup* ***of*** *coffee*
ein Kilo Kartoffeln	*a kilo* ***of*** *potatoes*
ein Liter Milch	*a liter* ***of*** *milk*
ein Stück Brot	*a piece* ***of*** *bread*
eine Portion Pommes frites	*an order* ***of*** *French fries*

Masculine and neuter nouns of measure *remain in the singular*, even following numerals greater than one.

See table of equivalent weights and measures on the inside of the back cover.

drei **Glas** Bier	*three glass**es** of beer*
zwei **Kilo** Kartoffeln	*two kilo**s** of potatoes*
vier **Stück** Brot	*four piece**s** of bread*

Feminine nouns of measure, however, *do* use their plural forms.

zwei Tass**en** Kaffee	*two cups of coffee*
drei Flasch**en** Wein	*three bottles of wine*
drei Portion**en** Pommes frites	*three orders of French fries*

Ordering in a restaurant is a communicative goal.

Variations: (1) Have students generate list of things one can drink (they know **Wasser, Milch, Bier, Wein, Kaffee**. You may want to add: **der Tee, der Saft**). Let one student be waiter, others place drink orders using **Tasse, Glas, Flasche** as appropriate.
(2) Make a shopping list together: **Was brauchen wir zum Abendessen?** This will generate amounts with **Liter, Kilo, Stück**.

Activities with destinations: use city map on p. 237 or photos in book for asking **Wohin gehen wir?**

Workbook Kap. 8, I.

■ 19 ■ Übung: Im Lokal Sie reisen mit einer Studentengruppe durch Deutschland und essen in einem Lokal. Die anderen in der Gruppe können kein Deutsch. Sie müssen der Kellnerin sagen, was sie bestellen wollen.

BEISPIEL: *I'd like a cup of coffee.*
Bringen Sie uns bitte eine Tasse Kaffee.

1. ... a glass of wine and two cups of coffee.
2. ... three glasses of water and two glasses of beer.
3. ... a bottle of wine and two orders of French fries.
4. ... three glasses of beer, two glasses of wine, and a cup of coffee.

Equivalents for English to

The all-purpose English preposition indicating destination is *to*: We're going *to Germany, to the ocean, to the train station, to the movies, to Grandma's.* German has several equivalents for English *to*, depending on the destination:

- Use **nach** with cities, states, and most countries.

Drill country and city destinations using endpaper maps. Books open, **Partnerarbeit** or instructor-directed **wohin** questions. Write exceptions with **in** on the board: **Schweiz, Türkei, Niederlande, Tschechische Republik**.

Wir fahren **nach Wien**.
nach Kalifornien.
nach Deutschland.
nach Europa.

and in the idiom: **nach Hause**.

Remember also that **an** + *acc.* signals motion toward a border, edge, or vertical surface: **Ich gehe ans Fenster/an die Tafel/an die Tür. Wir fahren ans Meer/an den See.** (Review p. 169.)

- Use **zu** with people and some locations.

Ich gehe **zu meinen Freunden**.
zu meiner Großmutter.
zum Arzt.
zum Bahnhof.
zur Buchhandlung.
zur Post (*to the post office*).

- Use **in** with countries whose names are feminine or plural, and with some locations.

Ich fahre **in die Schweiz**.
in die Bundesrepublik.
in die USA.

Wir gehen **ins Kino**.
ins Bett.
ins Konzert.
ins Museum.
ins Restaurant/ins Lokal.
ins Theater.
in die Stadt (*downtown*).
in die Kirche (*to church*).
in die Mensa.

With some destinations, **auf** + *acc.* is also used: **auf die Post, aufs Klo, auf mein Zimmer**.

Here is a rough rule-of-thumb for deciding whether to use **zu** or **in** with a destination within a city: **in** is usually used with destinations where one will spend a relatively long time (**ins Kino, in die Kirche, ins Bett**); **zu** is usually used with destinations involving a briefer visit (**zum Bahnhof, zur Post**).

■ 20 ■ **Übung: Wohin gehen Sie?** Antworten Sie auf Deutsch.

BEISPIEL: Wohin gehen Sie, wenn Sie einkaufen wollen?
Ich gehe in die Stadt.

1. Wohin gehen Sie, wenn Sie krank sind?
2. Wohin gehen Sie, wenn Sie mit der Bahn reisen?
3. Wohin gehen Sie, wenn Sie müde sind?
4. Wohin gehen Sie, wenn Sie Musik hören wollen?
5. Wohin gehen Sie, wenn Sie ein Buch kaufen wollen?
6. Wohin gehen Sie, wenn Sie Ihre Familie besuchen wollen?
7. Wohin gehen Sie, wenn Sie Hunger haben?
8. Wohin gehen Sie, wenn Sie einen Film sehen wollen?
9. Wohin gehen Sie, wenn Sie einen Brief schicken wollen?
10. Wohin gehen Sie, wenn Sie Kunst sehen wollen?

Vor dem Lesen

Tipps zum Lesen und Lernen

■ Tipp zum Vokabelnlernen

The topic of this chapter is **die Stadt**. Compound nouns with **Stadt** define various kinds of cities. You have already encountered, for example, **Altstadt**, the "old city" or medieval core of modern German cities. In the following reading, other kinds of cities are mentioned: **Großstadt**, **Kleinstadt**, and **Hafenstadt** (*port city*).

■ ■ ■ **Übung** Try to describe in German the following kinds of cities:

BEISPIEL: Industriestadt
Eine Stadt mit viel Industrie. (*oder*)
Eine Stadt, wo es viel Industrie gibt.

Touristenstadt
Universitätsstadt
Kulturstadt
Weltstadt
Ferienstadt

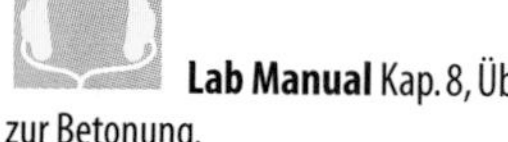

Lab Manual Kap. 8, Üb. zur Betonung.

■ Leicht zu merken

der **Aspekt, -e**	Aspekt
elegant	elegant
die **Generation, -en**	Generation
historisch	
katastrophal	katastrophal
die **Restauration, -en**	Restauration
der/die **Sozialarbeiter/in**	Sozialarbeiter
die **Tour, -en**	

■ Einstieg in den Text

The following reading is called **Aspekte der Großstadt**. In it, an American exchange student, a German social worker, and a German stone cutter talk about their lives in Hamburg, Munich, and Dresden. Before reading it, think about your own experiences in or impressions of cities. Write a few sentences in German about what you find good or bad about big cities.

Das Stadtleben

Das gefällt mir:	Das gefällt mir nicht:
______________________	______________________
______________________	______________________

Wortschatz 2

Verben

ärgern to annoy, offend
bauen to build
Rad fahren (fährt Rad), ist Rad gefahren to bicycle
Ski fahren (fährt Ski), ist Ski gefahren (*pronounced* „Schifahren") to ski
steigen, ist gestiegen to climb
zerstören to destroy

Substantive

der **Alltag** everyday life
der **Eindruck, ¨e** impression
der **Fußgänger, -** pedestrian
der **Hafen, ¨** port, harbor
der **Preis, -e** price

das **Jahrhundert, -e** century
(das) **München** Munich
das **Rad, ¨er** wheel; bicycle
das **Fahrrad, ¨er** bicycle
(das) **Russland** Russia

die **Ecke, -n** corner
an der Ecke at the corner
um die Ecke around the corner
die **Fußgängerzone, -n** pedestrian zone closed to vehicles
die **Großstadt, ¨e** large city (*over 500,000 inhabitants*)
die **Kleinstadt, ¨e** town (*5,000 to 20,000 inhabitants*)
die **Luft** air
die **Luftverschmutzung** air pollution

Adverbien

geradeaus straight ahead
links to *or* on the left
rechts to *or* on the right
trotzdem in spite of that, nevertheless

Andere Vokabeln

gar kein ... no . . . at all, not a . . . at all
obwohl (*sub. conj.*) although
viele (*pl. pronoun*) many people

Nützliche Ausdrücke

auf dem Land in the country (i.e., rural area)
aufs Land to the country
im Gegenteil on the contrary

Mit anderen Worten

riesengroß = sehr sehr groß

Ask students to guess the German word for *decade* (**das Jahrzehnt**), *millennium* (**das Jahrtausend**).

Links, **rechts**, and **geradeaus** are adverbs, *not* adjectives.

Aspekte der Großstadt

Learning about life in German cities is the cultural goal of this chapter.

Lab Manual Kap. 8, Lesestück.

Die meisten° Deutschen leben in Städten mit über 80 000 Einwohnern. Welche Vorteile und Nachteile° gibt es, wenn man in einer Großstadt wohnt?

Eindrücke eines Amerikaners

Mark Walker, Student: Dieses Jahr verbringe ich zwei Semester als Austauschstudent an der Universität Hamburg.[1] Da ich aus einer Kleinstadt in Colorado komme, schien° mir Hamburg zuerst riesengroß. Es war schwer zu verstehen, wie die Deutschen so dicht zusammengedrängt° leben können.

most
advantages and disadvantages
seemed
dicht zusammengedrängt = crowded together

1. A deep-water port on the Elbe River, population 1.7 million.

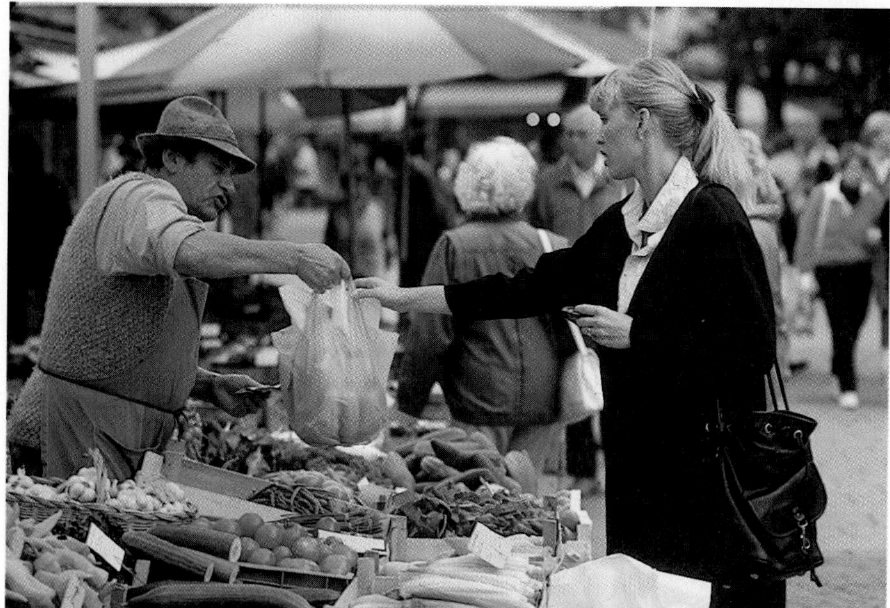

Einkaufen auf dem Markt (München)

Aber das heißt nicht, dass Hamburg mir nicht gefällt. Im Gegenteil! Ich finde es fantastisch, dass es in der Stadt so viel zu tun gibt. Wenn ich Lust habe, kann ich jeden Tag ins Konzert, ins Kino oder ins Museum gehen. Hamburg ist die zweitgrößte° Stadt der Bundesrepublik. Weil es eine Hafenstadt ist, gibt es seit Jahrhunderten Verbindungen° mit dem Ausland.

second largest

ties

Wenn das Stadtleben mir zu viel wird, dann ist es sehr leicht mein Fahrrad zu nehmen, in die Bahn zu steigen und aufs Land zu fahren. In der Lüneburger Heide[1] südlich von° Hamburg kann man schöne Radtouren machen. Dieser Kontrast zwischen Stadt und Land scheint mir typisch für Deutschland. Das Land ist den Einwohnern° der Städte sehr wichtig als Erholung° vom Stress des Alltags.

south of

inhabitants / relaxation

„Ich wohne gern hier"

Beate Kreuz, Sozialarbeiterin in München[2]: Ich arbeite mit Jugendlichen°. Sie haben oft keinen Schulabschluss° und können keine Arbeit finden. Ich sehe also jeden Tag die Probleme der Großstadt. Trotz dieser Probleme wohne ich sehr gerne hier. Obwohl die Wohnungsnot° schlimm ist, habe ich eine Wohnung in einem alten Gebäude finden können. Ich kann mit der S-Bahn° überall hinfahren° und brauche gar kein Auto. Im Sommer gehen wir in der Isar schwimmen oder im Englischen Garten[3] Rad fahren und im Winter fahren wir in den Alpen Ski. In der Kaufinger Straße gibt es eine große Fußgängerzone, wo viele gern einen Schaufensterbummel machen. An jeder Ecke gibt es ein elegantes Geschäft, aber in meinem Beruf sehe ich so viel Arbeitslosigkeit°, dass mich der Konsumzwang° und die hohen° Preise ärgern. Trotzdem kann man auch ohne sehr viel Geld in der Tasche relativ gut leben.

mit Jugendlichen = mit jungen Leuten / diploma

housing shortage

Stadtbahn = commuter rail service / **überall hin-** = everywhere

unemployment / pressure to buy / high

1. **Die Lüneburger Heide** (*heath*) is an extensive nature preserve on the North German plain between Hamburg and Hannover.
2. *Munich*: capital city of Bavaria (**Bayern**), population 1.2 million.
3. **Die Isar**: a tributary of the Danube. **Englischer Garten**: large park in the center of Munich designed by the American-born Benjamin Thompson, Count Rumford (1753–1814).

Aufbauarbeit° im Osten

Carsten Oberosler, 52; Steinmetz° in Dresden: Seit Generationen wohnen meine Vorfahren° in Sachsen°, aber meine Eltern sind erst nach dem Krieg nach Dresden[1] gekommen. Wie mein Vater bin ich Steinmetz und habe auch jahrelang° an der Restauration meiner Heimatstadt° gearbeitet.

Dresden war immer ein kunsthistorisches Juwel° Deutschlands, aber die eine Bombennacht° im Februar 1945 hat die ganze Innenstadt° zerstört. Bis heute haben wir immer noch nicht alles wiederaufgebaut° und dazu° bedroht° die katastrophale Luftverschmutzung Menschen und Gebäude. Ich bin aber optimistisch, weil die Stadt seit der Vereinigung Deutschlands 1990 endlich mehr Geld für die wichtige Restaurationsarbeit bekommt.

reconstruction work
stone cutter
Vorfahren = Eltern, Großeltern usw. / Saxony / for years / home town

jewel pronunciation: **Ju-wél**
night of bombing / center of the city / reconstructed / in addition / threatens

Nach dem Lesen

■ A ■ Antworten Sie auf Deutsch.

1. Woher kommt Mark Walker?
2. Wie gefällt ihm die Stadt Hamburg?
3. Was können die Menschen in der Stadt machen, wenn ihnen der Stress des Alltags zu viel wird?
4. Was ist Beate Kreuz von Beruf?
5. Warum braucht sie gar kein Auto?
6. Was macht sie in ihrer Freizeit im Sommer? im Winter?
7. Welche Probleme des Stadtlebens sieht sie in ihrer Arbeit?
8. Was ist Herr Oberosler von Beruf?
9. Warum ist seine Arbeit in einer Stadt wie Dresden besonders wichtig?

■ B ■ Wie ist es bei Ihnen zu Hause? Sie haben über drei deutsche Städte gelesen. Jetzt beschreiben Sie einem deutschen Freund den Ort, wo Sie wohnen. Geben Sie z.B. Informationen über diese Themen:

Größe (*size*)
Lage und Umgebung (*location and surroundings*)
Industrie
Kultur (Museen, Konzerte, Kinos usw.)
Geschäfte
Hochschulen

BEISPIEL: Boston ist eine Großstadt mit vielen Unis und Colleges. Es ist eine Hafenstadt und ist historisch sehr interessant. ...

Seals of the five new federal states created from the former German Democratic Republic; from left to right:
Mecklenburg-Vorpommern
Sachsen-Anhalt
Thüringen
Sachsen
Brandenburg

1. **Dresden** on the Elbe River is the capital of the federal state of Saxony (**Sachsen**). Under the 18th-century Saxon kings it reached its zenith as a center of art and culture. It is renowned for its beautiful public buildings and art treasures.

Situationen aus dem Alltag

Leave plenty of time for oral work with both parts of **Situationen aus dem Alltag**: city life & eating.

This vocabulary focuses on an everday topic or situation. Words you already know from **Wortschatz** sections are listed without English equivalents; new supplementary vocabulary is listed with definitions. Your instructor may assign some supplementary vocabulary for active mastery.

■ Unterwegs in der Stadt

Gebäude und Orte (*Buildings and places*)

die **Apotheke, -n**	*pharmacy*
die **Brücke, -n**	*bridge*
das **Café, -s**	*café*
die **Haltestelle, -n**	*streetcar or bus stop*
das **Kaufhaus, ¨er**	*department store*
die **Kirche, -n**	*church*
die **Konditorei, -en**	*pastry café*
die **Post**	*post office*
das **Rathaus, ¨er**	*city hall*

Verkehrsmittel (*Means of transportation*)

der **Bus, -se**	*bus*
das **Taxi, -s**	*taxicab*
die **Straßenbahn**	*streetcar*
die **U-Bahn**	*subway*

U-Bahn: short for **Untergrundbahn**.

City map provides a good review of equivalents of *to* (p. 231): **ins Hotel**, **zum Schwimmbad**, **zur Polizei**, **ins Kino**, etc.

Fragen wir nach dem Weg. (*Let's ask for directions.*)

Entschuldigung, wie komme ich **zur Post?**
... **zum Bahnhof?**

Das ist gleich in der Nähe.
Das ist nicht weit von hier.
Gehen Sie über die Straße und dann geradeaus.
... nach links.
... nach rechts.
... um die Ecke.

Asking directions is a communicative goal.

Assign one of these brief dialogues as written homework.

■ A ■ Partnerarbeit: Wie komme ich zu ... ? Partner A ist fremd in dieser Stadt. Er oder sie benutzt den Stadtplan, um nach dem Weg zu fragen. Partner B ist hier zu Hause und sagt Partner A den Weg durch die Stadt. Dann tauschen Sie die Rollen (**tauschen** = *exchange*).

1. Sie stehen vor der Post und wollen zum Marktplatz.
2. Sie sind im Museum und müssen zum Hotel zurück, um zu Mittag zu essen.
3. Sie sind in der Fußgängerzone und haben Hunger. Sie brauchen Hilfe (*help*), um ein Restaurant zu finden.

BAHNHOF
KAUFHAUS MEYER
POLIZEI
KONZERTHALLE
FUSSGÄNGERZONE
POST
RATHAUS
CAFÉ-KONDITOREI REIDEL
TAXI-STAND
ALTE BRÜCKE
MARKUS-KIRCHE
MARKTPLATZ
HOTEL SOMMERHOF
BUCHHANDLUNG TUCHOLSKY
KÖNIGSSTRASSE
SCHWIMMBAD (HIER KANN MAN SCHWIMMEN)
STADTMUSEUM
STRASSENBAHN LINIE 8
GLORIA-KINO
FLUSS
NEUE BRÜCKE
BUCHHANDLUNG STUDIOSUS
UNIVERSITÄT
RESTAURANT PRAGER HOF

■ B ■ Gruppendiskussion: Was machen wir denn morgen? Mit einer Studentengruppe machen Sie eine Reise durch Deutschland. Heute Abend sind Sie in einer Großstadt angekommen und übernachten im Hotel Sommerhof (siehe Stadtplan). Besprechen Sie, was Sie morgen machen wollen.

Wohin wollen wir gehen?
Was gibt es dort zu tun oder zu sehen?
Wo wollen wir essen?
Was machen wir denn am Abend?
Wie kommen wir hin (*get there*)? Zu Fuß, mit einem Taxi oder mit der Straßenbahn?

■ In der Konditorei

Am Tisch

Possible game: **Der Tisch ist gedeckt.** Have students look at the picture, learn the words for the objects on the table, then close their books and try to answer your questions: **Was liegt rechts vom Messer?** etc.

1. die Serviette, -n
2. die Gabel, -n
3. der Teller, -
4. das Messer, -
5. der Löffel, -
6. das Glas, ¨er
7. die Speisekarte, -n

Was gibt's zum Essen und zum Trinken?

Das wissen Sie schon:

das Bier
das Brot
das Brötchen, -
die Flasche, -n
der Kaffee
die Kartoffel, -n
der Käse
der Nachtisch
die Pommes frites
der Salat
die Tasse
das Wasser
der Wein
die Wurst

A **Konditorei** is a bakery-café serving pastries and sometimes light fare such as cold cuts and egg dishes.

Kaffee Hag is decaffeinated coffee; **Glühwein** is *hot mulled wine*; **Zitrone natur** is *fresh lemonade*; **Konfitüre** = **Marmelade**.

Auf der Speisekarte der Konditorei finden Sie auch:

die **Butter**	*butter*
das **Ei, -er**	*egg*
das **Eis**	*ice cream*
das **Kännchen, -**	*small (coffee or tea) pot*
der **Kuchen, -**	*cake*
die **Milch**	*milk*
die **Portion, -en**	*serving of, order of*
der **Saft, ¨e**	*juice*
die **Sahne**	*cream*
der **Schinken**	*ham*
der **Tee**	*tea*

❖ Café-Konditorei Reidel

Warme Getränke

Tasse Kaffee	2,30
Kännchen Kaffee	4,60
Tasse Mocca	4,40
Kännchen Mocca	5,40
Tasse Kaffee Hag.	2,40
Kännchen Kaffee Hag	4,80
Tasse Kakao mit Sahne	2,40
Kännchen Kakao mit Sahne	4,80
Glas Tee mit Milch oder Zitrone	2,30
Glas Tee mit Rum	4,50
Glas Pfefferminztee	2,30
Glas Grog von Rum 4 cl	5,00
Glas Glühwein 0,2 l	4,50
Glas heiße Zitrone	2,60

Eis und Eisgetränke

Portion gemischtes Eis	3,20
Portion gemischtes Eis mit Sahne	3,90
Früchte-Eisbecher „Florida"	6,50
Eis-Schokolade	4,00

Kalte Getränke

Flasche Mineralwasser	2,10
Flasche Coca Cola	2,10
Flasche Orangeade	2,10
Pokal Apfelsaft	2,40
Glas Orangensaft	2,80
Glas Tomatensaft	2,80
Glas Zitrone natur	2,60

Frühstück

Kleines Gedeck 1 Kännchen Kaffee, Tee od. Schokolade, 2 Brötchen, Butter, Konfitüre	6,00
Großes Gedeck 1 Kännchen Kaffee, Tee od. Schokolade, 2 Brötchen, Butter, Konfitüre, 1 gek. Ei, 1 Scheibe Schinken od. Käse	7,90

Ergänzung zum Frühstück

1 gekochtes Ei	1,00
1 Portion Konfitüre	0,80
1 Portion Butter	0,80
1 Scheibe Käse	1,60
1 Scheibe Schinken	1,80
1 Brötchen oder 1 Scheibe Brot	0,60

This should be a playful activity. Insist that students use no English and read the menu as well as they can. After five minutes, ask for each table's order from the waiters and waitresses.

Talking about food and ordering in a restaurant are communicative goals.

■ **C** ■ **Gruppenarbeit: In der Konditorei** (*3 oder 4 Personen*) Sie sitzen zusammen in der Café-Konditorei Reidel und bestellen etwas zu essen und trinken. Jemand in der Gruppe spielt den Kellner oder die Kellnerin. Die anderen bestellen von der Speisekarte.

Wo gehen wir hin?
Essen & Trinken · Freizeit & Unterhaltung

Zum Schluss

Lab Manual Kap. 8, Diktat.

Workbook Kap. 8, J–L.

You can also use phrases such as **nach meiner Vorlesung** and **vor dem Frühstück**.

Sprechen wir miteinander!

■ A ■ Übung: Wann machen Sie das? Ihr Professor fragt, wann Sie etwas machen. Die Liste der Zeitangaben (*time phrases*) hilft Ihnen mit der Antwort.

BEISPIEL: Wann haben Sie Zeit eine Reise zu machen?
Während der Ferien. / Im Sommer. / usw.

am	*im*	*während*
Morgen	Frühling	Woche
Abend	Herbst	Ferien
Wochenende	Winter	Vorlesung
Montag (usw.)	Januar (usw.)	Konzert

1. Wann gehen Sie zur Deutschstunde?
2. Wann haben Sie Zeit einzukaufen?
3. Wann schreiben Sie Briefe?
4. Wann schlafen Sie gern?
5. Wann haben Sie Lust ins Ausland zu fahren?
6. Wann haben Sie keine Zeit ins Kino zu gehen?

■ B ■ Partnerarbeit: Wie findest du das? On the left are some adjectives you can use to describe your attitude toward the activities listed on the right. Take turns telling each other what you think.

Stage 2: Students cover either right or left column and generate their own sentences. Left column covered: **Wie findest du es ins Museum zu gehen?** Right column covered: **Was findest du fantastisch?**

BEISPIEL: Ich finde es wunderschön schwimmen zu gehen.

altmodisch	einen Stadtbummel zu machen
bequem	Deutsch zu lernen
barbarisch	schwimmen zu gehen
blöd	Hausaufgaben zu schreiben
einfach	meine Eltern anzurufen
fantastisch	um 6 Uhr aufzustehen
furchtbar	Frühstück zu essen
gut	Romane zu lesen
interessant	ins Museum zu gehen
klug	Geld zu sparen
leicht	im Sommer zu arbeiten
nett	Freunde einzuladen
schwierig	Kaffee zu trinken
stinklangweilig	ein Zimmer zu finden

C. Variation: Use **Bruder** or **Eltern** as reference points: **Das ist das Fahrrad seiner Schwester. Das ist der Rucksack ihrer Tochter**, etc.

■ C ■ Partnerarbeit: Wessen ... ist das? Pictured below are Ute's family and some things that belong to them. Take turns asking what belongs to whom.

BEISPIEL: Wessen Buch ist das?
Das ist das Buch ihrer Schwester.

■ D ■ Gruppenarbeit: Warum tust du das? Ask each other why you do certain things. Answer with an **um ... zu** phrase.

BEISPIEL: A: Warum gehst du in die Altstadt?
B: Um einen Schaufensterbummel zu machen.

Implement as a **Kettenreaktion** or with one student asking the questions from open book.

1. Warum gehst du ins Wasser?
2. Warum lernst du Deutsch?
3. Warum fahren Studenten oft per Autostopp?
4. Warum bringt man eine Kamera mit, wenn man reist?
5. Warum fährt man im Winter in die Alpen?
6. Warum rufst du deine Freunde an?

■ E ■ Partnerarbeit: Warum machst du das gern? Jetzt fragen Sie andere Studenten in der Klasse, was sie gern machen und warum. Sie antworten mit **um ... zu** oder **weil**.

BEISPIEL: So fängt es an:
A: Was machst du denn gern?
B: Ich gehe oft gern in die Stadt.
A: Warum?
B: *Um* ins Kino *zu* gehen. (*oder*)
Weil ich gern ins Kino gehe.

Schreiben Sie zu Hause.

In exercises F and G avoid using adjectives attributively (before nouns). Attributive adjectives need endings that are taught in Kap. 9.

F **Die ideale Stadt** Sie sind Städteplaner/in von Beruf und kennen viele Städte. Einige haben Ihnen sicher gefallen, einige nicht. Jetzt dürfen Sie die ideale Stadt planen. Beschreiben Sie diese Stadt. Was würde sie haben, was würde sie nicht haben? Warum?

G **Ein Brief nach Hause** Sie kennen schon die Stadt auf Seite 237. Sie haben den Tag dort verbracht. Jetzt sitzen Sie am Abend im Hotel und schreiben einen Brief nach Hause. Beschreiben Sie Ihrer Familie, wie der Tag war. Was sind Ihre Eindrücke von der Stadt und von den Menschen?

H **Wie sagt man das auf Deutsch?**

With this chapter you have completed the second quarter of ***Neue Horizonte***. For a concise review of the grammar and idiomatic phrases in chapters 5–8, you may consult the **Zusammenfassung und Wiederholung 2** (*Summary and Review 2*) of your Workbook. The review section is followed by a self-correcting test.

1. Can you please tell me where the cathedral is?
2. It isn't far from here. If you go around the corner, you'll see it.
3. Thanks very much.

4. What do you do when city life gets too stressful for you?
5. Sometimes I go to the country and go for a walk.

6. Do I still have time to go shopping?
7. Yes, of course. If we can go right away, I'll come along.
8. My brother's girlfriend has a birthday tomorrow and I want to give her something.

9. During the week I don't have time to go to the museum.
10. Therefore I'd like to stay here until it closes.

In der Natur vergisst man den Stress des Alltags.

Videoecke

4 Gehen wir doch einkaufen! (13:19)

Die Metzgerei schließt um 18.00 Uhr.

*Katrin und Stefan müssen für ein Picknick Lebensmittel einkaufen. Das Wetter sieht aber nicht gut aus. Sie müssen laufen, denn es regnet vielleicht am Nachmittag. Sie gehen zuerst zum Tante-Emma-Laden (*Mom and Pop grocery store*) und finden dort fast alles. Es ist schon 18.00 Uhr und die Läden in der Stadt haben zugemacht. Also müssen sie zum Türkenmarkt (*open-air Turkish market*); dort kann man nach 18.00 Uhr noch einkaufen.*

Wortschatz zum Video

empfehlen	*to recommend*
probieren	*to sample, try*
schmecken	*to taste; to taste good*
wünschen	*to wish for, want to have*
die Flasche, -n	*bottle*
das Pfund	*500 grams (about 1 pound)*
die Tüte, -n	*paper bag; small cardboard carton*
welch-?	*which?*
Welchen Käse können Sie mir empfehlen?	*Which cheese can you recommend to me?*
Ich hätte gern ...	*I'd like to have . . .*
Könnt' ich ...	*Could I . . .*
Das war's.	*That's it. That's everything.*

A **Was sehen Sie im Video?** Watch the video episode (13:25–16:41) once without sound. Check off in the list below what you see in the video.

Das habe ich gesehen:

____ 1. einen Bus
____ 2. ein Kind auf einem Dreirad (*tricycle*)
____ 3. eine Bäckerei
____ 4. Zeitungen
____ 5. Frau Bachmann
____ 6. einen Regenschirm
____ 7. ein Computergeschäft
____ 8. Geld

B **Wer sagt das?**

Choose the person who says the following.

a. Katrin b. Stefan c. Verkäuferin im Laden
d. Verkäufer am Türkenmarkt

1. ____ sagt: „Ich komm' mit. Gehen wir doch zusammen einkaufen."
2. ____ sagt: „Du kaufst den Orangensaft, ich kaufe den Käse und die Leberwurst."
3. ____ fragt: „Welches Brot wünschen Sie bitte?"
4. ____ fragt: „Welcher Saft schmeckt besser?"
5. ____ sagt: „Das war's."
6. ____ sagt: „Wir gehen zum Türkenmarkt. Der hat länger offen."
7. ____ sagt: „Sechs Mark und achtzig."

C **Einkaufsliste** (Shopping list) Watch what Katrin and Stefan buy. Then fill in their shopping list with the amounts they need. What are these items in English?

	English
________ Brot	____________
________ Leberwurst	____________
________ Käse	____________
________ Orangensaft	____________
________ gegrilltes Hähnchen	____________

■ D ■ Die Metzgerei hat schon zugemacht. Use the shop sign pictured on page 243 to answer these questions.

1. An welchen Tagen kann man hier nicht einkaufen?
2. Wann macht das Geschäft am Mittwoch auf?
3. An welchem Tag macht das Geschäft um 13.00 Uhr zu?
4. Bis wann ist das Geschäft am Donnerstag auf?

■ E ■ Was haben Sie gesehen? Read through the list below. Then watch the **Welle Magazin** (16:43–18:14) and check off the words you have seen.

____ 1. Taxi
____ 2. Anprobe (*fitting room*)
____ 3. Lederjacke (*leather jacket*)
____ 4. Sparpreise (*low prices*)
____ 5. Parkhaus (*parking garage*)
____ 6. Ausgang (*exit*)
____ 7. Toiletten (*rest rooms*)
____ 8. Kasse (*cashier*)

See if students can read words printed in Fraktur.

SEIT 1390
HISTORICHES
Hotel-Restaurant
Goldener Adler
GOETHE-STUBE · BATZENHÄUSL
Besitzer · Familie Cammerlander
Direktion Karl Pokorny
6020 INNSBRUCK
Herzog Friedrich Str. 6. Tel. 26 3 34

Mit dem Bus durch Berlin

Most German cities have superb public transportation systems that make it easy to get around. Berlin, for instance, has a comprehensive system of subways, buses, streetcars, and commuter trains. These pages from a brochure give information about touring the city with the double-decker buses of the **BVG** (Berlin's public transportation authority). The map of bus line 100 (**die Hunderter Linie**) through the heart of Berlin (**Berlin Mitte**) and the accompanying photos show points of interest along the route. These include the Brandenburg Gate (**das Brandenburger Tor**) and Museum Island (**die Museumsinsel**).

Map activity: Students work in pairs. They are staying near the Klosterstr. subway station. They must decide how to reach Bus Line 100, what they want to see along the route, and where they need to get out. The descriptions of sights can be used as an exercise in extracting information from an advanced text. Students can correlate headwords and photos, then understand names like Mendelssohn-Bartholdy, words like **Rokoko**, and phrases like **Symbol für die Einheit Deutschlands** and **im Krieg zerstört**.

8

Brandenburger Tor

Wahrzeichen für die Stadt Berlin und seit dem Mauerfall auch Symbol für die Einheit Deutschlands. 1788-91 wurde das Brandenburger Tor von Langhans nach antikem Vorbild erbaut. 1793 wurde Schadows Quadriga mit der Siegesgöttin aufgestellt.

9

Staatsoper Unter den Linden

Die Lindenoper feierte 1992 ihr 250-jähriges Jubiläum. Mendelssohn-Bartholdy, Furtwängler und Richard Strauss feierten hier große künstlerische Triumphe. Der 1742 eingeweihte Knobelsdorf-Bau ist ein Zeugnis des norddeutschen Rokoko.

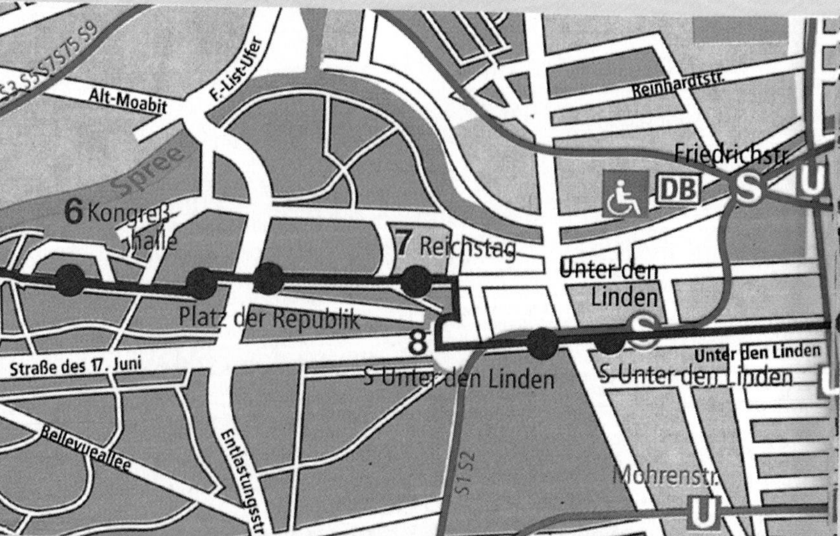

Berliner Dom

Im Stil der Neorenaissance wurde die Hofkirche der Hohenzollern in den Jahren 1893 bis 1905 erbaut. Im Krieg stark zerstört, wurde der größte Kirchenbau Berlins 1993 nach 18jähriger Renovierung wiedereröffnet. Hörenswert sind die Konzerte auf der historischen Orgel des Doms.

100% Berlin.
Auf der ganzen Linie.

BVG Gut für Sie. Und Berlin.

Museumsinsel

Zwischen dem Alten Museum und dem Bodemuseum erstreckt sich auf einer Insel zwischen Spree und Kupfergraben einer der weltweit bedeutendsten Museumskomplexe. Unter anderem befindet sich hier auch das Pergamonmuseum. Attraktionen sind der beeindruckende Pergamon-Altar und das berühmte Markttor von Milet. Nehmen Sie sich Zeit für einen Spaziergang in einer Welt von Kunst und Geschichte.

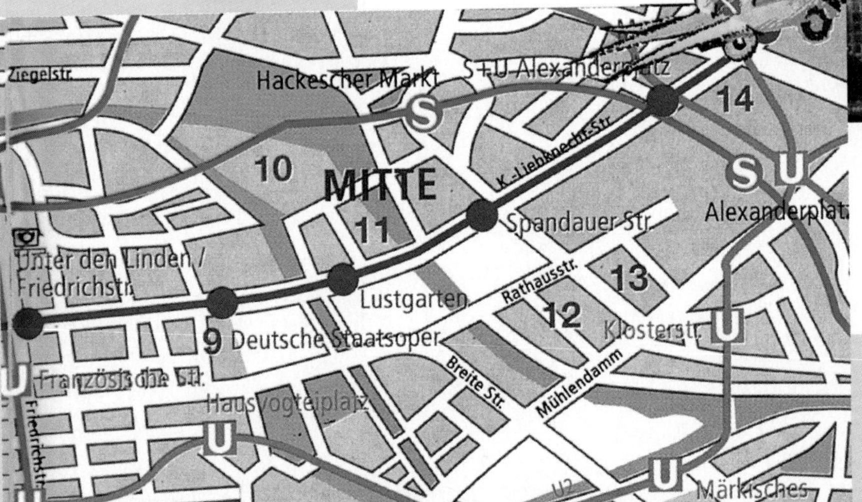

KAPITEL 9

Unsere Umwelt

Communicative Goals

- Using adjectives to describe things
- Giving the date
- Discussing ecology and recycling
- Talking about sports

Cultural Goal

- Learning about German and global environmental issues

Chapter Outline

- **Lyrik zum Vorlesen**
  Jürgen Werner, „Die Lorelei 1973"
- **Grammatik**
  Attributive adjectives and adjective endings
  Word order of adverbs: Time/manner/place
  Ordinal numbers and dates
- **Lesestück**
  Unsere Umwelt in Gefahr
- **Situationen aus dem Alltag**
  Der Sport
- **Almanach**
  Seid ihr schlaue Umweltfüchse?

Dialoge

Lab Manual Kap. 9, Dialoge, Fragen, Hören Sie gut zu!

Haus also = *apartment house, building*.

Discussing recycling is a communicative goal.

Pronunciation practice: Use dialogues to review voiced vs. unvoiced **s**: **Recycling; mit dem riesengroßen Sack; Altglas im Haus sammeln; alle Häuser; ein großer Fortschritt; Geburtstagsgeschenk; ein neues Fahrrad; sowieso; sag mal**.

Recycling in unserem Wohnhaus

Frau Berg trifft Herrn Reh auf der Treppe.

FR. BERG: Mensch, wohin mit dem riesengroßen Sack?
HR. REH: In den Keller. Die neuen Container sind da. Jetzt können wir Altglas und Altpapier hier im Haus sammeln.
FR. BERG: Na, endlich! Jetzt brauche ich meinen Müll nicht mehr zum Recycling zu schleppen.
HR. REH: Ja, das ist jetzt nicht mehr nötig. Wenn alle mitmachen, dann ist das ein großer Fortschritt.

Ein umweltfreundliches Geburtstagsgeschenk

DANIEL: Was hat dir Marianne zum Geburtstag geschenkt?
FRANK: Ein neues Fahrrad, weil wir unseren Zweitwagen verkauft haben.
DANIEL: Wieso denn?
FRANK: Er war ja sowieso kaputt, und da wir in die Stadt umgezogen sind, kann ich mit dem Rad zur Arbeit fahren.
DANIEL: Da sparst du aber viel Geld.
FRANK: Ja, und ich habe auch ein gutes Gefühl, weil ich etwas gegen die Luftverschmutzung mache.

Treibst du Sport?

Talking about sports is a communicative goal.

Point out the 9 noun phrases in the dialogues containing attributive adjective endings.

Dialogue 1: Point out that **da** often means *here* rather than *there*: **Da sind wir** = *Here we are*. ***Die Post ist schon da*** = *The mail is here*.

JUNGE: Sag mal, treibst du gern Sport?
MÄDCHEN: Klar. Ich verbringe das ganze Wochenende auf dem Tennisplatz. Spielst du auch Tennis?
JUNGE: Ja, das ist mein Lieblingssport, aber ich bin kein guter Spieler.
MÄDCHEN: Da kann ich dir einen wunderbaren Tennislehrer empfehlen.

Notes on Usage: Adverb **da** and flavoring particle **aber**

***The adverb* da** At the beginning of a clause, the adverb **da** often means *then, in that case, under those circumstances, for that reason*:

Da sparst du aber viel Geld.
Da kann ich dir einen wunderbaren Tennislehrer empfehlen.

***The flavoring particle* aber** As a flavoring particle, **aber** is often used to intensify a statement. It adds the sense of *really, indeed*.

Da sparst du **aber** viel Geld. — *Then you'll **really** save a lot of money.*

The particle **aber** can add a note of surprise or admiration:

Mensch, das ist **aber** teuer! — *Wow, that's **really** expensive!*

Wortschatz 1

Recycling: Model German pronunciation for students.

Verben

empfehlen (empfiehlt), hat empfohlen to recommend
mit·machen to participate, cooperate
sammeln to collect
schleppen (*colloq.*) to drag, lug (along), haul
treffen (trifft), hat getroffen to meet
treiben, hat getrieben to drive, force, propel
  Sport treiben to play sports
um·ziehen, ist umgezogen to move, change residence

Substantive

der **Container, -** large trash container
der **Fortschritt, -e** progress
der **Geburtstag, -e** birthday
  zum Geburtstag for (your/her/my/etc.) birthday
der **Junge, -n, -n** boy
der **Keller, -** cellar, basement
der **Müll** trash, refuse
der **Sack, ¨-e** sack
der **Sport** sport
der **Tennisplatz, ¨-e** tennis court
der **Zweitwagen, -** second car

das **Gefühl, -e** feeling
das **Geschenk, -e** present
das **Mädchen, -** girl
das **Papier, -e** paper
das **Recycling** recycling; recycling center
das **Tennis** tennis
das **Wohnhaus, ¨-er** apartment building

die **Treppe** staircase, stairs
  auf der Treppe on the stairs
die **Umwelt** environment
die **Verschmutzung** pollution

Fortschritt: Usually used in plural for progress of individual: **Du machst gute Fortschritte.**

Adjektive und Adverbien

ganz whole, entire
  das ganze Wochenende all weekend, the whole weekend
kaputt (*colloq.*) broken, kaput; exhausted
klar clear; (*colloq.*) sure, of course
nötig necessary
schmutzig dirty
sportlich athletic
umweltfreundlich environmentally safe, non-polluting
zweit- second

The word **kaputt** comes from a French cardplaying term, *être capot: "to lose all the tricks, be wiped out."*

zweit- must have an adjective ending. See pp. 253–256 below. It can also be a prefix, as in **Zweitwagen**.

Aktion Saubere Landschaft e. V.
Oskar-Walzel-Straße 17, 5300 Bonn

Note restricted meaning: *Container* is otherwise **der Behälter**. You may also want to teach: *wastebasket*, **der Papierkorb**; *garbage can*, **der Mülleimer**.

Recycling in Our Apartment Building

Ms. Berg meets Mr. Reh on the stairs.

MS. B: Wow, where to with that huge sack?
MR. R: To the cellar. The new trash containers are here. Now we can collect (old) glass and waste paper here in the building.
MS. B: At last! Now I don't have to haul my trash to the recycling center anymore.
MR. R: Yes, that's not necessary anymore. If everyone participates, then that's great progress.

An Ecological Birthday Present

D: What did Marianne give you for your birthday?
F: A new bicycle, because we sold our second car.
D: How come?
F: It was kaput anyway, and since we've moved to the city, I can ride my bike to work.
D: Then you're saving a lot of money.
F: Yes, and it also feels good to be doing something about air pollution.

Do You Play Sports?

BOY: Hey, do you like to play sports?
GIRL: Sure. I spend all weekend on the tennis court. Do you play tennis too?
BOY: Yes, that's my favorite sport, but I'm not a good player.
GIRL: Then I can recommend a wonderful tennis instructor to you.

Andere Vokabeln

Lieblings- (*noun prefix*) favorite
Lieblingssport favorite sport
was für ... ? what kind of . . . ?
wieso? How come? How's that? What do you mean?

Nützlicher Ausdruck

na endlich! at last! high time!

Gegensätze

nötig ≠ **unnötig** necessary ≠ unnecessary
schmutzig ≠ **sauber** dirty ≠ clean

Mit anderen Worten

dreckig (*colloq.*) = **schmutzig**

schmutzig: cognate is *smutty*.

Variationen

■ A ■ Persönliche Fragen

1. Ist man in Ihrem Studentenwohnheim umweltfreundlich? Was macht man da für die Umwelt?
2. Auch als Hobby kann man Dinge sammeln, z.B. Briefmarken (*stamps*), Münzen (*coins*) oder CDs. Sammeln Sie etwas? Was?
3. Frau Berg hat früher ihren Müll zum Recycling geschleppt. Was müssen Sie jeden Tag (z.B. in Ihrem Rucksack) mitschleppen?
4. Zum Geburtstag hat Frank ein neues Fahrrad bekommen. Was würden Sie gern zum Geburtstag bekommen?
5. Besitzt Ihre Familie einen Zweitwagen? Braucht sie wirklich zwei Wagen?
6. Fährt jemand in Ihrer Familie mit dem Rad zur Arbeit? Wenn nicht, warum nicht?
7. Meinen Sie, dass die Luftverschmutzung hier ein Problem ist? Wie ist die Luft bei Ihnen zu Hause?
8. Treiben Sie Sport? Wie oft in der Woche?
9. Was ist Ihr Lieblingssport? Lieblingsfilm? Lieblingsbuch? Und Ihre Lieblingsstadt?

■ B ■ Warum ich Geld brauche.

Sagen Sie, warum Sie Geld brauchen.

BEISPIEL: Warum brauchen Sie Geld?
Ich brauche Geld, *um* ein Rad *zu* kaufen.

Review colors introduced on p. 89 in preparation for adjective endings.

C **Welche Farbe hat das?** Sagen Sie, welche Farbe diese Dinge haben.

BEISPIEL: Welche Farbe hat Georgs Hemd?
Es ist rot.

Welche Farbe hat/haben ...

der Wald?
der Kaffee?
das Meer?
die Wände dieses Zimmers?
die Bluse dieser Studentin?
der Wein?
das Hemd dieses Jungen?
diese Landkarte?
die Bäume im Sommer? im Herbst?
Ihr Pulli?

Lyrik zum Vorlesen

Lab Manual Kap. 9, Lyrik zum Vorlesen.

Um diese Parodie zu verstehen muss man „Die Loreley" von Heinrich Heine schon kennen. Lesen Sie noch einmal Heines Gedicht (*poem*) auf Seiten 219–220 und dann diesen Text.

Many words are not glossed here because they are the same as in Heine's poem. Some new active vocabulary comes from **Wortschatz 2** of this chapter.

Albtraum (*nightmare*) is an old word related to English elf and suggesting a terrifying vision. It has nothing to do with the mountains (**die Alpen**).

Die Lorelei 1973

Ich weiß nicht, was soll es bedeuten,
dass ich so traurig bin;
ein Albtraum° aus unseren Zeiten, — nightmare
er geht mir nicht aus dem Sinn.

Die Luft ist schwül° und verdunkelt, — close, heavy
und dreckig fließt der Rhein;
kein Gipfel des Berges funkelt,
wo sollt' auch die Sonne sein?

Am Ufer° des Rheines sitzt sie, — bank
die deutsche Chemie-Industrie;
dort braut° sie gefährliche Gifte°, — brews / poisons
die Luft macht erstickend° sie. — suffocating

Sie kümmert sich nicht um° den Abfall°, — **kümmert ...** = doesn't care about / garbage
der° aus den Rohren° fließt; — / that / pipes
er kommt aus dem chemischen Saustall°, — pigsty
wo er in den Rhein sich ergießt°. — **sich ...** = pours

Dem Schiffer im Tankerschiffe,
ihm macht das Atmen Müh'°; — **ihm ...** = has trouble breathing
er schaut nicht die Felsenriffe,
er schaut nur die dreckige Brüh'°. — slop

Ich weiß, die Wellen verschlingen
einst° nicht nur Schiffer und Kahn; — some day
und das hat mit ihren Giften
die Industrie getan.

Jürgen Werner (geboren 1939)

Grammatik

Attributive adjectives and adjective endings

Predicate adjectives versus attributive adjectives

Adjectives in both English and German are used in one of two ways:

- They may follow "linking" verbs such as *to be, to become, to remain,* and *to seem* (**sein**, **werden**, **bleiben**, **scheinen**), in which case they are called *predicate adjectives* because they constitute the second part of the predicate. Most of the adjectives you have encountered in this book have been predicate adjectives.

Das Rad ist **neu**.	*The bicycle is* ***new****.*
Meine Großeltern werden **alt**.	*My grandparents are getting* ***old****.*
Der Kaffee ist **heiß**.	*The coffee is* ***hot****.*

  Predicate adjectives in German have *no endings.*

- Adjectives may also occur *before* a noun. In this position they are called *attributive adjectives.*

das **neue** Rad	*the* ***new*** *bicycle*
meine **alten** Großeltern	*my* ***old*** *grandparents*
heißer Kaffee	***hot*** *coffee*

  German attributive adjectives *always* have endings.

EIN NEUES DENKEN FÜR EINE NEUE ZEIT

The noun phrase

Attributive adjectives occur in noun phrases. A noun phrase consists of a noun and the words directly associated with it. English and German noun phrases have similar structures. They typically consist of three types of words: *limiting words, attributive adjectives*, and *nouns*.

Limiting words are the **der**-words and **ein**-words you already know:

Ein is both a limiting word (an indefinite article) and a cardinal number. Cardinal numbers from **zwei** on are *not* limiting words and thus are followed by primary endings: **Ich kenne zwei nette Studenten.**

der-*words*	**ein-*words***	
der	ein	
dieser	kein	
jeder	mein	possessive adjectives
welcher	dein	possessive adjectives
alle	sein	possessive adjectives
	ihr	possessive adjectives
	unser	possessive adjectives
	euer	possessive adjectives
	ihr	possessive adjectives

These words are called "limiting words" because they *limit* the noun in some way rather than describing it: ***dieses*** **Fahrrad** (***this*** *bicycle, not that one*), ***meine*** **Großeltern** (***my*** *grandparents, not yours*).

Here are some examples of noun phrases. Note that the noun phrase does not necessarily contain both a limiting word and an attributive adjective.

limiting word +	*attributive adjective* +	*noun*	
das	neue	Fahrrad	*the new bicycle*
jede		Woche	*every week*
alle	deutschen	Studenten	*all German students*
	heißer	Kaffee	*hot coffee*
meine	kleine	Schwester	*my little sister*

Alle is usually plural and takes the primary plural endings. Adjectives that follow it take the secondary plural endings: **alle deutschen Studenten**. When **alle** is followed by a second limiting word, however, they both take the same primary ending: **alle meine Freunde, alle diese Leute**.

German adjective endings have acquired the reputation of being a formidable obstacle for the learner. However, the system is conceptually quite simple and just requires practice until it becomes automatic in spoken German. To be able to use attributive adjectives, you need to know only two sets of endings—called the *primary endings* and the *secondary endings*—and three rules for their use. Half of the system is already familiar to you: the primary endings are simply the endings of the **der**-words that show gender, number, and case.

Primary Endings

	masc.	neut.	fem.	plur.
nom.	-er	-es	-e	-e
acc.	-en	-es	-e	-e
dat.	-em	-em	-er	-en
gen.	-es	-es	-er	-er

There are only two secondary endings, **-e** and **-en**. They occur in the following pattern:

Secondary Endings

	masc.	neut.	fem.	plur.
nom.	-e	-e	-e	-en
acc.	-en	-e	-e	-en
dat.	-en	-en	-en	-en
gen.	-en	-en	-en	-en

Note that the **-en** occurs *throughout the plural* as well as *throughout the dative and genitive cases.*

Rules for the use of adjective endings

1. Noun phrases with adjectives must have a primary ending, either on the limiting word, or on the adjective itself. When the limiting word takes a primary ending, the adjective that follows it takes a secondary ending.

limiting word with primary ending	+	*attributive adjective with secondary ending*	+	*noun*	
dies**es**		schön**e**		Bild	*this beautiful picture*
mit mein**er**		gut**en**		Freundin	*with my good friend*

2. If the noun phrase has no limiting word or has an **ein**-word without an ending, then the attributive adjective takes the primary ending.[1]

no limiting word or ***ein****-word without ending*	+	*attributive adjective with primary ending*	+	*noun*	
		alt**e**		Häuser	*old houses*
		heiß**er**		Kaffee	*hot coffee*
ein		alt**es**		Haus	*an old house*

The following examples contrast noun phrases with and without limiting words. Note how the primary ending shifts from the limiting word to the adjective when there is no limiting word:

dies**e** neu**en** Tennisplätze →	neu**e** Tennisplätze
mit mein**em** österreichisch**en** Geld →	mit österreichisch**em** Geld
welch**es** deutsch**e** Bier →	deutsch**es** Bier

3. Attributive adjectives in succession have the same ending.

ein groß**es** alt**es** Haus	*a large old house*
groß**e** alt**e** Häuser	*large old houses*
gut**er** deutsch**er** Wein	*good German wine*

Pay special attention to the three instances in which **ein**-words have no endings. They are the *only* instances in which **ein**-word endings differ from **der**-word endings.

masculine nominative	*neuter nominative and accusative*
ein alt**er** Mann	ein klein**es** Kind
but	*but*
d**er** alt**e** Mann	dies**es** klein**e** Kind

1. There is one exception to rule 2: In the masculine and neuter genitive singular, the attributive adjective not preceded by a limiting word takes the *secondary ending* **-en** rather than the primary ending.

trotz tief**en** Schnee**s**	*in spite of deep snow*
wegen schlecht**en** Wetter**s**	*because of bad weather*

Such phrases are quite rare. Moreover, note that the primary ending *is* present on the noun itself.

Adjectives whose basic forms end in unstressed **-er** (**teuer**) or **-el** (**dunkel**) drop the **-e-** when they take endings.

Die Theaterkarten waren **teuer**.	Das waren aber **teure** Karten!
Ist diese Farbe zu **dunkel**?	Ich mag **dunkle** Farben.

Let's summarize. The first table below shows the complete declension of an adjective following a **der**-word; the second, following an **ein**-word. The highlighted forms in the second table show the only instances in which the **ein**-word endings differ from the **der**-word endings. The third table shows adjective endings in noun phrases without a limiting word.

Adjective Endings Following a *der*-word

	masculine	neuter	feminine	plural
nom.	dies**er** jung**e** Mann	dies**es** jung**e** Kind	dies**e** jung**e** Frau	dies**e** jung**en** Leute
acc.	dies**en** jung**en** Mann	dies**es** jung**e** Kind	dies**e** jung**e** Frau	dies**e** jung**en** Leute
dat.	dies**em** jung**en** Mann	dies**em** jung**en** Kind	dies**er** jung**en** Frau	dies**en** jung**en** Leute**n**
gen.	dies**es** jung**en** Mann**es**	dies**es** jung**en** Kind**es**	dies**er** jung**en** Frau	dies**er** jung**en** Leute

Adjective Endings Following an *ein*-word

	masculine	neuter	feminine	plural
nom.	ein jung**er** Mann	ein jung**es** Kind	ein**e** jung**e** Frau	mein**e** jung**en** Leute
acc.	ein**en** jung**en** Mann	ein jung**es** Kind	ein**e** jung**e** Frau	mein**e** jung**en** Leute
dat.	ein**em** jung**en** Mann	ein**em** jung**en** Kind	ein**er** jung**en** Frau	mein**en** jung**en** Leute**n**
gen.	ein**es** jung**en** Mann**es**	ein**es** jung**en** Kind**es**	ein**er** jung**en** Frau	mein**er** jung**en** Leute

Adjective Endings Without a Limiting Word

	masculine	neuter	feminine	plural
nom.	kalt**er** Wein	kalt**es** Wasser	kalt**e** Milch	kalt**e** Suppen
acc.	kalt**en** Wein	kalt**es** Wasser	kalt**e** Milch	kalt**e** Suppen
dat.	kalt**em** Wein	kalt**em** Wasser	kalt**er** Milch	kalt**en** Suppen
gen.	kalt**en** Wein**es**	kalt**en** Wasser**s**	kalt**er** Milch	kalt**er** Suppen

Lab Manual Kap. 9, Var. zu Üb. 1, 3, 5, 6.

Workbook Kap. 9, A–H.

Using adjectives to describe things is a communicative goal.

Bring in objects or pictures for students to describe. Include plurals: **Welche Fenster sind das?** (Possible answer: **Das sind die *großen/hellen* Fenster.**) Proceed at first by gender; then repeat, eliciting responses with the indefinite article, or mix with both articles.

■ 1 ■ Übung: Welcher Tisch ist das? (*Mit offenen Büchern*) Below is a list of some people and classroom objects, arranged by gender, as well as a list of adjectives that you can use to describe them. Your instructor will ask you about them. Describe them with adjectives as in the example.

BEISPIEL: Welches Bild ist das?
Das ist *das neue Bild.*

Masculine	*Neuter*	*Feminine*	*Plural*	*Adjectives*
Bleistift	Bild	Gruppe	Bücher	alt
Junge	Buch	Hose	Jeans	billig
Kugelschreiber	Fenster	Jacke	Schuhe	blau, rot, grün *usw.*
Mantel	Foto	Kamera	Studenten	bunt
Pulli	Glas	Landkarte		fleißig
Radiergummi	Heft	Studentin		freundlich
Stadtplan	Hemd	Tafel		groß
Student	Kleid	Tasche		herrlich
Stuhl	Mädchen	Tür		höflich
	Papier	Uhr		kaputt
	Poster	Zeitschrift		kurz
	Wörterbuch	Zeitung		langweilig
				neu
				schrecklich
				toll
				typisch
				wunderbar

Students can use adjectives from list in **Üb. 1**. Continue with dative: **Was machen wir mit diesem Tisch? – Ja, was machen wir mit diesem hässlichen Tisch?**

■ 2 ■ Übung: Sehen Sie den Tisch? Now your instructor asks whether you see certain objects or people. You're not sure which ones are meant, so you ask for more information.

BEISPIEL: Sehen Sie den Tisch?
Meinen Sie den *grünen* Tisch?

Was für can also introduce exclamations: **Was für ein schöner Wagen!** (*What a beautiful car!*)

Point out that the **für** in **was für** is not the preposition requiring accusative case, and that **was für** is inserted into a prepositional phrase between the prep. and its object.

Students may still need list of adjectives from **Üb. 1**; work toward closed books. **Üb. 3** elicits plurals and some singulars without limiting words: **Was für Studenten sind das? Was für Wetter haben wir heute?**

Fragewort

Was für ... ? *What kind of . . . ?*

Was für ein Artikel ist das?	*What kind of article is that?*
Was für einen Wagen hast du?	*What kind of car do you have?*
Mit **was für** Menschen arbeitest du zusammen?	*What kind of people do you work with?*

3 **Übung: Was für ein Buch ist das?** Jetzt fragt Ihr Professor zum Beispiel, was für ein Buch das ist. Sie beschreiben das Buch.

BEISPIEL: Was für ein Buch ist das?
Das ist ein interessantes Buch.

4 **Partnerarbeit: Nicht wahr?** Respond to each other's impressions. One partner asks, the other responds, then switch roles.

BEISPIEL: Das Haus ist schön, nicht wahr?
Ja, das ist ein schönes Haus. (*oder*)
Nein, das ist kein schönes Haus.

1. Die Kneipe ist alt, nicht?
2. Der Junge ist klug, nicht wahr?
3. Das Hotel ist teuer, nicht wahr?
4. Der Automechaniker ist gut, nicht?
5. Das Kind ist müde, nicht wahr?
6. Die Buchhandlung ist fantastisch, nicht?
7. Das Bett ist bequem, nicht?
8. Der Tag ist warm, nicht?

Now create your own sentences on the same pattern.

Üb. 5: Be sure to include plurals. May continue with: **Was machen wir mit einem Tisch? – Ja, was machen wir mit einem alten Tisch?**

5 **Übung: Was für ein Buch brauchen Sie?** Jetzt möchte Ihre Professorin wissen, was für Sachen Sie brauchen, tragen usw. Sagen Sie es ihr.

BEISPIELE: A: Was für ein Buch brauchen Sie?
B: Ich brauche ein neues Buch.

A: Was für Schuhe tragen Sie heute?
B: Heute trage ich alte Turnschuhe.

6 **Übung: Wir haben keinen neuen Wagen.** Ihr Professor fragt Sie nach (*about*) etwas. Sie antworten, dass Sie es nicht haben.

BEISPIEL: Ist Ihr Wagen neu?
Nein, ich habe keinen neuen Wagen.

1. Ist Ihr Fahrrad neu?
2. Sind diese Bücher langweilig?
3. Ist der Tennislehrer wunderbar?
4. Ist der Kaffee heiß?
5. Ist die Wurst frisch?
6. Sind Ihre Freunde sportlich?
7. Sind diese Kleider schmutzig?
8. Ist Ihr Zimmer groß?
9. Ist Ihr Mantel neu?

Schwerindustrie im Ruhrgebiet.

Students may need books open when doing this exercise.

You can model dropping noun from noun phrase in answer: **Welches Hemd gefällt Ihnen besser? Das rote.** Eng. equivalent: *The red one.*

Students can now do **Zum Schluss** activities A and B, p. 270.

■ **7** ■ **Übung: Was machen Sie lieber?** Der Professor fragt Sie, was Sie lieber machen.

BEISPIEL: Dieser Zug fährt langsam, aber dieser fährt schnell.
Mit welchem Zug fahren Sie lieber?
Ich fahre lieber mit dem langsamen Zug.

1. Dieser Kaffee ist heiß, aber dieser ist kalt. Welchen trinken Sie lieber?
2. Dieses Hemd ist rot und dieses ist gelb. Welches gefällt Ihnen besser?
3. Diese Kartoffeln sind groß, aber diese sind klein. Welche nehmen Sie?
4. Dieser See ist warm, aber dieser ist kühl. In welchem würden Sie lieber schwimmen?
5. Diese Stadt ist schön, aber diese ist hässlich. In welcher würden Sie lieber wohnen?
6. Dieses Zimmer ist hell, aber dieses ist dunkel. Welches gefällt Ihnen?
7. Dieses Hotel ist alt, aber dieses ist neu. In welchem würden Sie lieber übernachten?
8. Diese Brezeln sind frisch, aber diese sind alt. Welche würden Sie lieber essen?

Word order of adverbs: Time/manner/place

You learned in **Kapitel 1** that adverb sequence in German is time before place.

	time	*place*
Ich fahre	**morgen**	**nach Kopenhagen.**
Wir bleiben	**heute**	**zu Hause.**

Place can be either location (**zu Hause**) or destination (**nach Kopenhagen**). Notice that prepositional phrases such as these function as adverbs.

If an adverb or adverbial phrase of manner (answering the question **wie?** or **mit wem?**) is also present, the sequence is *time—manner—place.*

	time	*manner*	*place*
Ich fahre	morgen	**mit der Bahn**	nach Kopenhagen.
Sie bleibt	heute	**allein**	zu Hause.

A good mnemonic device is that adverbs answer the following questions in alphabetical order:

wann? (morgen) **wie?** (mit der Bahn) **wo(hin)?** (nach Kopenhagen)

Workbook Kap. 9, I.

8 **Gruppenarbeit: Wie? Mit wem?** Create your own answers to these questions. Follow the example sentences.

1. Wie können wir morgen nach Berlin fahren?
   Wie viele Möglichkeiten gibt es für eine Reise nach Berlin?

   BEISPIEL: Wir können morgen *mit der Bahn* nach Berlin fahren.

2. Mit wem gehen Sie abends ins Kino?

   BEISPIEL: Ich gehe abends *mit meinem Freund* ins Kino.

Ordinal numbers and dates

The ordinal numbers (i.e., *first, second, third,* etc.) are adjectives and in German take the usual adjective endings.

German numbers up to **neunzehn** add **-t-** to the cardinal number and then the appropriate adjective ending. Note the three irregular forms in boldface.

In the new spelling, ordinals as adjectival nouns are capitalized: **Heute bin ich der *Erste* im Büro. Als *Drittes* müssen wir unsere Reise besprechen.**

der, das, die	**erste**	1st	elfte	11th
	zweite	2nd	zwölfte	12th
	dritte	3rd	dreizehnte	13th
	vierte	4th	vierzehnte	14th
	fünfte	5th	fünfzehnte	15th
	sechste	6th	sechzehnte	16th
	siebte	7th	siebzehnte	17th
	achte	8th	achtzehnte	18th
	neunte	9th	neunzehnte	19th
	zehnte	10th		

German numbers **zwanzig** and above add **-st-** and the adjective ending to the cardinal number.

der, das, die	zwanzigste	20th
	einundzwanzigste	21st
	zweiundzwanzigste	22nd
	dreiundzwanzigste	23rd
	usw.	
	dreißigste	30th
	vierzigste	40th
	hundertste	100th
	tausendste	1000th

In German, an ordinal number is seldom written out in letters. It is usually indicated by a period after the numeral.

der **10**. November = der zehnte November

The ordinal numbers are capitalized here (**die Erste, der Zweite**) because they are used as nouns. See **Kapitel 11**, pp. 322.

9 **Kettenreaktion: Ich bin die Erste. Ich bin der Zweite.** Count off using ordinal numbers. Males say **der** ... , females say **die** ...

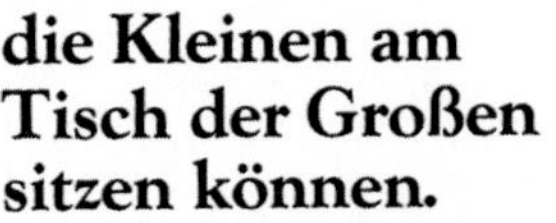

Immer auf der richtigen Höhe – damit die Kleinen am Tisch der Großen sitzen können.

Dates in German

In German, the full date is given in the order: day, month, year.

den 1.2.1999 *February 1, 1999*

To tell in what year something happened, English uses the phrase *in 1999.* The German equivalent is **im Jahre 1999** or simply **1999** (no **in**).
Here is how to say on what date something occurs or occurred:

Das war **am zehnten** August.	*That was on the tenth of August.*
Wir fliegen **am Achtzehnten.**	*We're flying on the eighteenth.*

Here is how to ask for and give the date:

Den Wievielten haben wir heute? *or* **Der Wievielte** ist heute?	*What's the date today?* (literally: *"The how manyeth do we have today/is today?"*)
Heute haben wir **den Dreizehnten.** *or* Heute ist **der Dreizehnte.**	*Today is the thirteenth.*

Lab Manual Kap. 9, Üb. 10, 11.

Workbook Kap. 9, J.

Giving the date is a communicative goal.

■ 10 ■ Übungen

A. Der Wievielte ist heute? Heute ist der ...

3. August
9. Februar
1. Mai
20. Juli
2. Januar
8. April

B. Den Wievielten haben wir heute? Heute haben wir den ...

5. März
13. Juni
11. November
19. September
7. Dezember
28. Oktober

Bring in calendar for more dates.

Kettenreaktion: **Wann hast du Geburtstag?**

■ 11 ■ Übung Wann kommt Frank? Er kommt am ...

4. Januar
30. September
5. April
25. Juli
31. Oktober
20. Februar
24. März

Assign as written homework, using perfect tense. In-class variation: Have students consult their own date books. **Was machen Sie diesen Monat? An welchem Tag?**

■ 12 ■ Partnerarbeit: Wann reist Susanne nach München?

Hier sehen Sie Susannes Terminkalender für Februar. Fragen Sie einander, wann sie alles macht.

BEISPIEL: A: Wann besucht sie Heinz?
B: Sie besucht ihn am Ersten.

FEBRUAR	
1 Heinz besuchen	**9** im Computerzentrum arbeiten
2	**10**
3 ins Theater gehen („Mutter Courage“)	**11** ins Kino („Das schreckliche Mädchen“)
4	**12** zum Recycling gehen
5	**13** Referat schreiben
6 mit Jörg und Katja essen gehen	...
7 schwimmen gehen (19 Uhr)	**20** Reise nach München
8	**21** in die Berge fahren

Lesestück

Vor dem Lesen

Tipps zum Lesen und Lernen

Tipps zum Vokabelnlernen

Identifying noun gender Now that you have acquired a German vocabulary of several hundred words, you can begin to recognize some patterns in the gender and formation of nouns. You have already learned that agent nouns ending in **-er** are always masculine (**der Lehrer**) and that the ending **-in** always designates a female (**die Lehrerin**).

The gender of many nouns is determined by a suffix. Here are some of the most common suffixes that form nouns.

- Nouns with the following suffixes are *always feminine* and *always* have the plural ending **-en**:

  -ung, -heit, -keit, -schaft, -ion, -tät

- **-ung** forms nouns from verb stems:

  lösen (*to solve*) → **die Lösung, -en** (*solution*)
  zerstören (*to destroy*) → **die Zerstörung** (*destruction*)
  verschmutzen (*to pollute*) → **die Verschmutzung** (*pollution*)

- **-heit** and **-keit** form nouns from adjective stems and from other nouns:

  frei → **die Freiheit, -en** (*freedom*)
  freundlich → **die Freundlichkeit** (*friendliness*)
  gesund → **die Gesundheit** (*health*)
  Mensch → **die Menschheit** (*humanity*)

- **-schaft** forms collective and more abstract nouns from concrete nouns:

  Studenten → **die Studentenschaft** (*student body*)
  Land → **die Landschaft, -en** (*landscape*)
  Freund → **die Freundschaft, -en** (*friendship*)

- **-ion** and **-tät**: Words with these suffixes are borrowed from French or Latin. Most have English cognates:

  die Diskussion, -en **die Generation, -en**
  die Universität, -en **die Elektrizität**

Humorous usage: **Tagchen** (no umlaut!), **Tschüsschen**, **Kataströphchen**, **Wehwehchen**; also intimate with proper names: **Peterchen**, **Gretchen**; also in southern dialects: **Hänsel und Gretel**.

- The suffixes **-chen** and **-lein** form diminutives. The stem vowel of the noun is umlauted wherever possible, and the noun automatically becomes *neuter*. The plural and singular forms are always identical.

  die Karte → **das Kärtchen, -** (*little card*)
  das Stück → **das Stückchen, -** (*little piece*)
  das Brot → **das Brötchen, -**
  die Magd (archaic: *maid*) → **das Mädchen, -**
  die Frau → **das Fräulein, -** (*Miss; young woman*)
  das Buch → **das Büchlein, -** (*little book*)

Übung: Raten Sie mal! (Take a guess!) Was bedeuten diese Wörter?

1. die Möglichkeit
2. die Wanderung
3. die Ähnlichkeit
4. die Mehrheit
5. die Meinung
6. die Lehrerschaft
7. die Wohnung
8. die Schönheit
9. die Dummheit
10. die Studentenschaft
11. die Radikalität
12. die Gesundheit
13. die Schwierigkeit
14. das Brüderlein
15. das Liedchen
16. das Städtchen
17. das Würstchen
18. das Häuschen
19. die Kindheit
20. die Menschheit

Lab Manual Kap. 9, Üb. zur Betonung.

■ Leicht zu merken

aktiv	aktiv
akut	
das **Atom, -e**	Atom
die **Basis**	
demonstrieren	demonstrieren
die **Elektrizität**	Elektrizität
die **Energie**	Energie
enorm	
die **Konsequenz, -en**	Konsequenz
der **Lebensstandard**	
die **Natur**	Natur
das **Ökosystem**	
das **Plastik**	
politisch	
produzieren	produzieren
das **Prozent** (%)	
radikal	radikal
sortieren	sortieren
sowjetisch	sowjetisch
der **Supertanker, -**	

das Plastik = der Kunststoff. die Plastik = die Skulptur

■ Einstieg in den Text

The following text discusses environmental problems. These issues concern people all over the globe. They are particularly crucial in densely populated Europe.

Look over **Wortschatz 2**, then read the following hypotheses about the environment. Do you agree or disagree with them? Compare your responses to the opinions expressed in the reading.

Have students read these statements aloud. Ask, **Stimmt das, oder nicht? Was ist Ihre Meinung?**

	Das stimmt.	*Das stimmt nicht.*
1. Wir sind heute immer noch sehr abhängig von der Natur.	☐	☐
2. Die Schwerindustrie ist für die Umweltverschmutzung verantwortlich.	☐	☐
3. Die Atomenergie ist eine gute Alternative zum Öl.	☐	☐
4. Der Durchschnittsbürger (*average citizen*) kann im Alltag viel gegen die Umweltverschmutzung tun.	☐	☐
5. Die Politiker müssen viel mehr für die Umwelt tun.	☐	☐

Wortschatz 2

Verben

führen to lead
lösen to solve
retten to rescue, save
verschmutzen to pollute; to dirty
verschwenden to waste
werfen (wirft), hat geworfen to throw
weg·werfen to throw away, discard

Substantive

der **Fisch, -e** fish
der **Politiker, -** politician
der **Unfall, ¨-e** accident
der **Vogel, ¨** bird

das **Beispiel, -e** example
das **Kraftwerk, -e** power plant
das **Atomkraftwerk** atomic power plant
das **Öl** oil
das **Tier, -e** animal

die **Chance, -n** chance
die **Dose, -n** (tin) can
die **Gefahr, -en** danger
die **Gesellschaft, -en** society

Model pronunciation: **Öl, Chance, Ware.**

die **Gesundheit** health
die **Jugend** (*sing.*) youth; young people
die **Kraft, ¨-e** power, strength
die **Lösung, -en** solution
die **Menschheit** mankind, human race
die **Partei, -en** political party
die **Pflanze, -n** plant
die **Politik** politics; policy
die **Technik** technology
die **Ware, -n** product

Adjektive und Adverbien

bereit prepared, ready
eigen- own
erstaunlich astounding
gefährlich dangerous
gesund healthy
hoch (*predicate adj.*), **hoh-** (*attributive adj.*) high
Das Gebäude ist **hoch**.
aber
Das ist ein **hohes** Gebäude.
jährlich annually
sauer sour; acidic
der saure Regen acid rain
stark strong

Andere Vokabeln

mancher, -es, -e many a (*in plural* = some)
manche Pflanzen some plants
solcher, -es, -e such, such a

Nützliche Ausdrücke

im Jahr(e) 1989 in 1989
nicht nur ... sondern auch not only . . . but also

im Jahre: Like the final **-e** in **nach/zu Hause,** this **-e** is an old dative ending.

Gegensätze

führen ≠ folgen (+ *dat.*) to lead ≠ to follow
gesund ≠ krank healthy ≠ sick
die **Gesundheit ≠** die **Krankheit** health ≠ sickness
hoch ≠ niedrig high ≠ low
sauer ≠ süß sour ≠ sweet
stark ≠ schwach strong ≠ weak

KATZEN
würden
GREENPEACE
wählen!

Lab Manual Kap. 9, Lesestück.

Learning about German environmental issues is the cultural goal of this chapter.

Unsere Umwelt in Gefahr

Das Problem: Der Mensch gegen die Natur?

Wir leben heute in Europa und Nordamerika in einer hoch industrialisierten° Welt. Wir lieben unseren Luxus° und brauchen die Technik, denn sie ist die Basis unseres hohen Lebensstandards. Aber unseren erstaunlichen Fortschritt haben wir teuer bezahlt°. Manchmal vergessen wir, dass wir immer noch von der Natur abhängig° sind.

Um unsere Lebensweise° möglich zu machen brauchen wir enorm viel Energie. Obwohl die Nordamerikaner und Westeuropäer nur zirka 15% der Weltbevölkerung° sind, verbrauchen° sie zirka 65% aller produzierten Energie. Spätestens° seit der Katastrophe im sowjetischen Atomkraftwerk in Tschernobyl am 26. April 1986 weiß man aber, wie gefährlich diese Energiequelle° für unser Ökosystem sein kann. Ein zweites Beispiel ist die Exxon-Valdez-Katastrophe vom Jahre 1989; das Öl aus diesem verunglückten° Supertanker hat das Meer verschmutzt und Fische und Vögel weit und breit° in Gefahr gebracht. Die schlimmen Folgen° von solchen Unfällen können jahrelang fortdauern°. Leider aber sind alle unsere Hauptenergiequellen (Öl, Kohle°, Atomkraft) schädlich° für die Natur und für unsere Gesundheit.

Aber nicht nur die Schwerindustrie muss für die Umwelt verantwortlich sein, sondern auch jeder einzelne° Mensch. Wir fahren zu viel Auto, wir essen zu viel in Fastfood-Restaurants, wir benutzen zu viele Spraydosen° und produzieren zu viel Müll. Die Konsequenzen sind: der saure Regen, Müllhalden° voll von unnötigen Plastikverpackungen° und die Zerstörung der Ozonschicht°. Das Problem ist im dicht besiedelten° Deutschland besonders akut. Dort wirft jeder Bürger jährlich zirka 300 bis 400 kg Müll weg! Man möchte wirklich fragen: Sind wir Menschen denn die Feinde° der Natur?

highly industrialized
luxury
teuer ... = paid a high price for / **von ...** = dependent on
way of life
world population
consume / at the latest
energy source
grounded
far and wide / consequences
jahrelang ... = persist for years / coal / harmful
individual
aerosol cans
trash dumps
plastic packaging / ozone layer / **dicht besiedelt** = densely populated
enemies

Pronunciation: **Schpree-** or **Schpreidosen**.

Die Lösung: aktiv umweltfreundlich sein!

Besonders die junge Generation in Deutschland zeigt für diese Probleme starkes Engagement°. Manche finden bei den Grünen[1] eine radikale Alternative zu der Umweltpolitik der großen Parteien. Viele demonstrieren gegen neue Atomkraftwerke und suchen auch in ihrem eigenen Leben Alternativen zu der Wegwerfgesellschaft. Aber nicht nur die umweltbewusste° Jugend, sondern auch Deutsche aus allen Altersgruppen° sind heute bereit ihr Leben zu ändern°, um Meere, Wälder, Tiere und Pflanzen zu retten.[2]

Model pronunciation of **Engagement**.

commitment
environmentally conscious
age groups / change

1. **Die Grünen**, the environmental and anti-nuclear party, first won seats in the **Bundestag** in 1983. Although they lost these seats in the 1990 federal elections, they regained them in 1994 and are also represented at the state level in some **Länder**.
2. In 1990 the Federal Republic became the first nation to ban the production and use of ozone-depleting chlorofluorocarbons.

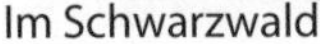

Im Schwarzwald

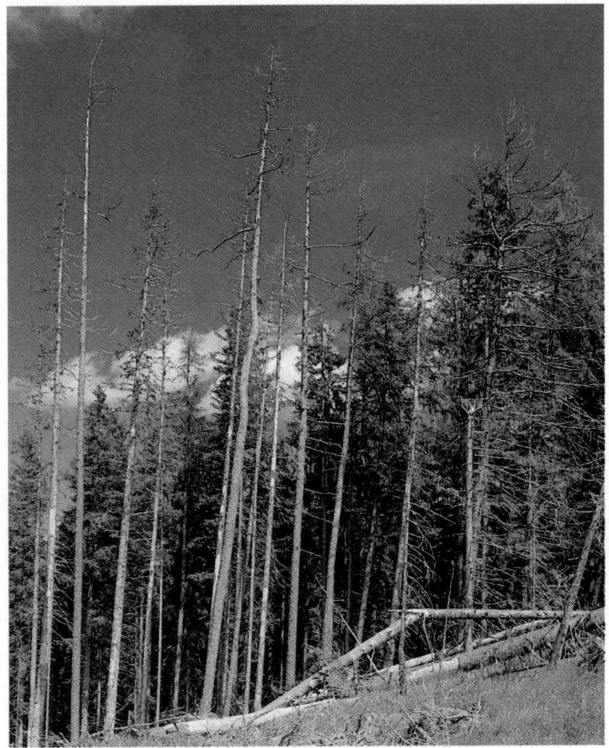

Waldsterben

Wie kann man denn ein umweltfreundliches Leben führen? Man kann z.B. mehr Rad fahren oder zu Fuß gehen und weniger° Auto fahren. Man sollte° nur Waren ohne unnötige Verpackung kaufen und den Hausmüll sortieren und zum Recycling bringen. Man kann auch so wenig Wasser und Elektrizität wie° möglich verschwenden. Diese Vorschläge° für den Alltag sind nur ein Anfang. Man muss natürlich auch von den Politikern mehr Umweltbewusstsein° fordern°. Die Menschheit hat nicht mehr viel Zeit. Nur wenn alle Länder politisch zusammenarbeiten, haben wir noch eine Chance unsere Umwelt zu retten.

less / should

so ... wie = as . . . as

suggestions

environmental awareness / demand

Nach dem Lesen

Discussing ecology and recycling is a communicative goal.

Optional: Use some of these questions as written assignments, e.g., 4, 7, 8.

■ A ■ Antworten Sie auf Deutsch.

1. Von welchen Umweltkatastrophen haben Sie schon gehört?
2. Wann war die Katastrophe in Tschernobyl?
3. Wie können Umweltkatastrophen für die Natur gefährlich sein?
4. Wer soll denn für die Umwelt verantwortlich sein?
5. Nennen Sie unsere Hauptenergiequellen.
6. Kennen Sie alternative Energiequellen?
7. Wie kann unser modernes Alltagsleben für die Umwelt gefährlich sein?
8. Wie können wir ein umweltfreundliches Leben führen?

Üb. B: Write question on board: **Benutzen Sie Dinge aus Plastik oder Styropor** (*styrofoam*) **im Alltag?**

Some objects students might generate: **Kugelschreiber, Gabeln, Löffel, Messer, Plastikteller, -flaschen, -becher, -tüten, -verpackung** usw.

■ B ■ Gruppenarbeit: Unsere Wegwerfgesellschaft? ***(4 oder 5 Personen)***

Jeden Tag benutzen wir viele Sachen. Aber wir verschwenden auch eine Menge, besonders Dinge aus Plastik. Machen Sie eine Liste von solchen Dingen aus Ihrem Alltag. Was haben Sie in den letzten Tagen wegwerfen müssen? Warum?

Liste: „Das haben wir in letzter Zeit weggeworfen."

**Die Wälder sterben-
nach den Wäldern
sterben die Menschen.**

Situationen aus dem Alltag

Talking about sports is a communicative goal.

This vocabulary focuses on an everyday topic or situation. Words you already know from **Wortschatz** sections are listed without English equivalents; new supplementary vocabulary is listed with definitions. Your instructor may assign some supplementary vocabulary for active mastery.

Some additional sports: **das Segeln, das Bergsteigen, das Klettern, der Basketball, der Volleyball, das Schlittschuhlaufen (das Eislaufen), die Leichtathletik** (*track and field*), **das Fechten, das Reiten, der Federball** (*badminton*), **der Ringkampf (das Ringen), das Boxen, das Gewichtheben, das Joggen, das Rudern, die Aerobik, das Krafttraining** (*weight training*).

■ Der Sport

„Wer Sport treibt, bleibt fit!" hört man oft. Was meinen Sie? Treiben Sie Sport, um fit und gesund zu bleiben, oder nur, weil es Ihnen Spaß macht? Hier sind einige nützliche Wörter für eine Diskussion über Sport.

Substantive

das **Spiel, -e** *game*
die **Mannschaft, -en** *team*
die **Konkurrenz** *competition*

Verben

gewinnen, hat gewonnen *to win*
schlagen, hat geschlagen *to beat*
trainieren *to train*

■ **A** ■ **Gruppenarbeit: Was spielst du gern?** Hier sind einige Piktogramme von den Olympischen Spielen. Welchen Sport treiben Sie gern?

BEISPIEL: A: Ich schwimme gern. Und du?
B: Ich ______ .

laufen
der **Läufer**
die **Läuferin**

schwimmen
der **Schwimmer**
die **Schwimmerin**

Ski fahren
der **Skifahrer**
die **Skifahrerin**

boxen
der **Boxer**

Volleyball spielen
der **Volleyballspieler**
die **Volleyballspielerin**

Fußball spielen
der **Fußballspieler**
die **Fußballspielerin**

Rad fahren
der **Radfahrer**
die **Radfahrerin**

(Eis)hockey spielen
der **Hockeyspieler**
die **Hockeyspielerin**

■ **B** ■ **Gruppenarbeit: Sprechen wir über Sport (*2 oder 3 Personen*)**

1. Welchen Sport treibst du?
2. Warum gefällt dir dieser Sport?
3. Treibst du an der Uni Sport? Hast du auch in der Schule Sport getrieben?

Klassendiskussion may be organized as debate.

■ **C** ■ **Klassendiskussion: Was meinen Sie?**

1. Kann man fit bleiben, ohne Sport zu treiben?
2. In Deutschland gibt es viele Sportklubs, aber nur wenige (*few*) Universitätsmannschaften. Finden Sie es gut, dass es solche Mannschaften an amerikanischen Unis gibt? Warum?

Zum Schluss

Sprechen wir miteinander!

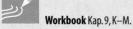

Lab Manual Kap. 9, Diktat.

Workbook Kap. 9, K–M.

■ A ■ Gruppenarbeit: Beschreiben wir das Klassenzimmer.

BEISPIEL: Dort hängt ein großes Bild an der Wand.
Dort steht ein kleiner Tisch.

Was sehen Sie sonst? Benutzen Sie Adjektive!

Üb. B: You may want to review clothing vocabulary first. You may also have students write descriptions in class, then hand them in or pass them to a neighbor who reads description aloud. Then proceed as in B.

■ B ■ Gruppenarbeit: Wer trägt was?

Benutzen Sie Adjektive, um die Kleider eines Studenten oder einer Studentin im Zimmer zu beschreiben. Die anderen müssen raten (*guess*), wen Sie meinen. Sie können auch Ihre eigenen Kleider beschreiben.

BEISPIEL: A: Wer trägt heute eine alte Hose und ein hässliches Hemd?
B: Meinst du Rick?

Using adjectives to describe things is a communicative goal.

Üb. C: Students should not read their descriptions of the pictures. Let them hand in written work and extemporize from memory. Written assignment can follow oral presentation. They can also use pictures from textbook.

■ C ■ Übung: Ich habe ein interessantes Bild gefunden.

Suchen Sie in einem Bilderbuch oder einer Zeitschrift ein interessantes Bild oder Foto. Beschreiben Sie es vor der Klasse. Benutzen Sie viele Adjektive!

BEISPIEL: Ich habe dieses schöne Bild in einem alten Buch gefunden. Hier sieht man viele Häuser in einem kleinen Dorf. In der Mitte des Bildes steht eine alte Kirche und vor dieser schönen Kirche geht ein alter Mann mit einem kleinen Kind spazieren. Hinter dem Dorf sieht man auch einen dunklen Wald usw.

Üb. D: Write on board: **Pfandflasche, Einwegflasche, die Mine** (*refill for ballpoint or mechanical pencil*).

■ D ■ Gruppenarbeit: Es gibt eine Alternative!

Hier sind einige Beispiele der Umweltverschmutzung. Können Sie Alternativen geben?

BEISPIEL: Einen Plastiklöffel wirft man meistens weg.
Alternative: Aber ich muss nicht mit Plastiklöffeln essen.

1. Meine Familie wirft jede Woche viele Flaschen weg.
2. Sonntags fahre ich gern im eigenen Auto aufs Land.
3. Im Supermarkt sind die Lebensmittel alle in Plastik verpackt.
4. Manchmal werfen Menschen Papier auf die Straße.
5. Wenn mein Kugelschreiber keine Tinte (*ink*) mehr hat, werfe ich ihn weg.
6. In unserem Studentenwohnheim gibt es keine Recyclingcontainer.

Schreiben Sie zu Hause.

E Combine elements of your choice from the following lists to write ten sentences that describe activities. Create both statements and questions and use both present and perfect tense.

Wann?	*Wie?*	*Wo(hin)?*	*Verben*
am 10. Oktober	mit meinen Freunden	ins Ausland	reisen
letzten Dienstag	allein	im Bett	liegen
morgen	mit dem Zug	in der Bibliothek	lesen
gestern	mit dem Auto	ins Kino	übernachten
1999	ziemlich schnell	in die Bibliothek	gehen
heute	gerne	in der Jugendherberge	essen
am Mittwoch	fleißig	im Tennisklub	joggen
nächsten Monat	zusammen	an der Uni	Sport treiben
dieses Semester	ohne mich	in der Mensa	Tennis spielen

BEISPIELE: Am Mittwoch esse ich mit meinen Freunden in der Mensa.

Wann habt ihr zusammen in der Jugendherberge übernachtet?

Üb. F: Have students write out entire narrative. May be read aloud in class.

F Rewrite this narrative, filling in each blank with an appropriate adjective. Don't forget to add the endings where they are needed.

Heute ist der ______ Mai und es ist ein ______ Tag. Ich bin mit meiner ______ Freundin Laura im ______ Wald spazieren gegangen. Die Sonne war ______ und im Wald war es sehr ______ . Wir haben unser Mittagessen mitgebracht und um ein Uhr waren wir schon hungrig. Aber wir haben vergessen eine Flasche Wein mitzubringen. Wir haben gewusst, dass es im Wald ein ______ Restaurant gibt, und bald haben wir es gefunden. Dort haben wir also eine ______ Flasche Wein gekauft. Die Kellnerin war eine sehr ______ Frau. Mit ihr haben wir über das ______ Wetter gesprochen. Sie hat auch ein ______ Kind gehabt und wir haben ein bisschen mit diesem ______ Mädchen gespielt. Später haben wir meinen ______ Freund Hannes getroffen. Er hat uns seinen ______ Wagen gezeigt. Am Ende dieses ______ Tages sind wir dann mit der Straßenbahn in die ______ Stadt zurückgefahren.

AUCH FÜSSE HABEN GEFÜHLE

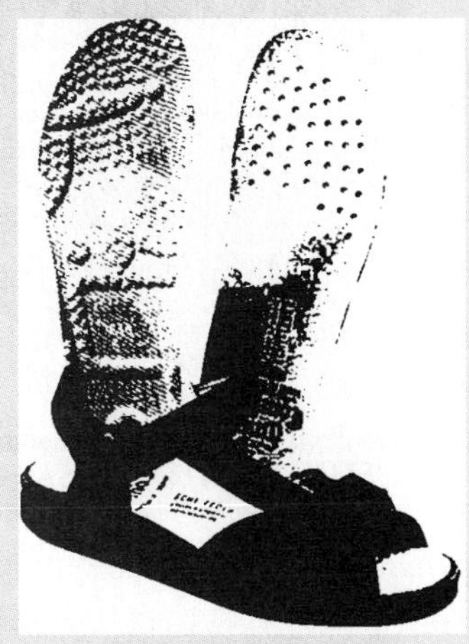

G Construct sentences from the elements provided. Be prepared to translate your sentences into English.

1. mein / umweltfreundlich / Mitbewohner / tragen / Müll / in / Keller
2. alle / neu / Einwohner / unser- (*gen.*) / Studentenwohnheim- / mitmachen
3. nach / unser / lang / Wanderung / können / wir / in / ein / billig / Restaurant / ein / kalt / Bier / trinken
4. das / riesengroß / Zimmer / ist / sonnig / und / ich / haben / mein / eigen / Schreibtisch
5. die / klein / Schüler / aus / d- / dritt- / Klasse / sammeln / leer / Flaschen / für / d- / Umweltaktion
6. ich / war / in / ein / fantastisch / Jugendherberge / in / d- / Schweiz, / wo / ich / in / ein / altmodisch / Bett / schlafen (*perfect tense*)
7. um / ein / lang, / gesund / Leben / haben, / sollen / jed- / Mensch / aktiv / bleiben
8. bei / dies- / schön / Wetter / wir / wollen / zusammen / zum / neu / Tennisplatz / gehen
9. ich / haben / ein / gut / Gefühl, / wenn / ich / mein- / schmutzig / alt / Dosen / zum / Recycling / schleppen

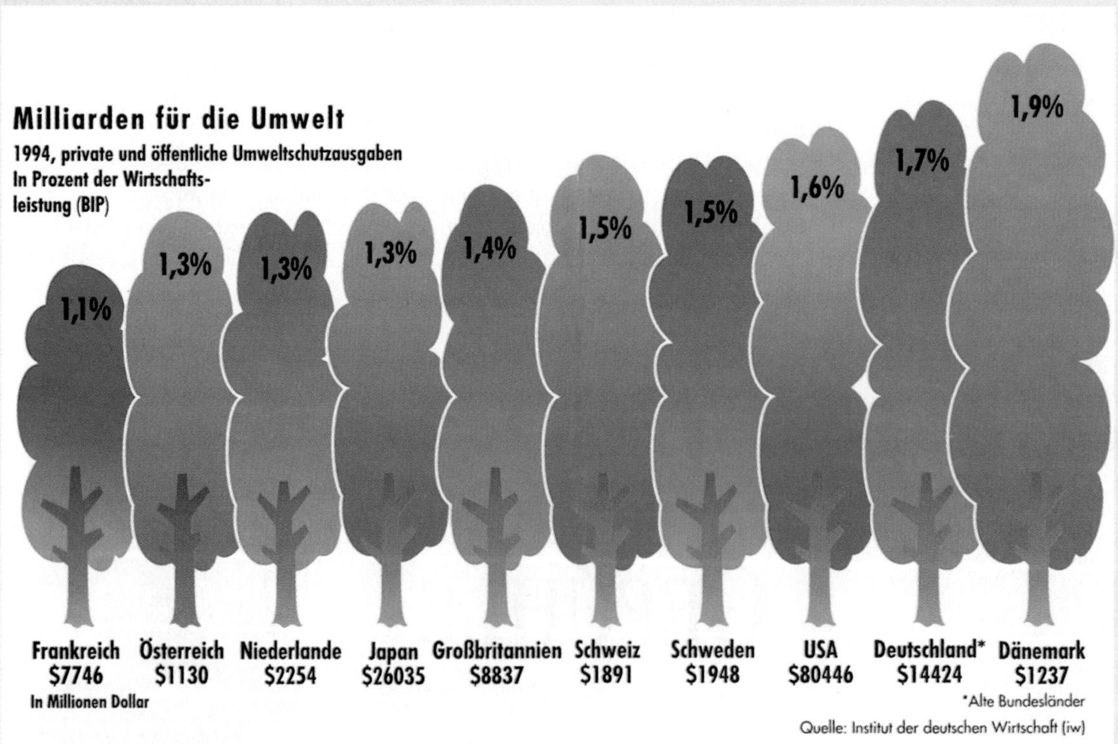

Üb. H: 1. Der Wievielte ist heute?/Den Wievielten haben wir heute? 2. Es ist der Fünfte/Wir haben den Fünften April. Warum fragst du? 3. Mein alter Freund Markus hat heute Geburtstag und ich habe ihn noch nicht angerufen. 4. Können Sie mir ein gutes Restaurant empfehlen? 5. Essen Sie gern französisch? 6. Natürlich. Kennen Sie ein gutes französisches Restaurant? 7. Ja, mein Lieblingsrestaurant ist in der Altstadt. 8. Werfen Sie diese alten Flaschen weg, Frau Schuhmacher? 9. Ja, ich habe keine Zeit, sie in den Keller zu tragen / schleppen. 10. Darf ich sie haben? Ich sammle Flaschen um Geld zu verdienen.

Use **Aufkleber** to practice pronunciation and guessing meaning from context cues. Note N-noun **Planet**.

H Wie sagt man das auf Deutsch?

1. What's the date today?
2. It's April 5th. Why do you ask?
3. My old friend Markus has a birthday today, and I haven't called him up yet.

4. Can you recommend a good restaurant to me?
5. Do you like to eat French food?
6. Of course. Do you know a good French restaurant?
7. Yes. My favorite restaurant is in the old part of town (**Altstadt**).

8. Are you throwing these old bottles away, Frau Schuhmacher?
9. Yes, I don't have time to carry them to the cellar.
10. May I have them? I'm collecting bottles to earn money.

BITTE VERLASSEN SIE DIESEN PLANETEN SO, WIE SIE IHN VORZUFINDEN WÜNSCHEN!

PVC = Polyvinylchlorid.

Seid ihr schlaue Umweltfüchse?

Der „Bund für Umwelt und Naturschutz Deutschland" ist eine Lobby von umweltfreundlichen Menschen. In einer Broschüre geben sie Tipps zum Schutz (*protection*) der Umwelt.

Umweltfüchse wissen, ...

- dass Wasser ein Lebensmittel ist.
- dass jeder Deutsche pro Tag zirka 150 Liter Trinkwasser benutzt.

Schlaue Umweltfüchse ...

- werfen keine Medikamente in die Toilette, sondern bringen sie zur Sammelstelle für Giftmüll.
- duschen lieber, als ein Vollbad zu nehmen, weil sie beim Duschen nur 50 bis 100 Liter Wasser benutzen, statt 200 Liter beim Baden.

Umweltfüchse wissen, ...

- dass die Bundesrepublik jedes Jahr einen Müllberg produziert, der so groß wie die Zugspitze ist.
- dass nur 11 Prozent dieses Mülls echter Müll sind. 89 Prozent wären recyclebar.

Schlaue Umweltfüchse ...

- kaufen Recyclingprodukte, z.B. Umweltschutzpapier.
- sortieren ihren Müll und bringen Glasflaschen, Metall und Papier zu Containern oder direkt zum Recycling.

Recyclingcontainer. (Garmisch-Partenkirchen, Bayern)

Help students figure out from context and visual clues the meanings of: **Fuchs (Füchse sind schlau=clever!** English cognates: *fox, vixen*); **Lebensmittel** (here, literally, "means of life"); **Gift** (ask: **Was für Müll ist Giftmüll?**). Using back endpaper table of equivalent measures, have students calculate how many gallons of water each German consumes. How many total liters per day are consumed in Germany? Ask about the pictures from brochure: **Was macht der Fuchs, warum ist das umweltfreundlich? (Er duscht statt zu baden, usw**.)

UMWELTTIPS

für jeden Tag

Haus · Garten · Verkehr

Bund für
Umwelt und
Naturschutz
Deutschland
e.V.

BUND

Note the old spelling in the brochure's title: **Tips** vs. **Tipps**.

KAPITEL 10

Deutschland im 20. Jahrhundert

Communicative Goals

- Narrating events in the past
- Describing objects
- Telling how long ago something happened
- Telling how long something lasted

Cultural Goal

- Learning about the Weimar Republic

Chapter Outline

- **Lyrik zum Vorlesen**
  Bertolt Brecht, „Mein junger Sohn fragt mich"
- **Grammatik**
  Simple past tense
  Equivalents for *when*: als, wenn, wann
  Past perfect tense
  More time expressions
- **Lesestück**
  Eine Ausstellung historischer Plakate aus der Weimarer Republik
- **Situationen aus dem Alltag**
  Die Politik
- **Videoecke**
  Treibst du gern Sport?
- **Almanach**
  German Politics and the European Union

Dialoge

Lab Manual Kap. 10, Dialoge, Fragen, Hören Sie gut zu!

Pronunciation practice: Use dialogues to contrast **v** and **w**: **Vorher habe ich in Mainz gewohnt; Als ich ein Kind war, habe ich den Sommer dort verbracht; Vor dem Krieg war die Stadt ganz anders; vor zwei Wochen; Was willst du wissen?**

Damals

Zwei Senioren sitzen nachmittags auf einer Bank.

HERR ZIEGLER: Wie lange wohnen Sie schon hier, Frau Planck?
FRAU PLANCK: Seit letztem Jahr. Vorher habe ich in Mainz gewohnt.
HERR ZIEGLER: Ach, das wusste ich ja gar nicht. Als ich ein Kind war, habe ich immer den ganzen Sommer dort bei meinen Großeltern verbracht.
FRAU PLANCK: Damals vor dem Krieg war die Stadt natürlich ganz anders.

The tag question ... **oder**? (here = *Did you?*) can follow either positive or negative statements. **Nicht wahr?** (p. 85) follows positive statements only.

Was ist denn los?

JÜRGEN: Heinz, was ist denn los? Du siehst so besorgt aus.
HEINZ: Ach, Barbara hat mir vor zwei Wochen ihren neuen Kassettenrecorder geliehen ...
JÜRGEN: Na und? Du hast ihn doch nicht verloren, oder?
HEINZ: Keine Ahnung. Ich hatte ihn in meiner Tasche, aber vor zehn Minuten konnte ich ihn dann plötzlich nicht mehr finden.
JÜRGEN: So ein Mist! Meinst du, jemand hat ihn dir geklaut?
HEINZ: Nee, denn mein Geldbeutel fehlt nicht.

Note that **eigentlich** in Dialogue 3 has the force of *anyway*: "While we're on the subject of your childhood, when were you born, *anyway*?"

Ask students: **Wann hat der Zweite Weltkrieg angefangen?** (1939) **Und wann war er zu Ende?** (1945)

Remember: English *in 1935* = **1935** (no *in*) or **im Jahre 1935**.

Schlimme Zeiten

Als Hausaufgabe muss Steffi (10 Jahre alt) ihre Oma interviewen.

STEFFI: Oma, für die Schule sollen wir unsere Großeltern über die Kriegszeit interviewen.
OMA: Nun, was willst du denn wissen, Steffi?
STEFFI: Also ... wann bist du eigentlich geboren?
OMA: 1935. Als der Krieg anfing, war ich noch ein kleines Mädchen.
STEFFI: Erzähl mir bitte, wie es euch damals ging.
OMA: Gott sei Dank lebten wir auf dem Land und zuerst ging es uns relativ gut, obwohl wir nicht reich waren.
STEFFI: Was ist dann passiert?
OMA: Das dauerte nur bis 1943. Dann ist mein Bruder in Russland gefallen und ein Jahr später starb meine Mutter.

Note the restricted meaning of **fallen** in this context: *to die in combat*. Proverb: **Generale siegen, Soldaten fallen** (**siegen** = *to be victorious*).

Contrast stress and meaning: Was ist *dann* passiert? / **Was ist denn** *passiert*?

Note on Usage: *doch*

In **Kapitel 4**, you learned that **doch** can soften a command to a suggestion. In a statement, **doch** adds emphasis in the sense of *surely, really*. In the second dialogue, Jürgen fears the worst and says to Heinz:

Du hast ihn **doch** nicht verloren, oder? — *(Surely) you haven't lost it, have you?*

Wortschatz 1

Verben

dauern to last; to take (time)
fallen (fällt), fiel, ist gefallen to fall; to die in battle
fehlen to be missing; to be absent
interviewen, hat interviewt to interview
leihen, lieh, hat geliehen to lend, loan; to borrow
passieren, passierte, ist passiert to happen
stehlen (stiehlt), stahl, hat gestohlen to steal
verlieren, verlor, hat verloren to lose

Substantive

der **Geldbeutel, -** wallet, change purse
der **Kassettenrecorder, -** cassette player
der **Monat, -e** month

Note: **verlieren** is a strong verb, not one of the weak **-ieren** verbs such as **passieren, studieren.**

der **Nachmittag, -e** afternoon
am Nachmittag in the afternoon
der **Senior, -en, -en** senior citizen
die **Bank, ¨-e** bench

Adjektive und Adverbien

besorgt worried, concerned
damals at that time, back then
letzt- last
plötzlich sudden(ly)
reich rich
vorher before that, previously

Andere Vokabeln

als (*sub. conj.*) when, as
doch (*flavoring particle,* *see p. 277*)
nachdem (*sub. conj.*) after
nun now; well; well now

Nützliche Ausdrücke

(Ich habe) keine Ahnung. (I have) no idea.

den ganzen Sommer (Tag, Nachmittag usw.) all summer (day, afternoon, etc.)
Na und? And so? So what?
So ein Mist! (*crude, colloq.*) What a drag! What a lot of bull!
Wann sind Sie geboren? When were you born?

Gegensätze

besorgt ≠ unbesorgt concerned ≠ carefree
reich ≠ arm rich ≠ poor
vorher ≠ nachher before that ≠ after that

Mit anderen Worten

klauen (*colloq.*) = stehlen

Model pronunciation and stress: **interv*í*ewen**.

Alert students that **So ein Mist** is considered somewhat vulgar.

Back Then

Two senior citizens are sitting on a bench in the afternoon.

Z: How long have you lived here, Mrs. Planck?
P: Since last year. Before that, I lived in Mainz.
Z: Oh, I didn't know that. When I was a child, I always spent the whole summer there with my grandparents.
P: Of course back then before the war the city was very different.

What's wrong?

J: Heinz, what's wrong? You look so worried.
H: Oh, Barbara loaned me her new cassette player two weeks ago . . .
J: So? You haven't lost it, have you?
H: No idea. I had it in my bag, but then ten minutes ago I suddenly couldn't find it.
J: What a drag! You think somebody ripped it off?
H: Nope, because my wallet's not missing.

Tough Times

As a homework assignment, Steffi (age 10) has to interview her grandmother.

S: Grandma, for school we're supposed to interview our grandparents about the war years.
O: Well, what do you want to know, Steffi?
S: Let's see . . . when were you born, anyway?
O: In 1935. When the war began I was still a little girl.
S: Please tell me what it was like for you back then.
O: Thank goodness we lived in the country, and at first things were relatively good, although we weren't rich.
S: What happened then?
O: That lasted only until 1943. Then my brother was killed in action in Russia and my mother died a year later.

Variationen

■ A ■ Persönliche Fragen

In A4, insist on the year without preposition or **im Jahre**.

1. Heinz sieht besorgt aus, weil er etwas verloren hat. Haben Sie je etwas verloren? Was?
2. Was machen Sie, wenn Sie etwas nicht finden können?
3. Würden Sie jemand Ihren Kassettenrecorder leihen? Warum oder warum nicht?
4. Wissen Sie, wann und wo Ihre Eltern geboren sind? Ihre Großeltern?
5. Wie lange wohnen Sie schon in dieser Stadt?
6. Herr Ziegler hat als Kind seine Sommerferien bei seinen Großeltern verbracht. Was haben Sie als Kind im Sommer gemacht?

Describing objects is a communicative goal.

Reviews adj. endings. First, model with a student.

■ B ■ Partnerarbeit: Fundbüro (Lost and found) Sie gehen zum Fundbüro, weil Sie etwas verloren haben. Unten ist eine Liste von Dingen im Fundbüro. Sagen Sie, was Sie verloren haben. Dann beschreiben Sie es.

BEISPIEL: A: Was haben Sie verloren?
B: Ich habe meine Kamera verloren.
A: Können Sie sie beschreiben?
B: Es war eine ________ Kamera.

Fahrrad
Kassettenrecorder
Jacke
Koffer
Tasche
Wörterbuch
Pulli
Turnschuhe
Geldbeutel

Elicit what *happened*, not what students *did*. Help with directed questions if necessary: **Was ist in der Welt / auf dem Campus / in der Stadt passiert?**

■ C ■ Übung: Was ist passiert? Gestern war sehr viel los. Sagen Sie, was passiert ist.

BEISPIEL: Können Sie uns sagen, was gestern passiert ist?
Ja, gestern ...

■ D ■ Übung: Den ganzen Tag How long did you do certain things? Answer that you did them all morning, all day, all week, all semester, and so on.

BEISPIEL: Wie lange sind Sie in Europa gewesen?
Ich war *den ganzen Sommer* da.

1. Wie lange haben Sie gestern Tennis gespielt?
2. Wie lange waren Sie in der Bibliothek?
3. Wie lange waren Sie mit Ihren Freunden zusammen?
4. Wie lange sind Sie im Bett geblieben?
5. Wie lange haben Sie an Ihrem Referat gearbeitet?

Lyrik zum Vorlesen

Bertolt Brecht fled Germany in 1933 to settle first in France, then in Scandinavia. This poem, written in Finland during World War II, is the sixth of the short cycle "1940." It reflects events of that year.

Lab Manual Kap. 10, Lyrik zum Vorlesen.

You may want to introduce **das Gedicht** as active vocabulary. This poem can be the basis for a brief discussion, in English or German, anticipating historical themes of Kap. 10 & 11. Emphasize that it was written during the war, in exile. What is the relation of the title "1940" to the content? Ask where the divisions of poem fall. Why does father first say it's pointless to study mathematics, French, and history, but then tell the son to study them after all?

Point out that familiar imperatives *with* **du** (**Reibe du nur ... , Lerne du nur ...**) are colloquial, not standard.

Mein junger Sohn fragt mich

Mein junger Sohn fragt mich: Soll ich
Mathematik lernen?
Wozu°, möchte ich sagen. Dass zwei
Stück Brot mehr ist als eines
Das wirst du auch so merken°.
Mein junger Sohn fragt mich: Soll
ich Französisch lernen?
Wozu, möchte ich sagen. Dieses Reich
geht unter°. Und
Reibe° du nur mit der Hand den Bauch°
und stöhne°
Und man wird dich schon verstehen.
Mein junger Sohn fragt mich: Soll
ich Geschichte lernen?
Wozu, möchte ich sagen. Lerne du nur
deinen Kopf in die Erde stecken°
Da wirst du vielleicht übrig bleiben°.

Ja, lerne Mathematik, sage ich
Lerne Französisch, lerne Geschichte!

Bertolt Brecht (1898–1956)

what for?

Das ... = you'll notice that anyway

Reich ... = empire will collapse

rub / belly
groan

deinen ... = to stick your head in the sand
wirst ... = will survive

›Der Klassiker der Vernunft‹
Bertolt Brecht
Große kommentierte Berliner und
Frankfurter Ausgabe in 30 Bänden
Suhrkamp

Grammatik

Narrating events in the past is a communicative goal.

Like German present tense (see Kapitel 1, p. 29), German past tense lacks progressive and emphatic forms (English: *was living, did live*).

Simple past tense

The simple past tense is used in written German to narrate a series of events in the past. Most literary texts are written in the simple past. In spoken German, however, the *perfect* tense is more commonly used to relate past events. Exceptions are **sein**, **haben**, and the modal verbs, which are used most frequently with the simple past in both conversation and writing. You learned the simple past tense of **sein** in **Kapitel 6**.

Weak verbs and strong verbs form the simple past tense in different ways. About 90 percent of German verbs are weak, but the strong verbs introduced in *Neue Horizonte* occur very frequently.

Simple past of weak verbs

The marker for the simple past of weak verbs is **-te**. Weak verbs form the simple past by adding endings to the verb stem as follows:

First- and third-person singular forms are identical: **ich wohnte**, **er wohnte**.

ich	wohn-**te**	*I lived*	wir	wohn-**ten**	*we lived*
du	wohn-**test**	*you lived*	ihr	wohn-**tet**	*you lived*
er, es, sie	wohn-**te**	*he, it, she lived*	sie, Sie	wohn-**ten**	*they, you lived*

Two other weak verbs that students already know with stems in **-t**: **warten, übernachten**. Have students conjugate a few of them so they get used to the stuttering sound of the simple past endings.

Verbs whose stems end in **-d** or **-t** add **-e-** between the stem and these endings:

ich	arbeit-**ete**	*I worked*	wir	arbeit-**eten**	*we worked*
du	arbeit-**etest**	*you worked*	ihr	arbeit-**etet**	*you worked*
er, es, sie	arbeit-**ete**	*he, it, she worked*	sie, Sie	arbeit-**eten**	*they, you worked*

For weak verbs, the only form you need to know to generate all other possible forms is the infinitive: **wohnen**, **wohnte**, **hat gewohnt**; **arbeiten**, **arbeitete**, **hat gearbeitet**.

Lab Manual Kap. 10, Var. zu Üb. 1, 2, 4–6.

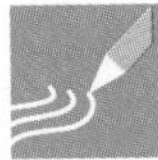

Workbook Kap. 10, A–E.

In short narratives like this, German uses the simple past rather than the perfect.

1 **Übung: Doras Einkaufstag** Here is a present-tense narrative of Dora's day in town. Retell it in the simple past tense.

Dora **braucht** Lebensmittel. Sie **wartet** bis zehn Uhr, dann **kauft** sie in einer kleinen Bäckerei ein. Sie **bezahlt** ihre Brötchen und **dankt** der Verkäuferin. Draußen **schneit** es und sie **hört** Musik auf der Straße. Sie **sucht** ein Restaurant. Also **fragt** sie zwei Studenten. Die Studenten **zeigen** ihr ein gutes Restaurant gleich in der Nähe. Dort **bestellt** sie etwas zu essen und eine Tasse Kaffee. Es **schmeckt** ihr sehr gut, aber die Menschen am nächsten Tisch **quatschen** zu laut und das **ärgert** sie ein bisschen.

Page 283 lists the 50 strong verbs introduced so far. The new simple past tense forms are boldfaced. Give yourself plenty of time to learn these and practice them aloud with a friend.

Simple past of strong verbs

Strong verbs do *not* have the marker **-te**. Instead, the verb stem is changed. The changed stem is called the *simple past stem*, e.g., nehmen, **nahm**, hat genommen. This new stem takes the following personal endings in the simple past tense:

ich	nahm	*I took*	wir	nahm-**en**	*we took*
du	nahm-**st**	*you took*	ihr	nahm-**t**	*you took*
er, es, sie	nahm	*he, it, she took*	sie, Sie	nahm-**en**	*they, you took*

Note that the **ich**- and the **er**, **es**, **sie**-forms of strong verbs have *no* endings in the simple past: **ich nahm**, **sie nahm**.

Tell students another reason to learn simple past stem: present subjunctive is formed from it.

Principal parts of strong verbs

The simple past stem is one of the *principal parts* of a strong German verb. The principal parts are the three (or sometimes four) forms you must know in order to generate all other forms of a strong verb. You have now learned all of them.

infinitive	*3rd-person sing. present*	*simple past stem*	*auxiliary + past participle*
nehmen	**(nimmt)**	**nahm**	**hat genommen**

The table on p. 283 contains the principal parts of all the strong verbs you have learned so far. As an aid to memorization, they have been arranged into groups according to the way their stem-vowels change in the past tenses. Memorize their simple past stems and review your knowledge of the other principal parts. Verbs formed by adding prefixes to these stems are not included in the table, e.g., **abfahren**, **aufstehen**, **beschreiben**, **verstehen**.

Wahlplakat der Grünen, Rheinland-Pfalz.

Verbs are arranged by **Ablautreihe** as an aid to memorization, with "orphans" at the end. There are 50 new past stems to learn (and participles and stem-vowel changes to review), and students should be given ample time to do so. Elicit principal parts of a few strong verbs orally in "spot quiz" fashion, perhaps in **Ablaut**-groups, at random times over the coming weeks. Perhaps test only 1/3 to 1/2 of the entire list at a time.

Principal Parts of Strong Verbs

Infinitive	3rd-sing. pres.	Simple past	Perfect	English
anfangen	fängt an	**fing an**	hat angefangen	*to begin*
fallen	fällt	**fiel**	ist gefallen	*to fall; to die in battle*
halten	hält	**hielt**	hat gehalten	*to hold; to stop*
schlafen	schläft	**schlief**	hat geschlafen	*to sleep*
verlassen	verlässt	**verließ**	hat verlassen	*to leave*
einladen	lädt ein	**lud ein**	hat eingeladen	*to invite*
fahren	fährt	**fuhr**	ist gefahren	*to drive*
tragen	trägt	**trug**	hat getragen	*to carry; to wear*
essen	isst	**aß**	hat gegessen	*to eat*
geben	gibt	**gab**	hat gegeben	*to give*
lesen	liest	**las**	hat gelesen	*to read*
sehen	sieht	**sah**	hat gesehen	*to see*
vergessen	vergisst	**vergaß**	hat vergessen	*to forget*
empfehlen	empfiehlt	**empfahl**	hat empfohlen	*to recommend*
helfen	hilft	**half**	hat geholfen	*to help*
nehmen	nimmt	**nahm**	hat genommen	*to take*
sprechen	spricht	**sprach**	hat gesprochen	*to speak*
stehlen	stiehlt	**stahl**	hat gestohlen	*to steal*
sterben	stirbt	**starb**	ist gestorben	*to die*
treffen	trifft	**traf**	hat getroffen	*to meet*
werfen	wirft	**warf**	hat geworfen	*to throw*
bleiben		**blieb**	ist geblieben	*to stay*
entscheiden		**entschied**	hat entschieden	*to decide*
leihen		**lieh**	hat geliehen	*to lend*
scheinen		**schien**	hat geschienen	*to shine; to seem*
schreiben		**schrieb**	hat geschrieben	*to write*
steigen		**stieg**	ist gestiegen	*to climb*
treiben		**trieb**	hat getrieben	*to drive, propel*
finden		**fand**	hat gefunden	*to find*
klingen		**klang**	hat geklungen	*to sound*
singen		**sang**	hat gesungen	*to sing*
trinken		**trank**	hat getrunken	*to drink*
beginnen		**begann**	hat begonnen	*to begin*
schwimmen		**schwamm**	ist geschwommen	*to swim*
liegen		**lag**	hat gelegen	*to lie*
sitzen		**saß**	hat gesessen	*to sit*
fliegen		**flog**	ist geflogen	*to fly*
fließen		**floss**	ist geflossen	*to flow*
schließen		**schloss**	hat geschlossen	*to close*
verlieren		**verlor**	hat verloren	*to lose*
ziehen		**zog**	hat/ist gezogen	*to pull; to move*
anrufen		**rief an**	hat angerufen	*to call up*
gehen		**ging**	ist gegangen	*to go*
hängen		**hing**	hat gehangen	*to be hanging*
heißen		**hieß**	hat geheißen	*to be called*
kommen		**kam**	ist gekommen	*to come*
laufen	läuft	**lief**	ist gelaufen	*to run*
sein	ist	**war**	ist gewesen	*to be*
stehen		**stand**	hat gestanden	*to stand*
tun		**tat**	hat getan	*to do*

■ **2** ■ **Übung** Change the following sentences to the simple past tense.

1. Mir gefällt sein neues Fahrrad.
2. Barbara ruft um halb fünf an.
3. Sie schwimmt das ganze Jahr, um fit zu bleiben.
4. Stefan findet seinen Geldbeutel nicht.
5. Jede Woche schreibt sie uns eine Postkarte.
6. Der Film beginnt um 20.30 Uhr.
7. Er hilft mir gern mit meinen Hausaufgaben.
8. Sie heißt Dora Schilling.
9. Um acht gehen die Senioren miteinander essen.
10. Er liegt immer gern im Bett und liest die Zeitung.
11. Ich finde es komisch, dass er nichts trinkt.
12. Am Montag kommt Bert zurück.
13. Sie kommt um 10 Uhr an und bleibt den ganzen Tag da.
14. Sie sieht ihren Freund und läuft schnell zu ihm.

In sentence 3, the infinitive construction **um fit zu bleiben** does not change tense.

■ **3** ■ **Übung: Ein Brief** Complete this letter by filling in the verbs in the simple past tense. Some of the verbs are strong and some are weak.

Liebe Martine,

weißt du, was dem armen Ulrich vorgestern passiert ist? Er hat mich gestern angerufen und ________ (erzählen) es mir. Er ________ (kennen lernen) im Park eine sympathische junge Studentin ________. Sie ________ (aussehen) ganz elegant und reich ________. Zusammen ________ (sitzen) sie auf einer Bank und ________ (sprechen) über das Studium. Ulrich ________ (tragen) eine Jacke, aber weil es sehr heiß war, ________ (legen) er sie auf die Bank. Alles ________ (scheinen) gut zu gehen und Ulrich ________ (einladen) sie in ein Konzert ________. Sie ________ (sagen) ja und ________ (geben) ihm ihre Adresse und Telefonnummer. Nach einer Stunde ________ (stehen) die Studentin auf und ________ (gehen) in die Bibliothek zurück. Am Abend ________ (kommen) er nach Hause und ________ (suchen) seinen Hausschlüssel in der Tasche seiner Jacke. Aber dort ________ (finden) er keinen Schlüssel und auch sein Geld ________ (sein) weg. Er ________ (rufen) die Nummer der Studentin an, aber sie ________ (wohnen) gar nicht da. So ein Mist, nicht?

Jetzt muss ich gehen. Viele Grüße,

deine

Annelies

■ Simple past of modal verbs

The modal verbs form their simple past with the **-te** marker, like the weak verbs. But those modals that have an umlaut in the infinitive *drop* it in the past tense.

müssen, **musste**			
ich muss**te**	*I had to*	wir muss**ten**	*we had to*
du muss**test**	*you had to*	ihr muss**tet**	*you had to*
er, es, sie muss**te**	*he, it, she had to*	sie, Sie muss**ten**	*they, you had to*

Similarly:

dürfen	ich **durfte**	*I was allowed to*
können	ich **konnte**	*I was able to*
mögen	ich **mochte**	*I liked*
sollen	ich **sollte**	*I was supposed to*
wollen	ich **wollte**	*I wanted to*

Note that **mögen** drops the umlaut and also has a consonant change in the simple past.

4 Übung

1. Sagen Sie, was Sie gestern machen mussten.

   BEISPIEL: Ich musste gestern zwei Bücher lesen.

2. Jetzt sagen Sie, was Sie und Ihre Freunde gestern machen wollten.

   BEISPIEL: Wir wollten gestern Ski fahren gehen.

3. Was durften Sie als Kind nicht machen?

   BEISPIEL: Ich durfte nie allein schwimmen gehen.

Simple past of mixed verbs

The mixed verbs (see p. 166) use the **-te** marker for the simple past but attach it to the *changed* stem, which you have already learned for the past participles:

wissen, **wusste**, hat gewusst			
ich wuss**te**	*I knew*	wir wuss**ten**	*we knew*
du wuss**test**	*you knew*	ihr wuss**tet**	*you knew*
er, es, sie wuss**te**	*he, it, she knew*	sie, Sie wuss**ten**	*they, you knew*

Remember that **wissen** is irregular in the present-tense singular: ich **weiß**, du **weißt**, er **weiß**.

Similarly:

bringen, **brachte**, hat gebracht
kennen, **kannte**, hat gekannt

Simple past of *haben* and *werden*

Students may forget that **er/sie hat** is present tense because it sounds like Engl. *had*. Contrast 3rd-pers. sing. forms:
I: *He's hungry.*
SI: **Er hat Hunger.**
I: *He was hungry.*
S2: **Er hatte Hunger.** (Vary with other 3rd-pers. subjects, **Angst haben.**)

Only **haben** and **werden** are irregular in the simple past tense.

haben, **hatte**, hat gehabt			
ich hatte	*I had*	wir hatt**en**	*we had*
du hatt**est**	*you had*	ihr hatt**et**	*you had*
er, es, sie hatte	*he, it, she had*	sie, Sie hatt**en**	*they, you had*

Work on pronunciation of **wurde** by having students first say **wu-**, then **wurde**. Especially when subjunctive is introduced, students tend to pronounce **wurde** as **würde** and **durfte** as **dürfte**.

werden, **wurde**, ist geworden			
ich wurd**e**	*I became*	wir wurd**en**	*we became*
du wurd**est**	*you became*	ihr wurd**et**	*you became*
er, es, sie wurd**e**	*he, it, she became*	sie, Sie wurd**en**	*they, you became*

5 **Übung** Retell the following short narrative in the simple past.

Andreas **kennt** Mainz sehr gut, weil seine Großeltern dort **wohnen**. Als er 11 Jahre alt **wird**, **darf** er allein mit dem Zug nach Mainz fahren. Er **verbringt** jeden Sommer dort. Die Großeltern **wissen** alles über die Stadt, denn sie **leben** seit Jahren in Mainz. Er **bringt** ihnen immer ein Geschenk mit und das **haben** sie immer gern.

Use of the simple past tense

In English there is a difference in *meaning* between past tense and perfect tense. Compare these sentences:

I saw Marion in the restaurant.
I have seen Marion in the restaurant.

I saw Marion refers to a unique event in the past, while *I have seen Marion* implies that Marion has been in the restaurant on several occasions and may be there again.

In German, there is *no* difference in meaning between simple past and perfect tense. They both simply convey that the action is in the past:

Ich **sah** Marion im Restaurant. Ich **habe** Marion im Restaurant **gesehen**.	*I saw Marion in the restaurant.*

The difference between German simple past and perfect tense is mainly one of *usage*: they are used under different circumstances. As you have already learned, the perfect tense is the *conversational past*, used in conversation to refer to events in the past. The simple past tense is regularly used in conversation only with frequently occurring verbs such as **sein**, **haben**, and the modal verbs.

Especially 2nd-pers. familiar forms would sound horribly stilted in conversation: **Kauftest du mir ein Geschenk? Gingst du gestern ins Kino? Fuhrt ihr mit dem Zug?**

A: Wo **warst** du denn gestern? Ich habe auf dich gewartet.	*Where were you yesterday? I waited for you.*
B: Ich **hatte** kein Geld mehr und **musste** nach Hause.	*I didn't have any more money and had to go home.*

The primary use of simple past tense is in *written* German (in letters, newspaper reports, short stories, novels, etc.) to narrate a series of events in the past. Here, for example, is the beginning of the fairy tale "Hänsel und Gretel":

Es war einmal ... is the formulaic beginning for most German fairy tales.

Es **war** einmal ein armer Holzhacker. Er **wohnte** mit seinen zwei Kindern vor einem Wald. Sie **hießen** Hänsel und Gretel. Sie **hatten** wenig zu essen und ihre Stiefmutter **wollte** sie los werden.	*Once upon a time there was a poor woodcutter. He lived at the edge of a forest with his two children. Their names were Hansel and Gretel. They had little to eat and their stepmother wanted to get rid of them.*

Simple past after the conjunction *als*

Clauses introduced by the subordinating conjunction **als** (*when* or *as* referring to a point or stretch of time in the past) require the simple past tense.

Hans hat uns oft besucht, **als** er in New York **wohnte**.	*Hans often visited us when he lived in New York.*
Als ich meinen Geldbeutel **suchte**, konnte ich ihn nicht finden.	*When I looked for my wallet I couldn't find it.*

■ 6 ■ Übung: Es war schon spät Sagen Sie, dass es schon spät war, als etwas passierte.

BEISPIEL: Das Konzert fing an.
Es war schon spät, als das Konzert anfing.

1. Ich fand den Laden.
2. Er ging endlich.
3. Wir kamen in München an.
4. Sie fuhr ab.
5. Das Telefon klingelte.
6. Meine Freunde kamen vorbei.

Üb. 7: After students work on sentences in class, have them submit as written homework.

■ 7 ■ Partnerarbeit: Wie geht's weiter? Take turns completing the following sentences with an als-clause.

1. Jürgen konnte seinen Schlüssel nicht finden, als ...
2. Herr Ziegler hat jeden Sommer seine Großeltern besucht, als ...
3. Es ging der Großmutter nicht gut, als ...
4. Ute lief schnell ins Haus, als ...
5. Alle Schüler lachten, als ...

Now restate the sentences, beginning with your **als**-clause.

BEISPIEL: *Als* Jürgen nach Hause kam, konnte er seinen Schlüssel nicht finden.

Equivalents for "when": als, wenn, wann

It is important to distinguish among three German subordinating conjunctions, each of which may be translated by English *when*.

- **als** = *when* (in the past); *as*
  Als refers to an event or state *in the past* and requires the simple past tense.

Als wir in Wien waren, haben wir Andreas besucht.	*When we were in Vienna, we visited Andreas.*

If necessary, remind students that **ob** = *if/whether*.

- **wenn** = *when/if; whenever*
  Wenn means *when* in reference to an event *in the present or future*. Since it can also mean *if*, clauses with **wenn** can be ambiguous.

Wenn wir in Wien sind, besuchen wir Andreas.	*When (If) we're in Vienna, we'll visit Andreas.*

  Wenn also means *whenever* in reference to repeated action in the past or present. To avoid confusion between *whenever* and *if*, add the adverb **immer** if you mean *whenever*.

Wenn Hans nach Wien kommt, geht er **immer** ins Kaffeehaus.	*Whenever Hans comes to Vienna, he always goes to a coffee house.*

  Note carefully the difference in meaning between **als** and **wenn** used with simple past tense.

Als sie das sagte, wurde er rot.	*When she said that, he turned red.*
Wenn sie das sagte, wurde er immer rot.	*Whenever she said that, he always turned red.*

Rule of thumb: For cases in which English *when* = *at what time*, use German **wann**. If *when* = *if* or *whenever*, use **wenn**.

- **Wann** = *when, at what time*
  Wann is always a question word, used both in direct questions and in indirect questions:

  Wann ist das passiert?
  When did that happen?

  Ich weiß nicht, **wann** das passiert ist.
  I don't know when that happened.

Workbook Kap. 10, F.

Üb. 8, Answers:
1. wann, Wenn
2. Wann, wann, wenn, als, wenn
3. Als, Wenn, wann.

■ 8 ■ Übung: Als, wenn oder wann? (*Mit offenen Büchern*)

1. Mutti, ________ darf ich spielen?
   ________ du das Altglas in den Keller getragen hast.
2. ________ fängt das Konzert an?
   Ich weiß nicht, ________ es anfängt.
   Karl kann es uns sagen, ________ er zurückkommt.
   Wir haben viele Konzerte gehört, ________ wir Berlin besuchten.
   Das möchte ich auch tun, ________ ich nächstes Jahr in Berlin bin.
3. ________ ich gestern an der Uni war, habe ich Angelika getroffen. Sie hat gesagt, sie kommt heute Abend mit.
   Gut! ________ Angelika mitkommt, macht es mehr Spaß.
   Sag mir bitte noch einmal, ________ die Party beginnt.

Üb. 9: Could also be a written assignment. Return to this later for more work on *when*.
Answers:
1. Wann, als, wenn, wann
2. Als, Wenn, Wann, Wenn

■ 9 ■ Partnerarbeit: Wie sagt man das auf Deutsch?

Sagen Sie diese Dialoge auf Deutsch.

1. A: When did you meet Claudia?
   B: I met her when I was studying in Vienna. Whenever I'm there, I always write her a postcard.
   A: I don't know when I'll go to Vienna again.

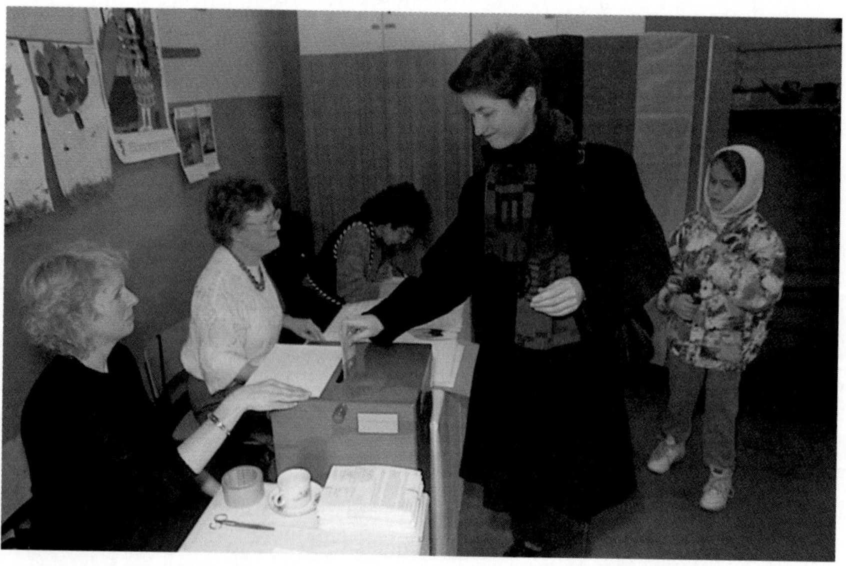

Die ersten freien Wahlen in der ehemaligen DDR.

2. A: When I was young I hitchhiked a lot.
   B: When I go to Europe, I'll do that too.
   A: When are you going to Europe?
   B: When I have enough money.

Past perfect tense

The past perfect tense is used for an event in the past that preceded another event in the past.

Als Hans aufstand, **hatte** Ulla schon **gefrühstückt**.	*When Hans got up, Ulla* ***had*** *already* ***eaten breakfast****.*

The form of the past perfect tense is parallel to that of the perfect tense, but the auxiliary verb (**haben** or **sein**) is in the past tense instead of the present (**haben** → **hatte**, **sein** → **war**).

ich **hatte gegessen**	*I had eaten*
du **hattest gegessen**	*you had eaten*
er **hatte gegessen**	*he had eaten*
wir **hatten gegessen**	*we had eaten*
ihr **hattet gegessen**	*you had eaten*
sie **hatten gegessen**	*they had eaten*
ich **war aufgestanden**	*I had gotten up*
du **warst aufgestanden**	*you had gotten up*
sie **war aufgestanden**	*she had gotten up*
wir **waren aufgestanden**	*we had gotten up*
ihr **wart aufgestanden**	*you had gotten up*
sie **waren aufgestanden**	*they had gotten up*

Look at the following timetable of morning events at Hans and Ulla's house, then at how they are combined in the sentences that follow.

8.00 Uhr: Ulla hat gefrühstückt.

9.00 Uhr: Hans ist aufgestanden.

10.00 Uhr: Ulla ist zur Uni gegangen.

11.00 Uhr: Hans hat gefrühstückt.

event 1 (8.00 Uhr)	event 2 (9.00 Uhr)
Ulla **hatte** schon **gefrühstückt**, *Ulla had already eaten,*	als Hans aufstand. *when Hans got up.*

The order of the clauses may of course be reversed:

event 2 (9.00 Uhr)	event 1 (8.00 Uhr)
Als Hans aufstand, *When Hans got up,*	**hatte** Ulla schon **gefrühstückt**. *Ulla had already eaten.*

Distinguish between the preposition **nach** (+ noun in the dative) and the conjunction **nachdem** (+ clause with the verb in final position). Both are translated *after*. **Nach der Deutschstunde** ... (after German class); **Nachdem wir das Essen bestellt hatten** ... (*After we had ordered the meal* ...).

The subordinating conjunction **nachdem** (*after*) is often used with the past perfect tense.

Nachdem Ulla gefrühstückt hatte, ging sie zur Uni. — *After Ulla had eaten breakfast, she went to the university.*

Lab Manual Kap. 10, Var. zur Üb. 10.

Workbook Kap. 10, G.

Üb. 10: Emphasize importance of **schon** in this exercise. Also good as written homework.

■ 10 ■ Übung: Als Ulla nach Hause kam Sie spielen die Rolle von Hans. Sie sind heute vor Ulla nach Hause gekommen und hatten viel Zeit eine Menge zu machen. Sagen Sie, was Sie schon gemacht hatten, als Ulla um 23.00 Uhr endlich nach Hause kam.

BEISPIEL: Lebensmittel eingekauft
Als Ulla nach Hause kam, hatte ich schon Lebensmittel eingekauft.

1. nach Hause gekommen
2. Kartoffeln gekocht
3. alles sauber gemacht
4. die Kinder abgeholt
5. einkaufen gegangen
6. den Kindern das Essen gegeben
7. die Zeitung gelesen
8. ein Glas Wein getrunken
9. die Kinder ins Bett gebracht
10. ein paar Briefe geschrieben
11. meine Kusine angerufen
12. ins Bett gegangen

Telling how long ago something happened is a communicative goal.

More time expressions

■ *vor* + dative = *ago*

The preposition **vor** is used with various time expressions in the dative case to mean *ago*.

vor fünf Minuten	*five minutes ago*
vor einer Stunde	*an hour ago*
vor drei Tagen	*three days ago*
vor vielen Wochen	*many weeks ago*
vor einem Monat	*a month ago*
vor hundert Jahren	*a hundred years ago*

■ **11** ■ **Übung: Wann war das?** Sagen Sie auf Deutsch, wann etwas passiert ist.

BEISPIEL: Wann ist das passiert?
(*two days ago*): Vor zwei Tagen.

1. a minute ago
2. an hour ago
3. three years ago
4. five months ago
5. ten days ago
6. a couple of weeks ago

„Vor 60 Jahren hast du mich hier ins Kino eingeladen. Nächstes Jahr lade ich dich ein."

■ **12** ■ **Partnerarbeit: Wann hast du zuletzt ... gemacht?** Ask each other when you last did these things.

BEISPIEL: A: Wann hast du zuletzt deine Großeltern besucht?
B: Ich habe sie vor drei Monaten besucht.

deine Oma besuchen
Geld ausgeben
einen Stadtbummel machen
einen langen Roman lesen
in ein neues Haus umziehen
Sport treiben
etwas für die Umwelt tun
einen Brief bekommen

■ Duration ending in the past

German and English differ in the way they show an action ending in the past versus an action continuing into the present. English makes this distinction by using different verb tenses:

*We **lived** in Berlin for three years.*	*Past tense* for a state ending in the past (i.e., we don't live there any more).
*We **have lived** in Berlin for three years.*	*Perfect tense* for a state continuing at the moment of speaking (i.e., we're *still* living there).

Telling how long something lasted is a communicative goal.

In German, however, both *the simple past* and *the perfect tense* are used for a state ending in the past.

Wir **wohnten** drei Jahre in Berlin.
Wir **haben** drei Jahre in Berlin **gewohnt**. } *We **lived** in Berlin for three years.*

■ Duration beginning in the past but continuing in the present

For a state beginning in the past but continuing at the moment of speaking, German uses *present tense* and one of these adverbial phrases:

You may also want to teach **schon seit** + *dative*.

schon (+ accusative) → **schon drei Jahre**
seit (+ dative) → **seit drei Jahren**

Wir **wohnen schon drei Jahre** in Berlin. Wir **wohnen seit drei Jahren** in Berlin.	} *We **have lived** in Berlin for three years.*

Note carefully the difference between verb tenses in the two languages!

Note on Usage: For a long time

Notice the different ways to express *for a long time.*

Ich hoffe, du kannst **lange** bleiben.	*I hope you can stay **for a long time.*** (continuing into the future)
Ich wohne **schon lange** hier. Ich wohne **seit langem** hier.	} *I've lived here **for a long time.*** (continuing from the past)

Lab Manual Kap. 10, Üb. 13.

Workbook Kap. 10, H.

■ 13 ■ Übung: Wie lange schon? Ihre Professorin möchte wissen, wie lange Sie etwas schon machen. Sagen Sie, Sie machen es schon zwei Jahre.

BEISPIEL: Wie lange arbeiten Sie schon hier?
Ich arbeite schon zwei Jahre hier.

Antworten Sie mit **schon**.

1. Wie lange studieren Sie schon hier?
2. Wie lange lernen Sie schon Deutsch?
3. Wie lange treiben Sie schon Sport?
4. Wie lange wohnen Sie schon im Studentenwohnheim?
5. Wie lange fahren Sie schon Rad?

Antworten Sie mit **seit**.

6. Seit wann kennen Sie mich?
7. Seit wann haben Sie kurze Haare?
8. Seit wann studieren Sie hier?
9. Seit wann sammeln Sie Altglas?
10. Seit wann spielen Sie ein Musikinstrument?

Üb. 14: Could be written assignment. Answers:
1. Wir kennen ihn seit einem (*or*: schon ein) Jahr.
2. Sie wohnt seit / schon 2 Wochen hier.
3. Er leiht mir seit langem / schon lange Geld.
4. Barbara ist (schon) seit 5 Tagen (*or*: schon 5 Tage) hier.
5. Sie studiert seit 2 Semestern / schon 2 Semester in Halle.
6. Seit 10 Jahren / Schon 10 Jahre gibt es hier ein ausgezeichnetes Restaurant.
7. Michael interviewt sie schon 3 Stunden / seit 3 Stunden.
8. Ich habe seit 2 Tagen / schon 2 Tage Hunger.

■ 14 ■ Partnerarbeit: Wie sagt man das auf Deutsch? Übersetzen Sie diese Sätze mit Ihrem Partner.

1. We've known him for a year.
2. She's lived here for two weeks.
3. He's been lending me money for a long time.
4. Barbara has already been here five days.
5. She has studied in Halle for two semesters.
6. For ten years there's been an excellent restaurant here.
7. Michael has been interviewing her for three hours.
8. I've been hungry for two days.

15 **Partnerarbeit: Wie lange machst du das schon?** Fragen Sie einander, wie lange oder seit wann Sie etwas machen. Unten (*below*) sind einige Ideen, aber Sie können auch Ihre eigenen Fragen stellen.

1. Wie lange studierst du schon hier?
2. Seit wann lernst du Fremdsprachen?
3. Wie lange lernst du schon Deutsch?
4. Seit wann gibt es diese Uni?
5. Wie lange kannst du schon Auto fahren?
6. Seit wann arbeitest du mit dem Computer?
7. Wie lange sind wir heute schon in der Deutschstunde?

Lesestück

Vor dem Lesen

Tipps zum Lesen und Lernen

Tipps zum Vokabelnlernen

Other examples: **Katholizismus, Protestantismus, Kapitalismus, Protektionismus, Sozialismus, Anarchismus, Modernismus, Expressionismus, Futurismus.**

The following reading mentions several concepts such as National Socialism, Communism, and anti-Semitism. English words ending in *-ism* denote a system of belief, a doctrine, or a characteristic. Their German equivalents end in the suffix **-ismus**. These words are all masculine in German and the stress is always on the penultimate syllable (**Optimismus**).

der Antisemitismus	der Kommunismus
der Extremismus	der Optimismus
der Idealismus	der Pessimismus

This is the origin of words like *hamburger*, *wiener*, *frankfurter*, *Budweiser*, and *pilsner* (from *Budweis* and *Pilsen*, German names for the Czech cities **České Budejovice** and **Plzeň**).

City names as adjectives The reading also mentions the *Weimar* Republic, the *Versailles* Treaty, and the *New York* Stock Exchange. When the names of cities are used as adjectives in German, they are capitalized and simply add the ending **-er** in all cases: **die Weimarer Republik**, **der Versailler Vertrag**, **die New Yorker Börse**.

Leicht zu merken

Lab Manual Kap. 10, Üb. zur Betonung.

Students should be able to guess the pronunciation of these cognates by now. Have them abstract some rules: (1) all adjectives ending in **-isch** stress penultimate syllable; (2) all nouns in **-tion** stress the final syllable and are feminine; (3) all **-ieren** verbs stress penultimate syllable.

die **Demokratie, -n**	Demokratie
demokratisch	
der **Direktor, -en**	
die **Epoche, -n**	Epoche
extrem	
die **Form, -en**	
ideologisch	
illegal	illegal
die **Inflation**	Inflation
manipulieren	manipulieren
die **Methode, -n**	Methode
die **Monarchie, -n**	Monarchie
die **Opposition, -en**	Opposition
die **Republik, -en**	Republik
die **Situation, -en**	Situation
symbolisch	
terroristisch	terroristisch

Einstieg in den Text

In the following reading, you will encounter quite a bit of factual historical information about an important period in modern German history: the Weimar Republic. Much of the information will probably be new to you, but you already know enough German to be able to understand complex issues.

When reading the text through for the first time, keep the following basic information questions in mind as a guide:

Was war die Weimarer Republik?
Wann war diese historische Epoche?
Wer hat damals eine Rolle gespielt?
Warum war diese Zeit so wichtig?

Before reading, also examine the illustrations that accompany and are referred to in the reading. These convey an impression of the content of the reading and will help you to understand the issues discussed.

Was für Plakate sind das?
Aus welcher Zeit kommen sie?
Was zeigen die Bilder?
Welche Wörter oder Namen können Sie schon verstehen?

Wortschatz 2

Verben

erklären to explain
nennen, nannte, hat genannt to name, call
stören to disturb
unterbrechen (unterbricht), unterbrach, hat unterbrochen to interrupt
versuchen to try, attempt
wachsen (wächst), wuchs, ist gewachsen to grow
wählen to choose; to vote
zählen to count

Substantive

der **Arm, -e** arm
der **Schriftsteller, -** writer (*m.*)
der **Staat, -en** state
der **Wähler, -** voter

das **Plakat, -e** poster
das **Reich, -e** empire, realm
das **Volk, ¨er** people, nation, folk

Wachsen: English cognate *to wax* (of the moon). Opposite is *to wane*, German cognate **wenig**.

die **Arbeitslosigkeit** unemployment
die **Ausstellung, -en** exhibition
die **Bedeutung, -en** meaning, significance
die **Dame, -n** lady
die **Idee, -n** idea
die **Schriftstellerin, -nen** writer (*f.*)
die **Wahl, -en** choice; election

Idea: **die Idee** is the most general equivalent: **Das ist eine gute Idee. Ahnung** means *inkling*: **Ich habe keine Ahnung.**

Adjektive und Adverbien

arbeitslos unemployed
ausländisch foreign
bekannt known; well known
hart hard; tough; harsh
unruhig restless, uneasy, troubled

das Reich: Originally from the Celtic, related to Latin *rex* (*king*). Preserved in names like Heinrich and Dietrich.

Andere Vokabel

bevor (*sub. conj.*) before

Nützliche Ausdrücke

zu Ende sein to end, be finished, be over
1918 war der Krieg zu Ende. The war ended in 1918.
eine Frage stellen to ask a question

Fragen takes a direct object of person (**Ich habe ihn gefragt**).

Gegensätze

bekannt ≠ unbekannt known ≠ unknown
unruhig ≠ ruhig restless ≠ calm, peaceful

Eine Ausstellung historischer Plakate aus der Weimarer Republik

Plakat is the term for informational posters, **Poster** for decorative posters (performers, vacation spots, etc.).

Im Hessischen Landesmuseum° gab es vor einiger Zeit° eine Ausstellung politischer Plakate aus der Weimarer Republik (1919–1933). Der Museumsdirektor führte eine Gruppe ausländischer Studenten durch die Ausstellung.

Hessian State Museum / **vor** ... = a while ago

Lab Manual Kap. 10, Lesestück.

„Meine Damen und Herren, herzlich willkommen im Landesmuseum! Bevor wir in die Ausstellung gehen, möchte ich Ihnen ein paar Worte über die Geschichte der Weimarer Republik sagen. Vielleicht ist Ihnen diese Epoche schon bekannt, aber wenn Ihnen etwas nicht klar ist, können Sie jederzeit° Fragen stellen – das stört mich gar nicht.

at any time

Learning about the Weimar Republic is the cultural goal of this chapter.

Was war das eigentlich, die Weimarer Republik? So nennen wir den deutschen Staat in der Zeit zwischen dem Ende des Ersten Weltkrieges 1918 und dem Anfang des Dritten Reiches[1] im Januar 1933. Es war Deutschlands erster Versuch° eine demokratische Staatsform zu entwickeln°. Unsere Plakate zeigen die extremen ideologischen Gegensätze° dieser Epoche. Aber sie zeigen auch, wie man gegensätzliche° Ideen oft mit ähnlichen Bildern darstellen° kann."

attempt
develop
polarities / contradictory
represent

Hier unterbrach ein Student mit einer Frage: „Entschuldigung, aber können Sie uns erklären, warum es die ‚Weimarer' Republik hieß? War Berlin nicht damals die Hauptstadt Deutschlands?"

German equivalents for *people*: **das Volk** (a people defined by a common language and culture: **das deutsche Volk**); **Menschen** (people in general: **die Menschen in dieser Stadt**); **Leute** (more restricted grouping: **die Leute hier im Zimmer**).

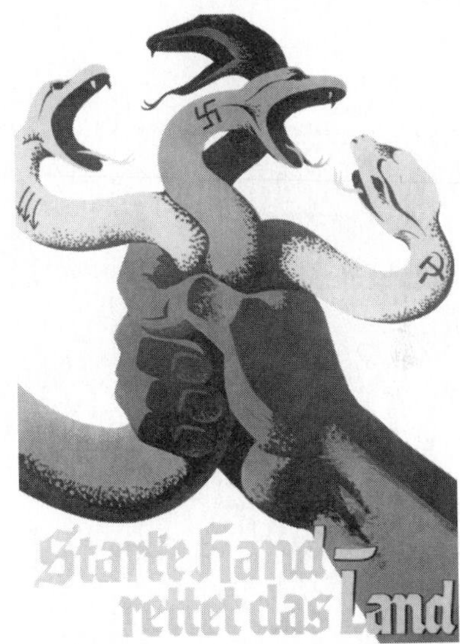

The symbols on the snakes from left to right identify the following parties: the Social Democrats (SPD), the Nazis (NSDAP), and the Communists (KPD). The fourth snake behind the others probably represents the right-wing German National People's Party (DNVP).

1. **Das Dritte Reich**: The Nazis' own name for their regime (1933–1945). The first empire was the Holy Roman Empire (962–1806). The second empire (**das Deutsche Reich**, 1871–1918) collapsed at the end of the First World War.

„Sicher. Berlin blieb auch die Hauptstadt, aber die Politiker kamen 1919 in der Stadt Weimar zusammen, um die neue demokratische Verfassung zu beschließen°. In Berlin war die politische Situation damals sehr unruhig und außerdem° hatte Weimar wichtige symbolische Bedeutung als die Stadt, wo die großen Schriftsteller Goethe und Schiller[1] früher gelebt und gearbeitet hatten.

Verfassung ... = ratify the constitution / moreover

Die ersten Jahre der Republik waren eine Zeit der Arbeitslosigkeit und der hohen Inflation. Deutschland hatte den Ersten Weltkrieg verloren und die Monarchie war zu Ende.[2] Unter dem harten Versailler Friedensvertrag musste der neue demokratische Staat 20 Milliarden° Goldmark an die Siegermächte° (besonders an Frankreich) zahlen. Unser erstes Plakat, aus der Zeit vor 1925, zeigt den deutschen Reichsadler° durch den Versailler Vertrag gefesselt°.

billion / victors
imperial eagle
fettered

SPD poster for the Reichstag election of May 1924 ("The Answer to the Hitler Trial")

After the failed Nazi putsch in Munich in November 1923, Hitler received a light prison sentence of 5 years, and his National Socialist Party was officially banned. The SPD made a weak showing in the election, while both the Communists and the radical Right gained strength.

Posters in this reading section are reprinted from exhibition catalogue: *Politische Plakate der Weimarer Republik 1918–1933* (Hessisches Landesmuseum Darmstadt, 1980).

1. Johann Wolfgang von Goethe (1749–1832); Friedrich von Schiller (1759–1805).
2. Kaiser Wilhelm II (1859–1941) abdicated in November 1918 and went into exile in the Netherlands. The Treaty of Versailles officially ended the First World War in 1919.

Als die New Yorker Börse° 1929 stürzte°, wurde die Wirtschaftskrise° in den Industrieländern Europas katastrophal. Man zählte im Februar 1930 schon mehr als° 3,5 Millionen arbeitslose Menschen in Deutschland.

Diese Wirtschaftskrise brachte die junge deutsche Demokratie in Gefahr, denn schon 1932 waren sieben Millionen Menschen arbeitslos. Es gab damals mehr als dreißig politische Parteien und besonders die antidemokratischen konnten schnell wachsen. Auf diesem zweiten Plakat sieht man, wie die ‚starke Hand' der katholischen Zentrumspartei[1] die extremen Parteien erwürgt°. In den Wahlen nach 1930 stieg aber die Macht der Nationalsozialistischen Deutschen Arbeiterpartei (NSDAP) – der Nazis – bis sie die stärkste° im Reichstag[2] wurde. Ihr Führer Adolf Hitler benutzte den Antisemitismus und Antikommunismus um die Ängste des Volkes zu manipulieren. Ein Plakat der Nazis zeigt den symbolischen ‚starken Mann', der° Deutschland retten soll. Die Opposition sehen Sie noch auf diesem Plakat von 1931, wo starke Arme versuchen, das Hakenkreuz° der Nazis zu zerreißen°."

Eine Studentin stellte eine Frage: „Ist denn Hitler nicht illegal an die Macht gekommen°?"

„Eigentlich nicht", antwortete der Museumsdirektor. „Nachdem die Wähler den Nazis die meisten Stimmen° gegeben hatten, musste man Hitler zum Reichskanzler ernennen°. Erst als er Kanzler geworden war, konnte er mit terroristischen Methoden die Republik in eine Diktatur verwandeln°. Deutschland ist also ein gutes Beispiel für die Zerstörung einer schwachen Demokratie durch wirtschaftliche Not° und politischen Extremismus."

stock market / crashed / economic crisis / **mehr als** = more than

strangles

strongest

who

swastika / rip apart

an ... = came to power

(*here*) votes

zum ... = appoint chancellor

in ... = transform into a dictatorship / **wirtschaftliche Not** = economic hardship

The problems introduced in the **Lesestück** are central to understanding modern German history and culture. Instructors are encouraged to augment this presentation as appropriate and to revisit the issue of the National Socialist past at higher levels in the curriculum.

1. The conservative Center Party, consisting mainly of Catholic voters.
2. The name of the German Parliament until 1945, now called **der Bundestag**. The parliament building in Berlin is still called the **Reichstag**.

Nach dem Lesen

This activity leads students from straightforward description to active engagement with historical issues raised in the **Lesestück**. You will need to supply or repeat some supplementary vocabulary: **Adler**, **gefesselt**, **Schlange**, **Hakenkreuz**, **Verfassung**, **Kette**.

■ A ■ Antworten Sie auf Deutsch.

1. Warum besuchte die Studentengruppe das Museum?
2. Aus welcher Zeit waren die Plakate dieser Ausstellung?
3. Wer führte die Gruppe durch die Ausstellung?
4. Was für Plakate haben die Studenten im Museum gesehen?
5. Warum hieß der deutsche Staat damals die „Weimarer" Republik?
6. Wie war die Situation in Deutschland nach dem Ersten Weltkrieg? Beschreiben Sie die Probleme.
7. Warum war die junge Demokratie in Gefahr?
8. Wann wurde Hitler Reichskanzler?
9. Wie ist er an die Macht gekommen?

■ B ■ Gruppendiskussion: Bilder erzählen Geschichte. Im Lesestück finden Sie fünf politische Plakate aus der Weimarer Republik. Besprechen Sie diese historischen Bilder.

1. Lesen Sie den Text auf dem Plakat vor.
2. Beschreiben Sie das Bild so ausführlich (*completely*) wie möglich.
3. Interpretieren Sie die Bilder: Was symbolisiert z.B. der Adler auf dem ersten Plakat? die Hand auf dem zweiten? die Kette auf dem letzten? usw.

Situationen aus dem Alltag

This vocabulary focuses on an everyday topic or situation. Words you already know from **Wortschatz** sections are listed without English equivalents; new supplementary vocabulary is listed with definitions. Your instructor may assign some supplementary vocabulary for active mastery.

■ Die Politik

In dem Lesestück haben Sie nicht nur etwas über Geschichte, sondern auch etwas über Politik gelernt. Was hat denn diese politische Diskussion mit unserem Leben zu tun? Wir sind alle politische Menschen und die Politik spielt eine Rolle in unserem Alltag, ob wir es wollen oder nicht.

Spielen wir jetzt ein bisschen mit der Sprache und den Bildern der Politik. Zuerst einige Wörter (viele sind Ihnen schon bekannt):

Politik also means *policy*: **Außenpolitik** (*foreign policy*), **Energiepolitik**, **Umweltpolitik** usw.

die Freiheit
der Frieden
der Krieg, -e
die Politik
der Politiker/die Politikerin
die Regierung, -en — *government in power, administration*

der Staat, -en
die Umwelt
das Volk, ¨-er
die Wahl, -en
wählen
der Wähler, -

Über Klimaschutz reden viele.
Wir tun etwas.

List specific issues on the board: **Umwelt, Bildung, Steuern, Dritte Welt, Atomenergie, Krankenversicherung, Asylpolitik** usw.

■ **A** ■ **Gruppenarbeit: Wir sind politisch aktiv (*in kleinen Gruppen*)** Gründen Sie (*found*) eine neue politische Partei.

Der Name unserer Partei: ____________
Unser Parteiprogramm:
Wir sind für ____________ , ____________ usw.
Wir sind gegen ____________ , ____________ usw.
Wir sehen viele Probleme in der modernen Welt:
____
Unsere Lösungen sind:
____
Unsere Parole (*slogan*) für die Wahlen:
____

Write other animal names on board as needed. **Hund** and **Katze** will be introduced in Kap. 11.

■ **B** ■ **Gruppenarbeit** Ihre politische Partei braucht auch ein Symbol für ihr Wahlplakat. Wie Sie gerade gelesen haben, waren Tiere wichtige Symbole auf den Plakaten in der Weimarer Republik. Sie können ein Tier als Symbol Ihrer Partei wählen, denn Tiere können Ideen symbolisieren.

der Adler, -	*eagle*
der Bär, -en, -en	*bear*
der Elefant, -en, -en	*elephant*
der Esel, -	*donkey*
der Fuchs, ¨-e	*fox*
der Löwe, -n, -n	*lion*
die Schlange, -n	*snake*
die Taube, -n	*dove*

Refer students to Weimar posters, where fam. pl. imperatives are used. If clear party differences emerge, 2 groups of students can prepare a debate. After each party has presented its platform, students can vote for the party they think best. They could fill out **Stimmzettel**. See **Almanach**, p. 306, for example.

■ **C** ■ **Gruppenarbeit: Wahlkampagne** (Election campaign) Jetzt zeigen Sie den anderen Studenten Ihr Wahlplakat. Erklären Sie, warum man Ihre Partei wählen soll. Die „Wähler" können natürlich Fragen stellen oder kritisieren.

Unser Plakat zeigt ...
Wählt unsere Partei, weil ...

Alternative activity for classes capable of more advanced discussion. Also good as written assignment.

■ **D** ■ **Gruppenarbeit: Zur Diskussion** Ist es wichtig für Politiker die Geschichte ihres Landes zu kennen? Was meinen Sie?

Zum Schluss

Sprechen wir miteinander!

Lab Manual Kap. 10, Diktat.

Workbook Kap. 10, Üb. I–K.

Chain drill to review primary plural endings. Once students have the adj. endings under control, they can invent their own sentences using adj. + pl. noun.

A **Kettenreaktion: Ich suche ... (*Mit offenen Büchern*)** Wählen Sie ein Adjektiv und ein Substantiv und sagen Sie dann, was Sie suchen. Der nächste Student sagt, er hat das nicht. Dann geht's weiter.

BEISPIEL: A: Ich suche deutsche Zeitungen.
B: Leider habe ich keine deutschen Zeitungen. *Ich* suche ...

Adjektive		*Substantive*	
amerikanisch	bunt	Romane	Fahrräder
kurz	frisch	Menschen	Alternativen
bekannt	freundlich	Pullis	Politiker
gesund	kostenlos	Geschenke	Restaurants
toll	leer	Brötchen	Arbeiter
deutsch	nagelneu	Rucksäcke	Gebäude
lang	riesengroß	Flaschen	Kleider
ehrlich	sportlich	Bücher	Wälder
besser	umweltfreundlich	Professoren	Plakate
interessant		Ideen	

Students must prepare Üb. B before class. They may want to use some vocabulary they have not yet had. Tell them to look up words they need, but keep it simple, and to use gestures as much as possible to make their meaning clear.

B **Gruppenspiel: Wer war ich?** Wählen Sie eine bekannte historische Person. Spielen Sie diese Person vor der Klasse. Geben Sie genug Information, so dass man Ihre Identität erraten (*guess*) kann.

BEISPIEL: Ich war im 18. Jahrhundert eine österreichische Prinzessin. Später wurde ich die Frau des Königs von Frankreich. Eigentlich habe ich nie gesagt: „Wenn das Volk kein Brot hat, dann soll es Kuchen essen." Während der Revolution verlor ich dann meinen Kopf. Wer war ich?

C **Partnerarbeit: Als meine Großeltern jung waren** Interviewen Sie einander über die Jugend Ihrer Großeltern. Füllen Sie den Fragebogen aus (*fill out the questionnaire*).

1. Wo sind deine Großeltern geboren? ____________________
2. Wo lebten sie als Kinder? ____________________
3. Kamen sie aus großen Familien? ____________________
4. Wo und wie lernten sie einander kennen? ____________________
5. Wie war ihre Kindheit und Jugend anders als heute? ____________________

Narrating events in the past is a communicative goal.

A useful phrase when composing your stories: **eines Tages** = *one day*.

D **Gruppenarbeit: Schreiben wir eine Geschichte zusammen (4–5 Personen)** Unten finden Sie eine Wortliste. Benutzen Sie diese Verben um zusammen eine kurze Geschichte zu schreiben. Sie brauchen einen Sekretär oder eine Sekretärin. Er oder sie soll die Geschichte aufschreiben (*write down*). Der erste Satz der Geschichte ist: „Vor vielen Jahren lebte ein armer Student in einem alten Gebäude in der Altstadt." Student A wählt ein Verb von der Liste und sagt den zweiten Satz. Studentin B sagt einen dritten Satz usw. Sie dürfen natürlich auch andere Verben benutzen und sollen auch viele Adjektive benutzen.

Expanded version can be assigned as written homework. See **Üb. G-2** on p. 302

aufstehen	aufmachen	aussehen	beginnen
benutzen	besitzen	bleiben	einkaufen
essen	dauern	frühstücken	heißen
hoffen	kochen	bekommen	liegen
machen	nehmen	schlafen	trinken
sitzen	spazieren gehen	klauen	lernen
verdienen	verlieren	sagen	zahlen
versuchen	helfen	sterben	übernachten

Lesen Sie einander Ihre Geschichten vor. (**vorlesen** = *to read aloud*)

Schreiben Sie zu Hause.

Üb. E reviews sentences with two objects. Variation: Before students hand in, ask them to read a sentence aloud, then substitute pronouns for dir. obj. and/or indir. obj.:
S1: Ich gebe meiner guten Freundin diesen neuen Roman.
I: Wem gibt er ihn?
S2: Er gibt ihn seiner guten Freundin.
I: Was gibt er ihr?
S3: Er gibt ihr diesen neuen Roman.

E Create sentences with a verb from column 1, an indirect object from column 2, and a direct object from column 3. Don't forget to change adjective endings where necessary.

BEISPIEL: Ich habe meinem lieben Onkel einen langen Brief geschrieben.

1	*2*	*3*
geben	mein lieber Onkel	ein langer Brief
schenken	die nette Austauschstudentin	das neue Restaurant
kaufen	die kleinen Kinder	unsere schöne Altstadt
zeigen	unsere neuen Freunde	unser großer Straßenatlas
erzählen	meine Großeltern	ein Geburtstagsgeschenk
schreiben	das sympathische Mädchen	neue Turnschuhe
beschreiben	mein sportlicher Freund	ein neuer Kassettenrecorder
empfehlen	die ausländischen Touristen	das alte Märchen
leihen	meine gute Freundin	dieser neue Roman

F Write a friend a note about your visit to the poster exhibition. Use the simple past and the past perfect tenses.

1. nachdem / ich / essen (*past perfect tense*) // ich / treffen / mein / Freunde / vor / Museum
2. dort / es / geben / interessant / Ausstellung / von / politisch / Plakate
3. wir / wollen / sehen / Ausstellung // um ... zu / lernen / über / modern / Geschichte
4. wir / unterbrechen / der Museumsdirektor // um ... zu / Fragen / stellen
5. Plakate / zeigen / die / viel / Partei / während / dies- / Zeit
6. nachdem / wir / verbringen / ganz / Nachmittag / dort (*past perfect tense*) // gehen / miteinander / in / Café

Üb. H: 1. Wie lange wohnen Sie schon in diesem Haus? 2. Wir sind seit zwei Jahren (schon zwei Jahre) hier. Es gefällt uns sehr. 3. Als wir in Rostock arbeiteten, hatten wir nur eine kleine Wohnung. 4. Du siehst besorgt aus. Ist dir etwas passiert? 5. Ich glaube, jemand hat mir meinen neuen Rucksack gestohlen / geklaut. 6. Ich hatte ihn neben mir im Restaurant, und plötzlich war er weg. 7. Hoffentlich hattest du deinen Ausweis und deinen Geldbeutel in der Tasche. 8. Wann warst du in Heidelberg? 9. Vor zwei Jahren, als ich Austauschstudent/in in Deutschland war. 10. Ich habe das ganze Jahr versucht, einen alten Freund von meinen Eltern zu finden, aber er war gestorben.

G Freies Schreiben

1. Können wir aus der Geschichte der Weimarer Republik etwas lernen?
2. Take the story you composed orally with your classmates in exercise D and polish it as a written assignment.

H Wie sagt man das auf Deutsch?

1. How long have you lived in this house?
2. We've been here for two years. We like it a lot.
3. When we worked in Rostock, we only had a small apartment.
4. You look worried. Did something happen to you?
5. I think that somebody stole my new backpack.
6. I had it beside me in the restaurant and suddenly it was gone.
7. I hope you had your ID and your wallet in your pocket.
8. When were you in Heidelberg?
9. Two years ago, when I was an exchange student in Germany.
10. I tried all year to find an old friend of my parents, but he had died.

Videoecke

5 Treibst du gern Sport? (18:18)

Stefan und Su-Sin machen eine Pause.

*Stefan fährt mit dem Fahrrad zum Park, wo er Su-Sin trifft. Sie wollen zusammen joggen gehen. Während Stefan sein Rad abschließt (*locks*), fällt ihm der Geldbeutel (*wallet*) aus der Tasche. Aber er merkt (*notices*) es nicht und sie laufen durch den Wald. Später machen sie eine Pause und Stefan merkt, dass sein Geldbeutel fehlt (*is missing*). Sie laufen schnell zurück und finden zwei ältere (*older*) Frauen bei den Rädern. Eine Frau hat den Geldbeutel gefunden, will aber wissen, ob er wirklich Stefan gehört. Also fragt sie ihn, was in seinem Geldbeutel war. Da er es ihr sagen kann, gibt sie ihm das Portemonnaie (= Geldbeutel) zurück.*

Wortschatz zum Video

verlieren, hat verloren	*to lose*
der **Geldbeutel, -**	*wallet*
bestimmt	**= sicher**
Los!	*Let's go!*
Schau mal, wie ...	*Look at how . . .*
Keine Ahnung.	*(I have) no idea.*
Wie ist Ihr Name?	**= Wie heißen Sie?**
Passen Sie auf.	*Be careful. Pay attention.*

A **Was haben Sie gesehen?** Watch the first minute of video Module 5 showing recreational activities (18:35–19:09). Then check off what you've seen in the video.

Das habe ich gesehen:

____ 1. Ein Vater spielt Fußball mit seinem Sohn.
____ 2. Eine Frau geht mit ihrem Dachshund spazieren.
____ 3. Kinder klettern (*are climbing*) auf einem Baum.
____ 4. Junge Leute fahren auf Fahrrädern.
____ 5. Ein Mann spielt Tennis.
____ 6. Zwei alte Menschen sprechen miteinander.

B **Was hat Stefan in seinem Geldbeutel gehabt?** Now watch the rest of video Module 5 (19:10–21:52). Check off the items that are in Stefan's wallet.

____ 1. Geld
____ 2. eine Einkaufsliste
____ 3. ein Schlüssel
____ 4. ein Foto von Katrin
____ 5. sein Studentenausweis
____ 6. eine Kreditkarte

C **Wer sagt das?** Choose the person who says the following.

a. Su-Sin   b. Stefan   c. Jogger   d. ältere Frau

1. ____ sagt: „Ich fahre jeden Tag mit dem Rad zur Uni."
2. ____ sagt: „Ich hab' einen gefunden, drüben bei den Rädern."
3. ____ sagt: „Ich bin jedes Wochenende auf dem Tennisplatz."
4. ____ sagt: „Schau mal, wie die Leute den Wald verschmutzen."
5. ____ sagt: „Ach, tut mir Leid. Keine Zeit!"
6. ____ sagt: „Wir nehmen sie mit und werfen sie weg."

D **Wie sehen sie aus?** Beschreiben Sie die Menschen im Video.

1. Su-Sin hat ________ Haare und trägt eine ________ Hose und einen ________ Pulli.
2. Stefan trägt ________ Schuhe und ein ________ Sweatshirt.
3. Die Frau mit dem Geldbeutel trägt einen ________ Mantel und einen ________ Pulli. Sie hat ________ Haare. Sie ist ungefähr (*about*) ________ Jahre alt und sieht ________ aus.
4. Die andere Frau trägt einen ________ Pulli und einen ________ Mantel.

Suggest alternatives: **nervös, freundlich, unfreundlich, sympathisch, skeptisch.**

E **Welle Magazin: Treibst du auch Sport?** Am Ende des Videos sehen Sie sich das Welle Magazin an (Sport in Berlin, 21:53–22:41). Sie sehen einige Sportarten. Sagen Sie jeweils (*in each case*), ob Sie einen Sport gern treiben, nicht gern treiben oder noch nie probiert (*tried*) haben.

Sportart	*gern*	*nicht gern*	*nie probiert*
Fußball	______	______	______
Rugby	______	______	______
Speerwurf (*javelin*)	______	______	______
Geländelauf (*cross-country*)	______	______	______
Tennis	______	______	______
Schwimmen	______	______	______
Rudern (*rowing*)	______	______	______
Windsurfing	______	______	______

German Politics and the European Union

On December 2, 1990, with the addition of the five new **Länder** (*states*) from the former German Democratic Republic, a united Germany held its first free elections in fifty-eight years. The last had been in November 1932, just before Hitler's seizure of dictatorial powers. In order to prevent the profusion of small parties that had weakened the Reichstag during the Weimar Republic, the framers of the post-war **Grundgesetz** (*Basic Law* or constitution of the Federal Republic of Germany) in 1949 added a requirement that a party must receive at least 5% of the popular vote to be represented in the **Bundestag** (*Federal Parliament*). This provision has effectively excluded small extremist parties of both the Right and the Left.

Stimmzettel

für die Wahl zum Deutschen Bundestag im Wahlkreis 63 Bonn

am ....

Sie haben 2 Stimmen

hier 1 Stimme
für die Wahl
eines/einer Wahlkreis-
abgeordneten

Erststimme

1	**Schmitz,** Mathias Werkmeister Bonn, Hohe Str. 30 **CDU** Christlich Demokratische Union Deutschlands	◯
2	**Kolven,** Franz Studienrat Bonn, Aachener Str. 29 **SPD** Sozialdemokratische Partei Deutschlands	◯
3	**Dr. Jansen,** Hildegard Ärztin Bonn, Wiener Platz 15 **F.D.P.** Freie Demokratische Partei	◯
4	**Anger,** Martin Kaufmann Bonn, Römerstr. 209 **GRÜNE** DIE GRUNEN	◯
5	**Müller,** Dietrich Journalist Bonn-Beuel, Rheinstr. 63 **DKP** Deutsche Kommunistische Partei	◯
7	**Linzbach,** Josef Bundesbeamter Bonn, Neumarkt 15 Wählergruppe Linzbach	◯

hier 1 Stimme
für die Wahl
einer Landesliste (Partei)
- maßgebende Stimme für die Verteilung der Sitze insgesamt auf die einzelnen Parteien -

Zweitstimme

◯	**CDU**	Christlich Demokratische Union Deutschlands Karl Minzenbach, Ute Krings, Paul Lammerich, Heinz Mewissen, Dr. Kurt Kuppers	1
◯	**SPD**	Sozialdemokratische Partei Deutschlands Hans Schmitz, Brigitte Nolden, Fritz Bitgenbach, Udo Walbrohl, Max Palm	2
◯	**F.D.P.**	Freie Demokratische Partei Bruno Meurer, Ernst Merten, Herbert Nettekoven, Renate Rotgen, Gustav Schlosser	3
◯	**GRÜNE**	DIE GRÜNEN Manfred Bauer, Inge Becker, Willi Geyer, Kathe Kohler, Axel Winter	4
◯	**DKP**	Deutsche Kommunistische Partei Peter Adam, Ursula Bartsch, Rudolf Hoffmann, Arthur Schulz, Alfred Sommer	5
◯	**NPD**	Nationaldemokratische Partei Deutschlands Jurgen Frank, Martina Gross, Otto Kraft, Alfons Sturm, Klaus Weber	6

Discuss in English differences between the German parliamentary system and the American system (Chancellor is not elected by popular vote, etc.). Ask them to read the names of the parties represented on the ballot and in the photos of this chapter.

The **CDU** (**Christlich-Demokratische Union**), with its Bavarian sister party the **CSU** (**Christlich-Soziale Union**), form the conservative end of the German political spectrum and have consistently received 45–50% of the popular vote. The **SPD** (**Sozialdemokratische Partei Deutschlands**) is the oldest party in the **Bundestag**, with a history stretching back to the beginnings of socialism in the 19th century. Today's SPD is dedicated to the welfare state, with only a minority supporting a program of more radical socialism. It traditionally receives 35–45% of the popular vote from industrial workers, students, and young professionals.

The small, liberal **FDP** (**Freie Demokratische Partei**) has had an influence out of proportion to its size because the larger parties need it as a coalition partner to achieve a majority in the **Bundestag**. The environmental and anti-nuclear party known as the Greens (**Die Grünen**) first won parliamentary representation in 1983 and has forced the traditional parties to adopt more environmentally-conscious platforms. The **PDS** (**Partei des Demokratischen Sozialismus**), successor to the former East German Communist Party, draws its votes largely from East Germans dissatisfied with the unemployment and social dislocations brought about by unification and integration into a free market economy.

Since the end of World War Two, the central concern of German foreign policy has been to insure Germany's integration into a peaceful Europe. The rabid nationalism that led to two disastrous wars in the first half of the 20th century was replaced by a firm commitment to European unity. France and Germany, archenemies since the 19th century, formed a coal and steel cooperative in 1950 that gradually grew into today's European Union. The 1992 Treaty of Maastricht commits the Union's 13 member nations to a central banking system and a common currency (the Euro) by the year 2000 and to increased political coordination, especially in the areas of foreign policy and security.

Germans have been more divided in their attitude toward their Eastern European neighbors, but since the early 1970s, the major parties of both the Right and the Left have recognized the need for increasing contact and dialogue with the East. Since the break-up of the Soviet Union in the late 1980s, many of its former satellite states are eager to apply for membership in both the European Union and NATO. Because of its history of division between West and East, its central location, and its strong economy, Germany will continue to play a leading role in the unification of Europe.

Wahlplakat in München

KAPITEL 11

Deutschland nach der Mauer

Communicative Goals

- Learning the parts of the body
- Describing morning routines
- Designating nationalities and saying where people are from

Cultural Goal

- Understanding Germany's role in Europe today

Chapter Outline

- **Lyrik zum Vorlesen**
  Hoffmann von Fallersleben, „Das Lied der Deutschen"
- **Grammatik**
  Reflexive verbs
  Dative pronouns with clothing and parts of the body
  Adjectives and pronouns of indefinite number: *einige, mehrere*, etc.
  Adjectival nouns
  More on *bei*
  Designating decades: The 90s, etc.
- **Lesestück**
  Deutschland im europäischen Haus
- **Situationen aus dem Alltag**
  Morgens nach dem Aufstehen
- **Almanach**
  Zeittafel, 1939–heute

Dialoge

Lab Manual Kap. 11, Dialoge, Fragen, Hören Sie gut zu!

Das Brandenburger Tor: The Brandenburg Gate is a triumphal arch built in the late 18th century. From 1961–1989 the Berlin Wall ran just west of it.

die neuen Bundesländer: The 5 new federal States created, after unification, from the former German Democratic Republic: Sachsen-Anhalt, Mecklenburg-Vorpommern, Sachsen, Thüringen, Brandenburg. More information on unification is found in the **Lesestück** in this chapter. See also map of Germany inside the front cover.

Pronunciation practice: Use dialogues to review glottal stop before vowels at the beginning of words or syllables: **aus den USA**, **mit Anke am Brandenburger Tor**; **die Mauer öffnete**; **war offen**; **die Beamten**; **zuerst**; **Beeilen wir uns**.

Preview reflexive verb forms in dialogues and **Wortschatz 1** in class before students work with them. Also explain term *adjectival noun* in **Wortschatz**.

Am Brandenburger Tor

aus den USA: Note dative plural.

Helen aus den USA war 1989 in Berlin. Jetzt ist sie wieder in Berlin, um ihre Bekannte Anke zu besuchen. Zusammen stehen sie am Brandenburger Tor.

ANKE: Weißt du noch, wie es am 9. November 1989 hier an der Mauer aussah?
HELEN: Als die DDR die Grenze öffnete? Das vergess' ich nie!
ANKE: Die Menschen haben sich so gefreut, sogar die Polizeibeamten waren freundlich!
HELEN: Du, von dieser Begeisterung merkt man aber heute nichts mehr. Man hört fast nur, wie schwierig und teuer die Vereinigung ist.
ANKE: Es stimmt: Deutschland ist wieder *ein* Land, aber es gibt noch starke Unterschiede zwischen den alten und den neuen Bundesländern.

Ein Unfall: Stefan bricht sich das Bein

23.00 Uhr. *Stefans Vater liegt schon im Bett. Seine Mutter spricht am Telefon. Plötzlich läuft sie ins Schlafzimmer.*

MUTTER: Markus, zieh dich schnell an und komm mit! Etwas Schlimmes ist passiert!
VATER: Was ist denn los?
MUTTER: Stefan hat sich beim Radfahren verletzt! Ich fürchte, er hat sich das Bein gebrochen.
VATER: Um Gottes Willen! Beeilen wir uns!

Anna besucht Stefan im Krankenhaus

ANNA: Wie geht's dir denn, du Armer?
STEFAN: Hallo Anna! Schön, dass du gekommen bist.
ANNA: Fühlst du dich heute besser oder tut dir das Bein noch weh?
STEFAN: Ach, es geht. Ich kann mich schon selber waschen, aber ich darf noch nicht aufstehen.
ANNA: Schade! Schau mal, ich habe dir Schokolade und Blumen mitgebracht.
STEFAN: Oh, die sind hübsch! Danke, das ist aber lieb von dir!
ANNA: Nichts zu danken! Gute Besserung!

Note on Usage: The definite article as pronoun

In colloquial spoken German, the definite article can replace the personal pronoun. This is somewhat more emphatic than the personal pronoun and usually comes at the beginning of the sentence.

Die (= sie) sind hübsch! *Those are pretty.*

Wortschatz 1

Verben

sich[1] etwas an·sehen (sieht an), sah an, hat angesehen to take a look at something
sich an·ziehen, zog an, hat angezogen to get dressed
sich beeilen to hurry
brechen (bricht), brach, hat gebrochen to break
sich erkälten to catch a cold
sich freuen to be happy
sich fühlen to feel (*intrans.*)
fürchten to fear
sich etwas leisten können to be able to afford something
Das kann ich mir nicht leisten. I can't afford that.
merken to notice
öffnen to open
schauen to look
schneiden, schnitt, hat geschnitten to cut
sich setzen to sit down
sich verletzen to injure oneself, get hurt
sich verspäten to be late
sich etwas vor·stellen to imagine something
waschen (wäscht), wusch, hat gewaschen to wash
weh tun, tat weh, hat weh getan (+ *dat. of person*) to hurt
Das tut (mir) weh. That hurts (me).

Compare: **Das tut mir weh** (*That hurts me*) with **Es tut mir Leid** (*I'm sorry*).

Substantive

der **Arzt, ⸚e** doctor (*m.*)
der **Beamte, -n** (*adj. noun*) official, civil servant (*m.*)
der/die[2] **Bekannte, -n** (*adj. noun*) acquaintance, friend
der **Finger, -** finger
der **Kopf, ⸚e** head
der **Mund, ⸚er** mouth
der **Unterschied, -e** difference
der/die **Verwandte, -n** (*adj. noun*) relative
der **Zahn, ⸚e** tooth

das **Auge, -n** eye
das **Bein, -e** leg
das **Bundesland, ⸚er** federal state (*in Germany and Austria*)
das **Gesicht, -er** face
das **Krankenhaus, ⸚er** hospital
das **Licht, -er** light
das **Ohr, -en** ear
das **Schlafzimmer, -** bedroom
das **Tor, -e** gate

die **Ärztin, -nen** doctor (*f.*)
die **Beamtin, -nen** official, civil servant (*f.*)
die **Begeisterung** enthusiasm
die **Blume, -n** flower
die **Deutsche Demokratische Republik (DDR)** the German Democratic Republic (GDR)
die **Grenze, -n** border
die **Mauer, -n** (*freestanding or outside*) wall

Stress German pronunciation of **Finger**.

1. **Sich** is a reflexive pronoun. This will be explained on pp. 313–314.
2. Inclusion of both masculine and feminine articles indicates that this is an adjectival noun. See p. 322.

At the Brandenburg Gate

Helen from the USA was in Berlin in 1989. Now she's in Berlin again to visit her friend Anke. They're standing together at the Brandenburg Gate.

A: Do you remember what it looked like here at the Wall on November 9, 1989?
H: When the GDR opened the border? I'll never forget it!
A: People were so happy, even the police officers were friendly.
H: You know, these days you don't see that enthusiasm anymore. Almost all you hear is how difficult and expensive unification is.
A: You're right: Germany is one country again, but there are still great differences between the old and the new *Bundesländer*.

An Accident: Stefan Breaks His Leg

11:00 P.M. Stefan's father is already in bed. His mother is talking on the telephone. Suddenly she runs into the bedroom.

M: Markus, get dressed quickly and come along! Something bad has happened.
F: What's wrong?
M: Stefan hurt himself riding his bike! I'm afraid he's broken his leg.
F: For heaven's sake! Let's hurry!

Anna Visits Stefan in the Hospital

A: How are you, you poor guy?
S: Hi, Anna! Nice of you to come.
A: Do you feel better today or does your leg still hurt?
S: Oh, it's all right. I can wash myself already, but they won't let me get up yet.
A: Too bad. Look, I've brought you chocolate and flowers.
S: Oh, those are pretty. Thanks, that's really nice of you!
A: Don't mention it. Get well soon!

die **Polizei** (*sing. only*) police
die **Schokolade** chocolate
die **Vereinigung** unification

Contrast **die Mauer** (*free-standing wall*) with **die Wand** (*interior wall*). The two words tell the cultural story of Roman innovations in building techniques. **Mauer** (from the Latin *murus*) was made of stone and capable of having windows (**Fenster** from Latin *fenestra*), whereas the Germanic **Wand** is related to the verb **winden**, and described a wall of woven twigs.

Adjektive und Adverbien

ander- other, different
genau exact, precise
hübsch pretty, handsome
mehrere several, a few
wenige few

Andere Vokabel

sich (*third-person reflexive pronoun, see pp. 313–314*)

Nützliche Ausdrücke

Gute Besserung! Get well soon!
schade too bad
Das ist schade! That's a shame! Too bad! What a pity!
Schau mal. Look. Look here.
Weißt du noch? Do you remember?

You may want to add **sich umziehen** (*to change*). Remind students of **um-** in **umsteigen** and **Umlaut**.

Gegensätze

sich anziehen ≠ sich ausziehen to get dressed ≠ to get undressed

Mit anderen Worten

schnell machen (*colloq.*) = **sich beeilen**

Wortschatz 1 introduces some vocabulary (parts of body) not occurring in the dialogues, but useful to learn at this point. Parts of body can be drilled by pointing to them:
I: **Was ist das?**
S1: **Das ist der Kopf.**
I: **Zwei ... ?**
S2: **Köpfe.**
Students already know: **Arm** (10–2), **Fuß** (3–2), **Hand** (5–1), **Nase** (5–1).

Variationen

■ A ■ Persönliche Fragen

1. Helen besucht ihre Bekannte in Berlin. Haben Sie Bekannte oder Verwandte im Ausland? Wo leben sie? Haben Sie sie schon einmal besucht?
2. Helen sagt, sie vergisst den 9. November 1989 nie. Gibt es einen Tag, den Sie nie vergessen können? Was ist an diesem Tag passiert?
3. Stefan hatte einen Unfall beim Radfahren. Haben Sie je einen Unfall gehabt? Mit dem Rad oder dem Auto?
4. Er hat sich verletzt. Ist Ihnen so was als Kind passiert? Wenn ja, wie?
5. Sind Sie je im Krankenhaus gewesen? Warum? Haben Ihnen Ihre Freunde etwas mitgebracht? Was denn?
6. Anna bringt Stefan Schokolade und Blumen mit. Was bringen Sie mir, wenn ich im Krankenhaus bin?

■ B ■ Übung: Ich habe etwas Interessantes gemacht! Choose from the list of adjectives below to characterize something you have done. Then say what it was you did.

BEISPIEL: A: Ich habe einmal etwas _____-es gemacht.
B: Wieso? Was hast du denn gemacht?
A: Ich habe (*oder* bin) _____ .

blöd	toll	wahnsinnig	intelligent
interessant	gefährlich	neu	furchtbar
wunderbar	schwierig	langweilig	schlimm

Üb. C can be assigned for preparation as homework.

■ **C** ■ **Partnerarbeit: Wie geht's denn weiter?** Take these two lines from the second dialogue and compose your own continuation. Then perform your dialogue for the class.

A: Zieh dich schnell an und komm mit!
B: Was ist denn los?
A: ______________________________
B: ______________________________
A: ______________________________
B: ______________________________

Lyrik zum Vorlesen

Play for the class the variations in the 2nd movement of Haydn's **Kaiserquartett**, Opus 76, No. 3 in C major; or Clara Schumann's Opus 9, **Variationen über „Gott erhalte Franz den Kaiser."**

The famous "Lied der Deutschen," also known as the "Deutschlandlied," is one of the most fervently nationalistic—and controversial—political songs ever composed. Although the first stanza is commonly associated with German military expansionism, the author was, ironically, an opponent of repressive government. His anti-authoritarian sentiments cost him his post as professor at the University of Breslau. The text proclaims abstract concepts ("unity, law, freedom") and calls for a unification of all German-speaking territories into one state. The idealistic dreams of unity were appropriate for Hoffmann's generation, which had survived the ravages of the Napoleonic Wars and was frustrated by the division of Germany into many small states.

Hoffmann wrote the text in 1841 to a favorite popular tune by Joseph Haydn in praise of the Austrian Emperor, "Gott erhalte Franz den Kaiser" (*God Preserve Kaiser Franz*, [1797]). Haydn also used this melody in his magnificent *Kaiserquartett* (Opus 76, No. 3, second movement). The song did not become the German national anthem until 1922, when it was chosen by the young Weimar Republic. In 1945 it was banned by the allied military government. In 1952, when no satisfactory substitute could be found, the third stanza alone became the national anthem of the Federal Republic of Germany.

Lab Manual Kap. 11, Lyrik zum Vorlesen.

die Maas = the Meuse River (Belgium); **die Memel** = the Nemunas River in Lithuania; **die Etsch** = the Adige River in South Tirol (Italy); **der Belt** = strait between two Danish islands in the Baltic Sea.

Das Lied der Deutschen

Deutschland, Deutschland über alles,
Über alles in der Welt,
Wenn es stets° zu Schutz und Trutze°
Brüderlich zusammenhält;
Von der Maas bis an die Memel,
Von der Etsch bis an den Belt:
Deutschland, Deutschland über alles,
Über alles in der Welt!

= **immer** / **Schutz ...** = protection and defiance

Deutsche Frauen, deutsche Treue°,
Deutscher Wein und deutscher Sang°
Sollen in der Welt erhalten°
Ihren alten, schönen Klang°,
Uns zu edler Tat begeistern°
Unser ganzes Leben lang:
Deutsche Frauen, deutsche Treue,
Deutscher Wein und deutscher Sang!

loyalty
song
preserve
sound
Uns ... begeistern = inspire us to noble deeds

Berlin, Potsdamer Platz: größte Baustelle (*construction site*) der Welt

Einigkeit° und Recht° und Freiheit
Für das deutsche Vaterland!
Danach lasst uns alle streben°
Brüderlich mit Herz und Hand!
Einigkeit und Recht und Freiheit
Sind des Glückes Unterpfand°:
Blüh° im Glanze° dieses Glückes,
Blühe, deutsches Vaterland!

August Heinrich Hoffmann von Fallersleben (1798–1874)

unity / justice

lasst ... = let us strive

des ... = guarantees of happiness

flourish / glow

Grammatik

Reflexive verbs

Reflexive verbs and pronouns

In most sentences with objects, the subject and the object are two different people or things.

subj. obj.
Ich habe **ihn** verletzt. *I injured **him**.*

Sometimes, however, a verb's subject and object are the *same* person or thing. The verb is then called *reflexive*. The object of a *reflexive verb* is always a pronoun called a *reflexive pronoun*.

subj. obj.
Ich habe **mich** verletzt. *I hurt **myself**.*

Reflexive pronouns in English end in *-self* or *-selves*, e.g., *myself, himself, herself, themselves*. German has both accusative and dative reflexive pronouns. Reflexive pronouns are identical to personal pronouns except in the third person and the formal second person, where the reflexive pronoun is **sich**.

Note on spelling: **sich** is not capitalized when used with the polite **Sie**: **Fühlen Sie sich heute besser?**

Reflexive Pronouns		
	accusative	dative
ich	**mich**	**mir**
du	**dich**	**dir**
er, es, sie	sich	sich
wir	uns	uns
ihr	euch	euch
sie, Sie	sich	sich

In the plural, the reflexive pronouns often denote reciprocity and are the equivalent of English *each other*.

Wir treffen **uns** morgen.	*We'll meet **each other** tomorrow.*
Kennt ihr **euch**?	*Do you know **each other**?*
Sie kennen **sich** seit langem.	*They've known **each other** for a long time.*
Wir verstehen **uns** gut.	*We understand **each other** well. (= We're on the same wavelength.)*

Note on Usage: *einander* (each other)

Plural reflexive pronouns used reciprocally may be replaced by the reciprocal pronoun **einander** (*each other*).

Kennt ihr **euch**? = Kennt ihr **einander**?

Remember that **einander** can also combine with prepositions.

miteinander	*with each other*
zueinander	*to each other*

■ Verbs with accusative reflexive pronouns

A transitive verb is a verb that takes a direct object (e.g., **sehen**, **tragen**, **verletzen**). An intransitive verb cannot take a direct object (e.g., **sein**, **werden**, **schlafen**).

Any transitive verb may be used reflexively. Here is a sample conjugation using **sich verletzen**.

Ich habe **mich** verletzt.	*I hurt **myself**.*
Du hast **dich** verletzt.	*You hurt **yourself**.*
Sie hat **sich** verletzt.	*She hurt **herself**.*
Wir haben **uns** verletzt.	*We hurt **ourselves**.*
Ihr habt **euch** verletzt.	*You hurt **yourselves**.*
Sie haben **sich** verletzt.	*They hurt **themselves**. (You hurt **yourself / yourselves**.)*

Lab Manual Kap. 11, Var. zu Üb. 1, 5, 8, 10.

Workbook Kap. 11, A–E.

Üb. 1: Point to individuals, groups, yourself, to cue responses. Expand: **Haben Sie sich schwer oder leicht verletzt?**

1 **Übung: Wer hat sich verletzt?** Die ganze Klasse war im Bus, als der Busfahrer einen kleinen Unfall hatte. Sagen Sie, wer sich verletzt hat.

BEISPIEL: Ich habe mich verletzt.

Note on Usage: *selber* and *selbst* as intensifiers

The words **selber** and **selbst** are often used to intensify or emphasize a reflexive pronoun:

Soll ich das Kind waschen?	*Should I wash the child?*
Nein, sie kann sich **selber** waschen.	*No, she can wash herself.*

Üb. 2: Point to indicate people intended.

2 **Übung: Er kennt nur sich selbst.** Answer these questions by saying that the person knows, sees, etc. only him- or herself.

BEISPIEL: Wen kennt er denn?
Er kennt nur sich selbst.

Proverb: **Liebe dich selbst, so hast du keine Rivalen.**

1. Wen sieht sie denn?
2. Wen versteht er denn?
3. Wen lieben Sie denn?
4. Wen brauche ich denn?
5. Wen haben Sie denn verletzt?
6. Wen hat er geärgert?
7. Wen haben sie gerettet?

3 **Partnerarbeit: Wir verstehen uns.** Use each of the verbs below in the following routine:

German transitive verbs *require* an accusative object even when that object is identical with the subject. Many English transitive verbs become intransitive when their subject performs an action on itself.

BEISPIEL:
A: *Verstehst* du mich?
B: Ja, ich verstehe dich. Verstehst du mich?
A: Ja, ich verstehe dich auch.
A & B: Wir verstehen uns! (Wir verstehen einander!)

verstehen	brauchen	morgen treffen
sehen	kennen	am Wochenende besuchen

German reflexive verbs that are not reflexive in English

Täglich sich waschen

Many German reflexive verbs are not reflexive in English. Their English equivalents often use *get*. Here are some examples.

sich anziehen	*to get dressed*
sich waschen	*to get washed*
sich setzen	*to sit down*
Sie wäscht **sich**.	*She's getting washed.*
Er zog **sich** an.	*He got dressed.*
Bitte, setzen Sie **sich**.	*Please sit down.* (literally: *Please seat yourselves.*)

Üb. 4: Model with 1 student, then run through it a few times. Other students can be asked: **Was hat er/sie gemacht?** Then ask several students to stand/sit down. Then choose student to run the same game with **du/ihr**-imperative. Next day, start class with all students standing. Tell one to sit down, who then tells another to sit down, etc.

4 **Übung: Bitte, setzen Sie sich!** Your instructor will tell you to stand up or sit down. Then say what you have done.

BEISPIEL:
A: Bitte stehen Sie auf!
B: (*Student/in steht auf.*) Ich bin aufgestanden.
A: Bitte setzen Sie sich.
B: (*Student/in setzt sich.*) Ich habe mich gesetzt.

■ Verbs requiring the accusative reflexive

Verbs like **anziehen** and **waschen** may be used either reflexively (**ich wasche mich**) or nonreflexively (**ich wasche den Wagen**). Some German verbs, however, must *always* be used with an accusative reflexive pronoun. Their English equivalents are *not* reflexive.

An analogous English verb is *to enjoy oneself. I enjoyed myself at the party* means I enjoyed the *party*, not literally *myself*. German: **sich amüsieren**.

sich beeilen	*to hurry*	**sich fühlen**	*to feel*
sich erkälten	*to catch cold*	**sich verspäten**	*to be late*
sich freuen	*to be happy*		

■ 5 ■ Gruppenarbeit: Wann freust du dich besonders? (*3 oder 4 Personen*) Alle müssen sagen, wann sie sich besonders freuen. Die Bilder geben Ihnen einige Ideen, aber Sie dürfen auch frei antworten.

Variation: **Ich fühle mich heute wunderbar. Wie fühlst du dich heute?**

BEISPIEL: Ich freue mich, wenn die Sonne scheint. Wann freust du dich?

■ 6 ■ Gruppenarbeit: Warum musst du dich beeilen? Jetzt sind Sie alle in Eile. Sagen Sie einander warum.

BEISPIEL: Ich muss mich beeilen, weil ich zur Uni muss. Warum musst du dich beeilen?

■ 7 ■ Gruppenarbeit: Warum hast du dich verspätet? Jeder verspätet sich manchmal. Erzählen Sie der Klasse, warum Sie sich einmal verspätet haben. Unten sind einige Möglichkeiten, aber Sie dürfen auch frei antworten.

BEISPIEL: Ich habe mich einmal verspätet, weil ...

krank sein	Fahrrad kaputt
spät aufstehen	die Deutschstunde vergessen
sich verletzen	die Uhr verlieren
einen Unfall haben	einen Freund im Krankenhaus besuchen

■ Verbs with dative reflexive pronouns

Verbs with dative objects Verbs such as **helfen** that require a dative object take a dative reflexive pronoun when they are used reflexively.

Ich kann **mir selber** helfen.	*I can help **myself**.*

Reflexive indirect object The subject and *indirect* object of a verb can be the same person. In this case the indirect object is a *dative* reflexive pronoun.

Note: Except for **mir** and **dir**, the dative reflexive pronouns are identical in form to the accusative reflexive pronouns.

Alert students that reflexive pronouns follow rules for pronoun word order **(p. 135): Was kaufen Sie sich?**

Ich kaufe **mir** Blumen.	*I'm buying **myself** flowers.*
Du kaufst **dir** Blumen. / Sie kaufen **sich** Blumen.	*You're buying **yourself** flowers.*
Er kauft **sich** Blumen.	*He's buying **himself** flowers.*
Wir kaufen **uns** Blumen.	*We're buying **ourselves** flowers.*
Ihr kauft **euch** Blumen. / Sie kaufen **sich** Blumen.	*You're buying **yourselves** flowers.*
Sie kaufen **sich** Blumen.	*They're buying **themselves** flowers.*

The dative reflexive makes explicit the fact that the subject is the beneficiary of its own action. It may be omitted without changing the basic meaning of the sentence.

Ich kaufe mir eine Jacke.	*I'm buying myself a jacket.*
Ich kaufe eine Jacke.	*I'm buying a jacket.*

Show analogy of reflexives with personal pronouns by asking: **Sie kaufen *sich* ein neues Hemd, aber was kaufen Sie *mir*? (Ihrem Freund Johann, Ihrer Mutter, etc.).** Once students can do this smoothly, repeat **Üb. 8** emphasizing attributive adjectives.

■ 8 ■ Übung: Einkaufsbummel Jetzt gehen wir zusammen einkaufen. Jeder hat DM 200 und darf sich etwas kaufen. Erzählen Sie den anderen, was Sie sich kaufen. Die Bilder geben Ihnen einige Ideen, aber Sie dürfen sich natürlich auch andere Sachen kaufen.

BEISPIEL: A: Was kaufen Sie sich, Robert?
B: Ich kaufe mir ein neues Hemd und eine Zeitung.

■ Verbs requiring the dative reflexive

There are some German verbs that must *always* be used with the dative reflexive pronoun. They all require a *direct object* (in the accusative) as well. Their English equivalents are *not* reflexive.

German: dative reflexive	*English: not reflexive*
sich etwas ansehen	*to take a look at, look over*
Ich wollte **mir** den Wagen ansehen.	*I wanted to take a look at the car.*
sich etwas leisten können	*to be able to afford*
Kannst du **dir** ein neues Fahrrad leisten?	*Can you afford a new bicycle?*
sich etwas vorstellen	*to imagine*
Das kann ich **mir** nicht vorstellen.	*I can't imagine that.*

Explain literal meaning of **sich etwas vorstellen**: *to place something in front of (your mind's eye)*. Make sure students understand how verbs with dative reflexive are presented in vocabularies.

Since the pronoun **sich** is both accusative and dative, how do you know which it should be with any particular reflexive verb? When a **Wortschatz** entry in this book includes the direct object **etwas**, it indicates that the reflexive pronoun is dative. If you look up **ansehen**, for example, you find **sich etwas ansehen**. This tells you that **etwas** is accusative and **sich** is dative. Any noun or pronoun in the accusative can replace **etwas**.

A parallel English structure is *to cook oneself something* (**sich etwas kochen**). I'm cooking myself (*ind. obj.*) an egg (*dir. obj.*). = **Ich koche mir ein Ei.**

sich (*dative*) **etwas** (*accusative*) ansehen

Ich möchte **mir** das **Auto** ansehen.

■ 9 ■ Kettenreaktion: Die armen Studenten Wie alle Studenten haben Sie nie genug Geld. Sagen Sie, was Sie sich nicht leisten können und dann fragen Sie weiter.

BEISPIEL: A: Ich kann mir keine Europareise leisten. Was kannst du dir nicht leisten?
B: Ich kann mir ...

Variation: Play the role of a German exchange student and ask your students: **Was soll ich mir in dieser Stadt ansehen?**

■ 10 ■ Partnerarbeit: Was wollen wir uns heute nachmittag ansehen? Sehen Sie sich den Stadtplan auf Seite 237 an. Sie verbringen den Nachmittag zusammen in dieser Stadt. Sagen Sie einander, was Sie sich ansehen möchten.

BEISPIEL: A: Ich möchte mir den Dom und ______ ansehen. Und du?
B: Ich möchte mir lieber ______ ansehen.

Dative pronouns with clothing and parts of the body

Learning the parts of the body is a communicative goal.

Unlike English, German does not usually use possessive forms with parts of the body, or with articles of clothing when they are being put on or taken off. German uses the personal dative instead.

Die Mutter wäscht **dem Kind** die Hände.	*The mother washes* ***the child's*** *hands.*
Meine Freundin schneidet **mir** die Haare.	*My girlfriend cuts* ***my*** *hair.*
Sie zog **ihm** den Mantel an.	*She put the coat on* ***him.***

Note that plural **die Haare** is more common than singular: **Sie hat dunkle Haare.**

If the subject is performing the action on itself, the dative pronoun is of course *reflexive.*

Ich habe **mir** die Hände gewaschen.	*I washed* ***my*** *hands.*
Sie zog **sich** den Mantel an.	*She put on* ***her*** *coat.*
Ich schneide **mir** selber die Haare.	*I cut* ***my*** *hair myself.*
Stefan hat **sich** das Bein gebrochen.	*Stefan broke* ***his*** *leg.*

You may want to add: **die Brust, das Knie, der Bauch (das Bauchweh), der Körper, das Kinn, der Hals** (neck *or* throat, **das Halsweh**), **die Wange, die Schulter, der Rücken.** Additional vocab.: **Hunde und Katzen *fressen*.**

Üb. 11 can also be used to review genitive case and possessive adjectives. (Students have trouble learning **ihr** = *her*):
I: **Nummer eins?**
S1: **Das ist der Kopf des Mannes.**
S2: **Ja, das ist sein Kopf.**
I: **Nummer 8?**
S3: **Das ist die Hand der Frau.**
S4: **Ja, das ist ihre Hand, etc.**

You can also introduce **recht-** and **link-** as attributive adjectives (**die linke Hand,** etc.).

■ **11** ■ **Übung: Körperteile** Review your knowledge of parts of the body by identifying them in the picture below.

Rätsel (Riddle)
Was ist das? Hat Arme, aber keine Hände, läuft und hat doch keine Füße.

Antwort: **der Fluss.**

die **Katze, -n** *cat* der **Hund, -e** *dog*

Lab Manual Kap. 11, Var. zur Üb. 12.

Cue body parts by pointing to them. Follow-up: **Oh, das tut mir aber Leid! Nehmen Sie 2 Aspirintabletten. Müssen Sie ins Krankenhaus?** usw. To drill 3rd-person, follow up by asking: **Wo tut es Richard/Anna weh?**

Ich ziehe **mich an.** = *I'm getting dressed.*
Ich ziehe **mir** ein Hemd an. = *I'm putting on a shirt.*

Point out that the two words that would frame this progression from few to many, **keine** at the top and **alle** at the bottom, *are* limiting words: **keine** is the all-exclusive class and **alle** the all-inclusive class. Thus: **keine** ≠ **alle alten Gebäude**, but **wenige alte Gebäude**.

For **limiting words**, see p. 253; for **primary and secondary endings**, see p. 254.

■ 12 ■ Übung: Wo tut es Ihnen weh? Stefan tut das Bein noch ein bisschen weh. Wo tut es Ihnen weh?

BEISPIEL: Wo tut es Ihnen weh?
Mir tut der Kopf weh.

■ 13 ■ Übung Sagen Sie Ihrem Professor, **wann** Sie sich heute angezogen haben, und dann, **was** Sie sich angezogen haben.

BEISPIEL: A: Um wie viel Uhr haben Sie sich heute angezogen?
B: Ich habe mich um halb acht angezogen.
A: Was haben Sie sich angezogen?
B: Ich habe mir ______, ______ und ______ angezogen.

Adjectives and pronouns of indefinite number

You have already learned as individual vocabulary words a group of adjectives used with plural nouns to indicate indefinite amounts.

wenige	*few*
einige	*some*
mehrere	*several*
andere	*other(s)*
viele	*many*

These adjectives are *not* limiting words. They are treated just like descriptive adjectives: when not preceded by a limiting word, they take *primary* endings.

Andere Leute waren da.	*Other people were there.*
Ich habe **viele** Freunde in Bonn.	*I have a lot of friends in Bonn.*

When a limiting word precedes them, they take *secondary* endings.

Die anderen Leute waren da.	*The other people were there.*
Meine vielen Freunde schreiben mir oft.	*My many friends often write to me.*

Remember that descriptive adjectives following the adjective of indefinite number *always* have the *same* ending as the adjective of indefinite number.

Ander**e** jung**e** Leute waren da.	*Other young people were there.*
Die ander**en** jung**en** Leute waren da.	*The other young people were there.*

■ 14 ■ Gruppenarbeit: Viele oder wenige? Choose a word from each column and state your opinion about a group of people. Begin with **Ich würde sagen, ...**

BEISPIEL: Ich würde sagen, viele sportliche Frauen sind gesund.

A	*B*	*C*	*D*
viele	jung	Menschen	Sport treiben
wenige	sportlich	Amerikaner	gesund sein
	reich	Professoren	Müll recyclen
	arm	Studenten	glücklich sein
	stark	Frauen	Deutsch sprechen
	sympathisch	Männer	gut verdienen
	verrückt	Eltern	gern trampen
	kreativ		

Lab Manual Kap. 11, Var. zur Üb. 15.

Workbook Kap. 11, F.

Üb. 15: May be assigned as written homework.

■ 15 ■ Übung Supply the correct adjective endings.

1. Darf ich mir einig___ schön___ Postkarten ansehen?
2. Sie hat schon mehrer___ deutsch___ Bücher gelesen.
3. Viel___ jung___ amerikanisch___ Schüler verstehen das nicht.
4. Haben Sie auch die ander___ neu___ Arbeiter kennen gelernt?
5. Ich habe mit viel___ interessant___ Menschen gesprochen.
6. Deine viel___ neu___ Ideen gefallen mir sehr.
7. Das sind die Probleme der ander___ jung___ Journalisten.
8. Ich kenne einig___ gut___ Restaurants in Hamburg.

■ Indefinite pronouns

When these words are not followed by nouns, they function as indefinite pronouns referring to human beings:

Viele sagen das.	*Many (people) say that.*
Einige gehen ins Kino, **andere** ins Theater.	*Some (people) are going to the movies, others to the theater.*

Üb. 16: Use a gesture to make clear that **Sie** refers to entire class, although you're asking only one student at a time. If you do this with closed books, write **einige** and **andere** on the board to guide student responses.

■ 16 ■ Übung: Einige und andere Not everyone in your class likes doing the same things. Answer the following questions by saying that *some* of you (**einige**) like doing one thing, *others* (**andere**) prefer something else.

BEISPIEL: A: Gehen Sie gern ins Kino?
B: *Einige* gehen gern ins Kino.
C: *Andere* gehen lieber ______ .

1. Spielen Sie gern Tennis?
2. Sprechen Sie gern über Politik?
3. Essen Sie gern Wurst?
4. Fahren Sie gern Ski?
5. Lesen Sie gern Zeitung?
6. Arbeiten Sie gern in der Bibliothek?
7. Trinken Sie gern Kaffee zum Frühstück?
8. Sitzen Sie gern vor dem Fernseher?

Adjectival nouns

■ Adjectival nouns referring to people

In English, adjectives such as *sick*, *rich*, and *famous* occasionally function as nouns referring *collectively* to a group of people.

> *Florence Nightingale cared for* ***the sick****.*
> *Lifestyles of* ***the rich and famous****.*

Adjectival nouns are more frequent in German than in English. Moreover, they can refer to individuals, not just to collective groups as in English. Masculine adjectival nouns denote men, feminine ones denote women, while plural adjectival nouns are not gender specific.

Colloquial **mein Alter/meine Alte** can mean *my father/my mother* or *my husband/my wife* (compare English *my old man/old lady*).

der Alte	*the old man*
die Alte	*the old woman*
die Alten	*the old people*

Realia on p. 261 has good examples of adjectival nouns in nominative and accusative plural.

Like other nouns in German, adjectival nouns are capitalized, but they *receive adjective endings* as though they were followed by the nouns **Mann**, **Frau**, or **Menschen**. Here are some examples that include these nouns in brackets to make the structure clear. *Note the adjective endings!* As in any noun phrase, these endings will change depending on whether or not the adjectival noun is preceded by a limiting word.

Die Alte [Frau] lag im Bett.	*The old woman was lying in bed.*
Kennst du **den Großen** [Mann] da?	*Do you know that tall man there?*
Hier wohnt **ein Reicher** [Mann].	*A rich man lives here.*
Er wollte **den Armen** [Menschen] helfen.	*He wanted to help the poor.*

In principle, any adjective can be used as an adjectival noun. Here are some common ones you should learn:

Only the masculine form **der Beamte** is an adjectival noun. The feminine form is **die Beamtin**.

der/die Deutsche is the *only* noun of nationality that is adjectival.

der/die **Alte, -n**	*old man/woman*
der/die **Arme, -n**	*poor man/woman*
der **Beamte, -n**	*official, civil servant*
der/die **Bekannte, -n**	*acquaintance, friend*
der/die **Deutsche, -n**	*German (man/woman)*
der/die **Grüne, -n**	*member of the Greens (the environmental political party)*
der/die **Kleine, -n**	*little boy/girl* or *short man/woman*
der/die **Kranke, -n**	*sick man/woman*
der/die **Verwandte, -n** (from **verwandt** = *related*)	*relative*

Lab Manual Kap. 11, Üb. 17.

Workbook Kap. 11, G, H.

■ 17 ■ Übung Complete each sentence with the appropriate form of **mein Bekannter** (*my acquaintance, friend* [m.]).

BEISPIEL: Das ist ______ .
Das ist *mein Bekannter.*

1. Heute zum Mittagessen treffe ich ______ .
2. Ich gehe oft mit ______ Volleyball spielen.

3. Das ist die Frau ____ .
4. ____ heißt Robert.

Add variations with **die Grünen**, **der/die Kleine/n**. If class has sense of humor, you can have students characterize each other: **Ist Robert fleißig? Ja, er ist ein Fleißiger! (faul, hübsch, sportlich, verrückt, stark, blond)**

Now use a form of **meine Bekannten** (*my friends*).

5. Das sind ____ .
6. Kennen Sie ____ ?
7. Helfen Sie bitte ____ !
8. Das sind die Kinder ____ .

Now use a form of **die Deutsche** (*the German* [f.]).

9. Wie heißt denn ____ ?
10. Meinst du ____ ?
11. Ich trampe mit ____ nach Italien.
12. Ist das der Rucksack ____ ?

Now use a form of **die Alten** (*the old people*).

13. Das haben wir von ____ gelernt.
14. Morgen kommen ____ .
15. Wer trägt denn die Koffer ____ ?
16. Machen wir etwas Schönes für ____ .

Now use a form of **unser Verwandter** (*our relative* [m.]).

17. Helmut ist ____ .
18. Kennst du ____ ?
19. Du sollst mit ____ sprechen.
20. Die Tochter ____ besucht uns morgen.

■ Neuter adjectival nouns referring to qualities

Neuter adjectival nouns are abstract nouns designating qualities (e.g., *something good, nothing new*). They occur only in the singular, most frequently after the indefinite pronouns **etwas**, **nichts**, **viel**, and **wenig**. Note that since these pronouns are *not* limiting words, the following adjectival noun has the *primary* neuter ending **-es**.

Concentrate on these as idioms, not on the grammar, since **etwas Neuem** is relatively rare.

etwas Herrliches	*something marvelous*
nichts Neues	*nothing new*
viel Gutes	*much that is good*
wenig Interessantes	*little of interest*

Etwas Unglaubliches
wird passieren:
Sie sitzen im Auto und
FAHREN.

You may want to introduce **alles Gute**. Superlatives such as **das Beste** are frequent, so review after comparison of adjectives in Kap. 12.

Include final line of thanks as in Dialogue 3: **Oh, wie hübsch**, etc.

■ **18** ■ **Rollenspiel: Was haben Sie mir mitgebracht? (*Mit offenen Büchern*)**

Ihre Professorin hatte einen Unfall und liegt im Krankenhaus. Sie besuchen sie und bringen ihr Geschenke mit. (*First choose an adjective from the left-hand column to describe your present, then tell her what it is.*)

BEISPIEL: A: Ich habe Ihnen etwas ________**-es** mitgebracht.
B: Oh, wie schön! Was denn?
A: Ein-_______ .

neu	Pflanze
schön	Kassettenrekorder
teuer	frische Brötchen
interessant	Schokolade
herrlich	Fotos von unserer Reise
klein	Stück von der Berliner Mauer
lecker	Flasche Wein
umweltfreundlich	Zeitschriften
wunderbar	Blumen

Show students the difference between an adjectival noun (**das Neue**) and an omitted redundant noun (**Das alte Haus gefällt dir, aber *das neue* gefällt mir**). Latter is *the new one* in English.

Neuter adjectival nouns can also occur after the definite article **das**. In this case, they are abstract nouns signaling the *quality* designated by the adjective. There are several English equivalents for this.

Das Moderne gefällt mir.	*I like modern things.* *I like what is modern.*
Sie sucht immer **das Gute**.	*She's always seeking the good.* *She's always seeking what's good.*

Compare the adjective endings in **etwas Modernes** (*something modern*) and **das Moderne** (*what is modern; modern things*).

More on bei

In **Kapitel 5** you learned that the dative preposition **bei** has the spatial meanings *in the home of* or *at*. Frequently, however, **bei** is used to set a scene. It then has the meanings *during, while . . . ing,* or *at* (an activity or someone's home or business). In this meaning, **bei** is often used with verbal nouns (p. 202).

You may also want to mention: **bei einer Tasse Kaffee**, **bei Tag**, **bei Nacht**.

Er hat sich **beim Radfahren** verletzt.	*He injured himself while riding his bicycle.*
Marion ist jetzt **bei der Arbeit**.	*Marion's at work now.*
Ich lese oft **beim Essen**.	*I often read while eating.*
Ich war gestern **beim Arzt**.	*I was at the doctor's yesterday.*

Lab Manual Kap. 11, Var. zur Üb. 19.

Üb. 19: Also good as written assignment. Remind students to capitalize verbal nouns.

■ 19 ■ Übung: Wann passiert das? Sagen Sie, wann etwas passiert oder nicht passiert. Benutzen Sie **bei** in Ihrer Antwort.

BEISPIEL: Ich falle nie, wenn ich Ski fahre.
Ich falle nie beim Skifahren.

1. Mein Mitbewohner stört mich, wenn ich lese.
2. Wir treffen uns oft, wenn wir Rad fahren.
3. Höfliche Kinder singen nicht, wenn sie essen.
4. Wenn wir spazieren gehen, können wir miteinander sprechen.
5. Ich höre gern Musik, wenn ich Auto fahre.
6. Wenn ich arbeite, ziehe ich mir die Schuhe aus.

■ 20 ■ Übung Antworten Sie mit **bei**.

BEISPIEL: Wie hat er sich denn verletzt? (*while skiing*)
Beim Skifahren.

1. Wie haben Sie sich erkältet? (*while swimming*)
2. Wo sind Sie morgens um zehn? (*at work*)
3. Wann lernt man viele Menschen kennen? (*while hitchhiking*)
4. Wann sprechen Sie nicht viel? (*when driving a car*)
5. Wo ist denn Ihre Frau? (*at the doctor's*)
6. Wie hast du so viel Geld verloren? (*playing cards*)

Designating decades: The 90s, etc.

These examples show how German designates decades (**das Jahrzehnt, -e**).

die 20er (Zwanziger) Jahre	*the 20s (Twenties)*
aus den 60er-Jahren	*from the 60s*
in den 90er-Jahren	*in the 90s*

Note that the cardinal number adds the ending **-er**. No other adjective ending is used, regardless of case.

■ 21 ■ Übung: Alte Briefmarken (stamps) Aus welchen Jahrzehnten kommen diese deutschen Briefmarken?

Lesestück

Designating nationalities and talking about where people are from are communicative goals.

Review adj. nouns, Eng. to Ger.: Robert is a German. Liese is a German. They are Germans. I know a German (man/woman). I know many Germans. I'm helping a German (man/woman). I'm helping the Germans. That's the suitcase of a German (man/woman). Those are the suitcases of the Germans.

Remind students of the invariant plural endings **-er** and **-erinnen**.

Vor dem Lesen

Tipps zum Lesen und Lernen

Tipps zum Vokabelnlernen

Country names; nouns and adjectives of nationality The only designation of nationality that is an adjectival noun is **der/die Deutsche**. Some other nouns of nationality have a masculine form ending in **-er** and a feminine in **-erin**. You already know some of these:

Country	*Male native*	*Female native*	*Adjective*
Amerika	der Amerikaner	die Amerikanerin	amerikanisch
England	der Engländer	die Engländerin	englisch
Italien	der Italiener	die Italienerin	italienisch
Kanada	der Kanadier	die Kanadierin	kanadisch
Österreich	der Österreicher	die Österreicherin	österreichisch
die Schweiz	der Schweizer	die Schweizerin	schweizerisch

Other nouns of nationality are N-nouns in the masculine that add **-in** (and sometimes an umlaut) in the feminine.

Country	*Male native*	*Female native*	*Adjective*
China	der Chinese, -n, -n	die Chinesin	chinesisch
Frankreich	der Franzose, -n, -n	die Französin	französisch
Russland	der Russe, -n, -n	die Russin	russisch

Variation: Also write a profession (p. 148) on the slip for each student. Students then also ask: **Was sind Sie von Beruf?** After mingling, students see if they can remember who comes from where and does what. This reviews omission of pronoun with both nationality and occupation: **Mike ist Franzose. Er ist auch Schriftsteller.**

Variation: Tell students to ask for more details: **Aus welcher Stadt in ... kommen Sie? Wie lange sind Sie schon in den USA? Wie lange sind Sie schon Ingenieur?**

Remember that when stating a person's nationality, Germans do *not* use the indefinite article.

Sind Sie Deutsche? — *Are you a German?*
Nein, ich bin Französin. — *No, I'm French.*

A **Gruppenarbeit: Woher kommst du?** Sie sind auf einer internationalen Studentenkonferenz. Sie bekommen vom Professor ein Stück Papier. Auf dem Papier steht der Name Ihrer Heimat (*native country*). Jetzt fragen Sie einander, woher Sie kommen.

BEISPIEL: A: Woher kommst du denn?
B: Ich komme aus England.
A: Ach, du bist Engländerin!

Lab Manual Kap. 11, Üb. zur Betonung.

Leicht zu merken

die **Demokratisierung**	
die **Demonstration, -en**	Demonstration
existieren	existieren
die **Integration**	Integration
investieren	investieren
der **Kapitalismus**	Kapitalismus
der **Kommunismus**	Kommunismus
der **Manager, -**	
die **Million, -en**	Million
modernisieren	modernisieren

Osteuropa	
der **Protest**	Protest
die **Reform, -en**	
reformieren	reformieren
das **Regime, -s**	
die **Revolution, -en**	Revolution
(das) **Rumänien**	
separat	separat
die **Sowjetunion**	Sowjetunion
stabil	stabil
das **Symbol, -e**	Symbol
zentral	zentral
die **Zone, -n**	

Einstieg in den Text

Word features such as prefixes and suffixes can help you build on your existing vocabulary and recognize new words in context.

***The negating prefix* un-** The prefix **un-** attached to a noun or adjective forms the antonym of that word. Guess the meanings of these words from the **Lesestück**:

die **Unsicherheit** (line 3)
ungelöste Probleme (line 36)

***The suffix* -los** The suffix **-(s)los** is attached to nouns and forms adjectives and adverbs, e.g., **arbeitslos**. It is the equivalent of the English suffix *-less*. Guess the meanings of these words from the **Lesestück**:

gewaltlos (from **Gewalt**: *force, violence*) line 27
hoffnungslos (from **Hoffnung**: *hope*) line 38

Past participles as adjectives Past participles of verbs are often used as attributive adjectives. They take regular adjective endings.

bauen → **gebaut-**	*to build* → *built*
Das ist das neu **gebaute** Studentenwohnheim.	*That's the newly built dormitory.*

The reading contains the following participles used as adjectives:

besiegen *to defeat*	→ **besiegt-** (line 9)
entnazifizieren *to denazify*	→ **entnazifiziert-** (lines 9–10)
vereinen *to unite*	→ **vereint-** (lines 32–33)
lösen *to solve*	→ **ungelöst-** (line 36)

B Übung Wie heißt das Adjektiv (mit Endung!)? Und wie heißt der neue Satz auf Englisch?

BEISPIEL: Jemand hat diese Waren gestohlen.
Die Polizei hat die *gestohlenen* Waren gefunden.
The police found the stolen goods.

1. Ich habe Altpapier gesammelt und jetzt schleppe ich das ________ Altpapier zum Recycling.
2. Eine Fabrik hat diesen Fluss verschmutzt und jetzt darf man in dem ________ Wasser nicht schwimmen.

3. Der Krieg hat viele deutsche Städte zerstört. Jetzt hat Deutschland seine __________ Städte wieder aufgebaut.
4. Wir hatten eine schöne Reise nach Schottland geplant, aber leider konnten wir uns die __________ Reise nicht leisten.
5. Ich habe meiner Mutter ein schönes Zimmer reserviert, aber das __________ Zimmer war ihr zu klein.

Wortschatz 2

Verben

ändern to change (*trans.*)
Sie hat ihr Leben geändert. She changed her life.
sich ändern to change (*intrans.*)
Ihr Leben hat sich geändert. Her life changed.
auf·geben (gibt auf), gab auf, hat aufgegeben to give up
aus·wandern to emigrate
rufen, rief, hat gerufen to call, shout
vereinen to unite
verschwinden, verschwand, ist verschwunden to disappear

Substantive

der Hass hatred
der Nachbar, -n, -n neighbor
der Schlüssel, - key
der Teil, -e part
der Tod death

das Mitglied, -er member

die Brücke, -n bridge
die Bundesrepublik Deutschland (BRD) the Federal Republic of Germany (FRG)
die Heimat homeland; native country
die Macht, ¨e power, might
die Regierung, -en government in power, administration
die Wirtschaft economy
die Zukunft future

Adjektive und Adverbien

beid- both
berühmt famous
europäisch European
offen open
tief deep
tot dead

Macht is usually the authority to exert control. **Kraft** (9–2) is usually physical power or energy. **Gewalt** is the power to force someone to do your will and also means *violence*.

verschieden various, different
wirtschaftlich economic

Compare **verschieden** (*various, different*) and **ander-** (*other, different*): **Ich kenne viele verschiedene Lieder** (*I know many different songs*) vs. **Ich kenne andere Lieder als du** (*I know different songs than you*).

Gegensätze

auswandern ≠ einwandern to emigrate ≠ to immigrate
der Hass ≠ die Liebe hatred ≠ love
offen ≠ geschlossen open ≠ closed
der Tod ≠ das Leben death ≠ life
die Zukunft ≠ die Vergangenheit future ≠ past

Change: Most general verb is **ändern**, *to alter part of a whole:* **Ändern Sie dieses Wort. Pläne, Meinungen werden geändert; das Wetter hat sich geändert.** Of people: Reflexive use shows change in character or attitude: **Sie ist heutzutage nicht mehr so sympathisch wie damals, sie hat sich geändert. Sich verändern:** Refers to the changing of external things, to change in appearance: **Die Stadt hat sich total verändert.**

Deutschland im europäischen Haus

Understanding Germany's role in Europe today is the cultural goal of this chapter.

Lab Manual Kap. 11, Lesestück.

Im Jahre 1989 ging mit dem Fall° der Berliner Mauer eine Epoche der europäischen Geschichte zu Ende: Die Nachkriegszeit war endlich vorbei°. Besonders für die Länder Osteuropas sind die 90er-Jahre eine Zeit der Unsicherheit, aber auch der neuen Hoffnungen. Mit seiner zentralen Lage° zwischen Ost und West und seiner starken Wirtschaft ist Deutschland in vieler Hinsicht° der Schlüssel zum neuen „europäischen Haus“.[1]

fall
over
location
in ... = in many respects

1. The common “European House” was envisioned by the former Soviet President Mikhail Gorbachev.

Historischer Hintergrund°: 1945 bis 1989

1945 teilten die vier Alliierten° – Amerika, England, Frankreich und die Sowjetunion – das besiegte° Hitlerreich in vier Zonen auf°, mit dem Ziel später einen neuen entnazifizierten° Staat zu bilden°. Aber bald änderte sich das politische Klima. Es begann der sogenannte° Kalte Krieg zwischen dem Kommunismus im Osten und dem Kapitalismus im Westen. Anstatt eines vereinten Landes gründete° man 1949 die Bundesrepublik Deutschland (BRD) und die Deutsche Demokratische Republik (DDR), zwei separate und sehr verschiedene Staaten.

Weil die Grenze zwischen Ost- und Westberlin bis 1961 offen blieb, konnten zirka 2,7 Millionen Menschen aus der DDR in den Westen auswandern.[1] Die DDR verblutete°. Um einen langsamen Tod zu verhindern° baute die ostdeutsche Regierung 1961 eine Mauer mitten durch° Berlin. Die Berliner Mauer, das berühmte Symbol des Kalten Krieges, existierte 28 Jahre, bis die zwei Supermächte USA und Sowjetunion endlich ihre Feindschaft° aufgaben.

background
allies
defeated / **teilten ... auf** = divided / denazified / form
so-called
founded
was bleeding to death / to prevent / **mitten ...** = through the middle of
enmity

November 1989: Die Grenze öffnet sich

In den 80er Jahren leitete die „Glasnost-Politik“[2] Michael Gorbatschows in der Sowjetunion eine Reform ein°, die° sich schnell auf die anderen Länder Osteuropas ausweitete°. Im Sommer 1989 gab es in Leipzig, Dresden und vielen anderen Städten der DDR riesengroße friedliche° Demonstrationen gegen den kommunistischen Staat. „Wir sind das Volk“, riefen die Demonstranten° und später: „Wir sind *ein* Volk“. Diese Demonstrationen leiteten die erste erfolgreiche gewaltlose Revolution der deutschen Geschichte ein°. Die Regierung musste die Grenze öffnen. Im März 1990 kamen dann die ersten freien Wahlen in der DDR und im Oktober die Vereinigung der beiden Teile Deutschlands.

leitete ... ein = initiated / that
sich ... ausweitete = spread
peaceful
demonstrators
leiteten ... ein = initiated

Deutschland im neuen Europa

Als Wirtschaftsmacht und größtes° Mitglied der Europäischen Union[3] spielt das vereinte Deutschland eine wichtige Rolle als Brücke zwischen Ost und West. Deutschland ist selber ein Spiegel der großen Unterschiede in Europa. Wie sieht denn die Zukunft des europäischen Hauses aus?

Es gibt natürlich noch ungelöste Probleme. Die Umwelt in Osteuropa war durch die Industrie viel mehr beschädigt° als° im Westen. Auch waren die meisten° Fabriken in den neuen Bundesländern und in anderen osteuropäischen Ländern hoffnungslos veraltet° und konnten mit der westeuropäischen Industrie nicht mehr konkurrieren°. Man musste sie entweder schließen oder° sehr viel investieren um sie zu modernisieren und umweltfreundlicher zu machen. Das bedeutete im Osten mehr Arbeitslosigkeit und Ressentiments° gegen die Manager aus dem Westen, die° die Marktwirtschaft° einführen° sollten.

biggest
damaged / than / most
hoffnungslos ... = hopelessly antiquated / compete
entweder ... oder = either . . . or
resentment / who
market economy / introduce

1. Although Berlin was located in the middle of the Soviet Occupation Zone, it too was divided among the Allies because of its importance as the capital. Air and highway corridors linked it to the West.
2. Mikhail Gorbachev initiated the internal reforms in the former Soviet Union known as *perestroika* (restructuring) and *glasnost* (openness). These changes eroded the Communist Party's centralized control and hegemony.
3. The European Union, a political and economic alliance of western European nations.

DDR-Wagen kurz vor der Wiedervereinigung. Was bedeutet „BRDDR"?

Die wirtschaftliche Situation in Osteuropa war nach der Auflösung° der Sowjetunion so prekär°, dass viele Menschen ihre Heimat verließen und nach Deutschland auswanderten.[1] Besonders die sogenannten° „Aussiedler" – d.h. Menschen deutscher Abstammung° aus Ländern wie Rumänien und Russland – stellten sich ein besseres° Leben in Deutschland vor. Obwohl die meisten° Deutschen diesen Menschen helfen wollen, gibt es auch eine rechtsradikale Minderheit°, die° Hass und Gewalt gegen Ausländer propagiert°. Im Ausland erwecken° solche Neonazis natürlich alte Ängste und Erinnerungen an die Hitlerzeit.

Es dauert wahrscheinlich noch lange, bis diese alten Ängste und die neuen politischen Probleme überwunden° sind. Aber die Demokratisierung und Integration Osteuropas mit dem Westen sind nicht mehr aufzuhalten°. Zwischen den neuen Nachbarn im Osten und den reichen Demokratien im Westen steht die politisch stabile und wirtschaftlich starke Bundesrepublik. Es ist sicher, dass sie in der Europäischen Union eine führende° Rolle zu spielen hat.

dissolution
precarious
so-called
deutscher ... = of German descent / better / most
rechtsradikale ... = radical right minority / who / spreads / awaken
overcome
sind ... = can no longer be stopped
leading

Nach dem Lesen

■ A ■ Antworten Sie auf Deutsch.

1. Wer hat zuerst von einem „europäischen Haus" gesprochen? Was bedeutet das?
2. Warum ist Deutschlands Rolle so wichtig im neuen Europa?
3. Wie kam es zu zwei deutschen Staaten?
4. Warum waren die beiden deutschen Staaten so verschieden?
5. Warum hat die Regierung der DDR die Mauer mitten durch Berlin gebaut?
6. Wie hat die friedliche Revolution in der DDR begonnen?
7. Wann hat die DDR-Regierung die Grenze ganz geöffnet?
8. Warum wollten Menschen aus Osteuropa nach Deutschland auswandern?

1. Until 1993 Germany had the most liberal asylum laws in the world. In January 1993 alone, 36,000 foreigners applied for asylum. Through a constitutional amendment that redefined application criteria, applications were reduced to 13,000 in January 1994.

■ B ■ Partnerarbeit: EU-Quiz

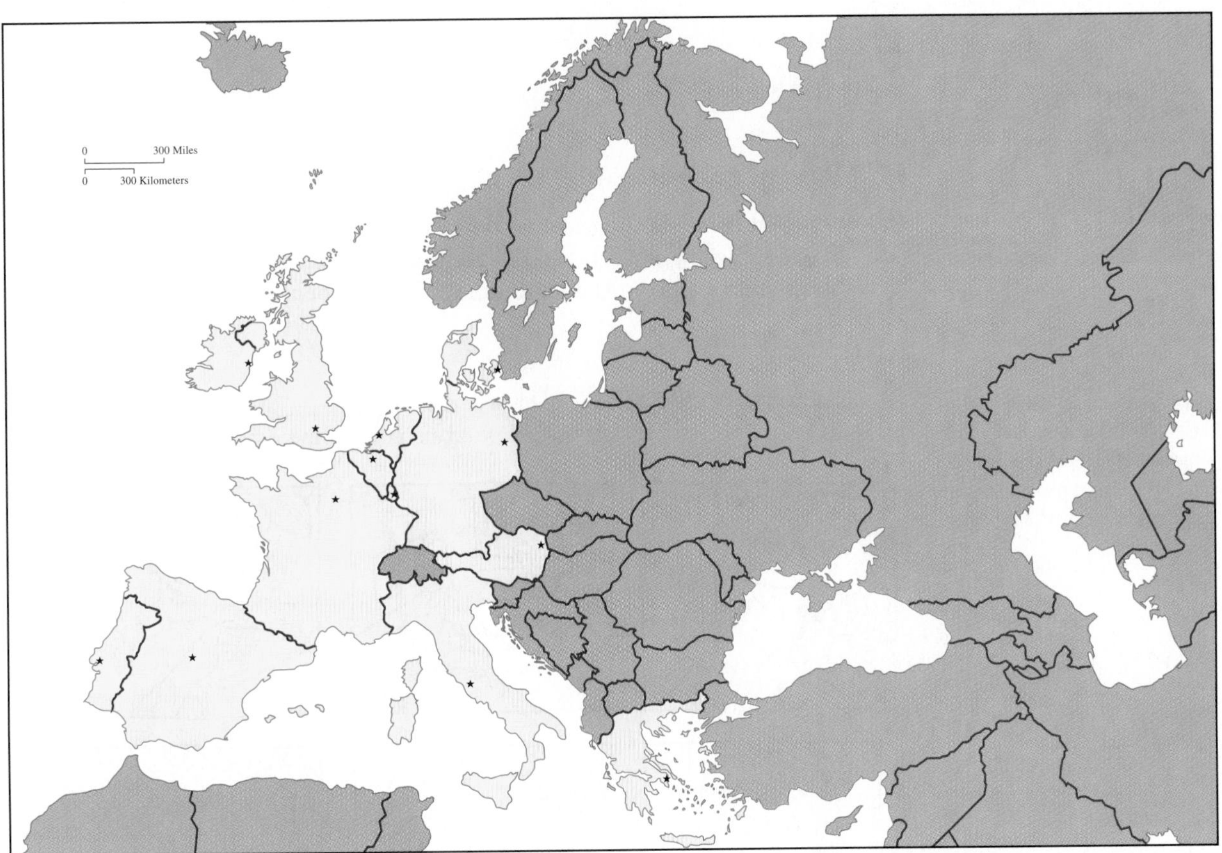

1. Tragen Sie die Namen der EU-Mitgliedstaaten und ihrer Hauptstädte auf die Karte ein. (**eintragen**: *to enter*)

Mitgliedstaaten		***Hauptstädte***	
Belgien	Italien	Athen	London
Dänemark	Luxemburg	Berlin	Luxemburg
Deutschland	Niederlande	Brüssel	Madrid
Finnland	Österreich	den Haag	Paris
Frankreich	Portugal	Dublin	Rom
Griechenland	Schweden	Helsinki	Stockholm
Großbritannien	Spanien	Kopenhagen	Wien
Irland		Lissabon	

2. Welche Kurzbeschreibung passt (*fits*) zu welchem Land?

   a. Wurde erst 1995 Mitglied der EU. Landessprache: Deutsch.
   b. Hat im 16. Jahrhundert Mexiko, Süd- und Mittelamerika kolonisiert.
   c. Der kleinste EU-Staat.
   d. Hier hatten die westliche Philosophie und die Demokratie ihren Anfang.
   e. Im 17. und 18. Jahrhundert eine große See- und Handelsmacht; hatte in Afrika, Indonesien und Nordamerika Kolonien.
   f. Halbinsel im Mittelmeer; historisches Zentrum eines alten Weltreichs.

Situationen aus dem Alltag

■ Morgens nach dem Aufstehen

Das Wochenende war herrlich, aber jetzt ist es wieder Montag. Sie müssen sich für den Tag fertig machen und gehen ins Badezimmer. Sie müssen eine Menge Reflexivverben benutzen um die Morgenroutine zu beschreiben.

With the help of the pictures, students should be able to guess the meaning of these verbs. Although vocabulary from **Situationen aus dem Alltag** is not for active use, you may want to require students to learn some of these high-frequency reflexives.

■ A ■ Übung: Welcher Satz gehört zu welchem Bild?

Er kämmt sich die Haare.
Sie badet sich.
Er rasiert sich.
Sie putzt sich die Zähne.
Sie schminkt sich.
Er duscht sich.

Preferred pronunciation: Short **u** for **duschen**.

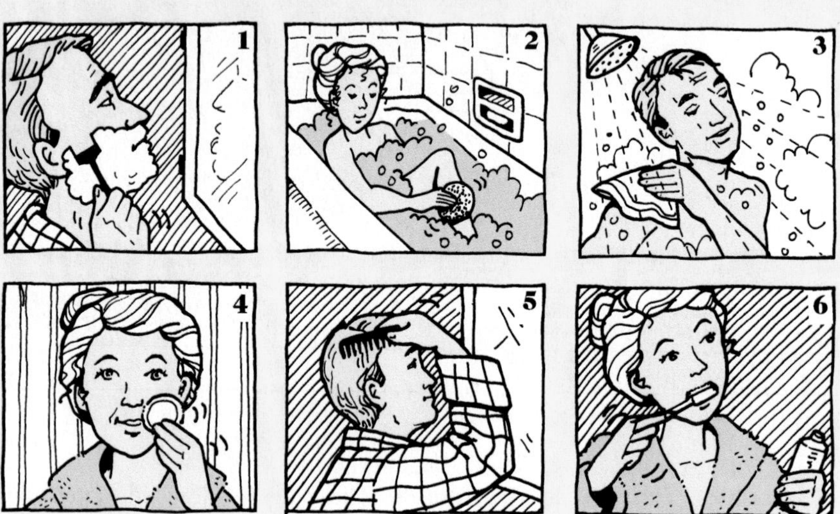

■ B ■ Übung: Was ist Ihre Morgenroutine?

In welcher Reihenfolge (*order*) machen Sie sich morgens fertig? Antworten Sie mit ganzen Sätzen.

frühstücken	1. Zuerst stehe ich auf.
Sachen in die Tasche packen	2. Dann ________________
aufstehen	3. ________________
zur Uni gehen	4. ________________
sich rasieren oder sich schminken	5. ________________
sich die Zähne putzen	6. ________________
eine zweite Tasse Kaffee trinken	7. ________________
sich anziehen	8. ________________
sich duschen oder baden	9. ________________
sich die Haare kämmen	10. ________________

Mit Inter Rail eröffnen sich neue Horizonte.

Zum Schluss

Lab Manual Kap. 11, Diktat.

Workbook Kap. 11, Üb. I, J, K.

Üb. B: **Bildbeschreibungen** also make good written assignments after having been discussed in class.

Üb. C, 1: Not meant as a history quiz, but rather a group effort at summarizing the most important developments from 1918–90. Suggest students look at the **Zeittafel** (**Almanach**, pp. 336–337) the night before. If students are slow in responding, write dates—e.g., 1918, 1933, 1945, 1989—on board and ask **Was ist 1918 passiert? Wissen Sie's noch?** Or approach it the other way by asking **In welchem Jahr ist Hitler an die Macht gekommen?** Try to work with books closed, giving students sense that they have mastered some new facts.

Sprechen wir miteinander!

■ A ■ Rollenspiel: Schade, dass du im Krankenhaus bist! (*3 Personen*) Lesen Sie zusammen diese Situation und dann spielen Sie sie miteinander:

Ein Student spielt einen Verletzten. Er hat einen Unfall gehabt und liegt jetzt im Krankenhaus. Die anderen zwei sind Freunde und besuchen ihn dort. Sie haben noch nichts Genaues über den Unfall gehört. (Sie wissen z.B. nicht, wie er sich verletzt hat.) Sie stellen ihm Fragen. Sie haben ihm natürlich auch Geschenke mitgebracht.

■ B ■ Gruppenarbeit: Sprechen wir über die Fotos in diesem Kapitel. Man sagt, ein Bild ist tausend Worte wert. Die Fotos in diesem Kapitel zeigen die menschliche Seite der Geschichte unserer Zeit. Sehen Sie sich diese Fotos noch einmal an und versuchen Sie so viel wie möglich auf dem Foto zu beschreiben. Dann stellen Sie sich vor, wie die Menschen auf diesen Fotos sich fühlen, was sie denken oder sagen.

■ C ■ Gruppendiskussion: Was hat sich geändert? Was muss sich noch ändern?

1. In Kapiteln 10 und 11 haben Sie eine ganze Menge über deutsche Geschichte im 20. Jahrhundert gelesen. Versuchen wir mal eine kurze Liste von einigen Tatsachen (*facts*) aus dieser Epoche an die Tafel zu schreiben. Was scheint Ihnen besonders wichtig zu sein? Warum?

Üb. C, 2: Warm up for this discussion by brainstorming a list of important issues (**Umwelt, Hunger in der Welt**, etc.) to be addressed. Write them on the board. Be sure **sich ändern** gets recycled. Other possibilities for the discussion: **Das ist eine gute Idee, aber können wir uns das leisten?**

2. Sie haben in diesem Kapitel über viele große Änderungen gelesen. Das Jahr 1989 bedeutete das Ende des Kalten Krieges. Müssen die USA heute immer noch so viel Geld wie früher für das Militär (*the military*) ausgeben? Stellen Sie sich mal vor, Sie sind Berater (*advisors*) des amerikanischen Präsidenten. Was würden Sie ihm sagen? Soll man dieses Geld jetzt für etwas anderes ausgeben? Was soll sich in unserem Land oder in der Welt ändern?

Helmut Kohl und Michael Gorbatschow bei den Gesprächen (*talks*) über die deutsche Vereinigung (1990)

Schreiben Sie zu Hause.

Write as a series of natural exchanges, beginning like this:

DR. BÜCHNER: **Guten Morgen, Herr Lenz!**
HERR LENZ: **Morgen, Herr Doktor.**
DR. BÜCHNER: **Es tut mir Leid, dass ich mich verspätet habe ...**

D **Gute Besserung!** Schreiben Sie diese Anekdote als Dialog zwischen Dr. Büchner und seinem Patienten Herrn Lenz. Der arme Herr Lenz liegt im Krankenhaus.

Dr. Büchner läuft morgens um 10.00 Uhr ins Krankenzimmer und sagt Herrn Lenz, es tut ihm Leid, dass er sich verspätet hat. Er würde gern wissen, wie es Herrn Lenz geht und ob er sich besser fühlt. Er fragt, wo es ihm noch weh tut und was er sonst noch braucht. Der Arzt sagt, dass er sich schon vorstellen kann, wie langweilig es ist, so lange im Bett liegen zu müssen.

Herr Lenz antwortet, dass es ihm nicht so gut geht, dass er noch sehr krank ist, dass es ihm überall weh tut, dass ihm das Essen im Krankenhaus nicht schmeckt und dass er das Fernsehen langweilig findet und einige neue Romane haben möchte.

Dr. Büchner sagt, es freut ihn zu sehen, dass Herr Lenz so viel besser aussieht. Er soll sich anziehen, denn er darf heute nach Hause.

E Complete the three mini-dialogues with appropriate nouns formed from adjectives. Choose from the following list:

gut	schön	verwandt	bekannt
deutsch	einfach	altmodisch	interessant
neu	kalt	toll	modern
besonder-	schlimm	herrlich	

1. A: Hast du etwas ______ zu berichten?
   B: Ja, in der Stadt habe ich heute etwas ganz ______ gesehen!
   A: Wirklich? In unserer langweiligen Stadt? Das ist schon etwas ______ !

The first sentence in dialogue 2 requires a designation of nationality (without article, see p. 326).

2. A: Kennst du Steffi Hartmann? Sie ist ______ und ist gerade aus Stuttgart angekommen.
   B: Wie nett dich kennen zu lernen, Steffi! Eine alte ______ von mir aus der Schulzeit heißt Hartmann und wohnt auch in Stuttgart.
   C: Ja, dann ist sie vielleicht sogar eine ______ von mir. Unsere Familie ist ziemlich groß.

3. A: Das ______ bei uns im Sommer ist nicht nur das Wetter, sondern auch die hohen Berge und die schöne Natur.
   B: Super. Für mich ist das etwas ______. Ich bin in der Großstadt zu Hause.
   A: Aber in unserem kleinen Dorf auf dem Lande ist das Leben manchmal noch wie im 19. Jahrhundert. Da gibt es wenig ______ zu tun.
   B: Das ist mir ja egal! So was gibt's in der Großstadt! Ich bin zu euch gekommen um das ______ zu sehen.

■ F ■ Machen Sie ganze Sätze. Vergessen Sie die Endungen nicht! (// = Komma)

1. (*perfect tense*) wegen / dies- / Situation / auswandern / viel- / Menschen
2. (*first clause: past perfect tense*) nachdem / man / Mauer / bauen // (*second clause: simple past tense*) können / wenig- / Menschen / nach Westen / reisen
3. (*simple past tense*) Mauer / müssen / 28 Jahre / existieren // bis / politisch / Situation / sich ändern
4. (*present tense*) nach / Vereinigung / beid- (*genitive*) / deutsch- / Staaten / aussehen / Zukunft / anders
5. (*present tense*) all- / Menschen / sich freuen // wenn / Völker / Europa (*genitive*) / in Frieden / miteinander / leben / können

Üb. G: 1. Wann sind Ihre Verwandten nach Amerika eingewandert? 2. Einige sind vor 60 Jahren aus Deutschland ausgewandert. 3. Andere sind am Anfang des 19. Jahrhunderts angekommen. 4. Ute hat mir gesagt, dass du dich verletzt hast. 5. Ja, ich habe mir letzte Woche den Arm gebrochen. 6. Wie ist denn das passiert? 7. Ich hatte einen Unfall mit meinem neuen Fahrrad. 8. Beeil dich, oder wir verspäten uns! 9. Ich muss mich noch waschen und anziehen. 10. Gott sei Dank können wir uns ein Taxi leisten. 11. Haben die Kinder schon gegessen? 12. Ja, und sie haben sich gewaschen und sind schon im Bett.

■ G ■ Wie sagt man das auf Deutsch?

1. When did your relatives immigrate to America?
2. Some emigrated from Germany sixty years ago.
3. Others arrived at the beginning of the 19th century.

4. Ute told me that you got hurt.
5. Yes, I broke my arm last week.
6. How did that happen?
7. I had an accident with my new bicycle.

8. Hurry up or we'll be late!
9. I still have to wash and get dressed.
10. Thank goodness we can afford a taxi.
11. Have the children already eaten?
12. Yes, and they've washed and are in bed already.

Zeittafel, 1939–heute

1939 Deutscher Einmarsch in Polen; Anfang des Zweiten Weltkriegs.

1945 9. Mai Kapitulation Deutschlands. Der Zweite Weltkrieg ist zu Ende.

1946 Erste demokratische Kommunalwahlen seit 1933.

1947 Marshall-Plan bringt den Westzonen ökonomische Hilfe. Der Wiederaufbau beginnt.

1948 Währungsreform im Westen. Berlin-Blockade durch die Sowjets, Berliner Luftbrücke.

1949 Gründung der BRD und der DDR, Deutschland in zwei Staaten geteilt.

1950

1953 Protestdemonstrationen in Ostberlin gegen zu hohe Arbeitsnormen.

1955 BRD wird Mitglied der NATO, DDR wird Mitglied des Warschauer Paktes

1960

1961 Bau der Mauer zwischen Ost-und West-Berlin

1989 Spätsommer Tägliche Flucht vieler DDR-Bürger über Ungarn. Erich Honecker tritt zurück. Millionen demonstrieren in Ostberlin, Leipzig und anderen Städten.
9. November Die Regierung öffnet die Grenzen.

1990 März Erste demokratische Wahlen in der DDR.
Juli Währungsunion der beiden deutschen Staaten.
Oktober Deutsche Vereinigung.
Dezember Erste gesamtdeutsche demokratische Wahlen seit 1932.

70er Jahre Willy Brandts Ostpolitik. Normalisierung der Beziehungen zwischen BRD und DDR.

1994
Die letzten alliierten Truppen verlassen Berlin.

1970  1980 1990 1994 1995

1963 Besuch des US-Präsidenten John F. Kennedy an der Mauer.

1982
Beginn der Kanzlerschaft Helmut Kohls.

1987
750-Jahr-Feier in beiden Teilen der Stadt Berlin.

1991
Berlin wird wieder die Hauptstadt Deutschlands.

1995
Österreich wird Mitglied der Europäischen Union.

KAPITEL 12

Erinnerungen

Communicative Goals

- Comparing things
- Saying how often things happen
- Talking about memories

Cultural Goal

- Applying your knowledge of twentieth-century Germany to an authentic German literary text

Chapter Outline

- **Lyrik zum Vorlesen**
  Joseph von Eichendorff, „Heimweh"
- **Grammatik**
  Comparison of adjectives and adverbs
  Relative pronouns and relative clauses
  The verb *lassen*
  Time phrases with *Mal*
  Parts of the day: *gestern früh*, etc.
- **Lesestück**
  Anna Seghers, „Zwei Denkmäler"
- **Situationen aus dem Alltag**
  Erinnerungen
- **Videoecke**
  Das vergesse ich nie.
- **Almanach**
  Four Modern Writers

Dialoge

Lab Manual Kap. 12, Dialoge, Fragen, Hören Sie gut zu!

Model German pronunciation of **Computer** and **Software**.

Use dialogues to review pronunciation of consonant clusters in compound nouns and adjectives: **idiotensicher**, **Haustür**, **Querstraße** (remind students of **Quatsch**), **Augenblick**, **knapp bei Kasse**, **gleichfalls**.

Idiotensicher

HANS-PETER: Du, Karin, hast du das Buch mit, das ich dir geliehen habe?
KARIN: Ach, tut mir Leid. Ich hab's wieder zu Hause gelassen. Ich arbeite noch an meinem Referat.
HANS-PETER: Ist ja egal. Du darfst es ruhig noch behalten. Hast du noch viel zu tun?
KARIN: Nein, ich bin fast fertig. Ich benutze zum ersten Mal meinen neuen Computer. Die Software ist wirklich idiotensicher.

Klatsch

PETRA: Wer war denn der Typ, mit dem Rita gestern weggegangen ist?
JÖRG: Der Mann, der so komisch angezogen war?
PETRA: Genau, den meine ich.
JÖRG: Das war der Rudi. Stell dir vor, sie hat sich mit ihm verlobt!
PETRA: Wenigstens sah er intelligenter aus als ihr letzter Freund.

Notice two N-nouns: **Nachbar** and **Herr**.

Vor der Haustür

Frau Schwarzer, die neulich ins Haus eingezogen ist, redet nach der Arbeit mit ihrem Nachbarn Herrn Beck.

FRAU SCHWARZER: Ach Herr Beck, ich wollte Sie etwas fragen. Wo kann ich am billigsten meinen VW reparieren lassen?
HERR BECK: In der nächsten Querstraße gibt's den besten Mechaniker in der Gegend, aber der ist leider nicht der Billigste.
FRAU SCHWARZER: Hmm ... Im Augenblick bin ich etwas knapp bei Kasse. Ich glaub', ich mache es diesmal lieber selber.
HERR BECK: Na, viel Spaß. Also, dann wünsche ich Ihnen einen schönen Abend noch.
FRAU SCHWARZER: Danke, gleichfalls!

Guten Abend is a greeting. (**Ich wünsche Ihnen einen**) **schönen Abend noch** is said when parting.

Contrast **gelassen** with **verlassen** (5–1). To practice, have students ask each other where things are; each answers, **Ich hab' ihn/es/sie zu Hause gelassen**.

Notes on Usage: *es* and *etwas*

In spoken German, the pronoun **es** is often contracted to **'s**.

Ich **hab's** wieder zu Hause gelassen.
In der nächsten Querstraße **gibt's** den besten Mechaniker.

etwas Note three different meanings:

Ich habe **etwas** vergessen.	*something*
Ich bin **etwas** müde.	*somewhat, a little*
Hast du **etwas** Geld?	*some*

Wortschatz 1

Tell students: **mit** meaning along with (*someone*), can be combined with many verbs: **ich fahre/esse/lese usw. mit**.

Verben

behalten (behält), behielt, hat behalten to keep, retain
erinnern an (+ *acc.*) to remind of
sich erinnern an (+ *acc.*) to remember
lassen (lässt), ließ, hat gelassen to leave (something or someone), leave behind; to let, allow; to cause to be done
reden to talk, speak
reparieren to repair
sich verloben mit to become engaged to
weg·gehen, ging weg, ist weggegangen to go away, leave
wünschen to wish

Substantive

der **Augenblick, -e** moment
im Augenblick at the moment
der **Besuch, -e** visit
der **Computer, -** computer
der **Klatsch** gossip
der **Typ, -en** (*slang*) guy

der Typ: Used colloquially for males (**ein sympathischer Typ**). For both male and female: **Er/sie ist nicht mein Typ.**

das **Mal, -e** time (*in the sense of "occurrence"*)
jedes Mal every time
zum ersten Mal for the first time
die **Erinnerung, -en** memory
die **Gegend, -en** area, region
die **Nacht, ¨-e** night
in der Nacht at night
Gute Nacht. Good night.
die **Querstraße, -n** cross street
die **Software** software

Adjektive und Adverbien

diesmal this time
einmal once
etwas somewhat, a little
fertig done, finished
idiotensicher foolproof
intelligent intelligent
knapp scarce, in short supply
knapp bei Kasse short of money
komisch peculiar, odd; funny
mit along with (someone)
nächst- nearest; next
neulich recently
ruhig (*as sentence adverb*) feel free to, go ahead and
Du kannst ruhig hier bleiben. Feel free to stay here.

Remember the basic meaning of **ruhig**: peaceful, calm. Cf. the cartoon on p. 78.

übermorgen the day after tomorrow
vorgestern the day before yesterday

Andere Vokabeln

als (*with adj. or adv. in comparative degree*) than
intelligenter als more intelligent than
na well . . .

Nützliche Ausdrücke

(Einen) Augenblick, bitte! Just a moment, please!
Danke, gleichfalls. Thanks, you too. Same to you.
Viel Spaß! Have fun!

Gegensätze

sich erinnern ≠ vergessen to remember ≠ to forget
reden ≠ schweigen, schwieg, hat geschwiegen to speak ≠ to be silent
reparieren ≠ kaputtmachen to repair ≠ to break
weggehen ≠ zurückkommen to go away ≠ to come back
die Nacht ≠ der Tag night ≠ day

Proverb: **Reden ist Silber, Schweigen ist Gold.**

Foolproof

H.-P: Karin, do you have the book with you that I lent you?
K: Oh, sorry. I left it at home again. I'm still working on my paper.
H.-P: Doesn't matter. Go ahead and keep it. Do you still have a lot to do?
K: No, I'm almost done. I'm using my new computer for the first time. The software is really foolproof.

Gossip

P: Who was the guy Rita left with yesterday?
J: The man who was dressed so funny?
P: Exactly. He's the one I mean.
J: That was Rudi. Just imagine, she's gotten engaged to him!
P: At least he looked more intelligent than her last boyfriend.

At the Front Door

Ms. Schwarzer, who has recently moved into the building, is talking after work to her neighbor, Mr. Beck.

MS. S: Oh Mr. Beck, I wanted to ask you something. Where can I get my VW repaired most cheaply?
MR. B: In the next cross street there's the best mechanic in the area, but he's unfortunately not the cheapest.
MS. S: Hmm . . . At the moment I'm somewhat short of cash. I think I'll do it myself this time.
MR. B: Well, have fun. Then I'll wish you a good evening.
MS. S: Thanks, you too.

Variationen

■ A ■ Persönliche Fragen

1. Schreiben Sie Ihre Referate mit dem Computer?
2. Leihen Sie Ihren Freunden Bücher oder nicht? Wie ist es mit CDs, Ihrem Fahrrad, oder mit Kleidern?
3. Was haben Sie heute zu Hause gelassen?
4. Jörg sagt, dass Rudi komisch angezogen war. Ziehen Sie sich manchmal komisch an? Was tragen Sie dann?
5. Wie alt soll man sein, bevor man sich verlobt? Was meinen Sie?
6. Besitzen Sie einen Wagen? Was für einen?
7. Sind Sie ein guter Mechaniker? Können Sie Ihr Auto selber reparieren?

Üb. B: Books closed.

■ B ■ Übung: Was braucht man? Um ihr Referat zu schreiben braucht Karin Bücher, einen Computer und vielleicht auch ein Wörterbuch. Was braucht man um …

einen Brief zu schreiben?
das Frühstück zu machen?
eine Urlaubsreise zu machen?
eine Fremdsprache zu lernen?
einkaufen zu gehen?
eine Radtour zu machen?
eine Wanderung in den Bergen zu machen?

■ C ■ Übung: Das Beste in der Gegend Herr Beck weiß, wer der beste Mechaniker in der Gegend ist. Wissen Sie, wo man das Beste in der Gegend findet? Wo ist hier in unserer Gegend …

das beste griechische Restaurant? das beste französische Restaurant?
das beste Kleidergeschäft?
das beste Hotel?
die beste Kneipe?
die beste Pizza?
das beste Sportgeschäft?
der beste Supermarkt?

Encourage students to use pronouns in their answers.

■ D ■ Übung: Sie dürfen das ruhig machen. Sie sagen, Sie würden gern etwas machen. Der/Die Nächste sagt, Sie dürfen es ruhig machen (oder) Sie können es ruhig machen.

BEISPIEL: Ich würde gern deinen Kuli benutzen.
Klar, du darfst ihn *ruhig* benutzen.

The sentence adverb **ruhig** goes immediately after the inflected verb and all personal pronouns.

1. Ich würde gerne deinen Wagen bis 3 Uhr behalten.
2. Heute Abend würde ich dich gerne besuchen.
3. Ich würde gern etwas Wichtiges sagen.
4. Ich würde meine Freunde gerne einladen.
5. Ich würde gern etwas essen.
6. Meinen Wagen würde ich gerne hier lassen.
7. Ich würde mir gerne die Kirche ansehen.
8. Ich würde gern meine Freundin Gertrud mitbringen.

Lyrik zum Vorlesen

Joseph von Eichendorff was one of the foremost poets of the Romantic movement in Germany. Reverence for nature, longing for one's beloved, and nostalgia for one's homeland are all typical themes for the Romantics. The poem "Heimweh" (*Homesickness*) is from Eichendorff's story ***Aus dem Leben eines Taugenichts*** (*From the Life of a Good-for-Nothing*), in which the hero, in Italy, yearns for Germany and his beloved.

Lab Manual Kap. 12, Lyrik zum Vorlesen.

Heimweh

Wer in die Fremde° will wandern
Der muss mit der Liebsten° gehn,
Es jubeln° und lassen die andern
Den Fremden alleine stehn.

= ins Ausland
beloved
rejoice

Zeichnung (*drawing*) von Ludwig Richter (19. Jhdt.)

Was wisset ihr, dunkele Wipfel°
Von der alten, schönen Zeit?
Ach, die Heimat hinter den Gipfeln°,
Wie liegt sie von hier so weit!

treetops
peaks

Return to poem after covering superlative (**die Liebste, am liebsten, der höchste Berg**). Explain poetic placement of genitive before its object in "**vor der Liebsten Tür.**" To help students appreciate prevalence of these themes in the Romantic era, show them picture of "**Der Wanderer über dem Nebelmeer**" (ca. 1815) by Caspar David Friedrich (1774–1840), which correlates visually with last strophe.

Am liebsten° betracht° ich die Sterne°,
Die schienen, wie° ich ging zu ihr,
Die Nachtigall° hör ich so gerne,
Sie sang vor der Liebsten Tür.

most of all / contemplate / stars / = **als**
nightingale

Der Morgen, das ist meine Freude°!
Da steig ich in stiller° Stund'
Auf den höchsten° Berg in die Weite°,
Grüß dich, Deutschland, aus Herzens
Grund°!

Joseph von Eichendorff (1788–1857)

joy
quiet
highest / distance
aus ... = from the bottom of my heart

Comparing things is a communicative goal.

Comparison of adjectives and adverbs

When adjectives or adverbs are used in comparisons, they can occur in three stages or degrees.

- Positive degree (*basic form*)

  so interessant wie = *as interesting as*

Jörg ist **so interessant wie** Dieter.	*Jörg is **as interesting as** Dieter.*
Jutta läuft **schnell**.	*Jutta runs **fast**.*

- Comparative degree (*marker*: **-er**)

  interessanter als = *more interesting than*

Jörg ist **interessanter als** Helmut.	*Jörg is **more interesting than** Helmut.*
Jutta läuft **schneller als** ich.	*Jutta runs **faster than** I do.*

Point out distinction between **Jutta läuft am schnellsten** and **Jutta ist die schnellste** (**Läuferin**). Confusing, because English permits *Jutta runs **the** fastest*.

- Superlative degree of attributive adjectives (*marker*: **-st**)

  der interessanteste Schüler = *the most interesting pupil*
  die schnellste Läuferin = *the fastest runner*

- Superlative degree of adverbs and predicate adjectives (*marker*: **am ______ -(e)sten**)

  am interessantesten = *most interesting*

Von allen Schülern ist Jörg **am interessantesten**.	*Of all the pupils, Jörg is **most interesting**.*
Jutta läuft **am schnellsten**.	*Jutta runs **fastest**.*

Die schnellsten Männer
der Welt starten nicht in Monza,
sondern im Büro.

Formation of comparative degree

- To form the comparative degree of any adjective or adverb, add the marker **-er** to the basic form:

Basic form	+ -er	= *Comparative degree*
schnell-	-er	**schneller**
dunkel-	-er	**dunkler**
interessant-	-er	**interessanter**

Spelling note: Adjectives ending in **-el** and **-er** drop the **-e-** in the comparative:
dunkel → **dunkler**
teuer → **teurer**

English adjectives longer than two syllables form their comparative with *more*: *interesting—more interesting*. German does not follow this pattern. Simply add **-er** to make the comparative, no matter how long the adjective is: **interessant—interessanter**.

- Attributive adjectives add the regular adjective endings *after* the comparative **-er-** ending.

Basic form	+ -er-	+ *Adjective ending*
schnell-	-er-	-en
interessant-	-er-	-es

Wir fuhren mit dem **schnelleren** Zug. — *We took the faster train.*
Ich lese ein **interessanteres** Buch. — *I'm reading a more interesting book.*

- **als** = *than* when used with the comparative.

Das Buch ist interessanter **als** der Artikel. — *The book is more interesting than the article.*

Lab Manual Kap. 12, Üb. 1 and Var. zu Üb. 3, 4, 6–11.

Workbook Kap. 12, A–F.

If you are directing **Üb. 1** and the class has a sense of humor, substitute students' names for **Jörg**.

1 Übung Everyone is praising Jörg, but you respond that you are *more* everything than he is.

BEISPIEL: A: Jörg ist interessant.
B: Aber ich bin interessanter als er.

1. Jörg ist hübsch.
2. Er ist ruhig.
3. Er läuft schnell.
4. Er ist ehrlich.
5. Jörg ist fleißig.
6. Er ist freundlich.
7. Er steht früh auf.
8. Er ist sportlich.

2 Übung: Vergleichen wir! (Let's compare!) Antworten Sie mit einem ganzen Satz.

BEISPIEL: A: Was fährt schneller als ein Fahrrad?
B: Ein Auto fährt schneller als ein Fahrrad.

1. Was fährt langsamer als ein Zug?
2. Was schmeckt Ihnen besser als Salat?
3. Was ist moderner als eine Schreibmaschine (*typewriter*)?
4. Wer ist reicher als Sie?
5. Welches Auto ist teurer als ein Volkswagen?
6. Welche Energiequelle (*energy source*) ist umweltfreundlicher als Öl?
7. Welche Stadt ist sauberer als New York?
8. Welche Länder sind kleiner als Deutschland?

Hier sehen Sie einen der größten Kohlendioxidfresser der Welt.

Üb. 3: Also possible as **Partnerarbeit**. Repeat using singular: **Dieses Hemd ist mir nicht dunkel genug. Hier haben wir ein dunkleres Hemd.**

■ 3 ■ Übung: Im Kaufhaus Sie sind Verkäufer im Kaufhaus. Ihr Professor spielt einen Kunden. Nichts scheint ihm zu gefallen. Sie versuchen ihm etwas Schöneres, Billigeres usw. zu zeigen.

BEISPIEL: A: Dieses Hemd ist mir nicht dunkel genug.
B: Hier haben wir dunklere Hemden.

1. Diese Blumen sind mir nicht schön genug.
2. Diese Brötchen sind mir nicht frisch genug.
3. Diese Taschen sind mir nicht leicht genug.
4. Diese Bücher sind mir nicht billig genug.
5. Diese Fahrräder sind mir nicht leicht genug.
6. Diese Computer sind mir nicht schnell genug.

■ Formation of the superlative

The superlative is formed in the following ways:

Adverbs All adverbs form their superlative using the following pattern:

Note on spelling: An extra **-e-** is added when the basic form ends in **-d**, **-t**, **-s**, **-ß**, or **-z**: **am mildesten**, **am heißesten**.

am ________-(e)sten
am schnellsten *most quickly*

Jutta läuft **am schnellsten**.	*Jutta runs **fastest**.*
Hans hat **am schönsten** gesungen.	*Hans sang **most beautifully**.*

German has no superlative marker like English *most*. No matter how long an adverb is, simply add **-sten**: **am interessantesten** = *most interestingly*.

Attributive Adjectives With attributive adjectives, add the regular adjective endings after the superlative **-(e)st-**, for example:

Basic form	+	-(e)st-	+	*Adjective ending*
interessant-		-est-		-e
schnell-		-st-		-en

Die **interessanteste** Studentin heißt Marianne.	*The **most interesting** student is named Marianne.*
Wir fuhren mit dem **schnellsten** Zug.	*We took the **fastest** train.*

Predicate Adjectives Predicate adjectives in the superlative may occur either in the **am ______-sten** pattern or with the definite article and regular adjective endings.

You can use the superlative only with the *definite* article, never with the *indefinite* article: **der tiefste See**, but not **ein tiefster See**.

Albert ist **am interessantesten**.	*Albert is **most interesting**.*
Albert ist **der Interessanteste**.	*Albert is **the most interesting person**.*
Diese Bücher sind die **interessantesten**.	*These books are **the most interesting (ones)**.*

■ 4 ■ Übung: Ich mache das am besten! A visitor is praising the whole class. You then praise yourself in the superlative.

BEISPIEL: A: Sie laufen alle schnell.
B: Aber ich laufe am schnellsten.

1. Sie sind alle freundlich.
2. Sie sind alle sehr fleißig.
3. Sie singen alle sehr schön.
4. Sie sind alle elegant angezogen.
5. Sie sind alle sehr sportlich.
6. Sie denken alle sehr kreativ.

Die besten Restaurants in Deutschland

Üb. 5: Variation: Try with English cues.
I: *Tell us you run fast.*
S1: **Ich laufe schnell.**
I: (to S2) *Tell us you do it better.*
S2: **Ich laufe schneller.**
I: (to S3) *Tell us you do it best.*

■ 5 ■ Gruppenarbeit: Ich bin der/die ______-ste! Here are some adjectives you can use to describe yourself. Choose the one that you think you exemplify the best of anyone in the class. (Don't take this too seriously!) Then say, **Ich bin der/die ______-ste.**

BEISPIEL: Ich bin der/die Schönste hier!

clever in German means *sly, ingenious*.

aktiv	elegant	hungrig
altmodisch	faul	modern
blöd	fleißig	radikal
clever	höflich	wahnsinnig

Üb. 6: Also possible as **Partnerarbeit**. Repeat, using singular (except for #1); note change in meaning in #6.

■ 6 ■ Übung: Im Laden Sie sind wieder Verkäufer und Ihre Professorin spielt eine Kundin. Sie sucht etwas und Sie sagen, Sie haben das Neueste, Billigste usw.

BEISPIEL: A: Ich suche billige Weine.
B: Hier sind die *billigsten* Weine.

1. Ich suche neue Schuhe.
2. Ich suche schöne Bilder.
3. Ich suche interessante Bücher.
4. Ich suche moderne Stühle.
5. Ich suche leichte Fahrräder.
6. Ich suche elegante Kleider.

Some comparative and superlative adjectives have two possible forms: **roter/röter**, **nasser/nässer**, **gesunder/gesünder**. **Gesund** is the only two-syllable adjective where umlaut is possible.

■ Umlaut in comparative and superlative

Many one-syllable adjectives and adverbs whose stem vowels are **a**, **o**, or **u** (but *not* **au**) are umlauted in the comparative and superlative degrees. Here is a list of adjectives and adverbs you already know. Some occur in easy-to-remember pairs of opposites.

old	alt	älter	am ältesten
young	jung	jünger	am jüngsten
dumb	dumm	dümmer	am dümmsten
smart	klug	klüger	am klügsten
cold	kalt	kälter	am kältesten
warm	warm	wärmer	am wärmsten
short	kurz	kürzer	am kürzesten
long	lang	länger	am längsten
strong	stark	stärker	am stärksten
weak	schwach	schwächer	am schwächsten
sick	krank	kränker	am kränksten
healthy	gesund	gesünder	am gesündesten
poor	arm	ärmer	am ärmsten
hard, harsh	hart	härter	am härtesten
often	oft	öfter	am öftesten
red	rot	röter	am rötesten
black	schwarz	schwärzer	am schwärzesten

Gruppenarbeit 7, Variation: Repeat with attributive adjs: **Ich habe eine kalte Wohnung**, etc.

■ 7 ■ Gruppenarbeit: kalt / kälter / am kältesten The first student reads a sentence, and the next two respond with the comparative and superlative.

BEISPIEL: A: Meine Wohnung ist kalt.
B: Meine Wohnung ist noch kälter.
C: Aber meine Wohnung ist am kältesten.

1. Mein Bruder ist stark.
2. Mein Auto ist alt.
3. Mein Referat ist lang.
4. Mein Freund ist krank.
5. Meine Schwester ist jung.
6. Mein Zimmer ist warm.
7. Mein Besuch war kurz.
8. Mein Beruf ist hart.

■ Irregular comparatives and superlatives

Some of the most frequently used adjectives and adverbs in German have irregular forms in the comparative and superlative.

Note: The superlative of **groß** adds **-t** (**größt-**) rather than **-est** to the stem.

Positive	*Comparative*	*Superlative*	
groß	größer	am größten	*big/bigger/biggest*
gut	besser	am besten	*good, well/better/best*
hoch, hoh-	höher	am höchsten	*high/higher/highest*
nahe	näher	am nächsten	*near/nearer/nearest; next*
viel	mehr	am meisten	*much, many/more/most*
gern	lieber	am liebsten	*like to/prefer to/most of all like to*

- The three degrees of **gern** are used to say how much you like to do things.

Ich gehe **gern** ins Kino.	*I like to go to the movies.*
Ich gehe **lieber** ins Theater.	*I'd rather* (or) *I prefer to go to the theater.*
Ich gehe **am liebsten** ins Konzert.	*Most of all, I like to go to concerts.*

Wenig, the antonym of **viel**, functions in the same way:
Ich esse **wenig** Brot.
Ich habe **wenige** Freunde.
Ich habe **weniger** Freunde als du.

- **Viel** means *much* or *a lot of* and it has *no adjective endings*. **Viele** means *many* and *does* have regular plural endings.

Ich esse **viel** Brot.	*I eat a lot of bread.*
Ich habe **viele** Freunde.	*I have many friends.*

The comparative degree **mehr** *never* has adjective endings.

Du hast **mehr** Freunde als ich.	*You have more friends than I.*

The superlative degree **meist-** *does* take endings; in addition, it is used with the definite article, in contrast to English *most*.

Die meisten Studenten essen in der Mensa.	***Most** students eat in the cafeteria.*

WENIGER IST MEHR.

Üb. 8: Also good as written homework.

■ 8 ■ Übung: gut, besser, am besten Rank the items on the right according to the criteria on the left.

BEISPIEL: schnell fahren — Bus, Fahrrad, Zug
Ein Fahrrad fährt schnell, ein Bus fährt schneller und ein Zug fährt am schnellsten.

1. gut schmecken — Schokolade, Wurst, Kartoffelsalat
2. hoch sein — Berg, Haus, Dom
3. nahe sein — Studentenwohnheim, Mensa, Bibliothek
4. viel wissen — Schüler, Professoren, Studenten

■ 9 ■ Gruppenarbeit: Was sind Ihre Präferenzen? Rank your preferences, as in the example.

BEISPIEL: trinken — Tee, Kaffee, Milch
Ich trinke gern Milch. Ich trinke lieber Kaffee. Aber am liebsten trinke ich Tee.

1. lesen — Zeitungen, Gedichte, Romane
2. hören — Rockmusik, Jazz, klassische Musik
3. wohnen — in der Stadt, auf dem Land, am Meer
4. spielen — Fußball, Tennis, Volleyball
5. bekommen — Briefe, Geschenke, gute Noten
6. essen — Pommes frites, Sauerkraut, Bauernbrot
7. schreiben — Briefe, Referate, Postkarten

■ Comparisons

genauso ... wie = *just as . . . as*
nicht so ... wie = *not as . . . as*

Heute ist es **genauso kalt wie** gestern. Aber es ist **kälter als** vorgestern.	*Today is **just as cold as** yesterday. But it's **colder than** the day before yesterday.*
Stuttgart ist **nicht so groß wie** Berlin. Aber es ist **größer als** Tübingen.	*Stuttgart is **not as large as** Berlin. But it's **bigger than** Tübingen.*

immer ________-er (shows progressive change)

Das Kind wird **immer größer**.	*The child's getting **bigger and bigger**.*
Sie liest **immer mehr** Bücher.	*She's reading **more and more** books.*

Üb. 10: Have students prepare as homework. Variation: Ask students to make statements about progressive change from their personal experience: **Diese Uni wird immer teurer, das Studium wird immer interessanter usw.**

■ 10 ■ Gruppenarbeit: Damals und jetzt Vergleichen wir (*Let's compare*) damals und jetzt. Jeder sagt, wie es früher war und wie sich alles immer mehr ändert.

BEISPIEL: Früher hatte man mehr Zeit, heute ist man immer mehr in Eile.
Früher war das Lebenstempo langsamer, jetzt wird es immer schneller.
Früher kostete das Studium ...

Üb. 11: Bring in pairs of similar objects (pieces of clothing, household items) and have students describe differences in free response.

■ 11 ■ Übung: Vergleiche (Comparisons) Bring in pictures or photos that you have drawn, taken, or found in books or magazines. Find similarities and differences in these pictures and compare them in German for the class.

BEISPIELE: Diese Bäume sind höher als diese hier, aber dieser Berg ist genauso hoch wie der andere.

Diese Mutter sieht nicht so jung aus wie diese hier, aber dieses Kind ist genauso alt wie das Kind da. Das dritte Kind ist das älteste.

Relative pronouns and relative clauses

A relative clause is a subordinate clause that modifies or further clarifies a noun. Relative clauses are introduced by relative pronouns. Compare the following sentences:

Das ist das **neue** Buch. — *That's the **new** book.*

	rel. pron.	
Das ist das Buch,	***das***	**du mir geliehen hast**.
That's the book	***that***	*you lent me.*

The relative clause **das du mir geliehen hast**, like the descriptive adjective **neue**, modifies **Buch** by telling *which* book is being talked about.

The relative pronouns in English are *who, whom, whose, that,* and *which*. The German relative pronoun is identical in most cases to the definite article, which you already know. Study the following table and note especially the forms in bold, which are *different* from the definite article.

Compare declension of definite article on p. 228. There are only three relative pronouns that are not identical to forms of the definite article: **denen**, **dessen**, and **deren**. These forms are printed in boldface in the table.

Relative Pronouns				
	masc.	neut.	fem.	plur.
nom.	der	das	die	die
acc.	den	das	die	die
dat.	dem	dem	der	**denen**
gen.	**dessen**	**dessen**	**deren**	**deren**

Sentences having a relative clause can be thought of as a combination of two separate sentences that share a common element (a noun and the pronoun representing it). This element in the main clause is called the *antecedent* because it *antecedes* (i.e., precedes) the relative pronoun. In the relative clause, the relative pronoun *relates* (i.e., refers) back to the antecedent. Here are some examples. Note how the antecedent and the relative pronoun always denote the same person or thing.

masc.
sing.
antecedent nom.

1. Das ist **der Typ**. **Er** war im Kino.

   Das ist der Typ, **der** im Kino war.
   rel. pron.
   That's the guy who was at the movies.

fem.
sing.
antecedent dat.

2. Kennst du **die Frau**? Ich arbeite mit **ihr**.

   Kennst du die Frau, mit **der** ich arbeite?
   rel. pron.
   Do you know the woman [whom] I work with?

masc.
sing.
antecedent gen.

3. Das ist **der Autor**. Die Romane **des Autors** sind berühmt.

   Das ist der Autor, **dessen** Romane berühmt sind.
   rel. pron.
   That's the author whose novels are famous.

acc.
antecedent plur.

4. Hast du **die Bücher**? Ich habe **sie** dir geliehen.

   Hast du die Bücher, **die** ich dir geliehen habe?
   rel. pron.
   Do you have the books [that] I lent you?

Rules for relative clauses

1. The relative pronoun is *never* omitted in German, as it often is in English (examples 2 and 4 above).
2. The relative pronoun *always* has the same gender and number as its antecedent.
3. The case of a relative pronoun is determined by its function in the relative clause.

   fem. sing. nom. — fem. sing. dat.

   Das ist **die Frau**, mit **der** ich arbeite.

In most of the following exercises, the antecedent is the last element, so word order is not a problem. Point out that in the last example, antecedent and relative clause are both in Ist position. Relative clause does not immediately follow antecedent if only one element like a participle or infinitive would be left at end: **Kannst du mir das Buch zurückgeben, das ich dir geliehen habe?**

4. If the relative pronoun is the object of a preposition, the preposition *always precedes* it in the relative clause (example 2 above). In English the preposition often comes at the end of the relative clause (e.g., *the woman I work **with***). This is *never* the case in German (die Frau, **mit** der ich arbeite).
5. The relative clause is *always a subordinate clause* with verb-last word order. The relative clause is *always* set off from the rest of the sentence by commas.
6. The relative clause is usually placed immediately after its antecedent.

   Das Buch, **das** du mir geliehen hast, hat mir geholfen. — *The book that you lent me helped me.*

Lab Manual Kap. 12, Üb. 12, 14, and Var. zu Üb. 17, 18.

Workbook Kap. 12, G–K.

12 **Kettenreaktion** Student A liest den ersten Satz auf Deutsch vor. Studentin B gibt eine englische Übersetzung und liest dann den nächsten Satz vor usw.

1. Das ist der Mann, der hier wohnt.
2. Das ist der Mann, den ich kenne.
3. Das ist der Mann, dem wir helfen.
4. Das ist der Mann, dessen Frau ich kenne.
5. Das ist das Fahrrad, das sehr leicht ist.
6. Das ist das Fahrrad, das sie gekauft hat.
7. Das ist das Fahrrad, mit dem ich zur Arbeit fahre.
8. Das ist das Fahrrad, dessen Farbe mir gefällt.
9. Das ist die Frau, die Deutsch kann.
10. Das ist die Frau, die wir brauchen.
11. Das ist die Frau, der wir Geld geben.
12. Das ist die Frau, deren Romane ich kenne.

Der Mann,
der alles kann.

13. Das sind die Leute, die mich kennen.
14. Das sind die Leute, die ich kenne.
15. Das sind die Leute, denen wir helfen.
16. Das sind die Leute, deren Kinder wir kennen.

Üb. 13: Also good as a written assignment.

In Europa ist nur die Wolga in Russland länger als die Donau (2.850 km). Die Zugspitze (2.692 m) ist der höchste Berg Deutschlands.

■ 13 ■ Übung Lesen Sie jeden Satz mit dem richtigen Relativpronomen vor.

1. Die Donau ist ein Fluss, ________ durch Österreich fließt. (*that*)
2. Der Berg, ________ man am Horizont sieht, ist die Zugspitze. (*that*)
3. Kennst du den Herrn, ________ dieser Wagen gehört? (*to whom*)
4. Der Professor, ________ Bücher dort liegen, kommt gleich zurück. (*whose*)
5. Das ist ein Schaufenster, ________ immer bunt aussieht. (*that*)
6. Mir schmeckt jedes Abendessen, ________ du kochst. (*that*)
7. Das Kind, ________ ich geholfen habe, ist wieder gesund. (*whom*)
8. Sie kommt aus einem Land, ________ Regierung undemokratisch ist. (*whose*)
9. Die Studentin, ________ neben mir saß, war im zweiten Semester. (*who*)
10. Beschreiben Sie mir die Rolle, ________ ich spielen soll. (*that*)
11. Christa, ________ der Computer gehört, leiht ihn dir gerne. (*to whom*)
12. Die Touristengruppe, ________ Gepäck dort steht, ist aus England. (*whose*)
13. Wer sind die Leute, ________ dort vor der Mensa stehen? (*who*)
14. Da sind ein paar Studenten, ________ du kennen lernen sollst. (*whom*)
15. Es gibt viele Menschen, ________ dieser Arzt geholfen hat. (*whom*)
16. Sind das die Kinder, ________ Hund gestorben ist? (*whose*)

Üb. 14 drills relative pronouns as objects of prepositions. Warm up with choral repetition of short phrases like **die Gegend, in der ich wohne**; **meine Freunde, von denen ich gehört habe**; **mein Vetter, an den ich schreibe**; **der Wald, durch den wir fahren**. Good as written homework.

■ 14 ■ Übung Antworten Sie wie im Beispielsatz.

BEISPIEL: Arbeiten Sie für *diesen* Chef?
Ja, das ist der Chef, für den ich arbeite.

1. Sind Sie durch *diese* Stadt gefahren?
2. Haben Sie in *diesem* Hotel übernachtet?
3. Haben Sie mit *diesen* Amerikanern geredet?
4. Haben Sie an *dieser* Uni studiert?
5. Erinnern Sie sich an *diesen* Roman?
6. Kommen Sie aus *dieser* Stadt?
7. Wohnen Sie bei *dieser* Familie?
8. Spricht er mit *diesen* Menschen?
9. Steht unser Wagen hinter *diesem* Gebäude?
10. Bekommst du Briefe von *diesen* Freunden?
11. Spielst du für *diese* Mannschaft?

Rosen an einer alten Mauer (Schloss Langenburg, Baden-Württemberg).

Üb. 15: May be assigned as written homework.

These sentences are paired as conversational exchanges. The relative clauses in numbers 4 and 10 begin with prepositions. In numbers 11 and 14, the relative pronoun is in the genitive case.

■ **15** ■ **Übung** Machen Sie aus den zwei Sätzen *einen* Satz. Machen Sie aus dem zweiten Satz einen Relativsatz.

BEISPIEL: Ich kenne die Frau. (Du meinst sie.)
Ich kenne die Frau, die du meinst.

1. Suchst du die Schokolade? (Sie war hier.)
2. Nein, ich habe selber Schokolade. (Ich habe sie mitgebracht.)
3. Ist das die Geschichte? (Horst hat sie erzählt.)
4. Ja, er erzählt Geschichten. (Man muss über seine Geschichten lachen.)
5. Das ist ein Buch. (Ingrid hat es schon letztes Jahr gelesen.)
6. Meinst du das Buch? (Es ist jetzt sehr bekannt.)
7. Ist das der Mann? (Sie haben ihm geholfen.)
8. Nein, ich habe einem anderen Mann geholfen. (Er war nicht so jung.)
9. Kennst du die Studenten? (Sie wohnen in der Altstadt.)
10. Ja, das sind die Studenten. (Mit ihnen esse ich zusammen in der Mensa.)
11. Wie heißt der Junge? (Sein Vater ist Professor.)
12. Er hat einen komischen Namen. (Ich habe ihn vergessen.)
13. Ist die Frau berufstätig? (Du wohnst bei ihr.)
14. Ja, sie ist eine Frau. (Ihre Kinder wohnen nicht mehr zu Hause.)

Üb. 16: Prepare by reviewing noun phrases of personal items: **eine neue Jacke** (**Rucksack**, **Turnschuhe**, **Kuli**, **Bleistift**, **Tasche**, **Buch**, **Armbanduhr**, **Bluse**, **Heft**, **Pulli**, **Sweatshirt**, etc.).

■ **16** ■ **Partnerarbeit: Ist das ein neuer Mantel?** Fragen Sie einander, ob Ihre Kleider und andere Sachen neu sind. Antworten Sie, dass Sie alles letztes Jahr gekauft haben. Benutzen Sie einen Relativsatz in Ihrer Antwort.

BEISPIEL: Ist das ein neuer Mantel?
Nein, das ist ein Mantel, *den* ich letztes Jahr kaufte.

The relative pronoun *was*

You may also want to mention **was** & **wer** as indefinite pronouns (*whatever, whoever*): **Nehmen Sie, was Sie wollen. Wer essen will, darf anfangen.**

A relative clause following the pronoun antecedents **das**, **etwas**, **nichts**, **viel**, **wenig**, and **alles** begins with the relative pronoun **was**. Note again that English often leaves out the relative pronoun, whereas German requires it.

Stimmt **das, was** er uns erzählte?	*Is what he told us right?* (literally: *Is that right what he told us?*)
Gibt es noch **etwas, was** Sie brauchen?	*Is there something else [that] you need?*
Nein, Sie haben **nichts, was** ich brauche.	*No, you have nothing [that] I need.*
Alles, was er sagt, ist falsch.	*Everything [that] he says is wrong.*

Was must also begin a relative clause whose antecedent is a neuter adjectival noun (see p. 323–324):

Was war **das Interessante, was** du mir zeigen wolltest?	*What was the interesting thing [that] you wanted to show me?*
Ist das **das Beste, was** Sie haben?	*Is that the best [that] you have?*

Was also begins a relative clause whose antecedent is an entire clause (English uses *which*):

Rita hat sich verlobt, was ich nicht verstehen kann.	*Rita got engaged, which I can't understand.*

Üb. 17: One student can read sentences. Others have books closed. Continue with students' own variations.

■ **17** ■ **Übung: Etwas, was mir gefällt. / Etwas, was mich ärgert.** Ihre Professorin sagt etwas und möchte Ihre Reaktion hören. Ist das etwas, was Sie ärgert, oder etwas, was Ihnen gefällt?

BEISPIEL: Die Umwelt ist sehr verschmutzt.
Das ist etwas, was mich ärgert!

1. Das Studium wird immer teurer.
2. Der Kalte Krieg ist zu Ende.
3. Ihr Mitbewohner spielt abends laute Rockmusik.
4. Heute Abend in der Mensa gibt es Pizza zum Abendessen.
5. Die Ferien beginnen bald.
6. Morgen kommen viele Verwandte zu Besuch.

Üb. 18: Students should prepare as homework in order to be able to answer these readily.

■ **18** ■ **Partnerarbeit: Was war das Tollste, was du je gemacht hast?** Below are cues for asking each other questions such as, "What's the greatest thing you've ever done?" Take turns asking each other the questions.

BEISPIEL: toll / machen
A: Was war das Tollste, was du je gemacht hast?
B: Ich habe 1989 auf der Berliner Mauer gesessen.

1. schwierig / machen
2. schön / sehen
3. gefährlich / machen
4. dumm / sagen
5. erstaunlich / hören
6. gut / essen
7. interessant / lesen
8. toll / bekommen

The verb lassen

Caution! Do not confuse these principal parts: **lassen (lässt), ließ, hat gelassen** and **lesen (liest), las, hat gelesen** (*to read*).

The verb **lassen** has several meanings in German:

- *to leave (something or someone), leave behind*

Lassen Sie uns bitte allein.	*Please leave us alone.*
Hast du deinen Mantel im Restaurant **gelassen**?	*Did you leave your coat in the restaurant?*

- *to allow, let:* **lassen** + infinitive

Man **lässt** uns **gehen**.	*They're letting us leave.*
Lass doch die Kinder **spielen**!	*Let the children play!*

- *to have or order something done:* **lassen** + infinitive

  In the following sentences **lassen** shows that the subject is not performing an action, but rather having it done by someone else.

Sie **lässt** ihren Wagen **reparieren**.	*She's having her car fixed.*

  The accusative case shows who performs the action:

Sie lässt **den Mechaniker** ihren Wagen reparieren.	*She's having the mechanic fix her car.*

Compare substandard English usage: *We're going to build us a house,* which retains reflexive.

  A dative reflexive pronoun shows explicitly that one is having something done for one's own benefit.

Ich lasse **mir** ein Haus bauen.	*I'm having a house built (for myself).*

When **lassen** is used with a dependent infinitive, it takes the double infinitive construction in the perfect tense. The structure is parallel to that of the modal verbs (see page 200).

double infinitive

Die Beamtin hat mich nicht **reden lassen**.
The official didn't let me speak.

Ich habe den Wagen **reparieren lassen**.
I had my car repaired.

Lab Manual Kap. 12, Var. zu Üb. 19, 21.

Workbook Kap. 12, L, M.

■ 19 ■ Übung: Warum ist das nicht hier? Sagen Sie, wo Sie diese Menschen oder Dinge gelassen haben. Rechts gibt es einige Möglichkeiten, aber Sie können auch frei antworten.

BEISPIEL: Warum haben Sie heute keine Jacke?
Ich habe sie zu Hause gelassen.

1. Warum sind Ihre Kinder nicht hier?	in der Schweiz
2. Warum tragen Sie heute keine Brille (*glasses*)?	im Rucksack
3. Warum haben Sie Ihr Referat nicht mit?	bei der Großmutter
4. Warum haben sie Ihren Ausweis nicht mit?	auf dem Bett
5. Warum haben Sie Ihren Wagen nicht mit?	zu Hause
6. Warum ist Ihre Tochter nicht hier?	in der Manteltasche

■ 20 ■ Partnerarbeit: Wo hast du das gelassen? Hat Ihre Partnerin heute etwas nicht mitgebracht? Fragen Sie sie, wo sie es gelassen hat.

BEISPIEL: A: Wo hast du heute deine grüne Jacke gelassen?
B: Ich habe sie im Zimmer gelassen.

lassen = *to have something done* needs most drilling. Students could build up to **Üb. 21** in 4 steps.
1. First generate infinitive + dir. obj. (good practice of "reverse" order of German infinitive): Instructor writes activities on board: **ein Haus bauen, den Wagen reparieren, den Koffer tragen**.
2. Students add **Ich lasse ...** : **Ich lasse ein Haus bauen.**
3. Add reflexive **mir**. (**Ich lasse mir ...**)
4. Vary subject: **Er lässt sich ...**

■ 21 ■ Übung: Er hat es machen lassen. Manchmal will man etwas nicht selber machen, sondern man will es lieber machen lassen. Was haben diese Leute machen lassen?

BEISPIEL: Hat Fritz das Mittagessen selber gekocht?
Nein, er hat es kochen lassen.

1. Hat Herr von Hippel sein Haus selber gebaut?
2. Hat Frau Beck ihren Wagen selber repariert?
3. Hat Oma ihren Koffer selbst getragen?
4. Hat deine Freundin sich die Haare selber geschnitten?
5. Hat Frau Schwarzer den Brief selbst abgeschickt (*sent off*)?
6. Hat Günter das Referat selbst geschrieben?
7. Hat Robert seine Schuhe selber geputzt (*cleaned*)?

Notes on Usage: German equivalents for English *to leave*

The equivalent you choose for the English verb *to leave* depends on whether it means *to go away* (intransitive) or *to leave something behind* (transitive), and also on what or whom you are leaving.

- Intransitive: **gehen**, **weggehen**, **abfahren** (= *leave by vehicle*)

Ich muss jetzt **gehen**.	*I have to leave now.*
Er **ging weg**, ohne etwas zu sagen.	*He left without saying anything.*
Um elf **fuhr** sie mit dem Zug **ab**.	*She left by train at eleven.*

Verlassen also means *abandon, forsake*.

- Transitive: **lassen** (= *leave something somewhere*); **verlassen** (= *leave a person or place for good*)

Ich habe meine Tasche zu Hause **gelassen**.	*I left my bag at home.*
Viele wollten ihre Heimat nicht **verlassen**.	*Many did not want to leave their homeland.*

For **Üb. 22**, #2: **gehen** or **weggehen**.

■ 22 ■ Übung: Wie sagt man das auf Deutsch?

1. Jörg left the house at seven.
2. Jörg left at seven.
3. Jörg's train left at seven.
4. Jörg left his book in the Mensa.
5. Jörg, please leave the room.
6. Jörg left his car in front of the hotel.
7. Jörg wants to leave school.

Time phrases with Mal

The English word *time* has two German equivalents, **die Zeit** and **das Mal**.

Zeit denotes time in general.

Ich brauche mehr **Zeit**.	*I need more time.*

Mal denotes an occurrence.

Wie viele Male = wie oft

Das erste **Mal** habe ich das Buch nicht verstanden.	*I didn't understand the book the first time.*
Wie viele **Male** hast du es gelesen?	*How many times did you read it?*

Learn the following idioms with **Mal**.

das erste Mal	*the first time*
zum ersten Mal	*for the first time*
zum zweiten Mal	*for the second time*
zum letzten Mal	*for the last time*
diesmal	*this time*
jedes Mal	*every time*
das nächste Mal	*(the) next time*

Saying how often things happen is a communicative goal.

Note on Usage: The suffix *-mal*

Note that **-mal** added as a suffix to cardinal numbers forms adverbs indicating repetition.

einmal	*once*
zweimal	*twice*
zwanzigmal	*twenty times*
hundertmal	*a hundred times*
zigmal	*umpteen times*

Note the new spelling with a hyphen when written with numerals: **2-mal, 20-mal, 100-mal.**

Workbook Kap. 12, N.

■ 23 ■ Übung: Wie oft haben Sie das schon gemacht? Fragen Sie einander, wie oft Sie etwas schon gemacht haben.

BEISPIEL: A: John, wie oft hast du schon dein Lieblingsbuch gelesen?
B: Ich habe es schon viermal gelesen.

1. Wie oft hast du schon deinen Wagen reparieren lassen?
2. Wie oft bist du dieses Jahr schon nach Hause gefahren?
3. Wie oft bist du dieses Semester schon ins Kino gegangen?
4. Wie oft hast du dieses Semester schon Referate schreiben müssen?
5. Wie oft hast du dieses Semester schon deinen besten Freund angerufen?
6. Wie oft bist du schon am Wochenende weggefahren?

Üb. 24: May be assigned as written homework.

■ 24 ■ Übung: Wie sagt man das auf Deutsch?

1. Please give me more time.
   Unfortunately, I don't have more time for you.
2. I'm trying it for the first time.
   The next time it's easier.
3. I need time and money.
   You say that every time.

ZEIT IN IHRER SCHÖNSTEN FORM.

■ 25 ■ Gruppenarbeit: Was haben Sie zum ersten Mal hier erlebt? Wenn man Student wird, erlebt (*experiences*) und lernt man viel Neues. Sagen Sie, was Sie hier an der Uni oder am College zum ersten Mal getan, erlebt, gelernt, gesehen, angefangen oder versucht haben.

BEISPIEL: Ich habe *zum ersten Mal* etwas über Astronomie gelernt.
Ich habe *zum ersten Mal* über Politik diskutiert.

Proverb: **Morgenstund' hat Gold im Mund** (*The early bird catches the worm*).

Parts of the day

German divides up the day in the following way:

gestern	früh *oder* Morgen Nachmittag Abend	*yesterday*	*morning* *afternoon* *evening*
heute	früh *oder* Morgen Nachmittag Abend	*this*	*morning* *afternoon* *evening*
morgen	früh Nachmittag Abend	*tomorrow*	*morning* *afternoon* *evening*

Most frequent student error: using **heute Nacht** for *tonight* (**heute Abend**). Tell them to use **heute Abend** for all evening activities prior to going to bed. **Gestern in der Nacht** = *during the night*. At the breakfast table, **heute Nacht** can mean *last night*: **Heute Nacht habe ich gut geschlafen.**

In addition, remember:

Workbook Kap. 12, O.

■ 26 ■ Übung: Gestern, heute und morgen Fragen Sie einander, wann Sie verschiedene Dinge zum letzten Mal gemacht haben.

BEISPIEL: A: Wann hast du zum letzten Mal Kaffee getrunken?
B: Gestern Abend. (*oder*) Heute früh.

1. Wann hast du zum letzten Mal deinen besten Freund gesehen?
2. Wann bist du zum letzten Mal einkaufen gegangen?

3. Wann hast du zum letzten Mal Hausaufgaben gemacht?
4. Wann bist du zum letzten Mal ins Kino gegangen?
5. Wann hast du zum letzten Mal telefoniert?

Jetzt fragen Sie, wann Sie verschiedene Dinge das nächste Mal machen.

6. Wann besuchst du das nächste Mal deine Eltern?
7. Wann gehst du das nächste Mal ins Konzert?
8. Wann gehst du das nächste Mal ins Museum?
9. Wann fährst du das nächste Mal Rad?
10. Wann triffst du das nächste Mal deine Freunde?

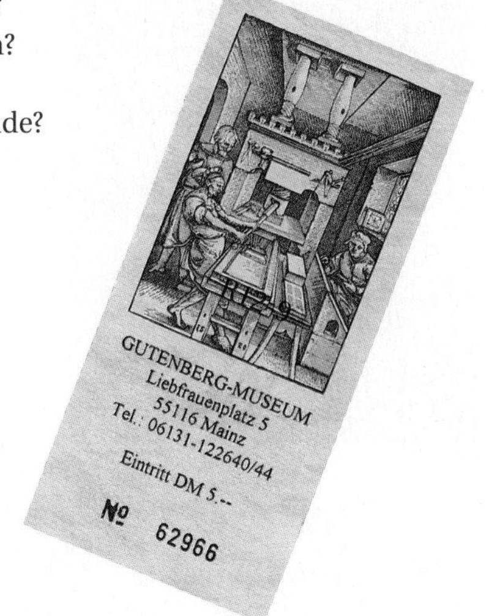

Lesestück

Lab Manual Kap. 12, Üb. zur Betonung.

Vor dem Lesen

Tipps zum Lesen und Lernen

■ Tipps zum Vokabelnlernen

***The prefix* irgend-** With question words like **wo**, **wie**, and **wann**, the prefix **irgend-** creates indefinite adverbs as does the English word *some* in *somewhere, somehow, sometime*, etc.

Similarly: **irgendwer** (= **irgendjemand**), **irgendwas** (= **irgendetwas**), **irgendwohin**, **irgendwoher**.

irgendwo	*somewhere (or other), anywhere*
irgendwie	*somehow (or other)*
irgendwann	*sometime (or other), any time*

Hast du meine Zeitung **irgendwo** gesehen?	*Have you seen my newspaper anywhere?*
Kommen Sie **irgendwann** vorbei?	*Will you come by sometime?*
Meinen Schlüssel habe ich **irgendwie** verloren.	*Somehow or other I've lost my key.*

Im Lesetext für dieses Kapitel schreibt Anna Seghers:

Der Dom hat die Luftangriffe ... **irgendwie** überstanden.	*The cathedral survived the air raids somehow or other.*

■ Einstieg in den Text

Like the poems in **Lyrik zum Vorlesen**, the following reading, "Zwei Denkmäler" by Anna Seghers, was written not for students learning German but rather for an audience of German speakers. Nonetheless, you have now learned enough German to read an authentic text with a little help from marginal glosses.

"Zwei Denkmäler" is not a story, but rather an essay *about* a story that Seghers never finished but could not "get out of her head" (**Das geht mir heute nicht aus dem Kopf**). She focuses on two monuments (**Denkmäler**)—one of grand cultural significance, the other of individual suffering.

Now that you have learned how relative clauses work in German, you will notice how frequent they are in expository prose like "Zwei Denkmäler." During your first reading of the text, be on the lookout for the eight relative clauses it contains. List each antecedent and relative clause. Here is the first one:

1. ... eine Erzählung, die der Krieg unterbrochen hat.
   . . . a story that the war interrupted.
2. ____
3. ____

etc.

Wortschatz 2

Verben

holen to fetch, get
vergleichen, verglich, hat verglichen to compare
wieder sehen (sieht wieder), sah wieder, hat wieder gesehen to see again, meet again
Auf Wiedersehen! Good-bye.

On the telephone one says **auf Wiederhören**.

Substantive

der **Stein, -e** stone
das **Denkmal, ¨-er** monument
das **Schiff, -e** ship
die **Erde** earth
die **Erzählung, -en** story, narrative
die **Freude, -n** joy
die **Größe, -n** size; greatness
die **Milch** milk

Adjektive und Adverbien

einzig- single, only
fern distant, far away

Contrast adjective **einzig-** with adverb **nur**. Covered in Kap. 13, p. 385.

grausam terrible, gruesome; cruel
jüdisch Jewish

Nützliche Ausdrücke

Das geht mir nicht aus dem Kopf. = Das kann ich nicht vergessen.
werden aus to become of
Was ist aus ihnen geworden? What has become of them?

Refer students to the photo of the Mainzer Dom on p. 338.

Zwei Denkmäler

Anna Seghers

Applying your knowledge of twentieth-century Germany to an authentic German literary text is the cultural goal of this chapter.

Anna Seghers is the pseudonym of Netty Reiling, who was born in Mainz in 1900. She studied art history and sinology. Because of her membership in the Communist Party, she was forced to flee Germany in 1933. She sought asylum in France and Mexico. Much of her writing in exile reflects the turbulent existence of a refugee and committed antifascist. In 1947 she moved to the GDR, where she died in 1983.

The opening sentence of Seghers's essay establishes the historical context of an exile from Hitler's Germany, writing during World War II about the horrors of World War I.

The writer addresses loss on many levels: of human life during wartime, of a literary manuscript, and of the memory of one woman's sacrifice. She suggests, however, that in the story she wanted to write, Frau Eppstein's daughter would have preserved that memory.

Lab Manual Kap. 12, Lesestück.

In der Emigration° begann ich eine Erzählung, die der Krieg unterbrochen hat. Ihr Anfang ist mir noch in Erinnerung geblieben. Nicht Wort für Wort, aber dem Sinn nach°. Was mich damals erregt° hat, geht mir auch heute nicht aus dem Kopf. Ich erinnere mich an eine Erinnerung.

In meiner Heimat, in Mainz am Rhein, gab es zwei Denkmäler, die ich niemals° vergessen konnte, in Freude und Angst, auf Schiffen, in fernen Städten. Eins° ist der Dom. Wie ich als Schulkind zu meinem Erstaunen° sah, ist er auf Pfeilern° gebaut, die tief in die Erde hineingehen° – damals kam es mir vor°, beinahe° so hoch wie der Dom hochragt°. Ihre Risse sind auszementiert worden° sagte man, in vergangener° Zeit, da, wo das Grundwasser Unheil stiftete°. Ich weiß nicht, ob das stimmt, was uns ein Lehrer erzählte: Die romanischen[1] und gotischen[2] Pfeiler seien haltbarer° als die jüngeren.

Dieser Dom über der Rheinebene° wäre mir in all seiner Macht und Größe geblieben°, wenn ich ihn auch nie wieder gesehen hätte°. Aber ebensowenig° kann ich ein anderes Denkmal in meiner Heimatstadt vergessen. Es bestand nur aus° einem einzigen flachen Stein, den man in das Pflaster° einer Straße gesetzt hat. Hieß die Straße Bonifaziusstraße? Hieß sie Frauenlobstraße? Das weiß ich nicht mehr. Ich weiß nur, dass der Stein zum Gedächtnis° einer Frau eingefügt wurde°, die im Ersten Weltkrieg durch Bombensplitter umkam°, als sie Milch für ihr Kind holen wollte. Wenn ich mich recht erinnere, war sie die Frau des jüdischen Weinhändlers° Eppstein. Menschenfresserisch°, grausam war der Erste Weltkrieg, man begann aber erst an seinem Ende mit Luftangriffen° auf Städte und Menschen. Darum hat man zum Gedächtnis der Frau den Stein eingesetzt, flach wie das Pflaster, und ihren Namen eingraviert°.

Der Dom hat die Luftangriffe des Zweiten Weltkriegs irgendwie überstanden°, wie auch° die Stadt zerstört worden ist°. Er ragt° über Fluss und Ebene. Ob der kleine flache Gedenkstein° noch da ist, das weiß ich nicht. Bei meinen Besuchen habe ich ihn nicht mehr gefunden.

In der Erzählung, die ich vor dem Zweiten Weltkrieg zu schreiben begann und im Krieg verlor, ist die Rede von° dem Kind, dem die Mutter Milch holen wollte, aber nicht heimbringen° konnte. Ich hatte die Absicht°, in dem Buch zu erzählen, was aus diesem Mädchen geworden ist.

here: in exile
dem ... = the sense of it / excited
niemals = nie
one of them
astonishment / pillars
go into / **kam ...** = it seemed to me / **beinahe = fast**
looms up / **Risse ...** = cracks have been patched
past / **Grundwasser ...** = groundwater caused damage
seien haltbarer = were more durable
Rheinebene = Rhine plain
wäre ... = would have remained / **wenn ...** = even if I had never seen it again
ebensowenig = no less
bestand ... = consisted of only
Pflaster = pavement
zum Gedächtnis = in memory of
eingefügt wurde = had been set in / **durch ...** = was killed by shrapnel
Weinhändler = wine merchant
Menschenfresserisch = cannibalistic
Luftangriffe = air raids
engraved
survived / **wie auch = obwohl** / **zerstört ...** = was destroyed / **ragt** = looms
Gedenkstein = commemorative stone
ist ... = the story is about
heimbringen = nach Hause bringen
Absicht = intention

1. **romanisch** Romanesque style (mid-11th to mid-12th century), characterized by round arches and vaults.
2. **gotisch** Gothic style (mid-12th to mid-16th century), characterized by pointed arches and vaults.

Some additional interpretive questions (good preparation for Aufsatzthemen G.): 1. Warum hat Anna Seghers die Erzählung nicht geschrieben? 2. Zu welcher Zeit würde diese Erzählung spielen? 3. Was ist die Funktion eines Denkmals? 4. Was sind die "zwei Denkmäler" im Titel, und was ist für jedes charakteristisch? (Eigenschaften in 2 Listen an die Tafel schreiben.) 5. Der Dom steht heute noch, aber wie ist es mit dem flachen Stein? Ist die Frau ganz vergessen, wenn der Stein nicht mehr da ist? Erklären Sie das.

Nach dem Lesen

■ A ■ Antworten Sie auf Deutsch.

1. Was hat Anna Seghers' Erzählung unterbrochen?
2. Welche Stadt war Anna Seghers' Heimatstadt?
3. Was konnte sie nie vergessen?
4. Über welche Denkmäler schreibt sie?
5. Vergleichen Sie diese zwei Denkmäler.
6. An wen sollte der Stein erinnern?
7. Hat Anna Seghers den Stein wieder gefunden?
8. Wann begann sie die Erzählung zu schreiben?
9. Was wollte sie erzählen?

■ B ■ Gruppenarbeit: Denkmäler und historische Gebäude Hier sehen Sie Fotos von berühmten Denkmälern und Gebäuden. Sehen Sie sich zusammen die Bilder an und beschreiben Sie sie auf Deutsch. Welche Denkmäler und Gebäude sind Ihnen schon bekannt? An welche Personen oder Ereignisse (*events*) erinnern sie? Was ist Ihre Reaktion auf diese Denkmäler?

1. Kaiser-Wilhelm-Gedächtniskirche (Berlin)

2. Vietnam-Krieg-Denkmal (Washington)

3. Arc de Triumphe (Paris)

4. Mozarts Geburtshaus (Salzburg)

5. Reste (*remains*) der Berliner Mauer

Situationen aus dem Alltag

Experience: **Erfahrung** refers to external happenings and the knowledge one draws from them: **Das weiß ich aus Erfahrung; Meine Erfahrungen als Kind haben mir gezeigt ... das Erlebnis**: an event lived inwardly and intensely. **Das Konzert war wirklich ein Erlebnis; Bildungserlebnis** (formative experience), **Kriegserlebnisse**.

■ „Das geht mir nicht aus dem Kopf"

In der kurzen Erzählung „Zwei Denkmäler" erinnert sich die Schriftstellerin an etwas, was vor vielen Jahren passiert ist. Sie sagt, sie erinnert sich „an eine Erinnerung". Am Anfang dieses Kapitels haben Sie das Gedicht „Heimweh" von Eichendorff gelesen, in dem er auch über Erinnerungen an die Heimat und die Geliebte spricht.

Jeder Mensch hat Erinnerungen, nicht nur Dichter und Schriftsteller. Sprechen wir jetzt ein bisschen über unsere eigenen Erinnerungen.

Neue Vokabeln

die **Erfahrung, -en**	*experience*
die **Gegenwart**	*present (time)*
das **Heimweh**	*homesickness*
der **Ort, -e**	*place; small town*

This vocabulary focuses on an everday topic or situation. Words you already know from **Wortschatz** sections are listed without English equivalents; new supplementary vocabulary is listed with definitions. Your instructor may assign some supplementary vocabulary for active mastery.

Diese Wörter und Ausdrücke kennen Sie schon.

Ich bin in ____________ (Heimatort) geboren.

sich erinnern an
alte Freunde
umziehen
die Vergangenheit
verlassen
wieder sehen

Point out that this is the same church as on p. 362. Built 1891–95 as the Kaiser-Wilhelm-Kirche. Destroyed in a bombing raid, Nov. 1943.

Berlin um 1900

■ A ■ Gruppendiskussion: Wo haben Sie als Kind gewohnt? Leben Sie noch in der Stadt, wo Sie geboren sind, oder sind Sie umgezogen? Gefällt es Ihnen besser, wo Sie jetzt wohnen? Besuchen Sie manchmal Ihren Geburtsort? Was wollen Sie dort sehen? Was hat sich dort geändert?

Discussing personal memories is a communicative goal.

Partnerarbeit: Good as written assignment after oral work in class.

■ B ■ Partnerarbeit: Ich erinnere mich an etwas Besonderes. Erzählen Sie einander eine wichtige Erinnerung aus Ihrer Kindheit. Gibt es z.B. einen besonderen Menschen, an den Sie sich erinnern? Oder einen Lieblingsort oder ein Gebäude, wo Sie gewohnt haben oder Zeit verbracht haben? Warum geht es Ihnen nicht aus dem Kopf?

Zum Schluss

Sprechen wir miteinander!

Lab Manual Kap. 12, Diktat.

Making comparisons is a communicative goal.

A **Gruppenarbeit: Vergleichen wir.** Sechs oder sieben Studenten kommen nach vorne (*to the front*). Zuerst sagen sie auf Deutsch, wann sie geboren sind. Dann antworten die Anderen auf die folgenden (*following*) Fragen.

1. Wer ist der/die Älteste?
2. Wer ist der/die Jüngste?
3. Wer ist der/die Größte?
4. Wer ist der/die Kleinste?
5. Wer hat die längsten/kürzesten Haare?
6. Wer ist heute am schönsten angezogen?

Variation: Compare classroom objects and/or objects you have brought in.

B **Partnerarbeit: Ich bin älter als du.** Jetzt vergleichen Sie sich mit Ihrem Partner. Seien Sie nicht zu ernst (*serious*)!

BEISPIEL: A: Ich bin intelligenter als du!
B: Vielleicht, aber ich habe schönere Augen als du!

Wer ist gesünder? müder? optimistischer? pünktlicher? sportlicher? usw.

Have students prepare the night before; they can use well-known sports records, first-time events, etc.

C **Weltrekorde** Jeder von Ihnen stellt den anderen eine Frage über einen Weltrekord. Die anderen müssen die Antwort erraten (*guess*).

BEISPIEL: Wie heißt der höchste Berg der Welt?
Wer ist die beste Tennisspielerin der Welt?

D **Gruppenarbeit: Was machen Sie selber? Was lassen Sie machen?** Sagen Sie, ob Sie etwas selber machen, oder ob Sie es lieber machen lassen.

BEISPIEL: den Wagen reparieren
Ich repariere den Wagen selber. (*oder*)
Ich lasse den Wagen lieber reparieren.

sich die Haare schneiden must have a dative reflexive, which is optional with the other verbs.

den Wagen reparieren	den Kaffee machen
die Haare schneiden	Lebensmittel einkaufen
das Mittagessen kochen	Referate schreiben

E **Spiel: Ratet mal, wen ich meine!** Choose another student in the room to describe, but don't tell anyone who it is. When your turn comes, say **Ich kenne eine Studentin, die ...** or **Ich kenne einen Studenten, der ...** and then add some description. The others must guess whom you mean.

BEISPIEL: Ich kenne eine Studentin, die heute eine gelbe Hose trägt.

Schreiben Sie zu Hause.

Tell students not to write relative clauses that are just substitutes for a descriptive adjective (**Ich wohne in einem Gebäude, das alt ist**), but to be ambitious and write more complex sentences. After students have prepared as written assignment, it can function as basis for more oral work in class. Ask similar personal questions with **mit/in/aus was für ...**?

With this chapter you have completed the third quarter of ***Neue Horizonte***. For a concise review of the grammar and idiomatic phrases in chapters 9–12, you may consult the **Zusammenfassung und Wiederholung 3** (*Summary and Review 3*) of your Workbook. The review section is followed by a self-correcting test.

Üb. H: 1. Kannst du deinen Wagen selber reparieren? 2. Nein, das habe ich nie gelernt. Ich lasse ihn immer reparieren. 3. Ein Deutscher, den ich kenne, ist der beste Mechaniker in der Stadt. 4. Sind deutsche Züge wirklich pünktlicher als amerikanische Züge? 5. Ja, aber französische Züge sind die schnellsten (am schnellsten). 6. Hast du den neusten Klatsch gehört? 7. Noch nicht. Was ist los? 8. Rita ist mit dem reichsten Typ im Büro weggegangen. 9. Sie hat den armen Rudi verlassen, der immer knapp bei Kasse war.

■ F ■ Antworten Sie mit Ihren eigenen Worten. Benutzen Sie in Ihrer Antwort einen Relativsatz (*relative clause*).

BEISPIEL: Mit was für Menschen verbringen Sie gern Ihre Freizeit?

Mögliche Antwort: Ich verbringe gern meine Freizeit mit Menschen, mit denen ich Sport treiben kann.

1. Was für Erzählungen würden Sie gern lesen?
2. Mit was für Menschen leben Sie gern zusammen?
3. Aus was für einer Familie kommen Sie?
4. Was für Städte gefallen Ihnen besonders gut?
5. In was für einem Gebäude wohnen Sie?
6. Mit was für Menschen verbringen Sie gern Ihre Freizeit?

■ G ■ Aufsatzthemen Anna Seghers hat eine Erzählung über das Mädchen begonnen, dessen Mutter im Ersten Weltkrieg Milch holen wollte, aber sie hat diese Erzählung nie zu Ende geschrieben. Wie würden Sie diese Geschichte erzählen? Schreiben Sie entweder den Anfang oder das Ende der Erzählung aus der Perspektive der Tochter.

1. Wie würde die Geschichte anfangen?
2. Schreiben Sie das Ende der Geschichte. Was ist aus dem Mädchen geworden?

■ H ■ Wie sagt man das auf Deutsch?

1. Can you repair your car yourself?
2. No, I never learned that. I always have it repaired.
3. A German I know is the best mechanic in the city.
4. Are German trains really more punctual than American trains?
5. Yes, but French trains are the fastest.
6. Have you heard the newest gossip?
7. Not yet. What's going on?
8. Rita went away with the richest guy in the office.
9. She left poor Rudi, who was always short of cash.

Videoecke

6 Das vergesse ich nie. (22:44)

Herzlichen Glückwunsch zum Geburtstag!

*Stefan und Katrin fahren zu Stefans Tante Waltraud, die heute Geburtstag feiert. Tante Waltraud wohnt in einem Dorf in der Nähe von Berlin. Bis 1990 lag dieser Ort in der DDR. Stefan und Katrin bringen der Tante Blumen und Geschenke mit. Sie sitzen zusammen im Wohnzimmer und sehen sich Familienfotos an, während ihnen Tante Waltraud über ihr Leben erzählt. Nachher kommt Stefans Familie auch zu Besuch, um ihr zum Geburtstag zu gratulieren (*congratulate*).*

Wortschatz zum Video

Herzlichen Glückwunsch!	*Congratulations! Best wishes!*
die **Decke, -n**	*blanket*
zufrieden	*satisfied*
Ich bin zufrieden.	*I can't complain.*
die **Hochzeit, -en**	*wedding*
die **Trümmer** (*pl.*)	*ruins, rubble*
der **Enkel, -**	*grandson*
die **Banane, -n**	*banana*

A **Tante Waltrauds Fotoalbum** Kreuzen Sie die Fotos an, die Sie in dem Fotoalbum sehen.

____ 1. das Geburtshaus
____ 2. der erste Schultag
____ 3. Tante Waltrauds zwei Brüder
____ 4. Tante Waltrauds Mutter
____ 5. Tante Waltraud an der Uni
____ 6. Fotos von ihrer Hochzeit
____ 7. das zerstörte Berlin
____ 8. Tante Waltraud auf Urlaub in Moskau
____ 9. der Enkel Markus
____ 10. Menschen auf der Berliner Mauer am 9. November 1989

B **Richtig oder falsch?** Indicate whether each statement is **richtig** (**R**) or **falsch** (**F**).

1. Stefan und Katrin fahren mit dem Bus zu Tante Waltraud. R F
2. Tante Waltraud freut sich sehr, sie zu sehen. R F
3. Sie bringen ihr Schokolade und Wein mit. R F
4. Tante Waltrauds Lieblingsfarbe ist grün. R F
5. Katrin schenkt ihr einen Pullover zum Geburtstag. R F
6. Katrin möchte wissen, was für ein Buch auf dem Tisch liegt. R F

C **Wer sagt das?** Choose the person who says the following.

a. Katrin b. Stefan c. Tante Waltraud d. Frau Bachmann

1. ____ sagt: „Bitte, kommt 'rein ins Wohnzimmer."
2. ____ sagt: „Die Eltern kommen später."
3. ____ sagt: „Ich stelle die Blumen in die Vase."
4. ____ fragt: „Wie geht es deinem Bein?"
5. ____ fragt: „Ist das nicht ein Bild vom 9. November?"
6. ____ sagt: „Hallo, liebes Geburtstagskind, hallo!"

D **Wie geht's weiter?** Choose the best completion for each sentence, based on the video episode.

1. Markus hat sich Bananen gekauft, ...
   a. weil er Hunger hatte.
   b. weil sie billig waren.
   c. weil sie für ihn etwas Herrliches waren.

2. Die Familie Bachmann kommt später zu Besuch, ...
   a. denn sie wollen bei Tante Waltraud übernachten.
   b. weil sie zusammen feiern wollen.
   c. um Stefan und Katrin mit dem Wagen abzuholen.

3. Tante Waltraud zeigt Katrin und Stefan ihr Fotoalbum und erzählt ihnen ...
   a. Erinnerungen aus ihrer Kindheit.
   b. von dem Krieg.
   c. von ihren Kindern.
4. Tante Waltraud ist sehr munter, ...
   a. aber sie hat sich erkältet.
   b. obwohl sie nicht gut geschlafen hat.
   c. obwohl ihr das Bein ein bisschen weh tut.

■ E ■ Welle Magazin: Was sehen Sie? Read through the list below. Then watch the **Welle Magazin** (Das Dorfleben, 26:34–27:31) and check off the people and things you see in the video.

Ich sehe ...

_____ 1. eine Bushaltestelle
_____ 2. einen Traktor
_____ 3. eine alte Kirche
_____ 4. Kinder auf einem Spielplatz
_____ 5. einen Bauern bei der Arbeit
_____ 6. Schweine und Kühe (*pigs and cows*)
_____ 7. eine alte Frau auf einem Fahrrad
_____ 8. ein Blumengeschäft
_____ 9. einen Supermarkt

Gestern Nachmittag haben wir das Baby bei Oma gelassen.

Four Modern Writers

A particular kind of memory has haunted German and Austrian writers of the past fifty years: the refusal to forget the Third Reich and the Second World War. For contemporary Germans, the act of recalling and interpreting this painful history has been termed **Vergangenheitsbewältigung**: *surmounting* (or) *overcoming the past.* These four writers all experienced National Socialism and war as children. They began writing after 1945 and earned international reputations. For them, there can be no question of repressing the past, for their literary works honor its memory, confront German guilt, and engage in **Trauerarbeit**, the *work of mourning.*

Günter Grass (b. 1927)

Günter Grass, the son of a grocer in Danzig (today Gdansk, Poland), was drafted out of school at the very end of the war and served briefly as a tank gunner. After the war he apprenticed to a stonecutter in Düsseldorf, and then studied graphic art and sculpture in Berlin. His first novel, *Die Blechtrommel* (*The Tin Drum*, 1959), was an instant international success. In it, the dwarf narrator Oskar Matzerath recounts with an outsider's black humor and wicked satire his life among the lower middle class of Danzig before, during, and after the war. Grass has continued to use his native city of Danzig/Gdansk as a setting for his fiction and to be an active voice for German-Polish reconciliation.

Ingeborg Bachmann (1926–1973)

Ingeborg Bachmann was born in Klagenfurt, Austria, and studied philosophy at the University of Vienna. Although she first gained fame as a lyric poet, she also wrote radio plays and short stories, an opera libretto, and the novel *Malina* (1972), which is the first volume of an unfinished trilogy entitled *Todesarten* (*Kinds of Death*). In her late prose Ingeborg Bachmann brilliantly exposes the tyranny and psychic violence that continue to lurk beneath the cultivated exterior of post-war Viennese society.

Jurek Becker (1937–1997)

Jurek Becker, born in Lodz, Poland, to Jewish parents, managed to survive imprisonment in Nazi concentration camps along with his father. Believing that anti-Semitism had been eliminated in Germany but not in Poland, they remained in what was to become the German Democratic Republic after the war. Becker's first novel, *Jakob der Lügner* (*Jakob the Liar*, 1969), is the story of a Jew who owns a clandestine radio and sustains the hopes of his fellow ghetto inhabitants by inventing stories of Allied victories. In *Bronsteins Kinder* (1986) he explores the complex relationship between a Holocaust survivor and his son.

Christa Wolf (b. 1929)

Christa Wolf's parents were shopkeepers in Landsberg, today Gorzów (Poland). She worked as an editor in the German Democratic Republic before publishing her first fiction in 1961. Since then, her works have been widely translated. Her autobiographical novel *Kindheitsmuster* (*Patterns of Childhood*, 1976) is an extended reflection on the psychic damage done to a child educated as a true believer in Nazism. *Kassandra* (1983) retells the story of the Trojan War from a feminist and antiheroic point of view.

KAPITEL 13

Die Schweiz

Communicative Goals

- Talking about the future
- Telling people you'd like them to do something
- Introducing yourself and others

Cultural Goal

- Learning about Switzerland

Anticipate cultural content with questions: **Was wissen Sie schon über die Schweiz? Ist sie ein großes Land (größer als Deutschland)? Klima? Geographie?** Turn to map, p. 397: **Was zeigt diese Karte, die Geographie des Landes? Was ist die größte Sprachregion?**

Chapter Outline

- **Lyrik zum Vorlesen**
  Eugen Gomringer, „nachwort"
- **Grammatik**
  Verbs with prepositional complements
  Pronouns as objects of prepositions: *da*- and *wo*-compounds
  Future tense
  Wanting X to do Y
- **Lesestück**
  Zwei Schweizer stellen ihre Heimat vor
- **Situationen aus dem Alltag**
  Wie stellt man sich vor?
- **Almanach**
  Profile of Switzerland

Dialoge

Lab Manual Kap. 13, Dialoge, Fragen, Hören Sie gut zu!

Ski is pronounced (and alternatively spelled) **Schi**. Note the colloquial contraction **vorm = vor dem**.

Point out verbal nouns in first dialogue: **Skifahren**, **Fliegen**.

Pronunciation practice: Use dialogues to review **z** versus voiced **s**: **zwei Wochen**, **Schweiz**, **Zürich**, **jetzt**; **sehr**, **Semesterferien**, **deine Sachen**, **seid**, **sagst du**, **Nase**, **Museum**.

Skifahren in der Schweiz

Kurz vor dem Semesterende sprechen zwei Studentinnen über ihre Ferienpläne.

BRIGITTE: Ich freue mich sehr auf die Semesterferien!
JOHANNA: Hast du vor wieder Ski zu fahren?
BRIGITTE: Ja, ich werde zwei Wochen in der Schweiz verbringen. Morgen früh flieg' ich nach Zürich.
JOHANNA: Da bin ich ja ganz baff! Früher hast du doch immer Angst vorm Fliegen gehabt!
BRIGITTE: Stimmt, aber ich habe mich einfach daran gewöhnt.

In der WG: Bei Nina ist es unordentlich.

UTE: Nina, hör mal zu, wann wirst du deine Sachen endlich aufräumen?
NINA: Ich mach' das gleich. Seid mir nicht böse–ich musste mich heute Morgen wahnsinnig beeilen.
LUTZ: Ja, das sagst du immer. Jetzt haben wir aber die Nase voll. Alle müssen doch mitmachen.
NINA: Ihr habt Recht. Von jetzt an werde ich mich mehr um die Wohnung kümmern.

Am Informationsschalter in Basel

TOURIST: Entschuldigung. Darf ich Sie um Auskunft bitten?
BEAMTIN: Gerne. Wie kann ich Ihnen helfen?
TOURIST: Ich bin nur einen Tag in Basel und kenne mich hier nicht aus. Was können Sie mir empfehlen?
BEAMTIN: Es kommt darauf an, was Sie sehen wollen. Das Kunstmuseum lohnt sich besonders. Wenn Sie sich für das Mittelalter interessieren, dürfen Sie die neue Ausstellung nicht verpassen.
TOURIST: Das interessiert mich aber sehr. Wie komme ich denn dahin?
BEAMTIN: Direkt vor dem Bahnhof ist die Haltestelle. Dort müssen Sie in die Straßenbahnlinie 2 einsteigen. Am Museum steigen Sie dann aus.
TOURIST: Das werde ich schon finden. Vielen Dank für Ihre Hilfe.
BEAMTIN: Bitte sehr.

Further practice on *must not*: **Wie sagt man das auf Deutsch?** You mustn't swim here / say that / drink the water / spend so much money. Encourage use of **man**.

Note on Usage: *nicht dürfen*

The equivalent for English *must not* is **nicht dürfen**.

Die Ausstellung dürfen Sie nicht verpassen.	*You mustn't (really shouldn't) miss the exhibit.*

Wortschatz 1

Verben

Angst haben vor (+ *dat.*) to be afraid of
auf·räumen to tidy up, straighten up
sich aus·kennen to know one's way around
  Ich kenne mich hier nicht aus. I don't know my way around here.
bitten, bat, hat gebeten um to ask for, request
sich freuen auf (+ *acc.*) to look forward to
sich gewöhnen an (+ *acc.*) to get used to
interessieren to interest
sich interessieren für to be interested in
sich kümmern um to look after, take care of; to deal with
sich lohnen to be worthwhile, worth the trouble
verpassen to miss (*an event, opportunity, train, etc.*)
sich vor·bereiten auf (+ *acc.*) to prepare for
vor·haben to plan, have in mind
warten auf (+ *acc.*) to wait for
zu·hören (+ *dat.*) to listen (to)
  Hören Sie gut zu! Listen carefully.
  Hör mir zu. Listen to me.

Substantive

der **Schalter, -** counter, window
das **Mittelalter** the Middle Ages
die **Auskunft** information
die **Haltestelle, -n** (streetcar or bus) stop
die **Hilfe** help
die **Linie, -n** (streetcar or bus) line
die **Straßenbahn, -en** streetcar

Adjektive und Adverbien

böse (+ *dat.*) angry, mad (at); bad, evil
  Sei mir nicht böse. Don't be mad at me.
direkt direct(ly)
unordentlich disorderly, messy

Nützliche Ausdrücke

von jetzt an from now on
Es kommt darauf an. It depends.
  Es kommt darauf an, was Sie sehen wollen. It depends on what you want to see.
Wie komme ich dahin? How do I get there?

Gegensätze

böse ≠ gut evil ≠ good
sich interessieren ≠ sich langweilen to be interested ≠ to be bored
unordentlich ≠ ordentlich disorderly, messy ≠ orderly, neat

Mit anderen Worten

baff sein (*colloq.*) = **sehr staunen, sprachlos sein**
schlampig (*colloq.*) = **unordentlich**

Skiing in Switzerland

Shortly before the end of the semester, two students are talking about their vacation plans.

B: I'm really looking forward to the semester break!
J: Do you plan to go skiing again?
B: Yes, I'll spend two weeks in Switzerland. Tomorrow morning I fly to Zürich.
J: I'm flabbergasted! Before, you were always afraid of flying!
B: True, but I've simply gotten used to it.

The **Wortschatz** sections of Kap. 13–16 are shorter than in previous chapters. Emphasis is on complex grammar rather than vocabulary acquisition.

In the Group Apartment: Nina's Place is Messy

U: Listen, Nina, when are you finally going to straighten up your things?
N: I'll do it right away. Don't be mad at me—I was in a big rush this morning.
L: Yeah, you always say that. Now we're really fed up. Everybody has to pitch in.
N: You're right. From now on I'll take more care of the apartment.

Tell students that *verb + prep.* is the major grammar topic of this chapter. It's vital for them to learn both verb and prep. Review lists of acc. and dat. prepositions, which they should know cold. With 2-way prepositions, they must also learn case, i.e., **sich vorbereiten auf** (+ *acc.*).

At the Information Window in Basel

T: Excuse me. May I ask you for information?
O: Sure. How can I help you?
T: I'm only in Basel for a day, and I don't know my way around here. What can you recommend to me?
O: It depends on what you want to see. The art museum is especially worthwhile. If you're interested in the Middle Ages, you mustn't miss the new exhibit.
T: That interests me a lot. How do I get there?
O: Right in front of the station is the streetcar stop. You have to get the number 2 streetcar. Then get out at the museum.
T: I'll find it all right. Thanks for your help.
O: You're welcome.

Variationen

Contrast German equivalent for *to ask*: **bitten** (*request*) vs. **fragen** (*inquire*). Ask students whether German would use **bitten** or **fragen** for these sentences:

1. She asked me for money. (**bitten**)
2. She asked me yesterday. (**fragen**)
3. He asked us to be quiet. (**bitten**)
4. They asked where the concert was. (**fragen**)
5. They asked what time it was. (**fragen**)
6. She asked me to come at 8:00. (**bitten**)

Üb. A: Sentences 1 & 7 can be used to anticipate **wo**-compounds. Write question words **worauf** and **wofür** on board. Then ask, **Worauf freuen Sie sich? Wofür interessieren Sie sich?**

■ A ■ Persönliche Fragen

1. Brigitte freut sich auf die Semesterferien. Freuen Sie sich auf etwas?
2. Sie hat vor Ski zu fahren. Was haben Sie am Wochenende vor?
3. Fahren Sie in den Semesterferien irgendwohin?
4. Bei Nina sieht's schlampig aus. Wie sieht es bei Ihnen im Zimmer aus?
5. Die anderen in der WG sind Nina böse, weil sie nicht aufräumt. Wann werden Sie böse?
6. Der Tourist kennt sich in Basel nicht aus, aber zu Hause kennt er sich natürlich sehr gut aus. In welcher Stadt kennen Sie sich besonders gut aus?
7. Der Tourist interessiert sich für das Mittelalter. Wann war denn das Mittelalter?
8. Der Tourist will die Ausstellung nicht verpassen. Haben Sie je etwas Gutes verpasst? Was denn?
9. Was machen Sie, wenn Sie sich in einer fremden Stadt nicht auskennen?

Üb. B answers:

1. knapp bei Kasse
2. die Nase
3. todmüde
4. stinklangweilig
5. riesengroß
6. blöd

■ B ■ Übung: Wie sagt man das mit anderen Worten?

1. Wenn man sehr wenig Geld hat, ist man ________ .
2. Wenn man zu viel von etwas gehabt hat, sagt man: „Ich habe ________ voll."
3. Jemand, der besonders müde ist, nennt man ________ .
4. Wenn Sie sich bei einer Vorlesung sehr gelangweilt haben, dann haben Sie sie ________ gefunden.
5. Etwas, was sehr groß ist, kann man auch ________ nennen.
6. Ein anderes Wort für *dumm* ist ________ .

Üb. C: Possible answers:

1. was Sie essen wollen
2. was Sie lesen wollen
3. was Sie hören wollen / was für Musik Sie mögen (usw.)
4. wohin Sie reisen wollen / was Sie sehen wollen
5. wie viel Geld Sie ausgeben wollen
6. was Sie trinken wollen
7. wie viel Geld Sie haben
8. wie viel Sie verdienen wollen / was Sie lieber machen

■ C ■ Übung: Es kommt darauf an. (It depends.)

Ihr Professor spielt die Rolle eines Freundes, dem Sie verschiedene Dinge empfehlen sollen. Sie sagen ihm jedes Mal, es kommt darauf an.

BEISPIEL: Können Sie mir etwas *in der Stadt* empfehlen?
Es kommt darauf an, *was Sie sehen wollen.*

1. etwas auf der Speisekarte
2. ein gutes Buch
3. eine neue CD
4. ein Reiseziel
5. ein ruhiges Hotel
6. einen guten Wein
7. einen guten Kassettenrekorder
8. einen neuen Beruf

■ **D** ■ **Rollenspiel: Am Informationsschalter** ***(Gruppen von 3 Studenten)***
Zwei von Ihnen sind Touristen und kennen sich in dieser Stadt nicht aus. Der/die Dritte arbeitet am Infoschalter und gibt Auskunft. Vergessen Sie nicht „Sie" zueinander zu sagen. Fangen Sie so an:

TOURISTEN: Entschuldigung, dürfen wir Sie um Auskunft bitten?
BEAMTER/BEAMTIN: Gerne. Wie kann ich Ihnen helfen?

Alpendorf im Winter (Kanton Graubünden)

Lyrik zum Vorlesen

Eugen Gomringer was born to Swiss parents in Bolivia. True to his typically polyglot Swiss background, he has written poems in German, Swiss-German dialect, French, English, and Spanish. Gomringer is a leading exponent of concrete poetry (**konkrete Poesie**), which rejects metaphor, radically simplifies syntax, and considers the printed page a visual as much as a linguistic experience. The following poem consists entirely of nouns followed by relative clauses in strict parallelism. Readers must work out the interrelationships for themselves. Pay particular attention to the verb tenses as you read this poem aloud.

Lab Manual Kap. 13, Lyrik zum Vorlesen.

The poem *nachwort* is an excellent review of relative clauses. Simple interpretive questions: **Worüber spricht der Dichter? Was hat er in seinem Leben gemacht? Warum heißt das Gedicht nachwort? Warum sind die letzten Zeilen im Präsens?** Some students may have fun translating this poem or writing their own in German or English.

nachwort°

das dorf°, das ich nachts hörte
der wald, in dem ich schlief

das land, das ich überflog°
die stadt, in der ich wohnte

das haus, das den freunden gehörte
die frau, die ich kannte

das bild, das mich wach hielt°
der klang°, der mir gefiel

nachwort: afterword
dorf: village
überflog: flew across
wach hielt: kept awake
klang: sound

das buch, in dem ich las
der stein, den ich fand

der mann, den ich verstand
das kind, das ich lehrte° — taught

der baum, den ich blühen° sah — blooming
das tier, das ich fürchtete

die sprache, die ich spreche
die schrift°, die ich schreibe — writing

Eugen Gomringer (geboren 1925)

Erstbesteigung (*first ascent*) des Matterhorns (4.478 m) im Jahre 1865

Grammatik

Verbs with prepositional complements

Many verbs use a prepositional phrase to complete, expand, or change their meaning. Such phrases are called *prepositional complements.*

Ich spreche.	*I'm speaking.*
Ich spreche **mit ihm**.	*I'm speaking **with him**.*
Ich spreche **gegen ihn**.	*I'm speaking **against him**.*

In the examples above, English and German happen to use parallel prepositions. In many cases, however, they do not. For example:

Er wartet **auf** seinen Bruder.	*He's waiting **for** his brother.*
Sie bittet **um** Geld.	*She's asking **for** money.*

For this reason, you must learn the verb and the preposition used with it *together*. For instance, you should learn **bitten (bat, hat gebeten) um**, *to ask **for***.

Here is a list of the verbs with prepositional complements that you have already learned in this and previous chapters.

Sometimes the complete verbal idea also involves a noun, as in **Angst haben vor.** Notice that most equivalent English verbs also have prepositional complements (*to look forward **to**, to wait **for***), but some do not (*to remember, to request*).

Angst haben vor (+ *dat.*) *to be afraid of*

Hast du Angst vorm Fliegen?	*Are you afraid of flying?*

bitten um *to ask for, request*

Sie bat mich um Geld.	*She asked me for money.*

erinnern an (+ *acc.*) *to remind of*

Das erinnert mich an etwas Wichtiges. — *That reminds me of something important.*

Some German speakers have begun to use **erinnern** (non-reflexive, *to remember*) as a transitive verb, even in print.

sich erinnern an (+ *acc.*) *to remember*

Sie hat sich an meinen Geburtstag erinnert. — *She remembered my birthday.*

sich freuen auf (+ *acc.*) *to look forward to*

Ich freue mich auf die Ferien! — *I'm looking forward to the vacation!*

sich gewöhnen an (+ *acc.*) *to get used to*

Sie konnte sich nicht an das kalte Wetter gewöhnen. — *She couldn't get used to the cold weather.*

sich interessieren für *to be interested in*

Interessieren Sie sich für moderne Kunst? — *Are you interested in modern art?*

sich kümmern um *to look after, take care of; to deal with*

Ich werde mich mehr um die Wohnung kümmern. — *I'll take more care of the apartment.*

sprechen (schreiben, lesen, lachen usw.) über (+ *acc.*) *to talk (write, read, laugh, etc.) about*

Er hat über seine Heimat gesprochen. — *He talked about his home.*

sich verloben mit *to get engaged to*

Rita hat sich mit Rudi verlobt. — *Rita got engaged to Rudi.*

Notice: Perfect tense of **sich vorbereiten** is **hat sich vorbereitet** (no **-ge-**).

sich vor·bereiten auf (+ *acc.*) *to prepare for*

Wir haben uns auf seinen Besuch gut vorbereitet. — *We prepared well for his visit.*

warten auf (+ *acc.*) *to wait for*

Auf wen warten Sie denn? — *Whom are you waiting for?*

■ Notes on verbs with prepositional complements

1. When a prepositional phrase is a verbal complement, it constitutes the second part of the predicate (see p. 77) and therefore comes at the end of the sentence or clause.

   Sie **schrieb** mir letzte Woche **über ihre neue Stelle**. — *She wrote me about her new job last week.*

2. When the preposition used with a verb is a two-way preposition, you must memorize the verb and the case it takes (dative or accusative). Don't just learn **warten auf**, *to wait for*, but rather **warten auf** + *accusative, to wait for*.

Pronouns as objects of prepositions: da-compounds and wo-compounds

da-compounds

When noun objects of prepositions are replaced by pronouns (e.g., **für meinen Freund** → **für ihn**), a distinction is made in German between nouns referring to people and nouns referring to inanimate objects.

- Nouns referring to people are replaced by personal pronouns, as in English.

Steht Christof hinter Gabriele?	*Is Christof standing behind Gabriele?*
Ja, er steht **hinter ihr**.	*Yes, he's standing **behind her**.*
Sprichst du oft mit den Kindern?	*Do you often talk with the children?*
Ja, ich spreche oft **mit ihnen**.	*Yes, I often speak **with them**.*
Wartet ihr auf Manfred?	*Are you waiting for Manfred?*
Ja, wir warten **auf ihn**.	*Yes, we're waiting **for him**.*

Da-compounds simplify things: they do not reflect case, number, or gender of the nouns they replace.

- Nouns referring to inanimate objects, however, are *not* replaced by personal pronouns. Instead, they are replaced by the prefix **da-** attached to the preposition (**da- + mit = damit**). If the preposition begins with a vowel, the prefix is **dar-** (**dar- + auf = darauf**).

Steht dein Auto vor oder hinter dem Haus?	*Is your car in front of the house or behind it?*
Es steht **dahinter**.	*It's **behind it**.*
Was machen wir mit diesen alten Maschinen?	*What shall we do with these old machines?*
Ich weiß nicht, was wir **damit** machen.	*I don't know what we'll do **with them**.*
Wie lange warten Sie schon auf den Zug?	*How long have you been waiting for the train?*
Ich warte schon 10 Minuten **darauf**.	*I've been waiting **for it** for 10 minutes.*

cell phone=**der Handy**

Damit haben Sie
das ganze Büro
in der Hand
ERICSSON

Lab Manual Kap. 13, Üb. 7, 8, and Var. zur Üb. 9.

Workbook Kap. 13, C–G.

7 **Übung** Antworten Sie wie im Beispielsatz.

BEISPIEL: A: Stand er neben dem Fenster?
B: Ja, er stand daneben.

1. Interessieren Sie sich für Fremdsprachen?
2. Hast du nach dem Konzert gegessen?
3. Fangt ihr mit der Arbeit an?
4. Hat er lange auf die Straßenbahn gewartet?
5. Hat sie sich an das Wetter gewöhnt?
6. Hat sie wieder um Geld gebeten?
7. Bereitest du dich auf die Deutschstunde vor?
8. Liegt meine Zeitung unter deinem Rucksack?
9. Erinnerst du dich an die Ferien?
10. Haben Sie vor der Bibliothek gewartet?

8 **Partnerarbeit** Diesmal kommt es darauf an, ob das Objekt ein Mensch ist. Wenn nicht, dann müssen Sie mit **da-** antworten.

BEISPIEL: A: Steht Ingrid neben *Hans-Peter*?
B: Ja, sie steht *neben ihm*.

A: Steht Ingrid neben dem *Wagen*?
B: Ja, sie steht *daneben*.

1. Hast du dich an das Wetter gewöhnt?
2. Bist du mit Ursula gegangen?
3. Erinnerst du dich an deine Großeltern?
4. Können wir über dieses Problem sprechen?
5. Wohnst du bei Frau Lindner?
6. Demonstrierst du gegen diesen Politiker?
7. Demonstrierst du gegen seine Ideen?
8. Interessierst du dich für Sport?
9. Gehst du mit Karin essen?
10. Hat er dir für das Geschenk gedankt?

■ *wo*-compounds

With questions beginning with a prepositional phrase, the same distinction between animate and inanimate objects is made. To ask a question about a person, German uses the *preposition* + **wen** or **wem**.

Auf wen warten Sie denn?	***Whom** are you waiting **for**?*
Mit wem spielen die Kinder?	***Whom** are the children playing **with**?*

When asking about a thing, use the **wo**-compounds you have already learned.

Worauf warten Sie denn?	***What** are you waiting **for**?*
Womit spielt das Kind?	***What** is the child playing **with**?*

■ 9 ■ Gruppenarbeit (*Mit geschlossenen Büchern*) Only student A has an open book. A reads each sentence aloud; B asks C for information about what was said, as in the examples.

BEISPIELE: A: Ich habe auf einen Brief gewartet.
B: Worauf hat sie gewartet?
C: Auf einen Brief.

A: Ich habe auf meine Kusine gewartet.
B: Auf wen hat er gewartet?
C: Auf seine Kusine.

1. Ich freue mich auf die Semesterferien.
2. Ich habe mit Professor Hauser gearbeitet.
3. Ich habe mich mit Rita/Rudi verlobt.
4. Ich muss mich um die Wohnung kümmern.
5. Ich interessiere mich für deutschen Wein.
6. Ich habe keine Angst vor Polizeibeamten.
7. Ich erinnere mich an meinen komischen Onkel.
8. Ich kann mich nicht an diese harte Arbeit gewöhnen.

Üb. 10 gets students used to the fact that the abbreviated answer to such a question is not simply **Das Mittelalter**, but rather the entire prepositional complement **Für das Mittelalter.** Give a further example: **Auf wen wartest du? Auf Maria** (not just **Maria**). Monitor students' use of cases.

■ 10 ■ Partnerarbeit: Persönliche Fragen Stellen Sie einander diese Fragen.

BEISPIEL: Wofür interessierst du dich besonders?
Für das Mittelalter. Und du?
Für ________ .

1. Wofür interessierst du dich besonders?
2. Wovor hast du manchmal Angst?
3. Worauf freust du dich besonders?
4. Worauf musst du dich im Moment vorbereiten?
5. Woran kannst du dich nicht gewöhnen?

Hildegard von Bingen
1098–1179

Hildegard von Bingen was a Benedictine nun and abbess. An early German mystic and author of numerous theological and spiritual works as well as sacred vocal music, Hildegard also wrote tracts on diet and health that are still read today.

Future tense

Talking about the future is a communicative goal.

■ Formation: *werden* + infinitive

The future is a compound tense, using an inflected form of the verb **werden** plus a dependent infinitive in final position:

ich	**werde schlafen**	*I shall sleep*	wir	**werden schlafen**	*we shall sleep*
du	**wirst schlafen**	*you will sleep*	ihr	**werdet schlafen**	*you will sleep*
sie	**wird schlafen**	*she will sleep*	sie, Sie	**werden schlafen**	*they, you will sleep*

Note: **Werden** as the auxiliary (helping) verb for future tense corresponds to *shall* or *will* in English. Do not confuse it with the modal verb **wollen**.

Er **wird** schlafen. *He* ***will*** *sleep.*
Er **will** schlafen. *He* ***wants to*** *sleep.*

Here is how the future tense of a modal verb is formed. Note that the order of the modal and its dependent infinitive is the reverse of English.

Wir werden es **tun müssen**.

We will ***have to do*** *it.*

■ Use of future tense

As you already know, German usually uses *present tense* to express future meaning, especially when a time expression makes the future meaning clear.

Sie kommt morgen zurück. *She's coming back tomorrow.*

Future tense makes the future meaning explicit, especially in the absence of a time expression such as **morgen**.

Sie wird selbstverständlich **zurückkommen**. *Of course she will come back.*

Lab Manual Kap. 13, Var. zur Üb. 11.

Workbook Kap. 13, H.

■ **11** ■ **Übung: Noch nicht, aber bald.** Sagen Sie, dass etwas noch nicht passiert ist, aber bald passieren wird.

BEISPIEL: A: Hast du schon gegessen?
B: Noch nicht, aber ich werde bald essen.

1. Hat es schon geregnet?
2. Hast du schon aufgeräumt?
3. Seid ihr schon Ski gefahren?
4. Ist er schon aufgestanden?
5. Haben sie sich schon vorbereitet?
6. Haben Sie das schon machen müssen?
7. Hat Susi schon angerufen?
8. Seid ihr schon essen gegangen?

Wanting X to do Y

Telling people you'd like them to do something is a communicative goal.

To express the idea that a person wants something to happen or be done, English uses a direct object and an infinitive phrase.

	d.o.	*infin. phrase*
She would like	***the music***	***to stop.***
I don't want	***him***	***to think that.***

German uses **wollen** or **möchten** followed by a **dass**-clause to express the same idea.

Sie möchte, **dass die Musik aufhört.**
Ich will nicht, **dass er das glaubt.**

Lab Manual Kap. 13, Üb. 12 and Var. zur Üb. 13.

Workbook Kap. 13, I.

■ 12 ■ Übung: Der Chef will das so. Sie arbeiten für einen Chef, der sehr streng (*strict*) ist. Heute zeigen Sie einem neuen Lehrling das Büro. Er fragt immer, ob man alles so machen *muss*. Sagen Sie ihm, der Chef *will*, dass man es so macht.

BEISPIEL: *Müssen* wir schon um acht im Büro sein?
Ja, der Chef will, dass wir schon um acht im Büro sind.

1. *Müssen* wir den ganzen Tag hier bleiben?
2. *Muss* ich immer pünktlich sein?
3. Dürfen wir erst um *zehn* Kaffee trinken?
4. *Müssen* wir diese alten Computer benutzen?
5. *Müssen* wir auch samstags arbeiten?
6. *Muss* man immer eine Krawatte tragen?

■ 13 ■ Übung: Ich möchte etwas ändern. Diese Situationen gefallen Ihnen nicht. Sagen Sie, wie Sie sie ändern möchten. Mehrere Antworten sind möglich.

BEISPIEL: Die Musik ist Ihnen zu laut.
Ich möchte, dass sie leiser wird.
..., dass sie aufhört.

1. Draußen regnet es.
2. Das Wetter ist Ihnen zu kalt.
3. Ihre Mitbewohner quatschen zu viel.
4. Ihr kleiner Bruder stört Sie bei der Arbeit.
5. Man verschwendet zu viel Glas und Papier.
6. Ihre Mitbewohner sind Ihnen zu schlampig.

Lesestück

Vor dem Lesen

Tipps zum Lesen und Lernen

■ Tipps zum Vokabelnlernen

Erst is introduced in Kap. 5, **Wortschatz 1**, but the **erst/nur** distinction is a second-year problem related to duration completed in the past vs. continuing in the present: **Wir haben *nur* 5 Monate in Berlin gewohnt.** vs. **Wir wohnen *erst* 5 Monate hier.**

***German equivalents for* only** When *only* is an adjective (meaning *sole* or *unique*), use **einzig-**. Otherwise use **nur**.

Er ist der **einzige** Mechaniker in der Gegend.	*He's the **only** mechanic in the area.*
Ich habe **nur** fünf Mark in der Tasche.	*I have **only** five marks in my pocket.*

Übung: Wie sagt man das auf Deutsch?

1. I have only one pencil.
2. My only pencil is yellow.
3. A cup of coffee costs only DM 1,00.
4. That was the only restaurant that was open.

Lab Manual Kap. 13, Üb. zur Betonung.

Leicht zu merken

die **Barriere, -n**	Barriere
(das) **Chinesisch**	
der **Dialekt, -e**	Dialekt
konservativ	konservativ
neutral	neutral
die **Neutralität**	Neutralität
offiziell	offiziell
das **Prozent**	
romantisch	
stabil	stabil
die **Stabilität**	Stabilität

Einstieg in den Text

In dem Lesestück auf Seite 387 sagt der Schweizer Dr. Anton Vischer, dass er sich manchmal über die Klischees ärgert, die er im Ausland über seine Heimat hört. Wenn man an die Schweiz denkt, denkt man z.B. automatisch an Schokolade, Schweizer Käse und gute Uhren. Diese Klischees sind Ihnen vielleicht auch bekannt. Aber interessanter ist sicher das Neue, was er über seine Heimat erzählt.

Nachdem Sie den Text gelesen haben, machen Sie sich eine Liste von wenigstens fünf neuen Dingen, die Sie über die Schweiz gelernt haben.

Wortschatz 2

Verben

antworten auf (+ *acc.*) to answer (something); to respond to
sich ärgern (über + *acc.*) to get annoyed (at), be annoyed (about)
auf·wachsen (wächst auf), wuchs auf, ist aufgewachsen to grow up

Use **antworten** + *dat.* for answering people (**Antworten Sie mir.**). Use **antworten auf** for answering questions (**Antworten Sie auf meine Frage.**).

denken, dachte, hat gedacht to think
denken an (+ *acc.*) to think of
sich erholen (von) to recover (from); to get well; to have a rest
reagieren auf (+ *acc.*) to react to
sich etwas überlegen to consider, ponder, think something over
Das muss ich mir überlegen. I have to think it over.

Contrast **vorstellen** with **sich etwas vorstellen** (Kap. 11).

vor·stellen to introduce; to present
Darf ich meine Tante vorstellen? May I introduce my aunt?
sich wundern (über + *acc.*) to be surprised, amazed (at)

Denken has been introduced late so students could get used to using **meinen** and **glauben**. Tell them that **denken** refers to the act of cogitation, whereas **glauben** and **meinen** denote having an opinion.

Substantive

der **Ort, -e** place; town
der **Rechtsanwalt, ¨-e** lawyer (*m.*)
der **Schweizer, -** Swiss (*m.*)

das **Gespräch, -e** conversation
das **Werk, -e** work (of art), musical composition

die **Firma, Firmen** firm, company
die **Rechtsanwältin, -nen** lawyer (*f.*)
die **Schweizerin, -nen** Swiss (*f.*)
die **Schwierigkeit, -en** difficulty

You may wish to introduce parallel phrases: **eines Morgens, eines Abends, eines Nachts**.

Adjektive und Adverbien

froh happy
stolz auf (+ *acc.*) proud of

Andere Vokabel

beides (*sing.*) both things

Nützliche Ausdrücke

eines Tages some day (*in the future*); one day (*in the past or future*)
in Zukunft in the future

Show students the parallelism in these pronouns: **alles** (*sing.*) = *everything*; **alle** (*pl.*) = *everyone*; **beides** (*sing.*) = *both things*; **beide** (*pl.*, Kap. 14) = *both people*.

Gegensatz

froh ≠ traurig happy ≠ sad

German equivalents for *happy*:
1. **Es freut mich, Sie kennen zu lernen**: equivalent of *Happy to meet you*.
2. **s. freuen:** *genuine, intimate feeling of joy*: Ich freue mich immer, wenn du da bist.
3. **froh:** *glad, relieved (that nothing bad has happened)*. Sei froh, dass du früh genug weggegangen bist. (**glücklich** = unidiomatic here)
4. **glücklich**: usually describes general state: Damals waren wir immer glücklich; also has meaning of *fortunate*.
BUT: **das Glück** = *happiness*; **Glück haben** = *to be lucky, have good fortune*.

Zwei Schweizer stellen ihre Heimat vor

Lab Manual Kap. 13, Lesestück.

Learning about Switzerland is the cultural goal of this chapter.

***Dr. Anton Vischer (45 Jahre alt), Rechtsanwalt aus Basel*[1]**

„In meinem Beruf bin ich für die Investitionen° ausländischer Firmen verantwortlich und reise darum viel im Ausland. Dort höre ich oft die alten Klischees über meine Heimat. Wenn man sagt, dass man aus der Schweiz kommt, denken viele Menschen automatisch an saubere Straßen, Schokolade, Uhren, Käse und an die Schweizer Garde[2] im Vatikan. Darüber ärgere ich mich immer ein bisschen. Ich möchte lieber, dass andere wissen, was für eine politische Ausnahme° die Schweiz in Europa bildet°. Ich werde versuchen Ihnen etwas davon zu beschreiben.

Schon seit dem 13. Jahrhundert hat die Schweiz eine demokratische Verfassung°[3]. Sie gehört also zu° den ältesten und stabilsten Demokratien der Welt. In beiden Weltkriegen ist die Schweiz neutral geblieben und sie hat ihre Neutralität und ihre politische Stabilität bis heute bewahrt°.

Einige werden unsere Gesellschaft wohl zu konservativ finden. In einem Kanton[4] war das Wahlrecht° der Frauen sogar bis 1992 beschränkt°. Aber man darf nicht vergessen, dass es in der Schweiz durchaus° auch einen Platz für soziale Kritik° gibt. Das zeigen die Werke unserer bekanntesten Schriftsteller wie Max Frisch und Friedrich Dürrenmatt[5].

investments
exception / constitutes
constitution
gehört ... = ist also eine von
hat ... bewahrt = preserved
suffrage / restricted
definitely / criticism

1. Basel (*French* Bâle), Swiss city on the Rhine.
2. The Vatican's Swiss Guards, founded in 1505 by Pope Julius II, are the remnant of the Swiss mercenaries who served in foreign armies from the 15th century on. The Vatican guards are recruited from Switzerland's Catholic cantons.
3. In 1991, Switzerland celebrated the 700th anniversary of the Oath of Rütli, the defense pact among the three original cantons against the Austrian Habsburgs. Wilhelm Tell is the legendary hero of this period of Swiss resistance to foreign power.
4. Switzerland is composed of twenty-three cantons, each with considerable autonomy. Women in the canton of Appenzell could not vote in local elections until 1992.
5. Max Frisch (1911–1991) and Friedrich Dürrenmatt (1921–1990) both wrote novels, essays, and plays.

„In den Bergen kann man sich körperlich und seelisch erholen."

Jemand fragte mich einmal, ob ich stolz bin, Schweizer zu sein. Darauf habe ich sofort mit Ja reagiert, aber in Zukunft werde ich mir die Antwort genauer überlegen. Ich werde einfach sagen, ich bin *froh* Schweizer zu sein, denn meine Heimat ist das schönste Land, das ich kenne. Da ich meine Freizeit immer auf Bergtouren verbringe, ist mein Leben mit der Alpenlandschaft eng verbunden°. Für mich sind die Alpen der einzige Ort, wo ich mich körperlich und seelisch° erholen kann. Das klingt vielleicht romantisch, aber eigentlich bin ich ein ganz praktischer Mensch."

eng verbunden = closely connected / **körperlich ...** = physically and emotionally

Nicole Wehrli (24 Jahre alt), Dolmetscherin° aus Biel

interpreter

„Ich bin in der zweisprachigen° Stadt Biel – auf Französisch Bienne – aufgewachsen, direkt an der Sprachgrenze zwischen der französischen und der deutschen Schweiz. Bei uns können Sie manchmal auf der Straße Gespräche hören, in denen die Menschen beides – Französisch *und* Deutsch – miteinander reden. In der Schule habe ich dann Latein°, Englisch und Italienisch gelernt. Sie werden sich also nicht wundern, dass ich mich für Fremdsprachen interessiere. Eines Tages möchte ich sogar mit Chinesisch anfangen.

bilingual

Latin

Die Eidgenossenschaft[1] ist wohl ein Unikum° in Europa, denn sie ist viersprachig. Die Sprachbarrieren waren lange Zeit ein großes Hindernis° für die politische Vereinigung der Kantone und machen uns heute noch manchmal Schwierigkeiten. 69% der Bevölkerung° hat Deutsch als Muttersprache, 18% spricht Französisch, 12% Italienisch und etwa° ein Prozent Rätoromanisch[2]. Unser „Schwyzerdütsch"[3]

something unique

obstacle

population

approximately

1. **Eidgenossenschaft** = Confederation. *Confoederatio Helvetica*: the official (Latin) name for modern Switzerland, hence CH on Swiss cars.
2. Rhaetoromansch, or simply Romansch. It is a Romance language, a linguistic remnant of the original Roman occupation of the Alpine territories, spoken by about 40,000 rural Swiss in the canton of Grisons (**Graubünden**). Long under threat of extinction, it was declared one of the four national languages in 1938.
3. **Schweizerdeutsch** (*Swiss-German dialect*). **Hochdeutsch** (*High German*) is the official, standardized language of German-speaking countries. It is the language of the media, the law, and education, and is based on written German (**Schriftdeutsch**). Educated native speakers are bidialectal, knowing their local dialect and High German, which they may speak with a regional accent.

können die meisten Deutschen nicht verstehen. Da unsere Kinder Schriftdeutsch° erst in der Schule lernen müssen, ist es für sie oft so schwer wie eine Fremdsprache. Die geschriebene und offizielle Sprache in den Schulen bleibt Schriftdeutsch, aber nach dem Unterricht° reden Lehrer und Schüler Schwyzerdütsch miteinander."

standard written German

nach ... = after class

Nach dem Lesen

■ A ■ Antworten Sie auf Deutsch.

1. Was ist Dr. Vischer von Beruf?
2. Welche Klischees hört er über die Schweiz, wenn er im Ausland ist?
3. Wie reagiert er darauf?
4. Seit wann hat die Schweiz eine demokratische Verfassung?
5. Was macht Herr Vischer in seiner Freizeit?
6. Warum ist die Stadt Biel, wo Nicole Wehrli aufgewachsen ist, besonders interessant?
7. Was war eine große Schwierigkeit bei der Vereinigung der Schweiz?
8. Wie viele Schweizer sind deutschsprachig?
9. Warum haben manche Deutschen Schwierigkeiten die Schweizer zu verstehen?

Frage #8: ungefähr 69% (siehe Zeile 35–36 im **Lesestück**).

Kinder mit Schlitten (*sleds*) in der Altstadt von Basel.

Ask students: **Was bedeutet dieses Bild? Was sagt es über die Mentalität der Schweizer aus?**

Lab Manual Kap. 13, Nach dem Lesen B.

■ **B** ■ In diesem Kapitel haben Sie über den Schweizer Dialekt – das Schwyzerdütsch – gelesen. Hier ist der Anfang eines Märchens auf Schwyzerdütsch mit einer Übersetzung ins Schriftdeutsche. Das Märchen kommt aus dem Kanton Aargau, westlich von Zürich. „Der Ma im Mond"[1] erzählt von einem Mann, der am Sonntag Holz (*wood*) stiehlt. Gott bestraft (*punishes*) ihn, indem er ihn zum Mann im Mond (*moon*) macht (*by making him . . .*).

Der Ma im Mond

Weisch, wer dört oben im Mond lauft? Das isch emol en usöde Ma gsi, de het nid umegluegt ob's Sunntig oder Wärchtig gsi isch; goht einisch am ene heilige Sunntig is Holz und fangt a e Riswälle zsämestäle; und won er fertig gsi isch, und die Wälle bunde gha het, nimmt er si uf e Rügge und isch e heimlige Wäg us, won er gmeint het, das ihm kei Mönsch begägni. Aber wer em do begägnet, das isch der lieb Gott sälber gsi.

1. From: *Kinder- und Hausmärchen aus der Schweiz.* Collected and edited by Otto Sutermeister, with drawings by J. S. Weißbrod. Aarau: H. R. Sauerländer, 1873.

Der Mann Im Mond

Weißt (du), wer dort oben° im Mond läuft? Das ist einmal ein böser Mann gewesen, der hat sich nicht umgesehen°, ob es Sonntag oder Werktag° gewesen ist; (er) geht einmal an einem heiligen° Sonntag ins Holz° und fängt an, ein Reisigbündel° zusammenzustehlen; und als er fertig gewesen ist und das Bündel gebunden hat°, nimmt er es auf den Rücken° und ist einen heimlichen Weg° hinausgegangen, wovon er gemeint hat, dass ihm kein Mensch begegnet°. Aber wer ihm dort begegnet, das ist der liebe Gott selber gewesen.

up there

sich ... = didn't pay attention / weekday / holy / woods / bundle of sticks / tied up

back / secret path

begegnen (+ dat.) = to encounter

Situationen aus dem Alltag

■ Wie stellt man sich vor?

Wie stellt man sich oder einen Bekannten auf Deutsch vor? Es kommt auf die Situation an. Unten sind vier verschiedene Situationen, aber zuerst ein paar Bemerkungen (*comments*).

Introducing yourself and others is a communicative goal.

Unter jungen Menschen ist es nicht so formell: Man sagt einfach seinen Namen und **Hallo** oder **Tag**, wie zum Beispiel in *Situation 1* (unten). Wie Sie schon wissen, sagen Studenten sofort **du** zueinander.

Go over grammar of **Ich möchte mich vorstellen.** vs. **Ich möchte Ihnen meinen Freund vorstellen.** Also point out that in *Situation 2*, Bernd's mother calls Theo by his first name, but says **Sie**.

Wenn man ältere Menschen zum ersten Mal kennen lernt, ist es formeller (*Situationen 2* und *3*). Man sagt **angenehm** oder **freut mich** oder **sehr erfreut** (alle drei = *pleased to meet you*). Natürlich sagt man **Sie** statt **du**.

In allen Situationen ist es höflich einander die Hand zu geben (*shake hands*). Das machen die Europäer viel öfter als die Amerikaner.

1. Die Studentin Sonja stellt ihrem Freund Wolfgang ihre Freundin Margaret aus Amerika vor.

SONJA: Hallo Wolfgang! Darf ich vorstellen? Das ist meine Freundin Margaret aus Chicago.
WOLFGANG: (*gibt ihr die Hand*) Hallo Margaret!
MARGARET: Hallo Wolfgang.
WOLFGANG: Nett, dich kennen zu lernen.
MARGARET: Danke, gleichfalls.

The descriptions of *Situations 1* and *2* illustrate the importance of case endings. Have students read them aloud and translate into English.

Greetings in Schwyzerdütsch: **Grüezi** für Sie; **Hoi** für du; **Grüezi mitenand** (Sie im Plural); **Hoi zäme** (zusammen) für ihr.

2. Bernd, 20, stellt seiner Mutter einen Freund vor.

BERND: Mutter, ich möchte dir meinen Freund Theo vorstellen.
FRAU RINGSTEDT: Freut mich, Sie kennen zu lernen, Theo.
THEO: Angenehm, Frau Ringstedt. (*Sie geben sich die Hand.*)

3. Der amerikanische Austauschstudent Michael Hayward stellt sich einem Professor in der Sprechstunde (*office hour*) vor.

MICHAEL HAYWARD: Guten Tag, Professor Mohr. Darf ich mich vorstellen? Mein Name ist Hayward. (*Gibt ihm die Hand.*)
PROF. MOHR: Guten Tag, Herr Hayward. Bitte nehmen Sie Platz.

4. Zwei Geschäftsleute treffen sich auf einer Konferenz.

FRAU MÜLLER: Guten Tag, mein Name ist Müller.
HERR BEHRENS: Freut mich, Frau Müller. Behrens.

Gruppenarbeit: Rollenspiele

1. Darf ich mich vorstellen?
Sie sind alle zusammen auf einer Studentenparty, wo sie einander noch nicht kennen. Stehen Sie alle auf und stellen Sie sich einander vor.

2. Ich möchte euch meine Freunde vorstellen.
Zwei Studenten spielen die Rollen der Eltern. Ein dritter Student bringt zwei Freunde nach Hause und stellt sie den Eltern vor.

3. Now pretend that you're all business people at a convention. Introduce yourselves to each other. (In this kind of situation, people usually give only their last names.)

Zum Schluss

Sprechen wir miteinander!

Lab Manual Kap. 13, Diktat.

Workbook Kap. 13, J, K.

Üb. B: Brainstorm topics and write on board, model future tense for students. Possible topics: **Arbeit**, **Arbeitszeit vs. Freizeit**, **die Umwelt**, **die Rolle des Computers im Leben**, **die Vereinigung Europas**.

A **Partnerarbeit: Was wird sein?** Lesen Sie die Zukunft Ihres Partners oder Ihrer Partnerin aus der Hand. Wie sieht die Zukunft aus?

BEISPIEL: Du wirst lange leben. Du wirst dich oft verloben und dreimal heiraten (*get married*). Du wirst ...

B **Gruppenarbeit: Seid ihr optimistisch oder pessimistisch?** Wie wird die Welt in fünfzig Jahren aussehen? Wird das Leben besser sein oder nicht? Werden die Menschen glücklicher sein? Sagen Sie Ihre eigene Meinung.

Üb. C, #10: Students may need help formulating **Worauf musst du dich vorbereiten?**

■ C ■ Partnerarbeit: Woran denkst du denn? Stellen Sie einander Fragen mit diesen Verben.

BEISPIEL: A: Woran denkst du denn?
B: Ich denke an unser Gespräch von gestern.

1. denken an
2. sich freuen auf
3. sich interessieren für
4. sich ärgern über
5. sich kümmern um
6. sich erinnern an
7. warten auf
8. Angst haben vor
9. sich wundern über
10. sich vorbereiten (müssen) auf

Üb. D: Write list of hobbies on board. Help students with new vocabulary. Stress **Wofür ... ?** and **Warum ... dafür?**

■ D ■ Gruppenarbeit: Was ist Ihr Hobby? Wie verbringen Sie Ihre Freizeit? Haben Sie ein Hobby? Sprechen wir ein bisschen darüber. Machen wir zuerst eine Liste von Möglichkeiten.

1. Was kann man sammeln? Zum Beispiel: Briefmarken (*stamps*).
2. Spielen Sie ein Musikinstrument? Welches? Zum Beispiel: Klavier (*piano*).
3. Machen Sie gern etwas Kreatives? Zum Beispiel: Fotografieren.
4. Spielen Sie gern etwas oder treiben Sie Sport? Zum Beispiel: Schach (*chess*).
5. Jetzt sprechen wir über unsere Hobbys. Stellen Sie einander Fragen darüber. Hier sind einige Möglichkeiten:

   A: Wofür interessierst du dich?
   B: Ich interessiere mich für ________.
   A: Warum interessierst du dich dafür? usw.

   A: Wie lange sammelst du schon ________?
   B: Seit ________.
   A: Kostet das viel Geld? usw.

■ E ■ Gruppenarbeit: Reaktionen: Das lohnt sich. / Das lohnt sich nicht. Wer hat etwas Interessantes vor? Sagen Sie, was Sie vorhaben. Die anderen müssen dann darauf reagieren.

BEISPIEL: A: Am Wochenende habe ich vor den neuen Film „________" zu sehen.
B: Ja, das lohnt sich! Ich habe ihn schon letzte Woche gesehen. (*oder*)
Das lohnt sich nicht. Ich habe gehört, er ist blöd.

Üb. F: Model this first for the whole class. Tell them they can be humorous: **Tom, ich möchte, dass Sie sich die Haare kämmen!** Brainstorm possible responses: **Ich habe mir doch die Haare gekämmt! / Warum denn? / OK, einverstanden.**

■ **F** ■ **Partnerarbeit: Ich will, dass du dich änderst.** Sagen Sie Ihrem Partner, wie er sein Leben ändern soll. Dann antwortet er darauf. (Das ist nur ein Spiel. Nehmen Sie es also nicht zu ernst!)

BEISPIEL: A: Ich will, dass du früher aufstehst!
B: Warum denn? Ich schlafe doch gern. *Ich* möchte, dass *du ...*

Schreiben Sie zu Hause.

Üb. G: Past participles as adjectives, introduced on p. 327 Kap. 11. This exercise reviews the concept and also adjective endings. Also prepares students for comprehension of extended modifiers (Kap. 16). This exercise may also be done orally.

■ **G** ■ For each pair of sentences below, fill in the past participle cued in English in the first sentence. In the second sentence, it is used as an attributive adjective. Don't forget the adjective ending!

1. Wer hat im Zimmer ________? (*straightened up*)
   Es ist schön in einem ________ Zimmer zu sitzen.
2. Letztes Jahr habe ich sehr viel Geld ________. (*saved*)
   Mit meinem ________ Geld will ich eine Reise ins Ausland machen.
3. Hat man dir den Rucksack ________? (*stolen*)
   Ja, und meine neue Kamera war leider im ________ Rucksack.
4. Ich habe meine Hemden ________. (*washed*)
   Die ________ Hemden hängen draußen hinter dem Haus.
5. Der Mann, mit dem sie sich verlobt hat, ist immer gut ________. (*dressed*)
   Sie geht nur mit gut ________ Männern aus.
6. Frau Schwarzer hat ihren Wagen selber ________. (*repaired*)
   Ihr ________ Wagen läuft jetzt gut.

■ **H** ■ **Aufsatzthemen** Wählen Sie eine Frage und schreiben Sie eine Seite darüber.

1. Gibt es Sprachbarrieren in Ihrer Heimat? Beschreiben Sie einige.
2. Kennen Sie Ausländer, deren Muttersprache nicht Englisch ist? Was für Schwierigkeiten gibt es wohl für solche Menschen? Vielleicht sind Sie selber Ausländer. Welche Schwierigkeiten haben Sie gehabt?

Üb. I answers: 1. Freust du dich auf das Ende des Semesters (auf das Semesterende)? 2. Ja, ich habe vor in der Schweiz Ski zu fahren (Ski fahren zu gehen). 3. Das klingt gut. Gute Reise! 4. Woran denkst du, wenn man über die Schweiz spricht? 5. Ich erinnere mich an die Tante meines Vaters, die aus der Schweiz kam.

■ **I** ■ **Wie sagt man das auf Deutsch?**

1. Are you looking forward to the end of the semester?
2. Yes, I'm planning to go skiing in Switzerland.
3. That sounds good. Have a good trip.
4. What do you think of when people talk about Switzerland?
5. I remember my father's aunt who came from Switzerland.

6. Entschuldigung, kennen Sie sich in der Bibliothek aus? 7. Ein bisschen. Wie kann ich Ihnen helfen? 8. Ich interessiere mich für Bücher über die Schweiz. Wissen Sie, wo sie sind? 9. Augenblick, bitte. Das muss ich mir überlegen. 10. Worüber ärgerst du dich so? 11. Meine Mitbewohnerin hat mich um Geld gebeten. 12. Sie will, dass ich es ihr bald gebe. 13. Wirst du es ihr geben? 14. Ich glaube nicht.

6. Excuse me, do you know your way around in the library?
7. A bit. How can I help you?
8. I'm interested in books on Switzerland. Do you know where they are?
9. Just a moment, please. I'll have to think it over.

10. What are you so annoyed about?
11. My roommate asked me for money.
12. She wants me to give it to her soon.
13. Will you give it to her?
14. I don't think so.

Almanach

Profile of Switzerland

Area: 41,288 square kilometers; 15,941 square miles (approximately the same area as the states of Massachusetts, Connecticut, and Rhode Island combined)

Population: 7,240,400; density 175 people per square kilometer (454 per square mile)

Currency: Swiss franc (**Schweizer Franken**); 1 sfr = 100 Rappen or Centimes

Major Cities: Berne (**Bern**, capital, pop. 130,000), Zürich (largest city, pop. 322,000), Basel, Geneva (**Genf**), Lausanne

Religions: 48% Roman Catholic, 44% Protestant, 8% other

Switzerland has one of the highest per capita incomes in the world, as well as one of the highest standards of living. The literacy rate is 99.5%. The beauty of the Swiss Alps has made tourism Switzerland's main service industry; the alpine rivers provide inexpensive hydroelectric power.

Switzerland has not sent troops into foreign wars since 1515. It guards its neutrality even to the extent of staying out of the European Union and the United Nations. It is, however, a member of several special U.N. agencies. The second headquarters of the U.N. are in Geneva, which is also the seat of the International Red Cross and the World Council of Churches.

Marktplatz und altes Rathaus (Basel)

ECOLE DE MUSIQUE
STADT MUSIKSCHULE

In der zweisprachigen Stadt Biel / Bienne

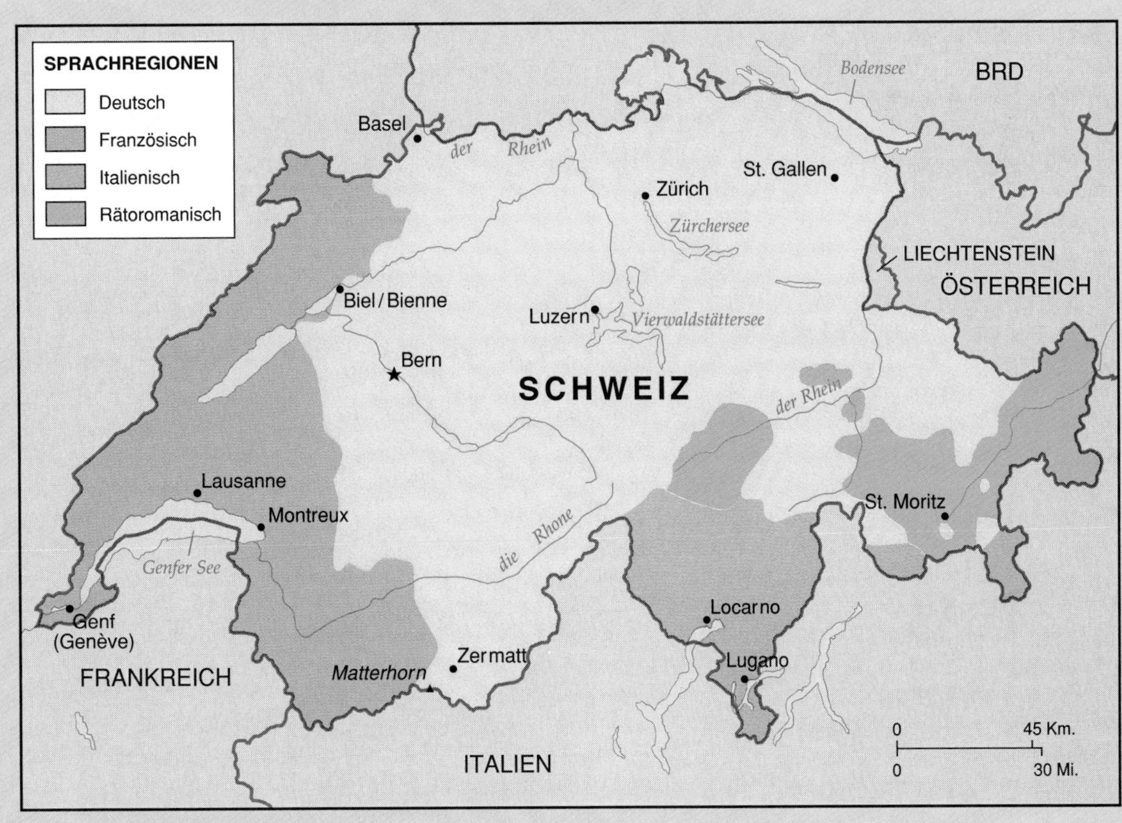
SPRACHREGIONEN
Deutsch
Französisch
Italienisch
Rätoromanisch
BRD
Bodensee
Basel
der Rhein
St. Gallen
Zürich
Zürchersee
LIECHTENSTEIN
ÖSTERREICH
Biel / Bienne
Luzern
Vierwaldstättersee
Bern
SCHWEIZ
der Rhein
Lausanne
Montreux
St. Moritz
die Rhone
Genfer See
Genf
(Genève)
Locarno
Lugano
Zermatt
Matterhorn
FRANKREICH
ITALIEN
0
45 Km.
0
30 Mi.

KAPITEL 14

Österreich

Vienna, Karlsplatz subway station (architect: Otto Wagner).

Communicative Goals

- Getting a room in a hotel
- Expressing wishes contrary to fact
- Talking about contrary-to-fact situations
- Making suggestions
- Making polite requests

Cultural Goal

- Learning about Austria

Anticipate cultural content with questions: **Was wissen Sie schon über Österreich? Ist es größer oder kleiner als Deutschland?** Turn to map, p. 427: **Was zeigt diese Karte? Wie heißt die Hauptstadt und wo liegt sie? Nennen Sie Österreichs Nachbarländer.**

Chapter Outline

- **Lyrik zum Vorlesen**
  Ernst Jandl, „ottos mops"
- **Grammatik**
  General subjunctive: Present tense
  Other uses of the general subjunctive
    - Conditions contrary to fact
    - Wishes contrary to fact
    - Hypothetical statements and questions
    - Polite requests
- **Lesestück**
  Zwei Österreicher stellen sich vor
- **Situationen aus dem Alltag**
  Im Hotel
- **Videoecke**
  Fährst du mit in die Schweiz?
- **Almanach**
  Profile of Austria

Dialoge

Lab Manual Kap. 14, Dialoge, Fragen, Hören Sie gut zu!

Austrian currency: **100 Groschen = 1 Schilling**.

Getting a room in a hotel is a communicative goal of this chapter.

Auf Urlaub in Österreich

Nach einem langen Tag in Salzburg will das Ehepaar Dietrichs aus Potsdam zum Abendessen ausgehen.

RICHARD: Ursula, hast du noch österreichisches Geld?

URSULA: Nein. Wieso, hast du auch keine Schillinge mehr?

RICHARD: Leider nicht. Wenn es nicht so spät wäre, könnte ich noch bei der Bank wechseln.

URSULA: Das macht ja nichts. An der Hotelkasse kannst du wechseln oder wir zahlen im Restaurant entweder mit Kreditkarte oder mit Reiseschecks.

heute Nacht = *tonight*, but also *last night* if said early in morning.

Emphasize **erst morgen** = *not until tomorrow*.

Most hotels in Europe include breakfast in the room price.

Note: **im ersten Stock** is the equivalent of American *on the second floor*.

An der Rezeption

TOURIST: Grüß Gott! Hätten Sie noch ein Zimmer frei für heute Nacht?

ANGESTELLTER: Wünschen Sie ein Einzelzimmer oder ein Doppelzimmer?

TOURIST: Am liebsten hätte ich ein Einzelzimmer mit Dusche.

ANGESTELLTER: Das könnte ich Ihnen erst morgen geben. Im Moment ist nur ein Doppelzimmer mit Bad frei.

TOURIST: Was würde das denn kosten?

ANGESTELLTER: 500 Schilling mit Frühstück.

TOURIST: Dürfte ich mir das Zimmer ansehen?

ANGESTELLTER: Selbstverständlich. (*Gibt ihm den Schlüssel.*) Das wäre Zimmer Nummer 14 im ersten Stock.

Heurige are taverns in and around Vienna, each originally belonging to a vineyard and serving wine (called **Heuriger**) pressed from the current harvest (**heuer** = *this year*). **Grinzing**, a suburb of Vienna, has many **Heurige**.

Pronunciation practice: Use dialogues to review **ä**, especially in subjunctive forms: **spät**, **wäre**, **hätten Sie**, **am liebsten hätte ich**, **selbstverständlich**, **das wäre Zimmer 14**. Some German speakers differentiate the long vowel **ä** (**Mädchen, bäte**) from **e** (**Meter, bete**).

Ausflug zum Heurigen

Zwei Freunde im ersten Semester in Wien wollen den neuen Wein probieren.

ANDREAS: Hast du heute Abend etwas Besonderes vor?

ESTHER: Nein, warum?

ANDREAS: Dann könnten wir endlich nach Grinzing zum Heurigen fahren.

ESTHER: Ja, höchste Zeit! Und es wäre auch schön dort zu essen.

ANDREAS: Gute Idee! Ich hab' schon Riesenhunger.

ESTHER: Dann sollten wir gleich losfahren.

Wortschatz 1

Verben

aus·gehen ging aus, ist ausgegangen to go out
los·fahren (fährt los), fuhr los, ist losgefahren to depart, start, leave
probieren to sample, try
wechseln to change (money)

Substantive

der/die **Angestellte, -n** employee
der **Ausflug, ⸚e** outing, excursion
der **Scheck, -s** check
der **Reisescheck, -s** traveler's check
der **Schilling** Austrian shilling
der **Stock** floor (*of a building*)
der **erste Stock** the second floor
im ersten Stock on the second floor

das **Bad, ⸚er** bath
ein Bad nehmen to take a bath
das **Badezimmer, -** bathroom
das **Doppelzimmer, -** double room
das **Ehepaar, -e** married couple
das **Einzelzimmer, -** single room
das **Erdgeschoss** first floor, ground floor

die **Bank, -en** bank
die **Dusche, -n** shower
die **Kasse, -n** cash register; cashier's office
die **Kreditkarte, -n** credit card
die **Nummer, -n** number
die **Rezeption** (hotel) reception desk

Contrast **die Bank, -en** (*bank*) vs. **die Bank, ⸚e** (*bench*: Kap. 10). **Bankarbeit** = *work in a bank or ironic pun*: **Bankarbeit machen** = *benchwarming*, **Ruhepause machen**.

Adjektiv

österreichisch Austrian

Andere Vokabel

entweder ... oder (*conj.*) either . . . or

Nützlicher Ausdruck

höchste Zeit high time

Gegensatz

entweder ... oder ≠ weder ... noch either . . . or ≠ neither . . . nor

Mit anderen Worten

der Riesenhunger = sehr großer Hunger

das Erdgeschoss, *synonym* = **das Parterre; im Erdgeschoss/Parterre**, *on the first (ground) floor*. **der Stock**, *synonym* = **die Etage**. Emphasize different usage: *first floor = the one above the ground floor*. Plural, **Stockwerke (Das Gebäude hat 4 Stockwerke.)**

On Vacation in Austria

After a long day in Salzburg, Mr. and Mrs. Dietrichs from Potsdam want to go out to dinner.

R: Ursula, do you have any more Austrian money?
U: No. Why? Don't you have any more shillings either?
R: Unfortunately not. If it weren't so late, I could still change money at the bank.
U: That doesn't matter. You can change money at the hotel cashier, or we'll pay in the restaurant, either with credit card or with traveler's checks.

At the Reception Desk

T: Hello, would you still have a room free for tonight?
E: Do you want a single or a double room?
T: I'd prefer a single room with shower.
E: I couldn't give you that until tomorrow. At the moment there is only a double room with bath available.
T: What would that cost?
E: Five hundred shillings with breakfast.
T: May I please have a look at the room?
E: Of course. (*Hands him the key*). That would be room number 14 on the second floor.

Outing to a *Heuriger*

Two friends in their first semester in Vienna want to try the new wine.

A: Have you got anything special planned for tonight?
E: No, why?
A: Then we could finally go to Grinzing to a *Heuriger*.
E: Yes, high time! And it would be nice to eat there too.
A: Good idea! I'm already famished.
E: Then we ought to leave right away.

Variationen

■ A ■ Persönliche Fragen

1. Haben Sie je Geld wechseln müssen? Wo?
2. Zahlen Sie im Restaurant mit Kreditkarte, Scheck oder Bargeld (*cash*)?
3. Haben Sie je in einem Hotel übernachtet? Wo war das?
4. Würden Sie lieber in Jugendherbergen oder in Hotels übernachten, wenn Sie nach Österreich reisen? Warum?
5. Haben Sie ein Doppel- oder ein Einzelzimmer im Studentenwohnheim?
6. Grinzing ist ein Ausflugsort in der Nähe von Wien. Kennen Sie in Ihrer Gegend einen schönen Ausflugsort?

German dormitories have only singles and doubles. A triple would be called **ein Dreibettzimmer**.

Stress: **Gó-liath**

Üb. B answers:
2. einen Riesenkoffer
3. eine Riesenfreude
4. eine Riesendemonstration
5. eine Riesenkatastrophe
6. ein Riesenhotel

■ B ■ Übung: Was ist ein Riese? Ein berühmter Riese in der Bibel hieß Goliath. Sie kennen schon das Wort „riesengroß". So nennt man etwas sehr Großes. Jetzt wissen Sie auch, wenn man sehr hungrig ist, sagt man: „Ich habe Riesenhunger!" Also:

1. Einen riesengroßen Hunger nennt man auch *einen Riesenhunger*.
2. Einen sehr sehr großen Koffer nennt man auch ________.
3. Eine ganz große Freude ist ________.
4. Wenn viele Menschen zusammen demonstrieren, dann hat man ________.
5. Wenn ein Supertanker einen Unfall hat und sein Öl ins Meer fließt, dann ist das ________.
6. Ein sehr großes Hotel kann man auch ________ nennen.

Üb. C: Students can generate list of positive and negative reactions. Write them on the board: **schön**, **gut**, **fantastisch**, **nett**, **interessant**, **langweilig**, **schrecklich**, **schlimm**.

■ C ■ Partnerarbeit: Wie wäre das? (How would that be?) Ihr Partner schlägt Ihnen etwas vor. Reagieren Sie darauf mit Ihren eigenen Worten: **Das wäre ... !** (Switch roles for second column.)

BEISPIEL: A: Sollen wir einen Ausflug machen?
B: Ja, das wäre toll!

ins Kino gehen?	uns die Stadt ansehen?
Geld wechseln?	zu Hause sitzen?
Freunde einladen?	das Zimmer aufräumen?
Ski fahren gehen?	im Restaurant essen?
Theaterkarten kaufen?	eine Radtour machen?

Drill **weder/noch** with students, letting them generate possibilities. I: **Ist er sympathisch und klug?** S: **Nein, er ist weder ... noch ...** (**sportlich/reich**; **höflich/glücklich**, **etc.**).

■ D ■ Übung: entweder ... oder Sagen Sie, Sie machen entweder **dies** oder **das**.

BEISPIEL: Was trinken Sie heute Abend?
Ich trinke entweder Tee oder Kaffee.

1. Wohin fahren Sie im Sommer?
2. Was möchten Sie gern essen?
3. Mit wem wollen Sie Tennis spielen?
4. Welche Fremdsprache werden Sie nächstes Jahr lernen?
5. Wer war denn das?
6. Wissen Sie, in welchem Stock Ihr Hotelzimmer ist?
7. Wie kann man im Hotel zahlen?
8. Wann wollen Sie das nächste Mal Ski fahren gehen?

Lyrik zum Vorlesen

The Austrian poet Ernst Jandl was born in Vienna. In the following poem, he shows that it is possible to tell a whole story using only one vowel. Reading it aloud will be a good review of the German long and short **o**! Like many other modern poets, Jandl does not capitalize nouns.

Lab Manual Kap. 14, Lyrik zum Vorlesen.

Students delight in this poem. Read aloud first, since nonstandard orthography may confuse them. Insist on good pronunciation of long and short **o.** Perhaps students want to try writing an English equivalent ("Pat's Cat"). Long **o's**: **otto**, ***soso***, **holt**, **koks**, ***obst***, ***ogott***.

ottos mops°

ottos mops trotzt°
otto: fort° mops fort
ottos mops hopst° fort
otto: soso

otto holt koks°
otto holt obst
otto horcht°
otto: mops mops
otto hofft

ottos mops klopft°
otto: komm mops komm
ottos mops kommt
ottos mops kotzt°
otto: ogottogott

Ernst Jandl (geboren 1925)

mops: mutt
trotzt: won't obey
fort: go away
hopst: hops
koks: charcoal briquettes
horcht: listens
klopft: knocks
kotzt: pukes

Caricature by Wilhelm Busch (1832–1908), German painter, satirist, humorist. As an artist and poet, Busch paved the way for modern comics. He told stories with line drawings captioned with his own humorous texts, the most famous of which is **Max und Moritz** (1865). This drawing is from 1870.

Grammatik

In addition to general subjunctive, German also has a "special" subjunctive that you will learn in Kap. 16.

The *imperative* (Kap. 4) is also a grammatical mood.

General subjunctive: Present tense

Language offers you the possibility of presenting information in various ways. On the one hand, you can present something as a fact. On the other hand, you can present it as hypothetical, conjectural, or contrary to fact. Both German and English have two different sets of verb forms for these two possibilities, called the *indicative* and the *subjunctive moods* (from Latin *modus*, "manner, mode, way").

Up to now, you have been using the *indicative mood* to talk about what is definite, certain, and real.

Barbara **ist** nicht hier.	*Barbara **isn't** here.*
Ich **habe** Zeit.	*I **have** time.*

The *subjunctive mood* (**der Konjunktiv**) is used to talk about hypothetical, uncertain, or unreal situations, and also to make polite statements and requests.

You've been using **würde**, the subjunctive form of **werden**, since Kap. 7.

Wenn Barbara nur hier **wäre**!	*If only Barbara **were** here!*
Wenn ich mehr Zeit **hätte** ...	*If I **had** more time . . .*
Würden Sie mir bitte helfen?	***Would** you please help me?*

A common subjunctive form in English is *were* in *if I were you*.

English *present* subjunctive is signalled by what look like *past-tense* forms or by ***would*** + a verb.

*If they **lived** nearby, we **would visit** them.*	(condition contrary to fact)
*If only I **had** more time!*	(wish contrary to fact)
*I **would like** to have a room.*	(polite request)

Note that the verbs *lived* and *had* in the examples above are identical to the past in *form*, but have present-tense meaning.

*If they **lived** nearby . . .*	(right now)
*If only I **had** more time!*	(right now)

Present subjunctive of weak verbs

The present tense of the general subjunctive in German is also based on past indicative forms. In the case of *weak* verbs (see p. 281), the present subjunctive is *identical* to the simple past indicative you have already learned.

wenn ich wohn**te**	*if I lived*	wenn wir wohn**ten**	*if we lived*
wenn du wohn**test**	*if you lived*	wenn ihr wohn**tet**	*if you lived*
wenn sie wohn**te**	*if she lived*	wenn sie, Sie wohn**ten**	*if they, you lived*

In Austria **Servus** means both *hello* and *so long*. It originally meant "Your servant" in Latin.

Expressing wishes contrary to fact is a communicative goal.

Note on Usage: Wishes contrary to fact

A contrary-to-fact wish is expressed in German by a **wenn**-clause in the subjunctive (verb last) with an added **nur**.

Wenn ich **nur** näher **wohnte**!	*If **only** I **lived** closer!*

The **nur** is placed after all personal and reflexive pronouns, but before **nicht**:

Wenn du es mir **nur** sagtest!	*If only you'd tell it to me!*
Wenn es **nur** nicht so spät wäre.	*If only it weren't so late.*

Lab Manual Kap. 14, Üb. 1, 3, 5, and Var. zu Üb. 4, 7–9.

Workbook 14, A–D.

Return to **Üb. 1** the next day as an English–German warm-up at start of class.
I: *If only she would buy that.*
S1: **Wenn sie das nur kaufte.**
Variation: switch to positive: **Hans-Peter wohnt hier. Wenn er nur *nicht* hier wohnte!**

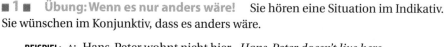

1 Übung: Wenn es nur anders wäre! Sie hören eine Situation im Indikativ. Sie wünschen im Konjunktiv, dass es anders wäre.

BEISPIEL: A: Hans-Peter wohnt nicht hier. *Hans-Peter doesn't live here.*
B: Wenn er nur hier wohnte! *If only he lived here!*

1. Petra kauft das nicht.
2. Georg beeilt sich nicht.
3. Der Urlaub dauert nicht länger.
4. Ich erhole mich nicht.
5. Die Gäste setzen sich nicht.
6. Maria macht die Tür nicht zu.
7. Robert bestellt nicht genug Bier.
8. Meine Freunde besuchen mich nicht.
9. Meine Großeltern wohnen nicht bei uns.
10. Inge wechselt ihr Geld nicht.

Present subjunctive of strong verbs

The present subjunctive of strong verbs is also based on their past indicative forms (see p. 282), but these forms are *modified* according to the following three-step procedure.

Step 1: Take the simple past stem of the verb:

fahren → **fuhr-** gehen → **ging-** laufen → **lief-** sein → **war-**

Remember that you can only add an umlaut to **a**, **o**, **u**, and **au**.

Step 2: Add an umlaut to the stem vowel whenever possible:

führ- **ging-** **lief-** **wär-**

Step 3: Add the following personal endings:

ich	wär**e**	*I would be*	wir	wär**en**	*we would be*
du	wär**est**	*you would be*	ihr	wär**et**	*you would be*
er	wär**e**	*he would be*	sie, Sie	wär**en**	*they, you would be*

Note the difference between the present subjunctive endings and the past indicative endings of strong verbs:

Present subjunctive (would go)		***Past indicative (went)***	
ich	ging**e**	ich	ging
du	ging**est**	du	ging**st**
sie	ging**e**	sie	ging
wir	ging**en**	wir	ging**en**
ihr	ging**et**	ihr	ging**t**
sie, Sie	ging**en**	sie, Sie	ging**en**

Only the **wir-** and the plural **sie-**endings are the same.

A complete list of the principal parts of strong and irregular verbs is in Appendix 2, pp. 486–487.

■ 2 ■ Übung Review the simple past stems of these strong verbs.

BEISPIEL: laufen *lief*

scheinen	finden
kommen	gehen
anfangen	fahren
gefallen	sein
tun	schlafen
aussteigen	bekommen

Üb. 3: Encourage students to replace nouns and names with pronouns in their answers. Also good as written assignment.

■ 3 ■ Übung: Wenn es nur anders wäre! Jetzt hören Sie eine Situation im Indikativ. Sie wünschen im Konjunktiv, dass es anders wäre.

BEISPIEL: Meine Gäste gehen nicht nach Hause.
Wenn sie nur nach Hause gingen!

1. Gabi läuft nicht schnell.
2. Die Sonne scheint nicht.
3. Robert kommt nicht um zwölf.
4. Karin geht nicht mit uns spazieren.
5. Wir sind nicht alt genug.
6. Das Kind schläft nicht länger.
7. Wir bekommen kein Doppelzimmer.
8. Laura findet ihre Kreditkarte nicht.
9. Die Uhr geht nicht richtig.
10. Unsere Freunde fahren nicht nach Australien.
11. Der Film fängt nicht an.
12. Die Wohnung gefällt uns nicht.
13. Das tut Marie nicht gern.
14. Hier steigen wir nicht aus.

Ohne Musik wäre das Leben ein Irrtum.
Friedrich Nietzsche

Once students learn the subjunctive **dürfte**, they tend to umlaut the indicative **durfte** as well. Correct as follows. Tell students to say **du**, then **durfte**.

Present subjunctive of modal verbs

To form the present subjunctive of modal verbs, take the past indicative, *including endings* (see pp. 284–285), and add an umlaut to the stem vowel of *only* those verbs that have an umlaut in their infinitive.

Infinitive		*Past indicative*	
dürfen	*to be allowed*	**ich durfte**	*I was allowed*

Present Subjunctive					
ich	**dürfte**	*I would be allowed*	wir	**dürften**	*we would be allowed*
du	**dürftest**	*you would be allowed*	ihr	**dürftet**	*you would be allowed*
er	**dürfte**	*he would be allowed*	sie, Sie	**dürften**	*they, you would be allowed*

Similarly:

Past indicative		*Present subjunctive*	
ich konnte	*I was able to*	ich **könnte**	*I could, would be able to*
ich mochte	*I liked*	ich **möchte**	*I would like to*
ich musste	*I had to*	ich **müsste**	*I would have to*

The present subjunctive of **sollen** and **wollen**, however, is *not* umlauted, and so looks just like the past indicative.

ich sollte	*I was supposed to*	ich **sollte**	*I ought to*
ich wollte	*I wanted to*	ich **wollte**	*I would want to*

Üb. 4: When students see the printed sentence, the drill is completely different. They must get used to distinguishing the forms aurally or "hearing the umlaut."

■ 4 ■ Übung: Hören Sie gut zu! (*Mit geschlossenen Büchern*) Listen to each pair of sentences, then say which one is past indicative and which present subjunctive. Then, with open books, repeat each sentence aloud and give the English equivalent.

1. Durfte sie das machen? / Dürfte sie das machen?
2. Wir könnten ihn abholen. / Wir konnten ihn abholen.
3. Sie müsste das wissen. / Sie musste das wissen.
4. Mochte er das Frühstück? / Möchte er das Frühstück?

Üb. 5: Note that #2 and #6 are positive, so the subjunctive wish will be negative. Also useful to have students give English translations and/or do as written homework.

■ 5 ■ Übung: Wenn es nur anders wäre! Ihre Professorin beschreibt wieder eine Situation im Indikativ. Sie wünschen im Konjunktiv, dass es anders wäre.

BEISPIEL: Christine kann kein Englisch.
Wenn sie nur Englisch *könnte*!

1. Wir können kein Französisch.
2. Die Gäste müssen nach Hause.
3. Wir dürfen nicht länger bleiben.
4. Esther will nicht nach Grinzing.
5. Die Kinder können nicht mitfahren.
6. Unsere Freunde müssen abfahren.
7. Sie dürfen nicht alles sagen.
8. Andreas will nicht helfen.

Making suggestions is a communicative goal.

Note on Usage: Using the subjunctive to make suggestions

Wir **könnten** zusammen ausgehen.	*We **could** go out together.*
Wir **sollten** eigentlich hier bleiben.	*We really **ought** to stay here.*

Ohne Zeitung hätten Sie weniger zu sagen.
DIE ZEITUNGEN IN DEUTSCHLAND.

6 **Partnerarbeit: Was könnten wir heute machen?** Partner A sagt etwas Schönes, was Sie machen **könnten**. Partner B sagt aber, Sie **sollten** eigentlich etwas anderes machen.

BEISPIEL: A: Wir *könnten* zusammen spazieren gehen.
B: Aber wir *sollten* eigentlich das Zimmer aufräumen.

Hier sind einige Möglichkeiten:

etwas Schönes	*etwas Wichtiges*
spazieren gehen	das Zimmer aufräumen
Karten spielen	Hausaufgaben machen
italienisch essen	Lebensmittel einkaufen
Musik hören	uns auf die Klausur vorbereiten

Present subjunctive of other mixed verbs should be covered at second-year level: **brennte**, **kennte**, **brächte**, **dächte**. **Brauchen** does not follow this model: **Wenn ich Geld brauchte, würde ich um 10 Mark bitten.** Many Germans, however, say **bräuchte**. Lower-frequency irregular forms: **hülfe**, **stürbe**, **stünde**.

Present subjunctive of *haben, werden,* and *wissen*

To form the present subjunctive of the verbs **haben**, **werden**, and **wissen**, take the past indicative, including endings (see pp. 285–286), and add an umlaut to the stem vowel:

Past indicative		*Present subjunctive*	
ich hatte	*I had*	ich **hätte**	*I would have*
ich wurde	*I became*	ich **würde**	*I would become, I would*
ich wusste	*I knew*	ich **wüsste**	*I would know*

Making polite requests is a communicative goal.

Note on Usage: Polite requests: Subjunctive + *gern*

Ich hätte gern ein Einzelzimmer mit Bad.	***I would like to have** a single room with bath.*
Ich wüsste gern, wo die Kasse ist.	***I would like to know** where the cashier is.*

7 **Kettenreaktion: Was hätten Sie gern?** Sagen Sie, was Sie gern hätten.

BEISPIEL: Ich hätte gern ein frisches Brötchen. Und du?
Ich hätte gern ein-________.

8 **Kettenreaktion: Was wüssten Sie gern?** Sagen Sie, was Sie gern wüssten.

BEISPIEL: Ich wüsste gern, wo ich Geld verdienen könnte. Und du?
Ich wüsste gern, ________.

■ Present subjunctive with *würden* + infinitive

In **Kapitel 7** you learned how to use the subjunctive construction **würden** + *infinitive* to express intentions, opinions, preferences, and polite requests. This construction is an alternative to the one-word present subjunctive forms you have been learning in this chapter.

There is no difference in meaning between the following clauses:

Er **käme ...** Er **würde kommen ...**	*He would come ...*

The present subjunctive with **würden** often replaces the one-word form of weak verbs which is indistinguishable from the past indicative:

Ich kaufte das nicht.	*I didn't buy that. (past indic.)* *I wouldn't buy that. (pres. subj.)*

is replaced by:

Ich **würde** das nicht **kaufen**.	*I wouldn't buy that.*

Tell students that they will gradually develop a feeling for which one-word forms are avoided in daily speech (**flöge**, **äße**, etc.).

Spoken German also replaces the one-word form of many strong verbs with **würden** + *infinitive* (but *not* in the case of the frequently used verbs **sein**, **haben**, and the modals).

Ich **tränke** Wein ...	is replaced by
Ich **würde** Wein **trinken ...**	*I'd drink wine . . .*

Üb. 9 can also be done as student exchanges in the **du**-form. Next stage: Have students invent their own questions based on this model.

■ 9 ■ Übung: Was würden Sie machen? Sagen Sie, was Sie in diesen Situationen machen würden.

BEISPIEL: Was würden Sie machen, wenn Sie diese Woche frei hätten?
Ich würde nach Hause fahren.

Was würden Sie machen ...

1. wenn Sie 500 Schilling hätten?
2. wenn Sie Hunger hätten?
3. wenn Sie Durst hätten?
4. wenn Sie Musik hören wollten?
5. wenn Sie Wanderlust hätten?
6. wenn Sie knapp bei Kasse wären?
7. wenn Sie Spaß haben wollten?
8. wenn Sie sich das Studium nicht leisten könnten?

Other uses of the general subjunctive

Talking about contrary-to-fact situations is a communicative goal.

■ Conditions contrary to fact: "If *X* were true, then *Y* would be true."

In **Kapitel 8** you learned about conditional sentences containing a **wenn**-clause (see p. 222). When the conditional sentence is describing a situation that is contrary to fact, the verbs must be in the subjunctive. Note the difference between the following sentences:

Indicative

Wenn der Junge schon dreizehn **ist**, **darf** er den Film sehen.	*If the boy is already thirteen he's allowed to see the movie.*

(*Implication*: The speaker doesn't know whether the boy is thirteen or not.)

Subjunctive

Wenn der Junge schon dreizehn **wäre**, **dürfte** er den Film sehen.	*If the boy were already thirteen, he would be allowed to see the movie.*

(*Implication*: The speaker knows the boy is not yet thirteen.)

A **wenn**-clause states the condition contrary to fact: "If X were true . . ."

Wenn wir jetzt in Deutschland wären ...	*If we were in Germany now . . .*
Wenn ich mehr Geld hätte ...	*If I had more money . . .*

The main clause (with an optional **dann** as the first word) draws the unreal conclusion: ". . . then Y would be true."

... (dann) würden wir sehr schnell Deutsch lernen.	*. . . (then) we would learn German very quickly.*
... (dann) müsste ich nicht so viel arbeiten.	*. . . (then) I wouldn't have to work so much.*

For word order in conditions beginning with **wenn**-clause, refer students to p. 224 in Kap. 8 (subordinating conj.): two inflected forms next to each other, separated by comma: **Wenn wir ... wären, würden wir ...**

Putting them together:

Wenn wir jetzt in Deutschland wären, würden wir sehr schnell Deutsch lernen.
Wenn ich mehr Geld hätte, dann müsste ich nicht so viel arbeiten.

Conditional sentences may begin either with the **wenn**-clause (as in the two previous examples) *or* with the conclusion clause.[1]

Wir **würden** sehr schnell Deutsch lernen, wenn wir jetzt in Deutschland **wären**.
Ich **müsste** nicht so viel arbeiten, wenn ich mehr Geld **hätte**.

1. The **wenn** is sometimes omitted from the **wenn**-clause. Its verb is then placed at the *beginning* of the clause. Compare the similar structure in English that omits *if*:
Hätte er das Geld, (dann) würde er mehr kaufen. ***Had** he the money, he would buy more.*

Lab Manual Kap. 14, Üb. 10, 14, and Var. zu Üb. 12–14.

Workbook 14, E–I.

Variation: Have students reverse order of clauses in **Üb. 10 & 11**. Also good as written assignments.

■ **10** ■ **Übung: Aber wenn es anders wäre ... (*Mit offenen Büchern*)** Ihr Professor beschreibt eine Situation im Indikativ. Sie sagen im Konjunktiv, wie es wäre, wenn die Situation *anders* wäre. (Note that the logic of these sentences demands changing positive to negative and vice versa.)

BEISPIEL: Weil es so kalt ist, können wir nicht schwimmen.
Aber wenn es *nicht* so kalt *wäre, könnten* wir schwimmen.

1. Weil es so weit ist, können wir nicht zu Fuß gehen.
2. Weil ich keine Lust habe, mache ich es nicht.
3. Weil dieses Buch langweilig ist, lesen wir es nicht.
4. Weil der Dom geschlossen ist, können Sie ihn nicht besuchen.
5. Weil ich keine Zeit habe, kann ich kein Bad nehmen.
6. Weil sie nicht aus Österreich kommt, sagt sie nicht „Grüß Gott".
7. Weil ich keinen Hunger habe, bestelle ich nichts.
8. Weil sie sich nicht für diesen Film interessiert, geht sie nicht mit.

■ **11** ■ **Übung (*Mit offenen Büchern*)** Wiederholen Sie, was Sie schon in **Übung 10** gemacht haben, aber diesmal beginnen Sie *nicht* mit **wenn**.

BEISPIEL: Wir kommen zu spät, weil du nicht schneller fährst.
Aber wir würden nicht zu spät kommen, wenn du schneller fahren würdest.

1. Wir bleiben hier, weil er uns braucht.
2. Ich muss jetzt wechseln, weil ich kein österreichisches Geld habe.
3. Wir gehen spazieren, weil die Sonne scheint.
4. Wir trampen nach Italien, weil wir keinen Wagen haben.
5. Ich lese die Zeitung nicht, weil ich so müde bin.
6. Er kann mir nicht danken, weil er meinen Namen nicht weiß.
7. Wir sehen uns nicht, weil er nicht mehr vorbeikommt.

Wenn ich fliegen könnte...

■ Wishes contrary to fact

There are two ways to form contrary-to-fact wishes:

Wenn sie nur hier wäre!	*If only she were here!*
Ich wünschte, sie wäre hier.	*I wish she were here.*

When you use the second expression, notice that *both* verbs are in the subjunctive (**wünschte, wäre**). The second clause of this construction *never* begins with **dass** but *always* has verb-second word order.

Üb. 12: Alternative: **Ich wollte, sie wäre hier.** Variation: Students may also begin with **Es wäre schön, wenn ...** Inflected verb then goes to end of **wenn**-clause.

Üb. 12: If necessary, put initial phrases on board: **Ich wünschte, ich hätte ... / ... ich könnte ... / ... wir würden ...** Encourage students to be playful: **Seien Sie kreativ! Wünschen Sie sich ruhig etwas Unmögliches!**

■ 12 ■ Gruppenarbeit: Buttje, Buttje, in der See Es gibt ein bekanntes norddeutsches Märchen („Der Fischer und seine Frau"), in dem ein großer Butt (*flounder*) einem Fischer seine Wünsche erfüllt (*grants*). Der Fischer ruft ihn immer wieder aus der See mit den Worten: „Buttje, Buttje, in der See", und sagt ihm, was er sich wünscht. Jetzt sagen Sie einander, was Sie sich wünschen. Antworten Sie, ob Sie den Wunsch erfüllen können oder nicht.

BEISPIEL: A: Ich wünschte, ich könnte wie ein Vogel fliegen!
B: Das kann ich dir leider nicht erfüllen!

■ Hypothetical statements and questions

German also uses subjunctive for hypothetical statements and questions, where English uses *would, could,* or *ought to*.

Du **solltest** daran denken.	*You **ought to** think of that.*
Wir **könnten** nach Grinzing fahren.	*We **could** drive to Grinzing.*
Das **wäre** schön!	*That **would be** nice!*
Was **würde** das kosten?	*What **would** that cost?*

Üb. 13: Remind students of range of possible reactions: **Gute Idee, toll, fantastisch, höchste Zeit usw.**

■ 13 ■ Partnerarbeit: Wie wäre das? Sie wollen heute irgendetwas zusammen machen. Partner A macht einen Vorschlag (*suggestion*). Partner B reagiert darauf.

BEISPIEL: A: Wir *könnten* eine Wanderung machen.
B: Ja, das *wäre* schön! (*oder*) Nein, das *wäre* mir zu schwierig.

Alt und Jung ruhen sich auf einer Bank aus. (Tirol, Österreich)

■ Polite requests

Note the difference in the tone of the following two requests:

> ***Can*** *you do this for me?* vs. ***Could*** *you do this for me?*

It is more polite to soften the request with the subjunctive, as in the second sentence.

German uses the subjunctive in the same way as English to make polite requests. These are sometimes in the statement form you have already used.

Ich **hätte** gern eine Tasse Kaffee.	*I'd like to have a cup of coffee.*
Ich **wüsste** gern, wo der Bahnhof ist.	*I'd like to know where the train station is.*

Sometimes polite requests are questions.

Könnten Sie mir bitte helfen?	*Could you please help me?*
Würden Sie mir bitte den Koffer tragen?	*Would you please carry my suitcase?*
Dürfte ich eine Frage stellen?	*Might I ask a question?*

■ 14 ■ Übung: Könnten Sie das bitte machen? Benutzen Sie den Konjunktiv statt des Indikativs um höflicher zu sein.

BEISPIEL: Können Sie mir bitte ein Einzelzimmer zeigen?
Könnten Sie mir bitte ein Einzelzimmer zeigen?

1. Können Sie mir bitte sagen, wann der Zug nach Berlin abfährt?
2. Haben Sie Zeit eine Tasse Kaffee mit mir zu trinken?
3. Darf ich mich hier setzen?
4. Tragen Sie mir bitte die Koffer? (Benutzen Sie *würden*!)
5. Ist es möglich eine Zeitung zu kaufen?
6. Können Sie mir meinen Platz zeigen?
7. Haben Sie ein Einzelzimmer mit Dusche?
8. Wissen Sie, wo man Karten kaufen kann?

Lesestück

Vor dem Lesen

Tipps zum Lesen und Lernen

Tipps zum Vokabelnlernen: Adverbs of time

Note spelling: **monatelang** but **zwei Monate lang**.

You can guess the meaning of **jahrzehntelang**.

Compare the Note on Usage on p. 292.

The suffix *-lang* To form the German equivalents of the English adverbial phrases *for days, for hours*, etc., add the suffix **-lang** to the plural of the noun.

minuten**lang**	*for minutes*	monate**lang**	*for months*
stunden**lang**	*for hours*	jahre**lang**	*for years*
tage**lang**	*for days*	jahrhunderte**lang**	*for centuries*
wochen**lang**	*for weeks*		

Also learn the phrase

eine Zeit lang *for a time, for a while*

In diesem Kapitel lesen Sie über Österreich. Das Lesestück spricht von der historischen Rolle Österreichs als Weltreich:

„Die Habsburger Dynastie regierte **jahrhundertelang** über Deutsche, Ungarn, Tschechen, Polen, Italiener, Serben und **eine Zeit lang** sogar über Mexikaner."

Übung: Wie lange hat's gedauert? Ihre Professorin möchte wissen, ob etwas lange gedauert hat. Wählen Sie ein Zeitadverb mit **-lang** für Ihre Antwort.

BEISPIEL: A: Haben Sie lange im Zug zwischen Paris und Berlin gesessen?
B: Ja, *stundenlang*.

Hat das elegante Abendessen lange gedauert?
Haben Sie lange auf den Bus warten müssen?
War's letzten Sommer sehr heiß?
War der Chef lange am Telefon?
Sind Sie manchmal schlechter Laune?
Waren die alten Römer lange Zeit in Nordeuropa?

Lab Manual Kap. 14, Üb. zur Betonung.

Contrast stress of Dynastie, Melancholie, Familie.

Leicht zu merken

analysieren	analysieren
die **Dynastie, -n**	Dynastie
der **Humor**	Humor
die **Ironie**	Ironie
der **Kontakt**	Kontakt
kreativ	kreativ
literarisch	literarisch
die **Melancholie**	Melancholie
der **Patient, -en, -en**	Patient
philosophieren	philosophieren
produktiv	produktiv
die **Psychoanalyse**	Psychoanalyse

Die Wiener Staatsoper

Einstieg in den Text

The two Austrians in the following reading selection use subjunctive mood mainly for conjectural and hypothetical statements. Below is one example of each type. After reading through the text once, write down other examples of subjunctive mood used for these purposes; be sure you understand them and can give English equivalents.

Hypothetical statements
Ich ... könnte ... bei meinen Eltern wohnen und an der Musikhochschule in Wien studieren.

Conjecture
... ohne Johann Strauß würde die Welt wahrscheinlich keine Walzer tanzen.

Wortschatz 2

Verben

erwarten to expect
sich konzentrieren auf (+ *acc.*) to concentrate on
statt·finden, fand statt, hat stattgefunden to take place
tanzen to dance
träumen to dream

Substantive

der **Künstler, -** artist (*m.*)
der **Spiegel, -** mirror
der **Witz, -e** joke; wit
das **Klavier, -e** piano
die **Gegenwart** present (time)
die **Gelegenheit, -en** opportunity, chance
die **Hochschule, -n** university; institution of higher learning
die **Künstlerin, -nen** artist (*f.*)

Hochschule corresponds roughly to college, not high school (generically called **die Oberschule**). **Musikhochschule** = *conservatory*; **Technische Hochschule** = engineering college.

Adjektive und Adverbien

außerdem (*adv.*) besides, in addition
begeistert von enthusiastic about, ecstatic about
ernst serious
etwas ernst nehmen to take something seriously
gemütlich cozy, comfortable; quiet, relaxed
witzig witty, amusing
zunächst first (of all), to begin with

Andere Vokabel

beide (*pl. pronoun*) both (people)

Nützlicher Ausdruck

eine Zeit lang for a time, for a while

Gegensätze

ernst ≠ heiter serious ≠ cheerful
gemütlich ≠ ungemütlich cozy ≠ unpleasant, not cozy

Point out again the parallelism in the pronoun pairs **alles** (sg.) = *everything* / **alle** (pl.) = *everyone* and **beides** (sg.) = both things / **beide** (pl.) = *both people.*

Zwei Österreicher stellen sich vor

Lab Manual Kap. 14, Lesestück.

Marie-Therese Werdenberg, Musikstudentin in Salzburg

„Ich heiße Marie-Therese Werdenberg und bin Musikstudentin. Ich komme aus Wien und könnte freilich° dort bei meinen Eltern wohnen und an der Musikhochschule in Wien studieren. Aber ich studiere lieber in Salzburg, weil ich mich hier besser auf das Klavierspielen konzentrieren kann. In Wien gäbe es zwar mehr Konzerte, in die man gehen könnte, aber hier ist es ruhiger und gemütlicher. Außerdem finden hier im Sommer die berühmten Festspiele[1] statt und da habe ich die Gelegenheit mit vielen Musikern° in Kontakt zu kommen.

Ja, was wäre Österreich ohne seine Musiktradition? Und umgekehrt°: Was wäre die Musikgeschichte ohne Österreich? Salzburg ist Mozarts Geburtsort°. Auch Haydn, Schubert, Bruckner, Mahler und Schönberg sind alle in Österreich geboren. Beethoven und Brahms – beides deutsche Komponisten° – haben in Wien ihre wichtigsten Werke geschrieben. Und ohne Johann Strauß würde die Welt wahrscheinlich keine Walzer° tanzen.

Aber ich sollte nicht nur über Musik reden, bloß° weil das meine Leidenschaft° ist. Die Kulturgeschichte Österreichs hat der Welt eine ganze Menge gegeben. In Wien um 1900 gab es z.B. ein besonders produktives und faszinierendes° Kulturleben. Die literarischen Werke von Hugo von Hofmannsthal und Arthur Schnitzler sind ein Spiegel dieser sehr kreativen Zeit. In der Malerei° arbeiteten Künstler wie Gustav Klimt und Oskar Kokoschka. Um diese Zeit gründete° Sigmund Freud die Psychoanalyse. Ich könnte noch viele Namen nennen, aber dann müssten wir fast den ganzen Tag hier sitzen."

= **natürlich**

Learning about Austria is the cultural goal of this chapter.

= **Menschen, die Musik, machen** / vice versa

= **Ort, wo man geboren ist**

= **Menschen, die Musik komponieren**

waltzes

= **nur** / passion

= **sehr interessantes**

painting

founded

The **Lesestück** contains the names of many famous Austrians. Have students look up information on them and report to class. Music majors can research the musicians, art majors the artists, etc.

Oskar Kokoschka (1886–1980), Selbstbildnis (*self-portrait*, 1917)

1. The **Salzburger Festspiele** are an annual summer festival of drama and classical music.

Blick auf Salzburg

Dr. Ulrich Kraus, Psychologe° aus Wien

psychologist

„Mein Name ist Kraus und ich bin Psychologe. Mit meinen Patienten und ihren Problemen habe ich mehr als genug zu tun; erwarten Sie also nicht von mir, dass ich den Durchschnittsösterreicher° analysiere. Ich könnte aber mindestens° versuchen diesen Menschen — den *homo austriacus* — ein bisschen zu beschreiben.

average Austrian / = **wenigstens**

Zunächst etwas Geschichte: Ich möchte Sie daran erinnern, dass wir Österreicher auf eine sehr alte und große Tradition stolz sind. Die Habsburger Dynastie regierte° jahrhundertelang über Deutsche, Ungarn, Tschechen, Polen, Italiener, Serben und eine Zeit lang sogar über Mexikaner.[1] Was man vom englischen Weltreich sagt, könnte man auch von Österreich sagen: Die Sonne ging nicht unter° über diesem Reich.

ruled

ging ... unter = set

Heute spielt unser kleines Land eine viel bescheidenere° politische Rolle. Und dieser Kontrast zwischen Vergangenheit und Gegenwart hat zu unserem Humor und unserer Selbstironie beigetragen°. Manchmal habe ich das Gefühl, wir Österreicher sind unglücklich über unsere verlorene Größe, aber wir sind wenigstens glücklich, dass wir unglücklich sind. Verstehen Sie diese witzige Melancholie, die sich selbst nicht ganz ernst nimmt?

more modest

contributed

Viele Österreicher würden den Unterschied zwischen sich und den Deutschen so ausdrücken: Die Deutschen sind fleißig, aber die Österreicher gemütlich. Die Wiener Kaffeehäuser könnten nicht existieren, wenn der Österreicher nicht gern stundenlang vor seinem Mokka[2] säße und träumte. Er philosophiert gern darüber, wie die Welt sein könnte. Darum nennt man Österreich manchmal das Land des Konjunktivs: ‚Alles würde hier besser gehen, wenn wir nur ...' oder ‚Das wäre möglich, wenn ... '"

1. The Habsburgs ruled the Holy Roman Empire from 1278 to 1806, and Austria (later Austria-Hungary) until 1918. The empire came to include Germans, Hungarians, Czechs, Poles, Italians, and Serbs. In 1864 Archduke Maximilian, brother of the Austrian Emperor, was made Emperor of Mexico. He was executed in 1867 by republican troops.
2. A strong aromatic coffee served in demitasse cups, named after a city in Yemen. The drink was introduced into Vienna during the Turkish siege of the city in 1683. Viennese cafés serve dozens of different types of coffee, each with its own name.

Im Café Central, Wien

Shown in photo is life-sized papier-mâché figure of Peter Altenberg (1859–1919), journalist, essayist, and habitué of the Café Central.

Poster designed by Oskar Kokoschka for a 1908 art show of the Viennese "Secession Movement"

Nach dem Lesen

■ A ■ Antworten Sie auf Deutsch.

1. Woher kommt die Musikstudentin im ersten Teil des Textes und was macht sie in Salzburg?
2. Warum studiert sie lieber dort als in Wien?
3. Nennen Sie einen berühmten Menschen, der in Salzburg geboren ist.
4. Kennen Sie andere berühmte Namen aus der Musikgeschichte Österreichs?
5. Warum war Wien um 1900 besonders interessant? Wer hat damals dort gelebt und gearbeitet?
6. Was wissen Sie von der Geschichte Österreichs?
7. Beschreiben Sie den größten Unterschied für die Österreicher zwischen der Vergangenheit und der Gegenwart ihres Landes.
8. Welche Unterschiede findet Dr. Kraus zwischen den Deutschen und seinen Landsleuten?
9. Warum nennt man Österreich manchmal das Land des Konjunktivs?

■ B ■ Gruppenarbeit: Im Café In einem Wiener Café darf man nicht einfach „eine Tasse Kaffee" bestellen, denn man hat eine riesengroße Auswahl von verschiedenen Kaffeegetränken. Von der Liste unten wählen Sie Ihren Lieblingskaffee. (Wenn Sie keinen Kaffee trinken wollen, gibt's natürlich auch Tee und Cola.) Lieben Sie Ihren Kaffee mit oder ohne Zucker? stark oder schwach? mit oder ohne Schlag (*whipped cream*)?

Kleiner Schwarzer	Demitasse of espresso.
Kleiner Brauner	**Kleiner Schwarzer** with a dash of milk.
Großer Schwarzer	Double shot of espresso.
Großer Brauner	A big **kleiner Brauner**.
Espresso	The universally-known strong black brew. If you'd like a weak one, ask for it "stretched": **gestreckt**.
Verlängerter	**Espresso gestreckt**, i.e., diluted with a shot of hot water.
Mokka	Synonymous with **Brauner** — a **Mokka** can be **klein** or **groß**.
Kapuziner	Dark coffee, the color of a Capuchin monk's robes.
Franziskaner	Dark coffee with a little more milk, the color of a Franciscan's robes.

Nussbraun	A little lighter: "nut brown."
Nussgold	Lighter still.
Gold	Very light.
Schwarzer	Black coffee (**klein** or **groß**).
Konsul	Black coffee with a dash of cream.
Melange	Espresso with steamed milk, sometimes with whipped cream (**Schlag** or **Schlagobers**).
Cappuccino	Espresso with foamed milk and a sprinkling of cinnamon.
Milchkaffee	Half coffee, half hot milk.
Einspänner	**Großer Mokka** with **Schlag** and a sprinkling of cocoa. Served in a tall glass.
Fiaker	Named after Vienna's horse-drawn carriages and their raucous drivers. Strong, black coffee laced with hot kirsch liqueur topped with Schlag and maraschino cherry.
Pharisäer	Strong black coffee with whipped cream, served with small liqueur glass of rum.
Türkischer	Black Turkish coffee served with traditional copper utensils.
Kaisermelange	Cup of black coffee served with raw egg yolk and brandy on the side.
Eiskaffee	Iced coffee with vanilla ice cream. Topped with **Schlag**.

C **Gruppenarbeit** (*3 Personen*) Jetzt sitzen wir gemütlich zusammen, trinken unseren Kaffee und spekulieren ein bisschen. Unten sind einige Situationen. Besprechen Sie miteinander, was Sie in diesen Situationen tun würden.

BEISPIEL: krank sein
Was würdest du tun, wenn du krank wärest?
Ich würde zunächst ins Bett gehen. Dann ...

reich sein
in Europa sein
kein Student sein
wenig Geld haben
viel Zeit haben
jetzt Ferien haben
Hunger haben
Politiker sein

Situationen aus dem Alltag

This vocabulary focuses on an everyday topic or situation. Words you already know from **Wortschatz** sections are listed without English equivalents; new supplementary vocabulary is listed with definitions. Your instructor may assign some supplementary vocabulary for active mastery.

Im Hotel

Auf Seite 419 sehen Sie die Rezeption in einem Hotel. Hier ist eine Liste von Vokabeln, die Ihnen zum größten Teil (*for the most part*) schon bekannt sind.

Die Hotelgäste
sich an·melden — *to register*
das **Gepäck**
der **Koffer, -**

der **Reisepass, -pässe** | *passport*
ein Zimmer reservieren
ein Taxi bestellen

An der Rezeption
der/die **Angestellte**
die **Kasse**
der **Zimmerschlüssel, -**
der **Stadtplan, ¨e**
der **Stadtführer, -** | *city guidebook*
der **Speisesaal** | *dining room*
der **Lift** | *elevator*

Im Hotelzimmer
das **Bad**
die **Dusche**
das **Telefon (telefonieren)**
sich um·ziehen | *to change clothes*

Gruppenarbeit: Also good as written assignment to review 2–way prepositions and hotel vocabulary.

■ **A** ■ **Gruppenarbeit** Beschreiben Sie dieses Bild. Wer steht wo? Wer tut was?

■ B ■ Rollenspiele (*Gruppen von 3 Personen*) Spielen Sie diese Situationen zusammen. Improvisieren Sie.

1. ***An der Rezeption*** Zwei Touristen kommen gerade vom Flughafen im Hotel an. Sie haben schon ein Zimmer reserviert. Sie melden sich an der Rezeption an und stellen Fragen über das Zimmer.
2. ***Eine Stunde später*** Die Touristen haben sich jetzt geduscht und umgezogen. Jetzt wollen sie ausgehen und sich die Stadt ansehen. An der Rezeption bitten sie um Auskunft. Der Angestellte gibt ihnen viele Informationen über die Stadt, z.B. über das kulturelle Leben, Verkehrsmittel, Restaurants usw. Bei ihm bekommen sie auch Stadtführer, Stadtpläne und Broschüren (*brochures*). Sie müssen auch Geld wechseln.

Zum Schluss

Lab Manual Kap. 14, Diktat.

Workbook 14, J–L.

Gruppenarbeit A reviews students' ability to discuss travel plans while focusing on the culture of Austria.

Partnerarbeit B: Stress use of polite requests; bring in a real or made-up menu. Work in pairs for 5–10 minutes, then select pairs to act out their situation for the class.

Üb. C: Encourage constructive criticism and serious discussion rather than mere complaint. Emphasize use of subjunctive. Prepares students for **Aufsatzthema H**, p. 422.

Sprechen wir miteinander!

■ A ■ Gruppenarbeit: Studentenreise nach Österreich (*4–5 Personen*) Sie reisen nächstes Jahr mit einer Studentengruppe nach Österreich. Sie müssen sich jetzt darauf vorbereiten.

1. Was sollte man mitbringen?
2. Was für Bücher könnte man über Österreich lesen?
3. Was sollte man dort sehen? (Die Fotos in diesem Kapitel geben Ihnen vielleicht einige Ideen.)
4. Was würden Sie am liebsten in Österreich machen?

■ B ■ Partnerarbeit: Rollenspiele Spielen Sie diese Situation zusammen. Seien Sie höflich und benutzen Sie den Konjunktiv! Seien Sie bereit Ihren Dialog vor der Klasse zu spielen.

Kellner und Gast im Lokal
Der Kellner fragt den Gast, was er (*oder* sie) bestellen möchte. Der Gast fragt, ob man verschiedene Gerichte (*dishes*) hat, und bestellt dann ein großes Essen. (You can use some food vocabulary from **Kapitel 8**, p. 239).

KELLNER/IN: Bitte sehr? Was hätten Sie gern?
GAST: Hätten Sie vielleicht ... ? Könnten Sie mir sagen ... ? Ich hätte gern ...

■ C ■ Gruppendiskussion: Wie könnten wir das ändern? An Ihrer Uni gibt es sicher Sachen, die Sie gern ändern würden. Machen Sie eine Liste von diesen Sachen. Dann diskutieren Sie, wie man sie ändern oder anders machen könnte.

BEISPIEL: Die Bibliothek schließt zu früh. Das müsste man ändern. Sie sollte länger offen bleiben, besonders am Semesterende. Ja, das wäre viel besser. Dann hätte man mehr Zeit zu lernen. Aber natürlich würde das mehr kosten. Wer würde das bezahlen?

Prepare by reviewing "Specifying time" in the **Zusammenfassung und Wiederholung 3** of your Workbook.

■ **D** ■ **Übung: Eine witzige Anekdote aus Österreich** Provide the missing time word or phrase (in parentheses) in the following anecdote.

_______ (*Many years ago*), _______ (*when*) noch relativ wenige Touristen nach Österreich kamen, erzählte man eine Anekdote über eine reiche Amerikanerin, die _______ (*one month*) in den österreichischen Alpen verbrachte. Sie wohnte in einem gemütlichen Hotel in einem kleinen Dorf, wo die Menschen sie sehr interessant fanden. _______ (*Each morning*), _______ (*when*) sie Frühstück aß, bestellte sie nur wenig zu essen: ein weich gekochtes Ei [*soft-boiled egg*] und eine Tasse Kaffee. _______ (*Whenever*) das Wetter gut war, verbrachte sie _______ (*the whole day*) draußen und aß Brot und Käse aus ihrem Rucksack, _______ (*when*) sie Hunger hatte. _______ (*When*) die Dame endlich wieder nach Hause musste, sagte sie dem Wirt [*innkeeper*] _______ (*on Sunday*), sie würde _______ (*day after tomorrow*) abfahren. _______ (*On Tuesday*) bestellte sie nach dem Frühstück die Rechnung [*bill*]. Zunächst las sie die Rechnung und sagte _______ (*for a while*) nichts. Darauf stand „für 28 Eier: 300 Schilling". Es stimmte, sie hatte _______ (*for weeks*) _______ (*every morning*) ein weiches Ei gegessen, aber sie konnte sich nicht erinnern, _______ (*when*) sie je in ihrem Leben so teure Eier gegessen hatte. Sie ließ sofort den Wirt kommen und bat ihn um eine Erklärung. „_______ (*When*) ich _______ (*every morning*) mein Ei bestellte," sagte sie, „wusste ich nicht, dass sie bei Ihnen so selten [*rare*] sind." Der Wirt antwortete: „Ja, wissen Sie, gnädige Frau [*Madame*], die Eier sind bei uns *nicht* so selten, aber *Amerikanerinnen* sehr." Sie lachte, bezahlte die Rechnung und sagte, sie würde _______ (*next year*) wieder kommen. „Hoffentlich sind _______ (*then*) Amerikanerinnen _______ (*no longer*) so selten und die Eier weniger teuer!"

Schreiben Sie zu Hause.

■ **E** ■ Schreiben Sie diese Sätze zu Ende.

1. Wenn ich Künstler/in wäre ...
2. Ich würde dich ernst nehmen, wenn ...
3. Wenn ich die Gelegenheit hätte, dann ...
4. Die Party könnte heute Abend stattfinden, wenn ...
5. Wenn du mit mir tanzen wolltest, ...
6. Wir würden in diesem Hotel übernachten, wenn ...
7. Wenn wir knapp bei Kasse wären, ...
8. Wenn ich morgen nichts Besonderes vorhätte, dann ...

■ **F** ■ Machen Sie ganze Sätze mit diesen Vokabeln. Vergessen Sie die Endungen nicht. (// = Komma)

1. wenn / ich / nur / können / Klavier / spielen! (*wish contrary to fact*)
2. wir / würd- / gemütlich / sitzen / zusammen // wenn / wir / haben / mehr Zeit (*condition contrary to fact*)
3. wenn / ich / haben / Zimmer / im / erst- / Stock // Straßenbahn / würd- / mich / stören (*condition contrary to fact*)
4. wenn / wir / können / nicht / wechseln / Geld // wir / können / immer / zahlen / mit / Reisescheck (*conditional sentence in the indicative*)
5. ich / wissen / gern // wie / kommen / man / zum Museum (*first clause: polite subjunctive*)
6. ich / wünschen // ich / sein / bei / mein- / Freunde / auf / Land (*wish contrary to fact*)

■ G ■ Wenn ich ein Vöglein wär' You have learned that the subjunctive is used to express wishes contrary to fact. As you might expect, this use of subjunctive occurs frequently in poems about love and longing. A well-known German folk song begins like this:

Wenn ich ein Vöglein wär'
Und auch zwei Flüglein° hätt' — little wings
Flög' ich zu dir.
Weil's aber nicht kann sein,
Bleib' ich allhier°. — = **hier**

Try creating a short poem of your own (either rhymed or not) in which you express such an unfulfillable wish.

Wenn ich ...
...
Dann ...

Üb. I answers: 1. Möchtest du morgen Abend mit uns tanzen gehen? 2. Das wäre toll, aber leider habe ich mir das Bein gebrochen. 3. Schade! Du könntest trotzdem mitkommen. 4. Dein alter Freund/Bekannter Rainer wird da sein. 5. Max ist schon wochenlang in Graz. 6. Es wäre nett ihm eine Postkarte zu schreiben. 7. Wenn ich nur wüsste, wo er jetzt wohnt. 8. Er ist entweder im Hotel Europa oder irgendwo in einer Jugendherberge. 9. Kannst du dich nicht auf dein Referat konzentrieren? 10. Nein, Marie stört mich immer mit ihrer lauten Musik. 11. Wenn ihr kein Klavier im Zimmer hättet, hättet ihr kein Problem (würdet ... haben). 12. Stimmt schon, aber dann müsste ich (mir) eine neue Mitbewohnerin suchen.

■ H ■ Aufsatzthema: Wenn ich die Welt regieren könnte Stellen Sie sich vor, Sie könnten eine Woche lang die Welt regieren. Was würden Sie für die Völker der Erde tun? Was würden Sie ändern? Schreiben Sie eine Seite darüber.

■ I ■ Wie sagt man das auf Deutsch?

1. Would you like to go dancing with us tomorrow night?
2. That would be great, but unfortunately I've broken my leg.
3. That's a shame! You could come along anyway.
4. Your old friend Rainer will be there.

5. Max has been in Graz for weeks.
6. It would be nice to write him a postcard.
7. If only I knew where he is living now.
8. He's either in the Hotel Europa or somewhere in a youth hostel.

9. Can't you concentrate on your paper?
10. No, Marie always disturbs me with her loud music.
11. If you didn't have a piano in your room, you wouldn't have a problem.
12. That's right, but then I would have to look for a new roommate.

Videoecke

7 Fährst du mit in die Schweiz? (27:32)

Fährst du mit in die Schweiz?

Katrin will in den Semesterferien in die Schweiz. Dort möchte sie ihre Tante in Zürich besuchen und auch ein bisschen in den Bergen wandern. Weil sie das Alpenland noch nicht gut kennt, geht sie zum Reisebüro. Die Angestellte im Reisebüro gibt ihr Auskunft darüber. Später ruft sie Su-Sin an um sie zu fragen, ob sie Lust hätte mitzukommen. Su-Sin muss sich diesen Plan überlegen, aber ruft dann bei Bachmanns an um zu sagen, dass sie gerne mitkommen würde.

Wortschatz zum Video

das **Reisebüro, -s**	*travel agency*
zunächst ... danach	*first . . . after that*
die **Ermäßigung**	*discount*
buchen	*to book (a flight, hotel, etc.)*
preiswert	= **billig**
die **Geduld**	*patience*
das **Bargeld**	*cash*

■ A ■ Verkehrsmittel (Means of transportation) Sehen Sie sich den Anfang des Abschnitts (*section*) (27:40–28:27) an. Welche öffentlichen (*public*) und privaten Verkehrsmittel sehen Sie? Kreuzen Sie sie an.

____ 1. Flugzeug
____ 2. Fahrräder
____ 3. Taxis
____ 4. die U-Bahn
____ 5. Autos
____ 6. Bus
____ 7. Straßenbahn
____ 8. Mopeds

■ B ■ Wörter im Kontext: Was könnte das bedeuten? Jetzt sehen Sie sich die ganze Episode an (28:27–31:34). Sie sehen oder hören die folgenden (*following*) Wörter. Wählen Sie das beste englische Äquivalent im Kontext.

1. Bahnsteig
   a. train information b. railroad crossing c. station platform
2. Reiseladen
   a. travel agency b. souvenir shop c. luggage shop
3. das Berner Oberland
   a. express train to Bern b. mountainous region in Switzerland
   c. a dog used for mountain rescue
4. Flugkarten
   a. flight itineraries b. postcards of airplanes c. airline tickets

■ C ■ Wer macht das? Wer sagt das? Choose the person who does or says the following.

a. Katrin b. die Angestellte im Reisebüro
c. ein Kunde im Reisebüro

1. ____ „Darf ich um Auskunft bitten?"
2. ____ „Da braucht man dann einen internationalen Jugendherbergsführer."
3. ____ unterbricht das Gespräch.
4. ____ findet einen Zettel (*note*) an der Tür.
5. ____ „Wie war Ihr Name bitte?"
6. ____ „Toll!"

■ D ■ Wie geht's weiter? Wählen Sie die beste Möglichkeit den Satz zu ergänzen (*complete*).

1. Katrins Tante lebt ...
   a. im Berner Oberland. b. in Leipzig. c. in Zürich.
2. Katrin hat es vor ...
   a. allein zu reisen. b. ihre Ferien mit einer Freundin zu verbringen.
   c. mit ihrer Tante zu wandern.

3. Die Angestellte sagt Katrin, sie kann Geld sparen, wenn sie ...
   a. in Jugendherbergen übernachtet. b. per Autostopp reist.
   c. nur Reiseschecks benutzt.
4. Der Kunde im Hintergrund ...
   a. spricht nur Französisch. b. scheint in Eile zu sein.
   c. will auch in die Schweiz.
5. Als Katrin auf dem Zettel liest, dass Su-Sin mitkommt, ...
   a. freut sie sich sehr. b. will sie sofort mit ihr telefonieren.
   c. ärgert sie sich.

E **Im Gespräch** For each sentence in the left column, find the appropriate response in the right column.

____ 1. Haben Sie vielleicht was zu schreiben?
____ 2. Entschuldigung, darf ich bitte unterbrechen?
____ 3. Dieser Prospekt informiert Sie über Sonderfahrkarten.
____ 4. Was empfehlen Sie, soll ich mir Reiseschecks kaufen?
____ 5. Ich fürchte, ich kann's mir nicht leisten.

a. Den nehme ich mit.
b. Ach, überleg's dir doch! Es ist bestimmt nicht teuer.
c. Da haben Sie Papier und einen Kugelschreiber.
d. Ja, das ist wohl sicherer als Bargeld.
e. Kleinen Moment Geduld bitte!

Das Hundertwasserhaus, Wien

Friedensreich Hundertwasser (b. 1928) is a painter, designer, and architect whose building designs incorporate bright color and flowing lines and often use trees and plants as integral elements. The Hundertwasserhaus is an apartment building finished in 1985.

Profile of Austria

Area: 83,855 square kilometers; 32,376 square miles (slightly smaller than the state of Maine)
Population: 8,132,500; density 97 people per square kilometer (251 people per square mile)
Currency: Schilling; 1 öS = 100 Groschen
Major Cities: Vienna (**Wien**, capital, pop. 1,597,000), Graz, Linz, Salzburg, Innsbruck
Religion: 85% Roman Catholic, 6% Protestant, 9% other

Austria consists of nine states (**Bundesländer**). It became a member of the European Union in 1995. In addition to basic industries such as machinery, iron and steel, and textiles and chemicals, tourism provides an important source of income. The literacy rate is 98%.

Austria plays a vital role in the United Nations, and Vienna is an important point of contact between eastern and western Europe. With the opening of the "UNO City" in 1979, Vienna became the third seat of the United Nations. It is also the headquarters for OPEC (the Organization of Petroleum Exporting Countries).

Straßenkonzert vor dem Stephansdom, Wien

Endlich ist der Frühling da. (Innsbruck mit Blick auf die Nordkette)

KAPITEL 15

Ausländer in Deutschland

Communicative Goals

- Using the post office
- Talking about what could or might have happened in the past
- Talking about houses and apartments

Cultural Goal

- Learning about the situation of foreigners in Germany

Anticipate topic of foreigners in Germany with questions in German (or English). Students' answers may reflect simplistic media coverage of the radical Right in Germany. **Was haben Sie über Ausländer in Deutschland schon gehört oder gelesen? Warum kommen sie nach Deutschland? Aus welchen Ländern kommen die meisten Ausländer? Gibt es eine ähnliche Situation in anderen Ländern?**

Chapter Outline

- **Lyrik zum Vorlesen**
  Clara Tauchert-da Cruz, „Über Grenzen",
  Şadi Üçüncü, „Integration"
- **Grammatik**
  General subjunctive: Past tense
  Passive voice
  The present participle
  Directional prefixes: *hin-* and *her-*
- **Lesestück**
  Şinasi Dikmen, „Wer ist ein Türke?"
- **Situationen aus dem Alltag**
  Wohnen und Wohnungen
- **Almanach**
  Foreigners Living and Working in Germany

Lab Manual Kap. 15, Dialoge, Fragen, Hören Sie gut zu!

Ich bin doch hier geboren: See p. 277 for flavoring particle **doch**.

Wo liegt die Heimat?

Demetra, Schülerin aus einer Gastarbeiterfamilie, wird für die Schülerzeitung interviewt.

INTERVIEWER: Es überrascht mich, dass du als Ausländerin so perfekt Deutsch kannst.
DEMETRA: Kein Wunder, ich bin doch hier geboren. Viele halten mich sogar für eine Deutsche.
INTERVIEWER: Aber ihr kommt doch aus Griechenland, nicht? Wo fühlst du dich eigentlich zu Hause?
DEMETRA: Das frag' ich mich auch. Hier kenne ich mich besser aus, aber mir ist klar, dass ich nicht von allen Deutschen akzeptiert werde.

verpasste: Notice the adjectival use of past participle.

Pronunciation practice: Use dialogues to review pronunciation of vocalic **r**, especially in forms of **werden**: **wird für die Schülerzeitung interviewt**, **kein Wunder**, **akzeptiert werde**, **Geburtstagsfeier**, **eingeladen worden**.

Die verpasste Geburtstagsfeier

LILLI: Bist du nicht zu Sonjas Geburtstagsfeier eingeladen worden?
FELIX: Doch, und ich wünschte, ich wäre dabei gewesen. Aber ich war auf Urlaub in Spanien.
LILLI: Du hättest wenigstens anrufen können, um ihr zu gratulieren.
FELIX: Da hast du Recht. Das hätte ich machen sollen.

Using the post office is a communicative goal.

drauf (*colloq.*) = **darauf**.

Vor der Post

Vor der Hauptpost sehen Herr und Frau Becker einen Briefkasten.

FRAU BECKER: Da kannst du deinen Brief einwerfen.
HERR BECKER: Augenblick. Hab' ich genug Briefmarken drauf? Vielleicht sollte ich hineingehen und ihn wiegen lassen.
FRAU BECKER: Zeig mal her – aber Hartmanns sind doch umgezogen! Das ist ihre alte Adresse.
HERR BECKER: Verflixt nochmal! Das hätte ich nicht vergessen sollen.
FRAU BECKER: Ach, reg dich nicht auf! Wir kaufen schnell einen neuen Umschlag.

Hans Becker
Kieler Straße 314
22083 Hamburg

Frau
Annemarie Hartmann
Vogelsangstraße 17
60327 Frankfurt

Wortschatz 1

Verben

akzeptieren to accept
sich auf·regen (über + *acc.*) to get upset (about), get excited (about)
dabei sein to be present, attend
ein·werfen to mail (a letter) (*literally*: to throw in)
sich fragen to wonder, ask oneself
 Ich frage mich, ob ... I wonder if . . .
gratulieren (+ *dat.*) to congratulate
 Ich gratuliere dir zum Geburtstag! Happy birthday!
halten für to take for, regard as, think X is
 Ich halte es für möglich. I think it's possible.
überraschen to surprise
wiegen, wog, hat gewogen to weigh (*trans. and intrans.*)

Substantive

der **Ausländer, -** foreigner (*m.*)
der **Briefkasten, ¨** mailbox
der **Gastarbeiter, -** foreign worker, guest worker (*m.*)
der **Umschlag, ¨e** envelope

(das) **Griechenland** Greece
(das) **Spanien** Spain

die **Adresse, -n** address
die **Ausländerin, -nen** foreigner (*f.*)
die **Briefmarke, -n** stamp
die **Feier, -n** celebration, party
 die Geburtstagsfeier birthday party
die **Gastarbeiterin, -nen** foreign worker, guest worker (*f.*)
die **Post** post office; postal service; mail

Gastarbeiter: Official designation of foreign workers is **ausländische Arbeitnehmer**.

Adjektiv oder Adverb

perfekt perfect(ly)

Andere Vokabel

hinein- (*prefix*) in, into (see pp. 441–443)

Nützliche Ausdrücke

Kein Wunder! No wonder!
Zeig mal her. Let's see. Show it to me.

Mit anderen Worten

Verflixt nochmal! (*colloq.*) = **So ein Mist!** (Das sagt man, wenn man sich über etwas sehr ärgert.)

Spanien: adj. **spanisch**. Idiom: **Das kommt mir spanisch vor** (*It's Greek to me*). The expression recalls the elaborate customs introduced to the Habsburg court from Spain in the 16th century.

Where Is Home?

Demetra, a student from a family of foreign workers, is being interviewed for the school newspaper.

I: I'm surprised that you, as a foreigner, speak such perfect German.
D: No wonder. After all, I was born here. Many people even think I'm a German.
I: But your family comes from Greece, don't they? Where do you actually feel at home?
D: I ask myself that too. I know my way around here better, but it's clear to me that I'm not accepted by all Germans.

The Missed Birthday Party

L: Weren't you invited to Sonja's birthday party?
F: Yes I was, and I wish I had been there. But I was on vacation in Spain.
L: At least you could have phoned to congratulate her.
F: You're right. I should have done that.

In Front of the Post Office

Mr. and Mrs. Becker see a mailbox in front of the main post office.

MRS.B: You can mail your letter there.
MR.B: Just a second. Do I have enough stamps on it? Maybe I should go in and have it weighed.
MRS.B: Let me see—but the Hartmanns have moved! That's their old address.
MR.B: Darn it all! I shouldn't have forgotten that.
MRS.B: Oh, don't get upset! We'll just buy a new envelope.

Variationen

A **Persönliche Fragen**

Üb. A, 4: If students ask, **Man schickt oder bekommt *eine* E-mail.**

Telefonieren = *to use the phone, talk on the phone* (intrans.): **Es ist billiger abends zu telefonieren.**
Anrufen = *to call up, telephone* (trans.): **Rufe mich morgen vor zehn an.**

1. Der Interviewer ist überrascht, dass Demetra so perfekt Deutsch spricht. Sind Sie auch manchmal überrascht? Was hat Sie zum Beispiel an dieser Uni überrascht, als Sie hier neu waren?
2. Die junge Griechin weiß nicht genau, wo sie sich eigentlich zu Hause fühlt. Wo fühlen Sie sich zu Hause: wo Sie jetzt wohnen, wo Ihre Eltern wohnen oder wo Sie geboren sind?
3. Felix hat Sonjas Geburtstagsfeier verpasst. Haben Sie je etwas Wichtiges verpasst? Erzählen Sie davon.
4. Schreiben Sie oft Briefe? An wen? Telefonieren Sie lieber oder benutzen Sie E-mail?
5. Wo ist hier der nächste Briefkasten?
6. Gehen Sie oft zur Post? Wann gehen Sie zur Post? Was lassen Sie dort machen?

Üb. B: Write list on board as students generate it.

B **Gruppenarbeit: Reg dich nicht auf!** (Take it easy!) Manchmal regt man sich unnötig auf. In welchen Situationen regen Sie sich besonders auf? Wenn Sie etwas vergessen haben? Wenn Sie etwas Wichtiges vorhaben? Machen Sie zusammen eine Liste von solchen Situationen.

BEISPIEL: Ich rege mich auf, wenn ich ein Referat halten muss.

Üb. C: Additional vocabulary: **einen runden Geburtstag feiern** (*decimal birthday*), **Geburtstagstorte, Kerzen, Sekt.** Today one hears Germans singing "Happy Birthday" in English; more traditional is **"Hoch soll er/sie leben."**

C **Klassendiskussion: Geburtstagstraditionen** Was macht man in Ihrer Familie, wenn jemand Geburtstag hat? Gibt es bestimmte Familientraditionen? Feiern Sie zu Hause oder im Restaurant? Lädt man viele Gäste ein oder ist es nur eine kleine Feier? Darf sich das Geburtstagskind (die Person, die Geburtstag hat) sein Lieblingsessen bestellen?

Lyrik zum Vorlesen

Lab Manual Kap. 15, Lyrik zum Vorlesen.

In diesen Gedichten beschreiben zwei Lyriker ihre Gefühle als Fremde in Deutschland. Obwohl diese Lyriker nicht in Deutschland geboren sind, leben sie jetzt dort und schreiben auf Deutsch. Clara Tauchert-da Cruz ist in Portugal geboren und studierte Germanistik. Şadi Üçüncü ist in der Türkei geboren und kam 1974 zum Studium der politischen Wissenschaften nach Deutschland.

Über Grenzen

Draußen
ist es leicht
die Grenzen zu überschreiten°.

Tief drinnen°
aber
sind die eigenen Grenzen
nicht zu überwinden°.

überschreiten: cross
drinnen: within
sind ... nicht zu überwinden = can't be conquered

Zu spät
kommt die Erkenntnis° — insight
— die Heimat ist schon
verloren
und keine neue gewonnen°. — gained

Clara Tauchert-da Cruz (geboren 1938)

Integration

ich bin glücklich,
wenn du mir „Guten Tag"
oder „Hallo" sagst;

ich bin froh,
wenn du mir freundlich
begegnest°; — **mir begegnest = mich grüßt**

ich freue mich,
wenn du mich fragst:
„Wie geht es dir";

ich finde es gut,
wenn du mit mir solidarisch° — supportive
und brüderlich° bist; — **brüderlich = wie ein Bruder**

es ist sehr nett
von dir,
wenn du mir hilfst;

es ist willkommen,
wenn du mich besuchst
ab und zu°; — now and then

dann fühle ich mich
in dieser fremden Gesellschaft,
in der Du und Ich
nebeneinander, miteinander
und
füreinander
leben,
nicht mehr
als Fremder, als Ausländer.

Şadi Üçüncü (geboren 1945)

Grammatik

Talking about what could or might have happened in the past is a communicative goal.

General subjunctive: Past tense

Past subjunctive is used to talk about hypothetical or contrary-to-fact situations *in the past* (e.g., "*I would have waited* for you yesterday"). Now that you have learned how to use present-tense subjunctive, past subjunctive will prove quite easy. Its form is similar to the *perfect tense* of the indicative. The only difference is that the auxiliary verb is in the *present subjunctive* (a form of **hätten** or **wären** instead of **haben** or **sein**).

Past Subjunctive			
ich **hätte** gewartet	*I would have waited*	wir **hätten** gewartet	*we would have waited*
du **hättest** gewartet	*you would have waited*	ihr **hättet** gewartet	*you would have waited*
sie **hätte** gewartet	*she would have waited*	sie, Sie **hätten** gewartet	*they, you would have waited*
ich **wäre** gekommen	*I would have come*	wir **wären** gekommen	*we would have come*
du **wärest** gekommen	*you would have come*	ihr **wäret** gekommen	*you would have come*
er **wäre** gekommen	*he would have come*	sie, Sie **wären** gekommen	*they, you would have come*

Caution! Note that English uses the word *would* in both the present and past subjunctive, while German uses **würden** *only* in the present subjunctive, *not* in the past.

Emphasize that there is only one past tense in subjunctive. Do not teach the rare **Er würde gewartet haben** in first year (*fut. perf. subj.*).

Present	Er **würde** mitkommen.	*He **would** come along.*
Past	Er **wäre** mitgekommen.	*He **would have** come along.*

Note also that the subjunctive mood has *only this one past tense*, unlike the indicative which has three past tenses (simple past, perfect, past perfect).

Lab Manual Kap. 15, Var. zu Üb. 1, 3, 4, 7.

Workbook Kap. 15, A–D.

■ 1 ■ Übung: Aber *ich* hätte das gemacht. Ihre Professorin sagt Ihnen, was sie nicht gemacht hat. Sie sagen, dass *Sie* es gemacht hätten.

BEISPIEL: Ich habe keinen Ausflug gemacht.
Aber *ich* hätte einen Ausflug gemacht.

1. Ich habe nicht um Auskunft gebeten.
2. Ich habe Anna nicht geholfen.
3. Ich habe die Adresse nicht gewusst.
4. Ich bin nicht Ski gefahren.
5. Ich habe mir die Haare nicht gekämmt.
6. Ich bin nicht lange geblieben.
7. Ich habe den Plan nicht verstanden.
8. Ich bin nicht tanzen gegangen.
9. Ich habe mich nicht verspätet.
10. Ich habe die Briefe nicht eingeworfen.

Üb. 2: Also good as a written assignment.

■ 2 ■ Übung Wie sagt man das auf Deutsch?

1. I would have hated that.
2. Bernd wouldn't have waited.
3. We would have bought stamps.
4. I would have gotten up earlier.
5. That would have lasted a long time.
6. That would have cost too much.
7. You wouldn't have been happy.
8. I would have gotten used to it.
9. They would have stayed longer.
10. They would have shown us a double room.
11. She would have congratulated me.
12. We would have gladly flown to Greece.

Üb. 3: Have several students respond to each situation.

3 **Gruppenarbeit (Phantasiediskussion): Was hätten Sie gemacht?** Sagen Sie, was *Sie* gemacht hätten ...

- wenn Sie letzten Sommer eine Million im Lotto (*lottery*) gewonnen hätten.
- wenn Ihr Professor sich gestern das Bein gebrochen hätte.
- wenn Sie vor 100 Jahren gelebt hätten.

Deutsche Post AG

Past subjunctive of modal verbs

The past subjunctive of modal verbs is also similar to the perfect indicative tense. Because modal verbs always use **haben** as their auxiliary, their past subjunctive is formed with **hätten** plus the *double infinitive*.

Review the double-infinitive construction in perfect indicative of modals, p. 200, and in perfect tense of **lassen**, pp. 355–356.

Du **hättest** doch **anrufen können**.	*You could have called.*
Das **hätte** ich **machen sollen**.	*I should have done that.*

In English, the past subjunctive of modal verbs uses *would have, could have* or *should have*. Notice how simple and consistent German modals are compared to English.

Ich **hätte** kommen **dürfen**.	*I **would have been allowed** to come.*
Ich **hätte** kommen **können**.	*I **could have** come.*
Ich **hätte** kommen **müssen**.	*I **would have had to** come.*
Ich **hätte** kommen **sollen**.	*I **should have** come.*
Ich **hätte** kommen **wollen**.	*I **would have wanted to** come.*

Note: When the double-infinitive structure occurs in a *subordinate* clause, the inflected auxiliary (**hätte** in the sentences above) must come *before* the double infinitive.

Dependent-clause word order is presented but not drilled. This word order can always be avoided in indicative by using simple past instead of perfect: **Es stimmt, dass ich es machen musste** (*instead of*: **habe machen müssen**), but cannot be avoided in past subjunctive.

Er sagte mir, dass ich mehr Geld **hätte** wechseln sollen

Ich fragte, wie ich das **hätte** wissen sollen

This is the *only* case in German where the inflected verb is not in final position in a subordinate clause.

4 **Übung: Das hätten Sie machen sollen** Ihr Professor hat vergessen viele wichtige Dinge zu machen. Sagen Sie ihm, er hätte sie machen sollen.

BEISPIEL: Ich habe vergessen meinen Regenschirm mitzubringen.
Sie hätten ihn doch mitbringen sollen.

1. Ich habe vergessen mein Bett zu machen.
2. Ich habe vergessen meine Bücher mitzubringen.
3. Ich habe vergessen meine Frau anzurufen.
4. Ich habe vergessen eine Zeitung zu kaufen.
5. Ich habe vergessen das Fenster zu schließen.
6. Ich habe vergessen den Witz zu erzählen.

Üb. 5: Also good as a written assignment.

■ 5 ■ Übung Wie sagt man das auf Deutsch?

1. We could have flown.
2. We would have had to buy tickets.
3. Frank should have come along.
4. He wouldn't have wanted to come along.
5. He wouldn't have been allowed to come along.

Üb. 6: Have several students respond to each situation.

■ 6 ■ Gruppenarbeit (Phantasiediskussion): Was hätten Sie machen müssen? Was hätten Sie machen müssen ...

- wenn Sie heute zu spät aufgestanden wären?
- wenn Sie Ihren Bus verpasst hätten?
- wenn Ihr Wagen kaputt gewesen wäre?
- wenn Sie sich das Bein gebrochen hätten?

■ 7 ■ Gruppenarbeit: Ich wünschte, ich hätte das nicht gemacht. Als Kinder haben wir alle viel gemacht, was wir lieber nicht gemacht hätten. Sagen Sie, was Sie lieber gemacht oder nicht gemacht hätten.

BEISPIELE: Ich wünschte, ich hätte meine ältere Schwester nicht so oft geärgert.
Ich wünschte, ich hätte mehr Klavier geübt.
Ich wünschte, ich wäre ...

At some point while working on passive, you may want to explain difference between "statal passive" and true passive, an issue for second year: **Die Fenster sind geschlossen** (*statal passive*: windows are in a closed state). **Die Fenster werden geschlossen** (*true passive*: windows are in *process* of being closed).

Passive voice

Compare the following sentences:

Die meisten Studenten lesen diesen Roman.	*Most students read this novel.*
Dieser Roman wird von den meisten Studenten gelesen.	*This novel is read by most students.*

Both sentences say essentially the same thing, but the first is in the *active voice* while the second is in the *passive voice*. The passive voice is used to emphasize that something is being *acted upon* (the *novel* is being read) rather than to emphasize the agent performing that action (the *students* are reading it).

In active sentences, the grammatical subject is also the agent or performer of the action.

Die Studenten lesen. — *The students read.*

In passive sentences, the grammatical subject is the *object* of the action.

Der Roman wird gelesen. — *The novel is read.*

Every passive sentence can be thought of as the transformation of an active sentence *with a transitive verb and a direct object*. The direct object (*acc.*) of the active sentence becomes the *subject* (*nom.*) of the passive sentence.

Since passive voice emphasizes the thing acted upon, most passive sentences do not express the agent at all. For passive sentences with an agent, see p. 440.

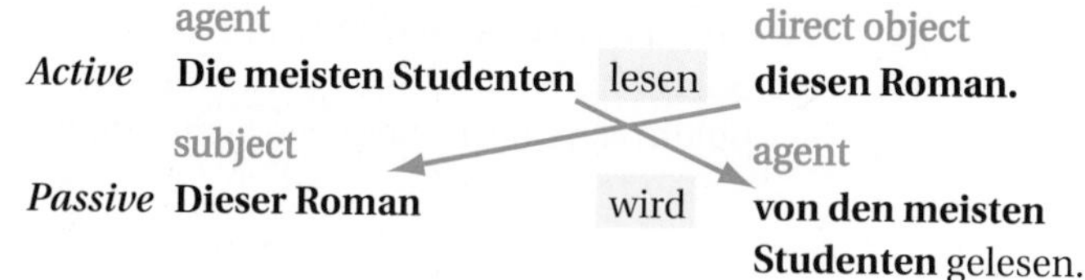
agent
direct object
Active **Die meisten Studenten** lesen **diesen Roman.**
subject
agent
Passive **Dieser Roman** wird **von den meisten Studenten** gelesen.

■ Formation of the German passive voice

The passive voice in English consists of the auxiliary verb *to be* plus a past participle.

Active voice	→ *Passive voice*	aux.	part.
They see him.	→ *He*	**is**	**seen**.
We never do that.	→ *That*	**is** *never*	**done**.
They drank coffee.	→ *Coffee*	**was**	**drunk**.

The passive voice in German consists of the auxiliary verb **werden** plus a past participle.

Active voice	→ *Passive voice*	aux.	part.
Sie sehen ihn.	→ Er	**wird**	**gesehen**.
Wir machen das nie.	→ Das	**wird** nie	**gemacht**.
Man trank Kaffee.	→ Kaffee	**wurde**	**getrunken**.

Here is a table showing the formation of all tenses of **gesehen werden** (*to be seen*).

Emphasize passive infinitive, since students need to understand it in order to use modal verbs in passive sentences.

Passive Voice		
passive infinitive	**gesehen** werden	*to be* ***seen***
present	Er wird **gesehen**.	*He is* ***seen***.
past	Er wurde **gesehen**.	*He was* ***seen***.
future	Er wird **gesehen** werden.	*He will be* ***seen***.
perfect	Er ist **gesehen** worden.	*He has been* ***seen***.
		or:
		He was ***seen***.
past perfect	Er war **gesehen** worden.	*He had been* ***seen***.

Use Appendix 2, pp. 486–487, to review the past participles of strong transitive verbs.

Note:

- In both German and English passive, the past participle (**gesehen**/*seen*) appears in all tenses. The auxiliary verb (**werden**/*to be*) is conjugated.
- The normal past participle of **werden** (**geworden**) is contracted to **worden** in the perfect tenses of the passive voice.
- The German passive infinitive is in the reverse order of English.

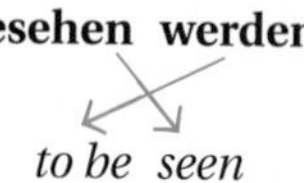
gesehen werden
to be seen

You should be able to understand the two passive structures in this advertisement.

Drill uses of **werden**: It's getting dark. The letter got mailed. We shall go to a concert. We were (got) surprised. We won't see you.

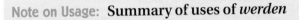

Note on Usage: Summary of uses of *werden*

Be careful not to confuse the three uses of **werden**.

- As main verb = *become, get*

  Sie **wird** alt. *She's **getting** old.*

- As auxiliary verb for future tense: **werden** + *infinitive*

  Sie **wird** sehen. *She **will** see.*

- As auxiliary verb for passive voice: **werden** + *past participle*

  Sie **wird** gesehen. *She **is** seen.*

Lab Manual Kap. 15, Üb. 9, 12, and Var. zu Üb. 8, 10.

Workbook Kap. 15, E–G.

Üb. 8, 9, 10: Each of these sentences in active voice has a personal pronoun or **man** as subject. These pronoun subjects disappear in the passive voice. Do not try to express agent in these passive sentences.

Üb. 8–10: Also good as written exercises to reinforce passive structures.

8 Übung Change the sentences from the active to the passive. Be careful to keep the same tense as in the active sentence.

Present tense

1. Man liest diese Romane oft.
2. Morgens kaufen wir die Zeitung.
3. Bei uns sieht man nicht viele Deutsche.
4. Ich rufe meine Eltern jedes Wochenende an.
5. Man versteht mich nicht!
6. Wir feiern morgen deinen Geburtstag.
7. Wir räumen die Schlafzimmer jeden Samstag auf.
8. Ich schicke dieses Paket nach Australien.

Simple past tense

9. Im 18. Jahrhundert schrieb man viele Briefe.
10. In der ganzen Welt las man seinen ersten Roman.
11. Man zeigte den Film in jedem Kino.
12. Man kaufte viele Bananen.

Future tense

13. Was wird man sagen?
14. Man wird dieses Wahlplakat nicht sehen.
15. Man wird neue Wohnungen für die Armen bauen.
16. Man wird dieses Thema besprechen.

Perfect tense

17. Man hat die alte Wohnung verkauft.
18. Man hat die Briefe eingeworfen.
19. Man hat den jungen Künstler eingeladen.
20. Man hat unsere Umwelt verschmutzt.

■ 9 ■ **Übung: Das wird sofort gemacht!** Sie sind Hotelangestellte/r. Ihre Professorin ist Gast im Hotel und bittet Sie etwas für sie zu machen. Sie sagen, alles wird sofort gemacht.

BEISPIEL: Können Sie mir bitte diese Uhr reparieren?
Ja, sie wird sofort repariert!

1. Können Sie mir bitte einen Brief einwerfen?
2. Können Sie mir bitte einen Tisch reservieren?
3. Können Sie mir bitte die Schuhe putzen?
4. Können Sie mir bitte das Zimmer aufräumen?
5. Können Sie mir bitte meine Kleider aufhängen?
6. Können Sie mir bitte das Bett machen?
7. Können Sie mir bitte das Frühstück bringen?
8. Können Sie mir bitte ein Taxi bestellen?

Welches Haus wurde früher gebaut? Fachwerk- (*half-timbered*) und modernes Einfamilienhaus

■ Passive voice with a modal verb

Often you need to say that something *must* be done, *should* be done, *can* be done, or *may* be done. In such cases, you must use the modal verb with the passive voice. Just keep in mind that the dependent infinitive is the two-word *passive infinitive* (e.g., **getan werden**) rather than the one-word active infinitive (**tun**).

Active	Er musste es **tun**.	*He had to do it.*
Passive	Es musste **getan werden.**	*It had to be done.*

Here is a table showing the formation of all tenses of a modal verb with the passive voice.

Passive with a Modal Verb		
present	Das muss **getan werden**.	*That has **to be done**.*
past	Das musste **getan werden**.	*That had **to be done**.*
future	Das wird **getan werden** müssen.	*That will have **to be done**.*
perfect	Das hat **getan werden** müssen.	*That had **to be done**.*
past perfect	Das hatte **getan werden** müssen.	*That had had **to be done**.*

Note: The modal verb is inflected. The passive infinitive remains unchanged throughout all tenses.

■ 10 ■ Übung Change the sentences from active to passive voice. Be sure to use the same tense as in the active sentence.

Future and the perfect tenses of modal verbs with the passive are not drilled.

Present

1. Wir müssen die Wohnung aufräumen.
2. Wir müssen noch den Wein kaufen.
3. Du darfst deine Freunde einladen.
4. Ich muss Oma nach Hause bringen.
5. Ich soll diese Briefe wiegen.

Past

6. Man musste die Fenster schließen.
7. Man musste die Kinder abholen.
8. Man konnte das Mädchen nicht interviewen.
9. Man durfte nichts kochen.
10. Ich durfte diesen Witz nicht erzählen.

■ 11 ■ Gruppenarbeit: Was muss gemacht werden? ***(Mit offenen Büchern)*** Sie diskutieren, was gemacht werden muss, um die Umwelt zu retten. Unten sind einige Möglichkeiten zum Kombinieren, aber Sie sollen auch Ihre eigenen Ideen benutzen.

BEISPIEL: Der Müll muss zum Recycling gebracht werden.

der Müll	schließen
das Altglas	finden
Alternativen	organisieren
Atomkraftwerke	zum Recycling bringen
Demonstrationen	ändern
unser Denken	bauen
umweltfreundliche Autos	sammeln

■ Passive voice with an agent

Most passive sentences make no mention of the agent performing the action.

Diese Häuser wurden sehr schnell gebaut.	*These houses were built very quickly.*
Das wird oft gesagt.	*That is often said.*

When the person performing the action *is* mentioned, **von** + *dative* is used.

Diese Häuser wurden **von türkischen Gastarbeitern** gebaut.	*These houses were built by Turkish foreign workers.*
Das wird **von vielen Menschen** gesagt.	*That is said by many people.*

Üb. 12: Also good as written homework.

■ 12 ■ Übung Restate the following sentences in the passive. Use the same tense as in the active sentence.

BEISPIEL: Meine Freundin liest jetzt den Roman.
Der Roman wird jetzt von meiner Freundin gelesen.

1. Fast alle Physikstudenten belegen dieses Seminar.
2. Viele deutsche Schüler tragen gern Turnschuhe.
3. Unser Professor empfahl dieses Buch.
4. Alle Schüler in der Schweiz müssen Fremdsprachen lernen.
5. Michael hat mich eingeladen.
6. Die Gruppe hat das Referat besprochen.
7. Mein Freund hat die Gäste abgeholt.
8. Die Kinder singen immer dieses Lied.
9. Der Gepäckträger schleppte den Koffer zum Taxi.
10. Die ganze Familie feiert Omas Geburtstag.

■ 13 ■ Übung: Von wem? Sagen Sie, von wem diese verschiedenen Dinge gemacht werden (oder gemacht wurden).

BEISPIEL: Von wem werden Brötchen gebacken?
Sie werden vom Bäcker gebacken.

1. Von wem wird das Essen im Restaurant gebracht?
2. Von wem werden Autos repariert?
3. Von wem werden Romane geschrieben?
4. Von wem wurde die Psychoanalyse gegründet?
5. Von wem wurde „Hamlet" geschrieben?
6. Von wem wurde Beethovens Neunte Symphonie komponiert?
7. Von wem wird eine Vorlesung an der Uni gehalten?
8. Von wem werden Zeitungsartikel geschrieben?

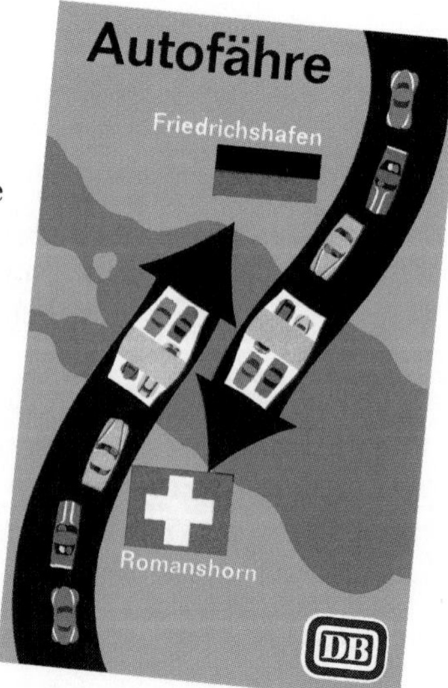

The present participle

To form the present participle (English: *sleep**ing***, *read**ing***, etc.) of a German verb, simply add **-d** to the infinitive.

schlafend	*sleeping*
feiernd	*celebrating*
denkend	*thinking*
lesend	*reading*

Remember that past participles can also be used as adjectives. See p. 327.

The present participle is used

- as an attributive adjective with the standard adjective endings:

Wir wollen das **schlafende** Kind nicht stören.	*We don't want to disturb the sleeping child.*
Lesen Sie die **folgenden** Seiten.	*Read the following pages.*

- occasionally as an adverb:

Das Kind lief **weinend** ins Zimmer.	*The child ran into the room crying.*

If students are confused, remind them that there is no German equivalent to English present progressive tense; *The child is sleeping* = **Das Kind schläft**.

The German present participle is *not* used as a verbal noun. German uses the infinitive for this purpose: *No Parking* = **Parken verboten** (see p. 202).

Lab Manual Kap. 15, Üb. 14.

Workbook Kap. 15, H.

Üb. 14: Two possibilities for no. 3: **Die wachsende Arbeitslosigkeit ... / ... ein wachsendes Problem.**

■ 14 ■ Übung Add the present participle of the cued verb as an adjective to each sentence.

BEISPIEL: Wir können die Preise nicht mehr zahlen. (steigen)
Wir können die steigenden Preise nicht mehr zahlen.

1. Jeder Mensch weiß das. (denken)
2. Was meinen die Politiker? (führen)
3. Die Arbeitslosigkeit ist ein Problem. (wachsen)
4. Sie hörte die Kinder. (lachen)
5. Bitte stören Sie meinen Mitbewohner nicht. (schlafen)

Directional prefixes: hin- *and* her-

German has two separable prefixes that combine with verbs of motion to show whether that motion is *toward the speaker* (**her-**) or *away from the speaker* (**hin-**). You are already familiar with these directional indicators from the question words **woher**? (*from where*?) and **wohin**? (*to where*?).

Können wir nicht **hin**fahren?	*Can't we go **there**?*
Komm doch mal **her**.	*Come **here** a minute.*
Wie komme ich (da)**hin**?	*How do I get **there**?*

Recall Herr Becker's line in the third dialogue, p. 429: **Vielleicht sollte ich hineingehen ...**

These directional indicators are often used in combination with other separable prefixes that indicate direction. Two sets of these are **auf und unter** (*up and down*) and **ein und aus** (*in and out*). The two elements combine to make one separable prefix that can be attached to any verb of motion.

hinausgehen

herauskommen

hereinkommen

hineingehen

heraufsteigen

hinuntergehen

Notice that the preposition **in** becomes the prefix **ein**: **hineingehen** = *to go in.*

The prefixes **hin-** and **her-** must be used when the sentence does not contain a directional phrase such as **in die Post** or **ins Haus**. It is *incorrect* to say „Gehen wir ein." Correct is: **Gehen wir hinein.**[1]

1. Even when a prepositional phrase is used, the directional prefixes are sometimes added:

Er ist aus dem Haus **heraus**gekommen.	*He came **out** of the house.*
Sie ging in die Kirche **hinein**.	*She went **into** the church.*

In spoken German, both directional prefixes are often replaced by initial **'r: Raus mit dir! Gehen wir rein/rauf/runter.**

Da ist die Hauptpost. Gehen wir **hinein**.	*There's the main post office. Let's go in.*
Draußen scheint die Sonne. Gehen wir **hinaus**.	*The sun is shining outside. Let's go out.*

Note: When someone knocks at the door, Germans simply say

Herein!	*Come in!*

Workbook Kap. 15, I.

In spoken German, both directional prefixes are often replaced by initial **'r: Raus mit dir! Gehen wir rein / rauf / runter.**

■ **15** ■ **Gruppenarbeit: Gehen wir hinein!** Complete these sentences by filling in the missing words.

You're standing ***outside*** *the house.*

1. Gehen wir ________ . (*in*)
2. Karl, komm doch ________ ! (*out*)
3. Anna ist vor einer Minute ________ . (*gone in*)
4. Bald kommen die Kinder aus dem Haus ________ . (*out*)

You're standing ***inside*** *the house.*

5. Kommt Grete bald ________ ? (*in*)
6. Es ist so schön, ich möchte jetzt ________ . (*go out*)
7. Wir sollten alle ________ . (*go out*)
8. (*Es klingelt.*) ________ ! (*"Come in!"*)

You're standing ***at the top*** *of the steps.*

9. Warum kommt ihr nicht ________ ? (*up*)
10. Jörg ist gerade ________ . (*gone down*)

You're standing ***at the bottom*** *of the steps.*

11. Susi, ich brauche Hilfe! Komm mal schnell ________ ! (*down here*)
12. Ich bin jetzt müde. Ich gehe ________ und lege mich aufs Bett. (*up*)

■ **16** ■ **Partnerarbeit: Wo kommt sie her? Wo geht er hin?** Beschreiben Sie, was diese Menschen machen.

Vor dem Lesen

Tipps zum Lesen und Lernen

■ Tipps zum Vokabelnlernen

***German equivalents for* to think** The English verb *to think* has several meanings, for which German has various verbs (rather than just one). You have already learned most of these verbs as separate vocabulary items.

- When *think = to have an opinion,* use **glauben**, **meinen**, or **finden**.

Ich **finde** das toll.	*I think that's great.*
Ich **meine**, das stimmt nicht.	*I think that's incorrect.*
Ich **glaube** schon.	*I think so.*
Ich **glaube** nicht.	*I don't think so.*

- When *think = to think of, keep in mind,* use **denken an**.

Er **dachte an** seine Jugend.	*He was thinking of his youth.*
Denken Sie **an** die anderen.	*Think of the others.*

In contemporary colloquial usage, **denken** is frequently used as a synonym for **meinen**.

- When *think = to think x is . . ., to take x for . . .,* use **halten für**.

Ich **hielt** sie **für** eine Deutsche.	*I thought she was a German.*
Ich **halte** das **für** zu schwer.	*I think that's too difficult.*

Synonyms for **halten für**: Ich **finde** das zu schwer. Ich **meine**, das ist zu schwer.

- When *think = to think about, ponder,* use **sich etwas überlegen**.

Das muss ich mir **überlegen**.	*I have to think about that.*
Ich werde mir die Alternativen **überlegen**.	*I'll think about the alternatives.*

Answers: 1. Ich denke oft an dich. 2. Ich halte sie für/Ich finde sie eine gute Ärztin. 3. Was meinst *du*? 4. Ich muss mir die Antwort überlegen. 5. Ich finde das/halte das für eine tolle Idee. 6. Hältst du mich für/Meinst du, ich bin verrückt? 7. Ich glaube nicht./Das finde ich nicht.

■ ■ ■ Übung: Wie sagt man das auf Deutsch?

1. I often think of you.
2. I think she's a good doctor.
3. What do *you* think?
4. I have to think about the answer.
5. I think that's a great idea!
6. Do you think I'm crazy?
7. I don't think so.

Lab Manual Kap. 15, Üb. zur Betonung.

■ Leicht zu merken

die **Anekdote, -n**	Anekdote
die **Arroganz**	Arroganz
die **Klinik, -en**	
die **Nationalität, -en**	Nationalität

Einstieg in den Text

Other passive constructions in lines 28–29, 33, 34–35.

Recognizing the passive voice in context The following text contains four passive constructions. You will recognize them by the fact that they all have some form of **werden** plus a past participle. Here is the first occurrence of passive voice (l. 7):

... der wegen seiner Nationalität nicht überall akzeptiert wird.

As you encounter the others, jot them down and make sure you understand them.

Leitfragen Im folgenden Lesestück beschreibt der Autor – ein Türke, der in Deutschland lebt –, was er eines Tages in einem Zugabteil erlebte (*experienced*). Die deutschen Mitreisenden halten ihn für einen Deutschen. Wenn dann ein „richtiger" Türke ins Abteil will, ist ihre Reaktion ganz anders. Die Sprache dieser Anekdote ist relativ einfach und direkt, aber auch witzig. Suchen Sie Antworten auf die folgenden Fragen, während Sie lesen:

1. Warum fühlt sich der Autor als Türke, obwohl er in Deutschland lebt und arbeitet?
2. Welche Klischees über die Türken und die Deutschen finden Sie in dieser Anekdote?
3. Was ist der Unterschied zwischen dem Erzähler und dem „richtigen" Türken? Zum Beispiel, wie sehen diese zwei Türken aus?

Wortschatz 2

Verben

an·schauen to look at
diskutieren to discuss
kontrollieren to check, inspect
schreien, schrie, hat geschrien to shout, yell
teil·nehmen (nimmt teil), nahm teil, hat teilgenommen an (+ *dat.*) to take part in
sich unterhalten (unterhält), unterhielt, hat sich unterhalten (mit) to converse with, talk to

Anschauen and its synonym **ansehen** = *to look at.* Contrast **sich etwas ansehen** = *to take a (good) look at something.*

Substantive

der **Pass, ¨-e** passport
der **Türke, -n, -n** Turk (*m.*)
das **Abteil, -e** railway compartment
das **Thema,** *pl.* **Themen** topic, subject, theme
(das) **Türkisch** Turkish (language)
die **Fahrt, -en** trip, ride
die **Türkei** Turkey
die **Türkin, -nen** Turk (*f.*)
die **Tüte, -n** (paper, plastic) bag

Die Türkei takes article, like **die Schweiz: Wir fahren in *die* Türkei. Er kommt aus *der* Türkei.**

Adjektive

angenehm pleasant
richtig true; real
türkisch Turkish

Andere Vokabel

so ein (*demonstrative*) such a

Gegensätze

angenehm ≠ unangenehm pleasant ≠ unpleasant
richtig ≠ falsch correct ≠ incorrect

Wer ist ein Türke?

Lab Manual Kap. 15, Lesestück.

Şinasi Dikmen ist 1945 in Ladik/Samsun in der Türkei geboren. Er besuchte in der Heimat eine Berufsschule für Gesundheitswesen°. Er arbeitete vier Jahre als Gesundheitsberater° in der Türkei. Dikmen lebt seit 1972 in der BRD. Dort arbeitete er zunächst als Fachkrankenpfleger° auf der chirurgischen° Intensivstation der Universitäts-Kliniken Ulm. Heute ist er freier Schriftsteller°.

In der folgenden Anekdote schreibt Dikmen mit Humor über ein ernstes soziales Thema. Als Ausländer, der wegen seiner Nationalität nicht überall akzeptiert wird, muss er sich fragen, was es denn bedeutet, ein Türke in Deutschland zu sein.

health professions
health consultant
nurse-specialist / surgical
freier ... = free-lance writer

Dikmen berichtet in heiterem Ton von Vorurteilen gegen Ausländer. Der **Almanach** (S. 454) behandelt (*treats*) die ernste Seite dieses Themas.

Wer ist ein Türke? Wie erkennt° man ihn, woher weiß man, ob jemand ein Türke ist? Diese Fragen beschäftigen° mich, seit ich in Deutschland bin. (...) Viele glauben, ein Türke sei[1] der°, der einen schwarzen Schnurrbart° und einen türkischen Pass hat. Es gibt in Europa aber viele Türken, die keinen türkischen Pass haben, darunter sogar etliche, denen gar der Schnurrbart fehlt°. Nichtsdestoweniger° sind es[2] Türken, denn sie sprechen Türkisch. Viele von ihnen sprechen aber auch Deutsch. Sind es[2] darum Deutsche? (...)

Ich bin in der Türkei geboren, mit türkischer Erziehung° aufgewachsen. Meine Eltern sind Türken wie meine Geschwister und meine Verwandten. Ich habe die türkische Schule besucht, als türkischer Gastarbeiter bin ich nach Deutschland gekommen, als Türke habe ich mich beim Ausländeramt gemeldet°. Meine Krankenversicherung°, meine Rente° und meine Autoversicherung° laufen unter der Nationalität „Türke" und ich spreche mit meinen Kindern, soweit° es möglich ist, zu Hause Türkisch, ich liebe türkisch°, ich hasse türkisch, ich esse türkisch (...), und ich glaubte fest daran, dass° ich ein Türke sei° – bis mir dieser Vorfall° passierte.

Vor zwei Jahren nahm ich an einer Lesung° in Hameln teil und stieg in Hannover in den Zug Richtung° Ulm.[3] Es war eine gute Lesung in Hameln. Das Publikum° war nett, wir unterhielten uns angenehm, diskutierten über die Situation der Türken und über die Deutschen, über Gott und die Welt°. Nach der Lesung gingen wir in ein griechisches Lokal, wo wir fast türkisch aßen. Am nächsten Tag wurde ich von einer Dame bis zum Bahnhof in Hannover gefahren. Ich betrat° ein Abteil, in dem nur ein älteres Ehepaar saß. Ich fragte sie höflich, ob ein Platz frei sei°, und sie antworteten höflich, ja, bitte; ich setzte mich hin, schlug „Die Zeit"[4] auf° und tat, was in Deutschland bei einer solchen° Fahrt verlangt° wird, nämlich° schweigen, schweigen, schweigen, nie etwas fragen, solange° du selbst nicht gefragt wirst. (...)

recognize
concern
sei der = ist jeder Mann / moustache
darunter ... = among them even many who have no moustache / **nichtsdestoweniger = trotzdem**
upbringing

habe ... = registered with the Resident Alien Office /
health insurance / pension /
car insurance / as far as
türkisch (*adv.*) = **als Türke**
glaubte ... = firmly believed that / = **war** / incident /
reading / in the direction of /
Publikum = Menschen, die zur Lesung gekommen waren / über Gott und die Welt = über alles
= ging in . . . hinein
= war
schlug ... auf = machte ... auf
einer solchen = such a / required / namely / as long as

1. **sei** (line 11): special subjunctive form of **sein** used to report speech and thoughts indirectly (= *is* or *was*).
2. **sind es Türken ... Sind es Deutsche?** The singular pronoun **es** used with plural **sind** is parallel to the phrase **das sind** (*those are*) and refers to people collectively.
3. **Hameln, Hannover**: Städte in Niedersachsen. Dikmen wohnt in **Ulm**.
4. **Die Zeit**: weekly newspaper with educated readership.

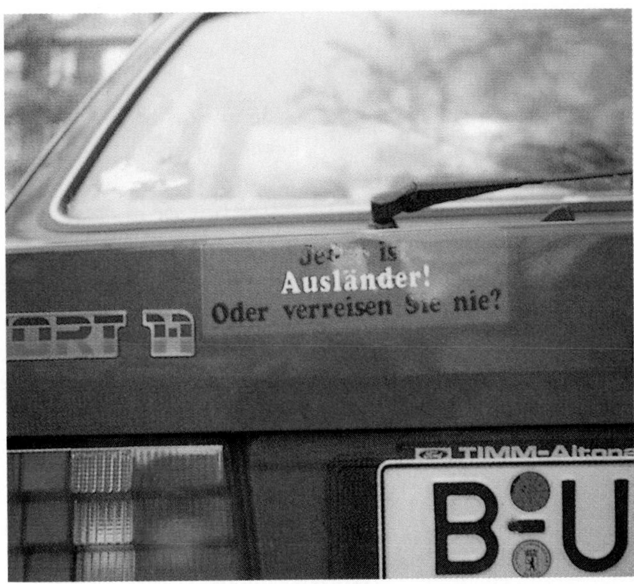

Autoaufkleber in Berlin

Ich (...) las weiter „Die Zeit", stellte niemandem Fragen, wurde auch nichts gefragt. (...) In Fulda[1] stieg ein richtiger Türke zu°, fragte das Ehepaar kurz und knapp°: „Frei?" Bevor er ausgesprochen hatte, schrie die Dame schon: „Nein, nichts frei!" Der Türke, klein, gedrungen°, mit handgestrickter Weste°, grün, ich würde sagen, Türkengrün[2], in beiden Händen Plastiktüten, ging nach dieser barschen° Antwort weiter.

Ich schaute ihn an, er schaute mich an, so als frage er°, hier sind doch drei Plätze frei; ich hatte das alles nicht richtig mitbekommen°, so schnell ging es. Der Zug war, soviel° ich sehen konnte, voll. Der Türke stellte sich genau vor unsere Tür – wie zum Trotz°. Ich fragte die Dame: „Hier sind doch noch drei Plätze frei. Warum sagten Sie dem Mann, dass nichts frei sei°?" Wie stets°, wenn Deutsche sich gegenseitig° taxieren°, antwortete die Dame mit einer Stimme, die zwar höflich war, aber° vom Gesprächspartner Abstand verlangte°, dass sie mit so einem Typen[3] nicht zusammen in einem Abteil fahren möchte.

Ich hakte nach°: „Was meinen Sie mit Typen? Mit einem türkischen Typen? Woher wissen Sie, dass er ein Türke ist?" „Das merkt man doch gleich", antwortete sie, ich solle° mal richtig hinschauen°, dieser finstere Blick° und diese Arroganz. Ich erwiderte°: „Der Mann hat doch nur höflich gefragt." „Das meinen Sie! Ich aber kenne diese Türkenblicke°!" Nein, ich könne° von der Dame nicht verlangen°, dass sie sich die Fahrt durch die Anwesenheit° eines Türken verderbe°. Sie möchte auf keinen Fall° mit einem Türken im Abteil sitzen. Ich ließ nicht locker°: „Sie fahren aber mit einem Türken im Abteil." „Nein", sagte sie, „nein, der ist mein Mann, ich fahre nicht und ich werde auch nicht fahren." „Doch, Sie fahren mit einem Türken, und zwar° mit mir!" Sie wusste zunächst nicht, was sie sagen sollte. Sie schaute ihren Mann an, bat ihn um Hilfe, aber der verlor kein Wort°, er kontrollierte seine Fußspitze°, tat so, als höre er nichts°. (...)

1. **Fulda**: Stadt im Bundesland Hessen.
2. **Türkengrün**: Wortspiel auf **Türkisgrün** (*turquoise*). Dieser Stein wurde zuerst in der Türkei gefunden.
3. Alternative usage of **Typ** as N-noun.

Niemandem (l. 34): If students ask, **niemand** has optional endings in the oblique cases.

ll. 35–38: Students may not be familiar with the stereotype of a „**richtiger**" **Türke** with his belongings in plastic bags instead of suitcases.

stieg ... zu = stieg auch ein

kurz und knapp = ohne viele Worte / stocky / hand-knit vest

= **unhöflich**

so ... = as if to ask

= **verstanden**

as far as

zum Trotz = out of defiance

= **ist** / = **immer** / = **einander**

"check out" / **zwar ... aber** = to be sure . . . but / **Abstand verlangte = Distanz erwartete** / **hakte nach** = followed up

= **sollte** / take a look / **finsterer Blick** = scowl / **erwiderte = antwortete** / "the way the Turks look at you" / = **konnte** / = **erwarten** / presence / ruin / **auf ... = nie** / **ließ ...** = didn't let up / namely

verlor ... = sagte nichts / tip of his foot / **tat ...** = acted as if he didn't hear anything

ll. 45–46: Help students with syntax of main clause: **antwortete die Dame ... dass sie ...**

„Ich bin aber Türke, und Sie fahren leider mit einem Türken zusammen." „Sie können doch kein Türke sein." „Warum nicht?" „Nur so°." „Ich bin Türke, soll ich Ihnen meinen Pass zeigen?" „Das brauchen Sie nicht, weil Sie kein Türke sind." "Warum sind Sie so sicher?" „Erstens°, ja, hmm, erstens, ich weiß nicht, aber, hmm, Sie sind auf alle Fälle kein° Türke." „Warum nicht?" „Weil, hmm, weil, wie soll ich sagen, hmm, weil Sie ‚Die Zeit' lesen."

"Just because."

first of all

auf ... = gar kein

Ich weiß nicht, wie viele „Zeit"-Leser es in Deutschland gibt, einhundert-, zweihundert-, drei-, vier-, fünfhunderttausend oder eine Million. In Deutschland leben 60 Millionen vermeintliche° Deutsche. Da nicht alle „Die Zeit" lesen, denke ich, dass die Deutschen, die keine „Zeit" lesen, keine Deutschen sind, sondern Türken.

putative, supposed

Nach dem Lesen

■ A ■ Antworten Sie auf Deutsch.

1. Wann und wo ist Şinasi Dikmen geboren?
2. Was hat er als Beruf gelernt? Wo wohnt er jetzt?
3. Was halten viele Deutsche für „typisch türkisch"?
4. Was identifiziert den Autor als Türken?
5. Was für einen Eindruck macht das deutsche Ehepaar im Abteil auf Dikmen? Was für einen Eindruck macht er auf sie?
6. Was hält er für „typisch deutsch"?
7. Warum wird der „richtige Türke" von der deutschen Dame nicht akzeptiert?
8. Warum hält die Dame den Autor für einen Deutschen?
9. Wo finden Sie Humor im Text? Geben Sie ein paar Beispiele.

Designate groups of 3 on day before doing this in class. Have students bring in interesting props to initiate conversation. You may assign students identities and specific props, e.g., first two are students from abroad on vacation, third is a musician carrying an instrument on his way to a concert. Other possible props: foreign-language newspaper or book, loaf of bread, small suitcase, stuffed animal, tennis racquet.

■ B ■ Rollenspiel: Begegnung [encounter] **im Zugabteil** ***(3 Personen)*** Zwei Personen sitzen im Zugabteil. Eine dritte Person kommt herein, fragt, ob hier ein Platz frei ist, und setzt sich. Die neue Person hat etwas Interessantes in der Hand und die ersten zwei fangen ein Gespräch mit der dritten Person an. Sprechen Sie zirka fünf Minuten zusammen und lernen Sie einander so gut wie möglich kennen.

Situationen aus dem Alltag

Refer to p. 179 for furniture vocabulary.

This vocabulary focuses on an everyday topic or situation. Your instructor may assign some supplementary vocabulary for active mastery.

If students don't notice, point out separate lavatory (**die Toilette, das Klosett**) and bath (**das Bad**). Bath might also contain shower. Living room in the rear, opening onto back garden.

■ Wohnen und Wohnungen

Hier ist der Grundriss (*floorplan*) vom Erdgeschoss einer typischen deutschen Wohnung. Wahrscheinlich gibt es auch noch einen ersten Stock mit mehr Schlafzimmern. Wie ist diese deutsche Wohnung anders als eine amerikanische? In Deutschland gibt es zum Beispiel keine eingebauten Schränke (*built-in closets*) wie in Amerika, sondern man hat einen großen Kleiderschrank (*wardrobe*) im Schlafzimmer. Merken Sie andere Unterschiede?

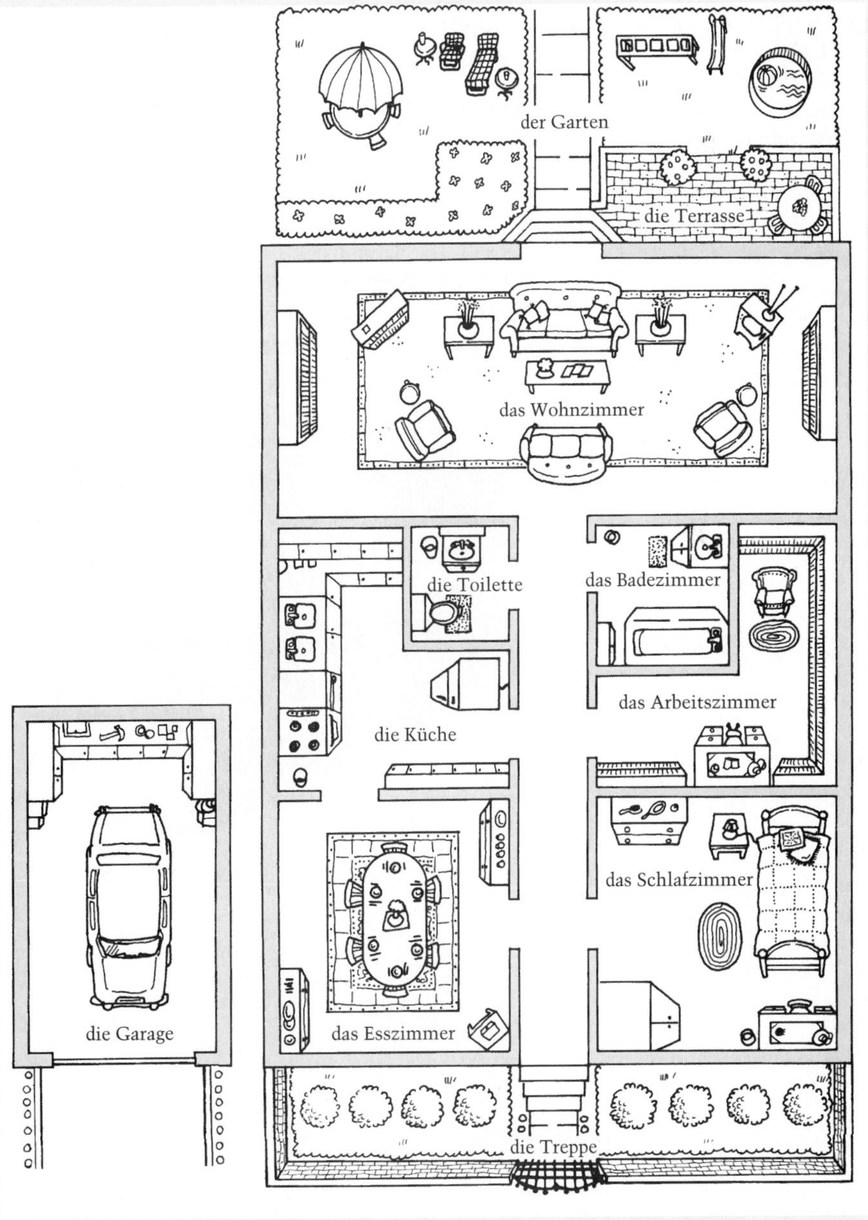

der Garten
die Terrasse
das Wohnzimmer
die Toilette
das Badezimmer
das Arbeitszimmer
die Küche
das Schlafzimmer
die Garage
das Esszimmer
die Treppe

Sentences 1–3 use passive.

■ **A** ■ **Übung: Zimmernamen** Um diese Übung zu machen müssen Sie zuerst die Namen der Zimmer wissen.

1. Wo wird das Essen gekocht?
2. Wo wird das Auto geparkt?
3. Wo werden Referate, Briefe usw. geschrieben?
4. Wo könnte man fernsehen und die Zeitung lesen?
5. Wo spielen die Kinder bei schönem Wetter?
6. Wo putzt man sich die Zähne?
7. Wo schläft man?
8. Wo nimmt man ein Bad?
9. Wo isst die Familie zusammen?
10. Wo könnte man bei gutem Wetter sitzen und Kaffee trinken?

Partnerarbeit: Model this first with one student. Be playful: **Du hast im Schlafzimmer endlich aufgeräumt!** Stress: **hinein, heraus, Treppe hinauf und hinunter, zum Garten hinaus**.

■ **B** ■ **Partnerarbeit: Ich möchte dir unsere Wohnung zeigen.** Partner A zeigt Partner B seine Wohnung.

A: Komm bitte herein. Gehen wir zuerst ins Esszimmer.
B: Oh, wie schön! Was ist denn das in der Ecke?

Gruppenarbeit: These topics can be assigned as written work after having been discussed in class.

■ **C** ■ **Gruppenarbeit: Zur Diskussion**

1. Wie wohnen Sie zu Hause? Beschreiben Sie das Haus oder die Wohnung Ihrer Familie.
2. Wie würde Ihr Traumhaus aussehen? Beschreiben Sie es.

Zum Schluss

Sprechen wir miteinander!

Lab Manual Kap. 15, Diktat.

Workbook Kap. 15, J–L.

A **Partnerarbeit: Was hättest du lieber gemacht?** In den Sommerferien hat man nie genug Zeit alles zu machen, was man machen möchte. Sagen Sie einander zuerst, was Sie letzten Sommer gemacht haben, und dann was Sie lieber gemacht hätten.

BEISPIEL: Ich musste den ganzen Tag im Büro arbeiten, aber ich hätte lieber eine lange Radtour gemacht.

B **Gruppenarbeit: Was hätten Sie gemacht, wenn ...** So ist es *nicht* gewesen, aber es hätte anders sein können. Was hätten Sie gemacht, ...

1. wenn Sie dieses Semester nicht studiert hätten?
2. wenn Sie letztes Jahr eine Million Dollar gewonnen hätten?
3. wenn Sie vor 10 000 Jahren gelebt hätten?
4. wenn Sie Beethoven gewesen wären?
5. wenn Sie gestern einen Autounfall gehabt hätten?

Üb. C: Also good as written assignment.

C **Übung** Erzählen Sie die „Lebensgeschichten" der folgenden Dinge im Passiv. Das wird so gemacht:

BEISPIEL: Zeitung: Journalisten / schreiben
Die Zeitung wird zuerst von Journalisten geschrieben.
(usw.)

You can connect your sentences with dann: **Die Zeitung wird zuerst von Journalisten geschrieben, *dann* wird sie ...**

1. die Zeitung: Journalisten / schreiben
   am Morgen auf der Straße / kaufen
   zwischen sieben und halb acht / lesen
   im Zug / vergessen
   alter Mann / finden und lesen
2. der Roman: Schriftsteller / schreiben
   in der Buchhandlung / kaufen
   zu Hause / lesen
   einem Freund / leihen
   vom Freund / verlieren
3. die Wurst: Metzger (*butcher*) / machen
   Hausfrau / kaufen
   im Wasser / kochen
   zum Mittagessen / essen
4. die Postkarte: in Italien / kaufen
   Barbara / schreiben
   zur Post / bringen
   in den Briefkasten / einwerfen
   Familie / lesen

Erzählen Sie weiter von den folgenden Gegenständen (*objects*): der Tisch, das Auto, das Brötchen, das Frühstück, das Gepäck, die Weinflasche, das Foto.

Set **Üb. D** up on previous class day as homework preparation. Each student brings in at least 2 written questions. Teacher acts as emcee. Offer useful new participles: **gemalt**, **komponiert**, **erfunden**.

■ **D** ■ **Gruppenarbeit: Trivial Pursuit** *(2 Mannschaften)* Jetzt spielen Sie ein bisschen „Trivial Pursuit". Jede Mannschaft stellt der anderen Fragen über Geschichte, berühmte Personen, Kunst, Literatur usw. Benutzen Sie das Passiv.

BEISPIELE: Von wem wurde *Faust* geschrieben?
Wo wurde Jazzmusik zuerst gespielt?

Schreiben Sie zu Hause.

■ **E** ■ Rewrite these sentences in passive voice. Keep the same tense.

1. Man akzeptiert mich fast überall.
2. Robert interviewt eine italienische Schülerin.
3. Man warf den Brief in den Briefkasten ein.
4. Die Studenten haben eine Europareise geplant.
5. Hat jemand die Wohnung im ersten Stock schon gekauft?
6. Dort sprach man nur Türkisch.
7. Man muss dieses Problem verstehen.
8. Die Gäste haben meine Großmutter überrascht.
9. Der Beamte muss das Gepäck kontrollieren.
10. Am Montag soll man dieses Thema diskutieren.

■ **F** ■ **Aufsatzthemen**

1. Was für Schwierigkeiten hätten Sie in einem Land, wo kein Englisch gesprochen wird? Beschreiben Sie einige typische Situationen.
2. Gibt es Gastarbeiter in Nordamerika? Wie ist die Situation anders als in Europa?

■ **G** ■ **Fantasiefrage** Wählen Sie eine historische Person und stellen Sie sich vor, Sie wären dieser Mensch gewesen. Wie hätten Sie gelebt? Hätten Sie etwas anderes gemacht?

BEISPIEL: Wenn ich Einstein gewesen wäre ...

Üb. H Answers:
1. Hätten Sie gern(e) im 19. Jahrhundert gelebt?
2. Das muss ich mir überlegen.
3. Wie wäre das Leben damals anders gewesen?
4. Sie hätten (man hätte) nicht mit einem Computer arbeiten können (*note position of* **nicht**).
5. Mein Referat muss bald geschrieben werden.
6. Wann wirst du anfangen?
7. Entweder heute oder übermorgen.
8. Worüber schreibst du denn?
9. Über Gastarbeiter in Österreich und der Schweiz.
10. Darüber sind viele Bücher geschrieben worden.
11. Da (dort) ist die (Haupt-) Post. Wolltest du deinen Brief nicht einwerfen?
12. Doch, gehen wir hinein. Ich könnte auch einige Briefmarken kaufen.

■ H ■ Wie sagt man das auf Deutsch?

1. Would you like to have lived in the 19th century?
2. I have to think about that.
3. How would life have been different back then?
4. You would not have been able to work with a computer.

5. My paper has to be written soon.
6. When are you going to start? (*Use future tense.*)
7. Either today or the day after tomorrow.
8. What are you writing about?
9. About foreign workers in Austria and Switzerland.
10. A lot of books have been written about that.

11. There is the post office. Didn't you want to mail your letter?
12. Yes, let's go in. I could also buy some stamps.

Almanach

Foreigners Living and Working in Germany

During the past 50 years, Germany has attracted large numbers of foreigners. In the economic recovery after World War II, manpower shortages existed in the industrialized countries of northern Europe. From the 1960s to the early 1970s, workers from Turkey, Yugoslavia, Italy, Greece, Spain, and Portugal were brought to West Germany. The Federal Republic still has the largest number of such so-called guest workers (**Gastarbeiter**) in Europe (1.9 million in West Germany in 1991), but has discouraged more from coming since the end of the labor shortage. Although many of these workers and their families have lived in Germany for years, German law makes it difficult for them to become citizens.

Another large class of foreigners in Germany are those seeking asylum from political persecution in their native countries. The German Basic Law (**Grundgesetz**) of 1949 stated that "those being persecuted politically have a right to asylum." But by the early 1990s, the densely populated country was finding it increasingly difficult to support large numbers of political refugees (438,000 in 1992). In 1993 the Basic Law was amended to make the requirements for asylum seekers much more strict.

The most acute immigration problem in the late 1980s and early 1990s resulted from the liberalization of Eastern Europe and the opening of what used to be called the "Iron Curtain." Ethnic Germans (**Volksdeutsche**) from Eastern European countries such as Poland, the Soviet Union, and Romania are entitled to citizenship under the German constitution. In 1992, over 230,000 of these Eastern European immigrants (the so-called **Aussiedler**) entered Germany. The government helps integrate these immigrants into German society with stipends, language courses, and temporary housing.

Dein Christus ein Jude
Dein Auto ein Japaner
Deine Pizza italienisch
Deine Demokratie griechisch
Dein Kaffee brasilianisch
Dein Urlaub türkisch
Deine Zahlen arabisch
Deine Schrift lateinisch
Und Dein Nachbar nur ein Ausländer?

Im BMW-Werk (München)

Die Frau: neue Wege und Rollen

Communicative Goals

- Reporting what others have said
- Expressing feelings

Cultural Goal

- Learning about women in Germany and the changing social roles of both men and women

Chapter Outline

- **Lyrik zum Vorlesen**
  Vier Gedichte von Mascha Kaléko
- **Grammatik**
  Subjunctive with *als ob* (as if, as though)
  Indirect quotation and special subjunctive
  Impersonal passive
  Subjective use of modal verbs
  Extended modifiers
- **Lesestück**
  Marie Marcks: Politik mit Witz
- **Situationen aus dem Alltag**
  Wie drückt man Gefühle aus?
- **Videoecke**
  Ich bezahle das Abendessen!
- **Almanach**
  Legal Protection During Pregnancy and Maternity

Dialoge

Lab Manual Kap. 16, Dialoge, Fragen, Hören Sie gut zu!

Pronunciation practice: Use dialogues to review difference between **u** and **ü**. Students tend to umlaut **u** incorrectly in the simple past of the passive: **Bei uns wurde ... gefeiert; was wurde denn gefeiert? Was würdest du gerne feiern? Ich würde auch feiern, wenn ich Zeit hätte.**

Return to first dialogue after students have read about indirect quotation in **Grammatik**. Note ambiguity in last sentence. Boss could have said either **Das geht** or **Das ginge**.

Kind oder Beruf?

Margarete ist bei ihrer alten Schulfreundin Martha zu Besuch. Sie sitzen im Garten bei einer Tasse Kaffee.

MARTHA: Wie schafft ihr das, wenn euer Kind da ist? Wirst du deine Stelle aufgeben?

MARGARETE: Nee, eine so gut bezahlte Stelle ist schwer zu finden. Rolf kann vormittags auf das Baby aufpassen und nachmittags an seiner Diss arbeiten.

MARTHA: Wer passt *dann* auf das Baby auf?

MARGARETE: Dann bin ich da. Ich habe meine Chefin schon gefragt, ob es möglich sei, halbtags zu arbeiten.

MARTHA: Was sagte sie dazu?

MARGARETE: Sie meinte, das ginge. Die ist ja selber verheiratet und hat Kinder.

Goldene Hochzeit

Am Morgen vor der Vorlesung treffen sich Heinrich und Liese im Studentencafé.

HEINRICH: Liese, du siehst aus, als ob du kaum geschlafen hättest.

LIESE: Stimmt schon. Bei uns wurde bis halb vier gefeiert.

HEINRICH: Was wurde denn gefeiert?

LIESE: Die goldene Hochzeit meiner Großeltern.

HEINRICH: Sagenhaft! Und sie sehen noch so jung aus!

Wortschatz 1

Verben

arbeiten an (+ *dat.*) to work on
auf·passen to pay attention; to look out
aufpassen auf (+ *acc.*) to look after
heiraten to marry, get married
verheiratet sein to be married

Substantive

der **Weg, -e** way; path

das **Baby, -s** baby

die **Hochzeit, -en** wedding
die **goldene Hochzeit** golden wedding anniversary

Hochzeit, which originally meant *celebration*, has become more specific since the Middle Ages and now refers to the "high times" enjoyed at a *wedding*.

Adjektive und Adverbien

golden golden
halbtags (*adv.*) half days
halbtags arbeiten to work part-time
kaum hardly, barely
vormittags (in the) mornings

Andere Vokabel

als ob (+ *subjunctive*) as if, as though

Nützliche Ausdrücke

Was sagen/meinen Sie dazu? What do you say to that?
sagenhaft incredible, marvelous

Gegensatz

verheiratet ≠ unverheiratet/ ledig married ≠ unmarried / single

Mit anderen Worten

die Diss = die Dissertation = die Doktorarbeit

Give students these examples: **Pass auf!** (*Look out!*) **Passen Sie gut auf** (*Pay close attention*); **Wer passt auf unsere Katze auf?** (*Who'll look after [take care of, keep an eye on] our cat?*).

Child or Career?

Margarete is visiting her old school friend Martha. They're having coffee in the garden.

M: How are you going to manage when your child is born? Will you quit your job?
M: No, such a well-paying job is hard to find. Rolf can look after the baby in the mornings and work on his dissertation in the afternoons.
M: Who'll look after the baby then?
M: Then I'll be here. I've already asked my boss whether it's possible to work part-time.
M: What did she say to that?
M: She thought it would work. She's married and has kids herself.

Golden Wedding Anniversary

In the morning before their lecture, Heinrich and Liese meet in the student café.

H: Liese, you look as though you had hardly slept.
L: That's right. Our party went on until 3:30.
H: What were you celebrating?
L: My grandparents' golden wedding anniversary.
H: Incredible! And they still look so young!

What were you celebrating? Good example of how English avoids passive where German uses impersonal passive.

Emphasize: **heiraten** refers to the act of marrying **(Wir haben letztes Jahr geheiratet); verheiratet sein** refers to the state of matrimony **(Wir sind seit letztem Jahr verheiratet)**.

Variationen

■ A ■ Persönliche Fragen

1. Margarete sagt, sie wird ihre Stelle nicht aufgeben, um auf das Baby aufzupassen. Was würden Sie in dieser Situation machen, wenn Sie gerade ein Kind bekommen hätten?
2. Haben Sie je eine gute Stelle aufgegeben? Warum?
3. Wollen Sie eines Tages Kinder haben? Wie stellen Sie sich Ihr Leben mit Kindern vor?
4. Liese sagt, dass sie bis halb vier gefeiert hat. Haben Sie je so lange gefeiert? Was wurde gefeiert?
5. Lieses Großeltern haben ihre goldene Hochzeit gefeiert. Nach wie vielen Jahren feiert man goldene Hochzeit?
6. Leben Ihre Großeltern noch? Wenn ja, wissen Sie, wie lange sie schon verheiratet sind?

Üb. A: Sentence 5 variation: **silberne Hochzeit?**

■ B ■ Gruppenarbeit: Was sagen Sie dazu?

Reagieren Sie auf die Sätze links mit einem passenden (*appropriate*) Ausdruck von der rechten Seite.

Review high-frequency idiomatic phrases like these in each **Zusammenfassung und Wiederholung** section. They are important for authentic conversational German.

Heute habe ich Geburtstag.	Das wäre nett!
Du sprichst ja perfekt Deutsch.	Gott sei Dank!
Gehen wir zusammen Ski fahren?	Doch.
Möchten Sie etwas trinken?	Natürlich.
Darf ich meinen Freund Gerd vorstellen?	Kein Wunder!
Morgen früh wasche ich mir die Haare.	Lieber nicht.
Stefan hat sich das Bein gebrochen.	Sehr angenehm.
Wollt ihr viele Kinder haben?	Höchste Zeit!
Wir bekommen einen neuen Professor.	Gerne!
Ich war bis halb vier auf.	Wie schade!
Kannst du mich nicht verstehen?	Verflixt nochmal!
Ich hab meinen Geldbeutel verloren!	Ich gratuliere!
	Danke gleichfalls!
	Bist du verrückt?

■ C ■ Übung: Das ist schwer zu finden

Margarete sagt, eine gute Stelle ist schwer zu finden. Antworten Sie auf die folgenden Fragen.

Number 1 will elicit an infinitive phrase (**Es ist schwer ein gutes Lokal zu finden**); 2 and 3 dependent clauses beginning with a question word (**Es ist schwer zu verstehen, wie/warum ...**).

1. Was ist in dieser Gegend schwer zu finden?
2. Was ist manchmal schwer zu wissen?
3. Was ist für Sie schwer zu verstehen?

Lyrik zum Vorlesen

Lab Manual Kap. 16, Lyrik zum Vorlesen.

Mascha Kaléko wurde 1907 als Tochter eines russischen Vaters und einer österreichischen Mutter geboren. Nach dem Ersten Weltkrieg zog die Familie nach Marburg. Kaléko studierte in Berlin, wo sie in den frühen 30er Jahren begann, für führende Zeitungen zu schreiben. 1938 verließ sie Hitlers Drittes Reich und ging nach New York ins Exil. 1966 zog sie nach Israel. Sie starb 1975.

Kalékos Gedichte, die oft in der Alltagssprache der Großstadt geschrieben sind, zeigen Witz, Ironie und manchmal etwas Melancholie. Diese vier kurzen Gedichte erschienen (*appeared*) zuerst in der Sammlung *Kleines Lesebuch für Große* (1934).

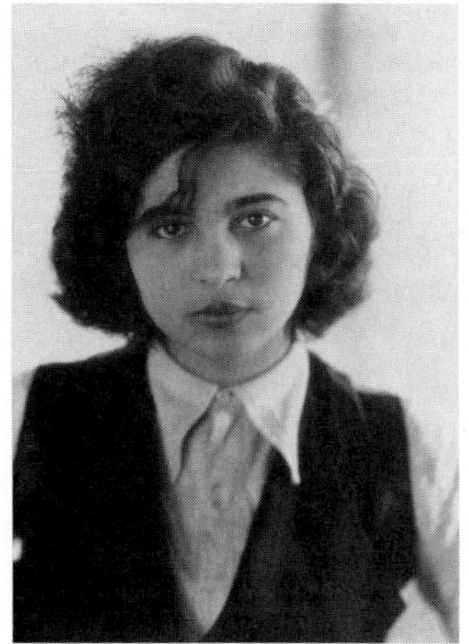

Mascha Kaléko als junges Mädchen

Von Mensch zu Mensch

Nun, da du fort° bist, scheint mir alles trübe°.
Hätt' ich's geahnt°, ich ließe dich nicht gehn.
Was wir vermissen°, scheint uns immer schön.
Woran das liegen mag° –. Ist das nun Liebe?

= **weg** / = **traurig**
foreseen
= **was uns fehlt**
woran ... = I wonder why that is.

Von Elternhaus und Jugendzeit

Jetzt bin ich groß. Mir blüht kein Märchenbuch°.
Ich muss schon oft „Sie" zu mir selber sagen.
Nur manchmal noch, an jenen° stillen Tagen,
Kommt meine Kindheit heimlich° zu Besuch.

Mir ... = Life's not going to be a fairy tale.
those
in secret

Von den Jahreszeiten

Der Frühling fand diesmal im Saale° statt.
Der Sommer war lang und gesegnet°.
– Ja, sonst gab es Winter in dieser Stadt.
Und sonntags hat's meistens geregnet ...

= **im Zimmer**
blissful

Von Reise und Wanderung

Einmal sollte man seine Siebensachen°
Fortrollen aus diesen glatten Geleisen°.
Man sollte sich aus dem Staube machen°
Und früh am Morgen unbekannt verreisen°.

Mascha Kaléko (1907–1975)

possessions
Fortrollen ... = roll off of these smooth tracks / **sich ...** = hit the road
= **wegreisen**

Grammatik

Point out parallel to English use of subjunctive after *as if*: You look as if you *were* sick.

Subjunctive with als ob (as if, as though)

The subordinating conjunction **als ob** (*as if, as though*) must be followed by a verb in the subjunctive.[1] Clauses with **als ob** are preceded by introductory phrases such as the following (note the special meaning of **tun** in the first example).

Du tust (so), als ob ...	*You act as though . . .*
Du siehst aus, als ob ...	*You look as if . . .*
Es war, als ob ...	*It was as if . . .*
Es klingt, als ob ...	*It sounds as if . . .*
Er tut, **als ob** er nichts **wüsste**.	*He acts as if he didn't know anything.*
Du siehst aus, **als ob** du krank **wärest**.	*You look as though you're ill.*
Es war, **als ob** wir uns immer **gekannt hätten**.	*It was as if we had always known each other.*
Es klingt, **als ob** du viel zu tun **hättest**.	*It sounds as if you have a lot to do.*

Lab Manual Kap. 16, Var. zur Üb. 1.

Workbook Kap. 16, A.

Üb. 1 also recycles antonyms.

1 Übung: Aber Sie tun doch, als ob Sie gesund wären! Ihr Professor erzählt Ihnen etwas über sich selbst. Sagen Sie ihm, er tut, als ob das Gegenteil stimmte.

BEISPIEL: Ich fühle mich heute krank.
Aber Sie tun doch, als ob Sie gesund wären.

1. Ich bin traurig.
2. Ich bin knapp bei Kasse.
3. Ich bin von Natur aus (*by nature*) faul.
4. Ich bin relativ altmodisch.
5. Ich bin eigentlich ein schlampiger Mensch.
6. Ich bin fast immer ernst.
7. Eigentlich bin ich dumm.

Sophie Scholl (1921–1943): leader of Munich student resistance to Hitler, executed with her brother Hans by the Nazis.
Nellie Sachs (1891–1970): poet, shared 1966 Nobel Prize for Literature.
Hannah Arendt (1906–1975): German-born political theorist, emigrated to the United States in 1941.

1. Either general *or* special subjunctive may be used. Sometimes this conjunction is used in the abbreviated form of **als** alone (without **ob**). In this case, the verb immediately follows it rather than coming at the end of the clause: Du siehst aus, als **wärest** du krank.

2 **Gruppenarbeit: Sie sehen aus, als ob ...** Sehen Sie sich die Menschen auf diesen Fotos an. Wie sehen sie aus? (Gefühle, Berufe usw.)

BEISPIEL: Sie sieht aus, *als ob* ...

Supplement with other photographs from book.

1.

2.

3.

4.

Indirect quotation and special subjunctive

Direct versus indirect quotation

Reporting what others have said is a communicative goal.

There are two basic ways to report what someone has said: directly or indirectly. One can quote directly, repeating the original speaker's exact words.

Note on punctuation: German uses a colon before a direct quotation, while English uses a comma.

Bernd sagte: „Ich muss heute in die Bibliothek.“	*Bernd said, "I have to go to the library today."*

It is much more common, however, to report speech in *indirect* quotation, either without a conjunction:

Bernd sagte, er muss heute in die Bibliothek.	*Bernd said he had to go to the library today.*

or with the conjunction **dass** (*that*):

Bernd sagte, dass er heute in die Bibliothek muss.	*Bernd said that he had to go to the library today.*

Note that in indirect quotation, pronouns often have to be changed: „**Ich** muss in die Bibliothek.“ — Er sagte, **er** muss in die Bibliothek.

In conversation many Germans simply use the indicative for indirect quotation, as in the previous examples and as we have done up to this point in this book. But it is also quite common to use *general subjunctive* for indirect quotation.

Bernd sagte, er **müsste** in die Bibliothek.	*Bernd said he had to go to the library.*
Meine Chefin meinte, das **ginge**.	*My boss thought it would work.*

In formal written and spoken German, however (for example, in a term paper, newspaper article, television news report, or speech), indirect quotation *must* be expressed with forms called the *special subjunctive.*

Er sagte, er **müsse** in die Bibliothek.
Die Chefin meinte, das **gehe**.

Notice that *thoughts* (**Die Chefin *meinte* ...**) can also be reported in indirect quotation.

■ Formation of the special subjunctive

To form the special subjunctive, add the endings from the general subjunctive of strong verbs (**-e**, **-est**, **-e**; **-en**, **-et**, **-en**) to the *unchanged infinitive stem* of the verb.

er, es, sie **gehe**, **laufe**, **könne**, **wisse**, **müsse**, **sehe** usw.

In practice, the special subjunctive occurs *almost exclusively* in the third person singular.[1] This form is immediately recognizable for the following reasons:

- It is built on the *infinitive* stem (**geh-**, **lauf-**), not on the past stem (**ging-**, **lief-**) like the general subjunctive.
- Special subjunctive ends in **-e (er, es, sie gehe)**, not in the indicative ending **-t (er, es, sie geht)**.

Fanny Mendelssohn-Bartholdy (1805–1847). Child prodigy at the piano, composer, diarist; sister of Felix Mendelssohn. Her music includes works for solo voice, chorus, piano, and chamber ensemble.

1. A note about forms. There are two reasons why special subjunctive occurs most often in the third person singular. First, any special subjunctive form that would be identical to an indicative form *does not exist.* Forms of the general subjunctive are used instead, as in the following paradigm:

ich	**liefe** (la~~uf~~e)	wir	**liefen** (la~~uf~~en)
du	**laufest**	ihr	**laufet**
er, es, sie	**laufe**	sie, Sie	**liefen** (la~~uf~~en)

Thus there is *no* **wir-** or **sie**-form in special subjunctive, because they would *always* be identical to indicative. An **ich**-form exists only for verbs with an irregular indicative singular, such as the modal verbs and **wissen**: **ich könne, ich wisse**.

The second reason for the high frequency of the third person singular is that special subjunctive is the *most formal* method for indirect quotation. As such, it is seldom used in the **ich-**, **du-**, or **ihr**-forms. It is usually used instead to quote formally some third person.

The *only* German verb with a complete set of forms in the special subjunctive is **sein**. Note that the **ich-** and **er-**forms lack endings.

ich	**sei**	wir	**seien**
du	**seiest**	ihr	**seiet**
er, es, sie	**sei**	sie, Sie	**seien**

The special subjunctive has only two additional tenses, future and past, each formed using the special subjunctive of the auxiliary verb.

Future	sie **werde** das **sagen**	*she will say that*
Past	er **habe** das **gewusst**	*he knew that*
	sie **sei** dort **gewesen**	*she was there*

In some cases the use of the general subjunctive has a different connotation than the more objective special subjunctive. E.g.: **Sie sagte, sie sei krank.** = objective restatement of what she said. But: **Sie sagte, sie wäre krank.** = the speaker does not necessarily believe this news. This is why journalistic style requires special subjunctive.

At this point remind students of first dialogue, p. 456: **„Ich habe meine Chefin schon gefragt, ob es möglich sei ...“** Also revisit Kap. 15 **Lesestück** for examples of indirect quotation.

■ Use of special subjunctive

You will encounter indirect quotation in special subjunctive introduced by a verb of saying or asking in the *indicative*. Once an environment of indirect quotation has been thus established, the economy of special subjunctive becomes evident: it makes explicit that the person is still being quoted indirectly, and no further verbs saying who is speaking are required, as they sometimes are in English. Here are some examples of the kind you might hear on the evening news or read in the paper:

Bei seinem Besuch in Rostock sagte der Bundeskanzler, er **wisse** noch nicht, wie man dieses Problem lösen **werde**, aber er **glaube**, dass etwas bald entschieden werden **müsse**. Man **habe** nicht mehr viel Zeit.	*On his visit to Rostock, the Chancellor said he didn't know yet how they would solve this problem, but he believed that something had to be decided soon. (He continued that) there wasn't much time left.*
In einem exklusiven Interview mit unserem Reporter sagte der junge Tennisstar, sie **hoffe** noch eine lange Karriere vor sich zu haben. Sie **sei** noch jung und **fühle** sich sehr fit, besonders seit sie sich von einer schlimmen Erkältung erholt **habe**.	*In an exclusive interview with our reporter, the young tennis star said that she hoped to have a long career still ahead of her. (She said) she was still young and felt very fit, especially since recovering from a bad cold.*

■ Tenses in indirect quotation

As you can see from the examples above, there is a difference in the way English and German handle tenses in indirect quotation. In English, the tense of the introductory verb of saying influences the tense of the indirect quotation.

Direct quotation
Barbara said, "I have to go to the library."

Indirect quotation: *Introductory verb in the present*
*She **says** she **has** to go to the library.*

Indirect quotation: *Introductory verb in the past*
*She **said** she **had** to go to the library.*

In German, the tense of the introductory verb of saying has *no influence* on the tense of the indirect quotation. The tense of the indirect quotation is *always the same as the tense of the direct quotation* from which it derives. If the tense of the direct quotation was *present*, use *present subjunctive* for the indirect quotation.

Bundeskanzler: „Ich **muss** mir das überlegen."

Der Bundeskanzler sagt, } er **müsse** sich das überlegen.
Der Bundeskanzler sagte, }

If the tense of the direct quotation was *future*, use *future subjunctive.*

Tennisstar: „Ich **werde** mehr spielen."

Der Tennisstar sagt, } sie **werde** mehr spielen.
Der Tennisstar sagte, }

If the tense of the direct quotation was *any past tense,* use *past subjunctive.*

Tennisstar: „Ich **habe** mich von der Erkältung **erholt**."

Der Tennisstar sagt, } sie **habe** sich von der Erkältung **erholt**.
Der Tennisstar sagte, }

If the original quotation is *already* in the subjunctive, the indirect quotation simply *remains* in the subjunctive.

Bundeskanzler: „Ich **möchte** nichts mehr darüber sagen."

Der Bundeskanzler sagt, } er **möchte** nichts mehr darüber sagen.
Der Bundeskanzler sagte, }

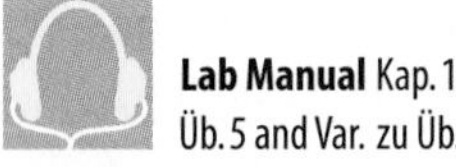

Lab Manual Kap. 16, Üb. 5 and Var. zu Üb. 3, 5.

Workbook Kap. 16, B–E.

Üb. 3: Also good as written assignment. Have students translate these into English.

■ 3 ■ Übung: Zeitungsartikel Here are two examples of indirect quotation one might encounter in a news report. Reconstruct the original direct quotations, changing pronouns as necessary.

1. Eine führende Politikerin berichtete, die Barrieren zur europäischen Vereinigung **seien** gefallen. Man **könne** jetzt beginnen dem Europa-Parlament in Straßburg mehr Autorität zu geben. Es **werde** wahrscheinlich noch ein paar Jahre dauern, bis alle Probleme gelöst **seien**. Sie persönlich **glaube** aber, dass man schon große Fortschritte gemacht **habe**.
2. Die Polizei meldete (*announced*) heute, ein schwerer Unfall auf der Autobahn zwischen Stuttgart und Heidelberg **habe** acht Verletzte und zwei Tote gekostet. Die Ursache (*cause*) des Unfalls **sei** das neblige Wetter im Neckartal gewesen. Alle Autofahrer **sollten** sich andere Routen nach Norden aussuchen.

The most polite form of address to someone with a professional title is **Frau Doktor Edenhof**, **Herr Professor Nolden**.

Our presentation of indirect quotation assumes that in most colloquial conversational situations, indicative will predominate, with some use of **sei**. The exercises that follow ask for special subjunctive *only* in the context of formal journalistic reports. In conversation we accept students' use of indicative. If you require use of special subjunctive, you may specify that before doing **Üb. 5** below.

■ 4 ■ Schriftliche Übung: Bericht über ein Interview As a reporter for the student newspaper, you interview Frau Dr. Edenhof, a visiting lecturer on international affairs. Below is a transcript from your tape recorder. Now report what she said to you in indirect quotation. Begin your report with „Frau Dr. Edenhof sagte, ... " and be careful to change pronouns and possessive adjectives as necessary.

„Ich freue mich sehr hier an der Uni zu sein. Ich war vor zehn Jahren zum letzten Mal hier und habe damals viele nette Menschen kennen gelernt. Ich finde diese Stadt wunderschön. Ich hoffe, ich werde diesmal mehr Zeit haben um mir die Stadt anzusehen. Mein Thema für heute Abend ist die Zukunft der NATO im neuen Europa. Ich weiß, dass es hier sehr viel Interesse für dieses aktuelle Problem gibt. Man kann natürlich in einer Stunde nicht alles darüber sagen. Ich hoffe, am Ende meines Vortrags (*lecture*) eine gute Diskussion mit Ihnen zu haben."

■ Questions and commands in indirect quotation

- Yes/no questions become **ob**-clauses in indirect quotation.

  Karin: „Hat Hans genug Geld?"

  Karin fragte, **ob** Hans genug Geld hat (habe, hätte).

- Information questions become subordinate clauses introduced by a question word.

  Tourist: „Wo ist der Bahnhof, bitte?"

  Der Tourist fragte, **wo** der Bahnhof ist (sei, wäre).

- Commands become statements with the verb **sollen**, with or without **dass**.

  Frau Henning: „Pass doch auf, Heinz!"

  Frau Henning sagte ihrem Mann, er **soll** (solle, sollte) aufpassen.

  Frau Henning sagte ihrem Mann, **dass** er aufpassen **soll** (solle, sollte).

Good example of indirect command with **sollen** in **Lesestück**, Kap. 15, p. 447, line 50.

Üb. 5: First example is in indicative. Specify if you prefer students to use only subjunctive in these conversational exchanges. Variation: Repeat statements, this time students use **Er/sie sagte, dass ...**

■ 5 ■ Übung: Was hat sie denn gesagt? Ihre Professorin fragt Sie etwas oder sagt, Sie sollen etwas machen. Erzählen Sie dem nächsten Studenten, was die Professorin gesagt hat.

BEISPIELE: A: Bitte leihen Sie mir einen Bleistift.
B: Sie sagte, ich soll ihr einen Bleistift leihen.

A: Wo ist Ihr Regenschirm?
B: Sie fragte, wo mein Regenschirm sei.

1. Wie fühlen Sie sich heute?
2. Arbeiten Sie oft mit dem Computer?
3. Was haben Sie zum Frühstück gegessen?
4. Empfehlen Sie mir bitte etwas Neues.
5. Helfen Sie mir bitte heute Nachmittag.
6. Können Sie sich auf Ihre Arbeit konzentrieren?
7. Können Sie sich ein neues Fahrrad leisten?
8. Haben Sie Ihren Studentenausweis mit?
9. Passen Sie gut auf!
10. Seien Sie froh!

Impersonal passive

One use of the German passive voice has no precise English equivalent. It is used to say that some human activity is going on, without mentioning who performs it. No subject is expressed at all, and the verb is *always* in the third person singular.

Bis halb vier **wurde gefeiert**.	*The party went on until 3:30.*
Hier **wird** bis zwei Uhr morgens **getanzt und gesungen**.	*There's dancing and singing here until 2:00 A.M.*

If no other element occupies first position in the sentence, an impersonal **es** is used to fill it. This **es** is not a real subject and disappears if any other element occupies first position.[1]

Es wurde bis halb vier gefeiert.
Es wird hier bis zwei Uhr morgens getanzt.

Lab Manual Kap. 16, Var. zur Üb. 6.

Workbook Kap. 16, F–H.

Note that impersonal passive is only passive in *structure*, not in *meaning*. The verb does not need to be transitive, but must designate a human activity. Impossible: **Hier wird geregnet** (not a human activity).

■ 6 ■ Übung: Anders gesagt Diese Sätze mit **man** kann man auch als unpersönliche Passivsätze formulieren.

BEISPIEL: Heute isst man um neun Uhr.
Heute wird um neun Uhr gegessen.

1. Hier singt man zu laut.
2. Beim Bäcker fängt man früh an.
3. In Leipzig demonstrierte man.
4. Damals arbeitete man schwer.
5. Morgen liest und schreibt man viel.
6. Jetzt kauft man ein.
7. Gestern tanzte man bis zwei Uhr.
8. In unserer Stadt baut man immer mehr.

Repeat **Üb. 6**, having students use initial **es: Es wird heute um neun Uhr gegessen.**

Was wird hier gemacht?

1. Similarly, when verbs with dative objects (see pp. 194–195) are used in the passive voice, their objects *remain* in the dative case and the passive is *always* in the third-person singular. An impersonal **es** is in the first position if no other element occupies it.

Active
Man hilft dem Alten. — *They're helping the old man.*

Passive
Dem Alten wird geholfen / Es wird dem Alten geholfen. } *The old man is being helped.*

Üb. 7 combines passive and impersonal passive with review of rooms of house. Students may open book to p. 449 if necessary.

■ 7 ■ Übung: Wo wird das in der Wohnung gemacht? Antworten Sie auf diese Fragen.

BEISPIELE: Wo wird in der Wohnung oder im Haus gekocht?
In der Küche.

Was wird im Arbeitszimmer gemacht?
Bücher werden dort gelesen.

1. Wo wird gegessen?
2. Was wird im Schlafzimmer gemacht?
3. Wo wird ferngesehen?
4. Was wird im Garten gemacht?
5. Wo wird der Wagen geparkt?

Und jetzt stellen Sie einander ähnliche Fragen.

Subjective use of modal verbs

If students are puzzled by the subjective/objective distinction, explain that objectively, the example sentence with **müssen** would mean: *The people over there are compelled to be tourists.*

The modal verbs are sometimes used to show speakers' subjective attitudes toward what they are saying. By and large, this subjective use of the modal verbs is parallel to English.

- **mögen** expresses *possibility*

Das **mag** sein.	*That may be.*

- **müssen** expresses *strong probability*

Die Menschen drüben **müssen** Touristen sein.	*The people over there must be tourists.*

The subjective modals also parallel English in the way they form their past tense: *objective:* **Er musste gestern in Wien sein** (*He had to be in Vienna yesterday*); *subjective:* **Er muss gestern in Wien gewesen sein** (*He must have been in Vienna yesterday*).

- **sollen** expresses *hearsay*

Sie **soll** eine gute Lehrerin sein.	*She's supposed to be a good teacher.*
Sie **sollen** so glücklich sein.	*They are said to be so happy.*

WIR MÜSSEN
VERRÜCKT SEIN:
NUR 75 PF/MIN.*
RUND UM DIE UHR.

- **können** expresses *fairly strong possibility*

Kann das Richard sein?	*Can that be Richard?*
Es **kann** sein, dass sie drei Wochen bleibt.	*It could be that she'll stay three weeks.*

- **wollen** casts *doubt on someone else's claim* (no parallel in English)

Er **will** viel über Musik wissen.	*He claims to know a lot about music.*

Workbook Kap. 16, I, J.

Üb. 8: To review subjective modals later, give these sentences in English and elicit German from students.

■ 8 ■ Übung: Kann das sein? Lesen Sie die folgenden Sätze laut vor. Dann geben Sie ein Äquivalent auf Englisch und sagen Sie, ob das Modalverb objektiv oder subjektiv gebraucht wird.

1. Kann das Utes Wagen sein?
2. Nein, das muss Richards Wagen sein.
3. Wieso, Ute wollte sich doch einen roten Wagen kaufen, nicht?
4. Mag sein. Wir müssen Ute fragen.
5. Ja, sie soll um drei wieder da sein.
6. Dann müssen wir zusammen in die Vorlesung.

Üb. 9: Also good as written assignment.

■ 9 ■ Übung: Wie sagt man das auf Deutsch?

1. She is supposed to be very famous.
2. That may be.

3. Hans-Peter must know a lot about politics.
4. He claims to know everything about politics.

5. It may be that they don't love each other any more.
6. But they are supposed to be so happy together!

Extended modifiers

Look at the following phrases:

diese deutsche Schriftstellerin	*this German writer*
diese bekannte deutsche Schriftstellerin	*this well-known German writer*
diese sehr bekannte deutsche Schriftstellerin	*this very well-known German writer*

Both German and English can extend noun phrases by inserting a series of adjectives and adverbs between a limiting word (**diese**, *this*) and its noun (**Schriftstellerin**, *writer*). In German, however, such a series can be continued much further than in English.

diese unter jungen Lesern sehr bekannte deutsche Schriftstellerin	*this German writer who is very well known among young readers*
diese unter jungen Lesern in Europa sehr bekannte deutsche Schriftstellerin	*this German writer who is very well known among young readers in Europe*
diese heute unter jungen Lesern in Europa sehr bekannte deutsche Schriftstellerin	*this German writer who is very well known among young readers in Europe today*

Students are not asked to generate extended modifiers, but they do have to recognize and transform them into relative clauses.

Such extended modifiers are encountered primarily in written German, and their use or avoidance is a matter of stylistic preference. You should not try to use this construction actively until you have had more experience with German, but you *should* be able to recognize and understand it.

The extended modifier is a substitute for a relative clause.

diese unter Studenten bekannte Schriftstellerin =
diese Schriftstellerin, **die unter Studenten bekannt ist**

Extended modifiers often contain a present or past participle functioning as an attributive adjective. This participle would be the conjugated verb in the corresponding relative clause.

Use of present participle means corresponding relative clause would be active; use of past participle means corresponding relative clause would be passive.

Die Schüler freuen sich auf **die in zwei Tagen *beginnenden* Ferien. =**
Die Schüler freuen sich auf die Ferien, **die in zwei Tagen *beginnen*.**

Eine so gut *bezahlte* Stelle ist schwer zu finden. =
Eine Stelle, **die so gut *bezahlt wird*,** ist schwer zu finden.

Moderne „Zusammenarbeit": So wird das Essen vorbereitet.

Sehen Sie sich das Foto genau an. Was weiß man über das Ehepaar?

Schauen Sie sich diese Briefmarken an. Was wird darauf als Beruf gewürdigt (*commemorated*)? Was meinen Sie: Kann man das einen Beruf nennen? Warum?

Üb. 10: You may choose to concentrate on translating extended modifiers into English rather than requiring students to transform them into relative clauses.

■ 10 ■ Übung: Die Schriftstellerin First read these sentences aloud. Then give their English equivalents. Finally, transform the extended modifiers into relative clauses.

BEISPIEL: Die in Hamburg geborene Schriftstellerin wohnt heute in Berlin.
The writer, who was born in Hamburg, lives in Berlin today.
Die Schriftstellerin, die in Hamburg geboren ist, wohnt heute in Berlin.

1. Ihr erstes, im Ausland kaum gelesenes Buch machte sie in Deutschland berühmt.
2. Ihre zwei Jahre jüngere Schwester ist Lehrerin in Düsseldorf.
3. In Berlin wohnt sie in einem alten, von Touristen kaum besuchten Stadtteil.
4. Aus ganz Deutschland bekommt sie Briefe von ihren oft sehr jungen Lesern.
5. Von ihr erwartet man Antworten auf viele für die Jugend immer ernster werdende Probleme.

Lesestück

Lab Manual Kap. 16, Üb. zur Betonung.

Vor dem Lesen

Tipps zum Lesen und Lernen

■ Leicht zu merken

ambivalent	ambivalent
die **Architektur**	
autobiographisch	
der **Autor, -en**	
der **Cartoon, -s**	
die **Emanzipation, -en**	Emanzipation
die **Frustration, -en**	Frustration
die Karikatur, -en	Karikatur
die **Karriere, -n**	Karriere
konfrontieren	konfrontieren
privat	privat
skeptisch	

Junge Managerin am Schreibtisch

Einstieg in den Text

Leitfragen Das folgende Lesestück präsentiert Zeichnungen von der Künstlerin Marie Marcks, in denen sie einen witzigen Blick auf die Rolle der Frau in der Gesellschaft und der Familie wirft. Durch verschiedene Situationen wird gezeigt, wie kompliziert das Leben der Frau in der modernen Welt geworden ist. Marcks zeigt, wie manche Frauen viele Rollen spielen müssen: Ehefrau, Mutter und berufstätigen Menschen.

Als Vorbereitung auf das Lesen sollen Sie über Ihre eigenen Meinungen zu diesem Thema nachdenken. Als Gruppendiskussion sollten Sie sich folgende Fragen stellen.

1. Ist Ihre Mutter Hausfrau?
2. Ist sie auch berufstätig?
3. Wie war es mit Ihrer Großmutter?
4. Vergleichen Sie das Leben Ihrer Mutter mit dem Leben Ihrer Großmutter.
5. Wollen Sie heiraten und Kinder haben? Wenn ja, wie stellen Sie sich Ihr Leben als Vater oder Mutter vor?

Identifying special subjunctive and extended modifiers in context The following reading contains examples of both indirect quotation in the special subjunctive and extended modifiers. After reading the text through once, first see if you understand why special subjunctive is used in lines 18 and 28. Then look closely at the two examples of extended modifiers and try to translate them into English. The marginal glosses will help you.

(lines 16–17)	**Eine zwischen Familie und Karriere hin- und hergerissene Frau** zeigt z.B. die folgende Zeichnung:
(lines 30–31)	**Jeder durch so viele verschiedene Pflichten gestresste Mensch** wird natürlich frustriert.

Wortschatz 2

Verben

bieten, bot, hat geboten to offer; to provide
blicken to gaze, look
brennen, brannte, hat gebrannt to burn
frustrieren to frustrate
sich lustig machen über (+ *acc.*) to make fun of
schützen vor (+ *dat.*) to protect from
zeichnen to draw
zu·schauen (+ *dat.*) to watch

Substantive

der **Blick, -e** view; gaze; glance
der **Ehemann, ¨er** married man; spouse
der **Zeichner, -** draftsman, graphic artist (*m.*)
das **Geschlecht, -er** sex, gender
das **Gesetz, -e** law
das **Vorurteil, -e** prejudice

die **Ehe, -n** marriage
die **Ehefrau, -en** married woman; spouse
die **Küche, -n** kitchen
die **Pflicht, -en** duty
die **Zeichnerin, -nen** graphic artist (*f.*)
die **Zeichnung, -en** drawing

Adjektive und Adverbien

alltäglich everyday
beliebt popular
deutschsprachig German-speaking
gesellschaftlich social
gestresst (*colloq.*) stressed out
gleich equal
gleichberechtigt enjoying equal rights
kritisch critical

Andere Vokabel

damit (*sub. conj.*) so that

Gegensätze

beliebt ≠ unbeliebt popular ≠ unpopular
privat ≠ öffentlich private ≠ public

Nützlicher Ausdruck

Es geht um ... It's a question of . . . ; It's about . . .
Worum geht es in dieser Zeichnung? What's this drawing about?
Es geht um Vorurteile. It's about prejudices.

Marie Marcks: Politik mit Witz

Die Zeichnerin und Autorin Marie Marcks ist 1922 in Berlin geboren und lebt heute in Heidelberg. Während der Schulzeit lernte sie Zeichnen und Schrift° bei ihrer Mutter, die eine private Kunstschule leitete°. In ihrem autobiographischen Werk *Marie, es brennt!* (1985) zeigt sie sich als kleines Mädchen, das seiner Mutter bei der Arbeit am Zeichentisch zuschaut.

lettering
directed

wackeln = jiggle

Am selben° Tisch arbeitet Marie Marcks noch heute.

Von 1942 bis 1944 studierte sie dann Architektur. Seit den 60er-Jahren erscheinen° ihre Zeichnungen regelmäßig° in deutschen Zeitungen und Zeitschriften. Sie hat auch Plakate gezeichnet und über zwanzig Bücher veröffentlicht°, die in der deutschsprachigen Welt sehr beliebt sind.

same
appear
regularly
published

Die Themen, für die Marie Marcks bei ihren Lesern besonders bekannt ist, spiegeln ihr Leben als Ehefrau und Mutter von fünf Kindern wider°. In ihrer Kunst geht es fast immer um die Rollen von Männern und Frauen in der Gesellschaft, ihre ambivalenten Gefühle in der Ehe, die Beziehungen° zwischen Eltern und Kindern und auch um die alltäglichen Frustrationen, mit denen Frauen zu Hause und in der Arbeitswelt konfrontiert werden. Eine zwischen Familie und Karriere hin- und hergerissene° Frau zeigt z.B. die folgende Zeichnung:

spiegeln ... wider = reflect
relations
hin- ... = pulled back and forth

Sozialleistungen = fringe benefits / **versteht sich = selbstverständlich**

Ein altes Klischee behauptet°, die Frau solle sich nur um Kinder, Küche und Kirche kümmern. Über diese traditionelle Rolle der Frau macht sich Marie Marks im nächsten Cartoon lustig. Hier schützt eine Frau ihren Mann vor den lauten Kindern, damit er „arbeiten" kann:

asserts

Es sieht aus, als ob diese beiden Frauen sich von ihren Familienpflichten nicht befreien° könnten. Aber es mag sein, dass in Zukunft Mädchen diese Rolle nicht mehr akzeptieren werden, wie die nächste Bilderfolge° zeigt.

= frei machen
series of pictures

= ein schlampiges Mädchen
kriegt = bekommt

Dass manche Männer wegen ihrer Vorurteile gar nicht merken, was Frauen schon leisten können, zeigt diese letzte Zeichnung:

sowas = that kind of thing

Im Grundgesetz[1] der BRD (Artikel 3) steht zwar°, dass alle Menschen vor dem Gesetz gleichberechtigt seien. Aber wie sieht es in Wirklichkeit aus? Manche berufstätigen Frauen müssen sich noch allein um den ganzen Haushalt° kümmern, obwohl sie oft den gleichen Arbeitstag haben wie ihre Ehemänner. Jeder durch so viele verschiedene Pflichten gestresste Mensch wird natürlich frustriert.

Mit kritischem Blick durchleuchtet° Marie Marcks diese Situation mit ihren Cartoons. Mit ihren Karikaturen blickt sie skeptisch, aber witzig auf das Leben der modernen Frau. Ihre Zeichnungen sind wohl immer autobiographisch, denn jede bietet ein Stück ihrer persönlichen Emanzipationsgeschichte.

zwar = to be sure
Haushalt = household work
durchleuchtet = illuminates

Nach dem Lesen

■ A ■ Antworten Sie auf Deutsch.

1. Welchen Einfluss (*influence*) hatte die Mutter auf Marie Marcks und ihre Berufswahl?
2. Wie alt war Marcks während des Krieges?
3. Was hat sie in den vierziger Jahren gemacht?
4. Was sind die Hauptthemen ihrer Zeichnungen?

1. The *Basic Law* or constitution of Germany.

B **Bildbeschreibung** Wählen Sie eine Zeichnung im Lesestück aus und beschreiben Sie sie so ausführlich (*completely*) wie möglich.

Use the already existing 3-picture series in the reading as a model.

C **Geschichte in Bildern** Nehmen Sie jetzt dieselbe Zeichnung oder eine andere. Diese Zeichnung soll das zweite Bild in einer Serie von drei Bildern sein. Beschreiben Sie (oder zeichnen Sie) nun Bild 1: Was passierte vorher? Dann beschreiben oder zeichnen Sie Bild 3: was wird nachher passieren?

Situationen aus dem Alltag

Expressing feelings is a communicative goal.

Mit Gefühl!

Sie haben schon viele Ausdrücke gelernt, mit denen Sie Gefühle und Reaktionen ausdrücken können. Die folgende Liste wiederholt solche Ausdrücke aus früheren Kapiteln.

***sich freuen (die Freude,** joy)*
Wunderbar!
Ich bin heute so glücklich!
Das ist ja wunderschön!
Ich gratuliere (dir)!
Ich bin begeistert!

***Mitleid ausdrücken (das Mitleid,** sympathy)*
Das tut mir Leid.
Gute Besserung!
Schade!
Du siehst traurig aus.
Was ist denn los?
Du Arme! Du Armer!

***sich ärgern (der Ärger,** annoyance, anger)*
Ich habe die Nase voll.
So ein Mist!
Verflixt nochmal!
Ich bin frustriert!

***enttäuscht sein (die Enttäuschung,** disappointment)*
Schade!
Ich habe Pech gehabt.
So ein Mist!

***überrascht sein (die Überraschung,** surprise)*
Um Gottes Willen!
Mensch!
So was!
Ich bin ganz baff!
Ich bin erstaunt!

Angst haben
Ich habe Angst vor ...
Ich fürchte ...
Hilfe!

■ A ■ Gruppenarbeit: Mensch, bin ich ...! Diese Zeichnungen zeigen Menschen, die starke Gefühle haben. Welche Emotion wird in jedem Bild gezeigt? (Es gibt natürlich verschiedene Möglichkeiten.)

Gruppendiskussion: Also good as written assignment.

■ B ■ Gruppendiskussion: Da war ich sehr aufgeregt. Alle Menschen haben manchmal starke Gefühle. Beschreiben Sie eine Situation aus Ihrem Leben, in der Sie ein Gefühl von Ärger, Freude, Überraschung, Enttäuschung, Mitleid oder Angst gehabt haben.

BEISPIEL: Ich war einmal besonders überrascht, als ...

Model **Partnerarbeit** with a student before partners begin work separately. Stress that these should be short exchanges: 2 utterances per speaker.

■ C ■ Partnerarbeit: Mini-Dialoge Unten werden verschiedene Situationen beschrieben. Erfinden Sie (*invent*) zu jeder Situation einen Mini-Dialog, in dem Sie Gefühle und Reaktionen ausdrücken. Spielen Sie dann einen von Ihren Dialogen vor der ganzen Klasse.

1. Sie wollen zusammen ausgehen. Ihre Freundin kann aber ihren Geldbeutel nicht finden.
2. Ein Partner ruft den anderen an und sagt, er müsse heute leider zu Hause bleiben, weil er sich erkältet habe.
3. Ein Partner arbeitet für die Lotterie (*lottery*) und ruft den anderen an um ihm zu gratulieren: Er habe DM 100 000 gewonnen.
4. Sie freuen sich schon seit Monaten auf eine Reise nach Spanien. Jetzt hören Sie plötzlich, dass die Reise nicht mehr stattfinden kann, weil die Reisegesellschaft (*travel agency*) bankrott (*bankrupt*) ist.
5. Sie verbringen einen langweiligen Nachmittag vor dem Fernseher und plötzlich klingelt es. Sie gehen an die Haustür und da steht Ihr Lieblingsonkel Max, den Sie seit vier Jahren nicht mehr gesehen haben.

Zum Schluss

Lab Manual Kap. 16, Diktat.

Workbook Kap. 16, K.

Casablanca (1942) was directed by Austrian emigré Michael Curtiz. It starred Humphrey Bogart, Ingrid Bergman, and Claude Rains as well as the German emigrés Peter Lorre and Conrad Veidt.

Sprechen wir miteinander!

A **Worum geht es?** Nennen Sie zuerst Filme oder Bücher, die Ihnen besonders gefallen. Dann sagen Sie bei jedem Werk, worum es geht.

BEISPIEL: Mein Lieblingsfilm heißt „Casablanca". In dem Film geht es um Liebe, aber auch um Politik.

B **Gruppenarbeit: Was wird hier gemacht?** Sagen Sie, was auf diesen Bildern gemacht wird.

BEISPIEL: Hier werden Bücher gelesen. (*oder*) Hier wird gelesen.

Rollenspiel: Students should prepare these in pairs as a homework assignment, then present them in class, without notes or with only key words on cards.

■ **C** ■ **Partnerarbeit: Rollenspiel** Wählen Sie eine Situation aus und seien Sie bereit sie vor der ganzen Klasse zu spielen.

1. ***Abends um 18 Uhr*** Margarete, die vor vier Monaten ein Baby bekommen hat, arbeitet wieder in ihrer alten Stelle. Ihr Mann Rolf schreibt an seiner Diss und bleibt bei dem Kleinen zu Hause. Margarete kommt nach einem harten Arbeitstag nach Hause.
2. ***Umziehen oder hier bleiben?*** Monika und Harald sind Studenten in ihrem letzten Semester an der Uni in München. Sie haben vor, bald zu heiraten. Harald hat gerade eine gut bezahlte Stelle an einem Gymnasium in Frankfurt bekommen. Monika hat noch keine Stelle gefunden und sie will München nicht verlassen.
3. ***Mutter und Tochter*** Anita (19 Jahre alt) fragt ihre Mutter (50), wie es damals war, als sie jung war. Frau Baumann erzählt ihrer Tochter, was sie als junge Frau gern gemacht hätte oder was sie heute anders machen würde.

Suggestion for **Üb. D**: One student stands at board and records words, phrases generated by group. Make two columns (**Mädchen/Jungen** or **Studenten/Studentinnen**) to show contrasts. Or: Students work in small groups for 5–10 minutes, then each group sends one student to board to record group's results. Compare the results of the groups' discussions.

■ **D** ■ **Klassendiskussion: Unterschiede und Ähnlichkeiten**

1. Besprechen Sie einige Unterschiede und Ähnlichkeiten
   - in der Erziehung (*upbringing*) von Mädchen und Jungen.
   - im Leben von Studenten und Studentinnen an dieser Uni.
2. An einigen privaten Hochschulen in Amerika studieren *nur* Frauen (ohne Männer). Halten Sie das für gut? Warum oder warum nicht?

Schreiben Sie zu Hause.

■ **E** ■ **Fernsehinterview** Im Fernsehen gab es neulich ein Gespräch zwischen einem Interviewer und der bekannten Feministin Elisabeth Schmidt-Baumann. Lesen Sie diesen Bericht über das Interview und schreiben Sie das Gespräch, das die beiden geführt haben, als Dialog.

Der Interviewer fragte Frau Schmidt-Baumann, wie lange sie wohl noch für die Emanzipation der Frau kämpfen müsse. Das sei schwer zu sagen, meinte sie. Sie werde einfach nicht aufgeben, bis alle Frauen gleichberechtigt seien. Der Interviewer unterbrach und sagte, dass die Gleichberechtigung (*equal rights*) schon seit Jahren im Grundgesetz stehe. Frau Schmidt-Baumann lachte und sagte, ja, das stimme schon und sei auch wichtig. Auf der anderen Seite seien das Grundgesetz und die Wirklichkeit leider oft zwei verschiedene Sachen. Die Frauenemanzipation dürfe nicht nur im Gesetz stehen. Man müsse auch das traditionelle Denken über die Rollen von Mann und Frau ändern. Der Interviewer dankte Frau Schmidt-Baumann für das Gespräch.

With this chapter you have completed the fourth quarter of ***Neue Horizonte***. For a concise review of the grammar and idiomatic phrases in chapters 13–16, you may consult the **Zusammenfassung und Wiederholung 4** (*Summary and Review 4*) of your Workbook. The review section is followed by a self-correcting test.

Üb. G answers:
1. Max sagte mir, es gebe ein neues Restaurant um die Ecke.
2. Ja, das Essen soll sehr gut sein.
3. Aber die Preise könnten niedriger sein.
4. Max hat schon dreimal da gegessen. Er hat es mir empfohlen.
5. Hast du Mimi gefragt, ob sie zur Hochzeit kommt (komme)?
6. Ja, aber sie tat, als ob sie nie davon gehört hätte.
7. Brigitte sagt, sie hat (habe, hätte) sie schon letzten Monat eingeladen.
8. Hallo, Ruth! Warum warst du am Freitag Abend nicht bei Linas Geburtstagsfeier?
9. Es tut mir Leid, aber ich war einfach zu müde.
10. Weißt du, ich habe eine neue Stelle gefunden und ich hatte viel zu tun.
11. Schade, dass du das verpasst hast.
12. Es wurde bis halb vier gefeiert.

■ F ■ Aufsatzthemen

1. Für Studenten: Was wäre in Ihrem Leben anders, wenn Sie eine Frau wären? Für Studentinnen: Was wäre in Ihrem Leben anders, wenn Sie ein Mann wären?

2. Wählen Sie ein Thema aus der Klassendiskussion D (S. 479) und schreiben Sie darüber.

■ G ■ Wie sagt man das auf Deutsch?

1. Max told me that there was a new restaurant around the corner.
2. Yes, the food is supposed to be very good.
3. But the prices could be lower.
4. Max has eaten there three times already. He recommended it to me.

5. Did you ask Mimi whether she were coming to the wedding?
6. Yes, but she acted as if she had never heard about it.
7. Brigitte says she invited her last month.

8. Hello, Ruth! Why weren't you at Lina's birthday party on Friday night?
9. I'm sorry, but I was simply too tired.
10. You know, I've found a new job and I had a lot to do.
11. Too bad you missed it.
12. We celebrated until 3:30. (Use impersonal passive.)

Videoecke

8 *Ich* bezahle das Abendessen! (32:33)

Katrin bezahlt das Essen.

*Stefan und Katrin sind im Restaurant in Kreuzberg, einem Stadtteil Berlins, wo viele Türken leben. Stefan hat Katrin ein Halstuch (*scarf*) geschenkt und sie dankt ihm dafür. Sie sprechen über die Türken, die sie heute auf dem Markt gesehen haben.*

Sie schauen sich die Speisekarte an und bestellen dann etwas zu essen und zu trinken. Während der Mahlzeit kommt das Gespräch auf die Rolle der Frau. Katrin sagt, sie finde es normal, wenn Frauen nicht nur Kinder haben, sondern auch berufstätig sind. So habe es ihre Mutter gemacht.

*Dann erzählen sie einander über ihre Ferienpläne. Katrin wird heute bei Su-Sin übernachten, denn sie fahren morgen zusammen in die Schweiz. Sie rufen den Kellner um zu zahlen. Jeder möchte den anderen einladen (*treat*), aber endlich gibt Stefan nach (*gives in*) und lässt Katrin zahlen.*

Wortschatz zum Video

das **Getränk, -e**	*drink*
die **Rechnung, -en**	*bill, check*
die **Speise, -n**	*food, dish (menu item)*
die **Nachspeise**	**= der Nachtisch**
das **Tuch, ¨er**	*scarf*
jemand anders	*someone else*
Prost! (*or*) **Prosit!**	*Cheers!*
Wie kommt das?	*How come? What's the reason for that?*

A **Was sehen Sie im Video?** Sehen Sie sich den Anfang des Abschnitts an (32:42–33:20). Hier sehen Sie den Kreuzberger Türkenmarkt am Maibachufer in Berlin. Kreuzen Sie in der Liste unten an, was Sie im Video sehen. Wenn Sie einen Preis sehen, schreiben Sie ihn auf.

____ 1. Bananen
____ 2. Würste
____ 3. Äpfel
____ 4. Salat
____ 5. Brötchen
____ 6. Gurken (*cucumbers*), Preis: DM ____
____ 7. Orangen
____ 8. Käse

B **Wer macht das? Wer sagt das?** Now watch the rest of video Module 8 (33:21–36:46). Choose the person who does or says the following.

a. Stefan b. Katrin c. der Kellner

1. ____ „Das letzte Mal hatte ich hier Eisbein mit Sauerkraut."
2. ____ „Getränke vielleicht erstmal?"
3. ____ bestellt sich ein Knoblauchrippchen (*pork chop with garlic*) mit Salat und Zwiebelbrot.
4. ____ „Ich würd' den Apfelstrudel empfehlen."
5. ____ trinkt Apollinaris (Mineralwasser).
6. ____ „Ich lade dich ein, zum Semesterabschluss."

C **Wie geht's weiter?** Wählen Sie die beste Möglichkeit um jeden Satz zu vervollständigen (*complete*).

1. Das Tuch, das Stefan Katrin geschenkt hat, ...
   a. ist ihr zu groß.
   b. gefällt ihr sehr.
   c. hat eine schöne rote Farbe.
2. Heute will Katrin das Essen bezahlen, denn ...
   a. Stefan hat kein Geld.
   b. es geht ihr um die Gleichberechtigung.
   c. das Essen war nicht sehr teuer.

3. Beide nehmen zum Nachtisch warmen Apfelstrudel, weil ...
   a. es sonst nichts Gutes gibt.
   b. sie immer noch Riesenhunger haben.
   c. es ihnen der Kellner empfohlen hat.
4. Katrins Mutter hat den ganzen Tag gearbeitet, während Katrin ...
   a. bei der Oma blieb.
   b. im Kindergarten war.
   c. in einer Fabrik arbeitete.

■ D ■ Im Gespräch For each sentence in the left column, find the appropriate response in the right column.

____ 1. Heute Abend möchte ich dich zum Abendessen einladen.
____ 2. Was darf's denn sein?
____ 3. Viele Gastarbeiter bleiben in der Bundesrepublik, nicht wahr?
____ 4. Herr Ober, zahlen bitte!
____ 5. Das macht zusammen DM 33,85 bitte.

a. Augenblick bitte, ich komme gleich.
b. Natürlich, viele sind sogar hier geboren.
c. Nee, heute bezahle *ich* das Abendessen.
d. Nehmen Sie bitte fünfunddreißig.
e. Wir möchten zweimal Espresso und zwei Stück Apfelstrudel bestellen.

Legal Protection During Pregnancy and Maternity

The laws known collectively as **Mutterschutz** (*Maternity Protection*) are a good example of the extensive social services available to German citizens. In 1992 this safety net served as a model for all countries in the European Union.

Mutterschaftsgeld A pregnant woman continues to receive the full amount of her previous pay (or disability pay, or a lump sum).

Mutterschaftsvorsorge All expenses for prenatal care and delivery are covered.

Gefahrenschutz A pregnant woman may not be forced to undertake tasks that would endanger her or her child.

Kündigungsschutz A woman cannot be fired during her pregnancy or in the four months following delivery (eight months if she chooses to take maternity leave).

Beschäftigungsverbot A pregnant woman cannot be forced to work in the six weeks prior to her delivery date, and may not work for eight weeks after delivery (twelve weeks for premature deliveries or multiple births).

Mutterschaftsurlaub Maternity leave at reduced salary for up to four months may be taken after the 8–12 week protective period has expired. 93 percent of mothers take advantage of this leave to care for their newborn children.

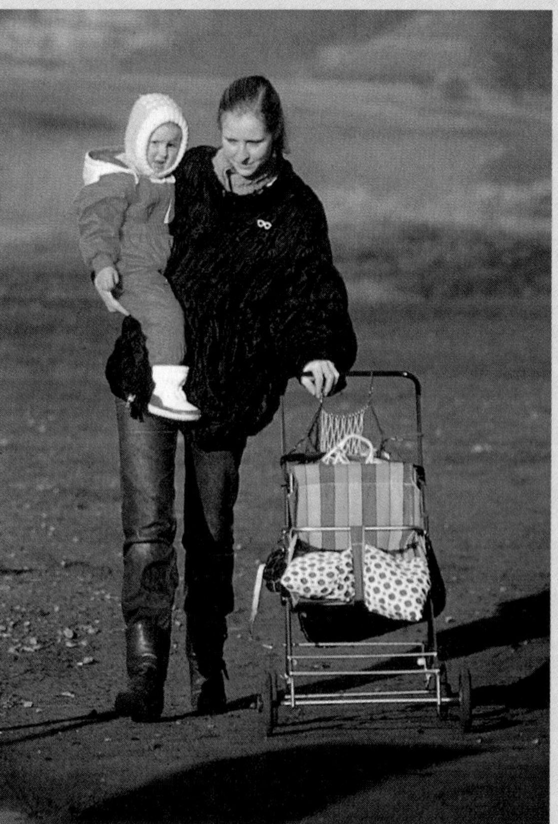

Appendix 1

Answer Key to Videoecke Exercises

Videoecke 1: *Ist das Zimmer noch frei?*

A. 1, 2, 4, 5, 6, 7, 8
B. 2, 3, 4, 7
C. 1. b; 2. c; 3. a; 4. b
D. 1. F; 2. R; 3. F; 4. F; 5. F; 6. R
E. 2, 3, 4, 5, 6, 7, 9, 11

Videoecke 2: *Ohne Frühstück geht's nicht!*

A. 1, 3, 4, 5, 6, 9
B. 2, 4, 5, 8
C. 1. b; 2. b; 3. c; 4. b; 5. b
D. 1. F; 2. R; 3. F; 4. R; 5. F; 6. F
E. 1. c; 2. b; 3. c; 4. c; 5. c
F. 1, 4, 5, 6

Videoecke 3: *Wie war deine Vorlesung?*

A. 1, 2, 5, 6
B. 1. in der Uni-Bibliothek; 2. aus China (aus Beijing); 3. Mathematik (Mathe); 4. langweilig; 5. ins Kino gehen
C. 1. a; 2. c; 3. c; 4. b; 5. b; 6. c
D. 1. R; 2. F; 3. R; 4. F; 5. F; 6. R
E. 1. b; 2. d; 3. a; 4. e; 5. c

Videoecke 4: *Gehen wir doch einkaufen!*

A. 1, 2, 4, 7, 8
B. 1. b; 2. a; 3. c; 4. b; 5. a; 6. b; 7. d
C. 1 Pfund Brot (*500 grams—about 1 pound—of bread*), 100 g Leberwurst (*100 grams of liverwurst*), 200 g Käse (*200 grams of cheese*), eine Flasche Orangensaft (*1 bottle of orange juice*), 1 gegrilltes Hähnchen (*1 grilled chicken*)
D. 1. sonntags und montags; 2. um 7.00 Uhr; 3. am Samstag; 4. bis 18 Uhr
E. 1, 2, 3, 4, 5, 8

Videoecke 5: *Treibst du gern Sport?*

A. 1, 3, 4, 6
B. 1, 3, 5
C. 1. a; 2. d; 3. b; 4. b; 5. c; 6. a
D. *Answers may vary.*
1. schwarze / dunkle / lange Haare; eine graue Hose; einen roten Pulli
2. weiße Schuhe; ein grünes Sweatshirt
3. einen roten Mantel; einen weißen / hellen Pulli; kurze / graue Haare; 60 bis 70 Jahre alt; sieht sympathisch / freundlich aus
4. einen roten Pulli; einen grauen Mantel

E. *Answers will vary.*

Videoecke 6: *Das vergesse ich nie.*

A. 1, 2, 4, 6, 7, 9, 10
B. 1. F; 2. R; 3. F; 4. F; 5. F; 6. R
C. 1. c; 2. b; 3. c; 4. b; 5. a; 6. d
D. 1. c; 2. b; 3. a; 4. c
E. 2, 3, 5, 7, 8

Videoecke 7: *Fährst du mit in die Schweiz?*

A. 1, 2, 3, 5, 6, 7
B. 1. c; 2. a; 3. b; 4. c
C. 1. a; 2. b; 3. c; 4. a; 5. b; 6. a
D. 1. c; 2. b; 3. a; 4. b; 5. a
E. 1. c; 2. e; 3. a; 4. d; 5. b

Videoecke 8: Ich *bezahle das Abendessen!*

A. 3; 5; 6 (Preis: DM 1,00 pro Stück); 7
B. 1. a; 2. c; 3. a; 4. c; 5. b; 6. a
C. 1. b; 2. b; 3. c; 4. b
D. 1. c; 2. e; 3. b; 4. a; 5. d

Appendix 2

Principal Parts of Strong and Irregular Verbs

The following table contains the principal parts of all the strong, mixed, and irregular verbs in *Neue Horizonte*. With a few exceptions, only the basic stem verbs are listed, e.g., **gehen**, **bringen**, and **kommen**. Verbs formed by adding a prefix—e.g., **weggehen**, **verbringen**, and **ankommen**—change their stems in the same way as the basic verb.

infinitive	3rd person sing. present	simple past	perfect	English
anfangen	fängt an	fing an	hat angefangen	*begin*
beginnen		begann	hat begonnen	*begin*
bieten		bot	hat geboten	*offer, provide*
bitten		bat	hat gebeten	*ask for, request*
bleiben		blieb	ist geblieben	*stay*
brechen	bricht	brach	hat gebrochen	*break*
brennen		brannte	hat gebrannt	*burn*
bringen		brachte	hat gebracht	*bring*
denken		dachte	hat gedacht	*think*
dürfen	darf	durfte	hat gedurft	*may, be allowed to*
einladen	lädt ein	lud ein	hat eingeladen	*invite*
empfehlen	empfiehlt	empfahl	hat empfohlen	*recommend*
entscheiden		entschied	hat entschieden	*decide*
essen	isst	aß	hat gegessen	*eat*
fahren	fährt	fuhr	ist gefahren	*drive*
fallen	fällt	fiel	ist gefallen	*fall*
finden		fand	hat gefunden	*find*
fliegen		flog	ist geflogen	*fly*
fließen		floss	ist geflossen	*flow*
geben	gibt	gab	hat gegeben	*give*
gehen		ging	ist gegangen	*go*
gewinnen		gewann	hat gewonnen	*win*
haben	hat	hatte	hat gehabt	*have*
halten	hält	hielt	hat gehalten	*hold, stop*
hängen[1]		hing	hat gehangen	*be hanging*
heißen		hieß	hat geheißen	*be called*
helfen	hilft	half	hat geholfen	*help*
kennen		kannte	hat gekannt	*know, be acquainted with*
klingen		klang	hat geklungen	*sound*
kommen		kam	ist gekommen	*come*
können	kann	konnte	hat gekonnt	*can, be able to*
lassen	lässt	ließ	hat gelassen	*leave; let; allow to; cause to be done*
laufen	läuft	lief	ist gelaufen	*run*

1. When it is transitive, **hängen** is weak: **hängte**, **hat gehängt**.

infinitive	3rd person sing. present	simple past	perfect	English
leihen		lieh	hat geliehen	*lend*
lesen	liest	las	hat gelesen	*read*
liegen		lag	hat gelegen	*lie*
mögen	mag	mochte	hat gemocht	*like*
müssen	muss	musste	hat gemusst	*must, have to*
nehmen	nimmt	nahm	hat genommen	*take*
nennen		nannte	hat genannt	*name, call*
raten	rät	riet	hat geraten	*guess*
rufen		rief	hat gerufen	*call, shout*
scheinen		schien	hat geschienen	*shine, seem*
schlafen	schläft	schlief	hat geschlafen	*sleep*
schlagen	schlägt	schlug	hat geschlagen	*hit, beat*
schließen		schloss	hat geschlossen	*close*
schneiden		schnitt	hat geschnitten	*cut*
schreiben		schrieb	hat geschrieben	*write*
schreien		schrie	hat geschrien	*shout, yell*
schweigen		schwieg	hat geschwiegen	*be silent*
schwimmen		schwamm	ist geschwommen	*swim*
sehen	sieht	sah	hat gesehen	*see*
sein	ist	war	ist gewesen	*be*
singen		sang	hat gesungen	*sing*
sitzen		saß	hat gesessen	*sit*
sollen	soll	sollte	hat gesollt	*should*
sprechen	spricht	sprach	hat gesprochen	*speak*
stehen		stand	hat gestanden	*stand*
stehlen	stiehlt	stahl	hat gestohlen	*steal*
steigen		stieg	ist gestiegen	*climb*
sterben	stirbt	starb	ist gestorben	*die*
tragen	trägt	trug	hat getragen	*carry, wear*
treffen	trifft	traf	hat getroffen	*meet*
treiben		trieb	hat getrieben	*drive, propel*
trinken		trank	hat getrunken	*drink*
tun		tat	hat getan	*do*
vergessen	vergisst	vergaß	hat vergessen	*forget*
vergleichen		verglich	hat verglichen	*compare*
verlassen	verlässt	verließ	hat verlassen	*leave*
verlieren		verlor	hat verloren	*lose*
verschwinden		verschwand	ist verschwunden	*disappear*
wachsen	wächst	wuchs	ist gewachsen	*grow*
waschen	wäscht	wusch	hat gewaschen	*wash*
werden	wird	wurde	ist geworden	*become*
werfen	wirft	warf	hat geworfen	*throw*
wiegen		wog	hat gewogen	*weigh*
wissen	weiß	wusste	hat gewusst	*know (a fact)*
wollen	will	wollte	hat gewollt	*want to*
ziehen		zog	hat/ist gezogen	*pull; move*

German–English Vocabulary

The following list contains all the words introduced in ***Neue Horizonte*** except for definite and indefinite articles, personal and relative pronouns, possessive adjectives, cardinal and ordinal numbers, and words glossed in the margins of the **Lesestücke**. The code at the end of each entry shows where the word or phrase is introduced in the text:

12-1	Kapitel 12, Wortschatz 1
9-2	Kapitel 9, Wortschatz 2
Einf.	Einführung (Introductory Chapter)
2-G	Kapitel 2, Grammatik
5-TLL	Kapitel 5, Tipps zum Lesen und Lernen (*in the section* Leicht zu merken)
10-SA	Kapitel 10, Situationen aus dem Alltag
2-VID	Video segment following Kapitel 2

Strong and irregular verbs are listed with their principal parts: **nehmen (nimmt), nahm, hat genommen**. Weak verbs using **sein** as their auxiliary are shown by inclusion of the perfect: **reisen, ist gereist**.

Separable prefixes are indicated by a raised dot between prefix and verb stem: **ab•fahren**. This dot is *not* used in German spelling.

When a verb has a prepositional complement, the preposition follows all the principal parts. If it is a two-way preposition, the case it takes with this verb is indicated in parentheses: **teil•nehmen (nimmt teil), nahm teil, hat teilgenommen *an*** (+ *dat.*).

Adjectival nouns are indicated thus: der / die **Verwandte**, **-n**.

Masculine N-nouns like **der Student** and irregular nouns like **der Name** are followed by both the genitive singular and the plural endings: der **Student**, ***-en***, **-en**; der **Name**, ***-ns***, **-n**.

Adjectives followed by a hyphen may only be used attributively: **eigen-**.

If an adjective or adverb requires an umlaut in the comparative and superlative degrees, or if these forms are irregular, this is indicated in parentheses: **arm (ärmer)**; **gern (lieber, am liebsten)**.

The following abbreviations are used here and throughout ***Neue Horizonte***.

acc.	accusative
adj.	adjective
adj. noun	adjectival noun
adv.	adverb
colloq.	colloquial
conj.	conjunction
coor. conj.	coordinating conjunction
dat.	dative
f.	feminine
gen.	genitive
intrans.	intransitive
m.	masculine
neut.	neuter
pers.	person
pl.	plural
prep.	preposition
sing.	singular
sub. conj.	subordinating conjunction
trans.	transitive
usw.	(= und so weiter) etc.

A

der **Abend, -e** evening, 7-2
am Abend in the evening, 7-2
Guten Abend! Good evening, *Einf.*
das **Abendessen, -** supper, evening meal, 8-1
zum Abendessen for supper, 8-1
abends (in the) evenings, 5-2
aber (1) but (*coor. conj.*), 1-1; (2) (*flavoring particle*), 9-1
ab·fahren (fährt ab), fuhr ab, ist abgefahren to depart, leave (by vehicle), 7-1
ab·holen to pick up, fetch, get, 5-2
das **Abi** (*slang*) = **Abitur,** 5-1
das **Abitur** final secondary school examination, 5-1
das **Abteil, -e** railway compartment, 15-2
ach oh, ah, 2-1
das **Adjektiv, -e** adjective
der **Adler, -** eagle, 10-SA
die **Adresse, -n** address, 15-1
das **Adverb, -ien** adverb
ähnlich (+ *dat.*) similar (to), 3-2
Sie ist ihrer Mutter ähnlich. She's like her mother.
die **Ähnlichkeit, -en** similarity, 11-2
die **Ahnung** notion, inkling, hunch
(Ich habe) keine Ahnung. (I have) no idea. 10-1
aktiv active, 9-TLL
aktuell current, topical, 5-2
akut acute, 9-TLL
akzeptieren to accept, 15-1
alle (*pl.*) all; everybody, 2-2
allein alone, 4-1
alles everything, 6-2
der **Alltag** everyday life, 8-2
alltäglich everyday, quotidian, 16-2
der **Almanach, -e** almanac
die **Alpen** (*pl.*) the Alps, 4-TLL
als (1) when (*sub. conj.*), 10-1; (2) as a, 5-1; (3) than (*with comparative degree*), 12-1
als ob (+ *subjunctive*) as if, as though, 16-1
also (1) well . . . 1-1; (2) thus, 3-2
alt (älter) old, 2-2
die **Alternative, -n** alternative, 2-TLL
altmodisch old-fashioned, 4-2
die **Altstadt, ⸚e** old city center, 8-TLL
ambivalent ambivalent, 16-TLL
(das) **Amerika** America, 3-2
der **Amerikaner, -** American (*m.*), 1-2
die **Amerikanerin, -nen** American (*f.*), 1-2
amerikanisch American, 3-2
an (*prep.* + *acc.* or *dat.*) to, toward; at, alongside of, 6-1
analysieren to analyze, 14-TLL
ander- other, different, 11-1
ändern to change (*trans.*), 11-2
sich ändern to change (*intrans.*), 11-2
anders different, 2-2
die **Anekdote, -n** anecdote, 15-TLL
der **Anfang, ⸚e** beginning, 6-1
am Anfang at the beginning, 6-1
an·fangen (fängt an), fing an, hat angefangen to begin, start, 5-1
der **Anfänger, -** beginner, 5-TLL
angenehm pleasant, 15-2; "pleasure to meet you," 13-SA
der/die **Angestellte, -n** (*adj. noun*) employee, 14-1
die **Anglistik** English studies, 6-SA
die **Angst, ⸚e** fear, 3-2
Angst haben to be afraid, 3-2
Angst haben vor (+ *dat.*) to be afraid of, 13-1
an·kommen, kam an, ist angekommen to arrive, 5-1
an·kommen auf (+ *acc.*) to depend on, be contingent on
Es kommt darauf an. It depends. 13-1
sich an·melden to register (at a hotel, at the university, etc.), 14-SA
an·rufen, rief an, hat angerufen to call up, 5-1
an·schauen to look at, 15-2
sich etwas an·sehen (sieht an), sah an, hat angesehen to take a look at something, 11-1
anstatt (*prep.* + *gen.*) instead of, 8-G
die **Antwort, -en** answer, 6-2
antworten (+ *dat.*) to answer (a person), 6-2
antworten auf (+ *acc.*) to answer (something), respond to, 13-2
an·ziehen, zog an, hat angezogen to dress, 11-1
sich anziehen to get dressed, 11-1
sich etwas anziehen to put something on
der **Anzug, ⸚e** suit, 3-SA
die **Apotheke, -n** pharmacy, 8-SA
der **Appetit** appetite
Guten Appetit! *Bon appétit!* Enjoy your meal! 8-SA
(der) **April** April, *Einf.*
die **Arbeit** work, 2-2
arbeiten to work, 1-1
arbeiten an (+ *dat.*) to work on, 16-1
der **Arbeiter, -** worker (*m.*), 5-2
die **Arbeiterin, -nen** worker (*f.*)
arbeitslos unemployed, 10-2
die **Arbeitslosigkeit** unemployment, 10-2
das **Arbeitszimmer, -** study, 15-SA
die **Architektur** architecture, 16-TLL
der **Ärger** annoyance, anger, 16-SA
ärgern to annoy; offend, 8-2
sich ärgern (über + *acc.*) to get annoyed (at), be annoyed (about), 13-2
arm (ärmer) poor, 10-1
der **Arm, -e** arm, 10-2
die **Armbanduhr, -en** wrist watch
die **Arroganz** arrogance, 15-TLL
der **Artikel, -** article, 2-1
der **Arzt, ⸚e** doctor (*m.*), 5-SA; 11-1
die **Ärztin, -nen** doctor (*f.*), 5-SA; 11-1
der **Aspekt, -e** aspect, 8-TLL
das **Atom, -e** atom, 9-TLL
das **Atomkraftwerk** atomic power plant, 9-2
auch also, too, 1-1
auf (*prep.* + *acc.* or *dat.*) onto; on, upon, on top of, 6-1

die **Aufgabe, -n** task, assignment, 16-2
auf·geben (gibt auf), gab auf, hat aufgegeben (*trans. & intrans.*) to give up, quit, 11-2
auf·hängen to hang up, 7-1
auf·hören (mit) to cease, stop (doing something), 5-1
auf·machen to open, 5-1
auf·passen to pay attention; to look out, 10-VID; 16-1
auf·passen auf (+ *acc.*) to look after, 16-1
auf·räumen to tidy up, straighten up, 13-1
sich auf·regen (**über** + *acc.*) to get upset (about), get excited (about), 15-1
der **Aufsatz, ¨-e** essay
das **Aufsatzthema, -themen** essay topic
auf·stehen, stand auf, ist aufgestanden (1) to stand up; to get up; (2) to get out of bed, 4-VID; 5-1
auf·wachen, ist aufgewacht to wake up (*intrans.*), 7-1
auf·wachsen (wächst auf), wuchs auf, ist aufgewachsen to grow up, 13-2
das **Auge, -n** eye, 11-1
der **Augenblick, -e** moment, 12-1
(Einen) Augenblick, bitte. Just a moment, please. 12-1
im Augenblick at the moment, 12-1
(der) **August** August, *Einf.*
aus (*prep. + dat.*) out of; from, 5-1
aus·brechen (bricht aus), brach aus, ist ausgebrochen to break out
der **Ausdruck, ¨-e** expression
der **Ausflug, ¨-e** outing, excursion, 14-2
aus·geben (gibt aus), gab aus, hat ausgegeben to spend (money), 6-2
aus·gehen, ging aus, ist ausgegangen to go out, 14-1
ausgezeichnet excellent, 8-1
sich aus·kennen, kannte aus, hat ausgekannt to know one's way around, 13-1
die **Auskunft** information, 13-1
das **Ausland** (*sing.*) foreign countries, 7-2
im Ausland abroad (*location*), 7-2
ins Ausland abroad (*destination*), 7-2
der **Ausländer, -** foreigner (*m.*), 15-1
die **Ausländerin, -nen** foreigner (*f.*), 15-1
ausländisch foreign, 10-2
aus·packen to unpack, 11-SA
aus·sehen (sieht aus), sah aus, hat ausgesehen to appear, look (like), 5-2
außer (*prep. + dat.*) besides; in addition to, 5-1
außerdem (*adv.*) besides, in addition, 14-2
aus·steigen, stieg aus, ist ausgestiegen to get out (of a vehicle), 7-2
die **Ausstellung, -en** exhibition, 10-2
der **Austauschstudent, -en, -en** exchange student, 6-1
aus·wandern, ist ausgewandert to emigrate, 11-2
der **Ausweis, -e** I.D. card, 6-2
aus·ziehen, zog aus, ist ausgezogen to move out, 6-1
sich ausziehen to get undressed, 11-1
das **Auto, -s** car, 2-2
die **Autobahn, -en** expressway, high-speed highway, 7-SA
autobiographisch autobiographical, 16-TLL
automatisch automatic, 6-TLL
der **Automechaniker, -** auto mechanic, 5-1
der **Autor, -en** author, 16-TLL
der **Autostopp** hitchhiking
per Autostopp reisen to hitchhike, 7-2

B

das **Baby, -s** baby, 16-1
der **Bäcker, -** baker, 5-1
die **Bäckerei, -en** bakery, 5-1
das **Bad** bath, 14-1
ein Bad nehmen to take a bath, 14-1
sich baden to take a bath, 11-SA
das **Badezimmer, -** bathroom, 14-1
baff sein (*colloq.*) to be flabbergasted, speechless, 13-1
die **Bahn** railroad, railway system, 7-2
der **Bahnhof, ¨-e** train station, 7-1
bald soon, 3-1
die **Banane, -n** banana, 12-VID
die **Bank, ¨-e** bench, 10-1
die **Bank, -en** bank, 14-1
der **Bär, -en, -en** bear, 10-SA
barbarisch barbaric, 4-TLL
das **Bargeld** cash, 14-VID
die **Barriere, -n** barrier, 13-TLL
die **Basis** basis, 9-TLL
bauen to build, 8-2
der **Bauer, -n, -n** farmer, 5-1
das **Bauernbrot** dark bread, 5-1
der **Baum, ¨-e** tree, 4-2
der **Beamte, -n** (*adj. noun*) official, civil servant (*m.*), 11-1
die **Beamtin, -nen** official, civil servant (*f.*), 11-1
bedeuten to mean, signify, 1-2
die **Bedeutung, -en** meaning, significance, 10-2
sich beeilen to hurry, 11-1
begeistert von enthusiastic about, 14-2
die **Begeisterung** enthusiasm, 11-1
beginnen, begann, hat begonnen to begin, 4-1
behalten (behält), behielt, hat behalten to keep, retain, 12-1
bei (*prep. + dat.*) (1) at the home of; near; at, 5-1; (2) during, while -ing, 11-G
beid- (*adj.*) both, 11-2
beide (*pl. pronoun*) both (people), 14-2

beides (*sing. pronoun*) both things, 13-2
das **Bein, -e** leg, 11-1
das **Beispiel, -e** example, 9-2
zum Beispiel for example, 1-2
bekannt known; well known, 10-2
der/die **Bekannte, -n** (*adj. noun*) acquaintance, friend, 11-1
bekommen, bekam, hat bekommen to receive, get, 4-1
belegen to take (a university course), 6-2
beliebt popular, 16-2
benutzen to use, 7-2
bequem comfortable, 7-2
bereit prepared, ready, 9-2
der **Berg, -e** mountain, 3-1
bergig mountainous, 4-SA
berichten to report, 5-2
der **Beruf, -e** profession, vocation, 2-2
Was sind Sie von Beruf? What is your profession? 5-SA
berufstätig employed, 2-2
berühmt famous, 11-2
beschreiben, beschrieb, hat beschrieben to describe, 4-2
besitzen, besaß, hat besessen to own, 2-2
besonders especially, 5-2
besorgt worried, concerned, 10-1
besprechen (bespricht), besprach, hat besprochen to discuss, 3-2
besser better, 12-G
die **Besserung: Gute Besserung!** Get well soon! 11-1
best- best, 12-G
bestellen to order, 8-1
bestimmt certainly, surely, 10-VID
der **Besuch, -e** visit, 12-1
besuchen to visit, 3-1
die **Betriebswirtschaft** management, business, 6-SA
das **Bett, -en** bed, 2-VID; 6-1
ins Bett gehen to go to bed, 7-1
bevor (*sub. conj.*) before, 10-2
bezahlen to pay, 6-2
die **Bibliothek, -en** library, 6-1
das **Bier, -e** beer, 4-2
bieten, bot, hat geboten to offer; to provide, 16-2
das **Bild, -er** picture; image, 5-2
billig inexpensive, cheap, 6-2
die **Biologie** biology, 6-SA
bis (*prep. + acc.*) until, *Einf.*; by, 1-1
bis dann until then, 1-1
ein bisschen a little; a little bit; a little while, 3-1
bitte (sehr) (1) you're welcome, 2-1; (2) please, 3-2; (3) here it is, there you are, 5-1
bitten, bat, hat gebeten um to ask for, request, 13-1
Er bittet mich um das Geld. He's asking me for the money.
blau blue, 3-2
bleiben, blieb, ist geblieben to stay, remain, 2-2
der **Bleistift, -e** pencil, *Einf.*
der **Blick, -e** view; gaze; glance, 16-2
blicken to gaze, look, 16-2
blitzschnell quick as lightning, 3-2
blöd dumb, stupid, 5-1
die **Blume, -n** flower, 11-1
die **Bluse, -n** blouse, 3-SA
böse (+ *dat.*) angry, mad (at); bad, evil, 13-1
boxen to box, 9-SA
brauchen to need, 2-1
braun brown, 3-2
die **BRD** (= **Bundesrepublik Deutschland**) the FRG (= the Federal Republic of Germany), 2-2
brechen (bricht), brach, hat gebrochen to break, 11-1
brennen, brannte, hat gebrannt to burn, 16-2
die **Brezel, -n** soft pretzel, 5-1
der **Brief, -e** letter, 6-2
der **Briefkasten, ¨** mailbox, 15-1
die **Briefmarke, -n** postage stamp, 15-1
der **Briefträger, -** letter carrier, mailman, 5-TLL
die **Brille** (*sing.*) (eye)glasses, 3-SA
bringen, brachte, hat gebracht to bring, 6-1
das **Brot, -e** bread, 5-1
das **Brötchen, -** roll, 4-1
die **Brücke, -n** bridge, 8-SA; 11-2
der **Bruder, ¨** brother, 2-1
das **Buch, ¨er** book, *Einf.*
buchen to book (a flight, hotel, etc.), 14-VID
das **Bücherregal, -e** bookcase, 6-SA
die **Buchhandlung, -en** bookstore, 5-2
die **Bude, -n** (*colloq.*) (rented) student room, 6-2
der **Bummel, -** stroll, walk, 8-1
einen Bummel machen to take a stroll, 8-1
das **Bundesland, ¨er** federal state (in Germany and Austria)
die **Bundesrepublik Deutschland** the Federal Republic of Germany, 2-2
bunt colorful, multicolored, 3-2
der **Bürger, -** citizen, 6-2
das **Büro, -s** office, 1-1
der **Bus, -se** bus, 7-SA
die **Butter** butter, 4-VID; 8-SA

C

das **Café, -s** café, 8-SA
campen to camp, 5-TLL
der **Cartoon, -s** cartoon, 16-TLL
die **CD, -s** CD (compact disk), 6-SA
der **CD-Spieler** CD player
die **Chance, -n** chance, 9-2
der **Chef, -s** boss (*m.*), 5-1
die **Chefin, -nen** boss (*f.*), 5-1
die **Chemie** chemistry, 6-SA
(das) **China** China, 11-TLL
der **Chinese, -n, -n** Chinese (*m.*), 11-TLL
die **Chinesin, -nen** Chinese (*f.*), 11-TLL
chinesisch Chinese (*adj.*), 11-TLL
der **Computer, -** computer, 6-SA; 12-1
der **Container, -** container, 9-1

D

da (1) there, 1-1; (2) then, in that case, 9-1; (3) since (*sub. conj., causal*), 8-G
da drüben over there, 2-1

dabei sein to be present, be there, 15-1
dahin: Wie komme ich dahin? How do I get there? 13-1
damals at that time, back then, 10-1
die **Dame, -n** lady, 10-2
damit (*sub. conj.*) so that, 16-2
danach (*adv.*) after that, 14-VID
der **Dank** thanks
vielen Dank thanks a lot, 2-1
danke thanks, thank you, *Einf.*; 1-1
Danke, gleichfalls. You too. Same to you. *Einf.*; 12-1
danken (+ *dat.*) to thank, 7-1
Nichts zu danken! Don't mention it! 2-1
dann then, 1-1
darf (*see* **dürfen**)
darum therefore, for that reason, 3-2
das sind (*pl. of* **das ist**) those are, 2-2
dass that (*sub. conj.*), 8-1
dauern to last; to take (time), 10-1
die **DDR (= Deutsche Demokratische Republik)** the GDR (= the German Democratic Republic), 11-1
die **Decke, -n** blanket, 12-VID
die **Demokratie, -n** democracy, 10-TLL
demokratisch democratic, 10-TLL
die **Demokratisierung** democratization, 11-TLL
die **Demonstration, -en** demonstration, 11-TLL
demonstrieren to demonstrate, 9-TLL
denken, dachte, hat gedacht to think, 13-2
denken an (+ *acc.*) to think of, 13-2
das **Denkmal, ¨er** monument, 12-2
denn (1) (*flavoring particle in questions*), 2-1; (2) (*coor. conj.*) for, because, 7-G
deutlich clear, 16-2
deutsch (*adj.*) German, 2-2
(das) **Deutsch** German language, 3-2
auf Deutsch in German, 1-2
der/die **Deutsche, -n** (*adj. noun*) German (person), 1-2
die **Deutsche Demokratische Republik** German Democratic Republic (GDR), 11-1
die **Deutsche Mark (DM)** German mark, 5-1
(das) **Deutschland** Germany, 1-2
deutschsprachig German-speaking, 16-2
die **Deutschstunde, -n** German class, 3-1
(der) **Dezember** December, *Einf.*
der **Dialekt, -e** dialect, 13-TLL
der **Dialog, -e** dialogue
der **Dichter, -** poet
(der) **Dienstag** Tuesday, *Einf.*
dieser, -es, -e; (*pl.*) **diese** this, these, 5-1
diesmal this time, 12-1
das **Ding, -e** thing, 7-2
direkt direct(ly), 12-1
der **Direktor, -en** director, 10-TLL
die **Diskussion, -en** discussion, 2-2
diskutieren to discuss, 15-2
die **Diss** (*university slang*) = **Dissertation,** 16-1
die **Dissertation, -en** dissertation, 16-1
DM *see* **Deutsche Mark**
doch (1) (*stressed, contradictory*) yes I do, yes I am, yes he is, etc., 3-1; (2) (*unstressed flavoring particle with commands*), 4-1; (3) (*unstressed flavoring particle with statements*), 10-1
die **Doktorarbeit, -en** dissertation, 16-1
der **Dom, -e** cathedral, 8-1
(der) **Donnerstag** Thursday, *Einf.*
das **Doppelzimmer, -** double room, 14-1
das **Dorf, ¨er** village, 5-2
dort there, 2-1
die **Dose, -n** (tin) can, 9-2
draußen outside, 1-1
dreckig (*colloq.*) dirty, 9-1
dritt- third, 9-G
drüben over there, 2-1
dumm (dümmer) dumb, 5-1
dunkel dark, 3-2
durch (*prep.* + *acc.*) through, 4-1
dürfen (darf), durfte, hat gedurft may, to be allowed to, 3-1
Was darf es sein? What'll it be? May I help you? 5-1
der **Durst** thirst
Durst haben to be thirsty, 8-1
die **Dusche, -n** shower, 14-1
sich duschen to take a shower, 11-SA
duzen to address someone with **du**, 1-2
die **Dynastie, -n** dynasty, 14-TLL

E

echt? (*colloq.*) really? 6-VID
die **Ecke, -n** corner, 8-2
an der Ecke at the corner, 8-2
um die Ecke around the corner, 8-2
egal wo, wer, warum usw. no matter where, who, why, etc., 7-2
Das ist (mir) egal. It doesn't matter (to me). I don't care. 7-1
die **Ehe, -n** marriage, 16-2
die **Ehefrau, -en** married woman; spouse, 16-2
der **Ehemann, ¨er** married man; spouse, 16-2
das **Ehepaar, -e** married couple, 14-1
ehrlich honest, 3-2
das **Ei, -er** egg, 4-VID; 8-SA
eigen- own, 9-2
eigentlich actually, in fact, 3-2
die **Eile** hurry
in Eile in a hurry, 1-1
einander (*pronoun*) each other, 1-2
der **Eindruck, ¨e** impression, 8-2
einfach simple, easy, 5-1
einige some, 6-2
ein·kaufen to shop for; to go shopping, 5-2
ein·laden (lädt ein), lud ein, hat eingeladen to invite, 8-1
einmal once, 4-1

noch einmal once again, once more, 4-1
eins one, 1-2
ein·schlafen (schläft ein), schlief ein, ist eingeschlafen to fall asleep, 7-1
ein·steigen, stieg ein, ist eingestiegen to get in (a vehicle), 7-2
der **Einstieg, -e** entrance, way in
einverstanden Agreed. It's a deal. O.K. 5-1
ein·wandern, ist eingewandert to immigrate, 11-2
ein·werfen (wirft ein), warf ein, hat eingeworfen to throw in; to mail (a letter), 15-1
das **Einzelzimmer, -** single room, 14-1
ein·ziehen, zog ein, ist eingezogen to move in, 6-1
einzig- single, only, 12-2
das **Eis** (1) ice; (2) ice cream, 8-SA
das **Eishockey** ice hockey, 9-SA
der **Elefant, -en, -en** elephant, 10-SA
elegant elegant, 8-TLL
die **Elektrizität** electricity, 9-TLL
die **Elektrotechnik** electrical engineering, 6-SA
der **Elektrotechniker, -** electrician; electrical engineer (*m.*), 5-SA
die **Elektrotechnikerin, -nen** electrician; electrical engineer (*f.*), 5-SA
die **Eltern** (*pl.*) parents, 2-1
die **Emanzipation** emancipation, 16-TLL
empfehlen (empfiehlt), empfahl, hat empfohlen to recommend, 8-VID; 9-1
das **Ende, -n** end, 6-2
am Ende at the end, 6-1
Ende Februar at the end of February, 6-2
zu Ende sein to end, be finished, be over, 10-2
endlich finally, 1-1
die **Energie, -n** energy, 9-TLL
der **Engländer, -** Englishman, 11-TLL
die **Engländerin, -nen** Englishwoman, 11-TLL
englisch English, 11-TLL
(das) **Englisch** English language, 3-2
der **Enkel, -** grandson, 12-VID
enorm enormous, 9-TLL
entscheiden, entschied, hat entschieden to decide, 3-2
Entschuldigung! Pardon me! Excuse me. 1-1
enttäuschen to disappoint, 6-2
die **Enttäuschung, -en** disappointment, 16-SA
entweder ... oder either . . . or, 14-1
die **Epoche, -n** epoch, 10-TLL
die **Erdbeermarmelade** strawberry jam, 4-VID
die **Erde** earth, 12-2
das **Erdgeschoss** ground floor, first floor, 14-1 (*see* **Stock**)
die **Erfahrung, -en** experience, 12-SA
erfinden, erfand, hat erfunden to invent
der **Erfolg, -e** success, 16-2
erfreut pleased
Sehr erfreut. Pleased to meet you. 13-SA
sich erholen (von) (1) to recover (from), get well; (2) to have a rest, 13-2
erinnern an (+ *acc.*) to remind of, 12-1
sich erinnern an (+ *acc.*) to remember, 12-1
die **Erinnerung, -en** memory, 12-1
sich erkälten to catch a cold, 11-1
erklären to explain, 10-2
die **Ermäßigung, -en** discount, 14-VID
ernst serious, 14-2
etwas ernst nehmen to take something seriously, 14-2
erst (*adv.*) not until; only, 5-1
erst- (*adj.*) first, 9-G
erstaunlich astounding, 9-2
erwarten to expect, 14-2
erzählen to tell, recount, 6-2
die **Erzählung, -en** story, narrative, 12-2
der **Esel, -** donkey, 10-SA
essen (isst), aß, hat gegessen to eat, 2-1
das **Essen** food; meal, 2-2
das **Esszimmer, -** dining room, 15-SA
etwas (1) (*pronoun*) something, 3-1; (2) (*adj. & adv.*) some, a little; somewhat, 12-1
(das) **Europa** Europe, 3-2
der **Europäer, -** European, 3-2
europäisch European, 11-2
existieren to exist, 11-TLL
extrem extreme, 10-TLL

F

die **Fabrik, -en** factory, 5-2
das **Fach, ⸚er** area of study; subject, 6-SA
fahren (fährt), fuhr, ist gefahren to drive, go (by vehicle), 3-1
die **Fahrkarte, -n** ticket (for bus, train, streetcar, etc.), 7-2
das **Fahrrad, ⸚er** bicycle, 8-2
die **Fahrt, -en** trip, ride, 15-2
fallen (fällt), fiel, ist gefallen (1) to fall; (2) to die in battle, 10-1
falsch false, incorrect, wrong, *Einf.*; 15-2
die **Familie, -n** family, 2-1
fantastisch fantastic, 2-1
die **Farbe, -n** color, 3-2
fast almost, 2-2
faul lazy, 5-2
(der) **Februar** February, *Einf.*
fehlen to be missing; to be absent, 10-1
die **Feier, -n** celebration, party, 15-1
feiern to celebrate, 6-2
das **Fenster, -** window, *Einf.*
die **Ferien** (*pl.*) (university and school) vacation, 6-2
fern distant, far away, 12-2
fern·sehen (sieht fern), sah fern, hat ferngesehen to watch TV, 5-2
der **Fernseher, -** television set, 2-2

fertig (mit) (1) done, finished (with), 12-1; (2) ready, 5-1
der **Film, -e** film, movie, 6-TLL
finanzieren to finance, 6-TLL
finden, fand, hat gefunden to find, 2-2
  Das finde ich auch. I think so, too. 3-2
der **Finger, -** finger, 11-1
die **Firma, Firmen** (*pl.*) firm, company, 13-2
der **Fisch, -e** fish, 9-2
fit in shape, *Einf.*; 3-1
flach flat, 4-2
die **Flasche, -n** bottle, 7-1; 8-VID
das **Fleisch** meat, 2-1
fleißig industrious, hard-working, 5-2
fliegen, flog, ist geflogen to fly, 1-1
fließen, floss, ist geflossen to flow, 4-2
der **Flughafen, ¨** airport, 7-SA
das **Flugzeug, -e** airplane, 7-2
der **Fluss, ¨e** river, 4-2
folgen, ist gefolgt (+ *dat.*) to follow, 9-2
die **Form, -en** form, 10-TLL
formell formal, 1-TLL
formulieren to formulate
der **Fortschritt, -e** progress, 9-1
das **Foto, -s** photograph, 6-TLL; 7-2
  ein Foto machen to take a picture, 7-2
die **Frage, -n** question, 2-1
  eine Frage stellen to ask a question, 10-2
der **Fragebogen** questionnaire
fragen to ask, 1-1
  fragen nach to inquire, ask about, 8-SA
  sich fragen to wonder, ask oneself, 15-1
(das) **Frankreich** France, 5-2
der **Franzose, -n, -n** Frenchman, 11-TLL
die **Französin, -nen** Frenchwoman, 11-TLL
französisch French, 5-2
die **Frau, -en** woman; wife, 1-1
  Frau Kuhn Mrs./Ms. Kuhn, *Einf.*
das **Fräulein, -** young (unmarried) woman
  Fräulein Schmidt Miss Schmidt, *Einf.*
frei free; unoccupied, 2-1
die **Freiheit, -en** freedom, 7-2
(der) **Freitag** Friday, *Einf.*
die **Freizeit** free time, leisure time, 5-2
fremd (1) strange; (2) foreign, 3-2
die **Fremdsprache, -n** foreign language, 3-2
die **Freude, -n** joy, 12-2
freuen
  Das freut mich. I'm glad. *Einf.*
  (Es) freut mich. Pleased to meet you. *Einf.*; 13-SA
  sich freuen to be happy, 11-1
  sich freuen auf (+ *acc.*) to look forward to, 13-1
der **Freund, -e** friend (*m.*), 2-1
die **Freundin, -nen** friend (*f.*), 3-1
freundlich friendly, 1-2
der **Frieden** peace, 6-2
frisch fresh, 5-1
froh happy, glad, 13-2
früh early, 3-1
der **Frühling** spring, 4-2
das **Frühstück** breakfast, 4-1
  zum Frühstück for breakfast, 4-1
frühstücken to eat breakfast, 4-1
die **Frustration, -en** frustration, 16-TLL
frustrieren to frustrate, 16-2
sich fühlen to feel (*intrans.*), 11-1
führen to lead, 9-2
für (*prep.* + *acc.*) for, 1-1
furchtbar terrible, *Einf.*
fürchten to fear, 11-1
der **Fuchs, ¨e** fox, 10-SA
der **Fuß, ¨e** foot, 3-2
  zu Fuß on foot, 3-2
der **Fußball** soccer; soccer ball, 5-2
der **Fußgänger, -** pedestrian, 8-2
die **Fußgängerzone, -n** pedestrian zone, 8-2

G

die **Gabel, -n** fork, 8-SA
ganz entire, whole, 9-1
  ganz gut pretty good, 1-1
  den ganzen Sommer (Tag, Nachmittag usw.) all summer (day, afternoon, etc.)
gar
  gar kein no . . . at all, not a . . . at all, 8-2
  gar nicht not at all, 3-2
die **Garage, -n** garage, 15-SA
der **Garten, ¨** garden, 2-VID; 15-SA
der **Gast, ¨e** guest; patron, 8-1
der **Gastarbeiter, -** foreign worker (*m.*), 15-1
die **Gastarbeiterin, -nen** foreign worker (*f.*), 15-1
das **Gebäude, -** building, 8-1
geben (gibt), gab, hat gegeben to give, 2-2
  es gibt (+ *acc.*) there is, there are, 2-2
gebildet educated, 16-2
das **Gebirge, -** mountain range, 4-TLL
geboren born
  Wann sind Sie geboren? When were you born? 10-1
der **Geburtstag, -e** birthday, 9-1
  Wann hast du Geburtstag? When is your birthday? *Einf.*
  zum Geburtstag for (one's) birthday, 9-1
der **Gedanke, -ns, -n** thought, 16-2
das **Gedicht, -e** poem
die **Geduld** patience, 14-VID
die **Gefahr, -en** danger, 9-2
gefährlich dangerous, 9-2
gefallen (gefällt), gefiel, hat gefallen (+ *dat. of person*) to please, appeal to, 7-1
das **Gefühl, -e** feeling, 9-1
gegen (*prep.* + *acc.*) (1) against, (2) around, about (*with time*), 4-1
die **Gegend, -en** area, region, 12-1
der **Gegensatz, ¨e** opposite
das **Gegenteil: im Gegenteil** on the contrary, 8-2
die **Gegenwart** present (time), 12-SA; 14-2

gehen, ging, ist gegangen (1) to go; (2) to walk, 1-1
Es geht. It's all right. 4-1
Es geht nicht. Nothing doing. It can't be done.
es geht um it's a question of . . . ; it's about . . . (*subject is always* **es**), 16-2
Wie geht es Ihnen/dir? How are you? *Einf.*
Wie geht's? How are you? *Einf.*
gehören (+ *dat. of person*) to belong to (a person), 7-1
gelb yellow, 3-2
das **Geld** money, 2-2
der **Geldbeutel, -** wallet, change purse, 10-1; 10-VID
die **Gelegenheit, -en** opportunity, chance, 14-2
das **Gemüse** vegetables, 2-1
gemütlich cozy, comfortable; quiet, relaxed, 14-2
genau exact, precise, 11-1
genauso ... wie just as . . . as, 12-G
die **Generation, -en** generation, 8-TLL
genug enough, 3-1
die **Geographie** geography, 4-TLL
geographisch geographical, 4-TLL
das **Gepäck** luggage, 7-1
gerade just, at this moment, 6-2
geradeaus straight ahead, 8-2
die **Germanistik** German studies, 6-SA
gern(e) (lieber, am liebsten) gladly, with pleasure, 2-VID; 4-1
etwas gern haben to like something, 4-1
gern + *verb* like to, 4-1
lieber + *verb* prefer to, would rather, 4-1
Lieber nicht. I'd rather not. No thanks. Let's not. 4-1
das **Geschäft, -e** business; store, 5-2
die **Geschäftsfrau, -en** businesswoman, 5-SA
der **Geschäftsmann, Geschäftsleute** (*pl.*) businessman, 5-SA
das **Geschenk, -e** present (*gift*), 9-1
die **Geschichte, -n** (1) story; (2) history, 6-2
das **Geschlecht, -er** sex, gender, 16-2
geschlossen closed (*see* **schließen**), 11-2
die **Geschwister** (*pl.*) siblings, 2-SA
die **Gesellschaft, -en** society, 9-2
gesellschaftlich social, 16-2
das **Gesetz, -e** law, 16-2
vor dem Gesetz under the law, in the eyes of the law, 16-2
das **Gesicht, -er** face, 11-1
das **Gespräch, -e** conversation, 13-2
gestern yesterday, 6-1
gestern Abend yesterday evening, 12-G
gestern früh yesterday morning, 12-G
gestresst (*colloq.*) stressed out, 16-2
gesund healthy, 9-2
die **Gesundheit** health, 9-2
das **Getränk, -e** drink, 16-VID
gewinnen, gewann, hat gewonnen to win, 9-SA
sich gewöhnen an (+ *acc.*) to get used to, 13-1
das **Glas, ¨er** glass, 8-1
glauben (+ *dat. of person*) (1) to believe; (2) to think, 4-1
Ich glaube nicht. I don't think so. 8-1
Ich glaube schon. I think so. 8-1
gleich (1) right away, immediately, 5-1; (2) equal, 16-2
gleichberechtigt enjoying equal rights, 16-2
die **Gleichberechtigung** (*sing.*) equal rights
das **Gleis, -e** track, 7-1
das **Glück** (1) happiness; (2) luck, 6-2
Glück haben to be lucky, 6-2
glücklich happy, *Einf.*
der **Glückwunsch: Herzlichen Glückwunsch!** Congratulations! Best wishes! 12-VID
golden golden, 16-1
die **goldene Hochzeit** golden wedding anniversary, 16-1
der **Gott, ¨er** god
Gott sei Dank thank goodness, 4-1
Grüß Gott hello (in southern Germany and Austria), *Einf.*
Um Gottes Willen! For heaven's sake! Oh my gosh! 3-1
das **Gramm** gram, 8-1
die **Grammatik** grammar
gratulieren (+ *dat. of person*) to congratulate, 15-1
grau gray, 3-2
grausam terrible, gruesome; cruel, 12-2
die **Grenze, -n** border, 11-1
(das) **Griechenland** Greece, 15-1
griechisch Greek, 8-1
groß (größer, am größten) big, tall, 2-1
die **Größe, -n** size; greatness, 12-1
die **Großeltern** (*pl.*) grandparents, 2-2
die **Großmutter, ¨** grandmother, 2-2
die **Großstadt, ¨e** large city (over 500,000 inhabitants), 8-2
der **Großvater, ¨** grandfather, 2-2
grün green, 3-2
der **Grund, ¨e** reason
die **Gruppe, -n** group, 1-2
grüßen to greet, say hello, 1-2
Grüß Gott hello (in southern Germany and Austria), *Einf.*
gut (besser, am besten) good, well, *Einf.*; 1-1
ganz gut pretty good, 1-1
Guten Abend! Good evening! *Einf.*
Guten Morgen! Good morning! *Einf.*
Gute Reise! Have a good trip! 1-1
Guten Tag! Hello! *Einf.*
Ist gut. (*colloq.*) O.K. Fine by me. 5-1
das **Gymnasium,** *pl.* **Gymnasien** secondary school (prepares pupils for university), 3-2

H

das **Haar, -e** hair, 6-2

sich die Haare kämmen to comb one's hair, 11-SA

haben (hat), hatte, hat gehabt to have, *Einf.*; 2-1

Ich hätte gern ... I'd like to have . . . 6-VID

der **Hafen, ¨** port, harbor, 8-2

halb (*adv.*) half

halb acht seven-thirty, *Einf.*

halbtags (*adv.*) half days, 16-1

halbtags arbeiten to work part time, 16-1

Hallo! Hello! *Einf.*

halten (hält), hielt, hat gehalten (1) to stop (*intrans.*); (2) to hold, 3-1

halten für (+ *acc.*) to take for, regard as, think X is, 15-1

die **Haltestelle, -n** (streetcar or bus) stop, 8-SA; 13-1

die **Hand, ¨e** hand, 5-1

der **Handschuh, -e** glove, 3-SA

hängen (*trans.*) to hang, 7-1

hängen, hing, hat gehangen (*intrans.*) to be hanging, 7-1

hart (härter) hard; tough; harsh, 10-2

der **Hass** hatred, 11-2

hassen to hate, 3-2

hässlich ugly, 1-1

Haupt- (*noun prefix*) main, chief, primary, most important, 4-TLL

das **Hauptfach, ¨er** major field (of study), 6-2

die **Hauptstadt, ¨e** capital city, 4-TLL

das **Haus, ¨er** house; building, 1-2

nach Hause home (as destination of motion), 3-1

zu Hause at home, 2-2

die **Hausaufgabe, -n** homework assignment, 3-2

die **Hausfrau, -en** housewife, 2-2

das **Heft, -e** notebook, *Einf.*

die **Heimat** native place or country, homeland, 11-2

das **Heimweh** homesickness, 12-SA

heiraten to marry, get married, 16-1

heiß hot, *Einf.*

heißen, hieß, hat geheißen to be called, 2-1

das heißt that means, in other words, 6-2

Ich heiße ... My name is . . . *Einf.*

Wie heißen Sie? What's your name? *Einf.*

heiter cheerful, 14-2

hektisch hectic, 7-TLL

helfen (hilft), half, hat geholfen (+ *dat.*) to help, 7-1

hell bright, light, 2-VID; 3-2

das **Hemd, -en** shirt, 3-2

her- (*prefix*) *indicates motion toward the speaker*, 15-G

der **Herbst** fall, autumn, 4-2

der **Herr, -n, -en** gentleman, 1-1

Herr Lehmann Mr. Lehmann, *Einf.*

herrlich great, terrific, marvelous, *Einf.*

Herzlich willkommen! Welcome! Nice to see you! 6-2

heute today, *Einf.*

heute Abend this evening, tonight, 1-1

heute Morgen this morning, 5-1

heute Nachmittag this afternoon, 12-G

hier here, 1-1

die **Hilfe** help, aid, 13-1

hin- (*prefix*) *indicates motion away from speaker*, 15-G

hinein- (*prefix*) in, into, 15-1

hinter (*prep.* + *acc.* or *dat.*) behind, 6-1

historisch historic, 8-TLL

hoch (*predicative adj.*), **hoh-** (*attributive adj.*) **(höher, am höchsten)** high, 4-2

höchste Zeit high time, 14-1

das **Hochland** highlands, 4-TLL

die **Hochschule, -n** university, institute of higher learning, 14-2

die **Hochzeit, -en** wedding, 12-VID; 16-1

die **goldene Hochzeit** golden wedding anniversary, 16-1

hoffen to hope, 7-2

hoffentlich (*adv.*) I hope, 4-1

höflich polite, 1-2

hoh-, höher (*see* **hoch**)

holen to fetch, get, 12-2

hören to hear, 3-2

der **Horizont, -e** horizon, 7-TLL

die **Hose, -n** trousers, pants, 3-2

das **Hotel, -s** hotel, 4-1

hübsch pretty, handsome, 11-1

der **Hügel, -** hill, 4-2

hügelig hilly, 4-SA

der **Humor** humor, 14-TLL

der **Hund, -e** dog, 11-G

hundert hundred, 2-G

der **Hunger** hunger, 8-1

Hunger haben to be hungry, 8-1

hungrig hungry, 4-1

der **Hut, ¨e** hat, 3-SA

I

die **Idee, -n** idea, 10-2

ideologisch ideological, 10-TLL

idiotensicher foolproof, 12-1

illegal illegal, 10-TLL

immer always, 1-2

immer größer bigger and bigger, 12-G

immer noch still, 4-2

in (*prep.* + *acc.* or *dat.*) in, into, 1-1

der **Indikativ** indicative

die **Industrie, -n** industry, 5-TLL

die **Inflation** inflation, 10-TLL

die **Informatik** computer science, 6-SA

der **Ingenieur, -e** engineer (*m.*), 5-SA

die **Ingenieurin, -nen** engineer (*f.*), 5-SA

die **Insel, -n** island, 4-TLL

das **Instrument, -e** instrument, 7-TLL

die **Integration** integration, 11-2

intelligent intelligent, 12-1

interessant interesting, 3-1

interessieren to interest, 13-1

sich interessieren für (+ *acc.*) to be interested in, 13-1

international international, 3-TLL

interviewen to interview, 10-1
investieren to invest, 11-TLL
irgend- (*prefix*)
irgendwann sometime or other, any time, 12-G
irgendwie somehow or other, 12-G
irgendwo somewhere or other, anywhere, 12-G
die **Ironie** irony, 14-TLL
(das) **Italien** Italy, 4-2
der **Italiener, -** Italian (*m.*), 11-TLL
die **Italienerin, -nen** Italian (*f.*), 11-TLL
italienisch Italian, 11-TLL

J

ja (1) yes; (2) (*unstressed flavoring particle*), 1-1
die **Jacke, -n** jacket, 3-2
das **Jahr, -e** year, 5-1
im Jahr(e) 1996 in 1996, 9-2
jahrelang (*adv.*) for years, 14-TLL
die **Jahreszeit, -en** season
das **Jahrhundert, -e** century, 8-2
jahrhundertelang (*adv.*) for centuries, 14-TLL
jährlich annually, 9-2
(der) **Januar** January, *Einf.*
je ever, 6-2
die **Jeans** (*pl.*) jeans, 3-TLL
jeder, -es, -e each, every, 5-1
jeder (*pronoun*) everyone
jemand somebody, someone, 2-2
jemand anders someone else, 16-VID
jetzt now, 3-1
von jetzt an from now on, 13-1
der **Journalist, -en, -en** journalist, 5-TLL
jüdisch Jewish, 12-2
die **Jugend** (*sing.*) youth; young people, 9-2
die **Jugendherberge, -n** youth hostel, 7-2
(der) **Juli** July, *Einf.*
jung (jünger) young, 2-2
der **Junge, -n, -n** boy, 9-1
(der) **Juni** June, *Einf.*
Jura (study of) law, 6-SA

K

der **Kaffee** coffee, 8-1
kalt (kälter) cold, *Einf.*
die **Kamera, -s** camera, 7-TLL
kämmen to comb
sich die Haare kämmen to comb one's hair, 11-SA
(das) **Kanada** Canada, 5-TLL; 6-1
der **Kanadier, -** Canadian (*m.*), 11-TLL
die **Kanadierin, -nen** Canadian (*f.*), 11-TLL
kanadisch Canadian (*adj.*), 11-TLL
das **Kännchen, -** small (coffee or tea) pot, 8-SA
der **Kapitalismus** capitalism, 11-TLL
das **Kapitel, -** chapter
kaputt (*colloq.*) (1) broken, kaput; (2) exhausted, 9-1
kaputt·machen to break, 12-1
die **Karikatur, -en** caricature, 16-TLL
die **Karriere, -n** career, 16-TLL
die **Karte, -n** (1) card; (2) ticket; (3) map, 4-1
die **Kartoffel, -n** potato, 8-1
der **Käse** cheese, 2-1
die **Kasse, -n** cashier; cashier's office, 14-1
der **Kassettenrecorder, -** cassette player, 10-1
katastrophal catastrophic, 8-TLL
die **Katastrophe, -n** catastrophe, 6-2
die **Katze, -n** cat, 11-G
kaufen to buy, 4-1
das **Kaufhaus, ¨-er** department store, 8-SA
kaum hardly, barely, 16-1
kein not a, not any, no, 3-1
kein ... mehr no more . . . , not a . . . any longer, 4-1
der **Keller, -** cellar, basement, 9-1
der **Kellner, -** waiter, 5-SA; 8-1
die **Kellnerin, -nen** waitress, 5-SA; 8-1
kennen, kannte, hat gekannt to know, be acquainted with, 2-1
kennen lernen to get to know; to meet, 5-1

die **Kette, -n** chain
die **Kettenreaktion, -en** chain reaction
das **Kilo** (*short for* das **Kilogramm**), 8-1
das **Kilogramm** kilogram, 8-1
der **Kilometer, -** kilometer
das **Kind, -er** child, 1-1
die **Kindheit, -en** childhood, 9-TLL
das **Kino, -s** movie theater, 6-2
die **Kirche, -n** church, 8-SA
klar (1) clear; (2) (*colloq.*) sure, of course, 9-1
die **Klasse, -n** class; grade, 1-2
der **Klatsch** gossip, 12-1
klauen (*colloq.*) to rip off, steal, 10-1
die **Klausur, -en** written test, 6-2
das **Klavier, -e** piano, 14-2
das **Kleid, -er** dress (*pl.* = dresses *or* clothes), 3-2
der **Kleiderschrank, ¨-e** clothes cupboard, wardrobe, 6-SA
die **Kleidung** clothing, 3-SA
klein little, small; short, 2-1
die **Kleinstadt, ¨-e** town (5,000 to 20,000 inhabitants), 8-2
das **Klima** climate, 4-2
klingeln to ring, 7-1
klingen, klang, hat geklungen to sound, 8-1
die **Klinik, -en** clinic, 15-TLL
das **Klischee, -s** cliché, 2-2
klischeehaft (*adj.*) clichéd, stereotyped, 13-SA
klug (klüger) smart, bright, 5-1
knapp scarce, in short supply, 12-1
knapp bei Kasse short of cash, 12-1
die **Kneipe, -n** tavern, bar, 6-2
kochen to cook, 2-2
der **Koffer, -** suitcase, 7-1
(das) **Köln** Cologne, 8-1
die **Kolonie, -n** colony, 4-TLL
komisch peculiar, odd; funny, 12-1
kommen, kam, ist gekommen to come, *Einf.*; 1-1
kommen aus to come from, *Einf.*

Wie kommt das? How come? What's the reason for that? 16-VID
der **Kommunismus** Communism, 11-TLL
die **Konditorei, -en** pastry café, 8-SA
der **Konflikt, -e** conflict, 2-TLL
konfrontieren to confront, 16-TLL
der **Konjunktiv** subjunctive
die **Konkurrenz** competition, 9-SA
können (kann), konnte, hat gekonnt can, be able to, 3-1
Ich kann Deutsch. I can speak German. 3-G
die **Konsequenz, -en** consequence, 9-TLL
konservativ conservative, 13-TLL
der **Kontakt, -e** contact, 14-TLL
der **Kontrast, -e** contrast, 4-TLL
kontrollieren to check, inspect, 15-2
sich konzentrieren auf (+ *acc.*) to concentrate on, 14-2
das **Konzert, -e** concert, 6-TLL
der **Kopf, ¨e** head, 11-1
Das geht mir nicht aus dem Kopf. I can't forget that. 12-2
der **Korrespondent, -en, -en** correspondent, 5-TLL
(das) **Korsika** Corsica, 5-TLL
kosten to cost, 2-VID; 5-1
Wie viel kostet das bitte? How much does that cost, please? 5-1
kostenlos free of charge, 6-2
die **Kraft, ¨e** power; strength, 9-2
das **Kraftwerk, -e** power plant, 9-2
krank (kränker) sick, *Einf.*
das **Krankenhaus, ¨er** hospital, 11-1
der **Krankenpfleger, -** nurse (*m.*), 5-SA
die **Krankenschwester, -n** nurse (*f.*), 5-SA
die **Krankheit, -en** sickness, 9-2
die **Krawatte, -n** tie, 3-SA
kreativ creative, 14-TLL
die **Kreditkarte, -n** credit card, 14-1
die **Kreide** chalk, *Einf.*
der **Krieg, -e** war, 6-2
kritisch critical, 16-2
die **Küche, -n** kitchen, 15-SA; 16-2
der **Kuchen, -** cake, 8-SA
der **Kugelschreiber, -** ballpoint pen, *Einf.*
kühl cool, *Einf.*
die **Kultur, -en** culture, 4-TLL
sich kümmern um (+ *acc.*) to look after, take care of, deal with, 13-1
der **Kunde, -n, -n** customer (*m.*), 5-1
die **Kundin, -nen** customer (*f.*), 5-1
die **Kunst, ¨e** art, 8-1
die **Kunstgeschichte** art history, 6-SA
der **Künstler, -** artist (*m.*), 5-SA; 14-2
die **Künstlerin, -nen** artist (*f.*), 5-SA; 14-2
kurz (kürzer) short; for a short time, 4-1
die **Kusine, -n** cousin (*f.*), 2-SA
die **Küste, -n** coast, 4-TLL

L

das **Labor, -s** laboratory, 6-SA
lachen to laugh, 3-2
der **Laden, ¨** shop, store, 5-1
die **Lampe, -n** lamp, 6-SA
das **Land, ¨er** country, 4-2
auf dem Land in the country, 8-2
aufs Land to the country, 8-2
die **Landkarte, -** map, *Einf.*
die **Landschaft, -en** landscape, 4-2
die **Landsleute** (*pl.*) compatriots
der **Landwirt, -e** farmer (*m.*), 5-SA
die **Landwirtin, -nen** farmer (*f.*), 5-SA
die **Landwirtschaft** agriculture, 6-SA
lang(e) (länger) long; for a long time, 4-1
langsam slow, *Einf.*; 3-2
sich langweilen to be bored, 13-1
langweilig boring, 3-1
lassen (lässt), ließ, hat gelassen (1) to leave (something or someone), leave behind; (2) to let, allow; (3) to cause to be done, 12-1
laufen (läuft), lief, ist gelaufen (1) to run; (2) (*colloq.*) to go on foot, walk, 3-1
die **Laune** mood
guter/schlechter Laune in a good/bad mood, *Einf.*
laut loud, *Einf.*
leben to live, be alive, 2-2
das **Leben** life, 4-2
die **Lebensmittel** (*pl.*) groceries, 5-2
der **Lebensstandard** standard of living, 9-TLL
die **Leberwurst, ¨e** liverwurst, 8-1
lecker tasty, delicious, 8-1
ledig single (= unmarried), 16-1
leer empty, 5-1
legen to lay, put down, 6-1
der **Lehrer, -** teacher (*m.*), *Einf.*
die **Lehrerin, -nen** teacher (*f.*), *Einf.*
der **Lehrling, -e** apprentice, 5-1
leicht (1) light (in weight); (2) easy, 3-1
Leid: Das tut mir Leid. I'm sorry about that. *Einf.*; 7-1
leider unfortunately, *Einf.*; 3-1
leihen, lieh, hat geliehen (1) to lend, loan; (2) to borrow, 10-1
leise quiet, soft, *Einf.*
leisten: sich etwas leisten können to be able to afford something, 11-1
die **Leitfrage, -n** guiding question
lernen to learn, 3-2
lesen (liest), las, hat gelesen to read, 2-1
lesen über (+ *acc.*) to read about, 2-1
das **Lesestück, -e** reading selection
letzt- last, 10-1
letzte Woche last week, 6-2
die **Leute** (*pl.*) people, 2-1
das **Licht, -er** light, 11-1
lieb dear; nice, sweet, 6-2
Lieber Fritz! Dear Fritz, (salutation in letter), 6-TLL
die **Liebe** love, 11-2
lieben to love, 3-2

lieber preferably, would rather (*see* **gern**), 4-1
Lieblings- (*noun prefix*) favorite, 9-1
liebsten: am liebsten most like to, like best of all to (*see* **gern**), 4-1
das **Lied, -er** song, 4-2
liegen, lag, hat gelegen to lie; to be situated, 4-2
der **Lift, -s** elevator, 14-SA
lila violet, lavender, 3-SA
die **Limnologie** limnology
die **Linguistik** linguistics, 6-SA
die **Linie, -n** (streetcar or bus) line, 13-1
links to the left; on the left, 8-2
die **Liste, -n** list
der **Liter** liter, 8-1
literarisch literary, 14-TLL
der **Löffel, -** spoon, 8-SA
der **Lohn, ¨-e** wage, 16-2
sich lohnen to be worthwhile, worth the trouble, 13-1
das **Lokal, -e** neighborhood restaurant or tavern, 8-1
los! let's go! 10-VID
Was ist los? (1)What's the matter? (2)What's going on? 3-1
lösen to solve, 9-2
los·fahren (fährt los), fuhr los, ist losgefahren to depart, start, leave, 14-1
die **Lösung, -en** solution, 9-2
der **Löwe, -n, -n** lion, 10-SA
die **Luft** air, 4-SA; 8-2
die **Luftverschmutzung** air pollution, 8-2
die **Lust** desire
Ich habe keine Lust. I don't want to. 3-1
Lust haben (etwas zu tun) to want to do (something), 8-1
lustig: sich lustig machen über (+ *acc.*) to make fun of, 16-2
die **Lyrik** poetry

M

machen (1) to make; (2) to do, 1-1
Das macht (mir) Spaß. That is fun (for me). 7-1
Das macht zusammen ... All together that comes to . . . 5-1
Es macht (doch) nichts. It doesn't matter. 7-1
die **Macht, ¨-e** power, might, 11-2
das **Mädchen, -** girl, 9-1
mag (*see* **mögen**)
(der) **Mai** May, *Einf.*
mal (*flavoring particle with commands, see* p. 104), 4-1
das **Mal, -e** time (in the sense of occurrence), 12-1
das nächste Mal (the) next time, 12-G
jedes Mal every time, 12-1
zum ersten Mal for the first time, 12-G
man one (*indefinite pronoun*), 1-2
der **Manager, -** manager, 11-TLL
mancher, -es, -e many a, 9-2
manche (*pl.*) some
manchmal sometimes, 2-2
manipulieren to manipulate, 10-TLL
der **Mann, ¨-er** (1) man; (2) husband, 2-1
die **Mannschaft, -en** team, 5-2
der **Mantel, ¨** coat, 3-2
das **Märchen, -** fairy tale, 4-2
die **Mark** (die **Deutsche Mark—DM**) mark (the German mark), 5-1
(der) **März** March, *Einf.*
die **Mathe** (*colloq.*) math, 6-VID
die **Mathematik** mathematics, 6-SA
die **Mauer, -n** (freestanding or exterior) wall, 11-1
der **Mechaniker, -** mechanic, 5-1
die **Medizin** (field of) medicine, 6-SA
das **Meer, -e** sea, 4-2
mehr more, 2-2
nicht mehr no longer, not any more, 2-2
mehrere several, 11-1
meinen (1) to be of the opinion, think, 1-2; (2) to mean, 2-1
Was meinen Sie dazu? What do you say to that? What do you think of that? 16-1
die **Meinung, -en** opinion
meist- most (*see* **viel**)
meistens mostly, usually, 5-2
die **Melancholie** melancholy, 14-TLL
die **Menge, -n** quantity; crowd
eine Menge a lot, lots of, 6-2
die **Mensa** university cafeteria, 1-1
der **Mensch, -en, -en** person, human being, 6-1
Mensch! Man! Wow! 3-1
die **Menschheit** mankind, human race, 9-2
merken to notice, 11-1
leicht zu merken easy to remember
das **Messer, -** knife, 8-SA
die **Methode, -n** method, 10-TLL
mieten to rent, 2-VID
die **Milch** milk, 8-SA; 12-2
mild mild, 4-TLL
die **Million, -en** million, 11-TLL
die **Minute, -n** minute, 3-1
minutenlang (*adv.*) for minutes, 14-TLL
Mist: So ein Mist! (*crude & colloq.*) (1) What a drag. (2) What a lot of bull. 10-1
mit (*prep. + dat.*) with, 2-1; (*adv.*) along with, 12-1
der **Mitbewohner, -** fellow occupant, roommate, housemate (*m.*), 3-1
die **Mitbewohnerin, -nen** fellow occupant, roommate, housemate (*f.*), 3-1
mit·bringen, brachte mit, hat mitgebracht to bring along, take along, 6-1
miteinander with each other, together, 1-2
das **Mitglied, -er** member, 11-2
mit·kommen, kam mit, ist mitgekommen to come along, 5-1
das **Mitleid** sympathy, 16-SA
mit·machen to participate, cooperate, pitch in, 9-1

mit·nehmen (nimmt mit), nahm mit, hat mitgenommen to take along, 7-2
das **Mittagessen** midday meal, lunch, 5-2
das **Mittelalter** the Middle Ages, 13-1
(der) **Mittwoch** Wednesday, *Einf.*
die **Möbel** (*pl.*) furniture, 6-SA
möbliert furnished, 6-SA
modern modern, 4-2
modernisieren to modernize, 11-TLL
mögen (mag), mochte, hat gemocht to like, 4-1
  möchten would like to, 3-1
  Das mag sein. That may be. 16-G
möglich possible, 6-1
der **Moment, -e** moment
  im Moment at the moment, 1-1
die **Monarchie, -n** monarchy, 10-TLL
der **Monat, -e** month, 10-1
monatelang (*adv.*) for months, 14-TLL
(der) **Montag** Monday, *Einf.*
morgen tomorrow, *Einf.*; 1-1
  morgen Abend tomorrow evening, 12-G
  morgen früh tomorrow morning, 12-G
  morgen Nachmittag tomorrow afternoon, 12-G
der **Morgen, -** morning, 1-1
  Guten Morgen! Good morning! 1-1
morgens (*adv.*) in the morning(s), 4-1
das **Motorrad, ¨er** motorcycle, 5-1
müde tired, weary, *Einf.*
der **Müll** trash, refuse, 9-1
(das) **München** Munich, 8-2
der **Mund, ¨er** mouth, 11-1
munter wide-awake, cheerful, *Einf.*
das **Museum,** *pl.* **Museen** museum, 8-1
die **Musik** music, 3-2
die **Musikwissenschaft** musicology, 6-SA
müssen (muss), musste, hat gemusst must, to have to, 3-1
die **Mutter, ¨** mother, 2-2
die **Muttersprache, -n** native language, 5-2
die **Mutti, -s** mama, mom, 2-2
die **Mütze, -n** cap, 3-SA

N

na well . . . 12-1
  Na endlich! At last! High time! 9-1
  Na und? And so? So what? 10-1
nach (*prep. + dat.*) (1) after, 5-1; (2) to (with cities and countries), 1-1
  nach Hause home (as destination of motion), 3-1
der **Nachbar, -n, -n** neighbor (*m.*), 11-2
die **Nachbarin, -nen** neighbor (*f.*), 11-2
nachdem (*sub. conj.*) after, 10-1
nachher (*adv.*) later on, after that, 4-1
der **Nachmittag, -e** afternoon, 10-1
  am Nachmittag in the afternoon, 10-1
nachmittags (in the) afternoons, 5-TLL
die **Nachspeise, -n** dessert, 16-VID
nächst- next; nearest, 12-1
  nächstes Semester next semester, 2-1
die **Nacht, ¨e** night, 1-1
  Gute Nacht. Good night. 12-1
  in der Nacht in the night, at night, 12-1
der **Nachtisch, -e** dessert, 8-1
  zum Nachtisch for dessert, 8-1
nachts at night, 5-TLL
nah(e) (näher, am nächsten) near, 8-1
die **Nähe** nearness; vicinity
  in der Nähe (von or + *gen.*) near, nearby, 7-2
der **Name, -ns, -n** name, 5-1
  Wie ist Ihr Name? What's your name? 10-VID
die **Nase, -n** nose, 5-1
  Ich habe die Nase voll. I'm fed up. I've had it up to here. 5-1
nass wet, damp, 4-2
die **Nationalität, -en** nationality, 15-TLL
die **Natur** nature, 9-TLL
natürlich natural, naturally; of course, 1-1
der **Nebel** fog, mist, 4-SA
neben (*prep. + acc.* or *dat.*) beside, next to, 6-1
das **Nebenfach, ¨er** minor field (of study), 6-2
neblig foggy, misty, *Einf.*
nee (*colloq.*) no, 6-1
nehmen (nimmt), nahm, hat genommen to take, 2-1
nein no, *Einf.*
nennen, nannte, hat genannt to name, call, 10-2
nett nice, 6-1
neu new, 3-2
neulich recently, 12-1
neutral neutral, 13-TLL
die **Neutralität** neutrality, 13-TLL
nicht not, *Einf.*; 1-1
  gar nicht not at all, 3-2
  nicht mehr no longer, not any more, 2-2
  nicht nur ... sondern auch not only . . . but also, 9-2
  nicht wahr? isn't it? can't you? doesn't she? etc., 3-1
nichts nothing, 3-1
  Nichts zu danken! Don't mention it! 2-1
  Es macht nichts. It doesn't matter. 7-1
nie never, 1-2
niedrig low, 6-2
niemand nobody, no one, 2-2
noch still, 2-2
  noch ein another, an additional, 2-2
  noch einmal once again, once more, 4-1
  noch etwas something else, anything more, 8-1
  noch immer still, 4-2
  noch jemand someone else

noch kein- not a . . . yet, not any . . . yet, 4-1
noch nicht not yet, 4-1
(das) **Nordamerika** North America, 2-TLL
der **Norden** the north, 4-2
normal normal, 2-TLL
die **Note, -n** grade, 5-1
nötig necessary, 9-1
(der) **November** November, *Einf.*
die **Nummer, -n** number, *Einf.*; 14-1
nun (1) now; (2) well . . . , well now, 10-1
nur only, 2-1
nützlich useful

O

ob (*sub. conj.*) if, whether, 8-1
oben (*adv.*) above; on top
das **Obst** fruit, 2-1
obwohl (*sub. conj.*) although, 8-2
oder (*coor. conj.*) or, 1-2
offen open, 11-2
öffentlich public, 16-2
offiziell official, 13-TLL
öffnen to open, 11-1
oft (öfter) often, 1-2
ohne (*prep. + acc.*) without, 4-1
ohne ... zu without . . . -ing, 8-G
das **Ohr, -en** ear, 11-1
das **Ökosystem, -e** ecosystem, 9-TLL
(der) **Oktober** October, *Einf.*
das **Öl** oil, 9-2
die **Oma, -s** grandma, 2-2
der **Onkel, -** uncle, 2-2
der **Opa, -s** grandpa, 2-2
die **Opposition, -en** opposition, 10-TLL
optimistisch optimistic, 3-TLL
ordentlich tidy, orderly, 13-1
der **Ort, -e** (1) place; (2) small town, 12-SA; 13-2
der **Osten** the east, 4-2
(das) **Österreich** Austria, 4-1
der **Österreicher, -** Austrian (*m.*), 11-TLL
die **Österreicherin, -nen** Austrian (*f.*), 11-TLL
österreichisch Austrian, 14-1
(das) **Osteuropa** Eastern Europe, 11-TLL

P

ein paar a couple (of), a few, 6-2
packen to pack, 7-TLL
die **Pädagogik** (field of) education, 6-SA
das **Papier, -e** paper, *Einf.*; 9-1
die **Partei, -en** political party, 9-2
der **Partner, -** partner, 5-TLL
die **Party, -s** party, 6-TLL
der **Pass, ¨-e** passport, 15-2
passieren, ist passiert to happen, 10-1
der **Patient, -en, -en** patient, 14-TLL
pauken (*student slang*) to cram, 6-VID
die **Pause, -n** break; intermission, 3-1
eine Pause machen to take a break, 3-1
Pech haben to have bad luck, be unlucky, 6-2
per by (means of)
per Autostopp reisen to hitchhike, 7-2
perfekt perfect, 15-1
die **Person, -en** person
persönlich personal
pessimistisch pessimistic, 3-TLL
die **Pflanze, -n** plant, 9-2
die **Pflicht, -en** duty, 16-2
das **Pfund** 500 grams, 8-VID
die **Philosophie** philosophy, 6-TLL
philosophieren to philosophize, 14-TLL
die **Physik** physics, 6-SA
das **Plakat, -e** (political) poster, 10-2
planen to plan, make plans, 7-1
das **Plastik** plastic, 9-TLL
der **Platz, ¨-e** (1) place; (2) space; (3) city square, 6-1; (4) seat, 7-2
plötzlich suddenly, 10-1
die **Politik** (1) politics; (2) policy, 9-2
der **Politiker, -** politician (*m.*), 5-SA; 9-2
die **Politikerin, -nen** politician (*f.*), 5-SA
die **Politikwissenschaft** political science, 6-SA
politisch political, 9-TLL
die **Polizei** (*sing. only*) the police
die **Pommes frites** (*pl.*) French fries, 3-2
die **Portion, -en** order, helping (of food), 8-SA
die **Post** (1) post office; postal service; (2) mail, 8-SA; 15-1
das **Poster, -** poster, *Einf.*
die **Postkarte, -n** postcard, 5-2
praktisch practical, 6-TLL
der **Präsident, -en, -en** president, 10-SA
der **Preis, -e** price, 8-2
preiswert inexpensive, 14-VID
prima terrific, great, *Einf.*; 1-1
privat private, 6-TLL
probieren to sample, try, 8-VID; 14-1
das **Problem, -e** problem, 2-2
produktiv productive, 14-TLL
produzieren to produce, 9-TLL
der **Professor, -en** professor (*m.*), *Einf.*
die **Professorin, -nen** professor (*f.*), *Einf.*
das **Programm, -e** program, 6-TLL
der **Programmierer, -** programmer (*m.*), 5-SA
die **Programmiererin, -nen** programmer (*f.*), 5-SA
Prost! (*or*) **Prosit!** Cheers! 16-VID
der **Protest, -e** protest, 11-TLL
das **Prozent** percent, 13-TLL
die **Prüfung, -en** examination
die **Psychoanalyse** psychoanalysis, 14-TLL
die **Psychologie** psychology, 6-SA
der **Pulli, -s** (*slang*) = **Pullover**, 3-2
der **Pullover, -** pullover, sweater, 3-2
pünktlich punctual, on time, 7-2
putzen to clean, 11-SA

Q

Quatsch! Nonsense! Baloney! 5-1

quatschen (*colloq.*) (1) to talk nonsense; (2) to chat, 7-2
die **Querstraße, -n** cross street, 12-1

R

das **Rad, ¨-er** (1) wheel; (2) bicycle, 8-2
Rad fahren (fährt Rad), ist Rad gefahren to bicycle, 8-2
der **Radiergummi** eraser, *Einf.*
radikal radical, 9-TLL
das **Radio, -s** radio, 6-SA
sich rasieren to shave, 11-SA
raten (rät), riet, hat geraten to guess
Raten Sie mal! Take a guess!
das **Rathaus, ¨-er** town hall, 8-SA
reagieren auf (+ *acc.*) to react to, 13-2
die **Reaktion, -en** reaction
realistisch realistic, 5-TLL
die **Rechnung, -en** bill, check, 16-VID
Recht: Recht haben (hat Recht), hatte Recht, hat Recht gehabt to be right, 4-1
rechts (*adv.*) to the right; on the right, 8-2
der **Rechtsanwalt, ¨-e** lawyer (*m.*), 5-SA; 13-2
die **Rechtsanwältin, -nen** lawyer (*f.*), 5-SA; 13-2
das **Recycling** recycling; recycling center, 9-1
reden to talk, speak, 12-1
das **Referat, -e** (1) oral report; (2) written term paper, 6-2
ein Referat halten to give a report, 6-SA
ein Referat schreiben to write a paper, 6-SA
die **Reform, -en** reform, 11-TLL
reformieren to reform, 11-TLL
das **Regal** shelf
der **Regen** rain, 4-SA
der **Regenschirm, -e** umbrella, 3-SA
die **Regierung, -en** government in power, administration (U.S.), 10-SA; 11-2
das **Regime** regime, 11-TLL
die **Region, -en** region, 4-TLL
regnen to rain, *Einf.*; 1-1
regnerisch rainy, 4-SA
reich rich, 10-1
das **Reich, -e** empire; realm, 10-2
die **Reise, -n** trip, journey, 3-2
eine Reise machen to take a trip, 3-2
Gute Reise! Have a good trip! 1-1
das **Reisebüro, -s** travel agency, 14-VID
der **Reiseführer, -** guide book, 5-1
reisen, ist gereist to travel, 5-2
per Autostopp reisen to hitchhike, 7-2
der **Reisepass, ¨-e** passport, 14-SA
der **Reisescheck, -s** traveler's check, 14-1
das **Reiseziel, -e** destination, 7-2
relativ (*adj. and adv.*) relative, 2-TLL
reparieren to repair, 12-1
die **Republik, -en** republic, 10-TLL
reservieren to reserve, 7-1
das **Restaurant, -s** restaurant, 8-1
die **Restauration, -en** restoration, 8-TLL
retten to save, rescue, 9-2
die **Revolution, -en** revolution, 11-TLL
die **Rezeption** hotel reception desk, 14-1
der **Rhein** the Rhine River, 4-TLL
richtig right, correct, *Einf.*; true, real, 15-2
der **Riese, -n, -n** giant
riesen- (*noun and adj. prefix*) gigantic
riesengroß huge, gigantic, 8-2
Ich habe Riesenhunger. I'm famished (*or*) hungry as a bear. 14-2
der **Rock, ¨-e** skirt, 3-SA
die **Rolle, -n** role, 2-2
der **Roman, -e** novel, 5-2
romantisch romantic, 13-TLL
rosa pink, 3-SA
rot (röter) red, 3-2
der **Rucksack, ¨-e** rucksack, backpack, 7-2
rufen, rief, hat gerufen to call, shout, 11-2
ruhig (1) calm, peaceful, 10-2; (2) (*as sentence adverb*) "feel free to," "go ahead and," 12-1
(das) **Rumänien** Romania, 11-TLL
der **Russe, -n, -n** Russian (*m.*), 11-TLL
die **Russin, -nen** Russian (*f.*), 11-TLL
russisch Russian, 11-TLL
(das) **Russland** Russia, 8-2

S

die **Sache, -n** (1) thing; item, 8-1; (2) matter, affair
der **Sack, ¨-e** sack, 9-1
der **Saft, ¨-e** juice, 8-SA
sagen to say; to tell, 1-2
Sag mal, ... Tell me, . . .
Was sagen Sie dazu? What do you say to that? What do you think of that? 16-1
sagenhaft! incredible! marvelous! 16-1
die **Sahne** cream, 8-SA
der **Salat, -e** (1) salad; (2) lettuce, 8-1
sammeln to collect, 9-1
(der) **Samstag** Saturday, *Einf.*
der **Satz, ¨-e** sentence; clause
sauber clean, 9-1
sauer (*colloq.*) (1) ticked off, sore, *Einf.*; (2) sour, acidic, 9-2
schade too bad, 11-1
Das ist schade! That's a shame! What a pity! 11-1
schaffen to handle, manage, get done, 3-1
der **Schalter, -** counter, window, 13-1
schauen to look, 11-1
Schau mal. Look. Look here. 10-VID; 11-1
das **Schaufenster, -** store window, 5-2
der **Scheck, -s** check, 14-1
scheinen, schien, hat geschienen (1) to shine; (2) to seem, 1-1
schenken to give (as a gift), 5-1
schicken to send, 6-2
das **Schiff, -e** ship, 12-2

der **Schilling, -e** Austrian shilling, 14-1
der **Schinken** ham, 8-SA
schlafen (schläft), schlief, hat geschlafen to sleep, 3-1
das **Schlafzimmer, -** bedroom, 11-1
schlagen (schlägt), schlug, hat geschlagen (1) to hit; (2) to beat, 9-SA
schlampig (*colloq.*) messy, disorderly, 13-1
die **Schlange, -n** snake, 10-SA
schlecht bad, *Einf.*; 1-1
schleppen (*colloq.*) to drag, lug (along), haul, 9-1
schließen, schloss, hat geschlossen to close, 5-2
schließlich (*adv.*) after all, finally, 15-1
schlimm bad, 5-2
der **Schluss, ⸚e** end, conclusion
  zum Schluss in conclusion, finally
der **Schlüssel, -** key, 6-SA; 11-2
schmecken (1) to taste (*trans. and intrans.*); (2) to taste good, 8-1; 8-VID
sich schminken to put on make-up, 11-SA
schmutzig dirty, 9-1
der **Schnee** snow, 4-2
schneiden, schnitt, hat geschnitten to cut, 11-1
schneien to snow, *Einf.*
schnell fast, *Einf.*; 3-2
  schnell machen (*colloq.*) to hurry, 11-1
das **Schnitzel, -** cutlet, chop, 8-1
die **Schokolade** chocolate, 11-1
schon (1) already, yet; (2) (*flavoring particle, see p. 73*), 3-1
  schon lange for a long time, 10-G
schön beautiful, 1-1
schrecklich terrible, 4-2
schreiben, schrieb, hat geschrieben to write, 3-2
  Wie schreibt man das? How do you write (spell) that? *Einf.*
der **Schreibtisch, -e** desk, 6-1
schreien, schrie, hat geschrien to shout, yell, 15-2
der **Schriftsteller, -** writer (*m.*), 10-2
die **Schriftstellerin, -nen** writer (*f.*), 10-2
der **Schuh, -e** shoe, 3-2
die **Schule, -n** school, 1-2
der **Schüler, -** grade school pupil or secondary school student (*m.*), *Einf.*
die **Schülerin, -nen** grade school pupil or secondary school student (*f.*), *Einf.*
das **Schulsystem, -e** school system, 3-TLL
schützen vor (+ *dat.*) to protect from, 16-2
schwach (schwächer) weak, 9-2
schwarz (schwärzer) black, 3-2
schweigen, schwieg, hat geschwiegen to be silent, 12-1
die **Schweiz** Switzerland, 4-2
der **Schweizer, -** Swiss (*m.*), 13-2
die **Schweizerin, -nen** Swiss (*f.*), 13-2
schweizerisch Swiss, 11-TLL
schwer (1) heavy; (2) hard, difficult, 3-1
die **Schwester, -n** sister, 2-1
schwierig difficult, 5-1
die **Schwierigkeit, -en** difficulty, 13-2
das **Schwimmbad, ⸚er** swimming pool, 8-SA
schwimmen, schwamm, ist geschwommen to swim, 4-1
der **See, -n** lake, 4-1
  am See at the lake
sehen (sieht), sah, hat gesehen to see, 2-1
sehr very, 1-1
sein (ist), war, ist gewesen to be, *Einf.*; 1-1
  dabei sein to be present, attend, 15-1
seit (*prep.* + *dat.*, *sub. conj.*) since, 5-1
  seit 5 Jahren for (the past) 5 years, 5-1
  seit langem for a long time, 10-G
die **Seite, -n** page; side
der **Sekretär, -e** secretary (*m.*), 5-SA
die **Sekretärin, -nen** secretary (*f.*), 5-SA
selber (*or*) **selbst** (*adv.*) by oneself (myself, yourself, ourselves, etc.), 6-2
selbstverständlich "It goes without saying that . . ." 4-1
selten seldom, 1-2
das **Semester, -** semester, 2-1
  nächstes Semester next semester, 2-1
die **Semesterferien** (*pl.*) semester break, 6-2
das **Seminar, -e** (university) seminar, 4-1
der **Senior, -en, -en** senior citizen, 10-1
separat separate, 11-TLL
(der) **September** September, *Einf.*
die **Serviette, -n** napkin, 8-SA
setzen to set (down), put, 7-1
  sich setzen to sit down, 11-1
sich (*3rd person reflexive pronoun*) himself, herself, themselves, (*formal 2nd person*) yourself, yourselves, 11-1
sicher certain, sure, 2-1
siebt- seventh, 9-G
siezen to address someone with **Sie**, 1-2
singen, sang, hat gesungen to sing, 3-2
die **Situation, -en** situation, 10-TLL
sitzen, saß, hat gesessen to sit, 6-2
(das) **Skandinavien** Scandinavia, 8-TLL
skeptisch skeptical, 16-TLL
Ski fahren (fährt Ski), ist Ski gefahren (*pronounced* "Schifahren") to ski, 8-2
so (1) like this, 1-2; (2) so, 7-2
  so ein (*demonstrative*) such a, 15-2
  so lange (*adv.*) for such a long time, 6-1
sofort immediately, right away, 6-2

die **Software** software, 12-1
sogar even, in fact, 2-2
der **Sohn, ¨-e** son, 2-1
solcher, -es, -e such, such a, 9-2
die **Solidarität** solidarity, 1-TLL
sollen (soll), sollte, hat gesollt should, be supposed to, 3-1
der **Sommer** summer, 4-2
das **Sommersemester** spring term (usually May–July), 6-SA
sondern (*coor. conj.*) but rather, instead, 7-1
nicht nur ... sondern auch not only . . . but also, 9-2
(der) **Sonnabend** Saturday, *Einf.*
die **Sonne** sun, 1-1
sonnig sunny, *Einf.*
(der) **Sonntag** Sunday, *Einf.*
sonst (*adv.*) otherwise, apart from that, 6-2
Sonst noch etwas? Will there be anything else? 5-1
sortieren to sort, 9-TLL
sowieso anyway, 7-1
die **Sowjetunion** Soviet Union, 11-TLL
sozial social, 2-TLL
der **Sozialarbeiter, -** social worker, 8-TLL
die **Soziologie** sociology, 6-SA
(das) **Spanien** Spain, 15-1
sparen to save (money *or* time), 7-2
der **Spaß** fun
Das macht (mir) Spaß. That is fun (for me). 7-1
Viel Spaß. Have fun. 12-1
spät late, 3-1
Ich bin spät dran. I'm late. 4-VID
Wie spät ist es? What time is it? *Einf.*
später later, 4-1
spazieren gehen, ging spazieren, ist spazieren gegangen to go for a walk, 5-2
die **Speise, -n** food, dish (menu item), 16-VID
die **Speisekarte, -n** menu, 8-SA
der **Speisesaal** (hotel) dining room, 14-SA
der **Spiegel, -** mirror, 14-2
das **Spiel, -e** game, 9-SA
spielen to play, 1-1
spontan spontaneous, 7-TLL
der **Sport** sport, 3-TLL; 9-1
Sport treiben to play sports, 9-1
sportlich athletic, 9-1
die **Sprache, -n** language, 3-2
sprechen (spricht), sprach, hat gesprochen to speak, talk, 2-1
sprechen über (+ *acc.*) to talk about, 2-1
der **Staat, -en** state, 10-2
stabil stable, 11-TLL
die **Stabilität** stability, 13-TLL
die **Stadt, ¨-e** city, 4-2
der **Stadtbummel, -** stroll through town, 8-1
der **Stadtführer, -** city guidebook, 14-SA
der **Stadtplan, ¨** city map, 5-2
stark (stärker) strong, 9-2
statt (*prep.* + *gen.*) instead of, 8-G
statt·finden, fand statt, hat stattgefunden to take place, 14-2
staunen to be amazed, surprised, 6-2
stehen, stand, hat gestanden to stand, 5-1
stehlen (stiehlt), stahl, hat gestohlen to steal, 10-1
steigen, stieg, ist gestiegen to climb, 8-2
steil steep, 3-1
der **Stein, -e** stone, 12-2
die **Stelle, -n** job, position, 2-2
stellen to put, place, 7-1
eine Frage stellen to ask a question, 10-2
sterben (stirbt), starb, ist gestorben to die, 5-2
die **Stimme, -n** voice, 5-2
stimmen to be right (*impersonal only*), 1-2
das stimmt that's right, that's true
Stimmt schon. That's right. 3-2
stinklangweilig (*colloq.*) extremely boring, 3-1
das **Stipendium,** *pl.* **Stipendien** scholarship, stipend, 6-2
der **Stock** floor (of a building), 14-2
der erste Stock the second floor (*see* **Erdgeschoss**)
im ersten Stock on the second floor
stolz auf (+ *acc.*) proud of, 13-2
stören to disturb, 10-2
die **Straße, -n** street; road, 1-1
der **Straßenatlas** road atlas, 7-1
die **Straßenbahn, -en** streetcar, 8-SA; 13-1
der **Stress** stress, 5-2
stressig stressful, 5-2
das **Stück, -e** piece, 5-1
ein Stück Kuchen a piece of cake, 8-G
sechs Stück six (of the same item), 5-1
der **Student, -en, -en** university student (*m.*), *Einf.*; 1-2
der **Studentenausweis, -e** student I.D., 6-2
das **Studentenwohnheim, -e** student dormitory, 6-1
die **Studentin, -nen** university student (*f.*), *Einf.*; 1-2
studieren to attend a university; to study (a subject); to major in, 1-2
studieren an (+ *dat.*) to study at, 6-SA
das **Studium** university studies, 6-2
der **Stuhl, ¨-e** chair, *Einf.*
die **Stunde, -n** (1) hour; (2) class hour, 3-1
stundenlang (*adv.*) for hours, 14-TLL
das **Substantiv, -e** noun
suchen to look for, seek, 2-1
der **Süden** the south, 4-2
super super, 4-1
der **Supermarkt, ¨-e** supermarket, 5-TLL
der **Supertanker, -** super tanker, 9-TLL
die **Suppe, -n** soup, 1-1
süß sweet, 9-2

das **Symbol, -e** symbol, 11-TLL
symbolisch symbolic, 10-TLL
sympathisch friendly, congenial, likeable, 7-2
das **System, -e** system, 3-TLL

T

die **Tafel, -n** blackboard, *Einf.*
der **Tag, -e** day, 1-1
eines Tages some day (in the future); one day (in the past or future), 13-2
Guten Tag! Hello! *Einf.*
jeden Tag every day, 5-2
Tag! Hi! Hello! *Einf.*
tagelang (*adv.*) for days, 14-TLL
das **Tal, ¨-er** valley, 4-2
die **Tante, -n** aunt, 2-2
tanzen to dance, 14-2
die **Tasche, -n** (1) pocket, (2) shoulder bag, 3-SA; 7-2
die **Tasse, -n** cup, 8-1
eine Tasse Tee a cup of tea, 4-VID
die **Taube, -n** dove, pigeon, 10-SA
tausend thousand, 2-G
das **Taxi, -s** taxicab, 8-SA
die **Technik** technology, 9-2
der **Tee** tea, 8-SA
der **Teil, -e** part, 11-2
teilen to divide, 11-2
teil·nehmen (nimmt teil), nahm teil, hat teilgenommen an (+ *dat.*) to take part in, 15-2
das **Telefon, -e** telephone, 6-SA; 7-2
telefonieren to telephone, make a phone call, 14-SA
die **Telefonnummer, -n** telephone number, *Einf.*
der **Teller, -** plate, 8-SA
das **Tempo** pace, tempo, 6-2
das **Tennis** tennis, 9-1
der **Tennisplatz, ¨-e** tennis court, 9-1
der **Teppich, -e** rug, 6-SA
der **Termin, -e** appointment, 6-2
die **Terrasse, -n** terrace, 15-SA
terroristisch terrorist (*adj.*), 10-TLL
teuer expensive, 6-2
der **Text, -e** text
das **Theater, -** theater, 3-TLL
das **Thema,** *pl.* **Themen** topic, subject, theme, 15-2
die **Thermosflasche, -n** thermos bottle, 7-1
das **Ticket, -s** (airline) ticket, 7-TLL
tief deep, 11-2
das **Tiefland** lowlands, 4-TLL
das **Tier, -e** animal, 9-2
der **Tipp, -s** tip, hint, suggestion
der **Tisch, -e** table, *Einf.*
die **Tochter, ¨** daughter, 2-2
der **Tod** death, 11-2
todmüde (*colloq.*) dead tired, 4-1
die **Toilette, -n** lavatory, 15-SA
toll (*colloq.*) great, terrific, 3-2
das **Tor, -e** gate, 11-1
tot dead, 11-2
die **Tour, -en** tour, 8-TLL
der **Tourist, -en, -en** tourist (*m.*), 1-TLL
die **Touristin, -nen** tourist (*f.*), 1-2
die **Tradition, -en** tradition, 11-TLL
traditionell traditional, 2-TLL
tragen (trägt), trug, hat getragen (1) to carry; (2) to wear, 3-1
trainieren to train, 9-SA
trampen, ist getrampt to hitchhike, 7-2
träumen to dream, 14-2
traurig sad, 13-2
treffen (trifft), traf, hat getroffen to meet, 9-1
treiben, trieb, hat getrieben to drive, force, propel, 9-1
Sport treiben to play sports, 9-1
die **Treppe** staircase, stairs, 9-1
auf der Treppe on the stairs, 9-1
trinken, trank, hat getrunken to drink, 4-2
trocken dry, 4-2
trotz (*prep.* + *gen.*) in spite of, despite, 8-G
trotzdem (*adv.*) in spite of that, nevertheless, 8-2
die **Trümmer** (*pl.*) ruins, rubble, 12-VID
Tschüss! So long! *Einf.*
das **T-Shirt, -s** T-shirt, 3-SA
das **Tuch, ¨-er** scarf; cloth, 16-VID
tun, tat, hat getan to do, 3-1
Das tut mir weh. That hurts (me). 11-1
Er tut, als ob ... (+ *subjunctive*) He acts as if . . . 16-G
Es tut mir Leid. I'm sorry (about that). 7-1
die **Tür, -en** door, *Einf.*
der **Türke, -n, -n** Turk (*m.*), 15-2
die **Türkei** Turkey, 15-2
die **Türkin, -nen** Turk (*f.*), 15-2
türkisch Turkish, 15-2
(das) **Türkisch** Turkish (language), 15-2
der **Turnschuh, -e** sneaker, gym shoe, 3-2
die **Tüte, -n** (paper, plastic) bag, 8-VID
der **Typ, -en** (1) type; (2) (*slang*) guy, 12-1
typisch typical, 1-1

U

die **U-Bahn** (= **Untergrundbahn**) subway train, 8-SA
üben to practice, *Einf.*
über (1) (*prep.* + *acc.*) about, 2-1; (2) (+ *acc.* or *dat.*) over, across; above, 6-1
überall everywhere, 2-2
sich etwas überlegen to consider, ponder, think something over, 13-2
übermorgen the day after tomorrow, 12-1
übernachten to spend the night, 7-2
überraschen to surprise, 15-1
die **Überraschung, -en** surprise, 16-SA
übersetzen to translate, *Einf.*
übrigens by the way, 1-1
die **Übung, -en** exercise
die **Uhr, -en** clock; watch, *Einf.*
9 Uhr 9 o'clock, *Einf.*; 5-1
Wie viel Uhr ist es? What time is it? 7-1
um (1) at (with times), 1-1; (2) around (the outside of), 4-1

um ... zu in order to, 8-1
der **Umschlag, ¨-e** envelope, 15-1
um·steigen, stieg um, ist umgestiegen to transfer, change (trains, buses, etc.), 7-SA
die **Umwelt** environment, 3-2
umweltfreundlich environmentally safe, non-polluting, 9-1
um·ziehen, zog um, ist umgezogen to move, change residence, 9-1
sich um·ziehen, hat sich umgezogen to change clothes, 14-SA
unangenehm unpleasant, 15-2
unbekannt unknown, 10-2
unbeliebt unpopular, 16-2
unbesorgt unconcerned, carefree, 10-1
und (*coor. conj.*) and, 1-1
der **Unfall, ¨-e** accident, 9-2
ungebildet uneducated, 16-2
ungemütlich unpleasant, not cozy, 14-2
die **Uni, -s** (*colloq.*) = **Universität**
die **Universität, -en** university, 5-TLL; 6-1
an der Universität/Uni at the university, 6-1
unmöglich impossible, 6-1
unnötig unnecessary, 9-1
unordentlich messy, disorderly, 13-1
unruhig restless, troubled, 10-2
unten (*adv.*) below, on the bottom
unter (+ *acc.* or *dat.*) (1) under, beneath; (2) among, 6-1
unterbrechen (unterbricht), unterbrach, hat unterbrochen to interrupt, 10-2
sich unterhalten (unterhält), unterhielt, hat sich unterhalten mit to converse with, talk to, 15-2
der **Unterschied, -e** difference, 11-1
unterwegs on the way, en route; on the go, 4-1
unverheiratet unmarried, 16-1
unwichtig unimportant, 2-2
uralt ancient, 3-2
der **Urlaub, -e** vacation (from a job), 4-1
Urlaub machen to take a vacation
auf (*or*) **im Urlaub sein** to be on vacation
in Urlaub gehen (*or*) **fahren** to go on vacation
die **USA** (*pl.*) the USA, 5-TLL
usw. (= **und so weiter**) etc. (= and so forth), 1-1

V

die **Variation, -en** variation
der **Vater, ¨** father, 2-1
der **Vati, -s** papa, dad, 2-2
(das) **Venedig** Venice (Italy), 7-1
verantwortlich für responsible for, 6-2
das **Verb, -en** verb
verboten forbidden, prohibited
verbringen, verbrachte, hat verbracht to spend (time), 7-2
verdienen to earn, 2-2
vereinen to unite, 11-2
die **Vereinigung** unification, 11-1
Verflixt nochmal! (*colloq.*) Darn it all! 15-1
die **Vergangenheit** past (time), 11-2
vergessen (vergisst), vergaß, hat vergessen to forget, 5-2
vergleichen, verglich, hat verglichen to compare, 12-2
verheiratet sein to be married, 16-1
verkaufen to sell, 4-1
der **Verkäufer, -** salesman, 5-SA
die **Verkäuferin, -nen** saleswoman, 5-SA
der **Verkehr** traffic, 7-SA
das **Verkehrsmittel, -** means of transportation, 8-SA
verlassen (verlässt), verließ, hat verlassen to leave (a person or place), 5-1
sich verletzen to injure oneself, get hurt, 11-1
verlieren, verlor, hat verloren to lose, 10-1; 10-VID
sich verloben mit (+ *dat.*) to become engaged to, 12-1
verpassen to miss (an event, opportunity, train, etc.), 13-1
verrückt crazy, insane, 7-2
verschieden different, various, 11-2
verschmutzen to pollute; to dirty, 9-2
die **Verschmutzung** pollution, 9-1
verschwenden to waste, 9-2
verschwinden, verschwand, ist verschwunden to disappear, 11-2
sich verspäten to be late, 11-1
verstehen, verstand, hat verstanden to understand, 3-1
versuchen to try, attempt, 10-2
der/die **Verwandte, -n** (*adj. noun*) relative, 11-1
der **Vetter, -n** cousin (*m.*), 2-SA
viel (mehr, am meisten) much, a lot, 1-1
viele many, 1-2; (*pronoun*) many people, 8-2
vielen Dank many thanks, 2-1
vielleicht maybe, perhaps, 1-1
das **Viertel** quarter
Viertel vor/nach sieben quarter to/past seven, *Einf.*
der **Vogel, ¨** bird, 9-2
die **Vokabel, -n** word
das **Volk, ¨-er** people, nation, folk, 10-2
das **Volkslied, -er** folk song, 4-2
voll full, 5-1
der **Volleyball** volleyball, 9-SA
von (*prep.* + *dat.*) from, 4-2; of; by, 5-1
vor (*prep.* + *acc.* or *dat.*) in front of, 6-1
vor einem Jahr a year ago, 10-G
vorbei·kommen, kam vorbei, ist vorbeigekommen to come by, drop by, 5-2
vor·bereiten to prepare
sich vor·bereiten auf (+ *acc.*) to prepare for, 13-1
vorgestern the day before yesterday, 12-1

vor·haben (hat vor), hatte vor, hat vorgehabt to plan, have in mind, 13-1
vorher (*adv.*) before that, previously, 4-VID; 10-1
vor·lesen (liest vor), las vor, hat vorgelesen to read aloud
die **Vorlesung, -en** university lecture, 6-1
das **Vorlesungsverzeichnis, -se** university course catalogue, 6-1
vormittags (*adv.*) (in the) mornings, 16-1
der **Vorschlag, ¨-e** suggestion
vor·stellen to introduce, present, 13-2
sich vor·stellen to introduce oneself, 13-2
sich etwas vor·stellen to imagine something, 11-1
das **Vorurteil, -e** prejudice, 13-SA, 16-2

W

wachsen (wächst), wuchs, ist gewachsen to grow, 10-2
der **Wagen, -** car, 3-1
die **Wahl, -en** (1) choice; (2) election, 10-2
wählen (1) to choose; (2) to elect, 10-2
der **Wähler, -** voter, 10-2
wahnsinnig (*adv. colloq.*) extremely, incredibly, 3-1
wahr true, 3-1
nicht wahr? isn't it? can't you? doesn't she? etc., 3-1
während (*prep. + gen.*) during, 8-G
die **Wahrheit, -en** truth, 13-SA
wahrscheinlich probably, 1-2
der **Wald, ¨-er** forest, 4-2
die **Wand, ¨-e** (interior) wall, *Einf.*
die **Wanderlust** wanderlust, 7-TLL
wandern, ist gewandert to hike, wander, 4-2
die **Wanderung, -en** hike, 5-2
der **Wandschrank, ¨-e** cupboard, 2-VID
wann? when? *Einf.*
die **Ware, -n** product, 9-2
warm (wärmer) warm, *Einf.*
warten to wait, 4-1
warten auf (+ *acc.*) to wait for, 13-1
Warte mal! Wait a second! Hang on! 4-1
warum? why? 1-1
was? what? *Einf.*
was für? what kind of? 9-1
Was ist los? What's the matter? What's going on? 3-1
waschen (wäscht), wusch, hat gewaschen to wash, 11-1
das **Wasser** water, 4-1
wechseln to change (money), 14-1
wecken to wake up (*trans.*), 4-VID
der **Wecker, -** alarm clock, 6-SA
weder ... noch neither . . . nor, 14-1
der **Weg, -e** way, path, 16-1
weg (*adv.*) away, gone, 4-1
wegen (*prep. + gen.*) because of, on account of, 8-G
weg·gehen, ging weg, ist weggegangen to go away, leave, 12-1
weg·werfen (wirft weg), warf weg, hat weggeworfen to throw away, 9-2
weh tun, tat weh, hat weh getan (+ *dat. of person*) to hurt, 11-1
weil (*sub. conj.*) because, 8-G
der **Wein, -e** wine, 4-2
weinen to cry, 3-2
weiß white, 3-2
weit far, far away, 8-1
weiter·gehen, ging weiter, ist weitergegangen to go on, continue
welcher, -es, -e which, 7-1; 8-VID
die **Welt, -en** world, 3-2
wem? (*dat.*) to whom? for whom? 5-1
wen? (*acc.*) whom? 2-1
wenig little bit, not much, 1-1
wenige few, 11-1
wenigstens at least, 2-2
wenn (*sub. conj.*) (1) if, 8-G; (2) when, whenever, 10-G
wer? (*nom.*) who? *Einf.*
werden (wird), wurde, ist geworden to become, get (*in the sense of* become), 4-1
werfen (wirft), warf, hat geworfen to throw, 9-2
das **Werk, -e** work (of art), musical composition, 13-2
wessen? whose? 2-1
der **Westen** the west, 4-2
das **Wetter** weather, *Einf.*; 1-1
die **WG, -s** (= **Wohngemeinschaft**) communal living group, shared apartment, 6-1
wichtig important, 2-2
wie (1) how, *Einf.*; (2) like, as, 1-1
Wie bitte? I beg your pardon? What did you say? *Einf.*
wie lange? how long? 3-1
wieder again, 1-1
wiederholen to repeat, *Einf.*
die **Wiederholung, -en** repetition; review
wieder sehen (sieht wieder), sah wieder, hat wieder gesehen to see again, meet again, 12-2
Auf Wiedersehen! Good-bye! *Einf.*
wiegen, wog, hat gewogen (*trans. and intrans.*) to weigh, 15-1
(das) **Wien** Vienna, 1-1
wieso? How come? How's that?; What do you mean? 9-1
wie viel? how much? 5-1
Wie viel Uhr ist es? What time is it? 7-1
wie viele? how many? 2-1
Wievielt-: Den Wievielten haben wir heute? What's the date today? 9-G
wild wild, 4-TLL
willkommen welcome, 6-2
Herzlich willkommen! Welcome! Nice to see you!, 6-2
der **Wind** wind, 4-SA
windig windy, *Einf.*
der **Winter, -** winter, 4-1
im Winter in the winter, 4-1
das **Wintersemester** fall term (usually Oct.–Feb.), 6-SA
wirklich real, 6-1
die **Wirtschaft** economy, 11-2
wirtschaftlich economic, 11-2
die **Wirtschaftswissenschaft** economics, 6-SA

der **Wischer, -** (blackboard) eraser, *Einf.*
wissen (weiß), wusste, hat gewusst to know (a fact), 2-1
Weißt du noch? Do you remember? 11-1
die **Wissenschaft, -en** (1) science; (2) scholarship; field of knowledge, 6-SA
der **Witz, -e** (1) joke; (2) wit, 14-2
witzig witty, amusing, 14-2
wo? where? *Einf.*
die **Woche, -n** week, 5-1
das **Wochenende, -n** weekend, 5-2
am Wochenende on the weekend, 5-2
Schönes Wochenende! (Have a) nice weekend! *Einf.*
wochenlang (*adv.*) for weeks, 14-TLL
woher? from where? *Einf.*
wohin? to where? 3-1
wohl probably, 6-2
wohnen to live, dwell, 1-1
die **Wohngemeinschaft, -en** communal living group, shared apartment, 6-1
das **Wohnhaus, ¨-er** apartment building, 9-1
die **Wohnung, -en** apartment, 6-2
das **Wohnzimmer, -** living room, 15-SA
die **Wolke, -n** cloud, 4-SA
wolkig cloudy, *Einf.*
wollen (will), wollte, hat gewollt (1) to want to, intend to, 3-1; (2) to claim to, 16-G
worden (*special form of the past participle of* **werden** *used in the perfect tenses of the passive voice*)
das **Wort** word (*2 plural forms:* die **Worte** = words in context; die **Wörter** = unconnected words, as in a dictionary), 5-2
das **Wörterbuch, ¨-er** dictionary, 5-2
der **Wortschatz** vocabulary
das **Wunder, -** miracle
Kein Wunder! No wonder! 15-1
wunderbar wonderful, 7-1
sich wundern (über + *acc.*) to be surprised, amazed (at), 13-1
wunderschön very beautiful, 1-1
wünschen to wish, 8-VID; 12-1
die **Wurst, ¨-e** sausage, 4-VID; 8-1
Das ist mir Wurst (*or* **Wurscht**). I don't give a darn. 7-1

Z

zahlen to pay, 8-1
Zahlen bitte! Check please! 8-1
zählen to count, 10-3
der **Zahn, ¨-e** tooth, 11-SA
sich die Zähne putzen to brush one's teeth, 11-SA
zeichnen to draw, 16-2
der **Zeichner, -** draftsman, graphic artist (*m.*), 16-2
die **Zeichnerin, -nen** graphic artist (*f.*), 16-2
die **Zeichnung, -en** drawing, 16-2
zeigen to show, 2-VID; 5-1
Zeig mal her. Let's see. Show it to me. 15-1
die **Zeile, -n** line (of text)
die **Zeit, -en** time, 3-2
höchste Zeit high time, 14-1
eine Zeit lang for a time, for a while, 14-2
die **Zeitschrift, -en** magazine, 5-2
die **Zeitung, -en** newspaper, 2-1
zentral central, 11-TLL
zerstören to destroy, 8-2
die **Zerstörung** destruction
ziehen, zog, hat gezogen to pull, 6-1
das **Ziel, -e** goal, 7-2
ziemlich fairly, quite, 1-2
zigmal (*adv.*) umpteen times, 12-G
das **Zimmer, -** room, 2-1
zirka circa, 4-TLL
die **Zone, -n** zone, 11-TLL
zu to; too, 1-1; (*prep.* + *dat.*) to, 5-1
zu Fuß on foot, 3-1
zu Hause at home, 2-2
zueinander to each other, 1-2
zuerst first, at first, 8-1
zufrieden satisfied
Ich bin zufrieden. I can't complain. 12-VID
der **Zug, ¨-e** train, 7-1
zu·hören (+ *dat.*) to listen (to), 13-1
die **Zukunft** future, 11-2
in Zukunft in the future, 13-2
zuletzt last of all, finally, 8-1
zu·machen to close, 5-1
zunächst first (of all), to begin with, 14-2
zurück back, 1-1
zurück·bringen, brachte zurück, hat zurückgebracht to bring back
zurück·kommen, kam zurück, ist zurückgekommen to come back, 1-1
zusammen together, *Einf.*; 4-1
die **Zusammenfassung** summary
zu·schauen (+ *dat.*) to watch, 16-2
zweimal twice, 12-G
zweit- second, 9-1
der **Zweitwagen, -** second car, 9-1
zwischen (*prep.* + *acc.* or *dat.*) between, 2-2

English–German Vocabulary

Strong and irregular verbs are marked by an asterisk: ***brechen, *können, *bringen**.
Their principal parts can be found in Appendix 2.

A

able: be able to *können
about über (*prep.* + *acc.*)
it's about X es geht um X
above oben (*adv.*); über (*prep.* + *dat.* or *acc.*)
abroad im Ausland (*location*); ins Ausland (*destination*)
absent: be absent fehlen
accept akzeptieren
accident der Unfall, ¨-e
account: on account of wegen (+ *gen.*)
acidic sauer
acid rain der saure Regen
acquaintance der/die Bekannte, -n (*adj. noun*)
acquainted: be acquainted with *kennen
across über (*prep.* + *dat.* or *acc.*)
act: He acts as if . . . Er tut, als ob ...
active aktiv
actually eigentlich
acute akut
address die Adresse, -n
address with *du* duzen
address with *Sie* siezen
adjective das Adjektiv, -e
administration, government in power die Regierung, -en
adverb das Adverb, -ien
affair, matter die Sache, -n
afford: be able to afford something sich etwas leisten können
afraid: be afraid (of) Angst haben (vor + *dat.*)
after nach (*prep.* + *dat.*); nachdem (*sub. conj.*)
after all schließlich
after that danach (*adv.*)
afternoon der Nachmittag, -e
in the afternoon am Nachmittag
(in the) afternoons nachmittags
this afternoon heute Nachmittag (*adv.*)
afterwards, after that nachher (*adv.*)
again wieder
against gegen (*prep.* + *acc.*)
ago vor (+ *dat.*)
a year ago vor einem Jahr
agreed einverstanden
agriculture die Landwirtschaft
ah ach
aid die Hilfe
air die Luft
air pollution die Luftverschmutzung
airplane das Flugzeug, -e
airport der Flughafen, ¨
alarm clock der Wecker, -
alive: be alive leben
all alle (*pl.*)
all summer (day, afternoon, etc.) den ganzen Sommer (Tag, Nachmittag usw.)
allow *lassen
allowed: be allowed to *dürfen
almanac der Almanach, -e
almost fast
alone allein
along with mit (*adv.*)
alongside of an (*prep.* + *acc.* or *dat.*)
a lot viel (mehr, am meisten); eine Menge
Alps die Alpen (*pl.*)
already schon
also auch
alternative die Alternative, -n
although obwohl (*sub. conj.*)
always immer
ambivalent ambivalent
amazed
be amazed staunen
be amazed (at) sich wundern (über + *acc.*)
America (das) Amerika
American amerikanisch (*adj.*); der Amerikaner, -; die Amerikanerin, -nen
among unter (*prep.* + *acc.* or *dat.*)
amusing witzig
analyze analysieren
ancient uralt
and und (*coor. conj.*)
anecdote die Anekdote, -n
anger der Ärger
angry (at) böse (+ *dat.*)
animal das Tier, -e
annoy ärgern
get annoyed sich ärgern
annoyance der Ärger
annually jährlich
another, an additional noch ein
answer die Antwort, -en
answer (a person) antworten (+ *dat.*)
answer (something) antworten auf (+ *acc.*)
anything
Anything more? (Sonst) noch etwas?
Will there be anything else? Sonst noch etwas?
anyway sowieso
anywhere irgendwo
apart from that sonst
apartment die Wohnung, -en
apartment building das Wohnhaus, ¨-er
appear *aus·sehen

appointment der Termin, -e
apprentice der Lehrling, -e
April (der) April
architecture die Architektur
area die Gegend, -en
arm der Arm, -e
around, about (with time) gegen (*prep.* + *acc.*)
around (the outside of) um (*prep.* + *acc.*)
arrive *an·kommen
arrogance die Arroganz
art die Kunst, ⸚e
  art history die Kunstgeschichte
article der Artikel, -
artist der Künstler, -; die Künstlerin, -nen
as wie
  as a als
ask fragen
  ask a question eine Frage stellen
  ask for *bitten um
  ask oneself sich fragen
aspect der Aspekt, -e
assignment die Aufgabe, -n
astounding erstaunlich
at bei (*prep.* + *dat.*); an (*prep.* + *acc.* or *dat.*); (*with times*) um (*prep.* + *acc.*)
  At last! Na endlich!
  at least wenigstens
athletic sportlich
atom das Atom, -e
atomic power plant das Atomkraftwerk, -e
attempt versuchen
attention: pay attention auf·passen
August (der) August
aunt die Tante, -n
Austria (das) Österreich
Austrian österreichisch (*adj.*); der Österreicher, -; die Österreicherin, -nen
author der Autor, -en; die Autorin, -nen
autobiographical autobiographisch
automatic automatisch
auto mechanic der Automechaniker, -; die Automechanikerin, -nen
automobile das Auto, -s; der Wagen, -
autumn der Herbst
away weg (*adv.*)

B

baby das Baby, -s
back zurück (*adv.*)
backpack der Rucksack, ⸚e
bad schlecht; schlimm; böse (*evil*)
bag die Tüte, -n
baker der Bäcker, -; die Bäckerin, -nen
bakery die Bäckerei, -en
ballpoint pen der Kugelschreiber, -
Baloney! Quatsch!
banana die Banane, -n
bank die Bank, -en
bar, tavern die Kneipe, -n
barbaric barbarisch
barely kaum
barrier die Barriere, -n
basement der Keller, -
basis die Basis
bath das Bad
  take a bath ein Bad *nehmen
bathroom das Badezimmer, -
be *sein
bear der Bär, -en, -en
beat *schlagen
beautiful schön
  very beautiful wunderschön
because weil (*sub. conj.*)
  because, for denn (*coor. conj.*)
  because of wegen (+ *gen.*)
become, get *werden
bed das Bett, -en
  get out of bed *auf·stehen
  go to bed ins Bett *gehen
bedroom das Schlafzimmer, -
beer das Bier, -e
before bevor (*sub. conj.*)
  before that vorher (*adv.*)
begin *an·fangen; *beginnen
  to begin with zunächst (*adv.*)
beginner der Anfänger, -
beginning der Anfang, ⸚e
  at/in the beginning am Anfang
behind hinter (*prep.* + *acc.* or *dat.*)
believe glauben (+ *dat. of person*)
belong to (a person) gehören (+ *dat.*)
below unten (*adv.*); unter (*prep.* + *acc.* or *dat.*)
bench die Bank, ⸚e
beneath unter (*prep.* + *acc.* or *dat.*)
beside neben (*prep.* + *acc.* or *dat.*)
besides außer (+ *dat.*)
best best-
  like best of all to am liebsten (+ *verb*)
better besser
between zwischen (*prep.* + *acc.* or *dat.*)
bicycle das Fahrrad, ⸚er; das Rad, ⸚er (*colloq.*)
  ride a bicycle Rad *fahren
big groß (größer, größt-)
bill die Rechnung, -en
biology die Biologie
bird der Vogel, ⸚
birthday der Geburtstag, -e
  for one's birthday zum Geburtstag
  When is your birthday? Wann hast du Geburtstag?
black schwarz (schwärzer)
blackboard die Tafel, -n
blanket die Decke, -n
blouse die Bluse, -n
blue blau
book das Buch, ⸚er; buchen (*verb*)
bookcase das Bücherregal, -e
bookstore die Buchhandlung, -en
border die Grenze, -n
bored: be bored sich langweilen
boring langweilig
  extremely boring stinklangweilig (*colloq.*)
born geboren
borrow *leihen
boss der Chef, -s; die Chefin, -nen
both beid-
  both (people) beide (*pl. pronoun*)
  both (things) beides (*sing. pronoun*)
bottle die Flasche, -n
bottom: at the bottom unten (*adv.*)

box boxen
boy der Junge, -n, -n
bread das Brot, -e
  dark bread das Bauernbrot
break, intermission die Pause, -n
  take a break eine Pause machen
break *brechen; kaputt machen
  break out *aus·brechen
breakfast das Frühstück, -e
  eat breakfast frühstücken
  for breakfast zum Frühstück
bridge die Brücke, -n
bright (light) hell
bright (intelligent) klug (klüger)
bring *bringen
  bring along *mit·bringen
  bring back *zurück·bringen
broken kaputt (*colloq.*)
brother der Bruder, ¨
brown braun
brush one's teeth sich die Zähne putzen
build bauen
building das Gebäude, -
burn *brennen
bus der Bus, -se
business das Geschäft, -e
  business (field of study) die Betriebswirtschaft
  business people die Geschäftsleute
  businessman der Geschäftsmann
  businesswoman die Geschäftsfrau
but aber (*coor. conj.*)
  but rather sondern (*coor. conj.*)
butter die Butter
buy kaufen
by
  by (a certain time) bis (*prep. + acc.*)
  by oneself (myself, yourself, etc.) selbst *or* selber (*adv.*)
  by the way übrigens

C

café das Café, -s
  pastry café die Konditorei, -en
cafeteria (at the university) die Mensa
cake der Kuchen, -
call *rufen
  be called *heißen
  call up *an·rufen
calm, peaceful ruhig
camera die Kamera, -s
camp campen
can, be able to *können
Canada (das) Kanada
Canadian kanadisch (*adj.*); der Kanadier, -; die Kanadierin, -nen
cap die Mütze, -n
capitalism der Kapitalismus
car das Auto, -s; der Wagen, -
card die Karte, -n
care
  I don't care. Das ist mir egal.
career die Karriere, -n
carefree unbesorgt
caricature die Karikatur, -en
carry *tragen
cartoon der Cartoon, -s
cash das Bargeld
cashier, cashier's office die Kasse, -n
cassette player der Kassettenrecorder, -
cat die Katze, -n
catalogue (university) das Vorlesungsverzeichnis, -se
catastrophe die Katastrophe, -n
catastrophic katastrophal
cathedral der Dom, -e
cause to be done *lassen (+ *infinitive*)
CD (compact disk) die CD, -s
  CD player der CD-Spieler, -
cease auf·hören (mit)
celebrate feiern
celebration die Feier, -n
cellar der Keller, -
central zentral
century das Jahrhundert, -e
  for centuries jahrhundertelang
certain, sure sicher; bestimmt
chain die Kette, -n
  chain reaction die Kettenreaktion, -en
chair der Stuhl, ¨e
chalk die Kreide
chance die Gelegenheit, -en; die Chance, -n
change ändern (*trans.*); sich ändern
  change (clothes) sich *um·ziehen
  change (money) wechseln
  change (trains, buses, etc.), transfer *um·steigen
change purse der Geldbeutel, -
chapter das Kapitel, -
chat quatschen (*colloq.*)
cheap billig
check der Scheck, -s (*bank check*); die Rechnung, -en (*restaurant bill*)
  Check please! Zahlen bitte!
check kontrollieren
cheerful munter; heiter
Cheers! Prost! *or* Prosit!
cheese der Käse
chemistry die Chemie
chief Haupt- (*noun prefix*)
child das Kind, -er
childhood die Kindheit, -en
China (das) China
Chinese (das) Chinesisch; der Chinese, -n, -n; die Chinesin, -nen
chocolate die Schokolade
choice die Wahl, -en
choose wählen
chop, cutlet das Schnitzel, -
church die Kirche, -n
circa zirka
citizen der Bürger, -
city die Stadt, ¨e
  capital city die Hauptstadt, ¨e
  city guidebook der Stadtführer, -
  city map der Stadtplan, ¨e
  large city (over 500,000 inhabitants) die Großstadt, ¨e
  old city center die Altstadt, ¨e
  small city (5,000 to 20,000 inhabitants) die Kleinstadt, ¨e
civil servant der Beamte (*adj. noun, m.*); die Beamtin, -nen (*f.*)
claim to *wollen

class die Klasse, -n
class hour die Stunde, -n
clean sauber (*adj.*); putzen (*verb*)
clear klar; deutlich
clerk der Verkäufer, -; die Verkäuferin, -nen
cliché das Klischee, -s
clichéd (*adj.*), **stereotyped** klischeehaft
climate das Klima
climb *steigen
clinic die Klinik, -en
clock die Uhr, -en
close *schließen, zu·machen
closed geschlossen
cloth das Tuch
clothes die Kleider (*pl.*)
clothes cupboard der Kleiderschrank, ¨-e
clothing die Kleidung
cloud die Wolke, -n
cloudy wolkig
coat der Mantel, ¨-
coffee der Kaffee
cold kalt (kälter)
catch a cold sich erkälten
collect sammeln
Cologne (das) Köln
colony die Kolonie, -n
color die Farbe, -n
colorful bunt
comb kämmen
comb one's hair sich die Haare kämmen
come *kommen
All together that comes to . . . Das macht zusammen ...
come along *mit·kommen
come back *zurück·kommen
come by *vorbei·kommen
I come from . . . Ich komme aus ...
Where do you come from? Woher kommst du?
comfortable bequem
communal living group die Wohngemeinschaft, -en; die WG, -s
Communism der Kommunismus
compare *vergleichen
compatriots die Landsleute (*pl.*)
competition die Konkurrenz
complain: I can't complain. Ich bin zufrieden.
computer der Computer, -
computer science die Informatik
concentrate on sich konzentrieren auf (+ *acc.*)
concerned besorgt
concert das Konzert, -e
conclusion der Schluss, ¨-e
in conclusion zum Schluss
conflict der Konflikt, -e
confront konfrontieren
congenial sympathisch
congratulate gratulieren (+ *dat. of person*)
Congratulations! Herzlichen Glückwunsch!
consequence die Konsequenz, -en
conservative konservativ
consider something sich etwas überlegen
contact der Kontakt, -e
contingent: be contingent on, depend on *an·kommen auf (+ *acc.*)
contrary: on the contrary im Gegenteil
contrast der Kontrast, -e
conversation das Gespräch, -e
converse with sich *unterhalten mit
cook kochen
cool kühl
cooperate mit·machen
corner die Ecke, -n
around the corner um die Ecke
at/on the corner an der Ecke
correct richtig
correspondent der Korrespondent, -en, -en
Corsica (das) Korsika
cost kosten
count zählen
counter, window der Schalter, -
country das Land, ¨-er
in the country auf dem Land
to the country aufs Land
couple
a couple (of) ein paar
married couple das Ehepaar, -e
cousin die Kusine, -n (*f.*); der Vetter, -n (*m.*)
cozy, relaxed gemütlich
cram pauken (*student slang*)
crazy verrückt
cream die Sahne
creative kreativ
critical kritisch
cross street die Querstraße, -n
crowd die Menge, -n
cruel grausam
cry weinen
culture die Kultur, -en
cup die Tasse, -n
current aktuell (*adj.*)
customer der Kunde, -n, -n; die Kundin, -nen
cut *schneiden
cutlet das Schnitzel, -

D

dad der Vati, -s
damp nass
dance tanzen
danger die Gefahr, -en
dangerous gefährlich
dark dunkel
darn
Darn it all! Verflixt nochmal!
I don't give a darn. Das ist mir Wurst (*or* Wurscht).
date: What's the date today? Der Wievielte ist heute? Den Wievielten haben wir heute?
daughter die Tochter, ¨-
day der Tag, -e
day after tomorrow übermorgen
day before yesterday vorgestern
for days tagelang
in those days damals
one day (in the past or future) eines Tages
some day (in the future) eines Tages
dead tot
deal with sich kümmern um
dear lieb

death der Tod, -e
December (der) Dezember
decide *entscheiden
deep tief
delicious lecker
democracy die Demokratie
democratic demokratisch
democratization die Demokratisierung
demonstrate demonstrieren
demonstration die Demonstration, -en
depart *ab·fahren; *los·fahren
department store das Kaufhaus, ¨-er
depend on *an·kommen auf (+ *acc.*)
describe *beschreiben
desire die Lust
desk der Schreibtisch, -e
despite trotz (+ *gen.*)
dessert der Nachtisch, -e; die Nachspeise, -n
for dessert zum Nachtisch
destination das Reiseziel, -e
destroy zerstören
destruction die Zerstörung
dialect der Dialekt, -e
dialogue der Dialog, -e
dictionary das Wörterbuch, ¨-er
die *sterben
die in battle *fallen
difference der Unterschied, -e
different, other ander- (*attributive adj.*); anders (*predicate adj.*)
different, various verschieden
difficult schwer; schwierig
difficulty die Schwierigkeit, -en
dining room das Esszimmer, -
dining room (hotel) der Speisesaal
direct(ly) direkt
director der Direktor, -en
dirty schmutzig; dreckig (*colloq.*)
disappear *verschwinden
disappoint enttäuschen
disappointment die Enttäuschung, -en
discount die Ermäßigung, -en
discuss diskutieren; *besprechen
discussion die Diskussion, -en
disorderly schlampig (*colloq.*); unordentlich
dissertation die Dissertation, -en; die Diss (*university slang*); die Doktorarbeit
distant fern
disturb stören
divide teilen
do machen; *tun
doctor der Arzt, ¨-e; die Ärztin, -nen
dog der Hund, -e
done fertig
donkey der Esel, -
door die Tür, -en
dove die Taube, -n
draftsman der Zeichner, -
drag schleppen (*colloq.*)
draw zeichnen
drawing die Zeichnung, -en
dream träumen
dress das Kleid, -er
dress, get dressed sich *an·ziehen
drink das Getränk, -e; *trinken (*verb*)
drive (a vehicle) *fahren
drive, force *treiben
drop by *vorbei·kommen
dry trocken
dumb, stupid dumm (dümmer); blöd
during während (+ *gen.*)
during, while . . . -ing bei ...
duty die Pflicht, -en
dwell wohnen
dynasty die Dynastie, -n

E

each jed-
each other einander
eagle der Adler, -
ear das Ohr, -en
early früh
earn verdienen
earth die Erde
east der Osten
easy, simple einfach; leicht
eat *essen
economic wirtschaftlich
economics die Wirtschaftswissenschaft
economy die Wirtschaft
ecosystem das Ökosystem, -e
educated gebildet
education (as field of study) die Pädagogik
egg das Ei, -er
either . . . or entweder ... oder
elect wählen
election die Wahl, -en
electrical engineer der Elektrotechniker, -; die Elektrotechnikerin, -nen
electrical engineering die Elektrotechnik
electrician der Elektrotechniker, -; die Elektrotechnikerin, -nen
electricity die Elektrizität
elegant elegant
elephant der Elefant, -en, -en
elevator der Lift, -s
emancipation die Emanzipation
emigrate aus·wandern
empire das Reich, -e
employed berufstätig
employee der/die Angestellte, -n (*adj. noun*)
empty leer
end das Ende, -n; der Schluss, ¨-e
at the end am Ende
at the end of February Ende Februar
end, be finished, be over zu Ende *sein
energy die Energie
engaged: become engaged to sich verloben mit
engineer der Ingenieur, -e; die Ingenieurin, -nen
English (*adj.*) englisch
English (language) (das) Englisch
English studies die Anglistik
Englishman der Engländer, -
Englishwoman die Engländerin, -nen
enormous enorm
enough genug
en route unterwegs
enthusiasm die Begeisterung
enthusiastic about begeistert von
entire ganz

entrance, way in der Einstieg, -e
envelope der Umschlag, ¨-e
environment die Umwelt
environmentally safe, non-polluting umweltfreundlich
epoch die Epoche, -n
equal gleich
equal rights die Gleichberechtigung (*sing.*)
enjoying equal rights gleichberechtigt
eraser der Radiergummi (*pencil*); der Wischer, - (*blackboard*)
especially besonders
essay der Aufsatz, ¨-e
essay topic das Aufsatzthema, -themen
etc. usw. (= und so weiter)
Europe (das) Europa
Eastern Europe (das) Osteuropa
European europäisch (*adj.*); der Europäer, -; die Europäerin, -nen
even, in fact sogar
evening der Abend, -e
evening meal das Abendessen
good evening guten Abend
in the evening am Abend
(in the) evenings abends
this evening, tonight heute Abend
ever je
every jed-
every time jedes Mal (*adv.*)
everybody alle (*pl. pron.*)
everyday (*adj.*) alltäglich
everyday life der Alltag
everyone jeder (*sing. pron.*)
everything alles
everywhere überall
evil böse (*adj.*)
exact genau
examination die Prüfung, -en; das Abitur (*final secondary school exam*); das Abi (*slang*)
example das Beispiel, -e
for example zum Beispiel
excellent ausgezeichnet
exchange student der Austauschstudent, -en, -en
excursion der Ausflug, ¨-e
Excuse me. Entschuldigung.
exercise die Übung, -en
exhausted kaputt (*colloq.*)
exhibition die Ausstellung, -en
exist existieren
expect erwarten
expensive teuer
experience die Erfahrung, -en
explain erklären
expression der Ausdruck, ¨-e
expressway die Autobahn, -en
extreme extrem
extremely wahnsinnig (*colloq. adv.*)
eye das Auge, -n
eyeglasses die Brille (*sing.*)

F

face das Gesicht, -er
fact
in fact eigentlich
in fact, even sogar
factory die Fabrik, -en
fairly ziemlich
fairy tale das Märchen, -
fall, autumn der Herbst
fall term das Wintersemester
fall *fallen
fall asleep *ein·schlafen
false, incorrect falsch
family die Familie, -n
famous berühmt
fantastic fantastisch
far, far away weit; fern
farmer der Bauer, -n, -n; der Landwirt, -e; die Landwirtin, -nen
fast schnell
father der Vater, ¨-
favorite Lieblings- (*noun prefix*)
fear die Angst, ¨-e; Angst haben (vor + *dat.*); fürchten
February (der) Februar
Federal Republic of Germany (FRG) die Bundesrepublik Deutschland (BRD)
fed up: I'm fed up. Ich habe die Nase voll.
feel sich fühlen (*intrans.*)
feeling das Gefühl, -e
fetch holen
fetch, pick up ab·holen
few wenige
a few ein paar
film der Film, -e
finally endlich; schließlich; zum Schluss; zuletzt
finance finanzieren
find *finden
Fine by me. Ist gut. (*colloq.*)
finger der Finger, -
finished with fertig mit
firm, company die Firma, *pl.* Firmen
first erst- (*adj.*); zuerst (*adv.*)
at first zuerst
first (of all) zunächst
fish der Fisch, -e
flabbergasted baff (*colloq.*)
flat flach
floor (of a building) der Stock
ground floor, first floor das Erdgeschoss
on the second floor im ersten Stock
second floor der erste Stock
flow *fließen
flower die Blume, -n
fly *fliegen
fog der Nebel
foggy neblig
folk das Volk, ¨-er
folk song das Volkslied, -er
follow folgen, ist gefolgt (+ *dat.*)
food das Essen; die Speise, -n (*dish, menu item*)
foolproof idiotensicher
foot der Fuß, ¨-e
on foot zu Fuß
for für (*prep.* + *acc.*)
for, because denn (*coor. conj.*)
for a long time lange; seit langem, schon lange
for years seit Jahren
forbidden verboten
force, propel *treiben
foreign ausländisch
foreign, strange fremd
foreign countries das Ausland (*sing.*)
foreign language die Fremdsprache, -n

foreign worker der Gastarbeiter, -; die Gastarbeiterin, -nen
foreigner der Ausländer, -; die Ausländerin, -nen
forest der Wald, ¨er
forget *vergessen
I can't forget that. Das geht mir nicht aus dem Kopf.
fork die Gabel, -n
form die Form, -en
formal formell
formulate formulieren
fox der Fuchs, ¨e
France (das) Frankreich
free
free, unoccupied frei
free of charge kostenlos
free time die Freizeit
freedom die Freiheit, -en
French (*adj.*) französisch
French fries die Pommes frites (*pl.*)
Frenchman der Franzose, -n, -n
Frenchwoman die Französin, -nen
fresh frisch
Friday (der) Freitag
friend der Freund, -e; die Freundin, -nen
friendly freundlich; sympathisch
from aus (+ *dat.*); von (+ *dat.*)
front: in front of vor (*prep.* + *dat.* or *acc.*)
fruit das Obst
frustrate frustrieren
frustration die Frustration, -en
full voll
fun der Spaß
Have fun. Viel Spaß.
make fun of sich lustig machen über (+ *acc.*)
That is fun (for me). Das macht (mir) Spaß.
funny, peculiar komisch
furnished möbliert
furniture die Möbel (*pl.*)
future die Zukunft
in the future in Zukunft

G

game das Spiel, -e
garage die Garage, -n
garden der Garten, ¨
gate das Tor, -e
gaze der Blick, -e
gaze, look blicken
gender das Geschlecht, -er
generation die Generation, -en
gentleman der Herr, -n, -en
geographical geographisch
geography die Geographie
German deutsch (*adj.*); der/die Deutsche, -n (*adj. noun*)
German class die Deutschstunde, -n
German Democratic Republic (GDR) die Deutsche Demokratische Republik (DDR)
German (language) (das) Deutsch
German mark, Deutschmark die Deutsche Mark
German studies die Germanistik
in German auf Deutsch
German-speaking deutschsprachig
Germany (das) Deutschland
get, receive *bekommen
get, become *werden
get, fetch holen
get, pick up ab·holen
get in (a vehicle) *ein·steigen
get out (of a vehicle) *aus·steigen
get there: How do I get there? Wie komme ich dahin?
get up, get out of bed *auf·stehen
giant der Riese, -n, -n
gigantic riesengroß; riesen- (*noun and adj. prefix*)
girl das Mädchen, -
give *geben
give (as a gift) schenken
give up *auf·geben
glad froh
I'm glad. Das freut mich.
gladly, with pleasure gern(e) (*adv.*)
glance der Blick, -e
glass das Glas, ¨er
glasses die Brille (*sing.*)
glove der Handschuh, -e
go *gehen
go (by vehicle) *fahren
go away *weg·gehen
go out *aus·gehen
let's go! los!
on the go unterwegs
goal das Ziel, -e
god der Gott, ¨er
golden golden
golden wedding anniversary die goldene Hochzeit
gone weg
good gut (besser, best-)
Good-bye! Auf Wiedersehen!
Good evening! Guten Abend!
Good morning! Guten Morgen!
Have a good trip! Gute Reise!
pretty good ganz gut
gossip der Klatsch
government in power die Regierung, -en
grade, class die Klasse, -n
grade (on a test, paper, etc.) die Note, -n
gram das Gramm
500 grams das Pfund
grammar die Grammatik
granddaughter die Enkelin, -nen
grandfather der Großvater, ¨
grandma die Oma, -s
grandmother die Großmutter, ¨
grandpa der Opa, -s
grandparents die Großeltern (*pl.*)
grandson der Enkel, -
graphic artist der Zeichner, - ; die Zeichnerin, -nen
gray grau
great, terrific herrlich; prima, toll (*colloq.*)
greatness die Größe
Greece (das) Griechenland
Greek griechisch (*adj.*)
green grün
greet grüßen
groceries die Lebensmittel (*pl.*)
group die Gruppe, -n
grow *wachsen
grow up *auf·wachsen
gruesome grausam
guess *raten

Take a guess! Raten Sie mal!
guest der Gast, ¨-e
guide book der Reiseführer, -
guy der Typ, -en (*slang*)
gym shoe der Turnschuh, -e

H

hair das Haar, -e
half halb (*adv.*)
half days halbtags (*adv.*)
ham der Schinken
hand die Hand, ¨-e
handsome hübsch
hang hängen (*trans.*); *hängen (*intrans.*)
hang up auf·hängen
happen passieren, ist passiert
happiness das Glück
happy glücklich, froh
be happy sich freuen
harbor der Hafen, ¨-
hard hart (härter)
hard, difficult schwer
hardly kaum
hard-working fleißig
harsh hart (härter)
hat der Hut, ¨-e
hate hassen
hatred der Hass
haul schleppen
have *haben
have in mind *vor·haben
have to, must *müssen
head der Kopf, ¨-e
health die Gesundheit
healthy gesund (gesünder)
hear hören
heaven: For heaven's sake! Um Gottes Willen!
heavy schwer
hectic hektisch
hello Grüß Gott! (*in southern Germany and Austria*); Guten Tag!; Hallo!
say hello to grüßen
help die Hilfe; *helfen (+ *dat.*)
helping, portion die Portion, -en
here hier (*location*); her (*destination*)
Here it is. Bitte.
Hi! Tag!
high hoch (*pred. adj.*), hoh- (*attributive adj.*) (höher, höchst-)
High time! Höchste Zeit! Na endlich!
highway die Autobahn, -en
hike die Wanderung, -en; wandern
hill der Hügel, -
hilly hügelig
hint der Tipp, -s
historic historisch
history die Geschichte, -n
hit *schlagen
hitchhike per Autostopp reisen; trampen
hitchhiking der Autostopp
hold *halten
home (as destination of motion) nach Hause
at home zu Hause
in the home of bei (+ *dat.*)
homeland die Heimat
homesickness das Heimweh
homework assignment die Hausaufgabe, -n
honest ehrlich
hope hoffen
I hope hoffentlich (*adv.*)
horizon der Horizont, -e
hospital das Krankenhaus, ¨-er
hot heiß
hotel das Hotel, -s
hour die Stunde, -n
for hours stundenlang
house das Haus, ¨-er
housemate der Mitbewohner, -; die Mitbewohnerin, -nen
housewife die Hausfrau, -en
how? wie?
How come? Wieso? *or* Wie kommt das?
how long? wie lange?
how many? wie viele?
how much? wie viel?
however aber
human being der Mensch, -en, -en
human race die Menschheit
humor der Humor
hunch die Ahnung, -en
hunger der Hunger
hungry hungrig
be hungry Hunger haben
hurry die Eile; sich beeilen, schnell machen (*colloq.*)
in a hurry in Eile
hurt weh *tun (+ *dat. of person*)
get hurt sich verletzen
That hurts (me). Das tut (mir) weh.
husband der Mann, ¨-er

I

ice das Eis
ice cream das Eis
ice hockey das Eishockey
idea die Idee, -n
(I have) no idea. Ich habe keine Ahnung.
I.D. card der Ausweis, -e
ideological ideologisch
if wenn (*sub. conj.*)
if, whether ob (*sub. conj.*)
illegal illegal
image das Bild, -er
imagine something sich etwas vor·stellen
immediately gleich; sofort
immigrate ein·wandern
important wichtig
most important Haupt- (*noun prefix*)
impossible unmöglich
impression der Eindruck, ¨-e
in, into in (*prep.* + *acc.* or *dat.*); hinein- (*prefix*)
incorrect, false falsch
incredible! sagenhaft!
incredibly wahnsinnig (*colloq. adv.*)
indicative der Indikativ
industrious fleißig
industry die Industrie, -n
inexpensive billig, preiswert
inflation die Inflation
information die Auskunft
injure oneself sich verletzen
inkling die Ahnung, -en
insane verrückt
inspect kontrollieren
instead sondern (*coor. conj.*)

instead of anstatt (+ *gen.*); statt (+ *gen.*)
instrument das Instrument, -e
integration die Integration
intelligent intelligent
intend to *wollen
interest interessieren
be interested in sich interessieren für
interesting interessant
intermission die Pause, -n
international international
interrupt *unterbrechen
interview interviewen
into in (*prep.* + *acc.*); hinein- (*prefix*)
introduce vor·stellen
introduce oneself sich vor·stellen
invent *erfinden
invest investieren
invite *ein·laden
irony die Ironie
Italian italienisch (*adj.*); der Italiener, -; die Italienerin, -nen
Italy (das) Italien

J

jacket die Jacke, -n
January (der) Januar
jeans die Jeans (*pl.*)
Jewish jüdisch
job, position die Stelle, -n
joke der Witz, -e
journalist der Journalist, -en, -en
journey die Reise, -n
joy die Freude, -n
juice der Saft, ¨-e
July (der) Juli
June (der) Juni
just, at the moment gerade
just as . . . as genau so ... wie

K

kaput kaputt (*colloq.*)
keep *behalten
key der Schlüssel, -
kilogram das Kilogramm; das Kilo (*colloq.*)
kilometer der Kilometer, -
kitchen die Küche, -n
knife das Messer, -
know (a fact) *wissen
get to know kennen lernen
know, be acquainted with *kennen
know one's way around sich *aus·kennen
known bekannt

L

lab(oratory) das Labor, -s
lady die Dame, -n
lake der See, -n
at the lake am See
lamp die Lampe, -n
landscape die Landschaft, -en
language die Sprache, -n
last letzt-
last of all zuletzt
last, take time dauern
late spät
be late sich verspäten
I'm late. Ich bin spät dran.
later on nachher (*adv.*)
laugh lachen
lavatory die Toilette, -n
lavender lila
law das Gesetz, -e
(study of) law Jura
under the law, in the eyes of the law vor dem Gesetz
lawyer der Rechtsanwalt, ¨-e; die Rechtsanwältin, -nen
lay, put down legen
lazy faul
lead führen
learn lernen
leave (something or someone), leave behind *lassen
leave (a person or place) *verlassen
leave (by vehicle) *ab·fahren; *los·fahren
leave, go away *weg·gehen
lecture (university) die Vorlesung, -en
left: to the left, on the left links (*adv.*)
leg das Bein, -e
leisure time die Freizeit
lend *leihen
let *lassen
let's go! los!
letter der Brief, -e
lettuce der Salat, -e
library die Bibliothek, -en
lie, be situated *liegen
life das Leben
light das Licht, -er
light (in color) hell
light (in weight) leicht
like *mögen; wie (*conj.*)
I like that. Das gefällt mir.
like something etwas gern haben; etwas mögen
like this so
like to (do something) gern (+ *verb*)
would like to möchten
likeable sympathisch
limnology die Limnologie
line (of text) die Zeile, -n
line (streetcar or bus) die Linie, -n
linguistics die Linguistik
lion der Löwe, -n, -n
list die Liste, -n
listen (to) zu·hören (+ *dat.*)
liter der Liter
literary literarisch
little klein (*adj.*); wenig (*pronoun*)
a little etwas
a little; a little bit; a little while ein bisschen
live leben
live, dwell wohnen
lively munter
liverwurst die Leberwurst, ¨-e
loan *leihen
long lang(e) (länger)
for a long time lange; (*stretch of time continuing in the present*) schon lange, seit langem
for such a long time so lange
no longer nicht mehr
look schauen, blicken
look after auf·passen auf (+ *acc.*); sich kümmern um
look, appear *aus·sehen
look at an·schauen
look for, seek suchen

look forward to sich freuen auf (+ *acc.*)
Look here. Schau mal.
look out (for) auf·passen (auf + *acc.*)
take a look at something sich etwas *an·sehen
lose *verlieren
lots of eine Menge; viel
loud laut
love die Liebe; lieben
low niedrig
luck das Glück
be lucky Glück haben
be unlucky, have bad luck Pech haben
lug (along) schleppen (*colloq.*)
luggage das Gepäck
lunch, midday meal das Mittagessen

M

magazine die Zeitschrift, -en
mail die Post
mail (a letter) *ein·werfen
mailbox der Briefkasten, ¨
mailman der Briefträger, -
main Haupt- (*noun prefix*)
major field (of study) das Hauptfach, ¨er
major in (a subject) studieren
make machen
make-up: put on make-up sich schminken
mama, mom die Mutti, -s
man der Mann, ¨er
Man! Mensch!
manage schaffen (*colloq.*)
management (field of study) die Betriebswirtschaft
manager der Manager, -
manipulate manipulieren
mankind die Menschheit
many viele (*adj.*)
many a manch-
many people viele (*pl. pron.*)
many things vieles (*sing. pron.*)
map die Karte, -n; die Landkarte, -n
March (der) März
mark (the German mark) die Mark
marriage die Ehe, -n
married man der Ehemann, ¨er
married woman die Ehefrau, -en
marry, get married heiraten
be married verheiratet sein
marvelous herrlich; sagenhaft
math die Mathe (*slang*)
mathematics die Mathematik (*sing.*)
matter, affair die Sache, -n
matter
It doesn't matter. Es macht (doch) nichts.
It doesn't matter to me. Das ist mir egal.
no matter where, who, why, etc. egal wo, wer, warum usw.
What's the matter? Was ist los?
May (der) Mai
may, be allowed to *dürfen
That may be. Das mag sein.
maybe vielleicht
meal das Essen
mean, signify bedeuten
mean, think meinen
that means, in other words das heißt
What do you mean? Wieso?
meaning die Bedeutung, -en
meat das Fleisch
mechanic der Mechaniker, -
medicine die Medizin
meet (for the first time) kennen lernen
meet again wieder *sehen
meet (by appointment) *treffen
melancholy die Melancholie
member das Mitglied, -er
mention: Don't mention it. Nichts zu danken.
menu die Speisekarte, -n
messy schlampig (*colloq.*); unordentlich
method die Methode, -n
Middle Ages das Mittelalter (*sing.*)
might die Macht
mild mild
milk die Milch
million die Million, -en
minor field (of study) das Nebenfach, ¨er
minute die Minute, -n
for minutes minutenlang
miracle das Wunder, -
mirror der Spiegel, -
Miss Fräulein
miss (an event, opportunity, train, etc.) verpassen
missing: be missing fehlen
mist der Nebel
misty neblig
modern modern
modernize modernisieren
mom, mama die Mutti, -s
moment der Augenblick, -e; der Moment, -e
at the moment im Augenblick; im Moment
at the moment, just gerade
Just a moment, please. (Einen) Augenblick, bitte.
monarchy die Monarchie, -n
Monday (der) Montag
money das Geld
month der Monat, -e
for months monatelang
monument das Denkmal, ¨er
mood die Laune, -n
in a good/bad mood guter / schlechter Laune
more mehr
not any more nicht mehr
morning der Morgen, -
Good morning! Guten Morgen!
in the morning(s) morgens (*adv.*); vormittags (*adv.*)
this morning heute Morgen
most meist-
most like to am liebsten (+ *verb*)
mostly meistens
mother die Mutter, ¨
motorcycle das Motorrad, ¨er
mountainous bergig
mouth der Mund, ¨er
move, change residence *um·ziehen
move in *ein·ziehen
move out *aus·ziehen
movie der Film, -e
movie theater das Kino, -s

Mr. Herr
Mrs. Frau
Ms. Frau
much viel (mehr, meist-)
  not much wenig
Munich (das) München
museum das Museum, *pl.* Museen
music die Musik
musicology die Musikwissenschaft
must *müssen

N

name der Name, -ns, -n; *nennen
  My name is . . . Ich heiße ...
  What's your name? Wie heißen Sie? *or* Wie ist Ihr Name?
napkin die Serviette, -n
nation, folk das Volk, ¨er
nationality die Nationalität, -en
native
  native language die Muttersprache, -n
  native place or country die Heimat
natural natürlich
nature die Natur
near nah (näher, nächst-)
  near, nearby in der Nähe (von *or* + *gen.*)
nearness die Nähe
necessary nötig
need brauchen
neighbor der Nachbar, -n, -n; die Nachbarin, -nen
neither . . . nor weder ... noch
neutral neutral
neutrality die Neutralität
never nie
nevertheless trotzdem
new neu
newspaper die Zeitung, -en
next nächst-
nice nett; lieb
night die Nacht, ¨e
  Good night. Gute Nacht.
  in the night, at night in der Nacht; nachts
no nein; nee (*colloq.*)
  no, not a kein (*negative article*)
  no more X kein X mehr
nobody, no one niemand
Nonsense! Quatsch!
normal normal
north der Norden
North America (das) Nordamerika
nose die Nase, -n
not nicht
  not a kein (*negative article*)
  not a . . . at all gar kein
  not an X any longer kein X mehr
  not any kein
  not any more, no longer nicht mehr
  not any X yet noch kein X
  not at all gar nicht
  not much wenig
  not only . . . but also nicht nur ... sondern auch
  not yet noch nicht
notebook das Heft, -e
nothing nichts
notice merken
notion die Ahnung, -en
noun das Substantiv, -e
novel der Roman, -e
November (der) November
now jetzt; nun
  from now on von jetzt an
number die Nummer, -n
nurse der Krankenpfleger, - (*m.*); die Krankenschwester, -n (*f.*)

O

object, thing die Sache, -n
objective objektiv
o'clock Uhr (3 o'clock = 3 Uhr)
October (der) Oktober
odd komisch
of von (*prep.* + *dat.*)
  of course natürlich
  of course, sure klar (*colloq.*)
offend ärgern
offer *bieten
office das Büro, -s
official offiziell (*adj.*); der Beamte (*adj. noun, m.*); die Beamtin, -nen (*f.*)
often oft (öfter)
oh ach
oil das Öl
O.K. Ist gut; okay (*colloq.*)
old alt (älter)
old-fashioned altmodisch
on auf (*prep.* + *acc.* or *dat.*)
once einmal
  once again, once more noch einmal
one (*indefinite pronoun*) man
oneself: by oneself (myself, yourself, etc.) selber, selbst
only nur (*adv.*)
  only, single einzig- (*adj.*)
onto auf (*prep.* + *acc.* or *dat.*)
open offen (*adj.*); öffnen (*verb*)
opinion die Meinung, -en
  be of the opinion, think meinen
opportunity die Gelegenheit, -en
opposite der Gegensatz, ¨e
opposition die Opposition, -en
optimistic optimistisch
or oder (*coor. conj.*)
order die Portion, -en (*of food*); bestellen
  in order to um ... zu
orderly ordentlich
other ander-
otherwise sonst
outing der Ausflug, ¨e
out of aus (*prep.* + *dat.*)
outside draußen (*adv.*)
over über (*prep.* + *dat.* or *acc.*)
  over there drüben; da drüben
own eigen- (*adj.*); *besitzen

P

pace das Tempo
pack packen
page die Seite, -n
pants die Hose, -n
papa der Vati, -s
paper das Papier, -e
  write a paper ein Referat schreiben
  written term paper das Referat
Pardon me. Entschuldigung.
  I beg your pardon? Wie bitte?
parents die Eltern (*pl.*)
part der Teil, -e
  take part in *teil·nehmen an (+ *dat.*)
participate mit·machen
partner der Partner, -

party die Party, -s
party (political) die Partei, -en
passport der Pass, ⸚e; der Reisepass, ⸚e
past (time) die Vergangenheit
path der Weg, -e
patience die Geduld
patient der Patient, -en, -en
patron der Gast, ⸚e
pay bezahlen; zahlen
pay attention auf·passen
peace der Frieden
peaceful, calm ruhig
peculiar komisch
pedestrian der Fußgänger, -
pedestrian zone die Fußgängerzone, -n
pen (ballpoint) der Kugelschreiber, -
pencil der Bleistift, -e
people die Leute (*pl.*)
people, nation, folk das Volk, ⸚er
percent das Prozent
perfect perfekt
perhaps vielleicht
person der Mensch, -en, -en; die Person, -en
personal persönlich
pessimistic pessimistisch
pharmacy die Apotheke, -n
philosophize philosophieren
philosophy die Philosophie
photograph das Foto, -s
physics die Physik (*sing.*)
piano das Klavier, -e
pick up ab·holen
picture das Bild, -er
take a picture ein Foto machen
piece das Stück, -e
pigeon die Taube, -n
pink rosa
pity: What a pity! Das ist schade!
place der Ort, -e; der Platz, ⸚e
place, put stellen
plan *vor·haben
plan, make plans planen
plant die Pflanze, -n
plastic das Plastik
plate der Teller, -
play spielen
play sports Sport *treiben
pleasant angenehm
please bitte
please, appeal to *gefallen (+ *dat.*)
Pleased to meet you. Sehr erfreut. *or* Es freut mich.
Pleasure to meet you. Angenehm.
pocket die Tasche, -n
poem das Gedicht, -e
poet der Dichter, -; die Dichterin, -nen
poetry die Lyrik
police die Polizei (*sing. only*)
policy die Politik
polite höflich
political politisch
political science die Politikwissenschaft
politician der Politiker, -; die Politikerin, -nen
politics die Politik
pollute verschmutzen
non-polluting, ecologically beneficial umweltfreundlich
pollution die Verschmutzung
ponder something sich etwas überlegen
poor arm (ärmer)
popular beliebt
port der Hafen, ⸚
portion die Portion, -en
position, job die Stelle, -n
possible möglich
postage stamp die Briefmarke, -n
postal service die Post
postcard die Postkarte, -n
poster das Poster, -
poster (political) das Plakat, -e
post office die Post
pot: small (coffee or tea) pot das Kännchen, -
potato die Kartoffel, -n
power die Kraft, ⸚e; die Macht, ⸚e
power plant das Kraftwerk, -e
practical praktisch
practice üben
precise genau
prefer (to do something) lieber (+ *verb*)
preferably lieber
prejudice das Vorurteil, -e
prepared, ready bereit
prepare for sich vor·bereiten auf (+ *acc.*)
present (gift) das Geschenk, -e
be present, be there dabei *sein
present (time) die Gegenwart
president der Präsident, -en, -en
pretty hübsch
pretzel die Brezel, -n
previously vorher
price der Preis, -e
primary Haupt- (*noun prefix*)
private privat
probably wahrscheinlich; wohl
problem das Problem, -e
produce produzieren
product, ware die Ware, -n
productive produktiv
profession der Beruf, -e
What is your profession? Was sind Sie von Beruf?
professor der Professor, -en; die Professorin, -nen
program das Programm, -e
programmer der Programmierer, -; die Programmiererin, -nen
progress der Fortschritt, -e
prohibited verboten
propel *treiben
protect (from) schützen (vor + *dat.*)
protest der Protest, -e
proud of stolz auf (+ *acc.*)
provide *bieten
psychoanalysis die Psychoanalyse
psychology die Psychologie
public öffentlich
pull *ziehen
pullover der Pullover, -; der Pulli, -s (*colloq.*)
punctual pünktlich
pupil der Schüler, -; die Schülerin, -nen
put stellen
put down, lay legen
put down, set setzen

Q

quantity die Menge, -n
quarter das Viertel, -

quarter to/past Viertel vor/nach
question die Frage, -n
ask a question eine Frage stellen
guiding question die Leitfrage, -n
it's a question of es geht um
questionnaire der Fragebogen
quick as lightning blitzschnell
quiet leise
quit, to give up *auf·geben
quite ziemlich
quotidian alltäglich

R

radical radikal
radio das Radio, -s
railroad, railroad system die Bahn
railway compartment das Abteil, -e
rain der Regen; regnen
rainy regnerisch
rather
I'd rather not. No thanks. Lieber nicht.
would rather (do something) lieber (+ *verb*)
reaction die Reaktion, -en
react to reagieren auf (+ *acc.*)
read *lesen
read aloud *vor·lesen
reading selection das Lesestück, -e
ready, finished fertig
ready, prepared bereit
real wirklich
really? echt? (*slang*)
realm das Reich, -e
reason der Grund, ¨-e
receive *bekommen
recently neulich
reception desk die Rezeption
recommend *empfehlen
recover (from) sich erholen von
recycling das Recycling
red rot (röter)
reform die Reform, -en; reformieren
refuse, trash der Müll
regard as *halten für
regime das Regime
region die Gegend, -en; die Region, -en
register (at a hotel, the university, etc.) sich an·melden
register for, take (a university course) belegen
relative relativ (*adj.* and *adv.*); der/die Verwandte, -n (*adj. noun*)
remain *bleiben
remember sich erinnern an (+ *acc.*)
Do you remember? Weißt du noch?
remind of erinnern an (+ *acc.*)
rent (from somebody) mieten
repair reparieren
repeat wiederholen
repetition die Wiederholung, -en
report berichten
give a report ein Referat *halten
oral report das Referat, -e
republic die Republik, -en
request *bitten um
rescue retten
reserve reservieren
respond to antworten auf (+ *acc.*)
responsible for verantwortlich für
rest: have a rest sich erholen
restaurant das Restaurant, -s; das Lokal, -e
restless unruhig
restoration die Restauration
retain *behalten
review die Wiederholung
revolution die Revolution, -en
Rhine River der Rhein
rich reich
right, correct richtig
be right Recht *haben (*with person as subject*); stimmen (*impersonal only*)
right away sofort; gleich
That's right. Das stimmt. Stimmt schon.
to the right, on the right rechts (*adv.*)
ring klingeln
rip off, steal klauen (*colloq.*)
river der Fluss, ¨-e
road die Straße, -n
road atlas der Straßenatlas
role die Rolle, -n
roll das Brötchen, -
Romania (das) Rumänien
romantic romantisch
room das Zimmer, -
dining room das Esszimmer, -
double room das Doppelzimmer, -
living room das Wohnzimmer, -
rented student room die Bude, -n (*colloq.*)
single room das Einzelzimmer, -
roommate der Mitbewohner, -; die Mitbewohnerin, -nen
rubble die Trümmer (*pl.*)
rucksack der Rucksack, ¨-e
rug der Teppich, -e
ruins die Trümmer (*pl.*)
run *laufen
Russia (das) Russland
Russian russisch (*adj.*); der Russe, -n, -n; die Russin, -nen

S

sack der Sack, ¨-e
sad traurig
salad der Salat, -e
salesman der Verkäufer, -
saleswoman die Verkäuferin, -nen
sample probieren
satisfied zufrieden
Saturday (der) Samstag, (der) Sonnabend
sausage die Wurst, ¨-e
save, rescue retten
save (money or time) sparen
say sagen
What did you say? Wie bitte?
What do you say to that? Was meinen/sagen Sie dazu?
scarce, in short supply knapp
scarf das Tuch, ¨-er
schilling (Austrian currency) der Schilling, -e
scholarship die Wissenschaft
scholarship, stipend das Stipendium, *pl.* Stipendien

school die Schule, -n; das Gymnasium, *pl.* Gymnasien (*prepares pupils for university*)
elementary school pupil or secondary school student der Schüler, -; die Schülerin, -nen
school system das Schulsystem, -e
science die Wissenschaft, -en
sea das Meer, -e
seat der Platz, ¨-e
second zweit-
second car der Zweitwagen, -
secretary der Sekretär, -e; die Sekretärin, -nen
see *sehen
Let's see. Zeig mal her.
see again wieder *sehen
seek, look for suchen
seem *scheinen
seldom selten
self: by oneself (myself, yourself, etc.) selbst *or* selber (*adv.*)
sell verkaufen
semester das Semester, -
semester break die Semesterferien (*pl.*)
seminar das Seminar, -e
send schicken
senior citizen der Senior, -en, -en
sentence der Satz, ¨-e
separate separat
September (der) September
serious ernst
take something seriously etwas ernst *nehmen
set (down) setzen
seventh siebt-
several mehrere, einige
sex, gender das Geschlecht, -er
shame: That's a shame! Das ist schade!
shape: in shape fit
shared apartment die Wohngemeinschaft, -en; die WG, -s
shave sich rasieren
shine *scheinen
ship das Schiff, -e
shirt das Hemd, -en
shoe der Schuh, -e
shop, store der Laden, ¨-
shop for, go shopping ein·kaufen
short kurz (kürzer); klein (*short in height*)
short of cash knapp bei Kasse
should *sollen
shoulder bag die Tasche, -n
shout *schreien
show zeigen
Show it to me. Zeig mal her.
shower die Dusche, -n
take a shower sich duschen
siblings die Geschwister (*pl.*)
sick krank (kränker)
sickness die Krankheit, -en
side die Seite. -n
significance die Bedeutung, -en
silent: be silent *schweigen
similar (to) ähnlich (+ *dat.*)
similarity die Ähnlichkeit, -en
simple, easy einfach; leicht
since (causal) da (*sub. conj.*)
since (temporal) seit (*prep. + dat. & sub. conj.*)
sing *singen
single, only einzig- (*adj.*)
single, unmarried ledig
sister die Schwester, -n
sit *sitzen
sit down sich setzen
situated: be situated *liegen
situation die Situation, -en
size die Größe, -n
skeptical skeptisch
ski Ski *fahren
skirt der Rock, ¨-e
sleep *schlafen
slow langsam
small klein
smart klug (klüger)
snake die Schlange, -n
sneaker der Turnschuh, -e
snow der Schnee; schneien
so so
So long! Tschüss!
so that damit (*sub. conj.*)
So what? Na und?
soccer der Fußball
soccer ball der Fußball, ¨-e
social gesellschaftlich; sozial
social worker der Sozialarbeiter, -; die Sozialarbeiterin, -nen
society die Gesellschaft, -en
sociology die Soziologie
soft, quiet leise
software die Software
solidarity die Solidarität
solution die Lösung, -en
solve lösen
some etwas (*sing.*); einige (*pl.*); manche (*pl.*)
somebody jemand
somehow or other irgendwie
someone jemand
someone else jemand anders
something etwas
sometime or other irgendwann
sometimes manchmal
somewhat etwas
somewhere or other irgendwo
son der Sohn, ¨-e
song das Lied, -er
soon bald
sore, ticked off sauer (*colloq.*)
sorry: I'm sorry about that. Das tut mir Leid.
sound *klingen
soup die Suppe, -n
sour, acidic sauer
south der Süden
Soviet Union die Sowjetunion
space der Platz, ¨-e
Spain (das) Spanien
speak reden; *sprechen
I can speak German. Ich kann Deutsch.
speechless baff (*colloq.*)
speed das Tempo
spell: How do you spell that? Wie schreibt man das?
spend (money) *aus·geben
spend (time) *verbringen
spend the night übernachten
spite
in spite of trotz (+ *gen.*)
in spite of that, nevertheless trotzdem (*adv.*)
spontaneous spontan
spoon der Löffel, -
sport der Sport
play sports Sport *treiben

spouse die Ehefrau, -en (*f.*); der Ehemann, ⸚er (*m.*)
spring der Frühling
spring term das Sommersemester
square: city square der Platz, ⸚e
stability die Stabilität
stable stabil
staircase die Treppe, -n
stairs die Treppe, -n
stamp die Briefmarke, -n
stand *stehen
stand up *auf·stehen
standard of living der Lebensstandard
start *an·fangen
start, depart (by vehicle) *los·fahren
state der Staat, -en; das Bundesland, ⸚er (federal state)
stay *bleiben
steal stehlen
steal, rip off klauen (*colloq.*)
steep steil
stereotyped, clichéd klischeehaft
still (*adv.*) noch; noch immer; immer noch
stipend das Stipendium, *pl.* Stipendien
stone der Stein, -e
stop (for streetcar or bus) die Haltestelle, -n
stop *halten (*intrans.*)
stop (doing something) auf·hören (mit)
store das Geschäft, -e
store, shop der Laden, ⸚
story die Geschichte, -n
story, narrative die Erzählung, -en
straighten up auf·räumen
strange, foreign fremd
strawberry jam die Erdbeermarmelade
street die Straße, -n
streetcar die Straßenbahn, -en
strength die Kraft, ⸚e
stress der Stress
stressed out gestresst (*colloq.*)
stressful stressig
stroll der Bummel, -
stroll through town der Stadtbummel, -
take a stroll einen Bummel machen
strong stark (stärker)
student (at university) der Student, -en, -en; die Studentin, -nen
student dormitory das Studentenwohnheim, -e
student I.D. der Studentenausweis, -e
studies (at university) das Studium
study das Arbeitszimmer, -
study (a subject), major in studieren
study at studieren an (+ *dat.*)
stupid blöd; dumm
subject, area of study das Fach, ⸚er
subject, topic das Thema, *pl.* Themen
subjective subjektiv
subjunctive der Konjunktiv
subway train die Untergrundbahn; die U-Bahn
success der Erfolg, -e
such a so ein(e)
suddenly plötzlich
suggestion der Vorschlag, ⸚e; der Tipp, -s
suit der Anzug, ⸚e
suitcase der Koffer, -
summary die Zusammenfassung, -en
summer der Sommer
sun die Sonne
Sunday (der) Sonntag
sunny sonnig
super super
supermarket der Supermarkt, ⸚e
super tanker der Supertanker, -
supper das Abendessen
for supper zum Abendessen
supposed: be supposed to *sollen
sure, certain sicher; bestimmt
sure, of course klar (*colloq.*)
surprise die Überraschung, -en; überraschen
be surprised staunen
be surprised (about) sich wundern (über + *acc.*)
sweater der Pullover, -; der Pulli, -s (*colloq.*)
sweet süß
swim *schwimmen
swimming pool das Schwimmbad, ⸚er
Swiss schweizerisch (*adj.*); der Schweizer, -; die Schweizerin, -nen
Switzerland die Schweiz
symbol das Symbol, -e
symbolic symbolisch
sympathy das Mitleid
system das System, -e

T

T-shirt das T-Shirt, -s
table der Tisch, -e
take *nehmen
take along *mit·bringen; *mit·nehmen
take (a university course) belegen
take for *halten für
take part in *teil·nehmen an (+ *dat.*)
take place *statt·finden
talk reden; *sprechen
talk nonsense quatschen (*colloq.*)
talk to sich *unterhalten mit
tall groß
task die Aufgabe, -n
taste; taste good schmecken
tasty lecker
tavern die Kneipe, -n; das Lokal, -e
taxicab das Taxi, -s
tea der Tee
teacher der Lehrer, -; die Lehrerin, -nen
team die Mannschaft, -en
technology die Technik
telephone das Telefon, -e; telefonieren
television set der Fernseher, -
watch television *fern·sehen
tell sagen
tell, recount erzählen
tell me sag mal

tempo das Tempo
tennis das Tennis
tennis court der Tennisplatz, ¨-e
term paper das Referat, -e
terrace die Terrasse, -n
terrible furchtbar; grausam; schrecklich
terrific herrlich; prima; toll (*colloq.*)
terrorist terroristisch (*adj.*)
test die Prüfung, -en
written test die Klausur, -en
text der Text, -e
than (*with comparative degree*) als
thank danken (+ *dat.*)
thank goodness Gott sei Dank
thanks der Dank
thanks, thank you danke
thanks a lot, many thanks vielen Dank
that dass (*sub. conj.*)
theater das Theater, -
theme das Thema, *pl.* Themen
then dann
then, in that case da (*adv.*)
there da, dort
How do I get there? Wie komme ich dahin?
there is, there are es gibt (+ *acc.*)
therefore darum
thermos bottle die Thermosflasche, -n
thing das Ding, -e
thing, item die Sache, -n
think *denken; meinen, glauben
I don't think so. Ich glaube nicht.
I think so. Ich glaube schon.
I think so too. Das finde ich auch.
think of *denken an (+ *acc.*)
think something over sich etwas überlegen
think X is *halten X für
What do you think of that? Was meinen/sagen Sie dazu?
third dritt-
thirst der Durst
thirsty Durst haben
this, these dies-
thought der Gedanke, -ns, -n
through durch (*prep.* + *acc.*)
throw *werfen
throw away *weg·werfen
Thursday (der) Donnerstag
thus also
ticked off, sore sauer (*colloq.*)
ticket die Karte, -n; die Fahrkarte, -n (*bus, train, streetcar*); das Ticket, -s (*airline*)
tidy ordentlich
tidy up auf·räumen
tie die Krawatte, -n
time die Zeit, -en
for a long time lange
for a short time, briefly kurz
for a time eine Zeit lang
for such a long time so lange
high time höchste Zeit
on time, punctual pünktlich
take time, last dauern
What time is it? Wie spät ist es? *or* Wie viel Uhr ist es?
time (in the sense of "occurrence") das Mal, -e
any time irgendwann
at that time, back then damals
for the first time zum ersten Mal
the next time das nächste Mal
this time diesmal (*adv.*)
umpteen times zigmal
tin can die Dose, -n
tip der Tipp, -s
tired, weary müde
dead tired todmüde
to (*prep.*) an (*prep.* + *acc.* or *dat.*); nach (+ *dat., with cities and countries*); zu (+ *dat., with people and some places*)
to each other zueinander
today heute
together zusammen; miteinander
tomorrow morgen
tomorrow afternoon morgen Nachmittag
tomorrow evening morgen Abend
tomorrow morning morgen früh
tonight heute Abend
too auch; zu
too bad schade
tooth der Zahn, ¨-e
top: on top oben (*adv.*)
topic das Thema, *pl.* Themen
topical aktuell
tough hart (härter)
tour die Tour, -en
tourist der Tourist, -en, -en; die Touristin, -nen
toward an (*prep.* + *acc.* or *dat.*)
town (5,000 to 20,000 inhabitants) die Kleinstadt, ¨-e
small town der Ort, -e
town hall das Rathaus, ¨-er
track das Gleis, -e
tradition die Tradition, -en
traditional traditionell
traffic der Verkehr
train der Zug, ¨-e
train station der Bahnhof, ¨-e
train (for a sport) trainieren
transfer *um·steigen
translate übersetzen
trash der Müll
trash container der Container, -
travel reisen
travel agency das Reisebüro, -s
traveler's check der Reisescheck, -s
tree der Baum, ¨-e
trip die Reise, -n; die Fahrt
Have a good trip! Gute Reise!
take a trip eine Reise machen
trousers die Hose, -n
true wahr; richtig
truth die Wahrheit, -en
try versuchen (*attempt*); probieren (*sample*)
Tuesday (der) Dienstag
Turk der Türke, -n, -n; die Türkin, -nen
Turkey die Türkei
Turkish türkisch
twice zweimal
type der Typ, -en
typical typisch

U

ugly hässlich
umbrella der Regenschirm, -e
unconcerned unbesorgt

under unter (*prep.* + *acc.* or *dat.*)
understand *verstehen
undress, get undressed sich *aus·ziehen
uneducated ungebildet
unemployed arbeitslos
unemployment die Arbeitslosigkeit
unfortunately leider
unification die Vereinigung
unimportant unwichtig
unite vereinen
university die Universität, -en; die Uni, -s (*colloq.*); die Hochschule, -n
  attend a university studieren
  at the university an der Uni(versität)
  university studies das Studium
unknown unbekannt
unmarried unverheiratet
unnecessary unnötig
unpack aus·packen
unpleasant ungemütlich; unangenehm
unpopular unbeliebt
until bis
  not until erst
upon auf (*prep.* + *acc.* or *dat.*)
upset: get upset (about) sich auf·regen (über + *acc.*)
USA die USA (*pl.*)
use benutzen
used to: get used to sich gewöhnen an (+ *acc.*)
useful nützlich
usually meistens

V

vacation (from university or school) die Ferien (*pl.*)
  be on vacation auf (*or*) im Urlaub sein
  go on vacation in Urlaub gehen/fahren
  take a vacation Urlaub machen
  vacation (from a job) der Urlaub, -e
valley das Tal, ¨er
variation die Variation, -en
various verschieden
vegetables das Gemüse (*sing.*)
Venice (Italy) (das) Venedig
verb das Verb, -en
very sehr
vicinity die Nähe
Vienna (das) Wien
view der Blick, -e
village das Dorf, ¨er
visit der Besuch, -e; besuchen
vocabulary der Wortschatz
voice die Stimme, -n
volleyball der Volleyball
voter der Wähler, -

W

wage der Lohn, ¨e
wait (for) warten (auf + *acc.*)
  Wait a second! Hang on! Warte mal!
waiter der Kellner, -
waitress die Kellnerin, -nen
wake up auf·wachen (*intrans.*); wecken (*trans.*)
walk der Bummel, -; *gehen; *laufen (*colloq.*)
  go for a walk spazieren *gehen
wall (freestanding or exterior) die Mauer, -n
  wall (interior) die Wand, ¨e
wallet der Geldbeutel, -
wander wandern
wanderlust die Wanderlust
want to *wollen
  I don't want to. Ich habe keine Lust.
  want to do something Lust haben, etwas zu tun
war der Krieg, -e
wardrobe der Kleiderschrank, ¨e
warm warm (wärmer)
wash *waschen
waste verschwenden
watch die Uhr, -en
watch zu·schauen (+ *dat.*)
  watch television *fern·sehen
water das Wasser
way der Weg, -e
  on the way unterwegs
weak schwach (schwächer)
wear *tragen
weary, tired müde
weather das Wetter
wedding die Hochzeit, -en
Wednesday (der) Mittwoch
week die Woche, -n
  for weeks wochenlang (*adv.*)
weekend das Wochenende, -n
  on the weekend am Wochenende
weigh *wiegen
welcome willkommen (*adj.*)
  Welcome! Nice to see you! Herzlich willkommen!
  You're welcome. Bitte (sehr).
well . . . also ... ; na ... ; nun ...
well (*adv.*) gut
  get well sich erholen von
  Get well soon. Gute Besserung.
  well known bekannt
west der Westen
wet nass
what? was?
  what kind of? was für?
wheel das Rad, ¨er
when als (*sub. conj.*); wann (*question word*); wenn (*sub. conj.*)
whenever wenn (*sub. conj.*)
where? wo?
  from where? woher?
  to where? wohin?
whether, if ob (*sub. conj.*)
which? welch-?
while während (*sub. conj.*)
  for a while eine Zeit lang
  while . . . -ing bei ...
white weiß
who? wer?
whole ganz
whose? wessen?
why? warum?
wild wild
win *gewinnen
wind der Wind
window das Fenster, -
  store window das Schaufenster, -
  window, counter der Schalter, -
windy windig
wine der Wein, -e
winter (der) Winter
  in the winter im Winter

wish wünschen
wit der Witz, -e
with mit
  with each other miteinander
without ohne
  without . . . -ing ohne ... zu
witty witzig
woman die Frau, -en
  young unmarried woman das Fräulein, -
wonder, ask oneself sich fragen
  No wonder! Kein Wunder!
wonderful wunderbar
word das Wort; *two plural forms*: die Worte (*in context*), die Wörter (*unconnected*); die Vokabel, -n
work die Arbeit
  work (of art) das Werk, -e
work arbeiten
  work on arbeiten an (+ *dat.*)
  work part time halbtags arbeiten
worker der Arbeiter, -; die Arbeiterin, -nen
world die Welt, -en
worried besorgt
worthwhile: be worthwhile, worth the trouble sich lohnen
Wow! Mensch!
write *schreiben
writer der Schriftsteller, -; die Schriftstellerin, -nen
wrong falsch

Y

year das Jahr, -e
  for years jahrelang
yell *schreien
yellow gelb
yes ja
  yes I do, yes I am, etc. doch
yesterday gestern
  yesterday evening gestern Abend
  yesterday morning gestern früh
young jung (jünger)
  young people die Jugend (*sing.*)
youth die Jugend
  youth hostel die Jugendherberge, -n

Z

zone die Zone, -n

Credits

Text

Page 252: "Die Lorelei 1973" by Jürgen Werner from *Gegendarstellungen: Autoren korrigieren Autoren: lyr. Parodien.* Edited by Manfred Ach & Manfred Bosch (Andernach: Atelier-Verlag, 1974). Reprinted by permission of Atelier Verlag Andernach. **280:** "Mein junger Sohn fragt mich" by Bertolt Brecht from *Gesammelte Werke,* Volume 9. Copyright © 1967, Suhrkamp Verlag Frankfurt am Main. Used by permission.
361: "Zwei Denkmäler" by Anna Seghers from *Atlaszusammengestellt von deutschen Autoren* (Berlin: Verlag Klaus Wagenbach, 1965). Copyright © by Anna Seghers. Reprinted by permission of Verlag Klaus Wagenbach. **376–377:** "nachwort" by Eugen Gomringer from *The Book of Hours/Stundenbuch.* Reprinted by permission of Eugen Gomringer. **402:** "ottos mops" by Ernst Jandl from *Der künstliche Baum,* 1970. Reprinted by permission of Luchterhand Literaturverlag GmbH. **431–432:** "Über Grenzen" by Clara Tauchert-da Cruz from *Über Grenzen,* edited by Karl Esselborn (Deutscher Taschenbuch Verlag, 1987). 432: "Integration" by Sadi Üçüncü from *Über Grenzen,* edited by Karl Esselborn (Deutscher Taschenbuch Verlag, 1987). **459:** From Mascha Kaléko, *Das lyrische Stenogrammheft,* © 1956. Reprinted by permission of Rowohlt Verlag GmbH.

Illustrations

Ruth J. Flanigan: 2–4, 6, 11–12, 14, 16–17, 24, 40–41, 50, 53, 64, 71, 82, 86, 92, 103, 114, 130, 162, 169–171, 179, 181, 199, 237–238, 241, 262, 289, 316–319, 332, 358, 419, 442–443, 449, 477–478.
Matthew Hansen: 129.
Joseph Scharl: 411. From *The Complete Grimm's Fairy Tales* by Jakob Ludwig Karl Grimm and Wilhelm Karl Grimm. Copyright © 1944 by Pantheon Books. Copyright renewed 1972 by Random House, Inc. Reprinted by permission of Pantheon Books, a division of Random House, Inc.
Marie Marcks: 78, 472–475. © Marie Marcks, Heidelberg.
Deutsche Schule Washington, D.C.: 147. Reproduced by permission.
„Studienzeiten": 185. From Zeitschrift „Deutschland". Reproduced by permission.

Photographs

Page 1: Farrell Grehan/Photo Researchers, Inc. **7:** David Simson/Stock Boston **12:** (*left*) Kevin Galvin/Stock Boston; (*right*) Beryl Goldberg **15, 16:** Andrew Brilliant; **21:** Palmer & Brilliant **22:** Beryl Goldberg **27:** Ulrike Welsch; **37:** (*left*) Granitsas/The Image Works; (*right*) Beryl Goldberg **40:** David Frazier **45:** Bob Krist **48:** Kees Van Den Berg/Photo Researchers, Inc. **56:** Palmer & Brilliant **58:** (*right*) Judy Poe **61:** Andrew Brilliant **70, 72, 90:** Ulrike Welsch **98:** Wolfgang Kaehler **99:** Tony Freeman/PhotoEdit **106:** Mike Mazzaschi/Stock Boston **112:** Wolfgang Kaehler **115:** Vandystadt/Photo Researchers, Inc. **116:** COMSTOCK/Sven Martsen **119:** (*left*) Judy Poe; (*center*) Ulrike Welsch; (*right*) Wolfgang Kaehler **126:** Jan Halaska/Photo Researchers, Inc. **132:** Palmer & Brilliant **142:** Beryl Goldberg **144:** Kevin Galvin/Stock Boston **148:** Kevin Galvin **155:** Beryl Goldberg **163:** Palmer & Brilliant **173:** Ulrike Welsch **176:** Kevin Galvin **186:** Carol Palmer **187:** David Simson/Stock Boston **194:** Kevin Galvin **201:** Ulrike Welsch **204:** Andrew Brilliant/Carole Palmer **205:** Ulrike Welsch **212:** Wolfgang Kaehler **215:** Palmer & Brilliant **222:** David Brilliant **234:** Kevin Galvin **242:** David Frazier **248:** Ulrike Welsch **259:** Helga Lade Fotoagentur **267:** (*left*) Marvullo/The Stock Market; (*right*) W. Geiersperger/Interfoto **268:** (*left*) Kevin Galvin/Stock Boston; (*right*) Interfoto **274:** Kevin Galvin **276:** Owen Franken/Stock Boston **282:** Beryl Goldberg **288:** Pierre Valette **307:** Beryl Goldberg **308:** Martin Specht/

Argus-Fotoarchiv GmbH/Peter Arnold, Inc. **313:** Francis Apesteguy/Gamma Liaison **330:** Margot Granitsas/The Image Works **334:** Reuters/Corbis-Bettmann **336:** (*top left and right*) Keystone Photo/The Image Works; (*bottom*) The Bettmann Archive **337:** (*top left*) The Bettmann Archive; (*top right*) Reuters/Bettmann Newsphotos; (*bottom*) The Bettmann Archive **338:** Mike Mazzaschi/Stock Boston; **353:** Margot Granitsas/ Photo Researchers, Inc. **360:** (*top*) Margot Granitsas/The Image Works; (*bottom*) Ullstein Bilderdienst **362:** (*left*) David Barnes/Tony Stone Images; (*right*) Joh Ortner/ Tony Stone Images **363:** (*top left*) John Lamb/Tony Stone Images; (*top right*) Francisco Hidalgo/The Image Bank; (*bottom*) Hans Wolf/The Image Bank **369:** Ulrike Welsch **370:** (*top*) Topham/The Image Works; (*bottom*) Ullstein Bilderdienst **371:** (top) Anita Schiffer-Fuchs/Ullstein Bilderdienst; (*bottom*) Ohlbaum/Interfoto **372:** Joyce Photographics/Photo Researchers, Inc. **376:** Ulrike Welsch **388:** Susan McCartney/Photo Researchers, Inc. **389:** Ulrike Welsch **396:** Judy Poe **397:** Judy and Thierry Lenzin **398:** D. Assmann/Helga Lade Fotoagentur **412:** Judy Poe **414:** Palmer & Brilliant **415:** Giraudon/Art Resource **416:** Ellen Crocker **417:** Blaine Harrington III/The Stock Market **425:** F. Hiersche/Interfoto **426:** Kevin Galvin **427:** Judy Poe **428:** David Simson/ Stock Boston **438:** (*left*) Thomas S. Hansen; (*right*) COMSTOCK/Stuart Cohen **447:** Thomas S. Hansen **454:** Owen Franken/Stock Boston **455:** Helga Lade Fotoagentur **459:** Ullstein Bilderdienst **461:** (*top left*) Kevin Galvin; (*top right*) Helen Marcus/Photo Researchers, Inc.; (*bottom left*) Stuart Cohen; (*bottom right*) Helga Lade Fotoagentur **469:** Pierre Valette **471:** Franklin Hollander/Argus-Fotoarchiv GmbH/Peter Arnold **484:** Owen Franken/Stock Boston

Index of Grammatical and Communicative Topics